In the Clinic

Practical Information about Common Health Problems

From the pages of *Annals of Internal Medicine*

Christine Laine, MD, MPH

David R. Goldmann, MD

ACP® PRESS

AMERICAN COLLEGE OF PHYSICIANS · PHILADELPHIA

Production Supervisor: Allan S. Kleinberg
Senior Production Editor: Karen C. Nolan
Editorial Coordinator: Angela Gabella
Cover Design: Lisa Torrieri

Printed in the United States of America
Printed by McNaughton & Gunn
Composition by Scribe, Inc. (www.scribenet.com)

ISBN: 978-1-934465-24-0

Library of Congress Cataloging-in-Publication Data is available from the Library of Congress.

The content of *In The Clinic* is drawn from the clinical information and education resources of the American College of Physicians (ACP), including PIER (Physicians' Information and Education Resource). *Annals of Internal Medicine* editors develop *In the Clinic* from these primary sources in collaboration with the ACP's Medical Education and Publishing Division and with the assistance of science writers and physician writers. Editorial consultants from PIER and MKSAP provide expert review of the content. Readers who are interested in these primary resourcees for more detail can consult http://pier.acponline.org and other resources referenced in each issue of *In the Clinic*.

The information contained herein should never be used as a substitute for clinical judgments.

The authors and publisher have exerted every effort to ensure that the drug selection and dosage set forth in this book are in accord with current recommendations and practice at the time of publication. In view of ongoing research, occasional changes in government regulations, and the constant flow of information relating to durg therapy and drug reactions, the reader is urged to check the package insert for each drug for any change in indications and dosage and for added warnings and precautions. This care is particularly important when the recommended agent is a new or infrequently used drug.

10 11 12 13 / 10 9 8 7 6 5 4 3 2

Preface

This book assembles the first two years of material from the "In the Clinic" section of *Annals of Internal Medicine*. If you are like many practicing physicians, you probably have a stack of unread journals accumulating dust somewhere in your home or office. You haven't tossed them in the recycle bin yet because you hope someday to find a few free minutes to look through them. You may also have this nagging sense that there probably is something buried in the stack that you should know. As journal editors, we would like to believe that our readers rush to read every *Annals* issue from cover to cover. As clinicians, however, we know that the realities of practice and life make that unlikely. We also know that, when practicing physicians do get to their journals, they too often find some articles irrelevant or at best tangential to their daily work of caring for patients. *Annals* developed "In the Clinic" to strengthen the connection between evidence and clinical practice.

"In the Clinic" appears monthly, and each installment focuses on a single common clinical condition relevant to internal medicine practice. The foundation for "In the Clinic" is the evidence-based content in PIER (Physicians' Information and Education Resource). PIER (http://pier.acponline.org) is a compendium of evidence-based clinical guidance presented in a unique telegraphic format designed for rapid access to clinical information at the point of care by physicians and other health care providers. "In the Clinic" emphasizes key knowledge that can readily be integrated into practice. Readers who desire greater detail can find it the source materials and evidence links in PIER.

The editors of "In the Clinic" carefully plan, closely direct and participate in writing "In the Clinic" to assure that it aligns with the evidence-based material from which it is derived. Science writers and physician writers help to transform the information in PIER into the question-answer based format that characterizes "In the Clinic." Outside experts review each piece to assure that it is accurate and current.

Generalists tell us that they find reading "In the Clinic" a good way to refresh their knowledge in core clinical topics. Subspecialist physicians find it a painless way to update themselves about clinical conditions outside of their area of expertise. We hope that you enjoy this collection and find information in it that will help you in the care of your patients.

Christine Laine, MD, MPH

David R. Goldmann, MD

Acknowledgments

In the Clinic has been edited collaboratively by Christine Laine, MD, MPH, and David Goldmann, MD, with two exceptions: Type 2 Diabetes was edited solely by Dr Laine; Harold C. Sox, MD, was a third editor on Hypertension.

The science/physician writers of *In the Clinic* are listed below. The editors gratefully acknowledge their contributions.

- *Type 2 Diabetes*—Jennifer F. Wilson

- *Smoking Cessation*—Jennifer F. Wilson

- *Peripheral Arterial Disease*—Jennifer F. Wilson

- *Allergic Rhinitis*—Christine Bahls

- *Depression*—Tonya Fancher, MD, and Richard Kravitz, MD

- *Asthma*—Reynold A. Panettieri, Jr., MD

- *Irritable Bowel Syndrome*—Jennifer F. Wilson

- *Osteoarthritis*—David J. Hunter, MD

- *Dyslipidemia*—Laurie A. Kopin, MS, ANP, and Thomas A. Pearson, MD, PhD

- *Influenza*—Margaret Trexler Hessen, MD

- *Migraine*—Jennifer F. Wilson

- *Heart Failure*—Jennifer F. Wilson

- *Insomnia*—Jennifer F. Wilson

- *Colorectal Cancer Screening*—David S. Weinberg, MD, MSc

- *Chronic Obstructive Pulmonary Disease*—Michael R. Littner, MD

- *Dementia*—David M. Blass, MD, and Peter V. Rabins, MD, MPH

- *Low Back Pain*—Jennifer F. Wilson

- *Hepatitis C*—Janice H. Jou, MD, and Andrew J. Muir, MD

- *Acne*—Susan V. Bershad, MD

- *Gastroesophageal Reflux Disease*—Jennifer F. Wilson

- *Deep Venous Thrombosis*—Steve Goodacre, MB, ChB, MSc, PhD

- *Obesity*—George A. Bray, MD, and Jennifer F. Wilson

- *Atrial Fibrillation*—David J. Callans, MD

- *Hypertension*—Debbie L. Cohen, MD, and Raymond R. Townsend, MD

Contents

Type 2 Diabetes

It is nearly impossible to be a practicing internist in the United States and have a day of clinical work pass without encountering at least 1 patient with type 2 diabetes. Currently, over 20 million Americans and over 150 million persons worldwide have type 2 diabetes. Models estimate that this number will nearly double by the year 2050 so that about one third of adult Americans will have the disease[1-3]. Unfortunately, although researchers are gaining new insights into the pathophysiology of the disease, including its genetic basis[4], and therapeutic options are expanding[5], many people with type 2 diabetes develop complications of the disease. A recent national analysis of diabetes care in the United States shows that despite improvements in processes of care and intermediate outcomes over the past decade, there remains much room for improvements in diabetes care[6]. Among adult Americans with diabetes, 2 in 5 have suboptimal lipid control, 1 in 3 has poor blood pressure control, and 1 in 5 has poor glycemic control.

Diagnosis

What are the diagnostic criteria for type 2 diabetes in nonpregnant adults?

Type 2 diabetes is often present at least 4 to 7 years before diagnosis[7]. Definitive diagnosis of type 2 diabetes is important because it allows attempts to improve glycemic control and to implement other interventions to improve clinical outcomes. Clinicians should confirm the diagnosis with laboratory testing when a patient presents with symptoms compatible with type 2 diabetes (polyuria, polydipsia, and unexplained weight loss), with evidence of possible diabetes complications (vision problems, retinopathy, impotence, renal dysfunction,

peripheral neuropathy, acanthosis nigricans, or frequent infections), or with elevated incidental blood glucose levels (≥126 mg/dL fasting or ≥200 mg/dL nonfasting). A fasting plasma glucose level that is 126 mg/dL or greater and is confirmed on repeated testing on another day is the current American Diabetes Association (ADA) preferred criterion for diagnosis (Table 1).

What alternative diagnoses should clinicians consider when a patient presents with hyperglycemia?

The differential diagnosis for type 2 diabetes is limited and includes type 1 diabetes, diabetes insipidus, and maturity-onset diabetes of the young.

1. Centers for Disease Control and Prevention. Diabetes Surveillance, 2005. Atlanta, GA, Department of Health and Human Services, 2005.
2. Honeycutt AA, Boyle JP, Broglio KR, Thompson TJ, Hoerger TJ, Geiss LS, et al. A dynamic Markov model for forecasting diabetes prevalence in the United States through 2050. Health Care Manag Sci. 2003;6:155-64. [PMID: 12943151]
3. Narayan KM, Boyle JP, Thompson TJ, Sorensen SW, Williamson DF. Lifetime risk for diabetes mellitus in the United States. JAMA. 2003;290:1884-90. [PMID: 14532317]
4. Hattersley AT. Beyond the beta cell in diabetes. Nat Genet. 2006;38:12-3. [PMID: 16380722]
5. Comi RJ. Treatment of type 2 diabetes mellitus: a weighty enigma [Editorial]. Ann Intern Med. 2005;143:609-10. [PMID: 16230728]
6. Saaddine JB, Cadwell B, Gregg EW, Engelgau MM, Vinicor F, Imperatore G, et al. Improvements in diabetes processes of care and intermediate outcomes: United States, 1988-2002. Ann Intern Med. 2006;v144:465-74. [PMID:16585660]
7. Harris MI, Klein R, Welborn TA, Knuiman MW. Onset of NIDDM occurs at least 4-7 yr before clinical diagnosis. Diabetes Care. 1992;15:815-9. [PMID: 1516497]

Table 1: Diagnostic Tests For Diabetes

Test	Threshold Value	Recommended Follow-up	Advantages	Disadvantages
Fasting plasma glucose (FPG)	· ≥126 mg/dL suggests diabetes · 100–125 mg/dL suggests prediabetes	· Confirm by repeated test on another day	· Time since last meal easily defined · Preferred American Diabetes Association criterion for diagnosis	· Less convenient to draw than a random glucose level
Random plasma glucose	· ≥200 mg/dL in setting of symptoms indicates diabetes	· Confirm with FPG or OGTT performed on another day	· Convenient	· Lower sensitivity and specificity than other tests · Least acceptable test for diagnosis
2–h oral glucose tolerance test (OGTT)	· ≥200 mg/dL diagnostic for diabetes · 140–199 mg/dL suggests prediabetes	· Confirm with FPG on another day	· None	· Less convenient and more costly to administer than other tests
Glycosylated hemoglobin	· Hemoglobin A_{1c} value >6% is suggestive of diabetes but not diagnostic	· Perform confirmatory testing with fasting glucose or OGTT measurement	· Convenient	· No universally implemented standard · Not an accepted diagnostic criterion for diabetes

Clinicians should consider type 1 diabetes when patients are younger than 40 years of age, have a history of ketoacidosis, or are of low or normal weight. Polyuria and polydipsia in the setting of confirmed normal plasma suggest diabetes insipidus. Strong familial transmission characterizes maturity-onset diabetes of the young, which is due to monogenetic defects in β-cell function.

> **Diagnosis...** Type 2 diabetes is common, and clinicians should consider the diagnosis when patients present with symptoms or signs of the disease or its complications. Fasting plasma glucose levels greater than 126 mg/dL on 2 occasions at least 1 day apart confirm the diagnosis and have the advantage of being relatively convenient to measure. However, random plasma glucose levels and oral glucose tolerance testing can also be used to establish the diagnosis of type 2 diabetes. Other forms of diabetes are much less common than type 2 diabetes, but clinicians should consider these alternatives and endocrinology consultation when the clinical picture is unclear.
>
> **CLINICAL BOTTOM LINE**

Screening

Should we screen for type 2 diabetes?

The natural history of type 2 diabetes includes an asymptomatic phase that is detectable only through screening or incidental testing. Because complications can occur before clinical symptoms, some groups advocate screening all primary care patients for the disease. However, no direct evidence proves that screening improves health outcomes. Further research is needed to define the effect of delaying the onset of frank diabetes on long-term outcomes and resource utilization and to determine whether there are potential harms of early treatment in patients with diabetes identified through screening. In the absence of such evidence, there is a lack of consensus about whether to screen all primary care patients, regardless of their underlying risk. Organizations have tended to advocate focusing screening on patients at high risk for diabetes or its complications.

Which patients are likely to benefit most from diabetes screening?

Several evidence-based guidelines advocate focusing screening efforts on patients with elevated risk for type 2 diabetes (Table 2), particularly those with cardiovascular disease, hypertension, or dyslipidemia.

Intensive glycemic control in people with type 2 diabetes reduces intermediate markers of microvascular complications but has not been convincingly shown to reduce end-organ complications or macrovascular disease. Yet fair evidence from observational studies[8-11] and a decision model[12] suggests that detecting diabetes improves estimates of cardiovascular risk and provides an opportunity for earlier and more aggressive interventions, such as more aggressive hypertension and lipid control, to reduce cardiovascular events in

8. Kannel WB, McGee DL. Diabetes and cardiovascular disease. The Framingham study. JAMA. 1979;241:2035-8. [PMID: 430798]
9. Kannel WB, McGee DL. Diabetes and glucose tolerance as risk factors for cardiovascular disease: the Framingham study. Diabetes Care. 1979;2:120-6. [PMID: 520114]
10. Haffner SM, Lehto S, Ronnemaa T, Pyoraia K, Laakso M. Mortality from coronary heart disease in subjects with type 2 diabetes and in nondiabetic subjects with and without prior myocardial infarction. N Engl J Med. 1998;339:229-34. [PMID: 9673301]
11. Evans JM, Wang J, Morris AD. Comparison of cardiovascular risk between patients with type 2 diabetes and those who had had a myocardial infarction: cross sectional and cohort studies. BMJ. 2002;324:939-42. [PMID: 11964337]
12. Goyder EC, Irwig LM. Screening for type 2 diabetes mellitus: a decision analytic approach. Diabet Med. 2000;17:469-77. [PMID: 10975217]
13. Standards of medical care in diabetes--2006. Diabetes Care. 2006;29 Suppl 1:S4-42. [PMID: 16373931]
14. Screening for type 2 diabetes mellitus in adults: recommendations and rationale. Ann Intern Med. 2003;138:212-4. [PMID: 12558361]

Table 2: Diabetes Screening Guidelines

Date	Organization (Reference)	Recommendations
2006	American Diabetes Association[13]	· For adults who do not have diabetes risk factors, consider screening every 3 y starting at age 45 y, particularly if body mass index >25 kg/m^2 · Screen adults < 45 y of age if they are overweight and have another diabetes risk factor
2003	U.S. Preventive Services Task Force[14]	· There is insufficient evidence to recommend for or against routine screening of asymptomatic adults · Fair evidence supports screening adults with hypertension or hyperlipidemia
2003	Canadian Diabetes Association[15]	· Evaluate all patients for type 2 diabetes risk annually · Screen patients without diabetes risk factors every 3 y starting at age 40 y · Consider earlier, more frequent screening for patients with diabetes risk factors

patients with diabetes and prevent common diabetes complications.

Although currently available guidelines (Table 2) differ in their recommendations for screening of patients with average cardiovascular risk and the ages at which to begin screening, they generally agree that clinicians should screen for diabetes in patients with elevated risk for cardiovascular disease.

Screening... Pending direct evidence of the benefits of early treatment for patients with type 2 diabetes identified through routine screening, screening for diabetes seems prudent for middle-aged patients with risk factors for cardiovascular disease, such as hypertension or dyslipidemia. Professional groups differ with respect to recommendations for screening in people without elevated cardiovascular risk.

CLINICAL BOTTOM LINE

Prevention

15. Canadian Diabetes Association Clinical Practice Guidelines Expert Committee. Canadian Diabetes Association 2003 Clinical Practice Guidelines for the Prevention and Management of Diabetes in Canada. Can J Diabetes. 2003;27(suppl 2).
16. Tuomilehto J, Lindstrom J, Eriksson JG, Valle TT, Hamalainen H, Ilanne-Parikka P, et al. Prevention of type 2 diabetes mellitus by changes in lifestyle among subjects with impaired glucose tolerance. N Engl J Med. 2001;344:1343-50. [PMID: 11333990]
17. Knowler WC, Barrett-Connor E, Fowler SE, Hamman RF, Lachin JM, Walker EA, et al. Reduction in the incidence of type 2 diabetes with lifestyle intervention or metformin. N Engl J Med. 2002;346:393-403. [PMID: 11832527]
18. Pan XR, Li GW, Hu YH, Wang JX, Yang WY, An ZX, et al. Effects of diet and exercise in preventing NIDDM in people with impaired glucose tolerance. The Da Qing IGT and Diabetes Study. Diabetes Care. 1997;20:537-44. [PMID: 9096977]

Can we prevent type 2 diabetes?
Before people develop type 2 diabetes, they almost always have "prediabetes." This condition is defined by hyperglycemia that does not meet the diagnostic criteria for diabetes. Whether this condition is called "impaired fasting glucose" or "impaired glucose tolerance" depends on whether the hyperglycemia was detected on measurement of fasting plasma glucose levels or an oral glucose tolerance test. Both impaired fasting glucose and impaired glucose tolerance are risk factors for future diabetes and cardiovascular disease[13]. Patients with prediabetes should undergo monitoring and should modify their risk factors for diabetes and cardiovascular disease if possible.

Prediabetes is identified by either of the following criteria:

· **Impaired fasting glucose:** fasting plasma glucose level 100 to 125 mg/dL (5.6 to 6.9 mmol/L)
· **Impaired glucose tolerance:** plasma glucose level 140 to 199 mg/dL (7.8 to 11.0 mmol/L) 2 hours after 75 g of glucose

---

In addition to observational studies, clinical trials document that dietary changes and regular exercise prevent or delay the development of overt diabetes in individuals at high risk for the disease, such as those with prediabetes.

In a randomized, unblinded, controlled trial of 522 overweight Finnish patients with impaired glucose tolerance (mean age, 55 years), an intervention aimed at a 5% reduction in weight decreased the incidence of newly diagnosed type 2 diabetes over 3 years from 23% to 11%[16]. The intervention involved personal counseling sessions to encourage a reduction in total and saturated fat intake to less than 30% and 10% of energy consumed, respectively; an increase in fiber intake; and moderate exercise for at least 30 minutes per day.

The Diabetes Prevention Project, a randomized, controlled trial that involved 3234 U.S. patients with prediabetes (mean age, 51 years; mean body mass index, 34 kg/m²), showed that a lifestyle modification program aimed at a 7% weight loss reduced the cumulative incidence of diabetes over 3 years from 29% to 14%[17] compared with placebo. The lifestyle intervention involved personal and group counseling sessions to encourage a low-calorie, low-fat diet and at least 150 minutes of moderate exercise (such as brisk walking) per week.

In a randomized, controlled trial that involved 577 Chinese adults with impaired glucose tolerance randomly assigned to diet, exercise, both, or neither, the incidence of diabetes over 6 years was 68% among persons in the "neither" group, 44% in the diet group, 41% in the exercise group, and 46% in the "both" group[18]. All 3 interventions resulted in statistically significant reductions in the progression to diabetes.

Clinical trials also show that certain medications can prevent type 2 diabetes in high-risk patients.

In the medication arm of the Diabetes Prevention Project, the trial that involved 3234 patients with prediabetes[18], metformin (850 mg twice daily) reduced the cumulative incidence of diabetes from 29% to 22% over

3 years. This reduction was significant but smaller than that observed with the lifestyle intervention in this trial.

In the randomized, double-blind, international Study to Prevent Non–Insulin-Dependent Diabetes Mellitus, which involved 1429 patients with impaired glucose tolerance, acarbose (100 mg three times daily) reduced the incidence of diabetes from 42% to 32% compared with placebo[19]. The relative risk reduction over 3 years was 25%.

The DREAM trial (Diabetes Reduction Assessment with ramiripril and rosiglitazone Medication) is a multinational study that, using a 2-by-2 factorial design, randomized 5269 adults without previous cardiovascular disease but with impaired fasting glucose, impaired glucose tolerance, or both to rosiglitazone 8 mg per day or placebo and to rosiglitazone up to 15 mg per day or placebo. After a median 3 years, 11.6% of patients who received rosiglitazone developed diabetes or died compared with 26.0% of patients who received placebo (hazard ratio, 0.40

[95% CI, 0.35 to 0.46]). In addition, patients who received rosiglitazone were more likely to achieve normoglycemia than patients in the placebo group (50.5% vs. 30.3%; P<0.001). Cardiovascular event rates were statistically similar in both groups[20]. Patients in the ramiripril group did not have a significantly reduced incidence of diabetes or death, but these patients were more likely to have regressed to normoglycemia than were those receiving placebo (42.5% vs. 38.2%; P=0.001)[21].

Prevention... High-quality evidence supports the recommendation of regular exercise, weight loss, and reduction in total and saturated dietary fat for patients with blood glucose levels that are higher than normal but that do not meet the diagnostic criteria for diabetes (prediabetes). In some circumstances, evidence supports the use of pharmacologic therapy (metformin, acarbose, or rosilgitazone) to reduce a patient's risk for type 2 diabetes. Clinicians should consider one of these interventions when they identify patients as having prediabetes.

CLINICAL BOTTOM LINE

Evaluation & Treatment

What should the initial evaluation of patients with newly diagnosed type 2 diabetes include?

The initial evaluation of a patient with newly diagnosed type 2 diabetes should include a detailed history, physical examination, and laboratory tests to establish baseline values of glycemic control, to assess risk factors for complications, and to screen for existing diabetes complications.

What are the components of non–drug therapy for patients with type 2 diabetes?

Diet and exercise with optimization of body weight are the cornerstones of the management of type 2 diabetes.

In a study of patients with newly diagnosed type 2 diabetes, diet initially improved hemoglobin A$_{1c}$ (HbA$_{1c}$) levels by 2.25 percentage points[22]. However, control deteriorated over time and most patients eventually required drug therapy.

A meta-analysis of 14 randomized trials that compared exercise with no exercise and involved a total of 377 patients with type 2 diabetes showed that exercise significantly improved glycemic control, reduced visceral adipose tissue, and reduced plasma triglycerides even in the absence of weight loss[23].

Physicians should initiate diet and exercise regimens as the first line of treatment for type 2 diabetes unless severe hyperglycemia necessitates immediate drug therapy. Even when drug therapy is necessary, diet and exercise remain essential components of diabetes management. Physicians need to recognize that no single diet applies to all patients with type 2 diabetes; instead, they should offer education about sensible dietary principles and an individualized strategy for optimization of body mass index.

What is the role of home glucose monitoring for patients with type 2 diabetes?

Physicians should consider home blood glucose testing for patients with type 2 diabetes. Although no studies have assessed whether home blood glucose monitoring leads to more favorable outcomes for patients receiving oral therapy, home monitoring can be helpful to guide oral medication adjustment, is essential for sensible adjustment of insulin dosage, and is valuable in determining whether symptoms are due to hypoglycemia or hyperglycemia. Urine

---

Initial Laboratory Evaluation of Patients with Type 2 Diabetes

· Fasting blood glucose level
· Glycosylated hemoglobin level
· Fasting lipid profile
· Serum electrolyte, blood urea nitrogen, and creatinine levels
· Urine dipstick for overt proteinuria, with confirmation of positive result. If no dipstick proteinuria, screen for microalbuminuria with a spot urinary albumin–creatinine ratio (>30 mg albumin/g creatinine is positive result)
· Electrocardiography

---

19. Chiasson JL, Josse RG, Gomis R, Hanefeld M, Karasik A, Laakso M, et al. Acarbose for prevention of type 2 diabetes mellitus: the STOP-NIDDM randomised trial. Lancet. 2002;359:2072-7. [PMID: 12086760]
20. The DREAM Trial Investigators. Effect of rosiglitazone on the frequency of diabetes in patients with impaired fasting glucose: a randomized controlled trail. Lancet. 2006; 368:1096-105. [PMID: 16997664]
21. The DREAM Trial Investigators. Effect of ramipril on the incidence of diabetes. N Engl J Med. 2006; 355:1551-62. [PMID: 16980380]
22. Intensive blood-glucose control with sulphonyl-ureas or insulin compared with conventional treatment and risk of complications in patients with type 2 diabetes (UKPDS 33). UK Prospective Diabetes Study (UKPDS) Group. Lancet. 1998;352:837-53. [PMID: 9742976]

glucose testing is not recommended because it does not adequately reflect current glycemic status.

Patients should generally test before a meal to reflect fasting glucose levels as closely as possible. However, measurement of postprandial levels may be informative, particularly for patients with elevated glycosylated hemoglobin values despite normal fasting glucose levels. Some experts now advocate postprandial monitoring to limit after-meal glucose excursions on the basis of observational data suggesting that postprandial glucose levels are associated with a degree of cardiovascular risk independent of fasting glucose levels[24–25]. Currently, however, the only studies that show improved outcomes with interventions based on postprandial glucose levels have been done in patients with gestational diabetes.

What target for glycemic control should physicians aim for in patients with type 2 diabetes?
Quality improvement efforts often define an HbA_{1c} value less than 7% as optimal control. It is clear that "tight" glycemic control reduces the risk for microvascular diabetic complications[22,26], and recent evidence shows that control also reduces the risk for macrovascular complications in type 1 diabetes[27]. However, tight control may not benefit patients with a limited life expectancy, substantial comorbidity, or a high risk for adverse hypoglycemic events. Clinicians and patients should consider these factors when setting targets for control.

When should the treatment of type 2 diabetes include drugs?
If diet and exercise fail to achieve the desired level of glycemic control, pharmacologic intervention is indicated. Patient characteristics and preferences should be used to set treatment goals in the initial choice of pharmacologic agent. In patients with severe hyperglycemia or marked symptoms, pharmacologic therapy may begin at the time of diagnosis. Some suggest that patients with fasting glucose levels greater than 250 to 300 mg/dL are reasonable candidates, although there are no clear data in this area. Patient preferences and shared decision making should be

23. Thomas DE, Elliot EJ, Naughton GA. Exercise for type 2 diabetes mellitus. Cochrane Database Syst Rev. 2006 Jul 19; 3:CD002968. [PMID: 16855995]
24. Gerich JE. The importance of tight glycemic control. Am J Med. 2005;118:7S-11S. [PMID: 16224937]
25. Ceriello A. Postprandial hyperglycemia and diabetes complications: is it time to treat? Diabetes. 2005;54:1-7. [PMID: 15616004]
26. Ohkubo Y, Kishikawa H, Araki E, Miyata T, Isami S, Motoyoshi S, et al. Intensive insulin therapy prevents the progression of diabetic microvascular complications in Japanese patients with non-insulin-dependent diabetes mellitus: a randomized prospective 6-year study. Diabetes Res Clin Pract. 1995;28:103-17. [PMID: 7587918]

Table 3: Oral Drug Therapies for Treating Type 2 Diabetes

Drug	Mechanism	Hemoglobin A_{1c} Reduction	Notes
Biguanides (metformin)	· Suppresses hepatic glucose production · Decreases intestinal absorption of glucose · Improves insulin sensitivity	· 1%–2% · May also reduce lipid and blood pressure levels, although blood pressure effect may not be clinically significant	· No weight gain · Gastrointestinal side effects · Increase in risk for lactic acidosis (avoid if creatinine level >1.4 mg/dL in women and >1.5 mg/dL in men, decompensated congestive heart failure, liver failure, or heavy alcohol use)
Sulfonylureas (glimepiride, glipizide, glyburide, acetohexamide, chlorpropamide)	· Increases pancreatic secretion of insulin	· 1%–2%	· Possible initial weight gain · Potential for hypoglycemia
Thiazolidinediones (rosiglitazone and pioglitazone)	· Increases sensitivity to insulin	· 1%–2% as monotherapy or when added to other agents	· Weight gain and edema · Avoid in New York Heart Association class III or class IV heart failure
α-Glucosidase inhibitors (acarbose and miglitol)	· Decreases postprandial hyperglycemia by reducing gastrointestinal carbohydrate absorption	· 0.5%–1.0%	· Gastrointestinal side effects · Acarbose contraindicated in cirrhosis and requires liver function monitoring
Meglitinides (repaglinide and nateglinide)	· Increases pancreatic secretion of insulin through a different glucose-binding site than used by sulfonylureas	· 0.5%–2%	· Compared with sulfonylureas: Shorter onset of action and half-life · Greater decrease in postprandial glucose level · Lower risk for hypoglycemia

prominent features in choosing the type of therapy.

How should physicians select therapies for a patient from among the many oral drug therapies available for type 2 diabetes?

Table 3 provides information on oral drug therapies for treating type 2 diabetes Given the minimal differences in efficacy and the limited data on long-term outcomes, use of oral agents should be based on patient preference, provider familiarity, and consideration of such issues as side effects and costs. Clinicians should consult with the patient and balance maximization of efficacy with minimization of weight gain, patient effort, hypoglycemia, other side effects, and cost.

Metformin and sulfonylureas are the mostly commonly used first-line agents. For overweight patients, metformin is often the preferred initial therapy since it causes less weight gain and is associated with a lower rate of hypoglycemia than other agents[28]. Sulfonylureas are a reasonable first choice for patients who are not very overweight, since these agents are associated with initial weight gain.

For obese patients who do not tolerate metformin or have renal insufficiency or another contraindication to metformin, thiazolidinediones are an alternative. Other alternatives include the nonsulfonylurea insulin secretagogues (nateglinide and repaglinide) and the α-glucosidase inhibitors (acarbose and miglitol) administerd before meals. They may be good choices for patients with irregular mealtimes, but they are more expensive than other oral diabetes drugs.

Most patients with diabetes have worsening glycemic control over time and are likely to need medication adjustment. When glucose control deteriorates with an oral agent, clinicians should consider increasing the dose, but the response to escalating from submaximal to maximal doses, particularly for metformin and sulfonylureas, is usually limited.

When glucose can no longer be controlled with a single oral agent, adding another oral agent with a different mechanism of action may help. The best-studied oral-agent combination is sulfonylurea compounds plus metformin, an approach that addresses both insulin deficiency and insulin resistance. Other combinations in common use are sulfonylurea compounds plus either α-glucosidase inhibitors or thiazolidinediones, and combinations of various insulin-sensitizing agents, such as biguanides and thiazolidinediones. Aggressive combination oral treatment may delay the need for insulin in patients with advancing type 2 diabetes, an option that may be preferable to many patients[29]. Combination medications (low doses of sulfonylurea plus metformin, metformin plus a glitazone, and glitazone plus sulfonylurea) are available, but there is limited evidence on improvements in effectiveness or safety with these treatment options.

When should physicians consider insulin therapy for patients with type 2 diabetes?

Patients who do not achieve adequate glycemic control with a combination of oral medications are candidates for insulin treatment. Other indications include:

- New diagnosis with severe, symptomatic hyperglycemia
- Comorbid illness, such as myocardial infarction, infection, or renal or hepatic disease, that makes control difficult with oral medications

---

General Advice about Diet and Exercise for Patients with Type 2 Diabetes

Diet
- Stress the importance of moderation
- Base calorie recommendations on the goal of achieving near-ideal body weight. A reasonable starting formula for weight maintenance is as follows: 10 calories per pound of current body weight, plus 20% for sedentary patients; 33% for those who engage in light physical activity; 50% for those who are moderately active; and 75% for heavily active patients
- Advise patient to avoid saturated fats
- Encourage regular meal schedule, particularly if patient is receiving insulin
- Inform patient that frequent, small meals might aid in weight loss and control of blood glucose levels
- Advise patient to choose complex carbohydrates (e.g., whole grains, cereals) over simple sugars (e.g., sweets).

Exercise
- Individualize exercise regimen, consider current level of activity, living situation, and comorbid conditions
- Consider beginning with 15 min of low-impact aerobic exercise 3 times per week for patients who can exercise and gradually increasing the frequency and duration to 30–45 min of moderate aerobic activity 3–5 d per week
- Caution patients receiving drug therapy about hypoglycemia during and after exercise

27. Nathan DM, Cleary PA, Backlund JY, Genuth SM, Lachin JM, Orchard TJ, et al. Intensive diabetes treatment and cardiovascular disease in patients with type 1 diabetes. N Engl J Med. 2005;353:2643-53. [PMID: 16371630]
28. Effect of intensive blood-glucose control with metformin on complications in overweight patients with type 2 diabetes (UKPDS 34). UK Prospective Diabetes Study (UKPDS) Group. Lancet. 1998;352:854-65. [PMID: 9742977]
29. Mooradian AD, Bernbaum M, Albert SG. Narrative review: a rational approach to starting insulin therapy. Ann Intern Med. 2006;145:125-34. [PMID: 16847295]

Table 4: Onset and Mechanisms of Action of Various Types of Insulin*

Type of Insulin	Onset and Mechanisms of Action
Lispro/aspart Glulisine	· Very short acting; onset of action within 15 min; peak action, 30–90 min; maximum, 5 h
Regular	· Short acting; onset of action within 1 h; duration, typically 4–8 h; maximum, 12 h
NPH	· Intermediate acting; onset within 2–3 h; duration, typically 8–12 h; maximum, 24 h
Lente	· Intermediate acting; onset within 2–3 h; duration, typically 8–12 h; maximum, 24 h
Glargine	· Long acting up to 24 h
Ultralente	· Longest acting up to 28 h
Premixed†	· Onset and duration are similar to those of the component parts

*NPH = neutral protamine Hagedorn.
†Regular and long acting (usually NPH); concentrations vary.

30. Yki-Jarvinen H, Kauppila M, Kujansuu E, Lahti J, Marjanen T, Niskanen L, et al. Comparison of insulin regimens in patients with non-insulin-dependent diabetes mellitus. N Engl J Med. 1992;327:1426-33. [PMID: 1406860]
31. Ratner RE, Want LL, Fineman MS, Velte MJ, Ruggles JA, Gottlieb A, et al. Adjunctive therapy with the amylin analogue pramlintide leads to a combined improvement in glycemic and weight control in insulin-treated subjects with type 2 diabetes. Diabetes Technol Ther. 2002;4:51-61. [PMID: 12017421]
32. Hollander PA, Levy P, Fineman MS, Maggs DG, Shen LZ, Strobel SA, et al. Pramlintide as an adjunct to insulin therapy improves long-term glycemic and weight control in patients with type 2 diabetes: a 1-year randomized controlled trial. Diabetes Care. 2003;26:784-90. [PMID: 12610038]

• Pregnancy
• Intolerance to oral medication.

Many different forms of insulin are available; all act directly on glucose metabolism (see Table 4)[30]. The starting dose for insulin varies widely and may be determined by weight-based algorithms. Randomized, controlled trials of different insulin regimens show that insulin can improve hemoglobin A_{1c} values by 1% to 2%, but there is no documented advantage of dosing insulin more than twice daily in type 2 diabetes[30]. Side effects include hypoglycemia and weight gain.

Insulin therapy may be combined with oral therapy to better achieve target glucose control. Options for combination therapy with insulin and oral agents include bedtime insulin (glargine or neutral protamine Hagedorn [NPH]) plus daytime sulfonylurea or bedtime insulin (glargine or NPH) plus metformin. Patients may discontinue other diabetes therapy before beginning these regimens. Glucose monitoring is essential to titrate the insulin dose to a morning fasting glucose level of 80 to 120 mg/dL.

After discontinuation of previous therapy, start with a dose of 0.10 to 0.15 U/kg divided into 2 daily doses (or with meals), then adjust dosages

(typically in 10% increments at 1-week intervals) based on results of home glucose monitoring. Metformin and glitazones can be continued for their insulin-sensitizing and insulin-sparing effects.

What other options are available if control is inadequate on traditional oral drugs or insulin?
If glycemic control remains inadequate, consider using either of these agents.

In 2005, the U.S. Food and Drug Administration (FDA) approved pramlintide for use with mealtime insulin when control is inadequate despite optimal insulin dosing. Exenatide is not for use with insulin.

Pramlintide
Pramlintide is a synthetic form of the hormone amylin, which is produced by the β cells in the pancreas along with insulin. Prescription should be as follows:

• Begin pramlintide at a dose of 60 µg subcutaneously just before each major meal.
• Reduce the dose of rapid-acting, short-acting, or fixed-mix premeal insulin by 50% to avoid risk for hypoglycemia.
• Monitor blood glucose frequently before and after meals and at bedtime.
• If the patient has no nausea, increase maintenance dose to 120 µg; if nausea develops and persists, decrease to 60 µg.
• When pramlintide dose is stabilized, adjust insulin dose to optimize.

In a multicenter, randomized, controlled trial, 538 insulin-treated patients with type 2 diabetes were given various doses of pramlintide or placebo for 52 weeks. In the 150-µg pramlintide group, 48% of patients achieved a reduction in both HbA$_{1c}$ and body weight from baseline to week 52 compared with 16% of patients on placebo[31].

In a similar study of 656 patients receiving insulin or insulin combined with metformin or a sulfonylurea, treatment with pramlintide, 120 µg twice daily, led to an HbA$_{1c}$ value less than 8% in 46% of patients compared with

28% of those receiving placebo. Patients in the pramlintide group had a mean weight loss of 1.4 kg, whereas those in the placebo group had a mean weight gain of 0.7 kg[32].

Exenatide

Exenatide, the first in a new class of medicines called incretin mimetics, exhibits many of the same glucoregulatory actions of glucagon-like peptide-1, a naturally occurring incretin hormone. It enhances glucose-dependent insulin secretion, suppresses inappropriately high glucagon secretion, slows gastric emptying, decreases food intake, promotes β-cell proliferation and neogenesis, reduces adiposity, and increases insulin-sensitizing effects in animal models. Patients who have not achieved adequate glycemic control with metformin, a sulfonylurea, or both may benefit from the addition of exenatide to their regimen. Nausea and vomiting are documented side effects of exenatide, but these may subside as treatment continues.

- The typical exenatide starting dose is 5 μg subcutaneously twice daily within 60 minutes before the morning and evening meal.
- For patients taking sulfonylureas, decrease sulfonylurea dose to reduce the risk for hypoglycemia; a reduction in metformin dose is usually not necessary.
- After 1 month of therapy, increase the dose of exenatide to 10 μg subcutaneously twice daily.

A randomized trial assigned 551 patients with type 2 diabetes and inadequate glycemic control despite combination metformin and sulfonylurea therapy to exenatide, 10 μg twice daily, or a titrated daily dose of insulin glargine. At week 26, both exenatide and insulin glargine reduced HbA$_{1c}$ levels by 1.11%. Exenatide reduced postprandial glucose excursions more than insulin glargine, while insulin glargine reduced fasting glucose concentrations more than exenatide. Body weight decreased 2.3 kg with exenatide and increased 1.8 kg with insulin glargine (difference, −4.1 kg [CI, −4.6 to −3.5 kg]). Rates of symptomatic hypoglycemia were similar, but nocturnal hypoglycemia occurred less frequently with exenatide. Gastrointestinal symptoms, including nausea (57.1% vs. 8.6%), vomiting (17.4% vs. 3.7%), and diarrhea (8.5% vs. 3.0%), were more common in the exenatide group than in the insulin glargine group[33].

In October 2006, the FDA approved sitagliptin as a monotherapy adjunct to diet and exercise or for use in combination with metformin or thiazolidinediones. Sitagliptin, a dipeptidyl peptidase 4 (DPP-4) inhibitor, is the first drug in a new class of oral therapy for type 2 diabetes. DPP-4 inhibitors block the breakdown of proteins that stimulate insulin synthesis and release when blood glucose rises. Further data, especially about long-term safety, is needed to determine the role of sitagliptin in the treatment of type 2 diabetes.

A randomized, controlled trial assigned 521 patients age 27 to 76 years with a mean baseline HbA$_{1c}$ of 8.1% in a 1:2:2 ratio to receive placebo, sitagliptin 100 mg once daily, or sitagliptin 200 mg once daily. After 18 weeks, HbA$_{1c}$ was significantly reduced with sitagliptin at both doses compared with placebo (placebo-subtracted HbA$_{1c}$ reduction, 0.60% for 100 mg and −0.48% for 200 mg)[34].

What are the novel therapeutic options on the horizon for patients with type 2 diabetes?

The FDA approved inhaled insulin in January 2006, providing patients with an alternative to injection as a mechanism of insulin delivery by enabling patients to breathe insulin into their lungs by using a special device[35].

A 2005 study involving 309 patients with type 2 diabetes who were taking oral drugs and had poorly controlled diabetes compared the results among those randomly assigned to continue taking the oral drugs, to add inhaled insulin to the pills before meals, or to stop taking the pills and take only inhaled insulin before meals. After 12 weeks, HbA$_{1c}$ level was most improved in the group that took inhaled insulin with the pills, second most improved in the group that took only inhaled insulin, and worst in the group that took only pills. The patients in the inhaled insulin groups experienced more mild weight gain, episodes of low blood glucose levels, and mild cough[35].

Whether patients will continue to show improved blood glucose levels or have side effects if they used inhaled insulin for longer periods is not known. It is also unclear how inhaled insulin compares with injected insulin over the long term. Injected insulin currently allows for finer dose adjustments than does inhaled insulin.

Possible insulin regimens include the following:
- Once-daily injection of insulin glargine with or without fast- or regular-acting insulin with meals
- Twice-daily NPH or Lente insulin injection (before breakfast and before dinner or at bedtime)
- Twice-daily split-mixed insulin (self-mixed NPH or Lente insulin with regular or premixed 70/30 solution) before breakfast and dinner
- Multiple daily injections of regular or very short–acting insulin.

33. Heine RJ, Van Gaal LF, Johns D, Mihm MJ, Widel MH, Brodows RG, for the GWAA Study Group/Exenatide versus insulin glargine in patients with suboptimally controlled type 2 diabetes: a randomized trial. Ann Intern Med. 2005;143:559-69. [PMID: 16230722]
34. Raz I, Hanefeld M, Xu L, Caria C, Williams-Herman D, Khatami H. Efficacy and safety of the dipeptidyl peptidase-4 inhibitor sitagliptin as monotherapy in patients with type 2 diabetes mellitus. Diabetologia. 2006 Sep 26; [Epub ahead of print]. [PMID: 17001471]
35. Rosenstock J, Zinman B, Murphy LJ, Clement SC, Moore P, Bowering CK, et al. Inhaled insulin improves glycemic control when substituted for or added to oral combination therapy in type 2 diabetes: a randomized, controlled trial. Ann Intern Med. 2005;143:549-58. [PMID: 16230721]

Table 5: Antihypertensive Agents in Type 2 Diabetes*

Antihypertensive Agent	Notes	Advantages	Disadvantages
ACE inhibitors	· ADA and ACP advocate as first-line agent	· Cardioprotective · Renoprotective	· Relatively expensive · Caution with advanced renal failure
ARBs	· ADA and ACP advocate as second-line agent	· Cardioprotective · Renoprotective	· Expensive · Caution with advanced renal failure
β–Blockers	· Use in patients with known CAD	· Cardioprotective · Most are inexpensive	· Can mask hypoglycemia · May be associated with weight gain and metabolic abnormalities
Thiazide diuretics	· Often used in combination with other agents to achieve blood pressure targets · ACP advocates as first-line agent	· May reduce CHF · Inexpensive · Cardioprotective	· May elevate blood glucose levels
α–Blockers	· Use only if target blood pressure cannot be reached with other agents	· Can help alleviate symptoms of benign prostatic hypertrophy	· Do not protect against CHF · Generally must be used with other agent
Calcium-channel blockers	· Use if target blood pressure cannot be reached with ACE inhibitors, ARBs, and thiazides	· Some evidence suggests this class is cardioprotective	· Appear to offer less cardioprotection than other antihypertensive agents

*ACE = angiotensin-converting enzyme; ACP = American College of Physicians; ADA = American Diabetes Association; ARB = angiotensin-receptor blocker; CAD = coronary artery disease; CHF = congestive heart failure.

Physicians should consider comorbidity, efficacy, and side effects when choosing antihypertensive agents (see Table 5).

Patients with known cardiovascular disease should receive lipid-lowering agents. For primary prevention of cardiovascular disease, patients with diabetes who are 40 years or older and have at least one additional cardiovascular risk factor should receive lipid-lowering therapy regardless of low-density lipoprotein cholesterol level[13]. Statins are generally the agents of choice, except for patients with low levels of both high-density lipoprotein and high triglycerides in whom fibrates with or without a statin may be a reasonable option. Caution is needed when combining statins and fibrates.

Physicians should consider aspirin 75 to 325 mg/day for all patients who have type 2 diabetes age >40 years, ≥1 additional risk factor, and no specific contraindication.

In addition to therapies aimed at glycemic control, what therapies should physicians consider to reduce the complications of type 2 diabetes?
Patients with hypertension should receive aggressive antihypertensive therapy to a blood pressure target <130/80 mm Hg. Some experts recommend <125/75 if proteinuria is present. Randomized controlled trials support the use of angiotensin-converting enzyme inhibitor or angiotensin-receptor blocker therapy for patients with type 2 diabetes regardless of blood pressure level.

36. Brown SA. Effects of educational interventions in diabetes care: a meta-analysis of findings. Nurs Res. 1988;37:223-30. [PMID: 3293025]
37. Franz MJ, Monk A, Barry B, McClain K, Weaver T, Cooper N, et al. Effectiveness of medical nutrition therapy provided by dietitians in the management of non-insulin-dependent diabetes mellitus: a randomized, controlled clinical trial. J Am Diet Assoc. 1995;95:1009-17. [PMID: 7657902]
38. Vijan S, Hayward RA. Treatment of hypertension in type 2 diabetes mellitus: blood pressure goals, choice of agents, and setting priorities in diabetes care. Ann Intern Med. 2003;138:593-602. [PMID: 12667032]

Table 6: Therapies To Decrease Neuropathy Symptoms

Agent	Notes
Tricyclic antidepressants	· Randomized, controlled trial (RCT) evidence shows effectiveness in neuropathic pain · Start with small bedtime dose (25 mg of nortriptyline) and titrate up · Watch for anticholinergic side effects
Duloxetine	· Recently approved by the U.S. Food and Drug Administration for diabetic neuropathy · Recommended dosage is 60 mg/d · Not appropriate if patient has liver disease or substantial alcohol use
Capsaicin cream	· RCTs show effectiveness in reducing pain and increasing function · May cause burning sensation
Antiepileptic agents	· Carbamazepine or gabapentin in patients unable to tolerate above options · RCTs support effectiveness

Table 7: Components of Follow-up Care for Type 2 Diabetes

Issue	Actions	How Often?
Glycemic control	· Ask about diet, exercise, results of home monitoring, and medications. Adjust medications.	· Each visit (at least quarterly)
	· Check hemoglobin A_{1c} values	· Quarterly
Weight control	· Weigh patient. Ask about diet and exercise.	· Each visit
Cardiovascular complications	· Ask about diet, smoking, and cardiac events in family members	· Each visit
	· Measure blood pressure, examine heart and peripheral pulses	· Each visit
	· Measure lipid levels	· Annually, or more frequently to monitor therapy
	· Consider performing other cardiac testing	· If patient has symptoms; has abnormal findings on examination or electrocardiography; or is sedentary and >35 y of age and plans vigorous exercise
	· Adjust therapy to achieve target lipid levels and blood pressure	· Each visit
Vision complications	· Ask about visual acuity, central vision loss, and eye pain	· At least annually; each visit once problem exists
	· Have specialist conduct eye examination	· At least annually; each visit once problem exists
Neurologic complications	· Ask about burning, tingling, numbness in extremities	· At least annually; each visit once problem exists
	· Conduct neurologic examination with monofilament testing	· At least annually; each visit once problem exists
Nephrologic complications	· Perform urinalysis; measure electrolytes, blood urea nitrogen, and creatinine; test urine for microalbuminuria	· At least annually, more frequently once problem exists
Infectious complications	· Ask about infections, including skin, dental, foot, genitourinary	· Each visit
	· Examine for periodontal disease, skin infection, and foot infection	· Each visit
Patient education	· Advocate diet, exercise, monitoring, and medication adherence	· Each visit

A variety of pharmacologic agents are effective in treating the symptoms of diabetic neuropathy (see Table 6).

How frequently should physicians see patients with type 2 diabetes, and what should physicians include in follow-up visits?

While no direct evidence suggests the ideal frequency of follow-up for patients with type 2 diabetes, expert opinion and the recommended frequency of monitoring HbA_{1c} levels and other aspects of routine diabetes care[13] suggest that quarterly visits are prudent (see Table 7).

When should generalist physicians consult specialists to assist in the care of patients with type 2 diabetes?

Meta-analyses have shown that diabetes education is effective in improving knowledge, skill, self-care behaviors, psychosocial outcomes, and metabolic control[36]. Data from randomized, controlled trials show that evaluation by a dietitian leads to improved glycemic control[37].

Endocrinology consultation can be helpful when the diagnosis is uncertain, management is complicated, glycemic control is elusive (persistent hyperglycemia, recurrent hypoglycemia, or ketoacidosis), or if the patient is pregnant or is contemplating pregnancy.

Nephrology consultation is prudent when a patient's glomerular filtration rate has decreased to <30 mL/min per 1.73 m², proteinuria persists, blood pressure control is difficult, or hyperkalemia occurs.

Cardiology consultation is appropriate for patients with cardiovascular symptoms or abnormal electrocardiography or stress test results.

Ophthalmology evaluation is recommended annually. Less frequent evaluation may be considered in the setting of repeated normal examinations.

Podiatry consultation is helpful when orthotic footwear is necessary to correct deformities and prevent foot ulcers.[38]

Treatment... Diet and exercise are the cornerstones for achieving glycemic control in patients with type 2 diabetes, and clinicians should stress the importance of lifestyle modification regardless of whether patients also require pharmacologic therapy. However, most patients with type 2 diabetes eventually require drug therapy to control glucose levels. Given the numerous oral and insulin-based therapies available and the limited data comparing 1 oral agent or combination of oral agents to another, clinicians should consider effectiveness, potential side effects, comorbid conditions, costs, and patient preferences when selecting treatment regimens for glycemic control.

CLINICAL BOTTOM LINE

Improving Practice

39. American College of Physicians. Pharmacologic lipid-lowering therapy in type 2 diabetes mellitus: background paper for the American College of Physicians. Ann Intern Med. 2004;140:650-8. [PMID: 15096337]

40. Snow V, Aronson MD, Hornbake ER, Mottur-Pilson C, Weiss KB. Lipid control in the management of type 2 diabetes mellitus: a clinical practice guideline from the American College of Physicians. Ann Intern Med. 2004;140:644-9. [PMID: 15096336]

What measures do U.S. stakeholders use to evaluate the quality of care for patients with type 2 diabetes?

In April 2005, The Ambulatory Care Quality Alliance (AQA) released a set of 26 health care quality indicators for use in quality improvement efforts, public reporting, and pay-for-performance programs (www.ambulatoryqualityalliance.org). In May 2005, the Centers for Medicare & Medicaid Services (CMS) endorsed the development of these indicators. Of the 26 indicators, 6 focus on the care of patients with diabetes (see Table 8). Three of the 6 diabetes-related indicators measure processes of care (HbA_{1c} measurement, lipid measurement, and eye examination by an eye specialist) and 3 measure intermediate outcomes (HbA_{1c}, blood pressure, and low-density lipoprotein cholesterol levels). It is important that clinicians be aware of these measures. AQA selected these measures because they have been linked to better clinical outcomes for patients with diabetes. Over the coming years, Medicare and other payers will increasingly link reimbursement to physician performance with respect to these quality indicators.

In addition to the 6 AQA measures, the CMS Physician Focused Quality Initiative's Doctors' Office Quality-Information Technology project (www.doqit.org) advocates the additional diabetes-related performance measures shown in Table 9.

What do professional organizations recommend regarding the care of patients with type 2 diabetes?

As noted in the preceding section on screening, several organizations offer recommendations about screening for type 2 diabetes. In addition, evidence-based guidelines are available to guide clinicians in the care of patients with the disease. A comprehensive listing of available guidelines is available through the National Guideline Clearinghouse (www.guidelines.gov). The following summarizes recently developed guidelines related to the care of type 2 diabetes.

American Diabetes Association
Every January, the ADA releases standards of diabetes care to provide clinicians, patients, and other stakeholders with tools to help in the provision and evaluation of diabetes

---

Table 8: Ambulatory Care Quality Alliance Diabetes-Related Quality Indicators*

Indicator	Description	Notes
HbA_{1c} management	· Percentage of patients with diabetes with ≥1 HbA_{1c} tests conducted during the previous year	· The higher the percentage, the better
HbA_{1c} control	· Percentage of diabetic patients with most recent HbA_{1c} value > 9.0%	· Measure of poor control · Denominator is all patients with diabetes (age 18–75 y) who had HbA_{1c} measured
Blood pressure management	· Percentage of patients with diabetes who had their blood pressure documented as < 140/90 mm Hg during the past year	· Refers to the last (most recent) blood pressure measurement · Denominator is all patients with diabetes who had blood pressure documented
Lipid measurement	· Percentage of patients with diabetes with ≥1 LDL cholesterol test or 1 all-component test	· All-component test refers to a lipid panel that includes LDL cholesterol, HDL cholesterol, and triglycerides separately · Measurement interval is the last 15 mo
LDL cholesterol level measurement	· Percentage of patients with diabetes with ≥1 LDL cholesterol level < 100 mg/dL or < 130 mg/dL	· Actually 2 measures reflecting moderately successful (<130 mg/dL) and optimal (<100 mg/dL) treatment outcomes · Measurement interval is the last 15 mo
Eye examination	· Percentage of patients with diabetes who had a retinal or dilated-eye examination by an optometrist or ophthalmologist during the reporting year or during the previous year if the patient is at low risk for retinopathy	· Patients are considered low risk if all 3 of the following criteria are met: 1) no insulin therapy, 2) HbA_{1c} value < 8%, and 3) no evidence of retinopathy in the previous year

*HbA_{1c} = hemoglobin A_{1c}; HDL = high-density lipoprotein; LDL = low-density lipoprotein.

Table 9: Additional Doctors' Office Quality-Information Technology Diabetes-Related Quality Indicators

Indicator	Description	Notes
Urine protein testing	· Denominator is all patients with diabetes age 18–75 y · Measurement interval is the last 15 mo	· Percentage of patients with ≥1 test for microalbuminuria during the measurement year or those who had evidence of existing nephropathy, microalbuminuria, or albuminuria
Foot examination	· Denominator is all patients with diabetes age 18–75 y · Measurement interval is the last 15 mo · Excludes patients with bilateral lower-extremity amputation	· Percentage of eligible patients receiving ≥1 complete foot examination (visual inspection, sensory examination with monofilament, and pulse examination)

care[13]. These standards address a broad range of issues in diabetes spanning from prevention to treatment for type 1, type 2, and gestational diabetes mellitus in a variety of settings. Complete ADA guidelines are available at www.diabetes.org/for-health-professionals-and-scientists/cpr.jsp.

American College of Physicians
The American College of Physicians (ACP) conducted systematic reviews[38, 39] of the evidence to develop guidelines on the management of hypertension[40] and lipids[41] in patients with type 2 diabetes, which were published in 2003 and 2004, respectively (Lipids: www.annals .org/cgi/reprint/138/7/587.pdf; and Hypertension: www.annals.org/cgi/ reprint/140/8/644.pdf).

American Association of Clinical Endocrinologists
The most recent guidelines for the management of diabetes mellitus from the American Association of Clinical Endocrinologists (AACE) are contained in the AACE System of Intensive Diabetes Self-Management – 2002 Update[42]. These guidelines include 3 phases. Phase 1 addresses the initial assessment of patients following the diagnosis of diabetes. Phase 2 addresses interim assessments of patients with diabetes. Phase 3 addresses ongoing assessment of the complications of diabetes and strategies for encouraging maintenance of patient enthusiasm for intensive control. The AACE guidelines include specific recommendations regarding

the frequency of follow-up and specific components of physical, psychosocial, and laboratory examinations. The AACE guideline is summarized at www.guideline.gov/summary/ summary.aspx?ss=15&doc_id= 3172&nbr=002398&string=AACE+ AND+guideline.

What tools are available to help clinicians adhere to performance standards?

Patient Registries
A registry is a system for tracking information about a specific group of patients. The Centers for Disease Control and Prevention (CDC) and the Bureau of Primary Health Care have developed several disease-specific electronic registries, including one for patients with diabetes, which are available free of charge. There are hardware, software, and staffing considerations for practices interested in using electronic registries. The CDC has developed a registry assessment tool to enable specific practices to evaluate the resources necessary to implement these registries (www .healthdisparities.net).

Flow Charts
Even practices that do not have the resources to implement electronic patient registries can avail themselves of "low-tech" tools to promote care in accordance with published, evidence-based recommendations. Such care will improve outcomes for patients with type 2 diabetes. In addition, the provision and documentation of such care will increasingly influence

Other Evidence-Based Clinical Guidelines Related to Type 2 Diabetes
Other organizations have developed guidelines relevant to specific elements of the care of patients with type 2 diabetes.

Eye Care
American Academy of Ophthalmology
Available at www.aao.org/ education/library/benchmarks/ loader.cfm?url=/commonspot/ security/getfile.cfm&PageID=13273

American Optometric Association
Available at www.aoa.org/ documents/CPG-3.pdf

Lipid Control
National Cholesterol Education Program—Adult Treatment Panel III
Available at www.nhlbi.nih.gov/ guidelines/cholesterol/index.htm

Hypertension
National Heart, Lung, and Blood Institute
Available at www.nhlbi.nih.gov/ guidelines/hypertension/jncintro .htm

Nephropathy
National Kidney Foundation
Available at www.kidney.org/ professionals/doqi/guidelineindex .cfm

41. Snow V, Weiss KB, Mottur-Pilson C. The evidence base for tight blood pressure control in the management of type 2 diabetes mellitus. Ann Intern Med. 2003;138:587-92. [PMID: 12667031]
42. American Association of Clinical Endocrinologists, American College of endocrinology. Medical guidelines for the management of diabetes mellitus: the AACE system of intensive diabetes elf-management—2002 update. Endo Pract. 2002;8(Suppl 1):40-82.

physician reimbursement over the coming years as pay for performance becomes a reality in the United States.

Reminder systems have been shown to improve the rates at which physicians provide recommended services. While electronic reminder systems can be particularly powerful, many physicians practice in settings in which electronic medical records and other high-technology systems are not yet available. Some evidence from a demonstration project done by the Diabetes Physician Committee of the Medical Society of Delaware suggests that "low-tech" paper flow sheets can also be effective in improving the rates of recommended care among patients with type 2 diabetes[43]. Flow charts can remind physicians and other caregivers about recommended interventions.

In addition, they can help to improve documentation of the provision of recommended care, which is important since many third parties consider the absence of documentation to indicate that a service was not rendered.

Many flow sheets are available, some locally developed and others developed by such organizations as the American Medical Association's Physician Consortium for Performance Improvement. The end of this section provides an example of a flow chart that focuses on the major performance measures discussed above and also provides space for noting current therapy. The ACP welcomes physicians to use or adapt this flow sheet for use in their own practices. A PDF file is available for free download at www.annals.org/intheclinic/.

43. Gill JM, DiPrinzio MJ. The Medical Society of Delaware's Uniform Clinical Guidelines for diabetes: did they have a positive impact on quality of diabetes care? Del Med J. 2004;76:111-22. [PMID: 15061458]

in the clinic
Tool Kit

Type 2 Diabetes

Chart Stickers
Reminder systems are built into many electronic health records but can also be implemented in practices without such systems. The ACP will provide Order Reminder and Check Results chart stickers that physicians and their staff can use to promote compliance with recommendations (www.acponline.org/provate/abimpim/diabetes/practicetools.html).

Diabetes Flow Sheet
To download an electronic copy of the flow sheet that appears at the end of this section for duplication and use in your office, go to www.annals.org/intheclinic/. Foot Examination Chart, Exercise Prescription, Patient Self-Management Check List, Worksheet, and Goal Contract (www.annals.org/intheclinic/)

Patient Education Brochures
ACP Special Reports are patient education brochures about c nditions, including diabetes. Brochures (in packs of 100) are available free to ACP members at www.acponline.org/catalog/campaign/special.htm.

Coming soon...Living with Diabetes is a practical guide for patients with diabetes that the ACP Foundation is developing in collaboration with health literacy experts, physicians, and patients with diabetes. The guide is designed for patients to use in concert with provider-delivered education. It will be available free to ACP members. Check www.foundation.acponline.org in April 2007.

Smoking Cessation Assistance
www.cdc.gov/tobacco/pubs1.htm#quit

Standard Orders Worksheet
Create a customized worksheet of standing orders for patients with diabetes (www.acponline.org/private/abimpim/diabetes/standing orders .html).

Tools To Promote Evidence-Based Immunization
Obtain reminders, wallet cards, vaccine records, posters, and educational flyers (www.acponline.org/aii/tools.htm).

Web Resources for Patients with Type 2 Diabetes
• American Diabetes Association: www.diabetes.org
• State-Based Diabetes Prevention and Control Programs: www.cdc .gov/diabetes/states/indec.htm
• American Association of Diabetes Educators: www.aadenet.org
• National Diabetes Education Program: www.cdc.gov.diabetes/ projects/ndeps.htm
• Take Charge of Your Diabetes: www.cdc.gov/diabetes/pubs/pdf/ tctd.pdf

Type 2 Diabetes Care Flow Sheet

Patient Name: _____ Date of Birth: _____

Date								
DIET AND EXERCISE								
Weight/BMI *frequency: every visit* *target: BMI <24*								
Diet counseling								
Exercise counseling								
Smoking cessation								
AQA MEASURES								
HbA1c *frequency: every 3-4 months* *target: <7%*								
Blood pressure *frequency: every visit* *target: <130/80*								
Lipids tested *frequency: yearly* *target: LDL <100mg/dL (lower is better)*								
COMPLICATIONS MONITORING								
Microalbumin *frequency: yearly*								
Specialist eye exam *frequency: yearly* *(more frequent when problem exisits)*								
Foot exam *frequency: yearly* *(more frequent when problem exisits)*								
DIABETES MEDICATIONS								
_____								
_____								
_____								
_____								
MEDICATIONS TO DECREASE RISK FOR CARDIOVASCULAR COMPLICATIONS								
Aspirin								
ACE or ARB								
β-Blocker								
Statin								
Other								
IMMUNIZATIONS								
Influenza *frequency: every year*								
Pneumonia *frequency: every 6-10 years*								

Smoking Cessation

According to the U.S. Centers for Disease Control and Prevention (1), 21% of American adults (44.5 million people) and 22% of American high school students (3.75 million people) smoke cigarettes. Although per capita tobacco use in the United States has decreased dramatically since the 1950s, it is unlikely that the United States will reach the Healthy People 2010 objectives of reducing smoking prevalence to less than 12% in adults and less than 16% in youth (2). Tobacco use is an even bigger public health threat in many regions outside of the United States. Many people who smoke wish that they could stop, but quitting is difficult and failure is common. Some, of course, do succeed in quitting permanently. In 2004, the CDC estimated that 45.6 million American adults were former smokers, representing half of all people who had ever smoked. Physicians play a critical role in reducing the burden of tobacco-related health problems by helping their patients who smoke to quit and by motivating their nonsmoking patients to remain nonsmokers. Unfortunately, many physicians report inadequate training in smoking cessation, and many smokers who see physicians do not receive assistance to quit.

Health Consequences of Smoking

Which health problems have definite links to tobacco use?
Smoking increases the risks of numerous diseases and associated illness and death. In general, smokers have a mortality rate approximately twice that of nonsmokers (3–5). Good evidence links smoking to cancer, cardiopulmonary disease, and complications of pregnancy. The risk for smoking-related disease increases with the amount a person smokes.

In a cohort study of 34 439 British male physicians, it was found after 40 years of follow-up that smokers had a mortality rate twice that of nonsmokers (40% vs. 20%), 13 times the risk for chronic obstructive lung disease, 15 times the risk for lung cancer, and 1.6 times the risk for ischemic heart disease (3).

In a study that followed 24 505 women and 25 034 men born between 1925 and 1941, 9% of female and 14% of male never smokers and 26% of female and 41% of male heavy smokers died in middle age. Smoking cessation decreased the risk of death during middle age (5).

Tobacco use accounts for 25% to 30% of all cases of cancer and approximately 170 000 cancer deaths every year in the United States. The types of cancer associated with tobacco use include those that affect the lung, mouth and pharynx, esophagus, stomach, pancreas, bladder, kidney, cervix, and possibly the colon in addition to acute myelogenous leukemia.

In particular, tobacco smoking has been linked to 90% of cases of lung cancer in males and 78% in females (6).

Smoking is the most important risk factor for chronic obstructive pulmonary disease (COPD). Only 5% to 10% of patients with COPD have never smoked. An estimated 12.5% of current smokers and 9.4% of former smokers have COPD (2), and an estimated 20% of regular cigarette smokers develop progressive COPD. Smokers are at least 4 times more likely to develop acute lung injury and the acute respiratory distress syndrome than people who do not smoke.

Smoking is a major cause of coronary artery disease, cerebrovascular disease, peripheral vascular disease, and abdominal artic aneurysm (AAA). An estimated 20% of all deaths from heart disease are attributable to cigarette smoking.

A case–control study of myocardial infarction that involved 27 809 participants in 52 countries found that current smokers were at substantially higher risk for nonfatal myocardial infarction than never-smokers (odds ratio [OR], 2.95 [95% CI, 2.77 to 3.14] (7).

Among 73 451 U.S. veterans aged 50 to 79 years without a history of AAA who were screened with ultrasound, smoking was strongly associated with an AAA (OR, 5.57 [CI, 4.24 to 7.31]) (8).

1. Cigarette Smoking Among Adults—United States, 2004. CDC. MMWR, November 11, 2005/54(44);1121-1124.
2. NIH State-of-the-Science Panel. National Institutes of Health State-of-the-Science Conference Statement: Tobacco Use: Prevention, Cessation, and Control. 2006. Ann Intern Med. 145:pages pending.
3. Doll R, Peto R, Wheatley K, et al. Mortality in relation to smoking: 40 years' observations on male British doctors. BMJ. 1994;309:901-11. [PMID: 7755693]
4. LaCroix AZ, Lang J, Scherr P, et al. Smoking and mortality among older men and women in three communities. N Engl J Med. 1991;324:1619-25. [PMID: 2030718]
5. Vollset SE, Tverdal A, Gjessing HK. Smoking and deaths between 40 and 70 years of age in women and men. Ann Intern Med. 2006;144:381-9. [PMID: 16549850]
6. Surgeon General. The Health Consequences of Smoking: Surgeon General's 2004 Report. Department of Health and Human Services (DHSS), Public Health Service (PHS), Center for Disease Control (CDC), Centre for Chronic Disease Prevention and Health Promotion, Office of Smoking and Health, DHSS Publication No. (CDC) 099-7830, 2004.
7. Teo KK, Ounpuu S, Hawken S, et al. Tobacco use and risk of myocardial infarction in 52 countries in the INTERHEART study: a case-control study. Lancet. 2006;368:647-58. [PMID: 16920470]

In a prospective analysis of 2174 patients over age 40, current smoking was highly correlated with an increased risk for peripheral arterial disease (OR, 4.5 [CI, 2.3 to 8.8]) after adjustment for confounding factors (9).

Babies born to women who smoke are more likely to have low birthweight and to be premature. Smoke exposure may increase the risk for miscarriage. Women, particularly those older than 35 years of age, who smoke and use birth control pills face an increased risk for heart attack, stroke, and venous thromboembolism.

Other conditions that affect smokers include cataract, chronic cough, respiratory infections, damage to skin, poor oral health, low bone density, gastroesophageal reflux, and fire-related injury or death (6).

Which health problems are associated with second-hand smoke exposure?

Second-hand smoke, also known as environmental tobacco smoke, presents a substantial health risk to nonsmokers. The National Cancer Institute considers any amount of exposure to second-hand smoke potentially unsafe, but nonsmokers who live or work with smokers in homes or workplaces where smoking is allowed are at the greatest risk.

Exposure to second-hand smoke is clearly linked to an increase in certain types of cancer among nonsmokers. Approximately 3000 lung cancer

deaths per year among adult nonsmokers in the United States are linked to second-hand smoke (10). Research also suggests associations between environmental tobacco exposure and cancer of the nasal sinus, cervix, breast, and bladder.

Those exposed to second-hand smoke are at increased risk for cardiopulmonary problems, including decreased lung function, chronic cough, and ischemic heart disease. Research has indicated that as many as 60 000 annual heart disease deaths in adult nonsmokers result from second-hand smoke (11).

Exposed children are more likely to have severe lower respiratory tract infections, severe asthma, and middle ear infections (12). In addition, the risk for sudden infant death syndrome is higher among babies exposed to smoke, and babies born to women exposed to second-hand smoke are more likely to have low birthweight and to be premature.

Health Consequences of Smoking... All people who smoke are at increased risk for several types of cancer (lung esophageal, oral, bladder, cervical, pancreatic, and possibly others), coronary artery disease, peripheral vascular disease, aortic aneurysm, stroke, chronic lung disease, poor pregnancy outcomes, and premature death. Environmental tobacco puts exposed nonsmokers at risk for many of these same health problems and contributes to childhood morbidity and mortality from infections and respiratory illness. Smokers and those that live with them are at risk for fire-realted injury and death.

CLINICAL BOTTOM LINE

What are the health benefits that smokers who quit can anticipate?

Smoking cessation provides meaningful health benefits, and people who quit smoking live longer on average than people who continue to smoke. Some benefits begin shortly after cessation (Figure 1). Smokers who quit decrease their risk for lung cancer and other types of cancer, heart attack, stroke, and chronic lung disease. The U.S. Surgeon General reports that people who quit smoking before age 50 have half the risk for dying within the

next 15 years compared with those who continue to smoke (6).

After 10 years of smoking cessation, the risk for lung cancer in former smokers was 30% to 50% less than that of current smokers. Individuals who quit smoking for 5 years have half the risk for cancer of the oral cavity and esophagus compared with continuing smokers. Smoking cessation also results in a 50% reduction in bladder cancer. Former smokers have a reduced risk for cervical cancer within a few years of smoking cessation and a

Prevention of Smoking-Related Disease

8. Lederle FA, Johnson GR, Wilson SE, et al. Prevalence and associations of abdominal aortic aneurysm detected through screening. Aneurysm Detection and Management (ADAM) Veterans Affairs Cooperative Study Group. Ann Intern Med. 1997;126:441-9. [PMID: 9072929]
9. Selvin E, Erlinger TP. Prevalence of and risk factors for peripheral arterial disease in the United States: results from the National Health and Nutrition Examination Survey, 1999-2000. Circulation. 2004;110:738-43. [PMID: 15262830]
10. National Cancer Institute. Cancer Progress Report. 2003. Public Health Service, National Institutes of Health, US Department of health and Human Services, 2004.
11. California Environmental Protection Agency. Health effects of Exposure to Environmental Tobacco Smoke, June 2005.
12. National Cancer Institute. Smoking and Tobacco Control Monograph 10: Health Effects of Exposure to Environmental Tobacco Smoke. Bethesda, MD: National Cancer Institute, 1999.

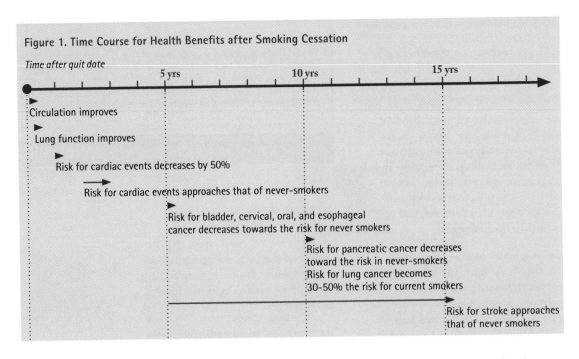

Figure 1. Time Course for Health Benefits after Smoking Cessation

Time after quit date

5 yrs — 10 yrs — 15 yrs

Circulation improves

Lung function improves

Risk for cardiac events decreases by 50%

Risk for cardiac events approaches that of never-smokers

Risk for bladder, cervical, oral, and esophageal cancer decreases towards the risk for never smokers

Risk for pancreatic cancer decreases toward the risk in never-smokers
Risk for lung cancer becomes 30–50% the risk for current smokers

Risk for stroke approaches that of never smokers

13. Negri E, La Vecchia C, D'Avanzo B, et al. Acute myocardial infarction: association with time since stopping smoking in Italy. GISSI-EFRIM Investigators. Gruppo Italiano per lo Studio della Sopravvivenza nell'Infarto. Epidemiologia dei Fattori di Rischio dell'Infarto Miocardico. J Epidemiol Community Health. 1994;48:129-33. [PMID: 8189165]

14. Dobson AJ, Alexander HM, Heller RF, et al. How soon after quitting smoking does risk of heart attack decline? J Clin Epidemiol. 1991;44:1247-53. [PMID: 1941018]

reduced risk for pancreatic cancer after 10 years of smoking cessation.

Observational studies suggest that there is a 50% reduction in cardiac events in the first year following smoking cessation and that the level of risk approaches that of persons who have never smoked after 2 to 3 years (13, 14). Circulation improves within just a few weeks of quitting. Within 5 to 15 years, stroke risk is reduced to that of a nonsmoker.

The chronic cough associated with smoking resolves or markedly decreases in 94% to 100% of patients when they quit, and in about half of these patients, cough resolution occurs within a few weeks. Lung function improves within 3 months, and shortness of breath improves within 1 to 9 months as lung function returns to normal.

Smoking cessation during the first 3 to 4 months of pregnancy reduces the risk for having a low-birthweight baby to that of women who never smoked.

Other benefits from smoking cessation include elimination of the damaging effects of tobacco on skin, breath, teeth, and gums. Cessation improves the sense of smell and taste. Everyday activities like climbing stairs or walking are less tiring. Smoking cessation eliminates the expense of cigarettes, as well as the higher costs of health and life insurance charged to smokers.

Which patients have the greatest potential to benefit from smoking cessation?

Patients with established coronary artery disease, COPD, and pregnant women and their babies are at the highest risk from smoking and thus benefit the most from quitting. Children also benefit significantly when smokers who they are living with quit.

Why is it difficult for smokers to quit?

Quitting smoking is hard for many reasons, but mostly because nicotine is highly addictive. It produces a mood-elevating physiologic response. Nicotine withdrawal symptoms include mild depression, anxiety, headaches, nausea, shakes, cough, hunger, fatigue, and insomnia. Typically, symptoms are most intense in the first 72 hours after quitting and last from 2 to 8 weeks. The craving for nicotine can last much longer.

Quitting smoking also requires behavior change. The habit of smoking is comforting to many smokers, and the act of reaching for, lighting, and smoking a cigarette becomes a routine part of life. Certain environments or social situations may cause relapse in people who quit smoking.

Is there an age after which smoking cessation fails to yield benefit?
Smoking cessation benefits people of all ages, regardless of the length of their smoking history.

Evidence for the benefits of smoking cessation in the elderly comes from a large study (4) involving men and women age 65 years or older. The study found that individuals who continued to smoke had significantly higher rates of mortality as well as cardiovascular and neoplastic disease than former smokers or nonsmokers after 5 years follow-up.

In a large, population-based study of Norwegian smokers 40 to 70 years of age (5), the mortality benefits of quitting were greatest for those who quit earliest, but benefits were clearly present for those who quit at age 60, the oldest age at which this study reported the effects of quitting.

How should clinicians screen for tobacco use and when should they provide tobacco cessation counseling?
Clinicians should ask all patients if they smoke, regardless of age, sex, or medical history. Since most adults who have ever smoked daily became daily users at or before age 18 years, the opportunities for primary smoking prevention are less for clinicians who care for adults than for those who care for children. However, all clinicians should send a clear message to patients that any amount of smoking is unhealthy and the best prevention is never to start.

Treatment

Can smokers quit without any intervention?
Some smokers do successfully stop smoking without any health care provider intervention, but intervention improves the success rate. Evidence documents that an intervention as simple as a single message from a physician to quit increases quit rates.

In a systematic review examining smoking cessation therapies with at least 6 months of follow-up (15), 17 randomized clinical trials included one episode of advice and encouragement from a physician. The summary absolute reduction in the rate of smoking was 2% (CI, 1 to 3). Ten trials of frequent encouragement found a reduction of 5% (CI, 1 to 8).

Another review of randomized, controlled trials examining smoking cessation advice from a medical practitioner found that brief advice increased smoking cessation rates (16). The OR for cessation was 1.69 (CI, 1.45 to 1.98) in favor of brief advice.

More intensive interventions can improve the smoking cessation success rates. Both behavioral therapy and pharmacotherapy can provide effective assistance, and the likelihood of

successful smoking cessation is increased when they are combined.

What behavioral interventions are effective in smoking cessation?
At every clinic visit, physicians should ask their patients about smoking, advise all smoking patients to quit, assess the smoking patients' willingness to change, assist them in their attempts to quit, and arrange follow-up to reassess willingness of patients unwilling to quit or to evaluate and support those who attempt to quit (Table 1) (17).

Behavioral interventions can range from briefly asking patients about smoking habits to multiple counseling sessions. Individual therapy, group therapy, and self-help therapy have all been found to help people stop smoking (Table 2). There is no apparent advantage of group therapy over individual therapy, nonspecific behavior modification over brief advice, or gradual cessation over abrupt cessation (16). While even brief interventions can work, high-intensity counseling (more than 10 minutes) is more

15. Law M, Tang JL. An analysis of the effectiveness of interventions intended to help people stop smoking. Arch Intern Med. 1995;155:1933-41. [PMID: 7575046]
16. Silagy C, Stead LF. Physician advice for smoking cessation. Cochrane Database Syst Rev. 2001;CD000165. [PMID: 11405953]
17. Clinical Practice Guideline. Treating Tobacco Use and Dependence. U.S. Department of Health and Human Services. Public Health Service. June 2000.

Table 1. U.S. Public Health Service Clinical Practice Guideline: 5-Step Brief Intervention for Smoking Cessation

5-As: For Patients Willing to Quit

Ask about tobacco use
Advise to quit
Assess willingness to make a quit attempt
Assist in quit attempt
Arrange follow-up

5-Rs: To Motivate Patients Unwilling to Quit

Encourage patient to think of **Relevance** of quitting smoking to their lives
Assist patient in identifying the **Risks** of smoking
Assist the patient in identifying **Rewards** of smoking cessation
Discuss with patient **Roadblocks** or barriers to attempting cessation
Repeat the motivational intervention at all visits

likely to succeed than low-intensity counseling (3 to 10 minutes), according to the Public Health Service (17). Additionally, programs with 8 or more sessions have provided greater benefit than those with 3 or fewer sessions.

Self-Help Therapy
Some patients may benefit from self-help therapy, but the magnitude of the benefit is likely to be small. Evidence suggests that standard self-help material provides no additional benefit when used with other interventions like clinician advice or nicotine replacement therapy (18). The Public Health Service guideline does not advocate the use of self-help interventions alone (17). There does not appear to be an advantage of group therapy over individual therapy, nonspecific behavior modification over brief advice, or gradual cessation over abrupt cessation.

Individual Therapy
Evidence suggests that individualized counseling by health care providers improves quit rates. One review found insufficient evidence to suggest that more intensive counseling was better than brief counseling (16), but the Public Health Service guideline states that "There is a strong dose-response relation between the intensity of tobacco dependence counseling and its effectiveness." In their review of the evidence they found an OR of 1.6 (CI, 1.2 to 2.0) for cessation with low-intensity counseling (i.e., 3 to 10 minutes) and an OR of 2.3 (CI, 2.0 to 2.7) with high-intensity

counseling (i.e., greater than 10 minutes). It was also determined that 8 or more sessions were more beneficial than programs with 3 or fewer sessions (17).

Some clinicians have reasoned that hospitalized individuals who smoke might be more responsive to smoking cessation interventions, but brief hospital smoking cessation programs have shown mixed results. Only intensive interventions consisting of inpatient contact plus follow-up for at least 1 month were associated with a higher quit rate than routine care (19). A brief intervention during hospital admission for smokers after myocardial infarction or bypass surgery, for instance, found no significant difference in abstinence at 6 weeks and 12 months (20).

Telephone Therapy
Consistent support and reminders to stay on track can be particularly helpful for people trying to quit. Individual telephone counseling is a popular way of administering such support and reinforcement. Research indicates that both proactive (initiated by patients) and reactive (arranged by clinicians) telephone counseling helps smokers interested in quitting (21). Quit rates are highest for those who receive more intensive therapy in the form of multiple sessions of call-back counseling.

A study of the effectiveness of the California Smokers Helpline (22) that randomized smokers to 7 telephone counseling sessions or to telephone counseling on an as-requested basis found a 2.2 increase in cessation in the intervention group at 1 year (P < 0.001).

A study of 837 smokers at Veterans Affairs medical centers (36) showed that telephone care, which combined phone counseling with provision of drug therapy, tripled long-term quit rates when compared with brief primary care intervention alone (13.0% vs. 4.1%; P < 0.001) (23).

Group Therapy
Group therapy provides smokers with mutual support as well as behavioral techniques for smoking cessation. Studies have found that group therapy

18. Lancaster T, Stead LF. Self-help interventions for smoking cessation. Cochrane Database Syst Rev. 2002;CD001118. [PMID: 16034855]
19. Rigotti NA, Munafo MR, Murphy MF, et al. Interventions for smoking cessation in hospitalised patients. Cochrane Database Syst Rev. 2003;CD001837. [PMID: 12535418]
20. Hajek P, Taylor TZ, Mills P. Brief intervention during hospital admission to help patients to give up smoking after myocardial infarction and bypass surgery: randomised controlled trial. BMJ. 2002;324:87-9. [PMID: 11786452]
21. Stead LF, Lancaster T, Perera R. Telephone counselling for smoking cessation. Cochrane Database Syst Rev. 2003;CD002850. [PMID: 12535442]

is more effective than self-help and about as effective as similar intensity individual therapy (24). Adding group therapy to other forms of treatment like nicotine replacement may provide additional benefit. Counseling that focuses on increasing cognitive and behavioral skills and on avoiding relapse appears to be most effective.

Exercise and Other Nondrug Therapies
Alternative behavioral interventions marketed for smoking cessation include exercise therapy, acupuncture, aversive smoking, and hypnosis. Systematic reviews have concluded that there is insufficient evidence to support their use. However, the Public Health Service acknowledges that some individuals might benefit from these techniques (18).

Which pharmacologic therapies are effective in smoking cessation?
Nicotine replacement therapies and bupropion are the most commonly used, effective forms of pharmacotherapy for smoking cessation. While smokers often use them alone for smoking cessation, combining pharmacotherapy with behavioral therapy increases success rates. Varenicline is a new drug for smoking cessation that received U.S. Food and Drug Administration approval in May 2006. Other pharmacologic therapies have limited evidence for benefit.

Nicotine Replacement
Nicotine replacement works by alleviating the symptoms of withdrawal. This therapy is available over-the-counter in gum, patch, and lozenge forms and by prescription in inhaler, nasal spray, and sublingual tablet forms. All forms increase the quit rate by about 1.5- to 2-fold at 6 months among motivated persons. This is equivalent to a smoking cessation rate of 17% among those using nicotine replacement compared with 10% among control groups (25). Nicotine therapy should not be used by people who continue to smoke. People planning to use nicotine medication should start using it on the day that they quit.

Given the lack of evidence that one form of nicotine replacement is more effective or safer than another, clinicians and patients should choose nicotine replacement therapy according to individual preferences, tolerability of the product, and financial cost (Table 3). When patients are paying out-of-pocket, the patch and gum are the least expensive nicotine replacement options and the nasal inhaler is the most expensive, costing as much as $15 per day. Side effects may be associated with the dose of nicotine, the duration of treatment, or the type of nicotine replacement used. For

Smoking cessation typically spans the following stages of change:

Precontemplative ("I don't want to quit")

Contemplative ("I am concerned but not ready to quit now")

Preparation ("I am ready to quit")

Action ("I just quit")

Maintenance ("I quit 6 months ago")

Table 2. Behavioral Interventions for Smoking Cessation

Self-help	Materials that smokers can access to learn about strategies to quit *Example:* *Good Information For Smokers: You Can Quit Smoking.* Consumer booklet, May 2003. U.S. Public Health Service. www.surgeongeneral.gov/tobacco/lowlit.htm
Individual therapy	Interventions that involve advice and encouragement that a provider (e.g., physician, nurse, psychologist, health educator) delivers to an individual smoker *Example:* Physician advice during an office visit, referal to a one-on-one visit with a nurse who delivers smoking cessation advice and follow-up
Group therapy	Interventions that involve advice and encouragement that a provider (e.g., physician, nurse, psychologist, health educator) delivers to a group of smokers *Example:* Employer or health plan–based classes on smoking cessation
Telephone therapy	Interventions that involve advice and encouragement delivered to an individual smoker during telephone calls *Example:* National smoking cessation hotline (1-800 QUIT NOW)

22. Zhu SH, Anderson CM, Tedeschi GJ, et al. Evidence of real-world effectiveness of a telephone quitline for smokers. N Engl J Med. 2002;347:1087-93. [PMID: 12362011]
23. An LC, Zhu SH, Nelson DB, et al. Benefits of telephone care over primary care for smoking cessation: a randomized trial. Arch Intern Med. 2006;166:536-42. [PMID: 16534040]
24. Stead LF, Lancaster T. Group behaviour therapy programmes for smoking cessation. Cochrane Database Syst Rev. 2002;CD001007. [PMID: 12137615]
25. Silagy C, Lancaster T, Stead L, et al. Nicotine replacement therapy for smoking cessation. Cochrane Database Syst Rev. 2002;CD000146. [PMID: 15266423]

Table 3. Commonly Used Pharmacologic Therapies for Smoking Cessation

Agent	Mechanism	Effectiveness	Initial prescription	Advantages	Disadvantages
Nicotine replacement* gum	Prevents nicotine withdrawal	Increases cessation rates about 1.5–2 times control at 6 months	1 piece (2 mg) whenever urge to smoke up to 30 pieces/day, continuous use for >3 months not recommended	• Less expensive than other forms of nicotine replacement • Chewing replaces smoking habit • No prescription required	• Some patients find taste unpleasant
Nicotine 24-hour patch†*	Prevents nicotine withdrawal	Increases cessation rates about 1.5–2 times control at 6 months	21-mg patch/day once daily for 4–8 weeks (remove and replace every 24 hours). Then 14-mg patch/day for 2–4 weeks followed by 7 mg patch/day for 2–4 weeks. *(Adults weighing less than 100 pounds, smoking fewer than 10 cigarettes/day and/or with cardiovascular disease: 14 mg patch/day for 4–8 weeks. Then 7-mg patch/day for 2–4 weeks.)*	• Less expensive than other forms of nicotine replacement • No prescription required	• Can cause skin irritation
Nicotine spray*	Prevents nicotine withdrawal	Increases cessation rates about 1.5–2 times control at 6 months	1 spray (0.5 mg nicotine) into each nostril 1–2 times each hour as needed whenever the patient feels the need to smoke up to a maximum of 5 doses (total of 10 sprays)/hour or 40 doses (total of 80 sprays)/day. Initially, encourage use of at least 8 doses (16 sprays/day), the minimum effective dose. Recommended duration is 3 months.	• Some patients prefer this delivery method	• More expensive than other forms of nicotine replacement • Prescription required • Safety not established for use longer than 6 months.
Nicotine inhaler*	Prevents nicotine withdrawal	Increases cessation rates about 1.5–2 times control at 6 months	24 to 64 mg (6 to 16 cartridges) per day for up to 12 weeks followed by a gradual reduction in dosage over a period of up to 12 weeks	• Some patients prefer this delivery method	• More expensive than other forms of nicotine replacement • Prescription required • Use for more than 6 months not recommended
Nicotine lozenges*	Prevents nicotine withdrawal	Increases cessation rates about 1.5–2 times control at 6 months	1 lozenge every 1–2 hours for 6 weeks, then 1 lozenge every 2–4 hours in weeks 7–9 and finally, 1 lozenge every 4–8 hours in weeks 10–12. Recommended duration of therapy is 12 weeks. *(Patients who smoke within 30 minutes of waking require 4 mg and those who have first cigarette later in the day require 2 mg lozenge.)*	• Some patients prefer this delivery method	• Some patients find taste unpleasant • Nausea, dyspepsia, mouth tingling can occur • Avoid acidic beverages (juice, soda) 15 minutes before use
Bupropion	Unclear	Increases cessation rates about 2 times control at 1 year	Begin 1–2 weeks before quit date 150 mg every day for 3 days then 150 mg twice daily through end of therapy (max 7–12 weeks)	• Some antidepressant activity, may be a good option for patients with history of depression	• Requires prescription • Avoid if seizure disorder or in patients at risk for seizure, eating disorders • Can interact with other drugs • Safety in pregnancy unclear • Associated with hypertension
Varenicline	Reduces cravings via nicotine receptor agonist	Increases cessation rates over 3.5 times control and almost 2 times bupropion at 12 weeks.	Begin 0.5 mg once daily on days 1–3, then 0.5 mg twice daily on days 4–7, then 1 mg twice daily through end of therapy (12 weeks, consider additional 12 weeks to prevent relapse)	• No hepatic clearance • No clinically significant drug interactions have been reported	• Requires prescription • Side effects include drowsiness, fatigue, nausea, sleep disturbance, constipation, flatulence • Safety in pregnancy unclear • Avoid in renal disease (adjust dose if creatine clearance ≤50 mL/min)

* Avoid nicotine replacement in patients with recent myocardial infarction, arrhythmia, and unstable angina. Safety of nicotine replacement in pregnancy unclear.
† Several formulations of patches are available. Dosing guidelines are for patches designed to stay in place for 24 hours and that come in doses of 21 mg, 14 mg, and 7 mg. Clinicians should check prescribing information on nicotine patches that come in other doses or that are designed for application for fewer than 24 hours/day.

instance, the patch can cause skin irritation while the gum and nasal spray can cause throat irritation.

Studies have found no significant difference between nicotine replacement therapy lasting 8 weeks or longer, or between abrupt withdrawal or gradual tapering. While no clear evidence has been found for high-dose nicotine replacement therapy (>22 mg/24 hours), it may be useful for selective smokers. Conversely, low-dependence smokers may be comfortable taking a lower-than-average starting dose.

Combination nicotine replacement therapy may be superior to monotherapy; however, research results are not clear on this issue. One trial that investigated the effects of combination therapy with the nicotine patch and nasal spray showed that this treatment regimen was more that twice as effective than the nicotine patch alone for smoking cessation at 1 year (27% vs. 11%; P = 0.001), and the trend persisted at 6 years (16% vs. 8%; P = 0.08) (26).

Bupropion

Bupropion, the first nonnicotine medication to be approved for smoking cessation, is known to inhibit serotonin, norepinephrine, and dopamine, but its mechanism of reducing cravings and enhancing smoking abstinence is unknown. Definitive head-to-head comparisons of bupropion to nicotine replacement are unavailable, but one study showed that bupropion use resulted in a 30% 1-year quit rate, about double that of nicotine replacement therapy (27).

Bupropion therapy, using the sustained-release formulation, usually begins 1 to 2 weeks before the quit date and continues for 8 to 12 weeks. Dosage for the first 3 days is 150 mg once daily followed by 150 mg twice daily for the duration of therapy. The optimal duration of bupropion therapy has not been fully assessed. The medication has been safely used for long periods in the treatment of depression. Side effects of use include insomnia and dry mouth. Bupropion can be used in combination with nicotine replacement for patients who do not quit with monotherapy, but definitive evidence about combination therapy is lacking.

Varenicline

Varenicline is a nonnicotine drug designed specifically for smoking cessation. It binds to a nicotine receptor associated with the relaxing effects felt with smoking, providing a less relaxing effect. It reduces the cravings felt by smokers who quit.

A recent randomized trial compared 12 weeks of treatment with varenicline, sustained-release bupropion, or placebo in 1025 smokers. During weeks 9 to 52, continuous abstinence rates were 21.9% for varenicline, 16.1% for bupropion, and 8.4% for placebo. Nausea was reported by 28.1% of patients on varenicline (28).

Another recent trial randomized 1236 smokers who achieved abstinence for at least 7 days after 12 weeks of open-label varenicline to either an additional 12 weeks of varenicline or placebo. The varenicline group had higher continuous abstinence rates than the placebo group at 13 to 24 weeks (70.5% vs. 49.6%) and 13 to 52 weeks (43.6% vs. 36.9%) (29).

Other Pharmacologic Therapies

Other therapies that have not been approved by the FDA for smoking cessation are sometimes used. Methods for which there is limited evidence for effectiveness include clonidine or nortriptyline or naltrexone to block nicotine withdrawal symptoms, alprazolam to treat withdrawal-related anxiety, silver acetate to give cigarettes a bad taste, mecamylamine to antagonize nicotine effects, and lobeline (an alkaloid derived from the leaves of an Indian tobacco plant). Clonidine and nortriptyline are recommended second-line therapies for treating nicotine-withdrawal symptoms, and naltrexone is under consideration. These alternate therapies may be used when first-line medications are contraindicated or ineffective. The antihypertertensive drug clonidine has the strongest evidence of benefit, but it has undesirable side effects like dry mouth, drowsiness, and dizziness.

26. Blondal T, Gudmundsson LJ, Olafsdottir I, et al. Nicotine nasal spray with nicotine patch for smoking cessation: randomised trial with six year follow up. BMJ. 1999;318:285-8. [PMID: 9924052]

27. Jorenby DE, Leishow SI, Nides MA, et al. A controlled trial of sustained release bupropion, a nicotine patch, or both for smoking cessation. N Engl J Med. 1999; 340:685-91. [PMID: 10053177]

28. Gonzales D, Rennard SI, Nides M, et al. Varenicline, an 4ß2 nicotinic acetylcholine receptor partial agonist, vs sustained-release bupropion and placebo for smoking cessation: a randomized controlled trial. JAMA. 2006;296:47-55. [PMID: 16820546]

29. Tonstad S, Tønnesen P, Hajek P, et al. Effect of maintenance therapy with varenicline on smoking cessation: a randomized controlled trial. JAMA. 2006;296:64-71. [PMID: 16820548]

30. Joseph AM, Norman SM, Ferry LH, et al. The safety of transdermal nicotine as an aid to smoking cessation in patients with cardiac disease. N Engl J Med. 1996;335:1792-8. [PMID: 8943160]
31. Greenland S, Satterfield MH, Lanes SF. A meta-analysis to assess the incidence of adverse effects associated with the transdermal nicotine patch. Drug Saf. 1998;18:297-308. [PMID: 9565740]

When should clinicians consider pharmacologic interventions for smoking cessation and how should they select from among the available therapies?

For patients ready to quit, support, behavioral therapy, and pharmacotherapy should be offered, since these interventions together provide the most benefit. Because of a lack of evidence to rank nicotine replacement, bupropion, and varenicline, the choice of a specific first-line pharmacotherapy should be guided by factors like clinician familiarity with the medications; contraindications for selected patients; previous patient experience with a specific pharmacotherapy; and patient characteristics, including concerns about weight gain or a history of depression (Table 3).

Are there conditions that contraindicate or caution against pharmacologic therapy for smoking cessation?

Nicotine Replacement
People using nicotine replacement therapy should not continue to smoke. Nicotine use is contraindicated in patients with a history of recent myocardial infarction, severe angina, and life-threatening arrhythmias. In these patients, the use of nicotine replacement therapy requires consideration of the potential adverse effects of the drug versus the risks associated with continued smoking. Nicotine replacement appears to be safe in persons with stable coronary disease, despite some theoretical concerns. Two randomized trials of nicotine replacement therapy in patients with stable ischemic heart disease found no increase in adverse cardiac events (30). A meta-analysis examining the incidence of adverse effects in individuals using the nicotine patch found no excess of cardiovascular outcomes in participants treated with the patch (31). At this time, the balance of risk and benefit from nicotine replacement therapy in pregnancy is unclear. Nicotine may be safer than smoking for pregnant women, but pregnant patients should use it only after failure of behavioral programs.

Bupropion
Bupropion is contraindicated in persons with a recent history of seizures, eating disorders, or other conditions that lower the seizure threshold. The seizure rate with bupropion is about 1 per 1000 persons treated. Drug interactions with antipsychotics and monoamine oxidase (MAO) inhibitors have been reported. Patients who are currently using or have used an MAO inhibitor or a drug with MAO inhibitor-like activity (e.g., furazolidone, linezolid, procarbazine, or selegiline) within the past 14 days should not receive bupropion. Similarly, other drugs that can lower the seizure threshold should be used with great caution or avoided in patients taking bupropion. Drugs that may lower the seizure threshold include some antidepressants, antipsychotics, cocaine, psychostimulants, sodium phosphate monobasic monohydrate, sodium phosphate dibasic anhydrous, theophylline, tramadol, and systemic corticosteroids. Blood pressure should be monitored in patients using bupropion as it has been associated with hypertension requiring treatment. Two forms of bupropion should not be administered together. Bupropion is a category B drug for pregnancy and should be considered only if behavioral interventions are unsuccessful.

Varenicline
Clinicians should use varenicline cautiously in patients with renal impairment. Dosage adjustments are necessary in patients with creatinine clearance ≤50 mL/min. The most common (>5%, and twice the rate seen in placebo) adverse reactions to varenicline were nausea/vomiting, sleep disturbance (insomnia, abnormal dreams, sleep disorder, nightmares), constipation, and flatulence. There are no adequate, well-controlled studies of varenicline in pregnant women (FDA pregnancy category C). Therefore, pregnant women should use varenicline only if the potential benefits outweigh the potential risk to the fetus. It is not known whether

varenicline is excreted in human milk, but it is excreted in animal milk.

How long should patients receive pharmacologic therapy for smoking cessation before declaring it ineffective?

Nicotine replacement therapy is typically prescribed for 12 to 16 weeks, but repeat courses may be necessary after failed quit attempts. The safety and effectiveness of long-term use is not known, although some people who quit smoking continue to use nicotine replacement for long periods to prevent relapse. Many clinicians encourage patients to use nicotine replacement for as long as needed to prevent relapse.

The optimal duration of bupropion or varenicline therapy has not been fully assessed. Bupropion is typically prescribed for 8 to 12 weeks. It is safely used for long periods in treatment of depression, and the FDA has approved its use for long-term maintenance. Current dosing recommendations for varenicline state to use it for 12 weeks with consideration of an additional 12 weeks to prevent relapse.

What strategies are effective for preventing relapse after quitting smoking?

Relapse is common, even among patients who succeed in quitting for extended periods. For instance, a follow-up study examined rates of smoking 8 years after enrollment in an RCT of the nicotine patch. The study found that 46% (CI, 38% to 54%) of those who had quit had relapsed, and relapse rates were similar in both treatment and control groups (32). Evidence about specific relapse prevention interventions to help smokers maintain abstinence as part of a smoking cessation program is lacking (33). The evidence to date, however, does not support skills training or other specific interventions to help individuals who have successfully quit smoking to avoid relapse. Clinicians and patients should not give up after failed quit attempts or relapse, as many patients require several attempts before achieving durable abstinence.

Should clinicians recommend that smokers switch to smokeless tobacco products if they are unable to cease tobacco use?

Chewing tobacco is the form of smokeless tobacco most widely available in the United States, but tobacco companies are developing new products, such as sachets and lozenges, that may appeal to groups, such as women, that currently have low rates of smokeless tobacco use. Smokeless tobacco products deliver the nicotine that smokers crave, but without exposing the lungs to the other harmful ingredients in cigarettes. As a result, some people perceive them as safer than cigarettes. However, smokeless tobacco products vary widely in the amount of nicotine, carcinogens, and other toxins that they contain and have clear associations with cancer of the oral cavity and pharynx, dental and periodontal disease, pregnancy-related health problems, and nicotine addiction. A recent National Health Institute State of the Science Conference concluded that high-quality studies comparing smokeless tobacco with proven pharmacologic and behavioral smoking cessation interventions are needed to help inform public health strategy about smokeless tobacco (2).

Are there adverse effects of smoking cessation, such as weight gain, that clinicians should prepare patients for?

Patients who stop smoking may gain weight and have depressive symptoms. However, the potential for these events should not discourage the initiation of smoking cessation interventions, but physicians should monitor for both.

Weight Gain

Weight gain is common among smokers who quit. Although the amount of weight gained is not usually more than a few pounds and it poses less of a health risk than continued smoking, it can trigger resumption

Varenicline dosage adjustments are necessary in patients with creatinine clearance ≤ 50 mL/min.

32. Yudkin P, Hey K, Roberts S, et al. Abstinence from smoking eight years after participation in randomised controlled trial of nicotine patch. BMJ. 2003;327:28-9. [PMID: 12842953]
33. Lancaster T, Hajek P, Stead LF, et al. Prevention of relapse after quitting smoking: a systematic review of trials. Arch Intern Med. 2006;166:828-35. [PMID: 16636207]

of smoking and many smokers use weight gain as an excuse not to quit.

One large study (34) found that adults who quit smoking were significantly heavier than patients who smoked. Men who were former smokers were on average 4.4 kg heavier than men who continued smoking. Women who were former smokers were on average 5.0 kg heavier than women who continued smoking.

Nicotine gum and bupropion have been shown to delay, but not prevent, the weight gain associated with smoking cessation. Recent research suggests that the antiopioid drug naltrexone may be an effective alternate therapy for smoking cessation, particularly for patients concerned about gaining weight. However, further evidence is needed to identify naltrexone's place among other therapies for smoking cessation.

Smokers who took 25-mg naltrexone daily with nicotine replacement therapy for 6 weeks gained 1.5 pounds compared with

4.2 pounds for the group that did not take the drug. While the 25-mg dose did not increase quit rates over nicotine replacement alone, a higher dosage—100 mg daily—raised 6-week abstinence rates to 71.6% compared with 48% for nicotine replacement alone. Nausea was a common side effect (35).

Depression

People who stop smoking may develop depressive symptoms. These symptoms may be severe enough to warrant treatment, particularly in persons with a history of major depression. For adherent patients who do not respond to nicotine replacement, it is important to consider a psychiatric problem, such as depression.

One study involving 100 smokers who were enrolled in a 2-month smoking cessation program and who had a history of major depression not currently requiring treatment found that the OR for an episode of major depression was 7.17 in patients who successfully quit compared with patients who did not (CI, 1.5 to 34.5) (36).

Bupropion and nortriptyline are recommended for smokers with depression who are trying to quit smoking. Both drugs provide efficacy for smoking cessation related to their antidepressant effects; more evidence supports the use of bupropion. Other antidepressants, particularly selective serotonin inhibitors, do not aid long-term smoking cessation.

34. Flegal KM, Troiano RP, Pamuk ER, Kuczmarski RJ, Campbell SM. The influence of smoking cessation on the prevalence of overweight in the United States. N Engl J Med. 1995;333:1165-70. [PMID: 7565970]

35. O'Malley SS, Cooney JL, Krishnan-Sarin S, et al. A controlled trial of naltrexone augmentation of nicotine replacement therapy for smoking cessation. Arch Intern Med. 2006;166:667-74. [PMID: 16567607]

36. Glassman AH, Covey LS, Stetner F, et al. Smoking cessation and the course of major depression: a follow-up study. Lancet. 2001;357:1929-32. [PMID: 11425414]

Practice Improvement

The United States' Healthy People 2010 initiative aims to reduce smoking prevalence to less than 12% in adults and less than 16% in youth. Currently, an estimated 21% of American adults and 22% of American high school students smoke. A concerted effort by health professionals will be critical in achievement of the Healthy People 2010 objectives.

Do U.S. stakeholders consider smoking cessation when evaluating the quality of care a physician delivers? In April 2005, The Ambulatory Care Quality Alliance (AQA) released a set of 26 health care quality indicators for clinicians, consumers, and health care purchasers to use in quality

improvement efforts, public reporting, and pay-for-performance programs (www.ahrq.gov/qual/aqastart.htm). In May 2005, the Centers for Medicare and Medicaid Services endorsed the development of these indicators. Of the 26 indicators, 7 focus on preventive care and 1 of these measures relates to smoking cessation. It is important that clinicians be aware of these measures for both clinical and administrative reasons. First, AQA selected these measures because they have been linked to better clinical outcomes for patients. Second, over coming years Medicare and other payers will increasingly link reimbursement to physician performance with respect to these quality indicators. AQA recommends that the

Table 4. U.S. Preventive Services Task Force (USPSTF) 2003 Recommendations: Counseling to Prevent Tobacco Use

The USPSTF strongly recommends that clinicians screen all adults for tobacco use and provide tobacco cessation interventions for those who use tobacco products.

- Good evidence supports brief smoking cessation interventions, including screening, brief behavioral counseling (less than 3 minutes), and pharmacotherapy delivered in primary care settings, are effective in increasing the proportion of smokers who successfully quit smoking and remain abstinent after 1 year.
- Good evidence documents that smoking cessation lowers the risk for heart disease, stroke, and lung disease.
- Good indirect evidence shows that even small increases in the quit rates from tobacco cessation counseling would produce important health benefits.

The USPSTF strongly recommends that clinicians screen all pregnant women for tobacco use and provide augmented pregnancy-tailored counseling to those who smoke.

- Good evidence supports that extended or augmented smoking cessation counseling (5–15 minutes) using messages and self-help materials tailored for pregnant smokers, compared with brief generic counseling interventions alone, substantially increases abstinence rates during pregnancy and leads to increased birth weights.
- Reducing smoking during pregnancy is likely to have substantial health benefits for both the baby and the expectant mother.

The USPSTF concludes that the evidence is insufficient to recommend for or against routine screening for tobacco use or interventions to prevent and treat tobacco use and dependence among children or adolescents.

- There is limited evidence that screening and counseling children and adolescents in the primary care setting are effective in either preventing initiation or promoting cessation of tobacco use.

see: *www.ahrq.gov/clinic/uspstf/uspstbac.htm*

The United States' Healthy People 2010 initiative aims to reduce smoking prevalence to less than 12% in adults and less than 16% in youth.

percentage of patients queried about tobacco use one or more times during a 2-year assessment period be a standard criterion to assess physician performance.

What do professional organizations recommend with regard to smoking cessation?

In 2003, the United States Preventive Services Task Force issued recommendations about counseling to prevent tobacco use (Table 4). Other professional organizations, particularly those that focus on cardiovascular or pulmonary diseases, or cancer, similarly advocate screening for tobacco use and promoting cessation.

Studies examining smoking cessation training programs found that these programs increased the likelihood that physicians would perform smoking cessation tasks. However, there was no strong evidence that training led to increased smoking cessation rates (37). Special training does not seem to be necessary if physicians wish to improve their effectiveness in helping their smoking patients to quit.

Practice Improvement... The Ambulatory Care Quality Alliance recommends that the percentage of patients queried about tobacco use one or more times during a 2-year assessment period be a standard criteria to assess physician performance. Special training does not appear to be necessary if physicians wish to improve their effectiveness in helping their patients to quit smoking. However, physicians must integrate routine assessment of smoking status, willingness to quit, and recommendation of cessation interventions into daily practice.

CLINICAL BOTTOM LINE

37. Lancaster T, Silagy C, Fowler G. Training health professionals in smoking cessation. Cochrane Database Syst Rev. 2000;CD000214. [PMID: 10908465]

Tool Kit

Smoking Cessation

Web Resources

Centers for Disease Control
http://cdc.gov/tobacco/
The CDC TIPS Web site contains a wealth of information for clinicians, smokers, and the public including the Surgeon General Reports and other publications, educational materials, research reports, and how-to-quit guides. Many of the materials are available in Spanish.

MedlinePlus
www.nlm.nih.gov/medlineplus/smokingcessation.html
Public-oriented information related to smoking cessation including information from the educational information from the National Institutes of Health, information about ongoing clinical trials, recent studies, and news. Includes material targeted to specific demographic groups.

Smoking Cessation Leadership Center
http://smokingcessationleadership.ucsf.edu/
The Smoking Cessation Leadership Center is a national program office of the Robert Wood Johnson Foundation that aims to increase smoking cessation rates by assisting health professionals in their efforts to help their patients quit smoking. The site includes information for health professionals and smokers.

Other Media

Information for Patients
www.annals/intheclinic/clinicaltools
Download a copy of the patient information sheet that appears on the next page for duplication and use in your practice.

http://foundation.acponline.org/hl/ht_smo_en.htm
Order pads of brief Health Tips on smoking cessation to distribute to patients

Office Posters
www.cdc.gov/tobacco/sgr/sgr_2004/sgrposters.htm
The CDC offers single, free copies of several posters promoting smoking cessation suitable for office display.

Cards to Refer Patients to National Telephone Quit Line
http://smokingcessationleadership.ucsf.edu/1800QuitNow.html
The Smoking Cessation Leadership Center offers a small, plastic card to help promote the quit line for 18 cents/card.

Counseling for Behavior Change Videotape
www.acponline.org/atpro/timssnet/catalog/electronic/behvchng.html
Order a videotape that demonstrates through office visit scenarios how to move patient through behavior change.

Tutorial on Counseling for Behavior Change
www.acponline.org/private/abimpim/diabetes/cardio_counsel.ppt
View a slide presentation that describes the stages of behavior change, diagnostic clues to each stage of change, and counseling strategies to help move a patient through the stages of change.

Pharmacological Therapies to Help Smokers Quit
www.acponline.org/private/abimpim/diabetes/quitsmoking.html
View a printable discussion of pharmacologic aids to smoking cessation.

Personalized Patient Educational Prescription
www.acponline.org/private/abimpim/diabetes/smoking.html
Follow this link to print out a personalized educational prescription to refer patients to the MedlinePlus materials on smoking cessation.

THINGS PEOPLE SHOULD KNOW ABOUT SMOKING

hatever your age, the amount you smoke, or when you started... quitting will improve your health.

Internet Sites with Good Information about How to Quit Smoking

Centers for Disease Control
http://cdc.gov/tobacco/

MedlinePlus
www.nlm.nih.gov/medlineplus/smokingcessation.html

Smoking Cessation Leadership (SLC)
http://smokingcessationleadership.ucsf.edu/

HEALTH TiPS*
WHAT YOU CAN DO

- Smoking can make you sick and shorten your life.
- If you quit now, you will be healthier.
- Quitting is hard work, but there are ways to help you.

- Smoking is dangerous, especially if you already have heart or lung disease or if you are pregnant.
- It increases the chances of your having a heart attack, stroke, lung disease, and cancer. When you smoke, you can make people around you sick—even your children.
- You can quit smoking even if you have smoked for a long time.
- When you quit smoking, it will change your life in a good way—you will feel better, live longer, and save money.

Ask your doctor
- Why it is important for you to quit
- How quitting can help you

Ask your doctor about what help you can get to stop smoking.
- Ways you can help yourself
- Treatment groups with other smokers

- Medicines to help stop the urge to smoke

After starting your program, set up times to see your doctor.

To help you fight the urge to smoke:
- Set a date in the next 2 weeks to stop smoking and stick to it.
- Throw away all your cigarettes *and* ashtrays
- Stay away from other smokers.
- Tell your family and friends you are quitting and ask for their help.
- See your doctor to keep track of your progress.
- Talk to your doctor if you are having trouble, especially if quitting makes you gain weight or feel depressed.
- Stick with your plan.
- If you fail, don't give up. Try again. Some people need to start over 3 or 4 times before they beat the habit.
- For extra help, call **1-800 QUIT NOW**

For free advice about quitting call: 1-800 QUIT-NOW

HEALTH TiPS are developed by the American College of Physicians Foundation and PIER

Patient Information

Peripheral Arterial Disease

The National Heart Lung and Blood Institute estimates that about 5% of U.S. adults older than 50 years of age and about 12% to 20% of adults older than 65 years have lower extremity atherosclerosis, commonly known as peripheral arterial disease (PAD). Despite the high prevalence, many patients and clinicians do not immediately consider PAD as a potential cause of leg pain in older people. The disease occurs equally in men and postmenopausal women, but men are more likely to have symptoms. Once recognized, modification of risk factors and therapeutic interventions can reduce PAD progression and improve symptoms and functional status. Some argue that even asymptomatic PAD warrants aggressive treatment to reduce cardiovascular risk factors because PAD can be a harbinger of other cardiovascular problems.

Prevention

What factors increase risk for PAD?

Many patients with PAD have systemic atherosclerosis, and risk factors for PAD are the same as those for other manifestations of atherosclerosis: smoking, hypertension, diabetes, and dyslipidemia. PAD is unusual in persons younger than 50 and becomes more common as people age. African Americans are at higher risk for PAD than whites (1).

Are there effective strategies to prevent the development of PAD?

Strategies aimed at reducing overall cardiovascular morbidity and mortality also prevent PAD. Tobacco use is highly associated with risk for PAD. On average, smokers who develop PAD have symptoms 10 years earlier than persons who do not smoke. Clinicians should encourage smoking cessation using a multifaceted approach that combines behavioral and pharmacologic interventions.

In a prospective analysis of 2174 patients older than age 40, the prevalence of PAD was found to be 4.3%. Correcting for age and other confounding factors, current smoking was strongly associated with increased risk for PAD (OR, 4.5 [CI, 2.3 to 8.8]) (2).

In the Framingham Offspring study, nearly 3300 patients with a mean age of 59 years were examined between 1995 and 1998. The prevalence of PAD was 3.9%. Controlling for confounding variables, smoking was associated with PAD (OR, 2.0 [CI, 1.1 to 3.4]) (3).

Hypertension, which is associated with systemic atherosclerosis and cardiovascular morbidity, is also associated with PAD (2). Although there is no direct evidence, experience with other forms of atherosclerosis suggests that keeping blood pressure within the normal range with standard antihypertensive therapy should reduce a patient's risk for PAD (4).

Type 1 and type 2 diabetes mellitus are associated with PAD. There is fair- to moderate-quality evidence that good glycemic control reduces the risk for macrovascular complications, including PAD. However, aggressive glycemic control may be less helpful after onset of the macrovascular complications (5). Diabetics with other risk factors, such as smoking or dyslipidemia, are at particularly high risk for PAD (6).

A meta-analysis of studies evaluating atherosclerotic manifestations showed a consistently strong correlation between diabetes mellitus and atherosclerotic manifestations, including PAD-related amputation (7).

Because PAD is a manifestation of systemic atherosclerosis, therapy for dyslipidemia that is beneficial in reducing atherosclerosis generally will also reduce the risk for PAD. The National Cholesterol Education Program–Adult Treatment Panel III guidelines provide specific information on dyslipidemia management in patients at risk for PAD (8).

1. Collins TC, Petersen NJ, Suarez-Almazor M, et. al. The prevalence of peripheral arterial disease in a racially diverse population. Arch Intern Med. 2003;163:1469-74. [PMID: 12824097]
2. Selvin E, Erlinger TP. Prevalence of and risk factors for peripheral arterial disease in the United States: results from the National Health and Nutrition Examination Survey, 1999-2000. Circulation. 2004;110:738-43. [PMID: 15262830]
3. Murabito JM, Evans JC, Nieto K, et al. Prevalence and clinical correlates of peripheral arterial disease in the Framingham Offspring Study. Am Heart J. 2002;143:961-5. [PMID: 12075249]
4. Joint National Committee on Prevention, Detection, Evaluation, and Treatment of High Blood Pressure. National Heart, Lung, and Blood Institute. Seventh report of the Joint National Committee on Prevention, Detection, Evaluation, and Treatment of High Blood Pressure. Hypertension. 2003;42:1206-52. [PMID: 14656957]

The Heart Protection Study random-ized patients with coronary artery disease, cerebrovascular disease, PAD, and/or dia-betes mellitus and a total cholesterol level >135 mg/dL to simvastatin or placebo. The *study included 6748 patients with PAD, in whom there was a 25% risk reduction in cardiovascular events over 5 years of fol-low-up (9).*

Prevention... The modifiable risk factors for PAD are the same as those for coronary and systemic atherosclerosis: smoking, hypertension, diabetes, and dyslipidemia. Strategies aimed at these risk factors to prevent atherosclerosis will reduce risk for PAD as well as other types of cardiovascular problems.

CLINICAL BOTTOM LINE

Screening

Should clinicians routinely screen primary care patients for PAD?
The U.S. Preventive Services Task Force (USPSTF) recommends against routine screening for PAD (www.ahrq.gov/clinic/uspstf/uspspard.htm). Although fair evidence shows that screening with an ankle–brachial index (ABI) can identify adults with asymptomatic PAD, there is little evidence that early detection of PAD in these patients results in more effective treatment of risk factors or better outcomes. Routine screening in primary care settings is likely to produce many false-positive results. Many interventions that might be prescribed after detecting asymptomatic PAD—smoking cessation, blood pressure control, and exercise—are of proven value in prevention of other atherosclerotic conditions. It seems reasonable that physicians should screen directly for these risk factors rather than screening for risk indirectly by screening for PAD.

However, screening for PAD has become a topic of some debate. Research clearly shows that PAD is significantly underdiagnosed and

that it increases the risk for death. Thus, screening for PAD in older patients with cardiovascular disease risk factors is advocated by some be-cause it could identify patients with systemic atherosclerosis who may benefit from risk factor reduction and medical therapies (10). Some would call this case-finding rather than screening. The USPSTF and other groups that do not advocate screening for PAD note that such individuals may be identified during recommended screening for cardio-vascular risk factors.

One prospective study evaluated history and ABI measurements in nearly 7000 pa-tients who were either >70 years of age or >55 years of age and had risk factors. The investigators detected PAD in 29% of these patients, and only 49% of their personal physicians were aware of the diagnosis. A classic history of claudication was present in only 11% (11).

A prospective study that followed 565 pa-tients (mean age, 66 y) for more than 10 years and identified PAD in 12% found that the risk for death was 3-fold greater for the patients with PAD than for those without (12).

5. Intensive blood-glucose control with sulfonylureas or insulin compared with conventional treatment and risk of complications in patients with type 2 diabetes (UKPDS 33). UK Prospective Diabetes Study (UK-PDS) Group. Lancet. 1998;352:837-53. [PMID: 9742976]
6. Kallio M, Forsblom C, Groop PH, et. al. Development of new peripheral arte-rial occlusive disease in patients with type 2 diabetes during a mean follow-up of 11 years. Diabetes Care. 2003;26:1241-5. [PMID: 12663604]
7. Beckman JA, Creager MA, Libby P. Diabetes and atherosclerosis: epi-demiology, patho-physiology, and management. JAMA. 2002;287:2570-81. [PMID: 12020339]
8. Coordinating Com-mittee of the Na-tional Cholesterol Education Program. Implications of recent clinical trials for the Na-tional Cholesterol Education Program Adult Treatment Panel III guidelines. Arterioscler Thromb Vasc Biol. 2004;24:e149-61. [PMID: 15297292]

Screening... There is no evidence to document that routine screening for PAD with ABI in asymptomatic adults improves patient outcomes. However, fair-to-moderate evidence suggests that clinicians should consider looking for history and physical examination evidence of PAD in patients at high risk for the disease (patients older than 65 years, smokers, African Americans, and patients with diabetes older than age 50).

CLINICAL BOTTOM LINE

Diagnosis

Which patient symptoms and signs should prompt clinicians to consider PAD?

Clinicians should consider PAD when a patient reports claudication, pain in the legs elicited by physical activity and subsiding with rest, particularly if it occurs in an older patient with risk factors for atherosclerosis. Patients with PAD sometimes report leg fatigue, numbness, heaviness, or weakness. Erectile dysfunction can also be a symptom of PAD. However, more than half of patients with PAD are asymptomatic. Even if patients with PAD have no exertional leg pain, any activity involving the legs tends to more difficult than for patients without PAD (13).

Signs on physical examination indicative of PAD include faint or absent pulses in the legs, femoral or lower extremity bruits, lower extremity ulcers, lower extremity hair loss and skin changes, and cool distal extremities. The legs of severely affected patients may become pale on elevation because of inadequate arterial pressure. However, these signs are neither highly sensitive nor highly specific for detecting PAD.

The absence of pedal pulses can rapidly focus the diagnostic evaluation. Palpation of arterial pulses, including the brachial, femoral, and pedal arteries, and auscultation of the abdominal aorta and femoral arteries for bruits should be done in all at-risk patients. The absence of a femoral pulse suggests in-flow disease of the aorta or iliac arteries, whereas in patients with a good femoral pulse, no femoral bruit, and an absent popliteal pulse, the disease is probably confined to the arteries in the leg. Table 1 links the site of claudication to the affected vasculature.

Which noninvasive diagnostic tests are useful in diagnosing PAD?

Ankle–Brachial Index

The ABI is the most commonly used and most useful diagnostic test for PAD. It is a simple test that can be done in the office in less than 15 minutes. The ABI compares blood pressure in the ankle with blood pressure in the arm (i.e., ankle pressure/brachial pressure) to estimate blood flow in the legs. Table 2 shows the interpretation of ABI results. An

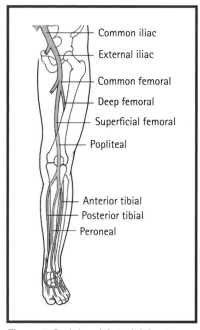

Figure 1. Peripheral Arterial Anatomy.

- Common iliac
- External iliac
- Common femoral
- Deep femoral
- Superficial femoral
- Popliteal
- Anterior tibial
- Posterior tibial
- Peroneal

From *The Merck Manual of Diagnosis and Therapy*, Edition 18, p. 755, edited by Mark H. Beers. Copyright 2006 by Merck & Co., Inc., Whitehouse Station, NJ.

Symptoms and Signs of PAD	
Symptoms	Claudication
	Lower extremity rest pain
	Lower extremity numbness
	Lower extremity fatigue
	Lower extremity heaviness
	Erectile dysfunction
Signs	Loss of lower extremity hair
	Lower extremity ulcers
	Bruits
	Absence of lower extremity pulses

Table 1. Claudication Site and Corresponding Location of Ischemia

Claudication Site	Vascular Territory
Buttock, hip	Aortoiliac
Thigh	Common femoral or aortoiliac artery
Upper calf	Superficial femoral artery
Lower calf	Popliteal artery
Foot	Tibial or peroneal artery

Table 2. Interpretation of Ankle–Brachial Index

Ankle–Brachial Index Result	Clinical Interpretation
>0.90 (with a range of 0.90 to1.30)	Normal lower extremity blood flow
<0.89 to >0.60	Mild PAD
<0.59 to >0.40	Moderate PAD
<0.39	Severe PAD

9. Heart Protection Study Collaborative Group. MRC/BHF Heart Protection Study of cholesterol lowering with simvastatin in 20, 536 high-risk individuals: a randomised placebo-controlled trial. Lancet. 2002;360:7-22. [PMID: 12114036]

10. ACC/AHA 2005 Practice Guidelines for the Management of Patients with Peripheral Arterial Disease (lower extremity, renal, mesenteric, and abdominal aortic). Circulation. 2006 ACC/AHA 2005 practice Guidelines for the Management of Patients With Peripheral Arterial Disease (Lower Extremity, Renal, Mesenteric, and Abdominal Aortic). Circulation. 2006;113:1474-1547. (PMID: 16549652)

ABI <0.90 has a sensitivity of 95% and a specificity of 100% for detecting arterial narrowing >50% when digital subtraction angiography is the gold standard. An ABI <0.90 is the commonly accepted definition of PAD from the Society for Vascular Surgery, the American Heart Association, and the Transatlantic Inter-Society consensus statements (10, 14).

Toe–Brachial Index

Particularly in patients with diabetes or kidney disease, arterial calcification can interfere with the accuracy of the ABI. Clinicians should suspect calcification if the ankle systolic blood pressure exceeds 290 mm Hg in any patient or 240 mm Hg in a patient whose brachial systolic blood pressure is <160 mm Hg. Calcification may also be present when the ABI is >1.3. In these cases, the toe–brachial index (TBI) may provide a more accurate result since toe arteries are rarely calcified. The TBI is the systolic blood pressures in the toe divided by the systolic blood pressures of the arms. A TBI less than 0.5 indicates the presence of PAD. Because the TBI requires a photoplethysmograph infrared light sensor and a small blood pressure cuff that can be placed around the toe, referral to a vascular laboratory may be necessary.

Exercise Ankle–Brachial Index

When patients have symptoms indicative of PAD, normal results on the ABI do not necessarily exclude the disease, since the body, while at rest, may compensate for long-standing aortoiliac disease. Exercise ABI may be useful if ABI results are normal but there is a high clinical suspicion of PAD. The normal response to exercise is decreased peripheral vascular resistance and increased blood flow to the active extremities, manifested by increased ABI (normal response) during exercise and subsequent recovery. An ABI that decreases 20% after exercise indicates PAD. Normal results on ABI after exercise

suggest another cause for the patient's symptoms. This test requires no special equipment beyond that required for an ABI.

Other Studies

For patients with an ABI below 0.90 or a TBI below 0.5, clinicians may order a duplex scan from an accredited vascular laboratory. This type of scan uses Doppler ultrasonography to measure blood velocity with spectral velocity and to evaluate plaque with B-mode imaging. The combination of techniques provides a visual image of the location, extent, and severity of PAD. However, the duplex scan is not always accurate (15).

Other vacular laboratory tests that can help identify PAD include Doppler ultrasonography alone and segmental blood pressure and pulse volume recordings. Angiography (discussed later) is generally used only when revascularization procedures are under consideration.

How should clinicians measure ankle–brachial index in the office setting?

To measure ABI, clinicians need a Doppler flow probe and appropriately sized blood pressure cuffs for each limb, including a cuff large enough for the thigh. The Doppler flow probe enables the clinician to audibly detect blood flow more easily than with a stethoscope. Figure 2 provides instructions for measurement of ABI.

When should clinicians consider invasive testing for patients with suspected PAD and what tests are useful?

Clinicians should consider invasive testing when considering interventions beyond risk factor and medical management. According to the American College of Cardiology/ American Heart Association (ACC/ AHA) clinical practice guidelines on PAD, decisions on whether revascularization will be useful requires a complete anatomical assessment of the affected arterial territory,

The absence of pedal pulses should rapidly focus the diagnostic evaluation on PAD.

11. Hirsch AT, Criqui MH, Treat-Jacobson D, et al. Peripheral arterial disease detection, awareness, and treatment in primary care. JAMA. 2001;286:1317-24. [PMID: 11560536]
12. PAD Criqui MH, Langer RD, Fronek A, et. al. Mortality over a period of 10 years in patients with peripheral arterial disease. N Engl J Med. 1992;326:381-6. [PMID: 1729621]
13. McDermott MM, Fried L, Simonsick E, et. al. Asymptomatic peripheral arterial disease is independently associated with impaired lower extremity functioning: the women's health and aging study. Circulation. 2000;101:1007-12. [PMID: 10704168]
14. Norgren L, Hiatt WR, Dormandy JA, et. al. Inter-Society Consensus for the Management of Peripheral Arterial Disease (TASC II). Eur J Vasc Surg. 2007;33:S1-S75.
15. Brown OW, Bendick PJ, Bove PG, et al. Reliability of extracranial carotid artery duplex ultrasound scanning: value of vascular laboratory accreditation. J Vasc Surg. 2004;39:366-71; discussion 371. [PMID: 14743137]

1. Patient should rest supine in a warm room for at least 10 minutes before testing.

2. Place blood pressure cuffs on both arms and ankles as illustrated, then apply ultrasound gel over brachial, dorsalis pedis, and posterior tibial arteries.

3. Measure systolic pressures in the arms
   - use Doppler to locate brachial pulse
   - inflate cuff 20 mm Hg above last audible pulse
   - deflate cuff slowly and record pressure at which pulse becomes audible
   - obtain 2 measures in each arm and record the average as the brachial pressure in that arm

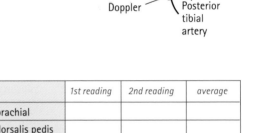

4. Measure systolic pressures in ankles
   - use Doppler to locate dorsalis pedis pulse
   - inflate cuff 20 mm Hg above last audible pulse
   - deflate cuff slowly and record pressure at which pulse becomes audible
   - obtain 2 measures in each ankle and record the average as the dorsalis pedis pressure in that leg
   - repeat above steps for posterior tibial arteries

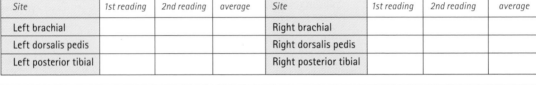

5. Calculate ABI

   Right ABI = $\dfrac{\text{highest right average ankle pressure (DP or PT)}}{\text{highest average arm pressure (right or left)}}$

   Left ABI = $\dfrac{\text{highest left average ankle pressure (DP or PT)}}{\text{highest average arm pressure (right or left)}}$

Site	1st reading	2nd reading	average	Site	1st reading	2nd reading	average
Left brachial				Right brachial			
Left dorsalis pedis				Right dorsalis pedis			
Left posterior tibial				Right posterior tibial			

Figure 2. How to Measure the Ankle–Brachial Index (ABI). DP = dorsalis pedalis, PT = posterior tibial.

including imaging of the occlusive lesions as well as arterial inflow and outflow (10). Various forms of arteriography are used to map the vasculature and determine the location and extent of lesions in patients who may be candidates for invasive intervention.

Digital subtraction arteriography (DSA) is the gold standard, but it is invasive and associated with risks, including bleeding, allergic reaction, and contrast nephropathy. In DSA, a radiograph is taken after the injection of dye into the arterial circulation.

Magnetic resonance angiography (MRA) may be used as the primary diagnostic imaging technique instead of DSA, particularly in patients at high risk for complications of contrast. MRA uses radiowave energy to image the vasculature. When done at experienced institutions, MRA is nearly as sensitive and accurate as DSA without the risks associated with iodinated contrast medium (16). MRA is not appropriate for patients with a metallic device like a pacemaker, prosthetic joint, mechanical heart valve, or some stents and surgical clips.

In some situations, such as when arterial access is difficult, computed tomography angiography (CTA) can aid the evaluation of peripheral arterial anatomy. This method uses computerized analysis of x-ray images to visualize arterial and venous blood flow. CTA has come to replace DSA in some centers and this trend is likely to increase as CT technology advances. As expected, MRA and CTA have lower estimated sensitivities and specificities than DSA, the gold standard (Table 3).

16. Koelemay MJ, Lijmer JG, Stoker J, Legemate DA, Bossuyt PM. Magnetic resonance angiography for the evaluation of lower extremity arterial disease: a meta-analysis. JAMA. 2001;285:1338-45. [PMID: 11255390]

17. Pararajasingam R, Nasim A, Sutton C, et al. The role of screening blood tests in patients with arterial disease attending vascular outpatients. Eur J Vasc Endovasc Surg. 1998;16:513-6. [PMID: 9894492]

Table 3. Useful Tests in the Evaluation of PAD*

Test	Sensitivity (%)†	Specificity (%)†	Notes
Ankle–brachial index	95	90	Reproducible, reliable, and minimal office cost.
Toe–brachial index	85–89	86–88	Good for patients with calcified arteries, especially those with longstanding diabetes mellitus.
Duplex arterial mapping and segmental pressure analysis	67–89	99	Requires a dedicated vascular ultrasound laboratory. More accurate for above the knee evaluation as tibial arteries are harder to image.
Magnetic resonance imaging	66–100	94–95	Nearly as accurate as digital subtraction arteriography, but may be limited by patient factors such as prior metal bioprostheses. Gadolinium, gadodiamide, and gadopentetate have similar contrast safety and enhancing properties.
Computed tomographic angiography	80	93	Newer imaging modality that may become a standard once many institutions acquire the newest generation of computed tomography scanners.
Digital subtraction arteriography	NA	NA	The gold standard, but invasive and associated with patient risk, including bleeding and contrast nephropathy.

*NA = not applicable.
†Digital subtraction arteriography is gold standard.

What blood tests are useful in evaluating patients with PAD?

When an intervention is being considered, concensus supports the performance of certain blood tests: complete blood count, electrolytes, creatinine, coagulation panel (pro-time, activated partial thromboplastin time, platelet count), urinalysis to evaluate for glycosuria and unsuspected infection, glycosylated hemoglobin, and lipid panel. The rationale for these tests is that patients with PAD often have comorbid conditions, such as anemia, hypertension, diabetes, and kidney disease that warrant evaluation and possible treatment in preparation for PAD intervention.

In a prospective study of new referrals for PAD, of 272 patients 21% had undiagnosed abnormalities in renal, glucose, or hematologic variables (17).

Underlying hypercoagulable disorders, including hyperhomocystinemia, activated protein C resistance, and elevated lipoprotein (a), may accompany early atherosclerosis and can cause graft failure, so clinicians may consider evaluating for hypercoagulable disorders in patients younger than 50 years of age and in those with a history of failed bypass.

In a prospective cohort of 50 young men with early PAD (age <45 years), the prevalence of hypercoagulable states was 2-fold higher than that of an age-matched cohort (P = 0.20) and lipoprotein (a) levels were associated with advanced disease (P <0.01) (18).

Other markers of systemic atherosclerosis, such as C-reactive protein, have been shown to be independently associated with PAD (19) and may be associated with graft occlusion (20). However, there is no evidence that measurement of this marker or others should change management beyond asessment and treatment of traditional risk factors.

What alternative diagnoses should clinicians consider when they suspect PAD?

Many causes of limb pain can be confused with PAD as well as occur in conjunction with it. A consensus document suggests a broad differential diagnosis for limb pain (21).

Nonvascular diagnoses that may mimic PAD include osteoarthritis, peripheral neuropathies, spinal stenosis, prolapsed intervertebral disc, restless legs syndrome, and such musculoskeletal diseases as fibromyalgia or polymyalgia rheumatica. Vascular disease that can present

18. Valentine RJ, Kaplan HS, Green R, et. al. Lipoprotein (a), homocysteine, and hypercoagulable states in young men with premature peripheral atherosclerosis: a prospective, controlled analysis. J Vasc Surg. 1996;23:53-61, discussion 61-3. [PMID: 8558743]
19. Ridker PM, Cushman M, Stampfer MJ, et. al. Plasma concentration of C-reactive protein and risk of developing peripheral vascular disease. Circulation. 1998;97:425-8. [PMID: 9490235]
20. Ouriel K, Green RM, DeWeese JA, et. al. Activated protein C resistance: prevalence and implications in peripheral vascular disease. J Vasc Surg. 1996;23:46-51, Discussion 51-2. [PMID: 8558741]
21. Dormandy JA, Rutherford RB. Management of peripheral arterial disease (PAD). TASC Working Group. TransAtlantic Inter-Society Consensus (TASC). J Vasc Surg. 2000;31:S1-296. [PMID: 10666287]

with symptoms that might suggest PAD include arterial embolus, deep venous thrombosis, venous insufficiency, popliteal entrapment syndrome, and chronic exertional compartment syndrome.

Thromboangiitis obliterans, also known as Buerger disease and a variant of PAD, is a rare cause of limb pain characterized by acute inflammation and thrombosis of the arteries and veins in the hands and feet. It occurs most commonly in men 20 to 40 years of age who use tobacco, but it may occur in women and men older than 50 years of age or in children with autoimmune diseases. Buerger disease is less common in the United States than in other countries, and the primary treatment is smoking cessation and wound care (22).

Diagnosis... Clinicians should consider PAD in older patients who present with leg pain, numbness, fatigue, or ulceration. Erectile dysfunction may also be a presenting symptom in patients with PAD. Pain while walking is a classic symptom of PAD, but symptoms can be atypical and some patients are asymptomatic. Absence of pedal pulses should rapidly focus the diagnosis on PAD. Ankle–brachial index is the standard test to confirm the presence and to evaluate the severity of PAD. Imaging studies, such as digital subtraction angiography, magnetic resonance angiography, or computed tomography angiography, are indicated to evaluate the location and extent of disease if invasive therapy is under consideration.

CLINICAL BOTTOM LINE

22. Olin JW, Shih A. Thromboangiitis obliterans (Buerger's disease). Curr Opin Rheumatol. 2006;18:18-24. [PMID: 16344615]
23. Gardner AW. The effect of cigarette smoking on exercise capacity in patients with intermittent claudication. Vasc Med. 1996;1:181-6. [PMID: 9546936]
24. Willigendael EM, Teijink JA, Bartelink ML, et al. Smoking and the patency of lower extremity bypass grafts: a meta-analysis. J Vasc Surg. 2005;42:67-74. [PMID: 16012454]
25. Giswold ME, Landry GJ, Sexton GJ, et al. Modifiable patient factors are associated with reverse vein graft occlusion in the era of duplex scan surveillance. J Vasc Surg. 2003;37:47-53. [PMID: 12514577]
26. Yusuf S, Sleight P, Pogue J, et al. Effects of an angiotensin-converting-enzyme inhibitor, ramipril, on cardiovascular events in high-risk patients. The Heart Outcomes Prevention Evaluation Study Investigators. N Engl J Med. 2000;342:145-53. [PMIDD: 10639539]

Treatment

Can risk factor modification prevent progression of or reverse PAD?
Modification of risk factors can greatly reduce progression of PAD and may even reverse it. Patients with extensive or early aggressive PAD may particularly benefit from a focused approach to risk factor modification.

Tobacco Control
Smoking cessation may reduce the progression of disease and is the most important intervention for limb salvage. Smokers with PAD have significantly worse claudication, reduced peripheral circulation, and worse exercise tolerance than nonsmokers with PAD (23). Smoking cessation is also critical to the success of angioplasty or vascular surgery and maintenance of patency. Continued smoking increases risk for PAD complications and death. Continued smoking in patients with PAD who require a surgical intervention results in a 3- to 4.7-fold increase in graft failure and an increased risk for amputation (24, 25).

Lipid Control
Aggressive lipid management is also imperative. Studies report that aggressive lipid management results in atherosclerosis regression, reduction in the rate of new or worsening intermittent claudication, and improvement in walking distance. Dietary modifications can significantly alter the lipid profile and decrease the progression of PAD and cardiovascular disease. Dietary habits are often hard to change, so clinicians may recommend that patients with PAD meet with a registered dietitian to set up a healthy eating plan. The Heart Protection Study showed that statin use in patients with PAD (with or without prior cardiac disease) reduced the risk for subsequent myocardial infarction (MI), stroke, and vascular death (9).

The current recommendation for patients with PAD is to achieve a low-density lipoprotein cholesterol level <100 mg/dL and a triglyceride level <150 mg/dL. However, patients with no contraindications to statins should receive them for secondary prevention of cardiovascular events regardless of lipid levels. Patients with hypertriglyceridemia may need an additional drug, such as niacin (8).

Blood Pressure Control
Hypertension treatment should take into account that patients with PAD are at particularly high risk for cardiovascular events. Data from the Heart Outcomes Prevention Evaluation Study suggest that angiotensin-converting enzyme inhibitors are particularly beneficial in patients with PAD to prevent MI, stroke, and death and to decrease blood pressure (26). Beta-blockers should be considered in patients undergoing vascular surgery because they reduce the risk for perioperative cardiovascular events. Beta-blockers were once thought to worsen symptoms of claudication, but critical review of the evidence concludes that PAD does not contraindicate their use (10).

Glucose Control
In patients with diabetes, intensive blood glucose control prevents microvascular complications, but the benefits on arterial disease are less certain. Several studies have shown that intensive therapy was associated with a trend toward fewer cardiovascular events, but the risk for PAD was not reduced because patients with PAD received less intensive treatment for lipid disorders and hypertension (11, 21).

What is the role of exercise in the treatment of patients with PAD?
Fair-to-moderate evidence shows that structured exercise programs benefit patients with mild-to-moderate PAD (27). Ambulation improves muscle efficiency and alters the pain threshold for distance traveled. Research involving patients with PAD found that exercise led to increases >120% in peak walking time and in pain-free walking compared with controls and led to increases in walking distance >180% that lasted at least 12 months (28, 29). While the best results are achieved with a motivated patient in a supervised setting, recent evidence suggests that unsupervised exercise can also benefit patients with PAD.

Among 417 patients with PAD followed for a median of 36 months, self-directed walking exercise at least 3 times per week was associated with less functional decline. These findings suggest benefit associated with unsupervised exercise (30).

Exercise benefits patients with all stages of PAD, including those who have developed critical leg ischemia. For these patients, exercise provides the additional benefits of helping to relieve ischemic rest pain, heal ischemic ulceration, and prevent limb loss (31). Clinicians should recommend that patients walk 30 to 40 minutes, stopping as necessary, at least 3 and preferably 4 to 5 times per week to improve walking distance.

Which pharmacologic therapy should clinicians consider for patients with PAD?
Medical therapy can reduce the pain associated with PAD and reduce the risk factors for PAD progression (Table 4). None of the available medications to treat PAD is a substitute for aggressive risk factor modification with pharmacologic therapy as needed for smoking cessation and control of hypertension, diabetes, and dyslipidemia.

Antiplatelet Therapy
All patients with PAD should receive antiplatelet therapy (10, 14). Aspirin (81 mg/d) is effective for all patients with PAD for prevention of cardiovascular events (including stroke and myocardial infarction) and to improve patency following revascularization procedures.

Clopidogrel (75 mg/d) is an acceptable alternative to antiplatelet therapy with aspirin. Clopidogrel has been found to reduce the risk for stroke and MI slightly more than aspirin,

27. Stewart KJ, Hiatt WR, Regensteiner JG, et. al. Exercise training for claudication. N Engl J Med. 2002;347:1941-51. [PMID: 12477945]
28. Hiatt WR, Wolfel EE, Regensteiner JG, et. al. Skeletal muscle carnitine metabolism in patients with unilateral peripheral arterial disease. J Appl Physiol. 1992;73:346-53. [PMID: 1506390]
29. Hiatt WR, Regensteiner JG, Hargarten ME, et al. Benefit of exercise conditioning for patients with peripheral arterial disease. Circulation. 1990;81:602-9. [PMID: 2404633]
30. McDermott MM, Liu K, Ferucci L, et. al. Physical performance in peripheral arterial disease: a slower rate of decline in patienst who walk more. Ann Intern Med. 2006:144:10-20.
31. Gardner AW, Katzel LI, Sorkin JD, Goldberg AP. Effects of long-term exercise rehabilitation on claudication distances in patients with peripheral arterial disease: a randomized controlled trial. J Cardiopulm Rehabil. 2002;22:192-8. [PMID: 12042688]

Table 4. Drug Treatment for PAD*

Agent	Mechanism of Action	Dosage	Benefits	Side Effects	Notes
Aspirin	Cyclooxygenase inhibitor	81 mg/d	Reduced risk for cardiovascular events, including stoke and MI	Bleeding, GI upset	Use for all patients with PAD for primary prevention and to improve revascularization patency
Clopidogrel	Inhibits platelet function	75 mg/d	Reduced risk for stroke and MI, slightly better than aspirin	Bleeding, rare bone marrow suppression	More expensive than aspirin; no definitive data for improvement in bypass patency over aspirin
Simvastatin, atorvastatin, lovastatin, pravastatin	Decreases cholesterol and has vascular anti-inflammatory effects	20–80 mg/d	Anti-inflammatory vascular effects independent of lipid lowering; improved walking distance	Myalgia, liver dysfunction	Use for all patients unless contraindications or intolerance; proven to slightly reduce claudication symptoms and to improve surgical bypass patency
Cilostazol	Vasodilates peripheral arteries; has mild antiplatelet effect	100 mg bid	Peripheral arteriolar dilator, decreased platelet aggregation	Tachycardia, headaches, precipitation of CHF	Proven to decrease claudication symptoms, but expensive and should not supersede diet, exercise, and smoking cessation
Ramipril	Vasodilation and decreased angiotensin II	10 mg/d	Increased pain-free and maximum walking time	Cough and renal dysfunction	One randomized, controlled trial supports this observation, but the cardiovascular benefits of ACE inhibitors are well documented, which makes this a reasonable first-line blood pressure medication
Pentoxifyl-line	Causes laxity of RBC membrane	400 mg tid	Improved blood flow through stenosed vessels	Headache, gastrointestinal upset	Less solid evidence of benefit, but worth considering in patients who do not tolerate cilostazol

*ACE = angiotensin-converting enzyme; bid = twice daily; CHF = congestive heart failure; GI = gastrointestinal; MI = myocardial infarction; RBC = red blood cell (erythrocyte); tid = three times daily.

32. Bhatt DL, Fox KA, Hacke W, Berger PB, Black HR, Boden WE, et al. Clopidogrel and Aspirin versus Aspirin Alone for the Prevention of Atherothrombotic Events. N Engl J Med. 2006;354:1706-17. (PMID: 16531616)
33. Hiatt WR. Medical treatment of peripheral arterial disease and claudication. N Engl J Med. 2001;344:1608-21. [PMID: 11372014]
34. Money SR, Herd JA, Isaacsohn JL, et al. Effect of cilostazol on walking distances in patients with intermittent claudication caused by peripheral vascular disease. J Vasc Surg. 1998;27:267-74; discussion 274-5. [PMID: 9510281]

but it is more expensive than aspirin. There are no definitive data on whether clopidogrel improves patency of vascular bypass procedures better than aspirin. Available data suggest that clopidogrel's safety profile is similar to that of aspirin except for a few reported cases of bone marrow suppression associated with clopidogrel.

A recent trial in patients with established cardiovascular disease including PAD or multiple cardiovascular risk factors compared aspirin plus clopidogrel to aspirin alone on myocardial infarction, stroke, and vascular death and found no differences (32). Thus the Inter-Society Concensus for the Management of Peripheral Arterial Disease (TASC II) does not recommend combination therapy for patients with stable PAD (14).

Therapy for Claudication

The phosphodiesterase inhibitor cilostazol (100 mg twice/d) is the recommended agent for treating lifestyle-limiting claudication symptoms in patients without heart failure. The drug's selective peripheral arterial vasodilatation with mild

antiplatelet activity improves ambulatory distance and time to fatigue. Several randomized, controlled trials have documented a benefit in terms of walking distance and quality of life (33).

A randomized, controlled trial evaluating the effect of cilostazol in 239 patients found that peak treadmill testing for total distance before claudication began was significantly improved with cilostazol (34).

In a similar randomized, controlled trial in 394 patients followed over 24 weeks, cilostazol was associated with 21% improvement in maximum walking distance and 22% net improvement in distance walked before onset of symptoms (35).

Another trial in 81 patients showed an increase in total walking distance and delay in claudication symptom onset (36).

Cilostazol is contraindicated in patients with heart failure because of the known association of this class of drugs with excess mortality from nonsustained ventricular tachycardia in patients with heart failure. Cilostazol is intended as an adjunctive treatment for claudication and not as a replacement for risk factor modification.

Other Medications
A recent, small, 24-week randomized trial compared ramipril 10 mg to placebo in 40 older adults with symptomatic PAD. This study found that ramipril improved pain-free and maximum walking time. However, generalizability of these preliminary findings is uncertain because the trial involved selected patients with limited exercise tolerance, ultrasound evidence of superficial femoral artery disease, no diabetes, and no hypertension (37).

Pentoxifylline, a drug that lowers blood viscosity, is approved by the U.S. Food and Drug Administration, but most patients may not notice an improvement in walking distance and it has not been shown to be more effective than placebo in several randomized, controlled studies. L-Carnitine may also be prescribed for improving skeletal muscle metabolism; however, its effectiveness in the treatment of claudication has not been established. Prostaglandin agonists (beraprost, iloprost) have little supportive evidence but may be considered in patients with no options other than amputation (14).

What are the indications and options for invasive revascularization therapy for patients with PAD?

Consideration of endovascular or surgical intervention is warranted in patients with PAD and severe, function-limiting symptoms, rest pain, or tissue loss. In such patients, revascularization will reduce symptoms and improve limb salvage.
In addition to disease extent and location, the choice of endovascular versus surgical intervention should also take into account comorbid conditions and local expertise. Angioplasty guidelines emphasize that more proximal lesions have better and more durable postprocedure patency rates than more distal, smaller artery lesions.

Endovascular Interventions
Endovascular procedures include angioplasty with stenting, subintimal recanalization, and atherectomy. Use of these less-invasive approaches as first-line therapy does not preclude surgical bypass procedures in the future. Although endovascular interventions are less invasive, durability in the infrainguinal location and cost-effectiveness have not been rigorously evaluated (38).

A retrospective study evaluated 329 patients with a mean follow-up of 1.8 years after infrainguinal angioplasty and stenting. Overall patency at 5 years was estimated at 52% and was negatively affected by long segment occlusions (39).

Surgical Bypass
Surgical bypass is indicated for long-segment lesions that are not amenable to endovascular intervention. In patients undergoing bypass, autologous tissue is always a better conduit than prosthetic material. Patients with renal failure are at high risk for patency failure and have higher short-term mortality (40, 41).

Revascularization interventions should be combined with adjunctive wound care treatment to improve limb perfusion. Beyond the tenets of standard wound care, each regimen should be individualized to take into account the patient's ability to perform wound care, with or without help from home care nursing.

What are the complications of revascularization interventions?

Complications are fairly common after both endovascular and surgical interventions because of both the underlying atherosclerosis and the associated comorbid conditions. The most common cause of acute arterial ischemia among patients with a bypass graft is occlusion, usually caused by local thrombosis. Other complications include lymph leakage, wound infection, hematoma, and pseudoaneurysm.

What are the indications for limb amputation?

For patients with poor functional status who have exhausted all potential

Clinicians should recommend that patients walk 30 to 40 minutes, stopping as necessary, at least 3 times per week to improve walking distance.

35. Strandness DE Jr, Dalman RL, Panian S, et al. Effect of cilostazol in patients with intermittent claudication: a randomized, double-blind, placebo-controlled study. Vasc Endovascular Surg. 2002;36:83-91. [PMID: 11951094]

36. Dawson DL, Cutler BS, Meissner MH, et al. Cilostazol has beneficial effects in treatment of intermittent claudication: results from a multicenter, randomized, prospective, double-blind trial. Circulation. 1998;98:678-86. [PMID: 9715861]

37. Ahimastos AA, Lawler A, Reid CM, et al. Brief communication: ramipril markedly improves walking ability in patients with peripheral arterial disease: a randomized trial. Ann Intern Med. 2006;144:660-4. [PMID: 16670135]

38. SchŸrmann K, Mahnken A, Meyer J, et al. Long-term results 10 years after iliac arterial stent placement. Radiology. 2002;224:731-8. [PMID: 12202707]

39. Surowiec SM, Davies MG, Eberly SW, et al. Percutaneous angioplasty and stenting of the superficial femoral artery. J Vasc Surg. 2005;41:269-78. [PMID: 15768009]

interventions, limb amputation is sometimes necessary. Amputation allows removal of the nonfunctional, painful limb and often allows return to premorbid activity with a prosthesis. Amputation might be a reasonable primary therapeutic option for patients with severe dementia, unacceptable surgical risk, very short life expectancy (<1 year), and disease anatomy that precludes bypass or interventional options for limb salvage.

When should clinicians consider hospitalization of patients with PAD?

Clinicians should consider hospitalizing patients with PAD if acute limb-threatening ischemia is present or if there are complications of arterial insufficiency or revascularization procedures.

Acute limb ischemia should be considered in patients with pain, poikilothermia pulselessness, paralysis, paresthesias, and pallor. The goal of hospitalization is to arrange emergent revascularization to salvage the limb. Unless a contraindication exists, patients with acute limb ischemia should receive intravenous heparin (100 U/kg bolus), which will decrease thrombus propagation in the setting of arterial embolic or thrombotic occlusion.

Complications related to revascularization procedures that require hospitalization include contrast nephropathy, symptomatic groin or arm hematoma, surgical wound infection, cardiovascular events (e.g., MI or stroke), pneumonia, and graft failure. Readmission to the hospital after an intervention for PAD is so common that clinicians should inform patients of this possibility before the intervention.

How should clinicians follow patients with PAD?

Patients with PAD should be followed periodically to assess disease progression and to monitor for complications of systemic atherosclerosis. Follow-up should include assessment of symptoms; physical examination with particular attention paid to any signs of PAD; ABI measurement; and evaluation of control of hypertension, lipids, glucose, and tobacco use.

Lifelong follow-up is required for patients with surgical arterial reconstructions. Postsurgical graft stenosis is the leading cause of longterm graft failure, and detection of subclinical graft stenosis can allow intervention before graft thrombosis occurs. However, primary bypass salvage is uncommon after thrombosis, and thrombolytics are often not efficacious. There are no prospective trials that provide data on the appropriate intervals of postprocedure evaluation. Consensus recommendations include an ABI and bypass graft interrogation with duplex ultrasonography to determine graft patency every 3 months for the first year, every 6 months for the next 2 years, then annually. Further evaluation by arteriography is indicated among patients with graft peak systolic velocities on duplex ultrasonography that are >300 cm/sec or have an at-site velocity ratio ≥3.5, or outflow velocities ≤45 cm/sec. There are no data to help determine whether reintervention is beneficial other than in patients with recurrent symptoms.

When should clinicians refer patients with PAD for specialty care?

Clinicians should consider involving a vascular specialist in the care of any patient with complex or severe PAD, particularly if invasive treatment is under consideration. Whether patients have better outcomes with specialty care than with generalist care is unknown, but some evidence suggests that vascular specialists are more likely to be aware of current therapies for atherosclerosis (42).

40. Feinglass J, Pearce WH, Martin GJ, et al. Postoperative and amputation-free survival outcomes after femorodistal bypass grafting surgery: findings from the Department of Veterans Affairs National Surgical Quality Improvement Program. J Vasc Surg. 2001;34:283-90. [PMID: 11496281]

41. O'Hare AM, Sidawy AN, Feinglass J, et al. Influence of renal insufficiency on limb loss and mortality after initial lower extremity surgical revascularization. J Vasc Surg. 2004;39:709-16. [PMID: 15071430]

42. McDermott MM, Hahn EA, Greenland P, et al. Atherosclerotic risk factor reduction in peripheral arterial diseasea: results of a national physician survey. J Gen Intern Med. 2002;17:895-904. [PMID: 12472925]

Consultation with a vascular specialist may also be appropriate if the patient has symptoms suggesting PAD but has a normal ABI, or when exercise stress ABI or reactive hyperemia testing is needed to assess blood flow under ambulatory conditions.

Plastic surgery consultation may be helpful in managing patients with complex wounds during or after the intervention to improve limb perfusion and in determining the need for reconstructive tissue flaps.

For patients who have had amputation, a multidisciplinary team of caregivers, including inpatient rehabilitation specialists and physiatrists, allows coordinated care to help these patients recover function and cope with life changes.

Treatment... Aggressive management of modifiable risk factors for atherosclerosis is essential in all patients with PAD. Clinicians should recommend an exercise program for patients with mild-to-moderate PAD, consider cilostazol in patients with moderate claudication, and prescribe antiplatelet therapy (aspirin or clopidogrel) for all patients with PAD in whom it is not contraindicated. Patients with severe claudication that limits function, rest pain, or tissue loss should undergo evaluation for endovascular or surgical revascularization.

CLINICAL BOTTOM LINE

Practice Improvement

Do U.S. stakeholders consider measures related to PAD when evaluating the quality of care a physician delivers?

In April 2005, The Ambulatory Care Quality Alliance released a set of 26 health care quality indicators for clinicians, consumers, and health care purchasers to use in quality improvement efforts, public reporting, and pay-for-performance programs (www.ahrq.gov/qual/aqastart.htm). Of the 26 indicators, none focuses directly on the care of PAD, but several relate to management of risk factors for atherosclerosis. These include measures of assessment of smoking status and cessation advice, control of lipids in patients with diabetes or coronary artery disease, and blood pressure and glucose control for people with diabetes.

What do professional organizations recommend regarding the management of patients with PAD?

In 2005, the ACC and the AHA (in collaboration with the American Association for Vascular Surgery/ Society for Vascular Surgery, Society for Vascular Medicine and Biology, and the Society of Interventional Radiology) published practice recommendations for the management of patients with PAD. This comprehensive document provides recommendations related to PAD diagnosis, risk factor management, treatment, and management of patients with critical and acute limb ischemia (10). The complete guideline is available for free at http://circ.ahajournals.org/cgi/reprint/113/11/e463.

TASC II is the work of representatives from 16 professional societies from North America, Europe, Australia, South Africa, and Japan (15). The consensus document covers diagnosis and management and updates TASC I, which was published in 2000. The document is available for purchase at www.sciencedirect.com.

Ankle–Brachial Index Calculation Tool
http://cpsc.acponline.org/enhancements/232abiCalc.html
A tool to assist in the calculation and interpretation of the ABI.

Ankle–Brachial Index Measurement Instructions and Worksheet
www.annals/intheclinic/tools
Download copies of the ABI measurement instructions and worksheet provided in Figure 2 of this article.

Patient Information Sheet
www.annals.org/intheclinic/tools
Download an electronic copy of the patient information sheet on the next page for duplication and use in your office.

Patient Education Pamphlet
www.acponline.org/catalog/campaign/special.htm
ACP Special Reports are patient education brochures (in packs of 100) about common conditions, including PAD. The brochures are free to ACP members.

Health Tips for Patients
http://foundation.acponline.org
Order pads of brief Health Tips on PAD to distribute to patients.

Standing Orders Worksheet
www.acponline.org/private/abimpim/cardiology/standing_order.html
Create a customized worksheet of standing orders for cardiac risk factor assessment for patients with PAD.

Exercise Prescription Form
www.acponline.org/private/abimpim/diabetes/exerciseprescription.pdf
Use this form to write an individualized exercise prescription for your patient.

CDC Smoking Cessation Materials
www.cdc.gov/tobacco/
Web site of the Centers for Disease Control and Prevention with information for clinicians, smokers, and the public, including the Surgeon General Reports and other publications, educational materials, research reports, and how-to-quit guides. Many materials are available in both English and Spanish.

MedlinePlus Smoking Cessation Materials
www.nlm.nih.gov/medlineplus/smokingcessation.html
Public-oriented information related to smoking cessation, including educational information from the National Institutes of Health, recent studies, and news. Includes materials targeted to specific demographic groups.

Things People Should Know About Peripheral Artery Disease (PAD)

Peripheral artery disease (PAD) is a form of atherosclerosis that involves the arteries of the legs. In atherosclerosis, the arteries become narrowed or clogged with a gradual buildup of fat and other substances. PAD can cause leg pain that can limit walking and sores on the legs or feet that are slow to heal.

Internet Sites with Good Information about PAD

Peripheral Arterial Disease (PAD) Coalition
www.padcoalition.org

MedlinePlus
www.nlm.nih.gov/medlineplus/ency/article/000170.htm

American Heart Organization
www.americanheart.org

HEALTH TiPS*
What You Can Do

- Having peripheral artery disease (PAD) means that not enough blood is flowing to your legs, feet, or toes.

- PAD can make your legs hurt when walking and can damage them if it gets worse.

Here's what you can do to help keep PAD from getting worse:

Don't smoke and stay away from those who do

- Smoking makes PAD worse.
- Breathing smoke from others is almost as bad smoking yourself.

Walk

- Walking is a good treatment for PAD.
- Start out slowly and walk a little more each week.
- A good goal is to walk 30 minutes, 5 days a week.
- If your legs hurt while walking, stop, rest, and start walking again.

Wear good shoes

- Wear shoes that are strong enough to keep your feet and toes safe if you bump them.
- Wear shoes that don't rub or hurt your feet.

Check your feet and toes every day

- Look for red spots, black spots or sores.

Call Your Doctor right away if you have:

- Pain in your legs when you are not walking
- No feeling in your feet
- Sores on the feet or legs

Things to ask your doctor about PAD:

- What might help me stop smoking?
- Is it OK to keep going even if my legs hurt when walking?
- Are there any medicines that can help? Will I need surgery?
- Can changing what I eat help? If so, what should I eat? Will losing weight help?
- Is my bad cholesterol high? (High levels of bad cholesterol make PAD worse.)
- Is my blood pressure OK? (High blood pressure makes PAD worse.)
- Is my blood sugar OK? (High blood sugar makes PAD worse.)
- Why is it so important to treat PAD? (Treating PAD can cut the risk of heart attack and stroke.)

*HEALTH TiPS are developed by the American College of Physicians Foundation and PIER

Patient Information

Allergic Rhinitis

Allergic rhinitis (AR), an inflammatory disease of the upper airways, is one of the most common problems seen in outpatient practice. Although sometimes trivialized by patients and physicians, AR is a major source of morbidity. According to the National Health Interview Survey, 18.6 million adults and 6.7 children were diagnosed with "hay fever" in 2004 (www.cdc.gov/nchs/fastats/allergies.htm), and the National Ambulatory Medical Care Survey showed that there were 14 million physician office visits for AR that year (www.cdc.gov/nchs/fastats/allergies.htm). Exact prevalence figures for AR are difficult to determine. A recent study estimated that it affects 23% of the population of Western Europe (1), and data from the third National Health and Nutrition Examination Survey (NHANES III) showed that about 55% of all U.S. citizens test positive to at least 1 allergen, a significant increase over the prevalence in the previous survey (2).

In addition to its effect on quality of life, AR imposes a significant economic burden on society. With an approximate 20% prevalence, it carries direct and indirect medical costs associated with diagnosis and treatment of about $2 billion a year (3). This figure more than doubles when indirect costs related to absence from work and decreased productivity at work largely due to the use of sedating antihistamines are added (3, 4).

Diagnosis

1. Bauchau V, Durham SR. Prevalence and rate of diagnosis of allergic rhinitis. Eur Respir J. 2004;24:758-64. [PMID: 15516669]
2. Arbes SJ Jr, Gergen PJ, Elliott L, Zeldin DC. Prevalences of positive skin test responses to 10 common allergens in the US population: results from the Third National Health and Nutrition Examination Survey. J Allergy Clin Immunol. 2005;116:377-83. [PMID: 16083793]
3. Fineman SM. The burden of allergic rhinitis: beyond dollars and cents. Ann Allergy Asthma Immunol. 2002;88(4 Suppl 1):2-7. [PMID: 11991546]
4. Crystal-Peters J, Crown WH, Goetzel RZ, Schutt DC. The cost of productivity losses associated with allergic rhinitis. Am J Manag Care. 2000;6:373-8. [PMID: 10977437]
5. Slavin RG, Reisman RE. Expert Guide to Allergy and Immunology. Philadelphia: American College of Physicians; 1999:23-40.

Which symptoms and signs should prompt clinicians to consider AR?

Clinicians can often make the diagnosis of AR from the patient's history (5). The symptoms of AR include sneezing, rhinorrhea, postnasal drainage, nasal congestion, and sometimes loss of sense of smell. Many patients also complain of itchy, watery eyes. The history should be used to estimate the frequency and severity of disease and how it affects the patient's quality of life. Validated questionnaires are also available to help measure these variables (see Practice Improvement).

Allergic rhinitis often first develops in childhood or in the teenage years (6). Personal and family histories are often positive for AR and other atopic diseases, such as eczema and asthma (7).

It is important to differentiate between seasonal and perennial AR. As the nomenclature implies, seasonal AR is most bothersome at certain times of the year when particular allergens—usually specific tree and grass pollens—are present in the environment. Perennial AR tends to cause symptoms on an ongoing basis whenever the patient is exposed to more common allergens, such as mold or dust mites.

Nasal obstruction, smell disturbance, chronic sinusitis, otitis media, and asthma are more common in perennial than in seasonal AR (8). Eye symptoms, including pruritus and conjunctival irritation, are more common in seasonal AR than in perennial AR. Both types of AR can present with malaise, weakness, and fatigue (7) (Table 1).

The history should be used to try to identify triggers for AR. The patient should be asked not only about specific symptoms and seasonal occurrence but also about home and workplace environments and specific events; for example: What changes, if any, have

Table 1. Characteristics of Allergic Rhinitis*

Characteristic	Seasonal	Perennial
Obstruction	Variable	Always, predominant
Secretion	Watery, common	Seromucous, postnasal drip, variable
Sneezing	Always	Variable
Smell disturbance	Variable	Common
Eye symptoms	Common	Rare
Asthma	Variable	Common
Chronic sinusitis	Occasional	Frequent

Data from reference 8.

occurred at home or at work? Has the patient recently moved or traveled? Did the patient visit a friend who has a pet? Can the patient identify any place, activity, or exposure that makes the rhinitis worse?

Triggers that may not be true allergens include irritating toxins, hormones, drugs, tobacco smoke, cold air, and hairspray (7); these triggers can cause symptoms in patients with AR as well as in others who do not have allergies. Persons in the latter group may have nonallergic noninfectious rhinitis.

Patients with AR frequently treat themselves either by avoiding situations that trigger symptoms or by using over-the-counter antihistamines and decongestants as needed. Estimating the severity of disease and determining what has or has not been useful in the past allows for optimum patient management. It is also important to ask about preexisting conditions and associated treatments. Such conditions as hypertension or glaucoma limit the use of drugs that are effective against AR, including oral decongestants or antihistamines.

On examination, the nasal mucosa is frequently edematous and pale but can be normal if the patient is asymptomatic. The nasal passages may be partially or completely obstructed. The patient should be evaluated for a deviated nasal septum, polyps, and ulceration. Injection and watering of the eyes suggest allergic conjunctivitis. Examination of the pharynx may reveal enlarged tonsils or pharyngeal injection from postnasal drip.

Look for otitis, sinus tenderness, and wheezing. Between 20% and 40% of patients with AR have asthma (9), and chronic sinusitis has been associated with AR in 40% to 80% of adult patients (10). Fever should be absent and, if present, suggests an upper respiratory infection.

What other similar conditions should clinicians consider in patients with symptoms suggestive of AR?

Nasal symptoms in patients with AR are nonspecific. Although a simple upper respiratory infection and AR are usually easily differentiated by history, more prolonged symptoms in a patient with a history of allergies may be more difficult. It is important to look for sinusitis in patients with purulent rhinorrhea, facial pain, and sinus tenderness. In fact, AR often precedes development of recurrent or chronic sinusitis because the accompanying nasal obstruction and inflammation interrupts normal mucociliary

6. Schoenwetter WF. Allergic rhinitis; epidemiology and natural history. Allergy Asthma Proc. 2000; 21:1-6. [PMID: 10748945]
7. Quillen M, Feller DB. Diagnosing Rhinitis: Allergic vs. Nonallergic. Am Fam Physician. 73:1-6. [PMID: 16719251]
8. van Cauwenberge P, Bachert C, Passalacqua G, et al. Consensus statement on the treatment of allergic rhinitis. European Academy of Allergology and Clinical Immunology. Allergy. 2000;55:116-34. [PMID: 10726726]
9. Palma-Carlos AG, Branco-Ferreira M, Palma-Carlos ML. Allergic rhinitis and asthma: more similarities than differences. Allerg Immunol (Paris). 2001; 33:237-41. [PMID: 11505808]
10. Spector SL, Bernstein IL, Li JT, Berger WE, et al. Practice Parameters for the Diagnosis and Management of Sinusitis - J. Allergic Rhinitis. J Allergy Clin Immunol. 1998;102: S107-44. [PMID: 9847450]

clearance, leading to retention of mucopurulent secretions within the sinuses (10).

It is also important to consider other nonallergenic, noninfectious, and mechanical causes of rhinitis in the differential diagnosis, including hormone changes in pregnancy and hypothyroidism causing nasal congestion. Vasomotor rhinitis—the cause of which is still unknown—may be a hypersensitive response to a dry atmosphere, air pollutants, spicy foods, alcohol, emotions, or some medications. Overuse of topical nasal decongestants containing oxymetazoline or phenylephrine can produce refractory nasal congestion and, consequently, rhinitis medicamentosa. Other medications that can cause rhinitis include angiotensin-converting enzyme inhibitors, chlorpromazine, aspirin and other nonsteroidal anti-inflammatory drugs, and cocaine.

Careful examination of the nose and rhinoscopy will help exclude mechanical causes of rhinitis (5), including nasal polyposis. A deviated nasal septum may cause unilateral symptoms. Foreign objects, particularly in children, may also be a cause.

Cystic fibrosis, although less common, is also in the differential diagnosis. A sweat chloride test should be considered if a young patient presents with nasal polyposis or chronic sinusitis. Other rare disorders that mimic AR include sarcoidosis, Wegener granulomatosis, and cerebral fluid rhinorrhea.

Which diagnostic tests are useful in confirming the diagnosis of AR?

Diagnosis of seasonal AR can usually be made clinically.

Medical history combined with a high baseline prevalence of AR support the common practice of empirical treatment since many of the medications used to treat AR have minimal toxicity and side effects (11).

Diagnostic testing is usually reserved for patients with more severe disease who do not respond to empirical avoidance of known allergens and pharmacologic treatment. Tests include allergy sensitivity testing to identify specific allergens, often in preparation for immunotherapy, and/or radiologic imaging to identify other underlying anatomical conditions.

Allergy sensitivity tests, including skin testing and IgE-specific antibody level determination, may be helpful in identifying allergens, confirming the diagnosis of AR, and choosing treatment. However, sensitivity to an allergen on testing does not necessarily mean that that allergen is causing clinical disease or can be easily avoided (8). Moreover, reported sensitivities and specificities of skin tests (which may sometimes not be well standardized) and serologic tests (of which there are many) vary widely; consequently, it may be difficult to confidently calculate the posttest probability of AR in some cases (11).

The 3 most frequently used skin testing methods are puncture, prick, or scratch; intradermal; and patch. In the first method, tiny drops of purified allergen extracts are pricked or scratched onto the skin's surface. Such allergens include pollen, mold, pet dander, dust mites, foods, and insect venom. In intradermal testing, the allergen is introduced under the skin using a syringe and a narrow-gauge needle. Patch testing, in

11. Gendo K, Larson EB. Evidence-based diagnostic strategies for evaluating suspected allergic rhinitis. Ann Intern Med. 2004;140:278-89. [PMID: 14970151]
12. Pumhirun P, Jane-Trakoonroj S, Wasuwat P,. Comparison of in vitro assay for specific IgE and skin prick test with intradermal test in patients with allergic rhinitis. Asian Pac J Allergy Immunol. 2000.3:157-60. [PMID: 11270471]
13. Sheikh A, Hurwitz B. House dust mite avoidance measures for perennial allergic rhinitis: a systematic review of efficacy. Br J Gen Pract. 2003;53:318-22. [PMID: 12879834]
14. Fuhlbrigge AL, Adams RJ. The effect of treatment of allergic rhinitis on asthma morbidity, including emergency department visits. Curr Opin Allergy Clin Immunol. 2003;3:29-32. [PMID: 12582311]

which an allergen is applied to a patch and then placed on the skin, is not usually used in patients with AR but is instead used to test for substances that cause contact dermatitis.

Medications taken for preexisting conditions can interfere with test results. These agents include the prescription antihistamines fexofenadine and cetirizine; over-the-counter antihistamines, such as diphenhydramine hydrochloride and chlorpheniramine; tricyclic antidepressants, such as amitriptyline and doxepin; and H_2-antagonists, such as cimetidine and ranitidine (11). Other factors can lead to false-positive and false-negative results (Table 2).

Administering skin tests if the patient has severe skin disease should be avoided, and in rare cases small amounts of substances administered to highly sensitive patients can lead to anaphylaxis.

Immunoglobulin E antibody testing, also referred to as radioallergosorbent testing (RAST), is recommended for patients who find skin tests impractical or who are taking medications that will interfere with the results. In vitro IgE-specific antibody testing is more expensive than skin testing but has a specificity of 80% to 90%. Although specific operating characteristics for skin prick testing and specific in vitro IgE antibody testing depend on the allergen used, they are generally similar and yield excellent results (12). Skin testing generally requires consultation with an allergist.

Unlike IgE-specific antibody testing, serum total IgE levels, although often elevated in patients with allergic disease, are not particularly helpful in confirming the diagnosis of AR. The same is true for eosinophilia in the peripheral blood count and for eosinophils on nasal cytology, which can be seen in patients with nonallergic rhinitis.

Radiologic studies may be valuable to confirm or exclude coexisting or complicating mechanical obstruction. Consider radiographs and computed tomography in patients with symptoms lasting for more than a few months to look for chronic sinusitis with obstruction, nasal polyps, or other anatomical abnormalities that require attention.

When should clinicians consider consultation with an allergist or otorhinolaryngologist to make an accurate diagnosis?

Clinicians should consider consulting an allergist if the cause of the patient's symptoms remains elusive, especially if skin testing may be useful or when rhinitis is

Diagnostic testing is usually reserved for patients with severe disease who do not respond to treatment.

Table 2. Causes of False–Positive and False–Negative Skin Test Results*

Causes of false-positive skin test results

Test sites too close together (<2 cm)
Dermatographism
Irritant reaction from testing solution
Contamination of testing solution with another allergen
Injecting >0.05 mL of testing solution (intradermal tests)
Using high-concentration testing solution (intradermal tests)

Causes of false-negative skin test results

Use of antihistamines, tricyclic antidepressants, long-term oral steroid therapy, or topical steroids
Insufficient penetration of skin with needle
Low potency of testing extract
Age >50 y
Chronic renal insufficiency
Spinal cord injury
Peripheral nerve injury
Testing in the week after anaphylaxis
Subcutaneous injection (intradermal tests)

* Data from reference 11.

15. Skoner DP, Rachelefsky GS, Meltzer EO, et al. Detection of growth suppression in children during treatment with intranasal beclomethasone dipropionate. Pediatrics. 2000;105:E23. [PMID: 10654983]
16. Schenkel EJ, Skoner DP, Bronsky EA, et al. Absence of growth retardation in children with perennial allergic rhinitis after one year of treatment with mometasone furoate aqueous nasal spray. Pediatrics. 2000;105:E22 [PMID: 10654982].
17. Weiler JM, Bloomfield JR, Woodworth GG, et al. Effects of fexofenadine, diphenhydramine, and alcohol on driving performance. A randomized, placebo-controlled trial in the Iowa driving simulator. Ann Intern Med. 2000;132:354-63. [PMID: 10691585]

associated with sinusitis, otitis media, or asthma.

An otorhinolaryngologist should be consulted for patients in whom nasal endoscopy or other diagnostic procedures requiring specialized instrumentation is needed to identify an underlying anatomical abnormality.

Diagnosis... Clinicians should base the initial clinical diagnosis of AR on the patient's history and consider laboratory testing to identify specific allergens if the diagnosis is unclear, symptoms are severe enough to affect quality of life, the patient does not respond to empirical drug therapy, and/or immunotherapy is being contemplated. Base the choice between skin testing and IgE-specific antibody testing on physician and patient preference. Obtain imaging studies only for patients in whom an underlying anatomical abnormality may influence management.

CLINICAL BOTTOM LINE

Treatment

Steps for Allergen Avoidance

- Reduce exposure to dust mites
- Remove carpeting from the home (especially the bedroom)
- Use allergy encasements for bedding
- Reduce the relative humidity in the home to <40%
- Wash bedding in hot (>120° F) water
- Control exposure to outdoor pollens and molds
- Close windows and doors
- Use an air conditioning system with a small-particle filter
- Control exposure to pets and animals

18. Condemi J, Schulz R, Lim J. Triamcinolone acetonide aqueous nasal spray versus loratadine in seasonal allergic rhinitis: efficacy and quality of life. Ann Allergy Asthma Immunol. 2000;84:533-8 [PMID: 10831008]
19. Weiner JM, Abramson MJ, Puy RM. Intranasal corticosteroids versus oral H$_1$ receptor antagonists in allergic rhinitis: systematic review of randomised controlled trials. BMJ.1998;317:1624-29 [PMID: 9848901].

What allergen control measures are effective in reducing symptoms of AR?

The most effective measure for reducing symptoms of AR would logically be to avoid offending allergens—which is probably easier for patients who are only seasonally affected than for those who are affected year-round.

Nearly all studies evaluate the effects of allergen avoidance in patients with asthma rather than in those with AR. A systematic review of 4 small studies suggested that air cleaners, vinyl mattress covers, and HEPA filtration systems reduce dust mite allergen burden but did not conclusively demonstrate long-term reduction in clinical symptoms of allergic rhinitis (13).

Current guidelines recommend allergen avoidance measures in patients with AR to improve symptoms and reduce the need for pharmacologic therapy and should avoid any other particular irritant or situation known to exacerbate symptoms (see the Box).

What pharmacologic measures should clinicians consider for patients with AR?

Most patients will not get complete relief from allergen-control measures and will need pharmacotherapy or immunotherapy. Physicians should base their choice of pharmacotherapy on effectiveness and safety as well as the patient's specific symptoms, severity, and duration. For nasal symptoms, physicians should also consider the patient's preference for oral or intranasal agents, comorbid conditions, and response to prior treatment. Observational studies of patients with both asthma and AR show that treating AR decreases asthma exacerbations by one third to one half (14).

In tailoring drug therapy, it is useful to determine which symptoms are most troublesome to the patient to decide which drugs are most likely to treat those symptoms and to classify symptom severity and frequency (see the Box on next page). For example, patients with mild seasonal AR may need to take an oral antihistamine for a few weeks at specific times during the year or may be able to control their symptoms with over-the-counter antihistamines or antihistamine–decongestant combinations. In persons with seasonal disease, it is sometimes helpful to start drug treatment a week or two before the beginning of allergy season. On the other hand, patients with perennial AR may require long-term multidrug therapy.

Available pharmacologic drug classes include oral, nasal, and ocular antihistamines; nasal, oral, and parenteral corticosteroids; nasal and ocular cromolyn; oral and nasal decongestants; nasal anticholinergics; and oral leukotriene-receptor agonists (Table 3). All nasal symptoms, including sneezing, rhinorrhea, nasal congestion, and nasal itch, can be treated with oral and nasal antihistamines, nasal steroids, nasal cromolyn, and oral antileukotrienes. Oral and nasal decongestants, however, treat only nasal congestion. In addition to the topical ocular agents, oral antihistamines, antileukotrienes, and even nasal steroids to some extent treat the eye symptoms.

A comprehensive evidence report from the Agency for Health Care Research and Quality in 2002 (www.ahrq.gov/clinic/tp/rhintp.htm) reviewed over 228 articles and found that nasal corticosteroids were most effective in the treatment of both seasonal and perennial AR. Sedating and nonsedating antihistamines were similarly effective, although less so than nasal corticosteroids. Cromolyn was also found to be effective in seasonal and perennial disease. None of the agents caused more than mild side effects, aside from sedation in first-generation antihistamines. No studies were identified comparing pharmacologic treatment with immunotherapy.

Treatment Based on Chronicity and Severity of Symptoms

- Mild, intermittent disease may require only monotherapy with nonsedating oral or nasal antihistamines or decongestants as needed.
- Mild but more persistent disease can be treated with monotherapy with a nonsedating oral or nasal antihistamine, nasal cromolyn, or an oral decongestant, depending on the predominant symptoms. A second of these agents can be added after a month if needed. Nasal decongestants should not be used for more than 3 days to avoid rhinitis medicamentosa.
- Treatment of moderate to severe, intermittent disease can begin with monotherapy with an oral or nasal antihistamine, oral decongestant, nasal cromolyn, or nasal steroid depending on specific symptoms.
- Patients with moderate to severe persistent disease are candidates for initial therapy with intranasal steroids. If symptoms do not improve within a month, consider adding an antihistamine for itching and sneezing, nasal ipratropium for rhinorrhea, an oral decongestant for congestion, or if necessary a short course of oral steroids (Table 4).

Intranasal Steroids

Intranasal corticosteroids, the drug class most effective for daily treatment of AR (especially in patients with significant persistent disease) (18), includes beclomethasone, ciclesonide, triamcinolone, budesonide, mometasone, flunisolide, and fluticasone. Comparative trials have not convincingly shown superiority of one over the other. However, several randomized trials and 2 systematic reviews attest to their superiority over both topical and oral antihistamines.

In a meta-analysis of 16 randomized, controlled trials including 2267 patients with AR, intranasal steroids provided greater relief than oral antihistamines of nasal blockage, nasal discharge, sneezing, postnasal drip, and total nasal symptoms. The odds ratio for the global rating for deterioration of symptoms was 0.26 (95% CI, 0.08 to 0.8). There were no differences between the treatments for nasal discomfort, resistance, or eye symptoms (19).

In another meta-analysis of 9 randomized, controlled trials including 648 patients with AR, intranasal steroids provided greater relief than topical antihistamines in total nasal symptoms, sneezing, rhinorrhea, itching, and nasal blockage but no difference in ocular symptoms (20).

20. Yáñez A, Rodrigo GJ. Intranasal corticosteroids versus topical H$_1$ receptor antagonists for the treatment of allergic rhinitis: a systematic review with meta-analysis. Ann Allergy Asthma Immunol. 2002;89:479-84. [PMID: 12452206]
21. Pullerits T, Praks L, Ristioja V, Lötvall J. Comparison of a nasal glucocorticoid, antileukotriene, and a combination of antileukotriene and antihistamine in the treatment of seasonal allergic rhinitis. J Allergy Clin Immunol. 2002;109:949-55. [PMID: 12063523]

Table 3. Drug Treatment for Allergic Rhinitis*

Agent*	Mechanism of Action	Dosage	Benefits	Side Effects	Notes
Intranasal corticosteroids					
Beclomethasone, triamcinolone, budesonide, fluticasone, mometasone flunisolide, and ciclesonide	Broad anti-inflammatory action	2 puffs each nostril once or twice per day	Effective agent for blockage, rhinorrhea, and sneezing	Should be used every day; small for corticosteroid side effects	Can be used as first-line agent; can stunt growth in children (15,16)
Oral antihistamines, first-generation					
Diphenhydramine	Blocks H$_1$-receptor	20–50 mg 3+ mg per day	Effective for rhinorrhea and sneezing; can be effective when used as needed or in conjunction with intranasal corticosteroids	Can be sedating or interfere with the ability to drive or operate machinery; less effective for congestion; not as effective as intranasal corticosteroids	First-generation antihistamines may cause driving impairment (17)
Chlorpheniramine and others	Blocks H$_1$-receptor	4 mg every 4–6 h	Effective for rhinorrhea and sneezing; can be effective when used as needed or in conjunction with intranasal corticosteroids	Can be sedating or interfere with the ability to drive or operate machinery; less effective for congestion	First-generation antihistamines may cause driving impairment (17)
Oral antihistamines, second-generation					
Loratadine, fexofenadine, and cetirizine	Blocks H$_1$-receptor	10 mg once per day 60 mg twice per day, or 180 mg once per day 5–10 mg once per day	Effective for rhinorrhea and sneezing; can be effective when used as needed or in conjunction with intranasal corticosteroids	Can be sedating or interfere with the ability to drive or operate machinery; less effective for congestion	Nonsedating antihistamines preferred
Oral decongestants					
Phenylephrine	Sympathomimetic	10 mg every 4–6 h	Effective for treating nasal blockage; can be used as needed or in conjunction with intranasal corticosteroids and/or antihistamines	Can cause sympathomimetic side effects; can cause bladder outlet obstruction in men; effective for only 1 symptom	Most often used in combination with antihistamines and/or nasal corticosteroids
Oral antihistamine/ decongestant combinations	H$_1$-antagonist/ sympathomimetic	Varies	Effective for nasal blockage, rhinorrhea, and sneezing; can be used as needed and in conjunction with intranasal corticosteroids	See adverse effects listed for antihistamines and decongestants	Many prescription and nonprescription products available
Oral montelukast	Leukotriene receptor antagonist	10 mg once per day	Effective for nasal blockage, rhinorrhea, and sneezing	Headache	
Intranasal cromolyn	Mast cell stabilizer	2 puffs, 3 or 4 times per day	Effective for nasal blockage, rhinorrhea, and sneezing; very low risk for adverse effects	Not as effective as intranasal corticosteroids; must be used every day, 4 to 6 times per day	Nonprescription
Intranasal antihistamines					
Azelastine hydrochloride	H$_1$ antagonist	2 puffs each nostril twice per day	As effective as oral antihistamines; some patients prefer as-needed nasal spray	Can be sedating	First-line therapy
Intranasal ipratropium	Anticholinergic	2 puffs each nostril 2 or 3 times per day	Effective for rhinorrhea; low risk for side effects	Not effective for symptoms other than rhinorrhea	Not considered first-line therapy
Systemic corticosteroids Prednisone	Broad anti-inflammatory	Varies; prednisone 40 mg daily for 5-7 days with tapering for acute, severe, allergic rhinitis	Highly effective for severe, acute allergic rhinitis	Risk for corticosteroid adverse effects	For severe, acute symptoms

* Not a comprehensive list.

Other trials have shown the superiority of intranasal steroids when used as monotherapy over antileukotriene agents, such as montelukast and antihistamine–antileukotriene combinations (21). Moreover, adding an antihistamine or an antileukotriene agent to fluticasone does not seem to be more effective than the intranasal steroid itself (22).

In a randomized, controlled study of 100 patients with seasonal AR, researchers compared fluticasone propionate aqueous nasal spray, given alone or with either cetirizine or montelukast, with a combination of the latter two. Patients treated with fluticasone alone and with fluticasone/cetirizine showed significantly better total symptom scores and less nasal itching than those treated with cetirizine/montelukast. Patients treated with fluticasone/cetirizine had significantly better total symptom scores, less nasal congestion on waking, less daily nasal congestion, less rhinorrhea, and less nasal itching. The authors concluded that fluticasone is highly effective for treating patients with AR and that efficacy exceeded that of cetirizine and montelukast. Combining fluticasone with either cetirizine or montelukast did not offer a substantial advantage over using fluticasone alone (25, 54).

When AR is being treated with intranasal steroids, the risk for such side effects as glaucoma and cataracts is small. However, nasal irritation and bleeding can occur with significant frequency, and it is wise to examine the nasal septum periodically in long-term users for erosions that may precede perforation. There are no data to suggest that intranasal steroids have a systemic effect in suppressing the hypothalamic–pituitary–adrenal axis. Unlike orally inhaled steroids used in asthma, mucosal candida infection is uncommon.

Antihistamines

Although they may not be as effective as intranasal steroids, oral antihistamines are often included in guidelines for use in combination with steroids in patients with moderate to severe persistent AR. More often they are used as monotherapy in patients with less severe disease and work rapidly to relieve symptoms. Antihistamines block the H_1-histamine receptor and are effective in treating rhinorrhea, nasal itching, sneezing, and eye symptoms but have little effect on nasal congestion.

The first-generation oral antihistamines, including diphenhydramine and chlorpheniramine, are widely available over the counter. However, because they are sedating, minimize reaction

22. Di Lorenzo G, Pacor ML, Pellitteri ME, et al. Randomized placebo-controlled trial comparing fluticasone aqueous nasal spray in monotherapy, fluticasone plus cetirizine, fluticasone plus montelukast and cetirizine plus montelukast for seasonal allergic rhinitis. Clin Exp Allergy. 2004;34:259-67. [PMID: 14987306]
23. Kakutani C, Ogino S, Ikeda H, Enomoto T. [Comparison of clinical efficacy and cost-quality of antihistamines in early treatment for Japanese cedar pollinosis]. Arerugi. 2006;55:554-65. [PMID: 16883093]
24. Rodrigo GJ, Yañez A. The role of antileukotriene therapy in seasonal allergic rhinitis: a systematic review of randomized trials. Ann Allergy Asthma Immunol. 2006;96:779-86. [PMID: 16802764]
25. Wilson AM, O'Byrne PM, Parameswaran K. Leukotriene receptor antagonists for allergic rhinitis: a systematic review and meta-analysis. Am J Med. 2004;116:338-44. [PMID: 14984820]

Table 4. Effects of Medications on Symptoms*

Medication	Symptoms				
	Sneezing	Rhinorrhea	Nasal Congestion	Nasal Itch	Eye Symptoms
Antihistamine, oral	++	++	+	+++	++
Antihistamine, nasal	++	++	+	++	0
Antihistamine, ocular	0	0	0	0	+++
Nasal steroids	+++	+++	+++	++	++
Cromolyn, nasal	+	+	+	+	0
Cromolyn, ocular	0	0	0	0	++
Decongestants, oral	0	0	+	0	++
Decongestants, nasal†	0	0	++++	0	0
Anticholinergics, nasal	0	++	0	0	0
Antileukotrienes	0	+	++	0	++

*Data from references 8 and 34. Note: Consult package insert for cautions and constraints. 0 = not effective for symptoms; + = mildly effective for symptoms; ++ = moderately effective for symptoms; +++ and ++++ = very effective for symptoms.

26. Plaut M, Valentine MD. Clinical practice. Allergic rhinitis. N Engl J Med. 2005; 18:1934-44 [PMID: 16267324].

27. Colás C, Monzón S, Venturini M, Lezaun A. Double-blind, placebo-controlled study with a modified therapeutic vaccine of Salsola kali (Russian thistle) administered through use of a cluster schedule. J Allergy Clin Immunol. 2006;117:810-6. [PMID: 16630938]

time, and are especially problematic in elderly patients, they should be avoided.

In 1 randomized crossover study comparing the effects of alcohol, diphenhydramine (a first-generation antihistamine), fexofenadine (a second-generation antihistamine), and placebo, participants in a driving simulation test performed worst after taking a single 50-mg dose of diphenhydramine (16).

The second-generation oral antihistamines, including loratadine, cetirizine, and fexofenadine, are less sedating because they are larger charged molecules that have a greater affinity for peripheral H_1-receptors and less readily penetrate the central nervous system. They include oral cetirizine, fexofenadine, loratadine, and astemizole. Astemizole and terbinafine, which was withdrawn from the market in the late 1990s, prolong the QT interval and may cause cardiovascular side effects.

Although numerous trials compare various oral antihistamines to other classes of drugs used to treat AR, there are few head-to-head trials comparing them to each other. Effectiveness is believed to be similar.

One randomized trial compared 175 patients with Japanese cedar pollinosis treated with 1 of 7 types of antihistamine monotherapy—azelastine, cetirizine, ebastine, epinastine, fexofenadine, loratadine, or oxatomide—with 510 patients who received placebo. There was no significant difference in sneezing, rhinorrhea, ocular itching, or overall health between the treated and the nontreated groups (23).

The topical antihistamine azelastine is available as a nasal spray for treating seasonal AR. However, it may cause drowsiness and anticholinergic side effects. Topical azelastine, olopatadine, and levocabastine can also be used to treat the ocular symptoms of seasonal allergic conjunctivitis. Allergic conjunctivitis can also be treated with the topical nonsteroidal anti-inflammatory agent ketorolac and the topical formulations of the mast cell stabilizers cromolyn and nedocromil.

Decongestants

Oral decongestants, such as pseudoephedrine, only treat nasal blockage; however, they cause sympathomimetic side effects, such as nervousness and tachycardia, and should be avoided in patients with hypertension and hyperthyroidism.

Nasal decongestants act by contracting the vascular sphincters near the venous plexuses of the turbinates. Although they are more effective than their oral counterparts, they should not be used more than once weekly because more frequent use can cause rhinitis medicamentosa.

Mast Cell Stabilizers

The mast cell stabilizers cromolyn and nedocromil work at the surface of the mast cell to inhibit degranulation and prevent release of histamine and other inflammatory mediators. They can be administered intranasally to patients with milder forms of AR to prevent and treat all manifestations and are best started early before seasonal triggers have caused symptoms. They must be used several times daily.

Cromolyn and nedocromil are also available as eye drops for treatment of ocular symptoms associated with allergic conjunctivitis.

Although there are relatively few data on use of these agents in patients with AR, neither appears to be as effective as intranasal steroids or antihistamines. They have few side effects.

Leukotriene Inhibitors

Release of leukotrienes from mast cells has been implicated in development of some of the symptoms of AR, such as sneezing, nasal itching, rhinitis, and late-stage congestion. Montelukast, usually used in asthma, is an oral leukotriene receptor antagonist that is available in oral form to treat these symptoms. Because they are less effective than intranasal steroids, antileukotrienes are usually reserved as second-line treatment for patients with milder AR who cannot tolerate other drugs.

In 1 systematic review of 17 studies including 6231 adults with seasonal AR, oral leukotriene antagonists improved daytime and nighttime nasal symptoms, eye symptoms, and overall quality of life compared with placebo. However, no differences were found when leukotriene antagonists were compared with histamine H_1-antagonists, and they were less effective in decreasing daytime and nighttime nasal symptoms than intranasal steroids. Intranasal steroids were also more effective than leukotriene antagonists combined with histamine H_1-antagonists (24).

In another systematic review of 11 randomized trials (8 evaluating leukotriene-receptor antagonists alone or in combination with other drugs vs. placebo or other treatments, and 3 evaluating leukotriene-receptor antagonists) plus an antihistamine, antihistamines reduced nasal symptoms scores 2% more than leukotriene-receptor antagonists, and nasal steroids improved the score by 12% more (25).

Other Agents

In patients with moderate to severe persistent AR, nasal ipratropium can be used to treat persistent rhinorrhea. It may also be useful in patients with vasomotor rhinitis.

When should clinicians prescribe systemic corticosteroids for patients with AR?

Patients with severe symptoms who do not respond to or are intolerant of other medications may be treated with either oral or injected systemic corticosteroids (26).

Systemic corticosteroids act quickly and effectively in reducing mucosal inflammation. A course of prednisone (40 mg/d for 5 to 7 days) is usually sufficient. Patients who respond quickly can be switched to long-term therapy with intranasal corticosteroids or other medications.

Continuous daily oral prednisone at a dose of 10 to 20 mg/d should be considered only when rhinitis does not respond to intranasal corticosteroids, oral antihistamines, oral decongestants, and immunotherapy. Although there are no studies on the long-term side effects of systemic corticosteroids in patients with AR, therapy with supraphysiologic doses of steroids should be avoided whenever possible.

What are the indications for allergen immunotherapy? What are the pros and cons of this type of treatment?

Allergen immunotherapy should be considered in patients who continue to have moderate-to-severe symptoms despite allergen avoidance and maximum pharmacologic therapy, in those who require courses of systemic corticosteroids, and in those who have such coexisting conditions as sinusitis, asthma, or both (26). Immunotherapy is more appropriate in patients with ongoing symptoms that affect quality of life than in those with relatively mild seasonal disease who are affected by a single allergen.

Immunotherapy comprises subcutaneous injections of allergenic extracts to which the patient has been shown to be sensitive during IgE-specific antibody testing. Injections are administered by gradually increasing the dose weekly and then continuing that dose every few weeks for about a year. If effective after that time, treatment is continued for a total of approximately 3 to 5 years.

Allergen immunotherapy should be considered in patients with moderate to severe symptoms despite allergen avoidance and maximum pharmacologic therapy.

28. Durham SR, Walker SM, Varga EM, et al. Long-term clinical efficacy of grass-pollen immunotherapy. N Engl J Med. 1999;341:468-75. [PMID: 10441602]
29. Immune Tolerance Network Group. Immunotherapy with a ragweed-toll-like receptor 9 agonist vaccine for allergic rhinitis. N Engl J Med. 2006;355:1445-55. [PMID: 17021320]

30. Omalizumab Seasonal Allergic Rhinitis Trail Group. Effect of omalizumab on symptoms of seasonal allergic rhinitis: a randomized controlled trial. JAMA. 2001;286:2956-67. [PMID: 11743836]

31. Huggins JL, Looney RJ. Allergen immunotherapy. Am Fam Physician. 2004;70:689-96. [PMID: 15338781]

32. Möller C, Dreborg S, Ferdousi HA, Halken S, Høst A, Jacobsen L, et al. Pollen immunotherapy reduces the development of asthma in children with seasonal rhinoconjunctivitis (the PAT-study). J Allergy Clin Immunol. 2002;109:251-6. [PMID: 11842293]

Some patients who complete a successful course of allergen immunotherapy find that AR symptoms do not worsen when the immunotherapy is discontinued. However, others benefit from more prolonged treatment. The magnitude of symptom reduction during immunotherapy varies but has been shown to be significant in some studies and is associated with improvement in quality-of-life measures.

In 1 double-blind, randomized, placebo-controlled study, 60 patients with moderately severe seasonal AR were randomly assigned to 1 or 2 doses of Alutard grass pollen or placebo over 1 allergy season. During the study, mean symptom and medication scores were 29% and 32% lower, respectively, in the high-dose group and 22% and 26% lower, respectively, in the low-dose group compared with placebo (P value for both < 0.001). In addition to reduced symptoms and medication use, quality of life improved (27).

Investigators randomly assigned patients who had been successfully treated with immunotherapy for 3 to 4 years to continue or to stop therapy. They followed the patients for 3 years, comparing them to a matched group who had not received immunotherapy. At the end of the study, symptom scores in both treatment groups for the 504 patients who discontinued therapy and the 921 patients who continued therapy were significantly lower than for those who

did not receive immunotherapy, suggesting induction of prolonged clinical remission even after immunotherapy is stopped (28).

More recently, newer approaches to immunotherapy have shown promise in small studies of patients with seasonal AR. Such approaches include conjugation of native allergens to other substances, such as immunostimulatory sequences of DNA (29), and use of recombinant monoclonal antibodies to form complexes with free IgE to block its interaction with mast cells and decrease symptoms (30).

Allergen immunotherapy should generally be avoided in elderly patients with significant cardiovascular or pulmonary disease and in those receiving β-blockers who may be less able to tolerate systemic reactions. It should always be managed by an experienced allergist or immunologist. The risk for systemic reactions to allergen immunotherapy ranges from 0.05% to 3.5%. Such reactions include increased nasal and ocular allergic symptoms, urticaria, angioedema, and hypotension (31). In addition, immunotherapy carries a small risk for anaphylaxis and should be administered in a setting by clinicians prepared to manage such reactions (Table 5).

Table 5. Pros and Cons of Allergen Immunotherapy for Allergic Rhinitis

Pros	Cons
Proven effective in reducing symptoms in most carefully selected patients	Requires allergy consultation and allergy testing
Proven effective in reducing medication use	Requires weekly or monthly travel to physician's office for injections
Effective for coexisting allergic asthma	Involves needles
Nonpharmacologic	Risk for systemic reaction 0.1%–1% per injection
Can reduce development of asthma in children (32)	Pharmacologic therapy easier to prescribe and administer

What should clinicians tell patients who ask about complementary-alternative medicine treatments for AR?

Although some complementary–alternative medicine methods for AR and asthma have been studied, evidence on efficacy and safety is insufficient.

A systematic review (33) of published randomized trials of complementary medicine treatments for AR and asthma from a search of MEDLINE and the Cochrane Library evaluated for quality found no clear evidence for the efficacy of acupuncture. Both positive and negative studies of homeopathy were found. There were too few studies on herbal remedies to make any recommendation.

When should clinicians consult an allergist or otorhinolaryngologist to help manage patients with AR?

Although most patients can be managed by generalist physicians with allergen avoidance and drug therapy, consider consulting an allergist or immunologist for patients who:

- Have had a suboptimum response to allergen avoidance and drug therapy
- Might benefit from skin testing or IgE-specific antibody testing to identify triggers
- Are candidates for allergen immunotherapy
- Require episodic systemic corticosteroid therapy
- Have such complications as sinusitis, otitis media, and/or asthma
- Have significant impairment in daily activities or decreased quality of life

The clinician should consult an otorhinolaryngologist when there are suspected anatomical abnormalities of the upper respiratory tract, such as nasal polyposis, nasal septal deformities, and/or recurrent sinusitis, that may require surgical intervention.

What is the appropriate follow-up for patients with AR?

Clinicians should see patients with AR at least once a year. Patients should be seen more frequently depending on disease severity, success of symptom control, and development of treatment side effects. The symptom assessment scales in the Practice Improvement section may be useful in following patients with AR.

Clinicians should tell patients who are receiving immunotherapy to report any reactions or changes in health status or medications, new upper respiratory tract infections, and development or worsening of other underlying diseases.

33. Passalacqua G, Bousquet PJ, Carlsen KH, Kemp J, Lockey RF, Niggemann B, et al. ARIA update: I-Systematic review of complementary and alternative medicine for rhinitis and asthma. J Allergy Clin Immunol. 2006;117: 1054-62. [PMID: 16675332]
34. World Health Organization. Allergic rhinitis and its impact on asthma. In collaboration with the World Health Organization. Executive summary of the workshop report. 7-10 December 1999, Geneva, Switzerland. Allergy. 2002;57:841-55. [PMID: 12169183]

Treatment... Drug options effective in treating 1 or more AR symptoms include oral second-generation or nasal antihistamines, intranasal corticosteroids, oral or nasal decongestants, intranasal cromolyn, or leukotriene-receptor antagonists. For patients with mild or intermittent AR, clinicians should base the choice on the predominant symptoms. Nasal decongestants and systemic steroids should be used for short duration and only in patients unresponsive to other interventions. Intranasal steroids should be the first-line therapy in patients with moderate to severe, or chronic AR and in those with asthma, rhinosinusitis, or otitis media. Immunotherapy may be useful in selected patients with moderate to severe AR unresponsive to drug therapy or with complicated asthma or sinusitis in whom allergy testing has identified specific inciting allergens.

CLINICAL BOTTOM LINE

Practice Improvement

What do professional organizations recommend regarding the care of patients with AR?

A comprehensive listing of available guidelines is available through the National Guidelines Clearinghouse (www.guidelines.gov). The following guidelines from the American Academy of Allergy, Asthma and Immunology are especially useful resources in caring for patients with allergic rhinitis:

www.aaaai.org/members/resources/practice_guidelines/rhinitis.asp *(a complete listing of professional guidelines for diagnosis and management of allergic rhinitis and information on pharmacotherapy)*

www.aaaai.org/professionals/resources/pdf/rhinitis_symptom_severity2003.pdf *(a full set of allergic rhinitis symptoms severity scales, including questionnaires about medications and quality of life)*

---

in the clinic
Tool Kit

Allergic Rhinitis

Additional Online Resources for Patients from The American Academy of Allergy, Asthma and Immunology

www.aaaai.org/patients/resources/easy_reader/rhinitis.pdf

A 2-page patient handout on the definition, causes, signs and symptoms, and treatment of AR.

www.aaaai.org/patients/publicedmat/tips/rhinitis.stm

Simple tips for patients on the treatment of allergic and nonallergic rhinitis.

Useful Online Material for Patients from MedlinePLUS

www.nlm.nih.gov/medlineplus/ency/article/00813.htm

in the clinic

Allergic Rhinitis Symptom Severity Scales*

The Joint Task Force on Practice Parameters of the American Academy of Allergy, Asthma and Immunology; the American College of Allergy, Asthma and Immunology; and the Joint Council on Allergy, Asthma and Immunology has developed 7-point visual analogue scales to assess individual nasal and nonnasal symptoms, global assessment of symptoms, quality of life, and effectiveness and side effects of present and past medications over specific time intervals. Part of this instrument is excerpted here and can be given to patients before and during treatment to assess symptoms at regular intervals. The complete instrument can be viewed at *www.aaaai.org/professionals/resources/pdf/rhinitis_symptom_severity2003.pdf*.

Assessment of Nasal Symptom Severity

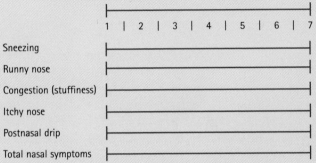

Assessment of Nonnasal Symptom Severity

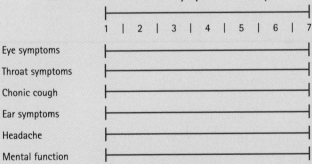

Global Assessment of Nasal and Nonnasal Symptom Severity

Key to symptoms
1 = None: No symptoms to an occasional limited episode
2
3 = Mild: Steady but easily tolerable symptoms
4
5 = Moderately bothersome: Symptoms hard to tolerate, may interfere with activities of daily living and/or sleep
6
7 = Unbearably severe: Symptoms so severe person cannot function all the time

*Reproduced with permission from Spector SL, Nicklas RA, Chapman JA, et al. Symptom severity assessment of allergic rhinitis: part 1. Ann Allergy Asthma Immunol. 2003;91:111–14.

Depression

D epression is common in primary care, affecting 5% to 10% of patients in this setting (1). Untreated depression may be a barrier to effective treatment of common co-occurring illnesses (e.g., diabetes and cardiovascular disease) (2). The disability associated with depression is similar to that of other chronic medical conditions (3). Depression is currently the fourth leading contributor to the global burden of disease (as measured using disability-adjusted life-years) and will move into second place by 2020 (4). Effective treatment of depression reduces symptoms and improves quality of life (5). Although sometimes viewed as "opening Pandora's box," primary care clinicians can efficiently identify and manage most cases of depression.

Screening

1. Pignone MP, Gaynes BN, Rushton JL, et al. Screening for depression in adults: a summary of the evidence for the U.S. Preventive Services Task Force. Ann Intern Med. 2002;136:765-76. [PMID: 12020146]
2. Katon WJ, Schoenbaum M, Fan MY, et al. Cost-effectiveness of improving primary care treatment of late-life depression. Arch Gen Psychiatry. 2005;62:1313-20. [PMID: 16330719]
3. Hays RD, Wells KB, Sherbourne CD, Rogers W, Spritzer K. Functioning and well-being outcomes of patients with depression compared with chronic general medical illnesses. Arch Gen Psychiatry. 1995;52:11-9. [PMID: 7811158]
4. Remick RA. Diagnosis and management of depression in primary care: a clinical update and review. CMAJ. 2002;167:1253-60. [PMID: 12451082]
5. Heiligenstein JH, Ware JE Jr., Beusterien KM, et al. Acute effects of fluoxetine versus placebo on functional health and well-being in late-life depression. Int Psychogeriatr. 1995;7 Suppl:125-37. [PMID: 8580388]
6. McDonald WM, Richard IH, DeLong MR. Prevalence, etiology, and treatment of depression in Parkinson's disease. Biol Psychiatry. 2003;54:363-75. [PMID: 12893111]
7. Beck CT. Predictors of postpartum depression: an update. Nurs Res. 2001;50:275-85. [PMID: 11570712]

Which patients are at especially high risk for depression?
Screening limited to high-risk adults (i.e., case-finding) may be more cost-effective than screening all adults. Risk factors for depression include older age (6) and associated neurologic conditions, recent childbirth (7), stressful life events (8), a personal or family history of depression, and selected medical comorbid conditions (9) (Table 1). Suicide rates are twice as high in families of suicide victims (10).

Should clinicians screen for depression?
A 2002 U.S. Preventive Services Task Force reviewed 14 randomized, controlled trials examining the effectiveness of screening for depression in primary care. This guideline recommends screening adults for depression in clinical practices that have "systems in place to assure accurate diagnosis, effective treatment, and follow-up" (1). Depression screening instruments do not diagnose depression but do accurately identify patients at risk. All positive screening tests should trigger a full diagnostic interview to determine the presence or absence of specific depressive disorders.

A meta-analysis of screening studies suggested that screening is associated with a 9% absolute reduction in the proportion of patients with persistent depression at 6 months. Assuming a prevalence of 10%, 110 primary care patients would need to be screened for depression to produce 1 additional remission (1).

How often should clinicians screen for depression?
The optimal interval for screening is unknown. Based on expert recommendations, clinicians should consider screening patients with identified risk factors (Table 1) and those with several unexplained or unrelated somatic symptoms, comorbid psychological conditions (e.g., panic disorder or generalized anxiety), substance abuse, chronic pain, or lack of response to usually effective treatments for comorbid medical conditions (11).

What methods should clinicians use to screen for depression?
A positive response to a 2-item instrument (see the Box on the next page) had a sensitivity of 96% and a specificity of 57%.

Table 1. Risk Factors for Depression

Risk Factor	
Older age (including associated neurologic conditions, such as Alzheimer disease and parkinsonism)	Prevalence 7% to 36% for persons over age 65 years; 40% for those with Alzheimer disease; 50% for those with Parkinson disease
Recent childbirth	13%
Recent stressful events	Variable
Personal or family history of depression	30% of patients experience recurrence within 2 years of initial diagnosis and 87% within 15 years
Comorbid conditions	2-fold increase in risk for depression among patients with diabetes, coronary artery disease, stroke, obesity, and HIV infection

Table 2. Screening Measures for Depression*

Screening Measure	Items, n	Time Frame	Available in Spanish	Administration Time, min
Primary Care Evaluation of Mental Disorders (PRIME-MD)	2	Past month	Yes	<2
Beck Depression Inventory (BDI)	21	Today	Yes	5–10
Center for Epidemiological Studies Depression Scale (CES-D)	20	Past week	Yes	5–10
General Health Questionnaire (GHQ)	28	Past few weeks	N/A	5–10
Medical Outcomes Study Depression Screen (MOS-D)	8	Past week	N/A	<2
Symptom-Driven Diagnostic System Primary Care (SDDS-PC)	5	Past month	N/A	<2
Zung Self-Depression Scale (SDS)	20	Recently	No	5–10
Hopkins Symptom Checklist-25	25	Past week	Yes and others	5–10
Geriatric Depression Scale (GDS)[†]	30	Past week	Yes	10–15
Cornell Scale for Depression in Dementia[†]	19	Past week	No	10–15
Hamilton Rating Scale for Depression[†]	21	N/A	No	10–15
Edinburgh Postnatal Depression Scale[‡]	10	Past week	Yes	5–10

* Adapted from Mulrow CD, Williams, JW Jr, Gerety MB, et al. Case-finding instruments for depression in primary care settings. Ann Intern Med. 1995;122:913-21. Sharp LK, Lipsky MS. Screening for depression across the lifespan: a review of measures for use in primary care settings. Am Fam Physician. 2002;66:1001-8.

† For use in elderly patients (>65 years of age).   ‡ For use in postpartum women.

Patients with a positive response to 1 or both questions (i.e., those with depressed mood and/or anhedonia) should undergo a full diagnostic interview to assess whether they meet the criteria for depression disorders as set forth in the *Diagnostic and Statistical Manual of Mental Disorders, fourth edition* (DSM-IV) (see Table 3 in Diagnosis).

A meta-analysis of 9 case-finding instruments in 18 studies and a head-to-head study of screening instruments showed that the 2-question instrument is as good as many of the longer instruments (12).

Many other screening tools, targeted to specific populations, are available (Table 2). The most commonly used screening tools in adults include the Beck Depression Inventory Scales II, the Center for Epidemiologic Studies Depression Scale-Revised, and the Zung Self-Rating Depression

---

Screening Questions for Depression

"Over the past 2 weeks have you felt down, depressed, hopeless?"

"Over the past 2 weeks have you felt little interest or pleasure in doing things?"

Scale. The Edinburgh Postnatal Depression Scale was specifically developed to assess postpartum depression (12–14). In the elderly, cognitive impairment can limit the utility of screening instruments and should be assessed with the Mini-Mental State Examination. In patients with cognitive deficits, clinicians should consider the interviewer-administered Cornell Scale for Depression in Dementia or the Hamilton Rating Scale (15, 16). Several tools are available in non-English versions. The Hopkins Symptom Checklist-25 has been validated in refugee populations and is available in many languages.

8. Person C, Tracy M, Galea S. Risk factors for depression after a disaster. J Nerv Ment Dis. 2006;194:659-66. [PMID: 16971817]
9. Kendler KS, Gardner CO, Prescott CA. Clinical characteristics of major depression that predict risk of depression in relatives. Arch Gen Psychiatry. 1999;56:322-7. [PMID: 10197826]
10. Runeson B, Asberg M. Family history of suicide among suicide victims. Am J Psychiatry. 2003;160:1525-6. [PMID: 12900320]
11. Terre L, Poston WS, Foreyt J, St Jeor ST. Do somatic complaints predict subsequent symptoms of depression? Psychother Psychosom. 2003;72:261-7. [PMID: 12920330]
12. Mulrow CD, Williams JW Jr., Gerety MB, et al. Case-finding instruments for depression in primary care settings. Ann Intern Med. 1995;122:913-21. [PMID: 7755226]
13. Beck AT, Steer RA, Brown GK. BDI-II, Beck Depression Inventory: Manual. 2nd ed. Boston: Harcourt Brace; 1996.

Screening... Clinicians should screen for depression as the first step in a systematic evaluation of mood disorders in all adults. Adults who are older, are postpartum, have a personal or family history of depression, or have comorbid medical illness are at increased risk. There is little evidence to recommend one screening method over another, so physicians can choose the method that best suits their patient population and practice setting. The 2-question instrument is more efficient and performs as well as longer instruments.

CLINICAL BOTTOM LINE

Diagnosis

What are the diagnostic criteria for depression?

Depression is diagnosed when 5 or more DSM-IV symptoms occur in the same 2-week period in conjunction with a change from previous functioning (Table 3) (17). At least one of the symptoms must be either depressed mood or anhedonia, as reflected in the 2-question depression screening model mentioned earlier.

An alternative strategy for diagnosing major depressive disorders is to follow the 2-item (mood and anhedonia) case-finding questions with assessment of the so-called SALSA inventory:

- Sleep disturbance
- Anhedonia
- Low Self-esteem
- Appetite disturbance

Patients with 2 of these 4 symptoms occurring nearly every day for at least 2 weeks are virtually identical to those diagnosed using the 5-out-of-9-symptom algorithm in Table 3. Over 97% of patients with major depression have at least 2 of the SALSA symptoms. Only 6% of persons who do not have major depression will have 2 of the SALSA symptoms (18).

How can clinicians determine the severity of depression?

Assessment of depressive symptom severity helps guide treatment. Mild to moderate depression responds equally well to either medication or psychotherapy (19). Patients with severe major depressive disorder benefit more from antidepressant medication or from medication combined with psychotherapy than from psychotherapy alone.

The self-administered 9-item Patient Health Questionnaire (PHQ-9) is easily scored to quantify the severity of depression (Table 4) (20). Items 1 through 9 are summed to yield a scale score ranging from 0 to 27.

On this scale, 0 to 4 is considered nondepressed, 5 to 9 mild depression, 10 to 14 moderate depression, 15 to 19 moderately severe depression, and 20 to 27 severe depression. The 9 items reflect the 9 DSM-IV criteria. Item 10 assesses functional impairment. Like symptom severity, severe functional impairment may suggest the need for hospitalization and psychiatric consultation (21).

How can clinicians and patients distinguish between normal reactions to life events and depression?

Situational adjustment reaction with depressed mood is subsyndromal depression with a clear precipitant. Subsyndromal (minor) depression is characterized by 2 to 4 DSM-IV depressive symptoms, including depressed mood or anhedonia, for more than 2 weeks (Table 3). Adjustment disorder usually abates with resolution of the stressor, but careful observation and supportive counseling are indicated.

Differentiating normal grieving and pathologic grief from depression can be difficult. The syndrome of major depression may be transiently present in normal grief; however, sadness without the complete syndrome is more common. Transient hallucinations (hearing or seeing the deceased person) or suicidal thoughts (feeling that one would be better off dead or should have died with the deceased person) are considered a normal part of grief. The boundaries of normal grief are affected by cultural and societal factors. Symptoms suggestive of depression include inappropriate guilt, persistent thoughts of death, morbid preoccupation with worthlessness, marked psychomotor retardation, prolonged functional impairment, and hallucinations. Patients whose symptoms persist beyond 2 months should be evaluated for depression.

14. Georgiopoulos AM, Bryan TL, Yawn BP, et al. Population-based screening for postpartum depression. Obstet Gynecol. 1999;93:653-7. [PMID: 10912961]
15. Alexopoulos GS, Abrams RC, Young RC, Shamoian CA. Cornell Scale for Depression in Dementia. Biol Psychiatry. 1988;23:271-84. [PMID: 3337862]
16. Hamilton M. A rating scale for depression. J Neurol Neurosurg Psychiatry. 1960;23:56-62. [PMID: 14399272]
17. Diagnostic and Statistical Manual of Mental Disorders (DSM-IV). 4th ed. Washington, DC: American Psychiatric Association; 1994.
18. Brody DS, Hahn SR, Spitzer RL, et al. Identifying patients with depression in the primary care setting: a more efficient method. Arch Intern Med. 1998;158:2469-75. [PMID: 9855385]

Table 3. Criteria for Major Depressive Episode on the Basis of the *Diagnostic and Statistical Manual of Mental Disorders**

Five or more of the following symptoms (one of which is depressed mood or loss of interest or pleasure) have occurred together for a 2-week period and represent a change from previous functioning:

Depressed mood most of the day, nearly every day as self-reported or observed by others

Diminished interest or pleasure in all or almost all activities most of the day, nearly every day

Significant weight loss when not dieting, or weight gain; or decrease or increase in appetite nearly every day

Insomnia or hypersomnia nearly every day

Psychomotor agitation or retardation nearly every day

Fatigue or loss of energy nearly every day

Feelings of worthlessness or excessive or inappropriate guilt nearly every day

Diminished ability to think or concentrate nearly every day

Recurrent thoughts of death, recurrent suicidal ideation without a specific plan.

The symptoms do not meet criteria for a mixed episode.

The symptoms cause clinically significant distress or impairment in social, occupational, or other areas of functioning.

The symptoms are not due to the direct physiologic effects of a substance (drug or medication) or a general medical condition (hypothyroidism).

The symptoms are not better accounted for by bereavement, or the symptoms persist for more than 2 months or are characterized by marked functional impairment, morbid preoccupation with worthlessness, suicidal ideation, psychotic symptoms, or psychomotor retardation.

* From American Psychiatric Association. Guidelines for the Treatment of Patients with Major Depressive Disorder. Washington, DC: American Psychiatric Publishing, Inc.; 1994. Reproduced with permission.

What alternative medical or psychiatric disorders should clinicians consider when evaluating patients with symptoms of depression?

Certain medications and comorbid conditions are known to be associated with clinical depression. Glucocorticoids, interferon, l-dopa, propanolol, and oral contraceptives are the most commonly implicated medications. Data on isotretinoin remain unclear (22). The clinical situation will guide the clinician in choosing to discontinue the suspected agent or to add antidepressant therapy.

Depression can be a manifestation of hypothyroidism, Cushing disease, or cobalamin deficiency, and depression

Table 4. Patient Health Questionnaire-9*

Over the last 2 weeks, how often have you been bothered by any of the following problems?
(0 = not at all; 1 = several days; 2 = more than one half the days; 3 = nearly every day)

1. Little interest or pleasure in doing things

2. Feeling down, depressed, or hopeless

3. Trouble falling or staying asleep or sleeping too much

4. Feeling tired or having little energy

5. Poor appetite or overeating

6. Feeling bad about yourself or that you are a failure or have let yourself or your family down

7. Trouble concentrating on things, such as reading the newspaper or watching television

8. Moving or speaking so slowly that other people have noticed or the opposite (i.e., being so fidgety or restless that you have been moving around a lot more than usual)

9. Thoughts that you would be better off dead or hurting yourself in some way

10. If you have checked off any problems, how difficult have these problems made it for you to do your work, take care of things at home, or get along with other people?

* The 9 items reflect the 9 DSM-IV criteria. Item 10 assesses functional impairment. Like symptom severity, severe functional impairment may suggest the need for hospitalization and psychiatric consultation. ©1999 Pfizer Inc. All rights reserved. Reproduced with permission.

19. Thase ME, Greenhouse JB, Frank E, et al. Treatment of major depression with psychotherapy or psychotherapy-pharmacotherapy combinations. Arch Gen Psychiatry. 1997;54:1009-15. [PMID: 9366657]

20. Löwe B, Unützer J, Callahan CM, Perkins AJ, Kroenke K. Monitoring depression treatment outcomes with the patient health questionnaire-9. Med Care. 2004;42:1194-201. [PMID: 15550799]

21. Depression Guideline Panel. Depression in Primary Care: Treatment for Major Depression, Volume 2. Clinical Practice Guideline No. 5. Rockville, MD: US Department of Health and Human Services Agency for Health Care Policy and Research; 1993.

Clinicians should assess for suicidal ideation at each visit for depression.

22. Marqueling AL, Zane LT. Depression and suicidal behavior in acne patients treated with isotretinoin: a systematic review. Semin Cutan Med Surg. 2005;24:92-102. [PMID: 16092797]
23. Frasure-Smith N. The Montreal Heart Attack Readjustment Trial. J Cardiopulm Rehabil. 1995;15:103-6. [PMID: 8542512]
24. House A, Dennis M, Mogridge L, et al. Mood disorders in the year after first stroke. Br J Psychiatry. 1991;158:83-92. [PMID: 2015456]
25. Popkin MK, Callies AL, Lentz RD, Colon EA, Sutherland DE. Prevalence of major depression, simple phobia, and other psychiatric disorders in patients with long-standing type I diabetes mellitus. Arch Gen Psychiatry. 1988;45:64-8. [PMID: 3257379]
26. Schleifer SJ, Macari-Hinson MM, Coyle DA, et al. The nature and course of depression following myocardial infarction. Arch Intern Med. 1989;149:1785-9. [PMID: 2788396]
27. Depression Guideline Panel. Depression in Primary Care: Detection and Diagnosis, Volume 1. Clinical Practice Guideline No. 5. Rockville, MD: US Department of Health and Human Services Agency for Health Care Policy and Research; 1993.
28. Geringer ES, Perlmuter LC, Stern TA, Nathan DM. Depression and diabetic neuropathy: a complex relationship. J Geriatr Psychiatry Neurol. 1988;1:11-5. [PMID: 3252874]
29. Moscicki EK. Identification of suicide risk factors using epidemiologic studies. Psychiatr Clin North Am. 1997;20:499-517. [PMID: 9323310]

can co-occur with diabetes, stroke, and myocardial infarction (23-28). It can also be associated with somatization, anxiety, domestic violence, cognitive dysfunction, and alcohol dependence.

How should clinicians assess a depressed patient's risk for self-harm, including suicide?

Each year, more than 30,000 Americans commit suicide. Mental and addictive disorders, such as alcohol abuse, are the most powerful risk factors for suicide in all age groups, accounting for over 90% of all suicides (29). In evaluating a patient with major depression, previous suicide attempts should be considered the best predictor of completed suicide (30). Most patients who commit suicide have seen a physician in the preceding months. Clinicians should assess for suicidal intent at each visit for depression.

Asking about and reducing access to lethal means (especially firearms) can reduce the risk for suicide (31). A recent report also suggests that close telephone follow-up by an experienced psychiatrist can reduce the risk for suicide after a prior suicide attempt (32). Accurate assessment of suicidal risk and consideration of hospitalization is critical. Clinicians should consult a psychiatrist if there is any uncertainty regarding suicidal risk. In patients with suicidal ideation, the "No Harm Contract" (33) is a verbal or written agreement in which suicidal patients are asked to agree not to harm or kill themselves for a particular period.

In the absence of exacerbating factors, if the patient has good social support and is able to make a contract for safety, the clinician can proceed with outpatient treatment and close follow-up. If the patient has poor social support, cannot contract for safety, or is currently intoxicated, the clinician should choose emergency referral for hospitalization and psychiatric assessment.

When should clinicians consult a mental health professional for help diagnosing depression or a related mood disorder?

While many mood disorders can be successfully managed by the primary care clinician, psychiatric consultation should be considered when diagnostic uncertainty, significant psychiatric comorbidity, or significant suicidal ideation is present. Common diagnostic consultations involve patients with prolonged grieving, atypical symptoms with significant functional impairment, patients with a history suggestive of bipolar illness, or those on multiple medications. Cultural consultations to aid in the diagnosis and treatment for depression in culturally diverse populations are available in some settings (34).

The syndrome of major depression can be a presenting feature of other mental disorders. Clinicians should assess patients for psychotic disorders (delusions, hallucinations, disorganized speech, or episodes of catatonia) and substance abuse. Patients with psychotic symptoms or comorbid substance abuse are at greater risk for suicide and warrant psychiatric evaluation (35).

It is important to screen patients for a history of manic episodes (periods of days to weeks marked by unusually high energy, euphoria, hyperactivity, or impaired judgment). Patients with undiagnosed bipolar affective disorder who present with depressed mood may convert to frank mania if they receive antidepressant medication without a concurrent mood-stabilizing medication. If a patient develops manic or hypomanic symptoms after starting an antidepressant, consulting a psychiatrist is recommended. Delays in initiation of mood-stabilizing drug therapy at illness onset in bipolar disorder, even for relatively mild symptoms, may confer elevated risk for suicidal behavior, poorer social adjustment, and more hospitalizations (36).

Treatment

How should clinicians decide whether to recommend psychotherapy, drug therapy, or both?

Patients with mild to moderate major depression will benefit equally from psychotherapy or medication (19); combined therapy offers no demonstrated short-term benefit in these groups. Informed patient preference should influence choice of initial therapy. In some areas, therapist availability and insurance policies remain barriers to care. Clinicians should help patients to identify appropriate psychotherapy providers and willingly reevaluate initiating pharmacotherapy if access is difficult.

Severely depressed patients benefit more from antidepressant medication than psychotherapy alone. The greatest benefit could be derived from combined medication and psychotherapy.

A meta-analysis of original data from 595 patients with major depression comparing interpersonal therapy or cognitive therapy alone with interpersonal therapy plus antidepressants showed that combined therapy was superior to psychotherapy alone in severely depressed patients (19).

What types of behavioral interventions and psychotherapy are most likely to be effective for depression?

Some patients with mild depression may prefer an initial trial of a self-help book on cognitive behavioral techniques, such as *Feeling Good: The New Mood Therapy* by David D. Burns (37).

A meta-analysis of so-called "bibliotherapy" found a large improvement at 4 weeks; however, the participants appeared to have a very high educational level (38).

Behavioral interventions and psychotherapy require specialized training. Three types of psychotherapeutic options have proven effective: cognitive behavioral therapy, interpersonal therapy, and problem-solving therapy. Cognitive behavioral therapy aims to modify thoughts and behaviors to yield positive emotions. This therapy has also been used to treat residual symptoms after drug therapy and may help prevent relapse in patients with recurrent depression (39). Interpersonal therapy targets such interpersonal events as conflicts and role transitions that seem to contribute to the current depressive episode. This therapy is useful only if the patient has the capacity for psychological insight and is committed to longer-term therapy. Problem-solving therapy teaches patients how to improve their ability to deal with their specific everyday problems. Therapists often use a combination of the 3 therapies.

How should clinicians select from among the many antidepressant drug therapies?

Clinicians face a wide array of antidepressant drug options (Table 5). The most commonly prescribed antidepressants are classified as selective serotonin reuptake inhibitors (SSRIs). Other agents include monoamine oxidase inhibitors (MAOIs), tricyclic antidepressants (TCAs), serotonin norepinephrine reuptake inhibitors (SNRIs), 5-HT_2–receptor antagonists, and dopamine reuptake inhibitors.

Generally, MAOIs are used infrequently, even by psychiatric specialists, because of the long list of dietary

30. Brody DS, Thompson TL 2nd, Larson DB, et al. Recognizing and managing depression in primary care. Gen Hosp Psychiatry. 1995;17:93-107. [PMID: 7789790]
31. Mann JJ, Apter A, Bertolote J, et al. Suicide prevention strategies: a systematic review. JAMA. 2005;294:2064-74. [PMID: 16249421]
32. Vaiva G, Vaiva G, Ducrocq F, et al. Effect of telephone contact on further suicide attempts in patients discharged from an emergency department: randomised controlled study. BMJ. 2006;332:1241-5. [PMID: 16735333]
33. Stanford EJ, Goetz RR, Bloom JD. The No Harm Contract in the emergency assessment of suicidal risk. J Clin Psychiatry. 1994;55:344-8. [PMID: 8071303]
34. Kirmayer LJ, Groleau D, Guzder J, Blake C, Jarvis E. Cultural consultation: a model of mental health service for multicultural societies. Can J Psychiatry. 2003;48:145-53. [PMID: 12728738]
35. Hofmann DP, Dubovsky SL. Depression and suicide assessment. Emerg Med Clin North Am. 1991;9:107-21. [PMID: 2001661]
36. Goldberg JF, Ernst CL. Features associated with the delayed initiation of mood stabilizers at illness onset in bipolar disorder. J Clin Psychiatry. 2002;63:985-91. [PMID: 12444811]
37. Burns DD. Feeling Good-The New Mood Therapy Revised and Updated. New York: Avon; 1999.
38. Anderson L, Lewis G, Araya R, et al. Self-help books for depression: how can practitioners and patients make the right choice? Br J Gen Pract. 2005;55:387-92. [PMID: 15904559]

Table 5. Drug Treatment for Depression*

Agent, Daily Dosage	Benefits	Side Effects	Notes
SSRI Citalopram, 20–60 mg (10–40 mg) Escitalopram, 5–20 mg (5–10 mg) Fluoxetine, 20–60 mg (5–40 mg) Fluvoxamine, 100–300 mg Paroxetine, 20–50 mg (5–40 mg) Sertraline, 50–200 mg (2.5–150 mg)	Effective, well tolerated, lower risk for overdose compared with TCAs	Nausea, diarrhea, decreased appetite, anxiety, nervousness, insomnia, somnolence, sweating, impaired sexual function	All contraindicated with MAOIs; all have potential for drug interactions with hepatically metabolized drugs Fluvoxamine: nausea common Paroxetine: withdrawal syndrome not uncommon; FDA advisory that it should generally not be initiated in women who are in their first trimester of pregnancy or in those planning to become pregnant, but for some, the benefits of continuing paroxetine may outweigh the potential risk to the fetus
SNRI Venlafaxine, 75–350 mg (50–225 mg) Duloxetine, 30–60 mg Mirtazapine, 15–45 mg (7.5–30 mg)	Venlafaxine: effective, well tolerated, lower risk for overdose than TCAs Mirtazapine may be effective when other agents have not been	Venlafaxine: nausea, dry mouth, anorexia, constipation, dizziness, somnolence, insomnia, nervousness, sweating, abnormalities of sexual function; cardiovascular effects Mirtazapine: high incidences of somnolence, dizziness, weight gain, increased cholesterol, elevated liver transaminases, orthostatic hypotension; possible agranulocytosis	Venlafaxine: contraindicated with MAOIs; may cause sustained treatment-emergent hypertension, nervousness, and insomnia Mirtazapine: use caution with renal impairment; do not use with MAOIs; avoid diazepam and similar drugs
Norepinephrine uptake inhibitor Maprotiline, 25–225 mg	Fewer side effects than TCAs	Dry mouth, drowsiness, dizziness, nervousness, constipation	Contraindicated with MAOIs; can cause seizures; use with caution in patients with cardiovascular disease and in those receiving sympathomimetics, anticholinergics, and thyroid hormone
Dopamine reuptake inhibitor Bupropion, 300–450 mg (75–225 mg)	Less weight gain, fewer adverse effects on sexual functioning; approved for smoking cessation	Lowers seizure threshold, may exacerbate eating disorders, anorexia, dry mouth, rash, sweating, tinnitus, tremor, abdominal pain, agitation, anxiety, dizziness, insomnia, myalgia, nausea, palpitation, pharyngitis, urinary frequency	Contraindicated in patients with history of seizures, family history of seizures, and head trauma; missed doses should not be taken with next dose; use with caution with other drugs that may lower seizure threshold and in patients with impaired hepatic function; do not use with MAOIs or in patients with anorexia and bulimia
5-HT$_2$–receptor agonist Nefazodone, 200–600 mg	Fewer adverse effects on sexual functioning; lower incidence of postural hypotension than TCAs but higher than that of SSRIs; low incidence of clinically significant ECG abnormalities	Liver failure in 1/250,000–300,000 patient-years; somnolence, dry mouth, nausea, dizziness, constipation, asthenia, lightheadedness, blurred vision, confusion, abnormal vision	Contraindicated with terfenadine, astemizole, cisapride, pimozide, or carbamazepine; do not use with triazolam, and alprazolam; use with caution in cardiovascular, cerebrovascular, and seizure disorders; drug removed from European market because of risk for liver failure
TCA Nortriptyline, 25–150 mg (10–100 mg) Desipramine, 25–300 mg Amitryptyline, 25–300 mg Doxepin, 25–300 mg Imipramine, 25–300 mg Amoxapine, 50–300 mg Clomipramine, 25–250 mg Protriptyline, 15–60 mg Trimipramine, 50–300 mg	Desipramine least sedating Amitryptyline and doxepin may be taken at bedtime to aid with sleep	Dry mouth, dizziness, nervousness, constipation, nausea, sedation, anticholinergic and orthostatic hypotension, may cause tardive dyskinesia and the neuroleptic malignant syndrome	Contraindicated with MAOIs; do not use in patients with prolonged QT interval or drugs that may prolong QT interval; use with caution in patients with cardiovascular disease and arrhythmia and patients prone to urinary retention and on thyroid medications; may precipitate attacks in narrow angle glaucoma; follow ECGs and orthostatic blood pressure changes
MAOI inhibitor, nonselective Isocarboxazid, 10–60 mg Tranylcypromine, 20–60 mg Phenelzine, 7.5–90 mg	May be effective when other agents have not been	Dizziness, headache, drowsiness, insomnia, hypersomnia fatigue, weakness, tremors, twitching, myoclonic movements, hyperreflexia, constipation, dry mouth, gastro-intestinal disturbances, elevated serum aminotransferases (without accompanying signs and symptoms), weight gain, postural hypotension, edema, sexual disturbances	Contraindicated in patients with cerebrovascular and cardiovascular disease, pheochromocytoma, liver disease; increases risk for hypertensive crisis and serotonin syndrome (hypertension, hyperthermia, tachycardia, death); many dietary (tyramine-containing foods) restrictions; interactions with many prescription and OTC drugs, also with alcohol, barbiturates, and cocaine; infrequently used in primary care; extensive patient education and caution in using with other medications are required

* Doses for geriatric patients are in parentheses. ECG = electrocardiogram; FDA = U.S. Food and Drug Administration; GI = gastrointestinal; MAOI = monoamine oxidase inhibitor; OTC = over the counter; SNRI = serotonin and noradrenaline reuptake inhibitor; SSRI = selective serotonin reuptake inhibitor; TCA = tricyclic antidepressant.

restrictions and potential for hypertensive crisis. However, MAOIs may be more effective in patients with atypical depression (characterized by hypersomnolence, hyperphagia, and rejection sensitivity) (40). Primary care clinicians should consult with a psychiatrist before considering MAOI therapy.

In contemporary practice, TCAs are also used less often because they may cause intolerable dry mouth, constipation, and dizziness and are relatively contraindicated in patients with coronary artery disease, congestive heart failure, and arrhythmias.

There are no important clinical differences in response rates among commonly prescribed antidepressants (including SSRIs, bupropion, duloxetine, mirtazapine, and venlafaxine) (41). Drug selection is based on tolerability, safety, evidence of effectiveness with the patient or first-degree relative, and cost. Regardless of the drug, therapy is effective. Within approximately 6 weeks, half of persons receiving antidepressants have at least a 50% reduction in symptoms (42).

How should clinicians monitor response to drug therapy?

Treatment for depression requires a minimum of 6 to 9 months of close follow-up. The first 2 weeks of drug therapy is often the most challenging for patients. The pessimism and hopelessness intrinsic to depression and the relatively rapid onset of adverse effects can lead to nonadherence: 28% of depressed primary care patients stop taking their medication during the initial month of treatment, and 44% stop within 3 months (43).

Clinicians should follow-up with patients within 1 to 2 weeks of initiation of therapy to ask about acceptance of medication, reinforce educational messages, reassess suicidality, and address adverse events. Telephone follow-up by a trained nurse is also effective (44). Addressing specific adverse effects as they emerge is critical to helping patients

continue medication until they respond. In addition, antidepressants may be associated with an increased risk for suicide in children, adolescents, and young adults.

A meta-analysis of 2741 patients age 6 to 18 years showed an increased relative risk for self-harm or suicide-related events among patients treated with newer-generation antidepressants compared with those given placebo (4.8% vs. 3.0%; P = 0.01; number needed-to-treat for harm, 55) (45).

The U.S. Food and Drug Administration (FDA) has issued a Public Health Advisory recommending close monitoring of all patients treated with antidepressants, particularly early in the course of treatment. A warning statement regarding a possible increased risk for suicide has been added to FDA Patient Information Sheets for citalopram, duloxetine, venlafaxine, escitalopram, fluvoxamine, paroxetine, fluoxetine, miratzapine, bupropion, and sertraline. However, the preponderance of evidence suggests that when properly administered, antidepressants avert many more suicides than they cause (46).

During the next 12 weeks, patients should be monitored in person or by phone on a monthly basis. Clinicians can use these encounters to assess adherence to medication and psychotherapy, emergence of adverse effects, symptom breakthrough, suicidality, and psychosocial stress.

Clinicians can also use a structured instrument, such as the PHQ-9, to assess changes in symptom severity by following changes in the score over time: A 50% decrease in symptoms constitutes an adequate response; a 25% to 50% response may indicate the need to modify treatment.

Recurrence of depression after a first episode is common. Clinicians should educate patients and their families to self-assess for symptoms and risk for recurrent episodes. Surveillance for recurrence or relapse should continue indefinitely.

Drug therapy for depression requires a minimum of 6 to 9 months with close follow-up.

39. Fava GA, Rafanelli C, Grandi S, Canestrari R, Morphy MA. Six-year outcome for cognitive behavioral treatment of residual symptoms in major depression. Am J Psychiatry. 1998;155:1443-5. [PMID: 9766780]
40. Thase ME, Trivedi MH, Rush AJ. MAOIs in the contemporary treatment of depression. Neuropsychopharmacology. 1995;12:185-219. [PMID: 7612154]
41. Kroenke K, West SL, Swindle R, et al. Similar effectiveness of paroxetine, fluoxetine, and sertraline in primary care: a randomized trial. JAMA. 2001;286:2947-55. [PMID: 11743835]
42. Williams JW Jr., Mulrow CD, Chiquette E, et al. A systematic review of newer pharmacotherapies for depression in adults: evidence report summary. Ann Intern Med. 2000;132:743-56. [PMID: 10787370]
43. Lin EH, Von Korff M, Katon W, et al. The role of the primary care physician in patients' adherence to antidepressant therapy. Med Care. 1995;33:67-74. [PMID: 7823648]
44. Wells KB, Sherbourne C, Schoenbaum M, et al. Impact of disseminating quality improvement programs for depression in managed primary care: a randomized controlled trial. JAMA. 2000;283:212-20. [PMID: 10634337]

45. Dubicka B, Hadley S, Roberts C. Suicidal behaviour in youths with depression treated with new-generation antidepressants: meta-analysis. Br J Psychiatry. 2006;189:393-8. [PMID: 17077427]
46. Grunebaum MF, Ellis SP, Li S, Oquendo MA, Mann JJ. Antidepressants and suicide risk in the United States, 1985-1999. J Clin Psychiatry. 2004;65:1456-62. [PMID: 15554756]
47. Pies RW, Rogers DP. Handbook of Essential Psychopharmacology. 2nd ed. Arlington, VA: American Psychiatric Publishing; 2005.
48. Trivedi MH, Fava M, Wisniewski SR, et al. Medication augmentation after the failure of SSRIs for depression. N Engl J Med. 2006;354:1243-52. [PMID: 16554526]

Consider long-term maintenance therapy for patients who have had 3 depressive episodes.

How long should clinicians treat depressed patients with drugs and when should they consider long-term maintenance on drug therapy?

The aim of therapy is complete remission of symptoms and return to normal functioning. In first episodes, treatment with antidepressant medication should be continued for 4 to 9 months after remission is achieved. Treatment to remission may take 1 to several months. While not strictly evidence-based, some clinicians advocate treatment for 1 year to maintain remission during 1 occurrence of every major holiday and anniversary. For patients with a history of depressive episodes, many experts advocate a "three-strikes-and-you're-on" strategy, meaning that after 3 depressive episodes, long-term maintenance therapy is recommended (47).

When should clinicians consider switching drugs because of a suboptimal response to initial drug therapy?

A minority of patients starting antidepressant therapy achieve complete remission, and increasing the dosage of the current medication or changing drugs is often necessary.

The STAR-D study randomly assigned 4041 patients to one of several treatment sequences, all starting with 12 weeks of citalopram. This landmark trial showed that 1) 30% of patients achieved complete remission after 12 weeks of treatment with citalopram; 2) of those in whom the first antidepressant failed, about 25% responded to a second alternative agent (sertraline, venlafaxine, or bupropion); 3) about one third of patients not achieving remission with citalopram responded to augmentation with bupropion (48).

The main message to clinicians and patients is not to give up, as both substitution and augmentation strategies may eventually be effective.

Complete intolerance or nonresponse should be addressed by a change in medication. Intolerance and lack of response to any particular antidepressant are common but not predictive of response to another antidepressant (49).

If response to treatment is not complete by week 6, clinicians have several treatment options (Table 6). If a partial response is observed, the dose of the initial agent should be maximized as tolerated before the medication is switched or another is added. If partial response continues, introduction of a second drug while maintaining the initial agent can be tried.

The advantages of combination therapy include faster effect than when 1 medication is withdrawn and another is started, potential for synergistic or complementary effect, and avoidance of withdrawal symptoms when the first agent is stopped. The disadvantages include the increased complexity of the regimen, increased opportunities for drug interactions, and adverse effects.

The addition of bupropion to an SSRI or venlafaxine therapy may enhance response or treat side effects in many patients (50). Similar response rates are found when adding mirtazapine to SSRI treatment (51). Combinations of MAOIs and either SSRIs or TCAs are not recommended because they may trigger the serotonin syndrome (marked by confusion, nausea, autonomic instability, and

---

Table 6. Treatment Options for Incomplete Response to Therapy*

Increase dose of the current medication

Switch to a different antidepressant

Add a second antidepressant (combination therapy; for example, an SSRI plus bupropion, a TCA, or mirtazapine)

Add an agent not typically used for depression (psychiatric consultation advised), e.g., lithium, liothyronine, risperidone, or pindolol

Add psychotherapy

---

* SSRI = selective serotonin reuptake inhibitor; TCA = tricyclic antidepressant.

hyperreflexia). There are no controlled studies of the use of stimulants (e.g., methyphenidate, dextroamphetamine) for augmentation (52). Adding psychotherapy to pharmacotherapy is another option.

What are the common adverse effects of antidepressant drugs and how should clinicians manage these effects?

Some specific side effects are more common with particular drugs and should guide choice of replacement medication (Table 5). Sexual side effects of SSRIs include decreased libido or interest (men and women), anorgasmia (women), and delayed ejaculation (men). Strategies for addressing these side effects include pretreatment counseling, switching to a drug with a different mechanism of action (e.g., bupropion or mirtazapine), or augmenting with sildenafil for SSRI-associated erectile dysfunction in the absence of contraindications (53). Switching to bupropion may also be helpful in patients who experience undesired weight gain. Agitation or excessive activation, seen most commonly with fluoxetine, warrants switching to another SSRI or adding a low-dose tricyclic agent or mirtazapine. During SSRI initiation, some clinicians provide a short course of benzodiazepines to counter short-term agitation.

When should clinicians consult a psychiatrist for help in managing drug therapy?

Treatment-resistant depression is a common clinical problem that may necessitate psychiatric consultation. Patients who have not responded to agents familiar to the primary care provider, who have experienced repeated failures, or who have side effects that are difficult to control should be referred for psychiatric consultation. The threshold for referral should be lower for more severely impaired patients. The Agency for Health Care Policy and Research recommends referral to a psychiatrist if the patient has severe symptoms, such as suicide risk; comorbid medical, psychiatric, or substance abuse problems; and lack of response to appropriate treatment (21).

Electroconvulsive therapy can be considered as first-line treatment for depressed patients with psychotic features, those with active suicidal thoughts, or those who have not responded to or who cannot tolerate antidepressants. Electroconvulsive therapy should be managed by a psychiatrist (4).

When should clinicians consider hospitalizing depressed patients?

Hospitalization is usually necessary when suicidal intent is significant but may also be warranted for suicidal ideation alone. Clinicians should consider hospitalization for patients: 1) with significant suicidal ideation or intent who do not have adequate safeguards in their family environment; 2) who express intent to hurt others; 3) who require close observation (to assess ability for self-care and adherence); 4) who are in need of detoxification or substance abuse treatment; 5) who are candidates for electroconvulsive therapy; or 6) who have dysfunctional family systems potentially exacerbating their depressive disorder or interfering with treatment. When life is in jeopardy, patients may be hospitalized against their wishes. The conditions of involuntary hospitalization are governed by legal requirements for corroborated documentation of risk and judicial review.

What should clinicians advise patients about complementary–alternative treatments for depression?

St. John's wort may be beneficial for patients who want to take something for subsyndromal depression or who are unwilling or cannot take conventional therapy for mild depression. St. John's wort has not been shown to benefit patients with moderate to severe major depression and is not indicated in these situations. Although St. John's wort has produced mixed results when studied in randomized, placebo-controlled trials, serious adverse effects are uncommon. Many trials with positive findings have used standardized doses of 0.3% hypericin, 300 mg three times a day (54).

There are several important caveats to the use of St John's wort. To avoid

Recognize the need for psychiatric consultation and/or hospitalization for patients with severe disease, treatment nonresponders, and those with suicidal ideation.

49. Fava M, Davidson KG. Definition and epidemiology of treatment-resistant depression. Psychiatr Clin North Am. 1996;19:179-200. [PMID: 8827185]
50. Spier SA. Use of bupropion with SRIs and venlafaxine. Depress Anxiety. 1998;7:73-5. [PMID: 9614595]
51. Carpenter LL, Jocic Z, Hall JM, Rasmussen SA, Price LH. Mirtazapine augmentation in the treatment of refractory depression. J Clin Psychiatry. 1999;60:45-9. [PMID: 10074878]
52. Nelson JC. Augmentation strategies in depression 2000. J Clin Psychiatry. 2000;61 Suppl 2:13-9. [PMID: 10714619]

53. Nurnberg HG, Hensley PL. Selective phosphodiesterase type-5 inhibitor treatment of serotonergic reuptake inhibitor antidepressant-associated sexual dysfunction: a review of diagnosis, treatment, and relevance. CNS Spectr. 2003;8:194-202. [PMID: 12595814]

54. Linde K, Mulrow CD, Berner M, Egger M. St John's wort for depression. Cochrane Database Syst Rev. 2005:CD000448. [PMID: 15846605]

55. Obach RS. Inhibition of human cytochrome P450 enzymes by constituents of St. John's Wort, an herbal preparation used in the treatment of depression. J Pharmacol Exp Ther. 2000;294:88-95. [PMID: 10871299]

56. de Maat MM, Hoetelmans RM, Math t RA, et al. Drug interaction between St John's wort and nevirapine. AIDS. 2001;15:420-1. [PMID: 11273226]

57. Ondrizek RR, Chan PJ, Patton WC, King A. Inhibition of human sperm motility by specific herbs used in alternative medicine. J Assist Reprod Genet. 1999;16:87-91. [PMID: 10079411]

Patients with recurrent depression should be carefully evaluated for long-term maintenance therapy.

symptoms of serotonin excess, it should not be used in conjunction with SSRIs. Through activation of the cytochrome P450 system, St. John's wort may reduce plasma concentration of such drugs as digoxin, theophylline, simvastatin, and warfarin (55). Severe drug interactions have also been reported with antiretroviral therapy; St. John's wort can decrease concentrations of protease inhibitors and nonnucleoside reverse transcriptase inhibitors (56). At high concentrations, St. John's wort has been shown to be harmful to sperm cells and may lead to decreased fertility (57). The National Institute of Health's National Center for Complementary and Alterative Medicine is a good resource for more information (http://nccam.nih.gov/health/stjohnswort).

If a patient relapses after cessation of depression treatment, should clinicians resume previously effective therapy or select a new therapy?

Recurrence of major depression should be treated with long-term maintenance therapy with the same antidepressant therapy that previously led to remission. Clinicians should consider lifetime maintenance therapy for patients who have had 3 or more episodes and for patients with a first recurrence and risk factors for further recurrences (family history of bipolar disorder, recurrence within 1 year, onset in adolescence, severe depression, suicidal attempt, and sudden onset of symptoms) (47).

How should clinicians advise women on drug therapy for depression who are or who wish to become pregnant?

The FDA has issued a warning concerning SSRI use during pregnancy (58). A case–control study showed that persistent pulmonary hypertension

(PPHN) was 6 times more common in babies whose mothers took an SSRI after the 20th week of gestation than in babies whose mothers did not take an antidepressant (59). The absolute risk for PPHN was low (about 6 to 12 per 1000 women). However, this study adds to concerns from previous reports that infants of mothers taking SSRIs late in pregnancy may have such problems as irritability; difficulty feeding; and in very rare cases, difficulty breathing.

The teratogenic potential of SSRIs is probably low overall, but 2 epidemiologic studies of paroxetine in early pregnancy prompted the FDA in late 2005 to order a change in labeling for this agent (www.fda.gov/cder/drug/advisory/paroxetine200512.htm). Paroxetine is the only SSRI with a class D rating for pregnancy; all others are class C. On the other hand, stopping antidepressants carries its own risks.

In a study of 201 pregnant women with a history of major depression before pregnancy, relapse of depression was more common among those who stopped their medication compared with those who maintained their medication (68% vs. 26%, hazard ratio 5.0, P < 0.001) (60).

Tricyclic antidepressants are not strictly contraindicated in pregnancy. However, the neonatal withdrawal syndrome may occur, and these drugs should be tapered before delivery (47). If a TCA is chosen, desipramine or nortriptyline may be preferred because they cause fewer side effects and drug levels can be monitored (61). Clinicians should help patients make an informed decision and remember to monitor for signs of postpartum depression 4 to 6 weeks after delivery.

Treatment... Primary care physicians play an increasingly important role in treating affective disorders. Depression is highly treatable and has many treatment options; clinicians familiar with 2 SSRIs, bupropion, and an SNRI (such as venlafaxine) are well equipped to treat most cases. Familiarity with local psychotherapy options is also helpful.

CLINICAL BOTTOM LINE

What can clinicians do to encourage adherence to therapy for patients with depression?

Patient education is the first line of defense against nonadherence to antidepressant therapy.

In 1 study of 155 depressed patients, those who received the following educational messages were more likely to comply with therapy during the first month: 1) take the medication daily; 2) antidepressants must be taken for 2 to 4 weeks for a noticeable effect; 3) continue to take medicine even if feeling better; 4) do not stop taking antidepressant medication without checking with the physician; 5) resolve questions regarding antidepressants and potential side effects with the physician (43).

Nonadherence often begins in the initial weeks of therapy. Reasons for nonadherence can include beliefs about the illness, concerns over side effects, ineffectiveness of treatment, cost of medications, and many other cultural and attitudinal factors (62). Clinicians should routinely ask patients and their families about their beliefs. Personalizing educational messages to the patient's actual beliefs will enhance the effect of patient education. When possible, family involvement may improve acceptance of and support for the patient's problems and enhance treatment. Clinicians should provide patients and their families with appropriate written and electronic patient education materials about depression and its management. Clinicians can improve the impact of printed material by intensive reinforcement of key educational messages (43).

Improving outcomes in depression care requires systems change. Evidence suggests that it is more likely that screening will actually take place if initiated by an automatic, nonphysician-triggered procedure (e.g., by nursing staff automatically assessing patients at visit entry rather than by procedures that rely on the physician's decision to initiate screening). Disease management "care pathways" address the multiple needs of patients with depression throughout the course of the illness. Programs that include coordination of care by care managers, provider education and feedback on performance, structured systematic assessment of patient response to treatment with feedback to the provider, stepped-care referrals for psychiatric consultation based on structured systematic assessment of patient progress, nurse-administered telephone support and education calls, or peer support are superior to usual care (2, 44).

What criteria are used to judge the quality of depression care?

In the era of quality performance, the AQA alliance has adopted 2 antidepressant medication management measures developed by the National Committee for Quality Assurance: antidepressant therapy for at least 12 weeks after the initial diagnosis and treatment; and continuous antidepressant therapy for at least 6 months after the initial diagnosis and treatment. For more information, see www.aqaalliance.org/performancewg.htm.

What do professional organizations recommend regarding screening for and managing depression?

In 2002, the United States Preventive Services Task Force issued guidelines on screening for depression (www.ahrq.gov/clinic/uspstf/uspsdepr.htm). The Task Force recommends screening adults in clinical practices that have systems in place to ensure accurate diagnosis, effective treatment, and follow-up. It does not recommend screening children or adolescents. The Task Force's guidelines are currently being updated. The Task Force also issued a guideline on screening for suicide risk in 2004 (www.ahrq.gov/clinic/uspstf/uspssuic.htm).

Patient education is the first line of defense against nonadherence to antidepressant therapy.

58. FDA Public Health Advisory: Treatment Challenges of Depression in Pregnancy. Rockville, MD: U.S. Food and Drug Administration; 2006.

59. Chambers CD, Hernandez-Diaz S, Van Marter LJ, et al. Selective serotonin-reuptake inhibitors and risk of persistent pulmonary hypertension of the newborn. N Engl J Med. 2006;354:579-87. [PMID: 16467545]

60. Cohen LS, Altshuler LL, Harlow BL, et al. Relapse of major depression during pregnancy in women who maintain or discontinue antidepressant treatment. JAMA. 2006;295:499-507. [PMID: 16449615]

61. Miller LJ. Psychiatric Medication During Pregnancy: Understanding and Minizing Risks. Psychiatric Annals. 1994;24:69-75.

62. Delgado PL. Approaches to the enhancement of patient adherence to antidepressant medication treatment. J Clin Psychiatry. 2000;61 Suppl 2:6-9. [PMID: 10714617]

The American Psychiatric Association published its Practice Guideline for the Treatment of Patients with Major Depressive Disorder in 2002, which contains useful algorithms for initial choice of treatment method and information on antidepressant medications (www.psych.org/psych_pract/treatg/pg/MDD2e_05-15-06.pdf). Updates to this guideline were published in 2005 (www.psych.org/psych_pract/treatg/pgMDD.Watch.pdf).

The MacArthur Initiative in Depression and Primary Care, in collaboration with Dartmouth College and Duke University, has expanded the work of the AHRQ and provides a comprehensive Web site that includes provider guidelines and patient education resources covering all aspects of depression management. It can be accessed at www.depression-primarycare.org.

Pharmacologic therapy of major depression and dysthymia is covered in clinical guidelines issued in 2000 from the ACP (www.annals.org/cgi/content/full/132/9/738).

in the clinic
Tool Kit

Depression

Depression Screening Instruments
www.chcr.brown.edu/pcoc/cesdscale.pdf
Center for Epidemiological Studies Depression Scale

http://healthnet.umassmed.edu/mhealth/ZungSelfRatedDepressionScale.pdf
Zung Self-Depression Scale

www.stanford.edu/~yesavage/GDS.html
Geriatric Depression Scale

www.nelmh.org/downloads/other_info/hopkins_symptom_checklist.pdf
Hopkins Symptom Checklist

www.aap.org/practicingsafety/Toolkit_Resources/Module2/EPDS.pdf
Edinburgh Postnatal Depression Scale

The American College of Physicians' PIER Depression Module
http://pier.acponline.org/physicians/public/d954/d954.html
PIER (the Physicians' Information and Education Resource) is an evidence-based, electronic resource for clinical recommendations and links to patient information materials at the point of care.

Pamphlet from the American College of Physicians
www.doctorsforadults.com/images/healthpdfs/depression.pdf
Downloadable brochure on depression and how internists can help.

MacArthur Initiative on Depression
www.depression-primarycare.org
Patient education handouts on depression symptoms, management, medications, and psychological counseling.

Patient Information Sheet
www.annals.org/intheclinic/tools
Download an electronic copy of the patient information sheet on the next page for duplication and use in your office

MedlinePLUS Depression Materials
www.nlm.nih.gov/medlineplus/depression.html
Public-oriented information on depression, including educational information from the National Institutes of Mental Health and other organizations, recent studies, and news. Many resources are available in Spanish.

Things People Should Know about Depression

HEALTH TiPS*

Depression makes you feel sad and makes it hard to do or enjoy anything. Talking to a therapist or taking the right medicine can make you feel better.

What You Can Do

- Don't be afraid to ask for help.
- If the doctor gives you medicine, take it every day.
- Don't expect your medicine to work for 2 to 4 weeks after you start it.
- Keep taking your medicine even if you feel better.
- Don't stop your medicine without checking with your doctor.
- Expect to take your medicine for at least 6 months.

See the doctor 1 to 2 weeks after you start medicine and then again in 6 weeks.

Ask your doctor about side effects--putting on weight, feeling nervous or having trouble with sex.

Ask your doctor about the right people to talk to and how your family can help you.

If you feel bad or need help, call your doctor or 911 or go to the emergency room right away.

Ask your doctor about seeing a specialist if:

- ❏ Your medicines don't seem to be working
- ❏ Your medicines have too many side effects
- ❏ You are having strange thoughts or big mood swings
- ❏ You feel you may hurt yourself or other people
- ❏ You are drinking too much or taking street drugs

The next visit with the doctor is _____

*HEALTH TiPS are developed by the American College of Physicians Foundation and PIER.

Web Sites with Good Information about Depression

MedlinePLUS
www.nlm.nih.gov/medlineplus/depression.html

National Alliance on Mental Illness
www.nami.org/Template.cfm?Section=By_Illness&Template=/TaggedPage/
TaggedPageDisplay.cfm&TPLID=54&ContentID=23039

National Institutes of Mental Health
www.nimh.nih.gov/publicat/depression.cfm

U.S. Food and Drug Administration
www.fda.gov/fdac/features/2003/103_dep.html

National Cancer Institute (Spanish)
www.cancer.gov/espanol/pdq/cuidados-medicos-apoyo/depresion/patient/

Asthma

Asthma, which is characterized by airway hyperresponsiveness and inflammation, is one of the most common respiratory illnesses. The global prevalence of asthma is increasing despite the development of new therapeutic approaches. Over the past 20 years, asthma mortality in the United States has declined; however, morbidity, as measured by hospitalizations and emergency department visits, continues to climb. Currently, about 1 in 20 Americans have asthma; in children, recent estimates suggest an incidence as high as 10%. In certain groups of Americans, such as persons of lower socioeconomic status and minority ethnicity, asthma morbidity and mortality are disproportionately high. Such trends are surprising, given the improvement in air quality in the United States and the availability of new pharmacologic therapies.

Diagnosis

What symptoms or elements of clinical history are helpful in diagnosing asthma?

Symptoms that should prompt clinicians to consider asthma are wheezing, dyspnea, cough, difficulty taking a deep breath, and chest tightness (1). Characteristically, asthma symptoms are intermittent and may remit spontaneously or with use of short-acting bronchodilators. Symptoms often vary seasonally or are associated with specific triggers, such as cold, exercise, animal dander, pollen, certain foods, aspirin or nonsteroidal anti-inflammatory drugs, or occupational exposures. Clinicians should also consider the diagnosis of asthma in all adults with chronic cough, especially if cough is nocturnal, seasonal, or related to the workplace or a specific activity.

What physical examination findings are suggestive of asthma?

A careful history to elicit the nature and timing of symptoms is paramount in diagnosing asthma. The physical examination is less helpful unless a patient is having an active exacerbation. The clinician should listen for wheezing during tidal respirations or prolonged expiratory phase of breathing and examine the chest for hyperexpansion. Studies suggest that respiratory signs (wheezing, forced expiratory time, accessory muscle use, respiratory rate, and pulsus paradoxus) may be useful to predict airflow obstruction, but clinicians often disagree about the presence and absence of these signs (1, 2).

The physical examination is sometimes most helpful in looking for evidence of alternative diagnoses. Persistent dry inspiratory crackles, focal wet crackles, or an abnormal cardiac examination all suggest diagnoses other than asthma.

How can clinicians determine whether asthma is the cause of chronic cough in adults?

Coughing may be the only manifestation of asthma in some patients (3). Up to 24% of patients presenting to a specialist with chronic cough after an initial evaluation by a primary care provider may have asthma. Although several protocols are available for the diagnosis of patients with chronic cough, it is not clear which is the best approach. Clinicians often use a trial of empirical asthma therapy, but national guidelines recommend pulmonary function tests for patients with chronic cough of unknown etiology.

What are the indications for spirometry in a patient whose clinical presentation is consistent with asthma?

Fair-quality evidence supports the performance of spirometry in all adult patients and older children suspected of having asthma. Initial pulmonary function testing should include spirometric measurements

1. Li JT, O'Connell EJ. Clinical evaluation of asthma. Ann Allergy Asthma Immunol. 1996;76:1-13; quiz 13-5. [PMID: 8564622]
2. National Heart, Lung, and Blood Institute, National Asthma Education and Prevention Program. Expert Panel Report 2: Guidelines for the diagnosis and management of asthma. Bethesda MD: US Department of Health and Human Services, National Institutes of Health, 1997; Publication 97-4051.
3. Corrao WM, Braman SS, Irwin RS. Chronic cough as the sole presenting manifestation of bronchial asthma. N Engl J Med. 1979;300:633-7. [PMID: 763286]
4. McFadden ER Jr. Exertional dyspnea and cough as preludes to acute attacks of bronchial asthma. N Engl J Med. 1975;292:555-9. [PMID: 1110670]
5. Hankinson JL, Odencrantz JR, Fedan KB. Spirometric reference values from a sample of the general U.S. population. Am J Respir Crit Care Med. 1999;159:179-87. [PMID: 9872837]

of the FEV_1, FVC, and the FEV_1–FVC ratio. If these measurements reveal airflow obstruction, then they should be repeated after administration of a bronchodilator to evaluate the reversibility of airflow obstruction. Reversibility of airflow obstruction defines asthma. Predicted normal values for spirometric measures are population-based and differ with age and ethnicity. Predictive tables are available (5, 6). Postbronchodilator improvement ≥ 12% of the FEV_1 or FVC indicates significant reversibility and therefore increases the likelihood of an asthma diagnosis.

Complete pulmonary function testing that includes lung volumes and diffusing capacity should be considered when there is evidence of a lack of airflow reversibility, or restrictive patterns with diminutions in the FEV_1 and FVC but a normal FEV_1–FVC ratio. These findings suggest chronic obstructive pulmonary disease (COPD) or interstitial lung disease (Table 1).

A number of studies show a poor correlation among the presence, severity, and timing of wheezing and the degree of airflow obstruction (7, 8). Patients vary in their degree of sensitivity to airflow limitations and can acclimate to the disability and thus become insensitive to airflow obstruction (9). Because of the disparity between patient and physician estimates of the severity of airflow obstruction and objective measures of obstruction, pulmonary function tests are important tools to characterize airflow obstruction and the degree and severity of asthma.

Spirometry should adhere to the standards of the American Thoracic Society (10). Of note, spirometry is effort-dependent, and many patients have difficulty with the FVC maneuver. In these patients (younger children, older adults, or patients with severe respiratory disease), alternative approaches, such as the FEV_6 may be an acceptable surrogate to the FVC, with a reduction in the FEV_1–FEV_6 ratio signifying obstruction (11).

Table 1. Laboratory and Other Studies for Asthma

Test	Notes
Spirometry	Abnormal spirometry (reversible obstruction) can help to confirm an asthma diagnosis, but normal spirometry does not exclude asthma.
Peak flow variability	A patient with normal spirometry but marked diurnal variability (based on a peak flow diary kept for >2 weeks) may have asthma, which may warrant an empirical trial of asthma mediations or further testing with bronchoprovocation.
Bronchoprovocation test	In a patient with a highly suggestive history of asthma and normal baseline spirometry, a low PC_{20} (the concentration of inhaled methacholine needed to cause a 20% drop in the FEV_1) on methacholine challenge testing supports a diagnosis of asthma. Cold air, exercise, and histamine are other types of provocative tests used. A normal bronchoprovocation test will almost definitively exclude asthma.
Chest radiography	Chest radiography may be needed to exclude other diagnoses but is not recommended as a routine test in the initial evaluation of asthma.
Complete blood count with differential	Although mild eosinophilia is not uncommon in persons with asthma, routine use of a CBC with leukocyte differential is not warranted in the initial evaluation.
Sputum evaluation	Routine sputum evaluation is not indicated for the initial evaluation of asthma.
IgE	Although elevated levels of IgE are not uncommon for persons with asthma, routine measurement of serum IgE is not warranted in the initial evaluation
Quantitative IgE antibody assays and skin testing for immediate hypersensitivity to aeroallergens	There is a strong association between allergen sensitization, exposure, and asthma. Allergy testing is the only reliable way to detect the presence of specific IgE to indoor allergens. Skin testing (or in vitro testing) may be indicated to guide the management of asthma in selected patients, but results are not useful in establishing the diagnosis of asthma.

6. Nunn AJ, Gregg I. New regression equations for predicting peak expiratory flow in adults. BMJ. 1989;298:1068-70. [PMID: 2497892]
7. McFadden ER Jr., Kiser R, DeGroot WJ. Acute bronchial asthma. Relations between clinical and physiologic manifestations. N Engl J Med. 1973;288:221-5. [PMID: 4682217]
8. Shim CS, Williams MH Jr. Relationship of wheezing to the severity of obstruction in asthma. Arch Intern Med. 1983;143:890-2. [PMID: 6679232]
9. Chetta A, Gerra G, Foresi A, Zaimovic A, Del Donno M, Chittolini B, et al. Personality profiles and breathlessness perception in outpatients with different gradings of asthma. Am J Respir Crit Care Med. 1998;157:116-22. [PMID: 9445288]
10. Standardization of Spirometry, 1994 Update. American Thoracic Society. Am J Respir Crit Care Med. 1995;152:1107-36. [PMID: 7663792]
11. Swanney MP, Jensen RL, Crichton DA, Beckert LE, Cardno LA, Crapo RO. FEV(6) is an acceptable surrogate for FVC in the spirometric diagnosis of airway obstruction and restriction. Am J Respir Crit Care Med. 2000;162:917-9. [PMID: 10988105]

Does normal spirometry rule out a diagnosis of asthma?

Abnormal spirometry (reversible obstruction) can confirm an asthma diagnosis, but normal spirometry does not rule out asthma. Clinicians should consider further studies in patients with normal spirometry who have a clinical history suggestive of asthma (Table 1). Bronchoprovocation with methacholine or histamine can be helpful in establishing a diagnosis in patients who report that they only have symptoms during exercise or at certain times of the year. Alternatively, marked diurnal variability based on measurements recorded in a peak flow diary kept for at least 2 weeks can help to establish asthma as the cause of symptoms. However, peak flow measurements are highly effort-dependent and may offer no opportunity for quality assurance of their accuracy.

When should clinicians consider provocative pulmonary testing?

A gold standard for diagnosis of asthma remains elusive. However, methacholine hyperresponsiveness in the pulmonary function laboratory has high reproducibility and accepted standardization (12). The test is safe but requires sophisticated instrumentation and is labor-intensive and expensive. In a patient with symptoms suggestive of asthma who has normal baseline spirometry, a low PC_{20} (the concentration of inhaled methacholine needed to induce a 20% decrease in the FEV_1) on methacholine challenge testing supports the diagnosis. Studies of methacholine challenge suggest that it is sensitive and has a high negative predictive value for the diagnosis of asthma (13, 14). Although cold air and exercise have been used in research to define mechanisms of bronchoconstriction, methacholine challenge remains the provocative test of choice in patients with normal pulmonary function tests who have symptoms consistent with asthma.

Spirometry before, during, or after exercise may be the only method to document bronchoconstriction in patients with exercise-induced asthma. As an alternative, monitoring peak flow is easy and inexpensive, but the measurement is less precise and limited in reproducibility and sensitivity (15). Because spirometry and peak flow have limitations in sensitivity and specificity, they are probably best used as part of a diagnostic strategy in conjunction with a comprehensive history, physical examination, and other laboratory data (16).

How should clinicians classify asthma severity?

The National Heart Lung and Blood Institute (NHLBI) Expert Panel Report 2 (2) defines asthma severity according to symptoms and spirometric measurements. As shown in Table 2, asthma severity is classified as intermittent, mild, moderate, and severe persistent. Each category is defined by the frequency of rescue inhaler use as well as nocturnal symptoms in conjunction with the FEV_1 or PEFR measurement. It is important to note that decrease in FEV_1 correlates with airflow obstruction and not with changes due to restrictive lung disease.

The initial determination of asthma severity should be made when the patient is receiving no medications. Asthma severity is dynamic—for example, patients who were initially diagnosed as having severe persistent asthma may have symptoms consistent with mild persistent asthma while receiving medication. The NHLBI Expert Panel Report 2 (2) suggests annual spirometry to aid in the classification of asthma, but high-quality studies are not available to support this recommendation.

12. Crapo RO, Casaburi R, Coates AL, Enright PL, Hankinson JL, Irvin CG, et al. Guidelines for methacholine and exercise challenge testing-1999. This official statement of the American Thoracic Society was adopted by the ATS Board of Directors, July 1999. Am J Respir Crit Care Med. 2000;161:309-29. [PMID: 10619836]

13. Cockcroft DW, Killian DN, Mellon JJ, Hargreave FE. Bronchial reactivity to inhaled histamine: a method and clinical survey. Clin Allergy. 1977;7:235-43. [PMID: 908121]

14. Hopp RJ, Bewtra AK, Nair NM, Townley RG. Specificity and sensitivity of methacholine inhalation challenge in normal and asthmatic children. J Allergy Clin Immunol. 1984;74:154-8. [PMID: 6747136]

15. Jain P, Kavuru MS, Emerman CL, Ahmad M. Utility of peak expiratory flow monitoring. Chest. 1998;114:861-76. [PMID: 9743179]

16. Perpiñá M, Pellicer C, de Diego A, Compte L, Macián V. Diagnostic value of the bronchial provocation test with methacholine in asthma. A Bayesian analysis approach. Chest. 1993;104:149-54. [PMID: 8325060]

Table 2. The Step Classification of Asthma Severity*

Classification	Symptoms[†]	Nocturnal Symptoms	Lung Function
Step 1: Mild intermittent	Symptoms ≤2 per week Asymptomatic and normal PEFR between exacerbations Exacerbations brief (a few hours to a few days); intensity may vary	2 per month	FEV_1 or PEFR ≥80% predicted PEFR variability <20%
Step 2: Mild persistent	Symptoms >2 per week but <1 per day Exacerbations may affect activity	>2 per month	FEV_1 or PEFR ≥80% predicted PEFR variability 20%–30%
Step 3: Moderate persistent	Daily symptoms Daily use of inhaled short-acting ß$_2$-agonist Exacerbations may affect activity Exacerbations ≥2 per week; may last days	>1 per week	FEV_1 or PEFR >60%–<80% predicted PEFR variability >30%
Step 4: Severe persistent	Continual symptoms Limited physical activity Frequent exacerbations	Frequent	FEV_1 or PEFR <60% predicted PEFR variability >30%

*Adapted from NHLBI Expert Panel Report. The presence of one of the features of severity is sufficient to place a patient in that category. Assign patient to the most severe grade in which any feature occurs. The characteristics noted in this Table are general and may overlap because of the high variability of asthma and because an individual's classification may change over time. PEFR = peak expiratory flow rate.

† Patients at any level of severity can have mild, moderate, or severe exacerbations. Some patients with intermittent asthma experience severe, life-threatening exacerbations separated by long periods of normal lung function and no symptoms.

What comorbid conditions and alternative diagnoses should clinicians consider in patients with suspected asthma?

The differential diagnosis of asthma includes the following conditions: COPD, interstitial lung disease, vocal cord dysfunction, congestive heart failure, medication-induced cough, bronchiectasis, pulmonary infiltration with eosinophilia syndromes, obstructive sleep apnea, mechanical airway obstruction, cystic fibrosis, and pulmonary hypertension. Clinicians should consider one of these alternative diagnoses when asthma is difficult to control or if the patient has atypical signs and symptoms. These conditions can also coexist in a patient who has asthma.

An important difference between asthma and COPD is the history of smoking. Although 30% of patients with asthma in the United States smoke, COPD, manifested by chronic bronchitis and emphysema, often occurs in older persons with a substantial history of cigarette smoking. Patients with COPD also do not demonstrate reversibility with bronchodilators on pulmonary function testing.

Lung imaging with radiography or computed tomography is helpful in identifying bronchiectasis or lung masses. Echocardiography can help to identify cardiovascular disorders, including ischemic heart disease, ventricular dysfunction, and pulmonary hypertension. Flow-volume loops and direct visualization of the larynx during an acute episode are useful in evaluating patients for vocal cord paralysis.

Chronic cough and dyspnea or recurrent wheezing are common signs of COPD, vocal cord dysfunction, cystic fibrosis, obstructive sleep apnea, Churg-Strauss syndrome, allergic bronchopulmonary aspergillosis, interstitial lung disease, bronchiectasis, congestive heart failure, and pulmonary hypertension, or may be side effects of

17. Irwin RS, Curley FJ, French CL. Difficult-to-control asthma. Contributing factors and outcome of a systematic management protocol. Chest. 1993;103:1662-9. [PMID: 8404082]
18. Althuis MD, Sexton M, Prybylski D. Cigarette smoking and asthma symptom severity among adult asthmatics. J Asthma. 1999;36:257-64. [PMID: 10350222]
19. Weiss ST, Utell MJ, Samet JM. Environmental tobacco smoke exposure and asthma in adults. Environ Health Perspect. 1999;107 Suppl 6:891-5. [PMID: 10592149]
20. Ostro BD, Lipsett MJ, Mann JK, Wiener MB, Selner J. Indoor air pollution and asthma. Results from a panel study. Am J Respir Crit Care Med. 1994;149:1400-6. [PMID: 8004290]

medications. Evidence shows that difficult-to-control asthma may be a result of comorbid conditions and that standardized evaluation of patients for comorbidity was associated with improved asthma control (17).

When should primary care clinicians consider referring patients with suspected asthma to specialists for diagnosis?

Consultation with a pulmonologist should be considered before ordering provocative pulmonary function testing because testing is time- and labor-intensive, requiring skilled performance and interpretation. Patients presenting with atypical symptoms, who have abnormal chest radiographs or unusual manifestations of the disease, or who display suboptimal response to therapy may benefit from referral to a pulmonologist. Referral to an allergist may be helpful for patients with asthma that seems to have an allergic component.

Diagnosis... A careful history focusing on the nature and timing of symptoms (wheezing, dyspnea, cough, chest tightness) and potential triggers is essential to the diagnosis of asthma. Moderate-quality evidence supports the use of spirometry in assessment of all adult patients and older children suspected of having asthma. However, normal spirometry does not definitively rule out asthma. Clinicians should consider provocative pulmonary testing for patients with normal spirometry but characteristic symptoms and no evidence of alternative diagnoses.

CLINICAL BOTTOM LINE

Treatment

21. Institute of Medicine Committee on the Assessment of Asthma and Indoor Air. Executive summary. In: Clearing the Air: Asthma and Indoor Air Exposures. Washington, DC: National Academy Pr; 2000.
22. National Heart, Lung, and Blood Institute, National Asthma Education and Prevention Program. Expert Panel Report: Guidelines for the Diagnosis and Management of Asthma—Update on Selected Topics 2002. Bethesda MD: US Department of Health and Human Services, National Institutes of Health, 2002; Publication 02-5075.
23. Aronson N, Lefevre F, Piper M, Management of Chronic Asthma. Summary, Evidence Report/Technology Assessment Number 44. Rockville, MD: Agency for Healthcare Research and Quality; 2001. AHRQ Publication 01-E044.

What advice about reducing allergen exposure should clinicians give patients?

Avoidance of triggers is the cornerstone of nonpharmacologic therapy of asthma. Clinicians should question the patient about triggers and provide strategies to diminish exposure to them (see box). Since many patients with asthma are atopic, reducing exposure to allergens can improve outcomes. Other common triggers of asthma include aspirin, nonsteroidal anti-inflammatory drugs, and sulfites in food preservatives. Limiting exposure to triggers is difficult to implement or sustain in some patients; however, in most cases such triggers are dose-dependent, so even modest remediation can be beneficial.

The NHLBI Expert Panel Report recognized environmental smoke exposure as a common cause of asthma exacerbations (2), and several studies have impugned active and passive cigarette smoking as a cause of decreasing lung function in adult asthma (18, 19).

One study considered associations between indoor air pollutants and symptoms in 164 adults with asthma and found an increase in days of restricted activity (odds ratio [OR], 1.61 [95% CI, 1.06 to 2.46]) and greater likelihood of increased asthma symptoms in patients exposed to a smoker at home (OR, 2.05 [CI, 1.79 to 2.40]) (20).

What evidence supports the use of indoor air-cleaning devices for patients with asthma?

Given the recognition that environment plays a critical role in airway hygiene, it may seem logical that indoor air-cleaning devices are beneficial. However, there is little evidence to suggest that HEPA filters, air duct cleaning, or dehumidifiers control asthma. Humidifiers may actually increase allergen levels and must be cleaned often. Keeping household humidity below 50% with dehumidifiers or air conditioners reduces dust mites and mold (21).

A multidisciplinary committee convened by the Institute of Medicine reviewed available evidence concerning the impact of ventilation and air cleaning on asthma (21). Although they concluded that particle air cleaning may reduce symptoms in certain situations, evidence is inadequate to broadly recommend air cleaning for patients with asthma.

How should clinicians select from among available drug therapy for asthma?

Table 3 summarizes drugs available to treat asthma. Table 4 presents a stepwise approach to using these drugs to maximize control of symptoms (2, 22).

Clinicians should tailor drug therapy to the severity of asthma (Table 2). Stepwise therapy consists of agents for acute relief of symptoms (rescue therapy) and for long-term control. Rescue therapy is critically important regardless of asthma severity. Patients with persistent symptoms require long-term control in addition to rescue therapy. If control is poor, stepping up to more intense therapy is indicated. If symptoms are well-controlled, stepping down to less intensive therapy is indicated.

Clinicians should review therapy every 1 to 6 months, depending on asthma severity. Asthma is a chronic disease that often requires long-term therapy. Given the complexity of airway inflammation, multiple drugs with different actions against the various aspects of the inflammatory response are often necessary.

Rescue Therapy
Patients with mild intermittent asthma may only need a quick relief medication (short-acting β-agonists) on an as-needed basis. Short-acting β-agonists are the drugs of choice for reversal of acute bronchospasm and are safe and well-tolerated. Patients with persistent asthma (mild, moderate, or severe)

should also receive a short-acting β-agonist and advice to keep the medication readily available for relief of acute symptoms.

Long-Term Controller Therapy
Patients with mild, moderate, or severe persistent asthma have abnormal baseline pulmonary function and require long-term controller therapy. Patients with mild persistent asthma should receive 1 long-term controller medication, usually a low-dose inhaled corticosteroid.

Compared with patients with mild intermittent asthma, patients with mild persistent asthma are more prone to underlying inflammation and disease exacerbations. Low-dose inhaled corticosteroids have been shown to reduce bronchial hyperresponsiveness, reduce rescue β-agonist use, and control symptoms. Secondary alternatives to inhaled corticosteroids are leukotriene-receptor antagonist medications (e.g., montelukast, zafirlukast) or cromolyn.

Patients with moderate persistent asthma will probably require 1 or 2 long-term controller medications in addition to short-acting rescue therapy. The therapy of choice in this group includes low-dose inhaled corticosteroids and a long-acting β-agonist or a moderate dose of a single long-term controller medication. Evidence suggests that patients who remain symptomatic while taking moderate doses of inhaled corticosteroids benefit from the addition of a long-acting bronchodilator such as theophylline, salmeterol, or formoterol. The additive effect of the long-acting bronchodilator improves lung physiology, decreases use of rescue β-agonists, and reduces symptoms better than doubling the dose of an inhaled corticosteroid (23–26). However, there is little evidence to guide the best choice of combinations. Clinicians and patients must weigh the reduced risk for adverse effects of steroids against the use of more complicated regimens. It is

Evidence is inadequate to broadly recommend air cleaning devices for patients with asthma.

24. Greening AP, Ind PW, Northfield M, Shaw G. Added salmeterol versus higher-dose corticosteroid in asthma patients with symptoms on existing inhaled corticosteroid. Allen & Hanburys Limited UK Study Group. Lancet. 1994;344:219-24. [PMID: 7913155]
25. Ukena D, Harnest U, Sakalauskas R, Magyar P, Vetter N, Steffen H, et al. Comparison of addition of theophylline to inhaled steroid with doubling of the dose of inhaled steroid in asthma. Eur Respir J. 1997;10:2754-60. [PMID: 9493656]
26. Woolcock A, Lundback B, Ringdal N, Jacques LA. Comparison of addition of salmeterol to inhaled steroids with doubling of the dose of inhaled steroids. Am J Respir Crit Care Med. 1996;153:1481-8. [PMID: 8630590]

Table 3. Drug Treatment for Asthma

Class/Agent	Mechanism of Action	Benefits	Side Effects	Notes
Short-acting ß-agonists: Albuterol Metaproterenol Terbutaline Pirbuterol	Relaxes bronchial smooth muscle, improves airflow	Fastest improvement in airflow physiology of all anti-asthma medications	Tachycardia, palpitations, tremors, hypokalemia	Should be carried by all patients with asthma at all times. Drug class of choice for acute bronchospasm. Use only as needed. Effective at preventing symptoms of asthma when used before exercise. Assessment of quantity of ß-agonist use may identify patients who require a "step-up" in therapy. Use of >1 canister during a 1-month period suggests inadequate control. Oral preparations available, but inhaled is preferred due to better side effect profile.
Inhaled corticosteroids: Beclomethasone dipropionate Beclomethasone hydrofluoroalkane Budesonide Flunisolide Fluticasone propionate Triamcinolone acetonide Ciclesonide Mometasone	Anti-inflammatory, blocks late reaction to allergen, and reduces airway hyperresponsiveness	Improved airflow physiology, reduced need for rescue medications (short-acting ß-agonists), prevents exacerbations and hospitalizations	Local: cough, dysphonia, and thrush. Systemic: cortisol suppression, adrenal suppression, potential osteoporosis, cataracts, glaucoma	Each type of inhaled corticosteroid has a different profile in terms of dosing potency and possible risks for any of the known side effects. Drug deposition in the lower airway and systemic absorption and toxicity are conditioned by the drug and preparation, inhalation technique, and use of a spacing chamber. There is little information on how to monitor effectiveness and toxicity of inhaled corticosteroids, especially considering the varying degrees of seasonal inflammations or following differing stimuli/exposures. Inhaled corticosteroids are the most potent and effective anti-inflammatory medications available for asthma.
Long-acting inhaled ß-agonists: Salmeterol Formoterol	Smooth muscle relaxation	Improved a.m. peak flow, improved nocturnal symptoms, effective in preventing symptoms of exercise-induced asthma for up to 12 hours after a single dose	Tachycardia, skeletal muscle tremor, prolongation of QT interval in overdose	Use only in conjunction with anti-inflammatory therapy. Protection against exercise-induced symptoms may decrease over time. Salmeterol has slower onset and both have longer duration of action compared with short-acting ß-agonists. May provide more effective symptom control when added to standard doses of inhaled corticosteroids compared to increasing corticosteroid dosage. The FDA has warned that these agents may increase the chances of a severe asthma episode. This seems more likely in blacks.
Combined fixed-agent controllers: Fluticasone and salmeterol Budesonide and formoterol	Anti-inflammatory moiety blocks late reaction to allergen, and reduces airway hyperresponsiveness, and long-acting ß-agonist leads to smooth muscle relaxation	Improved airflow physiology, reduced need for short acting ß-agonists, prevents exacerbations and hospitalizations; improved a.m. peak flow, improved nocturnal symptoms	Dysphonia, thrush, nausea, headaches	Should not be initiated in patients during rapidly deteriorating or potentially life-threatening episodes of asthma. Do not use in conjunction with inhaled long-acting ß-agonists. Combined preparations prevent the use of long-acting ß-agonists without inhaled corticosteroids.
Leukotriene modifiers: Montelukast Zafirlukast Zileuton	Work by inhibition of synthesis or antagonism of receptor site for cysteinyl leukotrienes	Improvements in symptoms and pulmonary function, decreased exacerbation rate, reduced need for rescue ß-agonist	Transient elevation in liver enzymes occurs with Zileuton and mandates monitoring of liver enzymes with initiation of therapy; there is controversy over possible link with Churg-Strauss angiitis (causation has not been established)	Oral tablets may be easier to use than inhaled medications and may enhance compliance; therapeutic benefits are less than those of inhaled corticosteroids. May be of particular benefit in patients with aspirin intolerance and/or nasal polyps. May allow for safe reduction in inhaled and oral corticosteroids. May be an alternative to increasing dose of inhaled corticosteroid.
Theophylline	Smooth muscle relaxation, may have secondary effects of inhibiting airway inflammation and enhancing diaphragm contractility	Modest improvement in expiratory flow rates	Dose-related acute toxicities include tachycardia, nausea vomiting, tachyarrhythmias (SVT), CNS stimulation, headache, seizures Sometimes adverse effects are seen at therapeutic levels	Studies show a benefit in the addition of theophylline to inhaled corticosteroids

Table 3. Drug Treatment for Asthma (continued)

Class/Agent	Mechanism of Action	Benefits	Side Effects	Notes
Mast cell stabilizers: Cromolyn Nedocromil	Anti-inflammatory, blocks early and late reaction to allergens, and stabilizes mast cell membranes; inhibits eosinophil activation and mediator release	Improved airflow physiology, reduced need for rescue medications (short-acting ß-agonists), prevents exacerbations	Cromolyn: no significant side effects Nedocromil: 15%–20% of users complain of unpleasant taste	The therapeutic response to this class of drugs is less predictable than to corticosteroids, but they continue to be used due to their safety profile
Systemic corticosteroids: Prednisone Prednisolone Methylprednisolone Triamcinolone	Anti-inflammatory, blocks late reaction to allergen, and reduces airway hyperresponsiveness	Improved airflow physiology, reduced need for rescue medications (short-acting ß-agonists), prevents exacerbations and hospitalizations	Short-term: increased appetite and weight gain, fluid retention, reversible abnormalities in glucose metabolism, mood alterations Long-term: dermal thinning, cortisol suppression, adrenal suppression, hypertension, diabetes mellitus, osteoporosis, avascular necrosis of femoral head, cataracts, glaucoma	Most effective medication for severe exacerbations and long-term control for patients with severe persistent asthma who are otherwise uncontrolled. Always seek lowest possible effective dose. Patients on corticosteroids (either daily or ≥2 corticosteroid prescriptions for 5-10 days/yr) and undergoing surgery or with acute severe illness should be assessed for adrenal reserve or treated presumptively with short-term systemic corticosteroid. Studies show that it is safe to give a short course of oral corticosteroids (7-10 days) without tapering.
Anticholinergic agents: Ipratropium bromide Glycopyrrolate otropium	Bronchodilation mediated by antagonism of muscarinic receptors of airway smooth muscle	Improved airflow physiology	Blurred vision if contact with eyes, dry mouth and respiratory symptoms	Treatment of choice in ß-blocker induced bronchospasm; may give added bronchodilation to ß-agonists. Meta-analysis of the use of ipratropium bromide in the treatment for acute severe asthma shows that there is a modest physiologic benefit in the addition of ipratropium to albuterol, with negligible risk of adverse side effects. Tiotropium has been suggested as an alternative to long-acting ß-agonists, but suitable effectiveness studies are lacking.
Intravenous magnesium sulfate	Smooth muscle relaxation	Bronchodilatation in acute severe asthma failing to respond to nebulized bronchodilators-	Minor effects; flushing, lethargy, nausea, or local reaction at the IV site	
Omalizumab	A monoclonal antibody that binds to IgE used in patients aged 12 years or older with moderate to severe persistent asthma, proven IgE-mediated sensitivity to perennial aeroallergens, and poor response to standard treatment. Binding of IgE by monoclonal antibody inhibits binding to high-affinity IgE receptors on mast cells and basophils	Reduction in exacerbations in patients with severe persistent asthma on the best available therapy	The main danger is anaphylaxis. Injections should be administered by trained personnel, and patients should be observed for 2 hours after every injection. Anaphylaxis has been reported up to 24 hours after injection, and patients receiving omalizumab treatment should be fully prepared to begin treatment for anaphylaxis with an epinephrine autoinjector	Anaphylaxis may occur after any dose of omalizumab (including the first dose), even if there was no adverse reaction to the first dose. The symptoms and signs of anaphylaxis include bronchospasm, hypotension, syncope, urticaria, and angioedema of the throat or tongue. In the major trials, there was a small increase in new or recurrent cancer compared to the control group

*Readers can access detailed information on dosing in PIER at http://pier.acponline.org/physicians/diseases/d146/drug.tx/d146-s7.html. CNS = central nervous system; FDA = Food and Drug Administration

unclear whether controlling the disease with high-dose inhaled corticosteroids or moderate-dose inhaled corticosteroids plus a long-acting bronchodilator results in a better long-term outcome.

In a 12-week, randomized, controlled trial of 447 patients who remained symptomatic on treatment with inhaled corticosteroids, a dry-powder inhaler containing salmeterol and fluticasone was more effective in improving physiologic endpoints, reducing rescue therapy use, and reducing exacerbations

Table 4. Stepwise Approach for Managing Asthma in Adults

STEP Classification	Long-Term Control	Quick Relief	Education
Step 1: Mild intermittent	No daily medication needed	Short acting bronchodilator: inhaled ß$_2$-agonists* as needed for symptoms	Teach basic facts about asthma; teach inhaler/spacer/holding chamber technique; discuss roles of medications; develop self-management plan; develop action plan for when to take rescue medications, especially for patients with a history of severe exacerbations; discuss appropriate environmental control measures to avoid exposure to known allergens and irritants
Step 2: Mild persistent	One daily medication: • Anti-inflammatory*: either inhaled corticosteroid (low doses) or cromolyn* or nedocromil* (children usually begin with a trial of cromolyn or nedocromil) • Sustained-release theophylline to serum concentration of 5-15 µg/mL is an alternative, but not preferred, therapy. • Montelukast, zafirlukast, or zileuton may also be considered for patients age 12 and older, although their position in therapy is not fully established	Short-acting bronchodilator: inhaled ß$_2$-agonists* as needed for symptoms	Step 1 actions, plus teach self-monitoring; refer to group education if available; review and update self-management plan
Step 3: Moderate persistent	Preferred treatment: • Low-to-medium dose inhaled corticosteroids and long-acting inhaled ß$_2$-agonists. Alternative treatment: Increase inhaled corticosteroids within medium-dose range OR • Low-to-medium dose inhaled corticosteroids and either leukotriene modifier or theophylline. OR • If needed (particularly in patients with recurring severe exacerbations): Increase inhaled corticosteroids within medium-dose range, and add long-acting inhaled ß$_2$-agonists. Alternative treatment: Increase inhaled corticosteroids to medium-dose range, and add either leukotriene modifier or theophylline	Short acting bronchodilator: inhaled ß$_2$-agonists* as needed for symptoms	Step 1 actions, plus teach self-monitoring; refer to group education if available; review and update self-management plan
Step 4: Severe persistent	Preferred treatment: High-dose inhaled corticosteroids AND Long-acting inhaled ß$_2$-agonists AND, if needed, Corticosteroid tablets or syrup long-term (2 mg/kg/d, generally do not exceed 60 mg/d). (Make repeated attempts to reduce systemic corticosteroids and maintain control with high-dose inhaled corticosteroids.)	Short-acting bronchodilator: inhaled ß$_2$-agonists* as needed for symptoms.	Step 2 and 3, plus refer to individual education/counseling

*Intensity of treatment depends on severity of exacerbation. Use of short-acting inhaled ß$_2$-agonists on a daily basis, or increasing use, indicates the need for additional long-term control therapy

than was the addition of montelukast to the inhaled corticosteroid fluticasone (27).

Long-acting β-agonists may help improve asthma symptoms, but they may also increase risks for adverse outcomes. Patients started on these medications should be followed closely.

A meta-analysis of 19 randomized, controlled trials found that, compared with placebo, long-acting ß-agonists increased severe exacerbations requiring hospitalization (OR, 2.6 [CI, 1.6 to 4.3]), life-threatening exacerbations (OR, 1.8 [CI, 1.1 to 2.9]), and asthma-related deaths (OR, 3.5 [CI, 1.3 to 9.3]; risk difference, 0.07%) (28). Risks were similar for salmeterol and formoterol and in children and adults. Several trials did not report information about potential harms, and the number of reported deaths was small. Black patients and patients not using inhaled corticosteroids seemed to be at high risk for these outcomes. These results suggest that long-acting ß-agonists should not be used alone in asthma (28).

27. Nelson HS, Busse WW, Kerwin E, Church N, Emmett A, Rickard K, et al. Fluticasone propionate/salmeterol combination provides more effective asthma control than low-dose inhaled corticosteroid plus montelukast. J Allergy Clin Immunol. 2000;106:1088-95. [PMID: 11112891]

Patients with severe persistent asthma may require 3 controller medications to adequately control symptoms. Patients with this level of disease are extremely prone to exacerbations and have profound underlying inflammation. Direct comparisons of high-dose inhaled corticosteroids to leukotriene-receptor modifiers (such as montelukast) revealed that the inhaled corticosteroids were more effective. The addition of montelukast to the regimen of a patient requiring high-dose inhaled corticosteroids, however, allowed a significant reduction in the dose of the inhaled corticosteroid while maintaining asthma control (29).

In a randomized, controlled study of patients with inadequate symptom control despite low- to moderate-dose inhaled corticosteroid, the addition of montelukast improved FEV$_1$ daytime symptoms and nocturnal awakenings (30).

A systematic review of trials comparing the addition of daily leukotriene-receptor antagonists or long-acting ß-agonists to inhaled corticosteroids in patients with severe asthma concluded that long-acting ß-agonists were better than leukotriene antagonists in preventing the need for rescue therapy and systemic steroids and improved lung function and symptoms (31, 32)

Omalizumab is a monoclonal antibody that binds to IgE that has been shown to reduce exacerbations in patients with severe persistent asthma despite best available therapy (33). However, severe anaphylaxis has been reported up to 24 hours after injection. Clinicians should view the drug as an option only in carefully selected cases of severe persistent asthma in patients with proven IgE-mediated sensitivity to perennial aeroallergens, and failure of other therapeutic options.

What therapeutic options are effective for patients with exercise-induced asthma?

In some patients, exercise exacerbates asthma. Symptoms often occur with vigorous exercise in cold, dry air. Patients who have more than 2 episodes of exercise-induced asthma per week are candidates for intervention. Patients who have normal baseline pulmonary function but experience exercise-induced symptoms can be treated effectively with albuterol, cromolyn sodium, or nedocromil 15 to 30 minutes before exercise.

If exercise-induced symptoms persist, addition of long-acting bronchodilators or leukotriene antagonists may be helpful. Recent evidence suggesting that monotherapy with long-acting bronchodilators may cause adverse outcomes in asthma cautions against using these agents as monotherapy in exercise-induced asthma (28, 34). Despite these concerns, evidence clearly suggests that formoterol or salmeterol is more effective than placebo in preventing exercise-induced bronchoconstriction (35, 36). In a study of patients with mild stable asthma, once-daily treatment with montelukast protected against exercise-induced bronchospasm (37).

The clinician should consider exercise-induced asthma in the context of the patient's overall therapy. Many patients who present with putative exercise-induced asthma may have abnormal pulmonary function tests at baseline. Such patients should be treated according to the NHLBI Expert Panel Report 2 regimen (2).

When should primary care clinicians refer patients with asthma to a specialist for treatment?

Although definitive evidence about the effect of specialty care on asthma outcomes is not available, according to consensus recommendations referral to a specialist may be useful in the following clinical situations:

- History of life-threatening exacerbations
- Atypical signs and symptoms
- Severe persistent asthma
- Need for continuous oral corticosteroids or high-dose inhaled steroids or more than 2 courses of oral steroids in a 1-year period

28. Salpeter SR, Buckley NS, Ormiston TM, Salpeter EE. Meta-analysis: effect of long-acting beta-agonists on severe asthma exacerbations and asthma-related deaths. Ann Intern Med. 2006;144:904-12. [PMID: 16754916]

29. Löfdahl CG, Reiss TF, Leff JA, Israel E, Noonan MJ, Finn AF, et al. Randomised, placebo controlled trial of effect of a leukotriene receptor antagonist, montelukast, on tapering inhaled corticosteroids in asthmatic patients. BMJ. 1999;319:87-90. [PMID: 10398629]

30. Laviolette M, Malmstrom K, Lu S, Chervinsky P, Pujet JC, Peszek I, et al. Montelukast added to inhaled beclomethasone in treatment of asthma. Montelukast/Beclomethasone Additivity Group. Am J Respir Crit Care Med. 1999;160:1862-8. [PMID: 10588598]

31. Coté J, Cartier A, Robichaud P, Boutin H, Malo JL, Rouleau M, et al. Influence on asthma morbidity of asthma education programs based on self-management plans following treatment optimization. Am J Respir Crit Care Med. 1997;155:1509-14. [PMID: 9154850]

32. Ducharme FM, Lasserson TJ, Cates CJ. Long-acting ß₂-agonists versus anti-leukotrienes as add-on therapy to inhaled corticosteroids for chronic asthma. Cochrane database Syst Rev. 2006:CD003137. [PMID: 17054161].

33. Humbert M, Beasley R, Ayres J, Slavin R, Hebert J, Bousquet J, et al. Benefits of omalizumab as add-on therapy in patients with severe persistent asthma who are inadequately controlled despite best available therapy (GINA 2002 step 4 treatment): INNOVATE. Allergy. 2005;60:309-16. [PMID: 15679715]

- Comorbid conditions that complicate asthma diagnosis or treatment
- Need for provocative testing or immunotherapy
- Problems with adherence or allergen avoidance
- Unusual occupational or other exposures.

Whether to consult an allergist or pulmonologist should reflect local availability and consideration of the predominant comorbid conditions and complicating features in asthma. For example, a patient with sleep apnea and asthma may benefit from a pulmonary consultation, whereas the patient who has asthma with an atopic component may benefit from referral to an allergist.

When is hospitalization indicated for a patient with asthma?

Patients who have a sustained response to treatment in outpatient settings do not need to be hospitalized if they understand the importance of continued anti-inflammatory therapy and close follow-up. The decision to hospitalize a patient with asthma should consider patient characteristics, severity of disease, and initial response to short-term therapy. Patients with an incomplete response to therapy during an exacerbation (PEFR >50% but <70% than patient's best or of the predicted value) may need hospitalization. When posttreatment PEFR remains <50% of the predicted value, intensive care unit admission may be warranted. However, data are insufficient to support the idea that adequate oxygen saturation and PEFR at the time of emergency department discharge predict a good outcome.

In a prospective cohort study of adults presenting with asthma to urban emergency departments in the United States, the PEFR of those who had a relapse did not significantly differ from those who did not have a relapse after discharge from the emergency department. However, such historical features as emergency department or urgent care visits (OR, 1.3 per 5 visits), use of a home nebulizer (OR, 2.2), multiple triggers (OR, 1.1 per trigger), and longer duration of symptoms (OR, 2.5 for 1 to 7 days) did predict relapse (38).

What factors identify patients with asthma at high risk for fatal or near-fatal events during an exacerbation?

Historical factors reflect the risk for fatal and near-fatal asthma-related events and should lower the threshold for hospitalization of a person when these factors are present. Such factors include asthma history, socioeconomic characteristics, and comorbid conditions (see Box).

Factors Associated with Poor Outcomes of Asthma Exacerbations

- Prior intubation
- Multiple asthma-related exacerbations
- Emergency room visits for asthma in the previous year
- Nonuse or low adherence to inhaled corticosteroids
- History of depression, substance abuse, personality disorder, unemployment, or recent bereavement

---

How often should clinicians see patients with asthma for routine follow-up?

No definitive studies are available to guide the frequency of asthma follow-up, but consensus suggests that for patients with newly diagnosed asthma, 2 to 4 visits during the 6 months after diagnosis can help to establish and reinforce the patient's basic knowledge and management skills. For patients with asthma who have shown maximum improvement in pulmonary function and have minimal to no related symptoms, the NHLBI Expert Panel Guide suggests routine follow-up every 1 to 6 months with annual pulmonary function tests (2); however, evidence documenting the benefit of this strategy is limited. The Report also suggests follow-up within 7 days for patients discharged from the hospital and within 10 days for patients treated as outpatients for an exacerbation. Studies have shown that relapse occurs in about 1% of patients per day until the follow-up visit (38–40).

34. SMART Study Group. The Salmeterol Multicenter Asthma Research Trial: a comparison of usual pharmacotherapy for asthma or usual pharmacotherapy plus salmeterol. Chest. 2006;129:15-26. [PMID: 16424409]

35. Nelson JA, Strauss L, Skowronski M, Ciufo R, Novak R, McFadden ER Jr. Effect of long-term salmeterol treatment on exercise-induced asthma. N Engl J Med. 1998;339:141-6. [PMID: 9664089]

36. Nightingale JA, Rogers DF, Barnes PJ. Comparison of the effects of salmeterol and formoterol in patients with severe asthma. Chest. 2002;121:1401-6. [PMID: 12006420]

37. Leff JA, Busse WW, Pearlman D, Bronsky EA, Kemp J, Hendeles L, et al. Montelukast, a leukotriene-receptor antagonist, for the treatment of mild asthma and exercise-induced bronchoconstriction. N Engl J Med. 1998;339:147-52. [PMID: 9664090]

38. Emerman CL, Woodruff PG, Cydulka RK, Gibbs MA, Pollack CV Jr, Camargo CA Jr. Prospective multicenter study of relapse following treatment for acute asthma among adults presenting to the emergency department. MARC investigators. Multicenter Asthma Research Collaboration. Chest. 1999;115:919-27. [PMID: 10208187]

Treatment... Patients should avoid asthma triggers. While air conditioners or de-humidifiers may be helpful, indoor air-cleaning devices are of unclear utility. All patients with asthma should have short-acting β-agonists available for relief of acute symptoms. For patients with persistent asthma, treatment with long-term controller medications should begin with low-dose inhaled corticosteroids and be stepped up to higher doses and/or additional agents according to asthma severity. Patients with severe persistent asthma may need as many as 3 long-term controller medications.

CLINICAL BOTTOM LINE

Practice Improvement

What do professional organizations recommend regarding the care of patients with asthma?

Many of the recommendations provided in this overview are from a guideline developed by the NHLBI that was most recently updated in 2002 (22). The guidelines were approved by the 40 organizations that comprise the National Asthma Education and Prevention Program. The document covers pathogenesis, medications, monitoring, and prevention and is available free at www.nhlbi.nih.gov/guidelines/asthma/asthgdln.htm.

Numerous other organizations have developed recommendations related to the care of patients with asthma, including the American Academy of Asthma, Allergy and Immunology (www.aaaai.org); the American Lung Association (www.lungusa.org); and the Asthma and Allergy Foundation of America (www.aafa.org). These organizations also provide demographically and culturally sensitive educational programs and teaching tools.

What is the role of patient education in optimizing the outcome of asthma care?

Asthma is a paradigm illness for patient self-management because of its intermittent and unpredictable nature. Patients and family members can recognize changes and initiate specific actions to minimize exacerbations. Clinicians should include asthma education as part of each office visit, and formal asthma education programs may be particularly helpful for patients who have had asthma hospitalizations, emergency department visits, or frequent exacerbations. Important elements of asthma education include basic information, the role of medications, inhaler and peak flow meter skills, environmental control measures, and appropriate use of rescue medications. Demographically and culturally appropriate educational materials can be used as an adjunct to one-on-one asthma education. Because many patients use metered-dose inhalers improperly, all patients should receive instruction on proper use.

Clinicians should develop individualized self-management plans for all patients, taking into consideration underlying disease severity and the patient's willingness and ability to manage the illness. For patients with mild disease, clinicians should consider providing a simple self-management plan that provides information on how to handle exacerbations, including health care contacts in case of emergency. For patients with moderate-to-severe disease, provide a self-management plan that incorporates a daily diary and a detailed written action plan with specific objective and subjective

39. McCarren M, McDermott MF, Zalenski RJ, Jovanovic B, Marder D, Murphy DG, et al. Prediction of relapse within eight weeks after an acute asthma exacerbation in adults. J Clin Epidemiol. 1998;51:107-18. [PMID: 9474071]
40. Rowe BH, Bota GW, Fabris L, Therrien SA, Milner RA, Jacono J. Inhaled budesonide in addition to oral corticosteroids to prevent asthma relapse following discharge from the emergency department: a randomized controlled trial. JAMA. 1999;281:2119-26. [PMID: 10367823]
41. Effectiveness of routine self monitoring of peak flow in patients with asthma. Grampian Asthma Study of Integrated Care (GRASSIC). BMJ. 1994;308:564-7. [PMID: 8148679]
42. Charlton I, Charlton G, Broomfield J, Mullee MA. Evaluation of peak flow and symptoms only self management plans for control of asthma in general practice. BMJ. 1990;301:1355-9. [PMID: 2148702]

markers for self-directed change in therapy.

Should all patients with asthma receive peak flow meters?

The precision of patients and physicians in estimating the degree of airflow obstruction based on symptoms alone varies greatly, so objective measurement of expiratory flow rates could in theory be useful to guide therapeutic strategies. However, studies that have randomly assigned patients to action plans that incorporate PEFR have not shown major improvements compared with action plans based on symptoms alone (41, 42).

Clinicians should ensure that all patients with persistent moderate-to-severe asthma have a peak flow meter at home and know how to use it. If patients are unwilling to measure peak flow, provide instruction in symptom-based monitoring.

Do U.S. stakeholders consider asthma care when evaluating the quality of care a physician delivers?

In April 2005, The Ambulatory Care Quality Alliance (AQA) released a set of 26 health care quality indicators for clinicians, consumers, and health care purchasers to use in quality improvement efforts, public reporting, and pay-for-performance programs (www.ahrq.gov/qual/aqastart.htm). In May 2005, the Centers for Medicare & Medicaid Services (CMS) endorsed the development of these indicators. Of the 26 AQA indicators, 2 focus on asthma care (see the Box).

As part of CMS's Physician Quality Reporting Initiative, physicians who successfully report a designated set of quality measures on claims for services provided July 1 to December 31, 2007, may earn a bonus payment. See the Box for the 2 CMS measures related to asthma (www.cms.hhs.gov/specifications_2007-02-04.pdf).

in the clinic
Tool Kit

Asthma

http://PIER.acponline.org
Asthma module of PIER, an electronic decision support resource designed for rapid access to information at the point of care.

http://pennhealth.com/ency/presentations/100200_1.htm
Tutorial on proper use of metered dose inhalers.

http://pier.acponline.org/qualitym/asm.html
Tool to assist clinicians in developing strategies to improve adherence to the AQA asthma performance measures.

www.annals/intheclinic/tools
Download copies of the patient information sheet that appears on the following page for duplication and distribution to your patients.

THINGS PEOPLE SHOULD KNOW ABOUT ASTHMA

Asthma causes a squeezing of the muscle in the walls of the tubes (airways, bronchi) that bring air to the lungs. Breathing becomes difficult when this happens.

Web Sites with Good Information about Asthma

MedlinePLUS
www.nlm.nih.gov/medlineplus/asthma.html

American Lung Association
www.lungusa.org

How to Use a Metered Dose Inhaler

Inhalers deliver a specific dose of medicine to the lungs in a spray form.

1. Take off the cap and shake the inhaler hard.
2. Breathe out all the way.
3. Hold the inhaler about 2-fingers width from your mouth.
4. Start to breath in slowly through your mouth as you press down on the inhaler once and keep breathing in slowly until you can't breathe in any more.
5. Hold your breath and count to 10 slowly.
6. Repeat steps 1 to 5 if your doctor has prescribed more than 1 puff of medicine, wait about 1 minute between puffs.

HEALTH TiPS*
WHAT YOU CAN DO

Asthma makes you cough and wheeze and can make it hard to breathe.

Here's what you can do to feel better.

Stay away from what makes your asthma worse:

- Dust
- Smoke
- Animals
- Cold or dry air

Don't smoke and stay away from people who do

Asthma-proof your home:

- Get special mattress and pillow covers
- Get rid of old carpets and drapes
- Use air conditioners and dehumidifiers

Use your medicines the right way:

- Take medicines that prevent attacks every day
- Take medicines that stop attacks when you need them
- Learn the right way to use your inhalers

Call your doctor or go to the hospital if it is hard to breathe and your medicines are not helping

Things to ask your doctor:

Which medicines are to keep attacks from happening?

Which medicines are to stop attacks when they come on?

Can you show me the right way to use my inhaler?

Can I use my inhalers more often if I need to?

What are the side effects of my inhalers and my other medicines?

Do I need a special meter to check my breathing at home? How do I use it?

How long should I wait to call the doctor or go to the hospital if I am having trouble breathing?

*HEALTH TiPS are developed by the American College of Physicians Foundation and PIER

Irritable Bowel Syndrome

I rritable bowel syndrome (IBS) is a common but poorly understood disorder that interferes with normal colon function, resulting in abdominal pain, bloating, constipation, and diarrhea. No specific biological biomarker, physiologic abnormality, or anatomical defect has been discovered. Psychosocial stress may exacerbate symptoms.

IBS is 1 of 28 adult and 17 pediatric functional gastrointestinal disorders. These disorders are symptom-based and not explained by other pathologically defined diseases. IBS appears to be linked to motor and sensory physiology and brain–gut interaction (1). Emerging theories suggest that alteration of intestinal bacteria may also play a role in the condition. IBS affects as many as 1 in 5 U.S. adults, occurs more often in women than in men, and begins before the age of 35 in about half of all people who develop the disorder. IBS is recognized worldwide, but prevalence varies geographically.

Diagnosis

What symptoms should prompt a clinician to consider IBS?
Symptoms of IBS vary from person to person, but clinicians should consider IBS if abdominal discomfort or pain associated with bowel dysfunction is present. Other symptoms that suggest IBS include prominent gastrocolic reflex, alternating constipation and diarrhea, and excess gas and flatulence. Gastrointestinal symptoms that wax and wane for more than 2 years and those that are exacerbated by psychosocial stress should raise suspicion for IBS over other diagnoses.

Three general patterns of bowel symptoms are common in IBS: diarrhea-predominant, constipation-predominant, and mixed (alternating diarrhea and constipation). Determining a patient's predominant symptom pattern can be useful in guiding management because the different subgroups respond differently to the various therapeutic options. Because an individual patient's symptom pattern can change over time, it is debatable whether symptom pattern clearly demarcates patients with different IBS subtypes.

Certain clinical features, often called alarm features or red flag symptoms, suggest that the diagnosis is something other than IBS (2) (see Box). Alarm features include weight loss, nocturnal awakening because of gastrointestinal symptoms, blood in the stool, family history of colon cancer or inflammatory bowel disease, recent use of antibiotics, and fever.

What are the accepted diagnostic criteria for IBS?
History is the main diagnostic tool for IBS. There are 2 sets of symptom-based diagnostic criteria to help discriminate IBS from other disorders: the Manning criteria and the Rome criteria (Table 1). These criteria were developed for use in clinical studies, but can be helpful in clinical settings.

Alarm Features That Suggest Possible Organic Disease

Symptoms
- Weight loss
- Frequent nocturnal awakenings due to gastrointestinal symptoms
- Fever
- Blood mixed in stool

History
- New onset, progressive symptoms
- Onset of symptoms after age 50
- Recent antibiotic use
- Family history of colon cancer or inflammatory bowel disease

Physical Findings
- Abdominal mass
- Stool positive for occult blood
- Enlarged lymph nodes

---

1. Drossman DA. The functional gastrointestinal disorders and the Rome III process. Gastroenterology. 2006;130:1377-90. [PMID: 16678553]
2. Longstreth GF. Irritable bowel syndrome. Diagnosis in the managed care era. Dig Dis Sci. 1997;42:1105-11. [PMID: 9201069]
3. Manning AP, Thompson WG, Heaton KW, Morris AF. Towards positive diagnosis of the irritable bowel. Br Med J. 1978;2:653-4. [PMID: 698649]

Manning and colleagues (3) proposed the first widely used IBS criteria in 1978 based on the symptoms listed in Table 1.

In 1989, a group of experts met in Rome and developed another set of consensus-based criteria known as the Rome criteria to assist in the diagnosis of IBS and other functional gastrointestinal disorders (4). The Rome criteria, which are also displayed in Table 1, were based on a broader array of symptoms than the Manning criteria and explicitly considered both duration and frequency of symptoms. In 1999, the same group of experts developed the Rome II criteria, a modified version of the earlier criteria intended to be more adaptable to clinical practice (5).

The group released the most recent version of the Rome criteria, Rome III, in 2006. Rome III did not change the basic diagnostic criteria for IBS but modified the time frame for symptoms and description of IBS subtyping (6). Rome III specifies that symptoms must have begun at least 6 months before the diagnosis can be established and that patients have fulfilled the Rome criteria for at least 3 months before IBS can be diagnosed. Rome III

recommends that clinicians base classification of IBS symptoms as diarrhea-prominent; constipation-prominent; or mixed, based on stool consistency. Rome criteria are dynamic, and future studies are needed to confirm the validity of recent changes intended to increase the usefulness of the criteria in research and clinical settings (1).

When diagnostic criteria are satisfied; warning symptoms are absent; the history and physical examination suggest IBS; and the occult blood test, complete blood count (CBC), and erythrocyte sedimentation rate (ESR) are normal, the risk for overlooking organic disease may be as low as 1% to 3%. Thus, expert consensus is that physicians should limit evaluation to fulfillment of the Rome or Manning criteria if no alarm symptoms are present.

Even without exclusion of alarm features, the presence of at least 3 of the 6 Manning criteria has an average sensitivity of approximately 60% and specificity of approximately 80%. The criteria's sensitivity and specificity vary by study; however, the diagnostic accuracy is known to be better in women, younger patients, and when more criteria are fulfilled (7).

When Rome criteria have been satisfied, warning symptoms are absent; the history and physical examination suggest IBS; and the occult blood test, complete blood count, and erythrocyte sedimentation rate are normal, the risk for overlooking organic disease may be as low as 1% to 3%.

Table 1. Symptom Criteria for Irritable Bowel Syndrome

Rome III*

Recurrent abdominal pain or discomfort at least 3 days per month in the past 3 months associated with 2 or more of the following:

1. Improvement with defecation
2. Onset with change in frequency of stool
3. Onset associated with a change in the form and appearance of stool

Criteria must be fulfilled for at least the past 3 months with symptom onset at least 6 months before diagnosis.

Manning†

Pain relief with defecation, often

Looser stools at pain onset, often

More frequent stools at pain onset, often

Visible abdominal distention

Mucus per rectum

Feeling of incomplete evacuation

†To establish IBS diagnosis, patient must meet 3 or more criteria.

4. Thompson WG, Dotewall G, Drossman DA, et al. Irritable bowel syndrome: guidelines for the diagnosis. Gastroenterol Int. 1989;2:92-95.
5. Thompson WG, Longstreth GF, Drossman DA, et al. Functional bowel disorders and functional abdominal pain. Gut. 1999;45 Suppl 2:II43-7. [PMID: 10457044]
6. Longstreth GF, Thompson WG, Chey WD, et al. Functional bowel disorders. Gastroenterology. 2006;130:1480-91. [PMID: 16678561]
7. Talley NJ, Phillips SF, Melton LJ, et al. Diagnostic value of the Manning criteria in irritable bowel syndrome. Gut. 1990;31:77-81. [PMID: 2318433]

Tolliver and coworkers showed that the Rome criteria had a positive predictive value of 98.5%—out of 196 patients, they excluded 1 case of colon cancer, 1 of colitis, and 1 of peptic ulcer (8).

Vanner and colleagues prospectively studied 95 patients who met the Rome criteria and lacked red flags and found the positive predictive value was 98% (9).

Investigators conducted interviews with a large, community-based sample of U.S. women diagnosed with IBS, and they found that Rome I was significantly more sensitive than Rome II (84% vs. 49%; P < 0.001). Only 58% of patients who had IBS according to Rome I criteria had IBS according to Rome II criteria; 17.7% did not meet the criteria for either Rome I or II (10).

What is the utility of the physical examination in diagnosing IBS?

The physical examination is usually normal in IBS, except for mild abdominal tenderness or a palpable, tender loop of colon. However, neither is sensitive or specific for IBS. Physical findings that are not associated with IBS but that are notable because they indicate the need to seek other diagnoses include fever, weight loss, lymph node enlargement, abdominal mass, and hepatosplenomegaly. The physical examination should include testing the stool for occult blood.

Which diagnostic tests are useful in diagnosing IBS?

There are no specific diagnostic tests for IBS. Tests that may be helpful for ruling out diagnoses other than IBS include endoscopy, blood tests, evaluation of stool samples, and imaging studies. Clinicians should use these tests with discretion depending on the patient's age, history, and symptom pattern, and on the presence of alarm features for organic disease.

Endoscopy
Flexible sigmoidoscopy may be helpful in excluding colitis or obstructive lesions of the colon. However, if patients are young, fulfill the Rome criteria, and have no alarm features, a presumptive diagnosis of IBS can be made without endoscopy but should be reevaluated depending on the course of symptoms over time. Because patients with IBS have abnormally sensitive gastrointestinal tracts, they may find endoscopy more uncomfortable than do patients without this condition. Rectal and colonic balloon studies have shown hypersensitivity of the intestines in 55% to 93% of patients with IBS (11). Thus, normal endoscopy can be particularly indicative of IBS when it causes more pain than expected or when it reproduces the patient's symptoms.

Blood Tests
A CBC and an ESR are reasonable to evaluate for anemia, elevated sedimentation rate, or leukocytosis because these findings are not compatible with IBS. Serum amylase and liver enzyme levels may be useful if pancreatic or biliary disease is suspected.

Evaluation of Stool Samples
Evaluation of stool for *Clostridium difficile* may be helpful if the patient has recently taken antibiotics. Examination of stool for ova and parasites may be helpful in patients with diarrhea-predominant symptoms, especially if travel history suggests potential exposure to parasites. In general, bacterial cultures are unlikely to be helpful in the diagnosis of chronic diarrhea. However, there is a form of IBS in which patients develop typical IBS symptoms after resolution of an acute episode of dysentery. This condition may take 6 months to resolve and can lead to chronic IBS. Factors associated with post infectious IBS include age, female sex, severity of infection, and possibly psychological predisposition. Awareness of the condition can limit the search for persistent infection.

8. Tolliver BA, Herrera JL, DiPalma JA. Evaluation of patients who meet clinical criteria for irritable bowel syndrome. Am J Gastroenterol. 1994;89:176-8. [PMID: 8304298]
9. Vanner SJ, Depew WT, Paterson WG, et al. Predictive value of the Rome criteria for diagnosing the irritable bowel syndrome. Am J Gastroenterol. 1999;94:2912-7. [PMID: 10520844]
10. Chey WD, Olden K, Carter E, et al. Utility of the Rome I and Rome II criteria for irritable bowel syndrome in U.S. women. Am J Gastroenterol. 2002;97:2803-11. [PMID: 12425552]

Stool collection over a 24-hour period for quantification of volume may be helpful in patients who report large-volume or watery diarrhea. Normal stool volume is 200 mL or less per day. Volumes over 350 to 400 mL suggest etiologies other than IBS.

Measurement of fecal calprotectin in stool samples can help to identify patients with intestinal inflammation as an organic cause of symptoms mimicking IBS. In one study, the positive predictive value of fecal calprotectin for organic disease was 76% and the negative predictive value was 89% (12).

A spot or 24-hour fecal fat test can show malabsorption. Screening for celiac sprue with antigliadin and antiendomysial antibodies is both sensitive and specific (13). If no fat malabsorption is detected, clinicians may still consider these antibody tests in patients with unexplained anemia or weight loss.

Imaging Studies
Imaging studies should be used judiciously, but the following tests may help to exclude conditions that could mimic IBS. A flat and upright abdominal radiograph during an episode of pain may show unrecognized bowel obstruction, aerophagia, or retained stool. A small bowel barium radiograph can diagnose ileal and jejunal Crohn disease, and dilatation or diverticula favoring small bowel overgrowth. Computed tomography (CT) scanning will have low yield if there are no alarm symptoms.

What is the differential diagnosis that clinicians should consider when evaluating a patient for possible IBS?
The differential diagnosis of a patient presenting with symptoms of IBS is extensive (Table 2). Thus, some clinicians feel obligated to perform a wide variety of diagnostic tests before attributing a patient's symptoms to IBS. However,

no definitive data support routine performance of any diagnostic tests in patients with potential IBS. Clinicians should consider symptom patterns when trying to exclude serious diagnoses that can masquerade as IBS.

Patients with Constipation-Prominent Symptoms
In patients with constipation, clinicians should consider partial colonic obstruction or non-IBS causes of colonic dysmotility. Nonobstructive causes of colonic symptoms may be because of dysmotility secondary to medications, neurologic disease, hypothyroidism, pelvic floor dysfunction, or colonic inertia (colon transit > 5 days). The diagnosis is not IBS if colonic dysmotility is present without pain or if there is another explanation for symptoms, such as neurologic disorder, pelvic floor disorder, or colonic inertia (transit through colon > 72 hours, with predominantly right colon delay). In patients younger than 45 years of age with mild, chronic constipation-predominant symptoms, normal CBC, and no alarm features, treatment with fiber or an osmotic laxative should be offered before additional diagnostic testing.

Patients with Diarrhea-Predominant Symptoms
The differential in patients with diarrhea-predominant symptoms includes inflammatory bowel disease, infection, malabsorption, and effects of medication and diet. For younger patients with mild, chronic diarrhea-predominant symptoms, clinicians should consider flexible sigmoidoscopy, CBC, and examination of stools for ova and parasites. For patient older than 45 years or those with refractory, severe, or new-onset symptoms, evaluating the entire colon may be warranted to exclude neoplasm. However, clinicians must keep in mind that non-IBS disease is unlikely if the patient satisfies

11. Mertz H, Naliboff B, Munakata J, Niazi N, Mayer EA. Altered rectal perception is a biological marker of patients with irritable bowel syndrome. Gastroenterology. 1995;109:40-52. [PMID: 7797041]
12. Tibble JA, Sigthorsson G, Foster R, Forgacs I, Bjarnason I. Use of surrogate markers of inflammation and Rome criteria to distinguish organic from nonorganic intestinal disease. Gastroenterology. 2002;123:450-60. [PMID: 12145798]
13. Bürgin-Wolff A, Gaze H, Hadziselimovic F, et al. Antigliadin and antiendomysium antibody determination for coeliac disease. Arch Dis Child. 1991;66:941-7. [PMID: 1819255]

Table 2. Differential Diagnosis of Irritable Bowel Syndrome*

Disease	Clinical Characteristics	Diagnostic Strategy
Constipation-predominant symptoms		
Strictures due to inflammatory bowel disease, diverticulitis, ischemia, or cancer	Obstipation	Colonoscopy vs. barium enema and flexible sigmoidoscopy
Colonic inertia	Very infrequent bowel movements	Sitzmark transit study
Pelvic floor dysfunction[†]	Straining, self-digitation	Rectal examination, balloon expulsion study, anoretal manometry, defecography
Neurologic disease[†]	Concurrent Parkinson disease, autonomic dysfunction (Shy-Drager), multiple sclerosis	History and neurologic examination
Medication[†]	Opiates, cholestyramine, calcium-channel blockers, anticholinergic medications	Medication history
Hypothyroidism[†]	Other hypothyroid symptoms and signs	Serum thyroid-stimulating hormone
Diarrhea-predominant symptoms		
Crohn disease	Diarrhea may be from inflammatory exudate, motility changes, small bowel overgrowth, or bile salt malabsorption	Colonoscopy, small bowel barium radiograph
Ulcerative colitis	Likely to have rectal bleeding	Colonoscopy
Microscopic colitis[†]	Generally middle-aged and older women with autoimmune disease (especially thyroiditis)	Colonoscopy/flexible sigmoidoscopy and biopsy
Parasites	*Giardia lamblia* (stream and well water); *Ascaris lumbricoides*, *Entamoeba histolytica* (travel to developing world); *Strongyloides stercoralis* (travel to developing world, Kentucky, or Tennessee)	O + P x 3, stool *Giardia* antigen, metronidazole trial
Clostridium difficile	Recent antibiotics taken	Stool ELISA, flexible sigmoidoscopy for pseudomembranes
Other bacteria	IBS after dysentery may persist for months after infection with bacteria	Compatible history, possible initial positive stool culture
Small bowel overgrowth	Due to severe small bowel dysmotility, partial obstruction, blind loop, or jejunal diverticulosis	Abdominal radiograph, small bowel barium radiograph, lactulose breath hydrogen test, antibiotic trial
Sprue[†] (gluten-sensitive enteropathy)	May present with diarrhea, usually steatorrhea	Usually steatorrhea, positive gliadin, endomysial serum antibodies; endoscopy with small bowel biopsy is gold standard
Lactose intolerance[†]	Symptoms worse with lactose consumption	Avoidance trial, lactose breath test
Postgastrectomy syndrome	Postprandial symptoms	History of problems worse after gastric surgery
HIV enteropathy	May have chronic GI infections, such as with cryptosporidium, CMV, *Blastocystis hominis*, amoeba	Clinical suspicion, HIV test, low CD4
Gastrointestinal endocrine tumor	Carcinoid, gastrinoma, VIPoma	Urine 5HIAA, fasting gastrin (followed by secretin stimulation test), serum VIP
Pain-predominant symptoms		
Aerophagia, bloating	Patient may be anxious (nervous air swallowing), can be exacerbated by antireflux surgery	Abdominal radiograph with pain
Intermittent small bowel	More likely with history of previous abdominal surgeries	Abdominal radiograph with pain, small bowel barium radiograph

Table 2. Differential Diagnosis of Irritable Bowel Syndrome* (continued)

Disease	Clinical Characteristics	Diagnostic Strategy
Crohn disease	Small intestine or colon involvement	Small bowel barium radiograph colonoscopy
Acute intermittent porphyria	Rare; may have elevated liver enzymes and neurologic symptoms	Serum and urine porphyrins, especially porphobilinogen, and delta aminolevulinic acid
Ischemia	Intestinal angina especially in vasculopaths, food aversion, weight loss, pain 15–40 min after meals	Mesenteric angiogram
Chronic pancreatitis	Alcohol abuse, pain usually more persistent than with usual IBS	Abdominal radiograph for calcifications, CT scan, ERCP, endoscopic ultrasonography
Lymphoma of GI tract	Generally, weight loss	CT scan, small bowel radiograph
Endometriosis	Menstrual-associated symptoms, pelvic symptoms	Laparoscopy

*CMV = cytomegalovirus; CT = computed tomography; ELISA = enzyme-linked immunosorbent assay; ERCP = endoscopic retrograde cholangiopancreatography; GI = gastrointestinal; IBS = irritable bowel syndrome; O + P = ova and parasites; VIPoma = vasoactive intestinal peptide-producing tumor.

†Unlikely alone to cause abdominal pain.

Rome criteria and lacks alarm symptoms.

Patients with Pain-Predominant Symptoms

In patients with refractory, pain-predominant symptoms, a flat and upright abdominal radiograph during a pain episode can be helpful in revealing unrecognized bowel obstruction, aerophagia, or retained stool. Serum amylase and liver enzyme levels may diagnose pancreatic and biliary disease if symptoms suggest these diagnoses. CT scanning for neoplasms will have low yield if there are no alarm symptoms. Other rare conditions that may cause pain-predominant abdominal symptoms with some bowel dysfunction include intestinal angina (generally associated with weight loss and occult blood) and endometriosis (in general cyclic with menses).

Clinicians should use clinical judgment to modify these general guidelines to allow less or more evaluation.

Under what circumstances should clinicians consider consultation with a gastroenterologist?
Gastroenterologists often work with primary care physicians and patients to diagnose IBS and to exclude relevant disorders. Consultation is warranted in the following cases of diagnostic uncertainty: when patients do not fit Rome or Manning criteria, when patients have alarm symptoms, and when patients do not respond to initial management. Consultation is also necessary if specialized diagnostic procedures, such as endoscopy, are needed.

Diagnosis... Clinicians should base the diagnosis of IBS on history and physical examination, paying careful attention to fulfillment of the Rome or Manning criteria and exclusion of alarm features. Patients who fulfill the criteria and have no alarm features may need no additional testing other than a complete blood count and test for fecal occult blood to establish a presumptive diagnosis of IBS. Diagnostic testing should be judicious and focus on exclusion of specific non-IBS conditions that are consistent with the individual patient's clinical presentation.

CLINICAL BOTTOM LINE

Treatment

14. Prior A, Whorwell PJ. Double blind study of ispaghula in irritable bowel syndrome. Gut. 1987;28:1510-3. [PMID: 3322956]

15. Müller-Lissner SA. Effect of wheat bran on weight of stool and gastrointestinal transit time: a meta analysis. Br Med J (Clin Res Ed). 1988;296:615-7. [PMID: 2832033]

16. Brandt LJ, Bjorkman D, Fennerty MB, et al. Systematic review on the management of irritable bowel syndrome in North America. Am J Gastroenterol. 2002;97:S7-26. [PMID: 12425586]

17. Colwell LJ, Prather CM, Phillips SF, Zinsmeister AR. Effects of an irritable bowel syndrome educational class on health-promoting behaviors and symptoms. Am J Gastroenterol. 1998;93:901-5. [PMID: 9647015]

18. Owens DM, Nelson DK, Talley NJ. The irritable bowel syndrome: long-term prognosis and the physician-patient interaction. Ann Intern Med. 1995;122:107-12. [PMID: 7992984]

19. Creed F, Craig T, Farmer R. Functional abdominal pain, psychiatric illness, and life events. Gut. 1988;29:235-42. [PMID: 3345935]

20. Bennett EJ, Tennant CC, Piesse C, Badcock CA, Kellow JE. Level of chronic life stress predicts clinical outcome in irritable bowel syndrome. Gut. 1998;43:256-61. [PMID: 10189854]

21. Drossman DA, Sandler RS, McKee DC, Lovitz AJ. Bowel patterns among subjects not seeking health care. Use of a questionnaire to identify a population with bowel dysfunction. Gastroenterology. 1982;83:529-34. [PMID: 7095360]

22. Drossman DA, Leserman J, Nachman G, et al. Sexual and physical abuse in women with functional or organic gastrointestinal disorders. Ann Intern Med. 1990;113:828-33. [PMID: 2240898]

Is dietary modification effective in the management of IBS?

Dietary modification is not proven to reduce IBS symptoms, and major exclusion diets are not recommended. However, it may be reasonable to consider dietary modification for individual cases in which specific foods seem to trigger symptoms. In addition, common-sense dietary recommendations directed at the predominant symptom can help to minimize symptoms. Clinicians should talk with patients about their dietary habits to:

- Evaluate for lactose intolerance
- Evaluate consumption of caffeine, fructose, or artificial sweeteners, all of which can have laxative effects
- Inquire about laxative-containing herbal products
- Determine whether patients with gas and bloating are drinking excess carbonated beverages, drinking with a straw, or chewing gum, all of which can lead a person to swallow too much air
- Advise against excess intake of fats, which can lead to gas retention
- Advise avoidance of certain carbohydrates, such as beans, cabbage, broccoli, and cauliflower, if they trigger symptoms. They may be difficult to digest and lead to fermentation and gas in the colon.

Inadequate dietary fiber may cause constipation, and clinicians often encourage patients with constipation-predominant IBS to increase fiber intake. Studies suggest that fiber is helpful for relief of constipation, but not for relief of pain (14, 15). Fiber is not effective for patients with diarrhea-predominant IBS and may even exacerbate symptoms. Achieving constipation relief with fiber may require high-dose therapy, which patients are often unable to tolerate.

A systematic review studied the role of bulking agents in IBS (wheat bran, corn fiber, calcium polycarbophil, ispaghula husk, and psyllium) and concluded that they were no more effective than placebo in providing global symptom relief of IBS . However, the authors deemed all of the trials inadequate because of methodological flaws or small sample size (16).

Are there nonpharmacologic interventions aside from diet that are useful in the management of IBS?

In addition to advice about diet, important nonpharmacologic aspects of IBS care include reassurance, education with advice about trigger avoidance, stress management, and exercise. Clinicians must reassure patients that their symptoms are not because of a life-threatening disorder and assist them in developing effective self-management strategies. Patients do better and use health care more efficiently when it is acknowledged that their symptoms are not imagined, that the symptoms have physiologic causes that are poorly understood but real, and that they can themselves control some symptom triggers.

In an uncontrolled study, advice about diet and exercise, stress management, and appropriate use of medications was associated with alleviation of IBS symptoms in 80% of patients (17).

Retrospective analysis of outpatient charts at a referral center showed a correlation between patient education, including discussion of psychosocial stressors, and reduced future visits(18) .

It may be helpful to ask patients to complete daily diaries of symptoms, including entries for stressors, mood, events, thoughts, and diet. Clinicians should use the diary information to help patients understand the role of psychosocial stressors and to help them develop self-management strategies.

What is the role of psychotherapy in the care of patients with IBS?

Psychosocial stressors are associated with symptoms (19–21). Patients with IBS are more likely to have had early life or current trauma, including losses or abuse (22), and are more likely to have generalized anxiety disorder and worry (23). Psychological distress is associated with IBS after dysentery (24). Psychological therapy to minimize anxiety can reduce symptoms.

One randomized, controlled trial (RCT) involving patients whose symptoms had not improved with standard medical treatment for at least 6 months showed that two thirds of the patients receiving psychotherapy had less diarrhea but not less constipation; they also had less intermittent pain, but those with constant abdominal pain did not improve (25).

Other research has found that psychotherapy also results in decreased use of health care resources. So while psychotherapy has costs on the front end, it may reduce long-term medical costs (26). However, trials of psychological treatment in IBS have methodological inadequacies, mostly because of difficulties in creating a true control group or in adequately blinding trials (27). Consequently, it has not been definitively determined whether psychotherapy is any more beneficial for IBS than other interventions.

Which pharmacologic therapies are effective in IBS?

The choice of drug therapy depends on an individual's symptoms, and effectiveness varies from patient to patient (28). Drugs used in management of patients with IBS include antispasmodics, laxatives, antidiarrheals, antidepressants, and antibiotics. IBS drugs are described in Table 3. Limited effectiveness of conventional treatment options is frustrating for patients but also common.

In a study of 350 IBS patients, more than half of patients (55%) taking prescription drugs for IBS felt that they were ineffective or only somewhat effective, more than 60% reported adverse effects from these medications, and 40% of patients taking over-the-counter medications reported that they were ineffective (29).

> **Stress management options include the following:**
>
> - Stress reduction training and relaxation therapies, such as meditation
> - Counseling and support
> - Regular exercise, such as walking or yoga
> - Changes to the stressful situations in your life
> - Adequate sleep
> - Hypnotherapy.

The U.S. Food and Drug Administration (FDA) has approved only 2 drugs to treat IBS: tegaserod maleate, a $5\text{-}HT_4$–receptor agonist that increases intestinal motility, and alosetron hydrochloride, a $5\text{-}HT_3$–receptor antagonist medication that decreases abdominal sensitivity. However, tegaserod was taken off the market in March 2007 because of safety concerns, and use of alosetron has been restricted.

Antispasmodics

Antispasmodics are indicated on an as-needed basis as a first-line treatment for IBS pain. The 2 antispasmodics available in the United States, dicyclomine and hyoscyamine, block the action of acetylcholine at parasympathetic sites in secretory glands, smooth muscle, and the central nervous system. The effect is reduced contractions in the colon. The drugs are particularly helpful when taken before meals if postprandial urgency, diarrhea, and cramping are a problem. Adverse reactions increase as dose increases.

23. Hazlett-Stevens H, Craske MG, Mayer EA, Chang L, Naliboff BD. Prevalence of irritable bowel syndrome among university students: the roles of worry, neuroticism, anxiety sensitivity and visceral anxiety. J Psychosom Res. 2003;55:501-5. [PMID: 14642979]
24. Gwee KA, Leong YL, Graham C, et al. The role of psychological and biological factors in postinfective gut dysfunction. Gut. 1999;44:400-6. [PMID: 10026328]
25. Guthrie E, Creed F, Dawson D, Tomenson B. A controlled trial of psychological treatment for the irritable bowel syndrome. Gastroenterology. 1991;100:450-7. [PMID: 1985041]
26. North of England IBS Research Group. The cost-effectiveness of psychotherapy and paroxetine for severe irritable bowel syndrome. Gastroenterology. 2003;124:303-17. [PMID: 12557136]
27. Talley NJ, Owen BK, Boyce P, Paterson K. Psychological treatments for irritable bowel syndrome: a critique of controlled treatment trials. Am J Gastroenterol. 1996;91:277-83. [PMID: 8607493]
28. Jailwala J, Imperiale TF, Kroenke K. Pharmacologic treatment of the irritable bowel syndrome: a systematic review of randomized, controlled trials. Ann Intern Med. 2000;133:136-47. [PMID: 10896640]
29. International Foundation for Functional Gastrointestinal Disorders. IBS in the real world survey. Milwaukee, WI: International Foundation for Functional Gastrointestinal Disorders; 2002:1-19.

Table 3. Drugs Commonly Used in the Treatment of Irritable Bowel Syndrome*

Class/Agent	Mechanism of Action	Dosing	Benefits	Side Effects	Notes
Antispasmodics (Dicycolime, hyocsyamine)	Reduce contractions in colon and small bowel that may produce diarrhea and cramps	Generally given as needed, especially before meals	Reduce pain	Dry mouth, somnolence, constipation, urine retention, diplopia; side effects usually minor	Effective to blunt gastrocolonic response if diarrhea/urgency or postprandial pain; first-line agents for pain
Combination antispasmodics/sedatives Clidinium, bromide/chlordiazepoxide, phenobarbital, hyocsyamine, atropine/scopolamine	Additive effect of sedative to reduce GI motility	Generally given as needed, especially before meals	Useful for pain, especially if patient anxious and antispasmodics alone have failed	Drowsiness, additive effect with alcohol; other side effects similar to those of antispasmodics; do not take before driving or tasks requiring alertness	Potential for abuse minimized by anticholinergic component
Laxatives PEG solution, magnesium citrate, sodium phosphate, sorbitol	Draw water into colon	Titrate to effect	Reduce distention of colon due to retained stool; PEG-based lavage solutions useful for severe constipation when a few glasses are taken at bedtime	Hypermagnesemia, hyperphosphatemia if renal insufficiency; can cause gas and bloating	Less cramping and probably safer long-term than stimulant cathartics (which may cause tachyphylaxis and "cathartic colon"); first-line agents after fiber in constipation-predominant IBS; avoid in IBS with gas and bloating
Antidiarrheals Loperamide, diphenoxylate/atropine	μ-Opiate agonists have primarily gut effect to increase segmenting contractions and decrease propulsive ones	Titrate to effect	Reduce diarrhea but not pain	Can cause constipation; atropine can give dry mouth, urine retention, tachycardia	No known long-term sequelae from repeated use; loperamide has no CNS penetration; abuse of diphenoylate prevented by combination with atropine
Antidepressants Tricyclics, SSRIs	Mechanism is uncertain	Lower doses than needed to treat depression	Reduce pain	Anticholinergic effects with tricyclics, diarrhea with SSRIs	Tricyclics are first-line agents in patients with pain and diarrhea, no definitive data on SSRIs
Antibiotics Neomycin, rifaximin	Aims to restore normal intestinal bacteria	Rifaximin 400 mg 3 times/d for 10 days in recent trial	Symptom improvement correlates with normalization of intestinal bacteria	Antibiotic resistance; ototoxicity and CNS symptoms with neomycin	Resistance is less of a concern with rifaximin because it is not absorbed

*CNS = central nervous system; GI = gastrointestinal; IBS = irritable bowel syndrome; PEG = polyethylene glycol; SSRIs = selective serotonin reuptake inhibitors.

30. Poynard T, Naveau S, Mory B, Chaput JC. Meta-analysis of smooth muscle relaxants in the treatment of irritable bowel syndrome. Aliment Pharmacol Ther. 1994;8:499-510. [PMID: 7865642]
31. Drossman DA, Whitehead WE, Camilleri M. Irritable bowel syndrome: a technical review for practice guideline development. Gastroenterology. 1997;112:2120-37. [PMID: 9178709]

For patients who are anxious or for whom antispasmodics alone are not successful, clinicians should consider a sedative–antispasmodics combination. The risk for abuse of sedative–antispasmodics is low because of the small dose of sedatives in most formulations and because of the unpleasant anticholinergic side effects that occur with dose elevation.

A meta-analysis of 26 RCTs with antispasmodics supports their utility in the management of IBS symptoms. The study, which incorporated only trials of antispasmodics that are not approved by the FDA (cimetropium bromide, pinaverium bromide, trimebutine, octilium bromide, and mebeverine), found that the drugs were significantly better than placebo for improving overall symptoms and pain. Patients receiving active drugs had more adverse effects (6% mean difference; P < 0.01) than those receiving placebo, but the adverse reactions were not serious (30).

Laxatives

Expert consensus suggests osmotic-type laxatives if fiber is unsuccessful for initial therapy of constipation (31). Osmotic laxatives, like magnesium citrate or sodium phosphate, are used to rapidly empty the lower intestine and bowel.

Although not usually used for long-term or repeated correction of constipation, they are considered safe and effective for severe constipation when used daily or as needed. Low-dose daily administration of another type of hyperosmotic laxative, polyethylene glycol, increases bowel frequency and decreases symptoms in chronic constipation in which fiber supplementation is not successful (32). Polyglycol is a large molecule that causes water to be retained in the stool, which softens the stool and increases the number of bowel movements.

Patients with IBS should avoid regular use of stimulant cathartics, such as senna, cascara, and phenolphthalein. Stimulant cathartics increase the risk for cramps and tachyphylaxis and may lead to a markedly slow "cathartic colon."

Antidiarrheals
Nonabsorbable synthetic opioids can be useful to treat patients with diarrhea-predominant IBS. These antidiarrheal agents work by peripheral μ-opioid receptors to reduce visceral nociception via afferent pathway inhibition. The effect is to reduce propagating contractions and to increase segmenting contractions in the bowel, which slows transit and allows more time for water absorption.

Loperamide is the first-line agent for diarrhea. It can be taken as needed or on a scheduled basis depending on the severity and frequency of symptoms. Two RCTs (33, 34) showed that loperamide is effective for diarrhea; however, it did not significantly relieve pain in either study. There are no identified safety concerns associated with repeated use of loperamide.

Other opioid antidiarrheal agents are also likely to be effective. Diphenoxylate hydrochloride combined with atropine sulfate is used in IBS to slow gastrointestinal transit. Diphenoxylate is a constipating meperidine congener that reduces excessive gastrointestinal propulsion and motility, and atropine discourages abuse by speeding up the heart rate. Diphenoxylate may exacerbate constipation.

5-HT Antagonists
Tegaserod, a $5-HT_4$–receptor agonist, was the only drug approved by the FDA for relief of abdominal discomfort, bloating, and constipation in patients with IBS (35). However, on March 30, 2007, the FDA requested that the manufacturer withdraw tegaserod from the market because of an association between use of the drug and myocardial infarction and stroke. In an analysis of over 18 000 patients, adverse cardiovascular events occurred in 13 of 11 614 patients (0.11%) receiving tegaserod compared with 1 of 7031 patients (0.01%) receiving placebo (www.fda.gov/cder/drug/advisory/tegaserod.htm).

Alosetron, a $5-HT_3$–receptor antagonist that can provide relief in diarrhea-predominant IBS, increases colonic compliance, reduces intestinal transit, and reduces pain and diarrhea (36). It was withdrawn from the market in 2000 because of the occurrence of serious life-threatening gastrointestinal effects and was reintroduced in 2002 with restricted availability and use. Alosetron carries a 1 in 700 risk of ischemic colitis and thus should be reserved for women with severe, refractory IBS symptoms causing significant impairment in quality of life. Prescribing physicians must register with the manufacturer (phone: 888-825-5249), and patients must sign a consent form to begin therapy. Three separate double-blind, randomized, placebo-controlled

32. Andorsky RI, Goldner F. Colonic lavage solution (polyethylene glycol electrolyte lavage solution) as a treatment for chronic constipation: a double-blind, placebo-controlled study. Am J Gastroenterol. 1990;85:261-5. [PMID: 2178398]
33. Cann PA, Read NW, Holdsworth CD, Barends D. Role of loperamide and placebo in management of irritable bowel syndrome (IBS). Dig Dis Sci. 1984;29:239-47. [PMID: 6365490]
34. Efskind PS, Bernklev T, Vatn MH. A double-blind placebo-controlled trial with loperamide in irritable bowel syndrome. Scand J Gastroenterol. 1996;31:463-8. [PMID: 8734343]
35. Talley NJ. Serotoninergic neuroenteric modulators. Lancet. 2001;358:2061-8. [PMID: 11755632]
36. Watson ME, Lacey L, Kong S, et al. Alosetron improves quality of life in women with diarrhea-predominant irritable bowel syndrome. Am J Gastroenterol. 2001;96:455-9. [PMID: 11232690]
37. Camilleri M, Northcutt AR, Kong S, et al. Efficacy and safety of alosetron in women with irritable bowel syndrome: a randomised, placebo-controlled trial. Lancet. 2000;355:1035-40. [PMID: 10744088]
38. Camilleri M, Chey WY, Mayer EA, et al. A randomized controlled clinical trial of the serotonin type 3 receptor antagonist alosetron in women with diarrhea-predominant irritable bowel syndrome. Arch Intern Med. 2001;161:1733-40. [PMID: 11485506]

39. Camilleri M, Mayer EA, Drossman DA, et al. Improvement in pain and bowel function in female irritable bowel patients with alosetron, a 5-HT3 receptor antagonist. Aliment Pharmacol Ther. 1999;13:1149-59. [PMID: 10468696]
40. Jackson JL, O'Malley PG, Tomkins G, et al. Treatment of functional gastrointestinal disorders with antidepressant medications: a meta-analysis. Am J Med. 2000;108:65-72. [PMID: 11059442]
41. Myren J, Løvland B, Larssen SE, Larsen S. A double-blind study of the effect of trimipramine in patients with the irritable bowel syndrome. Scand J Gastroenterol. 1984;19:835-43. [PMID: 6151243]
42. Greenbaum DS, Mayle JE, Vanegeren LE, et al. Effects of desipramine on irritable bowel syndrome compared with atropine and placebo. Dig Dis Sci. 1987;32:257-66. [PMID: 3545719]
43. Drossman DA, Toner BB, Whitehead WE, et al. Cognitive-behavioral therapy versus education and desipramine versus placebo for moderate to severe functional bowel disorders. Gastroenterology. 2003;125:19-31. [PMID: 12851867]
44. Pimentel M, Chow EJ, Lin HC. Eradication of small intestinal bacterial overgrowth reduces symptoms of irritable bowel syndrome. Am J Gastroenterol. 2000;95:3503-6. [PMID: 11151884]
45. Pimentel M, Chow EJ, Lin HC. Normalization of lactulose breath testing correlates with symptom improvement in irritable bowel syndrome. A double-blind, randomized, placebo-controlled study. Am J Gastro-enterol. 2003;98:412-9. [PMID: 12591062]
46. Attar A, Flourié B, Rambaud JC, et al. Antibiotic efficacy in small intestinal bacterial overgrowth-related chronic diarrhea: a crossover, randomized trial. Gastroenterology. 1999;117:794-7. [PMID: 10500060]

trials have shown that alosetron for diarrhea-predominant IBS had an overall "adequate response" rate of nearly 60%. Improvement over placebo was approximately 15% (37–39).

Antidepressants

Antidepressants can be helpful in alleviating IBS symptoms. According to a recent meta-analysis of 12 studies, the number needed to treat for benefit in 1 person was 3.2 (40).

Clinicians should consider tricyclic antidepressants to reduce pain and diarrhea. The mechanism of action of these drugs in IBS is unclear, but it is known that they act primarily by blocking the uptake of neurotransmitters at specific presynaptic nerve endings in the central nervous system. As a result, they prevent synaptic receptor overstimulation. The benefit of tricyclics in IBS seems to be independent of the anticholinergic effects or antidepressant effects. The required dosage is less than that required for the treatment of depression. Several studies have shown benefits for tricyclic use (41–43). Tricyclics can be used in combination with antispasmodics.

Use of selective serotonin reuptake inhibitors (SSRIs) is not well-studied in patients with IBS, but early findings suggest that SSRIs can improve the quality of life in patients who have severe IBS with associated psychological stress. This may be primarily a psychological effect. Patients may also benefit from pain alleviation; however, a cohort study that associated paroxetine with improved quality of life in IBS did not find any association with alleviated abdominal pain (26).

SSRIs might be a consideration for older patients or in persons with constipation because they lack anticholinergic side effects. SSRIs may trigger episodes in patients with diarrhea-predominant IBS while being helpful for patients with constipation.

Antibiotics

Alterations in gut flora have been identified in patients with IBS, and some hypothesize that intestinal bacterial overgrowth may play a role in symptoms. The antibiotic neomycin has been shown to improve IBS symptoms. This effect seems to correlate with normalization of intestinal bacterial flora (44, 45). However, neomycin effectively eliminates bacterial overgrowth in only about 25% of patients (45), and side effects limit its use. Low efficacy, side effects, and concerns about antimicrobial resistance also apply to other antibiotics that have been previously investigated for treating bacterial overgrowth (46). For this reason, researchers have been seeking an antibiotic for IBS that is not systemically absorbed, has minimal adverse effects, and effectively eliminates bacterial overgrowth. One drug that meets these criteria is rifaximin.

An RCT assigned 87 patients who met the Rome I criteria for IBS to receive either 400 mg of rifaximin 3 times daily for 10 days or placebo. A questionnaire was administered before treatment and 7 days after treatment. The primary outcome was global improvement in IBS. Patients were then asked to keep a weekly symptom diary for 10 weeks. Over the 10 weeks of follow-up, rifaximin resulted in greater improvement in IBS symptoms than placebo. In addition, rifaximin recipients had a lower bloating score after treatment. This preliminary, short-duration trial suggests that rifaximin improves IBS symptoms for up to 10 weeks after discontinuation of therapy (47).

What are some possible future treatments for IBS?

Several new drugs are being studied for the treatment of IBS. IBS therapy is moving from "symptom-based" therapy to "hypthesis-based" therapy. Rather than treating symptoms, new IBS approaches aim to treat the underlying pathophysiology.

Trials are currently underway for treating IBS with renzapride, a $5\text{-}HT_3$–receptor antagonist and a $5\text{-}HT_4$–receptor agonist (48, 49). Tachykinin antagonists, like substance P and neurokinin A, might also be useful for treating IBS. Tachykinins are present in the gastrointestinal tract and are involved in such functions as gastrointestinal motility, visceral sensitization, and autonomic reaction to stress. Studies in animals and healthy humans have yielded promising results (50, 51). Neutrophins, a family of neuropeptides that includes neutrophin-3, are also undergoing preclinical study as potential therapeutic agents for functional gastrointestinal disorders. Studies have shown that recombinant human neutrophin-3 increased stool frequency; facilitated stool passage in patients with constipation; and accelerated gastric, small bowel, and colonic transit in healthy persons (52, 53). Antibiotics and probiotics aim to normalize intestinal bacteria.

Is there evidence to support the effectiveness of complementary and alternative medicine treatments for IBS?

Patients with IBS frequently try nontraditional therapies, particularly if traditional approaches to treatment do not relieve their symptoms. While some patients have some relief with such therapies, data to support their use are sparse (54) (Table 4).

What components of care should clinicians integrate into follow-up of patients with IBS?

There are no specific data on which to base a recommendation on the frequency or the components of follow-up for patients with IBS. However, a common-sense approach includes monitoring for alarm features, progression of symptoms, and management of psychosocial stressors. The typical symptom course in IBS is chronic and fluctuating. Clinicians should consider additional diagnostic tests or referral if alarm features develop or if symptoms are refractory and persistent. Clinicians should emphasize to patients that the long-term prognosis is good. Carefully explaining the prognosis can significantly reduce patient distress.

47. Pimentel M, Park S, Mirocha J, Kane SV, Kong Y. The effect of a nonabsorbed oral antibiotic (rifaximin) on the symptoms of the irritable bowel syndrome: a randomized trial. Ann Intern Med. 2006;145:557-63. [PMID: 17043337]
48. Meyers NL, Tack J, Middleton S, et al. Efficacy and safety or renzapride in patients with constipation-predominant irritable bowel syndrome [Abstract]. Gut. 2002;51(suppl III): A10.
49. George A, Meyers NL, Palmer RMJ. Efficacy and safety of renzapride in patients with constipation-predominant IBS: a phase IIB study in the UK primary healthcare setting [Abstract]. Gut. 2003;52:A91.
50. Julia V, Morteau O, Buéno L. Involvement of neurokinin 1 and 2 receptors in viscerosensitive response to rectal distension in rats. Gastroenterology. 1994;107:94-102. [PMID: 7517374]
51. Lördal M, Navalesi G, Theodorsson E, Maggi CA, Hellström PM. A novel tachykinin NK2 receptor antagonist prevents motility-stimulating effects of neurokinin A in small intestine. Br J Pharmacol. 2001;134:215-23. [PMID: 11522614]
52. Coulie B, Szarka LA, Camilleri M, et al. Recombinant human neurotrophic factors accelerate colonic transit and relieve constipation in humans. Gastroenterology. 2000;119:41-50. [PMID: 10889153]
53. Coulie B, Lee JS, Lyford G, et al. Recombinant human neurotrophin-3 increases noncholinergic smooth muscle contractility and decreases nonadrenergic (NANC) inhibition of myenteric neurons in guinea-pig colon [Abstract]. Gastroenterology. 2000;118:A710.
54. Spanier JA, Howden CW, Jones MP. A systematic review of alternative therapies in the irritable bowel syndrome. Arch Intern Med. 2003; 163:265-74. [PMID: 12578506]

Table 4. Alternative and Complementary Therapies Used by Patients with Irritable Bowel Syndrome

Therapy	Proposed Action	Notes
Acupuncture	Relief of chronic pain	No definitive studies available; results of existing studies are mixed
Hypnosis	Relief of chronic pain	No definitive studies available
Peppermint oil	Natural antispasmodic believed to relax intestinal smooth muscle	Ineffective in 2 crossover trials; some effect noted in one parallel trial
Ginger	Natural antispasmodic believed to relax intestinal smooth muscle	No evidence from high-quality trials
Aloe	Natural antispasmodic believed to relax intestinal smooth muscle	No evidence from high-quality trials
Chinese herbal therapy	Natural antispasmodic believed to relax intestinal smooth muscle	Global improvement noted in 1 study
Probiotics	Aim to replenish the beneficial intestinal bacteria that may be lacking in patients with IBS	*Bifidobacteria infantis* showed symptom improvement in early clinical studies

When should clinicians consider consulting a specialist for treatment?

When management strategies are not effective, clinicians should consider consulting a gastroenterologist. Gastroenterologists may have greater knowledge of treatment options because of increased familiarity with the disorder. Clinicians should consider referral to a mental health professional for patients with refractory symptoms leading to impaired quality of life or major depression, anxiety disorder, bipolar disorder, or other serious psychological disease.

Treatment... Dietary advice, patient education, and stress management are essential to effective IBS management. Drug therapy should target the individual patient's symptom pattern, and options include antispasmodics, laxatives, antidiarrheals, 5-HT antagonists, antidepressants, and antibiotics. Of the many non-traditional therapies that patients use to treat IBS, clinical trial data best support a clinical benefit of probiotics.

CLINICAL BOTTOM LINE

Practice Improvement

Do professional organizations offer recommendations for the care of patients with IBS?

In 2003, the American Gastroenterological Association developed clinical practice guidelines for IBS based on a comprehensive review (31).

Are there performance measures related to the care of patients with IBS?

Current proposed performance measures in the United States do not include any measures specifically related to the care of patients with IBS. However, the quality of the doctor–patient interaction is paramount in the care of patients with IBS.

A survey developed by the American Gastrointestinal Association may be useful for evaluating a patient's satisfaction with his or her care (www.gastro.org/wmspage.cfm?parm1=3266). However, the survey has not yet been validated.

---

in the clinic
Tool Kit

Irritable Bowel Syndrome

www.pier.acponline.org
IBS module of PIER, an electronic decision support resource designed for rapid access to information at the point of care.

www.annals/intheclinic/tools
Download copies of the Patient Information sheet that appears on the following page for duplication and distribution to your patients.

www.gastro.org/wmspage.cfm?parm1=3266
Patient satisfaction surveys to enable the physician to quantitatively measure the patient care experience as well as physician–patient communication.

in the clinic

THINGS PEOPLE SHOULD KNOW
ABOUT IRRITABLE BOWEL SYNDROME

- IBS causes pain, cramping, bloating, gas, diarrhea, and constipation. Another name for the condition is spastic colitis.
- The cause of IBS is believed to be intestines that are overly sensitive to normal intestinal movement, gas, some foods, and stress.
- There is no test for IBS, so doctors make the diagnosis by carefully evaluating symptoms and excluding other conditions.
- There is no cure, but people with IBS can control symptoms by healthy diet and exercise, managing stress, avoiding things that trigger symptoms, and taking medications to treat symptoms.

Web Sites with Good Information about Irritable Bowel Syndrome

MedlinePLUS
www.nlm.nih.gov/medlineplus/irritablebowelsyndrome.html

National Institute of Diabetes and Digestive and Kidney Diseases
http://digestive.niddk.nih.gov/ddiseases/pubs/ibs_ez/

International Foundation for Functional Gastrointestinal Disorders
www.aboutibs.org/

Mayo Clinic
www.mayoclinic.com/health/irritable-bowel-syndrome/MM00461 (a short video clip that provides information about irritable bowel syndrome)

HEALTH TiPS*

Irritable bowel syndrome (IBS) is a common problem that can cause constipation, diarrhea, or both. Sometimes there is stomach pain or gas. IBS comes and goes but never goes away for good. IBS does not cause cancer.

What You Can Do:

Find out what makes your IBS symptoms worse

- Stress at home or work
- Some foods

Write down when your IBS symptoms happen

- Get help to deal with stress
- Stay away from too much caffeine, soda, fatty foods, and laxatives

See your doctor often to keep your IBS on track. Next doctor's visit _____

Things to Ask your Doctor:

What causes IBS?

Do I need any tests?

Why do I have problems if all my tests are normal?

How can I deal with stress?

Do I need medicine for my IBS?

Why doesn't medicine always work for my IBS?

What are the side effects of my medicines for IBS?

*HEALTH TiPS are developed by the American College of Physicians Foundation and PIER and are designed to be understood by most patients.

Patient Information

Osteoarthritis

1. Prevalence of disabilities and associated health conditions among adults—United States, 1999. MMWR Morb Mortal Wkly Rep. 2001;50:120-5. [PMID: 11393491]
2. Lawrence RC, Helmick CG, Arnett FC, et al. Estimates of the prevalence of arthritis and selected musculoskeletal disorders in the United States. Arthritis Rheum. 1998;41:778-99. [PMID: 9588729]
3. Badley E, DesMeules M. Arthritis in Canada: An Ongoing Challenge. 2003. Ottawa, Canada.
4. Arthritis prevalence and activity limitations—United States, 1990. MMWR Morb Mortal Wkly Rep. 1994;43:433-8. [PMID: 8202076]
5. Nuki G. Osteoarthritis: a problem of joint failure. Z Rheumatol. 1999;58:142-7. [PMID: 10441841]
6. Eyre DR. Collagens and cartilage matrix homeostasis. Clin Orthop Relat Res. 2004:S118-22. [PMID: 15480053]
7. Guccione AA, Felson DT, Anderson JJ, et al. The effects of specific medical conditions on the functional limitations of elders in the Framingham Study. Am J Public Health. 1994;84:351-8. [PMID: 8129049]
8. Hannan MT, Felson DT, Pincus T. Analysis of the discordance between radiographic changes and knee pain in osteoarthritis of the knee. J Rheumatol. 2000;27:1513-7. [PMID: 10852280]
9. Felson DT. An update on the pathogenesis and epidemiology of osteoarthritis. Radiol Clin North Am. 2004;42:1-9, v. [PMID: 15049520]
10. Tetsworth K, Paley D. Malalignment and degenerative arthropathy. Orthop Clin North Am. 1994;25:367-77. [PMID: 8028880]
11. Sharma L, Song J, Felson DT, Cahue S, Shamiyeh E, Dunlop DD. The role of knee alignment in disease progression and functional decline in knee osteoarthritis. JAMA. 2001;286:188-95. [PMID: 11448282]

Osteoarthritis (OA) is the leading cause of disability in elderly persons (1). Recent estimates suggest that symptomatic OA of the knee occurs in 13% of persons 60 years of age and older (2). The prevalence of OA is expected to increase as the U.S. population ages and the prevalence of obesity rises. By 2020, the number of people with OA may double (3, 4). Despite its growing prevalence, OA remains poorly understood, and recent concerns about the safety of several medications that are commonly prescribed for treatment have highlighted the deficiencies in OA management.

OA can be viewed as the clinical and pathologic outcome of a range of disorders that causes structural and functional failure of synovial joints with loss and erosion of articular cartilage, subchondral bone alterations, meniscal degeneration, limited synovial inflammatory response, and bone and cartilage overgrowth (osteophytes) (5). OA occurs when the dynamic equilibrium between the breakdown and repair of joint tissues become unbalanced (6). This progressive joint failure can cause pain and disability (7), although many persons with structural changes consistent with OA are asymptomatic (8).

OA can occur in any synovial joint in the body but is most common in the knees, hips, and hands. OA may affect 1 or several joints. A diagnosis is usually made by assessing the constellation of presenting clinical features on the history and physical examination. The diagnosis can be confirmed by imaging.

This article will primarily emphasize prevention, diagnosis, and treatment of OA of the knee, but many of the diagnostic and therapeutic recommendations also apply to OA of the hip and hand.

Prevention

What are the major risk factors for OA?

OA is perhaps best understood as resulting from excessive mechanical stress applied in the context of systemic susceptibility. Susceptibility to OA may be increased in part by genetic inheritance (a positive family history increases risk), age, ethnicity, and female gender (9).

Although OA has worldwide distribution, geographic and ethnic differences have been reported and can provide further insights into disease etiology (10). For example, the prevalence of hand and knee OA is similar among Europeans and Americans. However, there is great variation in the distribution of hip OA, with markedly lower rates in African blacks, Asian Indians, and Chinese persons from Beijing and Hong Kong.

In persons vulnerable to knee OA, local mechanical factors, such as malalignment, muscle weakness and alterations in the structural integrity of the joint environment (such as meniscal damage), facilitate the progression of OA. Loading can also be affected by obesity and joint injury, both of which may increase the likelihood of development or progression of OA.

As few as 5 degrees of genu varum (bow-legged) malalignment results in an estimated 70% to 90% increase in compressive loading of the medial knee compartment (10). This increase corresponds to a 4-fold increase in the risk for worsening OA of the medial knee over 18 months (11). Conversely, genu valgum (knock-kneed) malalignment markedly increases compressive load on the lateral compartment of the knee, elevating the risk for lateral OA progression 5-fold (11).

What should clinicians advise patients about diet and physical activity to prevent OA of the knee?

Obesity is the single most important modifiable risk factor for severe OA of the knee (12, 13). Obesity has also been increasing in prevalence in the United States over the past 4 decades (14, 15). Thus, it is critical to counsel patients to lose weight, particularly women with a body mass index (BMI) of 25 or more.

In the Framingham study, among women with a baseline body mass index (BMI) > 25, weight loss was associated with a significantly lower risk for knee OA. For a woman of normal height, for every 11-lb weight loss (approximately 2 BMI units), risk for knee OA dropped > 50%. A similar weight gain was associated with an increased risk for knee OA (odds ratio, 1.28 for weight gain of 2 BMI units). If obese (BMI > 30) elderly men lost enough weight to fall into the overweight category (BMI 26–29.9) and overweight men lost enough weight to move into the normal-weight category (BMI <26), the incidence of knee OA would decrease by 21.5%. Similar changes in weight category in women would result in a 33% decrease in knee OA (16).

Before age 50, OA is more common in men than in women. This is attributed to joint injury. In an effort to reduce the potential for injury and subsequent OA, sports participants should be advised to use graduated training schedules, participate in appropriate conditioning programs, and avoid intense loading of previously injured joints (17). Persons involved in contact sports are at greater risk for meniscal tears and cruciate ligament injury, which are known to predispose to OA (18, 19).

Quadriceps weakness decreases the ability of muscle to distribute load across the knee joint and maintain joint stability. Quadriceps weakness may result from the pain of OA (20); however, some have suggested that quadriceps weakness precedes the onset of knee OA and is itself a risk factor for knee OA, particularly in women (21, 22). Patients should be encouraged to maintain quadriceps muscle strength through strengthening exercise, as this may diminish the risk for both radiographic knee OA and symptomatic knee OA (22).

> **Prevention...** Obesity is the single most important modifiable risk factor for OA of the knee. People participating in sports should be advised to engage in proper training and conditioning to avoid injury, and all patients should be encouraged to exercise to maintain quadriceps strength.
>
> **CLINICAL BOTTOM LINE**

Diagnosis

What are the characteristic symptoms that should alert clinicians to the diagnosis of OA?

OA typically presents with joint pain. During a 1-year period, 25% of people over 55 years have a persistent episode of knee pain, and 1 in 6 consult their general practitioner about it (23). Approximately 50% of these persons have radiographic

knee OA (24). Symptomatic knee OA, defined as pain on most days and radiographic features consistent with OA, occurs in approximately 12% of persons older than 55 years (23).

OA of the hand usually affects the distal and proximal interphalangeal joints and the base of the thumb.

12. Coggon D, Reading I, Croft P, McLaren M, Barrett D, Cooper C. Knee osteoarthritis and obesity. Int J Obes Relat Metab Disord. 2001;25:622-7. [PMID: 11360143]
13. Felson DT, Zhang Y. An update on the epidemiology of knee and hip osteoarthritis with a view to prevention. Arthritis Rheum. 1998;41:1343-55. [PMID: 9704632]
14. Flegal KM, Carroll MD, Ogden CL, Johnson CL. Prevalence and trends in obesity among US adults, 1999-2000. JAMA. 2002;288:1723-7. [PMID: 12365955]
15. Ogden CL, Carroll MD, Curtin LR, McDowell MA, Tabak CJ, Flegal KM. Prevalence of overweight and obesity in the United States, 1999-2004. JAMA. 2006;295:1549-55. [PMID: 16595758]
16. Felson DT, Zhang Y, Hannan MT, Naimark A, Weissman B, Aliabadi P, et al. Risk factors for incident radiographic knee osteoarthritis in the elderly: the Framingham Study. Arthritis Rheum. 1997;40:728-33. [PMID: 9125257]
17. Felson DT, Lawrence RC, Dieppe PA, et al. Osteoarthritis: new insights. Part 1: the disease and its risk factors. Ann Intern Med. 2000;133:635-46. [PMID: 11033593]
18. Englund M, Roos EM, Lohmander LS. Impact of type of meniscal tear on radiographic and symptomatic knee osteoarthritis: a sixteen-year followup of meniscectomy with matched controls. Arthritis Rheum. 2003;48:2178-87. [PMID: 12905471]
19. Roos H, Laurén M, Adalberth T, Roos EM, Jonsson K, Lohmander LS. Knee osteoarthritis after meniscectomy: prevalence of radiographic changes after twenty-one years, compared with matched controls. Arthritis Rheum. 1998;41:687-93. [PMID: 9550478]

20. Hurley MV, Scott DL, Rees J, Newham DJ. Sensorimotor changes and functional performance in patients with knee osteoarthritis. Ann Rheum Dis. 1997;56:641-8. [PMID: 9462165]

21. Slemenda C, Brandt KD, Heilman DK, et al. Quadriceps weakness and osteoarthritis of the knee. Ann Intern Med. 1997;127:97-104. [PMID: 9230035]

22. Slemenda C, Heilman DK, Brandt KD, et al. Reduced quadriceps strength relative to body weight: a risk factor for knee osteoarthritis in women? Arthritis Rheum. 1998;41:1951-9. [PMID: 9811049]

23. Peat G, McCarney R, Croft P. Knee pain and osteoarthritis in older adults: a review of community burden and current use of primary health care. Ann Rheum Dis. 2001;60:91-7. [PMID: 11156538]

24. Cibere J. Do we need radiographs to diagnose osteoarthritis? Best Pract Res Clin Rheumatol. 2006;20:27-38. [PMID: 16483905]

25. Zhang Y, Niu J, Kelly-Hayes M, et al. Prevalence of symptomatic hand osteoarthritis and its impact on functional status among the elderly: The Framingham Study. Am J Epidemiol. 2002;156:1021-7. [PMID: 12446258]

26. Cunningham LS, Kelsey JL. Epidemiology of musculoskeletal impairments and associated disability. Am J Public Health. 1984;74:574-9. [PMID: 6232862]

27. Armstrong AL, Hunter JB, Davis TR. The prevalence of degenerative arthritis of the base of the thumb in postmenopausal women. J Hand Surg [Br]. 1994;19:340-1. [PMID: 8077824]

When symptomatic, especially at the base of thumb, hand OA is associated with functional impairment (25, 26). OA of the thumb carpometacarpal joint is a common condition that can lead to substantial pain, instability, deformity, and loss of motion (27). Approximately 5% of women and 3% of men over the age of 70 years have symptomatic OA affecting this joint with impairment of hand function (25).

The prevalence of hip OA is about 9% in Caucasian populations (14). In contrast, studies in Asian, black, and East Indian populations indicate a very low prevalence of hip OA (28). The prevalence of symptomatic hip OA is approximately 4% in those populations (2).

The joint pain of OA is typically exacerbated by activity and relieved by rest. More advanced cases of OA can cause rest and night pain. The source of pain is not particularly well understood and is best framed in a biopsychosocial framework in which biological, psychological, and social factors all play a significant role (29). Of the local events in the joint, cartilage loss itself probably does not contribute directly to pain because cartilage is not innervated. In contrast, the exposed subchondral bone, periosteum, synovium, and joint capsule are all richly innervated and can be the sources of nociceptive stimuli in OA.

What physical examination findings should clinicians look for in diagnosing OA?

The features on physical examination that suggest a diagnosis of OA are shown in Table 1. In addition to evaluation of the joint, it is important to assess muscle strength and ligament stability of the joints. Evaluation of joint involvement of the lower limb should include assessment of body weight and BMI and postural alignment during standing and walking (30).

To assess alignments, a goniometer can be used to visually bisect the thigh and lower leg along their lengths. The centers of both the patella and ankle should be located and marked with a pen. The center of the goniometer is placed on the center of the patella, and the arms of this goniometer are extended along the center of the thigh and along the axis of the lower leg to the center of the ankle.

When should clinicians order imaging studies and other diagnostic studies in patients with suspected OA?

Bearing in mind that radiographs are notoriously insensitive to the early pathologic features of OA, the absence of positive radiographic findings does not rule out symptomatic disease. Conversely, the presence of positive radiographic findings does not guarantee that an osteoarthritic joint is the active source of the patient's current knee or hip symptoms; other sources of pain, including periarticular sources, such as pes anserine bursitis at the knee and trochanteric bursitis at the hip, often contribute (8).

According to the American College of Rheumatologists (ACR) criteria for classification of OA, radiographs are less sensitive and specific than physical examination in the diagnosis of symptomatic hand OA, but more so for OA of the hip

> **Common Symptoms of Osteoarthritis**
>
> - Pain (typically described as activity-related or mechanical, may occur with rest in advanced disease; often deep, aching, and not well-localized; usually insidious in onset).
> - Stiffness of short duration, also termed "gelling," (i.e., short-lived) stiffness after inactivity.
> - Reduced movement, swelling, and crepitus in the absence of systemic features, such as fever.

and knee (31). When disease is advanced, it is visible on plain radiographs, which show narrowing of joint space, osteophytes, and sometimes changes in the subchondral bone (Figure 1).

In clinical practice, OA should be diagnosed on the basis of history and physical examination. Radiography should be used only to confirm clinical suspicion and exclude other conditions.

Magnetic resonance imaging (MRI) can be used to facilitate diagnosis of other causes of joint pain that can be confused with OA, such as osteochondritis dissecans and avascular necrosis. An unfortunate consequence of frequent use of MRI in clinical practice is the frequent detection of meniscal tears. Meniscal tears are nearly universal in persons with knee OA and are not necessarily a cause of increased symptoms (32). Removal of menisci should be avoided unless there are symptoms of locking or significantly decreased knee extension (33).

Do not rely on laboratory testing to establish the diagnosis of OA. Because OA is relatively noninflammatory, laboratory findings should be normal. Instead, use tests to detect conditions that therapy could worsen. Consider obtaining a blood count, creatinine level, and liver function tests before initiating nonsteroidal antiinflammatory drugs (NSAIDs) for OA, especially in elderly persons or those with other chronic illnesses. Laboratory testing

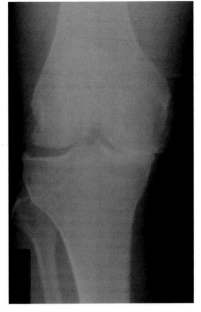

Figure 1. A weight-bearing plain radiograph of the knee depicting the characteristic features—joint space narrowing, osteophytosis, and subchondral sclerosis—of osteoarthritis.

should otherwise be reserved to exclude other types of arthritis when the diagnosis is uncertain.

What clinical factors should clinicians consider in deciding whether to perform diagnostic arthrocentesis?

Consider aspirating a joint if effusion is present and a diagnosis other than OA is suspected. Synovial fluid from osteoarthritic joints is clear, viscous, and noninflammatory; leukocyte count is less than 2000/mm^3. Always perform diagnostic aspiration to look for septic arthritis, gout, and pseudogout if the joint is red, hot, and swollen. If a diagnosis other than OA is sus-

28. Nevitt MC, Xu L, Zhang Y, et al. Very low prevalence of hip osteoarthritis among Chinese elderly in Beijing, China, compared with whites in the United States: the Beijing osteoarthritis study. Arthritis Rheum. 2002;46:1773-9. [PMID: 12124860]
29. Dieppe PA, Lohmander LS. Pathogenesis and management of pain in osteoarthritis. Lancet. 2005;365:965-73. [PMID: 15766999]
30. Kraus VB, Vail TP, Worrell T, McDaniel G. A comparative assessment of alignment angle of the knee by radiographic and physical examination methods. Arthritis Rheum. 2005;52:1730-5. [PMID: 15934069]
31. Altman RD. Classification of disease: osteoarthritis. Semin Arthritis Rheum. 1991;20:40-7. [PMID: 1866629]
32. Bhattacharyya T, Gale D, Dewire P, et al. The clinical importance of meniscal tears demonstrated by magnetic resonance imaging in osteoarthritis of the knee. J Bone Joint Surg Am. 2003;85-A:4-9. [PMID: 12533565]
33. Englund M, Lohmander LS. Risk factors for symptomatic knee osteoarthritis fifteen to twenty-two years after meniscectomy. Arthritis Rheum. 2004;50:2811-9. [PMID: 15457449]

Table 1. Physical Findings Suggestive of a Diagnosis of Osteoarthritis*

Tenderness, usually over the joint line

Crepitus with movement of the joint

Bony enlargement of the joint (e.g., Heberden and Bouchard nodes at the DIP and PIP joints, squaring of the first CMC joint), typically along the affected joint line in the knee

Restricted joint range of motion

Pain on passive range of motion

Deformity (e.g., angulation of the DIP and PIP joints, varus deformity of the knees [bowed legs])

Joint instability

CMC = carpometacarpal; DIP = distal interphalangeal; PIP = proximal interphalangeal.

34. Altman R, Asch E, Bloch D, et al. Development of criteria for the classification and reporting of osteoarthritis. Classification of osteoarthritis of the knee. Diagnostic and Therapeutic Criteria Committee of the American Rheumatism Association. Arthritis Rheum. 1986;29:1039-49. [PMID: 3741515]

35. Calmbach WL, Hutchens M. Evaluation of patients presenting with knee pain: Part II. Differential diagnosis. Am Fam Physician. 2003;68:917-22. [PMID: 13678140]

36. Tallon D, Chard J, Dieppe P. Relation between agendas of the research community and the research consumer. Lancet. 2000;355:2037-40. [PMID: 10885355]

37. Glazier RH, Dalby DM, Badley EM, et al. Management of common musculoskeletal problems: a survey of Ontario primary care physicians. CMAJ. 1998;158:1037-40. [PMID: 9580733]

38. Standing Committee for International Clinical Studies Including Therapeutic Trials ESCISIT. EULAR Recommendations 2003: an evidence based approach to the management of knee osteoarthritis: Report of a Task Force of the Standing Committee for International Clinical Studies Including Therapeutic Trials (ESCISIT). Ann Rheum Dis. 2003;62:1145-55. [PMID: 14644851]

39. EULAR Standing Committee for International Clinical Studies Including Therapeutics (ESCISIT). EULAR evidence based recommendations for the management of hip osteoarthritis: report of a task force of the EULAR Standing Committee for International Clinical Studies Including Therapeutics (ESCISIT). Ann Rheum Dis. 2005;64:669-81. [PMID: 15471891]

pected, the specimen should be sent for crystal analysis, Gram stain, and culture in addition to cell count.

What are the diagnostic criteria for OA?

When diagnosing OA of the knee, consider using the criteria from the ACR based on clinical, radiologic, and synovial fluid anaylsis data (31, 34) (Table 2). Similar criteria are available for classification of OA of the hip and hand.

What is the differential diagnosis of OA?

Other forms of arthritis may present with hand, knee, or hip pain, including rheumatoid arthritis, psoriatic arthritis, other seronegative spondyloarthropathies (e.g., ankylosing spondylitis, arthritis associated with inflammatory bowel disease, and reactive arthritis), and sarcoidosis. The prognosis and treatment for inflammatory arthropathy are quite different from those of OA. If a patient presents with features suggestive of inflammatory arthritis, such as prolonged early morning stiffness, symmetrical peripheral polyarthropathy, prominent soft tissue swelling, or extensive

axial (spine and sacroiliac joint) involvement, consider these alternate diagnoses and investigate them appropriately.

Many diseases can predispose a person to OA, including metabolic diseases like hemochromatosis, Wilson disease, and ochronosis; endocrine diseases like acromegaly and hyperparathyroidism; hypermobility due to the Ehlers-Danlos syndrome; crystal arthropathy due to gout or calcium pyrophosphate dihydrate crystal deposition disease; neuropathic joints; and chondrodysplasias. Patients may also present with knee pain due to pes anserine bursitis, iliotibial band friction syndrome (runner's knee), patella tendonitis, patellofemoral pain syndrome, prepatellar bursitis, and semimembranosus bursitis (35).

Under what circumstances should clinicians consider consultation with a rheumatologist or an orthopedist for diagnosis?

Patients should be referred to a rheumatologist for diagnostic consultation if the pattern of joint involvement is atypical, if the patient has symptoms that suggest an

---

Table 2. 1986 Criteria for Classification of Idiopathic Osteoarthritis of the Knee*

Clinical and laboratory	Clinical and radiographic	Clinical†
Knee pain + at least 5 of 9: - Age > 50 years - Stiffness <30 minutes - Crepitus - Bony tenderness - Bony enlargement - No palpable warmth - ESR <40 mm/hour - RF <1:40 - SF OA	Knee pain + at least 1 of 3: - Age > 50 years - Stiffness <30 minutes - Crepitus + Osteophytes	Knee Pain + at least 3 of 6: - Age > 50 years - Stiffness <30 minutes - Crepitus - Bony tenderness - Bony enlargement - No palpable warmth
92% sensitive 75% specific	91% sensitive 86% specific	95% sensitive 69% specific

*ESR = erythrocyte sedimentation rate (Westergren); RF = rheumatoid factor; SF OA = synovial fluid signs of OA (clear, viscous, or white blood cell count <2000/mm³).

† Alternative for the clinical category would be knee pain + 4 of 6, which is 84% sensitive and 89% specific.

R. Altman, E. Asch, D. Bloch, G. Bole, D. Borenstein, K, Brandt, et al. The American College of Rheumatology criteria for the classification and reporting of osteoarthritis of the knee. Arthritis Rheum 1986;29:1039–49.

©2006 American College of Rheumatology

inflammatory arthropathy with prolonged morning stiffness and soft tissue swelling, or if the patient has severe or atypical polyarticular OA. Patients with atypical joint involvement or inflammatory symptoms may not have OA but rather another type of arthritis, or they may have a secondary cause of OA. Similarly, if a patient presents with features less consistent with OA and more consistent with a periarticular source of pain, such as pes anserine bursitis or trochanteric bursitis, consider referral to an orthopedist or rheumatologist if advice is needed. A red, hot, and swollen joint requires immediate joint aspiration. If synovial fluid cannot be obtained promptly, seek specialist consultation right away.

Diagnosis... In clinical practice, the diagnosis of OA should be made on the basis of history and physical examination. Reserve radiography and diagnostic joint aspiration to confirm suspicion in atypical cases and to exclude other conditions as needed.

CLINICAL BOTTOM LINE

Treatment

How should clinicians manage OA?
Management of OA should be individualized to address specific findings on clinical examination, including obesity, malalignment, and muscle weakness in addition to joint pain. Comprehensive management always includes a combination of treatment options directed toward the common goal of alleviating pain and increasing tolerance for functional activity. Treatment plans should not be defined rigidly according to the radiographic appearance of the joint because structural alterations on radiographs often correlate poorly with pain and functional limitation. Treatment should instead remain flexible so that it can be altered according to functional and symptomatic responses.

Most interventions currently prescribed for knee OA involve either drugs or surgery (36), and options for conservative care of patients with knee OA are often overlooked (37). In addition, because of the known toxicity and adverse event profiles of such therapies as NSAIDs, cyclooxygenase (COX)-2 inhibitors, and total joint replacement, primary care for OA should place greater emphasis on nonpharmacologic treatments. Only when more conservative efforts fail to improve function should pharmacologic agents be offered. Surgery should be a last resort. Consult guidelines from professional organizations for OA management that are based on evidence from trials; expert consensus supports this approach (38–40).

The nonpharmacologic approach includes education, weight loss, exercise, physical therapy and braces, and orthotics and other assistive devices.

What should clinicians tell their patients about OA?
Education should be an integral part of treatment for any chronic disease and can affect disease outcome. All patients with OA should be encouraged to participate in self-management programs, such as those conducted by the Arthritis Foundation, or to consult videos, pamphlets, and newsletters that provide information about the natural history of the disease, resources

40. Recommendations for the medical management of osteoarthritis of the hip and knee: 2000 update. American College of Rheumatology Subcommittee on Osteoarthritis Guidelines. Arthritis Rheum. 2000;43:1905-15. [PMID: 11014340]
41. Superio-Cabuslay E, Ward MM, Lorig KR. Patient education interventions in osteoarthritis and rheumatoid arthritis: a meta-analytic comparison with nonsteroidal antiinflammatory drug treatment. Arthritis Care Res. 1996;9:292-301. [PMID: 8997918]
42. Marks R, Allegrante JP, Lorig K. A review and synthesis of research evidence for self-efficacy-enhancing interventions for reducing chronic disability: implications for health education practice (part I). Health Promot Pract. 2005;6:37-43. [PMID: 15574526]
43. Messier SP, Loeser RF, Miller GD, et al. Exercise and dietary weight loss in overweight and obese older adults with knee osteoarthritis: the Arthritis, Diet, and Activity Promotion Trial. Arthritis Rheum. 2004;50:1501-10. [PMID: 15146420]
44. Ettinger WH Jr, Burns R, Messier SP, Applegate W, Rejeski WJ, Morgan T, et al. A randomized trial comparing aerobic exercise and resistance exercise with a health education program in older adults with knee osteoarthritis. The Fitness Arthritis and Seniors Trial (FAST). JAMA. 1997;277:25-31. [PMID: 8980206]
45. Roddy E, Zhang W, Doherty M. Aerobic walking or strengthening exercise for osteoarthritis of the knee? A systematic review. Ann Rheum Dis. 2005;64:544-8. [PMID: 15769914]
46. Roddy E, Zhang W, Doherty M, et al. Evidence-based recommendations for the role of exercise in the management of osteoarthritis of the hip or knee—the MOVE consensus. Rheumatology (Oxford). 2005;44:67-73. [PMID: 15353613]

47. Deyle GD, Henderson NE, Matekel RL, et al. Effectiveness of manual physical therapy and exercise in osteoarthritis of the knee. A randomized, controlled trial. Ann Intern Med. 2000;132:173-81. [PMID: 10651597]

48. Standing Committee for International Clinical Studies Including Therapeutic Trials ESCISIT. EULAR Recommendations 2003: an evidence based approach to the management of knee osteoarthritis: Report of a Task Force of the Standing Committee for International Clinical Studies Including Therapeutic Trials (ESCISIT). Ann Rheum Dis. 2003;62:1145-55. [PMID: 14644851]

49. Recommendations for the medical management of osteoarthritis of the hip and knee: 2000 update. American College of Rheumatology Subcommittee on Osteoarthritis Guidelines. Arthritis Rheum. 2000;43:1905-15. [PMID: 11014340]

50. Neumann DA. Biomechanical analysis of selected principles of hip joint protection. Arthritis Care Res. 1989;2:146-55. [PMID: 2487719]

51. Lindenfeld TN, Hewett TE, Andriacchi TP. Joint loading with valgus bracing in patients with varus gonarthrosis. Clin Orthop Relat Res. 1997:290-7. [PMID: 9372780]

52. Kirkley A, Webster-Bogaert S, Litchfield R, et al. The effect of bracing on varus gonarthrosis. J Bone Joint Surg Am. 1999;81:539-48. [PMID: 10225800]

53. Pincus T, Swearingen C, Cummins P, Callahan LF. Preference for nonsteroidal anti-inflammatory drugs versus acetaminophen and concomitant use of both types of drugs in patients with osteoarthritis. J Rheumatol. 2000;27:1020-7. [PMID: 10782831]

for social support, and instructions on coping skills (41, 42).

A meta-analysis showed that various educational interventions provided additional pain relief in persons with OA who were using NSAIDs (41).

How effective is weight loss?

Overweight patients should be encouraged to lose weight through a combination of diet and exercise.

In The Arthritis, Diet, and Activity Promotion Trial, participants in an 18-month program of exercise and a calorie-restricted diet showed a 24% improvement in physical function and a 30.3% decrease in knee pain. These improvements were far superior to those seen in patients relegated to exercise only or to diet only as well as those seen in the control group. The greatest benefits were obtained after 6 months, and the diet-plus-exercise group maintained these benefits for an additional year, with no regression toward baseline values (43).

What kind of exercise should clinicians recommend for patients with OA of the knee or hip?

Exercise increases aerobic capacity, muscle strength, and endurance and facilitates weight loss (44). All persons capable of exercise should be encouraged to participate in a low-impact aerobic exercise program, such as walking, biking, or swimming (45). Quadriceps strengthening exercises also lead to improvements in pain and function. (46)

Most strengthening exercise regimens should begin with isometric exercises, then advance to isotonic resistance exercises as tolerated. Both aerobic walking and home-based quadriceps strengthening reduce pain and disability from OA.

It is important to individualize exercise therapy and provide adequate advice and education to promote increased physical activity (46). As adherence is the main predictor of long-term outcome from exercise in knee and hip OA, adopt strategies to improve adherence, such as long-term monitoring. Similarly,

encourage patients to do exercise they enjoy to promote long-term participation. Some exercises can be harmful over time to an already-injured joint, particularly those that involve high-velocity impact, such as running and step aerobics. These activities should be actively discouraged.

When should clinicians prescribe formal physical and occupational therapy?

Refer patients with knee or hip OA to a physical therapist for active and passive range of motion exercise, muscle strengthening, instruction on joint protection principles, and manual therapy when you feel they are not obtaining maximum benefit from their own exercise program.

A randomized, controlled trial (RCT) that compared manual therapy (passive, physiologic and accessory joint movements, muscle stretching, and soft tissue mobilization) and a standardized knee exercise program to subtherapeutic ultrasound found that patients receiving manual therapy improved more than controls. The average distance walked in 6 minutes at 8 weeks among patients in the treatment group was 170 m (95% CI, 71 to 270 m) more than in the placebo group and the average Western Ontario and McMaster Universities (WOMAC) scores were 599 mm higher (CI, 197 to 1002 mm). At 1 year, patients in the treatment group had clinically and statistically significant gains over baseline WOMAC scores and walking distance; 20% of patients in the placebo group and 5% of patients in the treatment group had undergone knee arthroplasty (47).

Some patients with hand OA may benefit from referral to an occupational therapist for range of motion exercises, joint protection instruction, and splinting of the first carpometacarpal joint, preferably with prefabricated neoprene (48, 49).

When should clinicians prescribe devices?

Consider a cane, used in the hand contralateral to the painful joint, in patients with persistent ambulatory pain from hip or knee OA. A cane reduces loading force on the joint and is associated with decreased pain in patients with hip and knee OA (50).

The importance of mechanical factors may explain why knee OA occurs more often in the medial compartment, presumably because of its increased loading during gait (51). Specially designed knee braces have been shown to realign the knee, thereby reducing transarticular loading on the medial compartment with marked improvements in pain in persons with medial tibiofemoral OA (52).

Therapeutic taping of the knee may also be helpful in relieving pain and disability.

In an RCT found of therapeutic taping in patients with knee OA, at 3 weeks, 73% (21 of 29) of patients in the therapeutic tape group reported improvement compared with 49% (14 of 29) of the control tape group and 10% (3 of 29) of the no tape group (52).

Which analgesic should clinicians prescribe first?

Acetaminophen in doses up to 4 g/day is the oral analgesic of choice for mild to moderate pain in OA. Table 3 presents pharmacologic treatment options for OA.

Nonsteroidal antiinflammatory drugs (NSAIDs) may be added or substituted in patients who do not respond adequately to acetaminophen. NSAIDs are considered by many physicians to be the preferred first-line agents for pharmacologic management of OA based on greater efficacy and patient preference (53, 54). However, there are disadvantages of routinely using NSAIDs in OA. For example, all NSAIDs, both nonselective and COX-2–selective, are associated with significant potential toxicity, particularly in elderly people (55). NSAIDs alone cause over 16 500 deaths and over 103 000

hospitalizations per year in the United States, predominantly related to gastrointestinal toxicity (56). Use both COX-2–selective and nonselective NSAIDs with caution in light of concern about cardiovascular risk (57). Rofecoxib and valdexocib, two COX-2-selective inhibitors, were withdrawn from the US market in 2005 for this reason.

When are topical analgesics useful?

Topical NSAIDs have been reported to be effective in relieving pain when compared with placebo for both hand and knee OA (58, 59), but they are not widely available. This route may reduce gastrointestinal adverse reactions by maximizing local delivery and minimizing systemic toxicity but is associated with more local side effects, such as rash, itching, and burning.

Topical capsaicin can be used as an alternative to systematic pharmacologic therapy or as an adjunct when response to conservative therapy has been suboptimal. Capsaicin in a concentration of 0.025% is better tolerated than 0.075%. It should be applied 3 to 4 times per day for at least 3 to 4 weeks.

In a study of patients with knee OA, 80% of capsaicin (0.025%)–treated patients had pain relief after 2 weeks compared with those randomized to placebo (60).

What are the best strategies for avoiding drug toxicity in patients who require NSAIDs, especially those with comorbid conditions?

Patients at high risk for peptic ulcer disease or gastrointestinal bleeding include those older than 65 years, those taking anticoagulants, and those with comorbid medical conditions, or a history of peptic ulcer disease or gastrointestinal bleeding.

In patients with increased gastrointestinal risk, nonselective NSAIDs plus a gastroprotective

54. Pincus T, Koch GG, Sokka T, et al. A randomized, double-blind, crossover clinical trial of diclofenac plus misoprostol versus acetaminophen in patients with osteoarthritis of the hip or knee. Arthritis Rheum. 2001;44:1587-98. [PMID: 11465710]
55. Felson DT, Lawrence RC, Hochberg MC, et al. Osteoarthritis: new insights. Part 2: treatment approaches. Ann Intern Med. 2000;133:726-37. [PMID: 11074906]
56. Wolfe MM, Lichtenstein DR, Singh G. Gastrointestinal toxicity of nonsteroidal antiinflammatory drugs. N Engl J Med. 1999;340:1888-99. [PMID: 10369853]
57. McGettigan P, Henry D. Cardiovascular risk and inhibition of cyclooxygenase: a systematic review of the observational studies of selective and nonselective inhibitors of cyclooxygenase 2. JAMA. 2006;296:1633-44. [PMID: 16968831]
58. Bookman AA, Williams KS, Shainhouse JZ. Effect of a topical diclofenac solution for relieving symptoms of primary osteoarthritis of the knee: a randomized controlled trial. CMAJ. 2004;171:333-8. [PMID: 15313991]
59. Lin J, Zhang W, Jones A, Doherty M. Efficacy of topical non-steroidal anti-inflammatory drugs in the treatment of osteoarthritis: meta-analysis of randomised controlled trials. BMJ. 2004;329:324. [PMID: 15286056]
60. Deal CL, Schnitzer TJ, Lipstein E, et al. Treatment of arthritis with topical capsaicin: a double-blind trial. Clin Ther. 1991;13:383-95. [PMID: 1954640]
61. Spiegel BM, Farid M, Dulai GS, Gralnek IM, Kanwal F. Comparing rates of dyspepsia with Coxibs vs NSAID+PPI: a meta-analysis. Am J Med. 2006;119:448.e27-36. [PMID: 16651060]

Table 3. Drug Treatment for Osteoarthritis*

Agent	Mechanism of Action	Dosage	Benefits	Side Effects	Notes
Acetaminophen	Exact mechanism is unknown but thought to block pain-impulse generation in peripheral nervous system and to inhibit CNS prostaglandin synthesis	500–1000 mg qid	Reduces pain	Hepatotoxicity if maximum daily dose exceeded or if used with ethanol	Safe for elderly patients, patients with renal disease, and patients at high risk for or who have a history of upper GI bleeding, although high doses may be associated with adverse GI effects; does not inhibit platelet function. Use with caution in patients with preexisting liver disease and those who drink ethanol regularly. Use with high-dose warfarin may increase INR.
NSAIDs: naproxen, ibuprofen, diclofenac	Inhibit COX-1 and COX-2	Naproxen, 250 mg bid; ibuprofen, 400 mg tid or qid; diclofenac, 50 mg bid or tid	Reduces pain and inflammation	Peptic ulcer disease, renal insufficiency, edema, hyperkalemia	Use lowest dose needed to control symptoms; pain relief does not appear to increase with higher doses. Use analgesic, not anti-inflammatory, doses. Higher doses may be associated with greater toxicity.
COX-2 inhibitors: celecoxib, valdecoxib	Selectively inhibit COX-2	Celecoxib, 200 mg once daily or 100 mg bid	Reduces pain and inflammation	Edema, hypertension, renal insufficiency	May increase risk for myocardial infarction and stroke in patients at high risk; celecoxib and valdecoxib are contraindicated in patients with sulfonamide allergies. Valdecoxib may cause serious skin reactions, including exfoliative dermatitis, the Stevens–Johnson syndrome, and toxic epidermal necrolysis.
Nonacetylated salicylates: choline magnesium trisalicylate; salsalate	Decrease PMN aggregation, activation, and chemotaxis	1000–1500 mg bid for both drugs	Reduces pain and inflammation	Tinnitus, CNS toxicity	No effect on platelet aggregation.
Capsaicin	Depletes substance P from neurons	Apply 0.025% cream tid or qid	Reduces pain	Local pain and redness	Effective for hand and knee OA; assess efficacy after a 4-wk trial.
Intraarticular glucocorticoids: methylprednisolone acetate; triamcinolone hexacetonide; triamcinolone acetonide; betamethasone sodium phosphate-sodium acetate	Multiple inhibitory effects on inflammatory cells and mediators	Methylprednisolone acetate, triamcinolone hexacetonide, triamcinolone acetonide: 20–40 mg; betamethasone sodium phosphate–sodium acetate: 6 mg	Reduces pain and swelling quickly but only for a short time	Postinjection flare, transient flushing	Usually reserved for patients with exacerbations of knee pain who also have effusions. Hips are not usually injected.
Intraarticular HA: hylan G-F 20; sodium hyaluronate	May restore viscoelasticity of synovial fluid, augment flow of synovial fluid, and normalize HA synthesis and/or inhibit hyaluronan degradation	Intraarticular injection for 3 or 5 consecutive wk	Reduces pain and improves function	Injection site reaction	Expensive; improvement may not occur for several weeks; no data indicate which patients might best respond.

Table 3. Drug Treatment for Osteoarthritis (Continued)

Agent	Mechanism of Action	Dosage	Benefits	Side Effects	Notes
Tramadol, tramadol–acetaminophen	μ-opioid receptor agonist, weakly blocks reuptake of serotonin and norepinephrine	Tramadol, 50 mg every 6 h; tramado–acetaminophen, (37.5 mg/325 mg), 2 every 6 h	Reduces pain	Nausea, drowsiness, may potentiate or cause seizures especially with concomitant use of tricyclic anti-depressants, SSRIs, and narcotic analgesics	More expensive than narcotic analgesics and may have abuse potential. Nausea can be reduced if the dose is escalated slowly.
Narcotic analgesics: codeine–acetaminophen; hydrocodone–acetaminophen; SR morphine; oxycodone–acetaminophen; SR oxycodone	Opioid receptor agonists	Starting dosages: codeine/acetaminophen (30 mg/300 mg), 1–2 every 4–6 h; hydrocodone–acetaminophen (5 mg/500 mg), 1–2 every 6 h; oxycodone–acetaminophen (5 mg/325 mg) 1-2 every 4–6 h; SR oxycodone, 10 mg q 12 h	Reduces pain	Nausea, sedation, dizziness, constipation, pruritus, respiratory depression, tolerance	SR oxycodone has significant abuse potential and is more expensive than SR morphine or short-acting narcotics. Dose should be titrated upward until pain is controlled. Maximum dose is largely determined by the amount of acetaminophen in these agents. The dose should be increased with extreme caution in elderly patients because their susceptibility to side effects is greater.

*bid = twice daily; CNS = central nervous system; COX = cyclooxygenase; GI = gastrointestinal; HA = hyaluronan; INR = international normalized ratio; NSAID = nonsteroidal anti-inflammatory drug; OA = osteoarthritis; PMN = polymorphonuclear neutrophil; qid = 4 times daily; SR = sustained release; SSRI = selective serotonin reuptake inhibitor; tid = three times daily.

agent, or a selective COX-2 inhibitor, should be used. COX-2 inhibitors appear to have a similar gastrointestinal safety profile to an NSAID plus a proton pump inhibitor (PPI) (61).

A meta-analysis of 26 studies comparing dyspepsia between COX-2 inhibitors and NSAIDs revealed a 12% relative risk reduction for COX-2 inhibitors with an absolute risk reduction of 3.7%. A comparison of patients with dyspepsia receiving an NSAID plus a PPI compared with patients receiving an NSAID alone revealed a 66% relative risk reduction for the NSAID–PPI combination and an absolute risk reduction of 9%. Compared with the NSAID strategy, the number needed to treat to prevent dyspepsia was 27 for COX-2 inhibitors and 11 for the NSAID–PPI combination (61).

Concomitant use of low-dose aspirin may partially abrogate the protective gastrointestinal effect of the COX-2 inhibitors (62); thus, if patients require treatment with low-dose aspirin, it may be more cost-effective to use a non-selective NSAID with a PPI.

Caution should be exercised when using COX-2 inhibitors and certain NSAIDs in patients with cardiac risk factors. Evidence suggests that patients with cardio-vascular disease who must take NSAIDs should be offered anti-platelet agents when there are no contraindications.

In a study of NSAID use among 181 441 Tennessee Medicaid recipients with heart disease age 50 to 84 years NSAIDs for a mean 1.5 years was not associated with an increased or a reduced risk for serious coronary heart disease or stroke when compared with controls (63).

Another study, however, suggested that ibuprofen given before aspirin may limit the cardioprotective effect of aspirin as assessed

62. Silverstein FE, Faich G, Goldstein JL, et al. Gastrointestinal toxicity with celecoxib vs nonsteroidal anti-inflammatory drugs for osteoarthritis and rheumatoid arthritis: the CLASS study: A randomized controlled trial. Celecoxib Long-term Arthritis Safety Study. JAMA. 2000;284:1247-55. [PMID: 10979111]
63. Ray WA, Stein CM, Hall K, Daugherty JR, Griffin MR. Nonsteroidal anti-inflammatory drugs and risk of serious coronary heart disease: an observational cohort study. Lancet. 2002;359:118-23. [PMID: 11809254]
64. Catella-Lawson F, Reilly MP, Kapoor SC, et al. Cyclooxygenase inhibitors and the antiplatelet effects of aspirin. N Engl J Med. 2001;345:1809-17. [PMID: 11752357]

65. Bellamy N, Campbell J, Robinson V, Gee T, Bourne R, Wells G. Intraarticular corticosteroid for treatment of osteoarthritis of the knee. Cochrane Database Syst Rev. 2005:CD005328. [PMID: 15846755]

66. Lo GH, LaValley M, McAlindon T, Felson DT. Intra-articular hyaluronic acid in treatment of knee osteoarthritis: a meta-analysis. JAMA. 2003;290:3115-21. [PMID: 14679274]

67. Morelli V, Naquin C, Weaver V. Alternative therapies for traditional disease states: osteoarthritis. Am Fam Physician. 2003;67:339-44. [PMID: 12562155]

68. Towheed TE, Maxwell L, Anastassiades TP, et al. Glucosamine therapy for treating osteoarthritis. Cochrane Database Syst Rev. 2005:CD002946. [PMID: 15846645]

69. McAlindon TE, LaValley MP, Gulin JP, Felson DT. Glucosamine and chondroitin for treatment of osteoarthritis: a systematic quality assessment and meta-analysis. JAMA. 2000;283:1469-75. [PMID: 10732937]

70. Reichenbach S, Sterchi R, Scherer M, et al. Meta-analysis: chondroitin for osteoarthritis of the knee or hip. Ann Intern Med. 2007;146:580-90. [PMID: 17438317]

71. Clegg DO, Reda DJ, Harris CL, et al. Glucosamine, chondroitin sulfate, and the two in combination for painful knee osteoarthritis. N Engl J Med. 2006;354:795-808. [PMID: 16495392]

72. Vas J, Méndez C, Perea-Milla E, Vega E, et al. Acupuncture as a complementary therapy to the pharmacological treatment of osteoarthritis of the knee: randomised controlled trial. BMJ. 2004;329:1216. [PMID: 15494348]

73. Berman BM, Lao L, Langenberg P, Lee WL, Gilpin AM, Hochberg MC. Effectiveness of acupuncture as adjunctive therapy in osteoarthritis of the knee: a randomized, controlled trial. Ann Intern Med. 2004;141:901-10. [PMID: 15611487]

by impact on serum thromboxane B_2 formation and platelet aggregation (64).

Nonacetylated salicylates such as salsalate and choline magnesium trisalicylate inhibit prostaglandin synthesis less than other NSAIDs and can be considered in patients with mild renal insufficiency. They do not inhibit platelet aggregation and may be used if the risk of gastrointestinal bleeding is considered to be increased. Tramodol or opiates are options for patients in whom NSAIDs are contraindicated.

When are intraarticular glucocorticoids or hyaluronan indicated?

In patients who present with acute exacerbations of pain and signs of local inflammation with joint effusion but no evidence of infection or inflammatory arthritis on synovial fluid analysis, intraarticular corticosteroids are of short-term (about 1 week) benefit in improving pain and function (65). Do not use intraarticular steroids more often than once every 4 months because repeated use can cause cartilage and joint damage, resulting in disease progression.

Hyaluronan (hyaluronic acid) is a high-molecular-weight polysaccharide found in the extracellular matrix of connective tissue. Pain relief from hyaluronan injection is equivalent to that from athrocentisis.

While meta-analyses of the efficacy of hyaluronan are not in complete agreement largely because of varied study selection methods, most suggest that the effects are moderate. The pooled effect size for hyaluronic acid is 0.32 (CI, 0.17 to 0.47), despite significant evidence of heterogeneity, publication bias, and a significant placebo response (66).

Note that 2 preparations of intraarticular hyaluronan are available in the United States: sodium hyaluronate (5 weekly injections) and hylan G-F 20 (3 weekly injections). There are no data supporting the use of one preparation over another. These compounds are only approved for use in the knee.

What is the role of glucosamine-chondroitin, acupuncture, and other complementary–alternative therapies?

Glucosamine compounds in particular have attracted a great deal of attention, mostly in the lay press. Possibly as a function of this publicity, OA is the leading medical condition for which persons use alternative therapies (67) and the use of glucosamine is particularly widespread. However, two meta-analyses on glucosamine (69,70) and a recent one on chondroitin point out the defects of available studies. They suggest that these agents seem to have a symptom-modifying effect similar to placebo (68-70), but their structure-modifying benefits at this point are not clear.

The Glucosamine/Chondroitin Arthritis Intervention Trial assessed the efficacy of glucosamine and chondroitin sulfate alone or in combination and found that they were equal to placebo in persons with OA of the knee. Compared with the rate of response to placebo (60.1%), the rate of response to glucosamine was 3.9% higher (P = 0.30), the rate of response to chondroitin sulfate was 5.3% higher (P = 0.17), and the rate of response to combined treatment was 6.5% higher (P = 0.09). The rate of response in the celecoxib control group was 10.0% higher than that in the placebo control group (P = 0.008) (71).

There is growing evidence that acupuncture used as complementary therapy for treatment of OA of the knee shows benefit in relieving pain. Acupuncture plus diclofenac is more effective than placebo acupuncture plus diclofenac for symptomatic treatment for OA of the knee (72). Acupuncture seems to improve function and relieve pain as an adjunctive therapy (73), although it may be a placebo effect (74).

When should clinicians consider joint lavage, debridement, or joint replacement?

Surgery should be reserved for patients in whom symptoms can no longer be managed with other treatments. Typical indications for surgery are debilitating pain and major limitations in such functions as walking, working, or sleeping.

The role of arthroscopic debridement of the knee is controversial. In a well-designed placebo surgery trial, improvement in symptoms could be attributed to a placebo effect (75). However, for a subgroup of knees with loose bodies, flaps of meniscus, or cartilage causing mechanical symptoms (especially locking or catching of the joint), arthroscopic removal of these unstable tissues may improve joint function and alleviate mechanical symptoms.

Osteotomy, in which a wedge of bone is removed from the tibia to improve leg alignment, may delay the need for total joint replacement for 5 to 10 years, although there are no data to suggest that osteotomy is more effective than conservative treatment or other surgical options (76). The relative merits of osteotomy versus unicompartmental knee replacement are currently being debated (77), and the subject warrants further investigation.

A recent systematic review of osteotomy suggested that this intervention improves pain and function in patients with malaligned knees. (78).

Currently, the most common indication for knee and hip replacement (approximately 85% of all cases) is OA. The consensus among orthopedic surgeons on indications for surgery, carried out by a postal survey, was severe daily pain and radiographic evidence of joint space narrowing (79); however, there are no evidence-based guidelines to support this. With proper patient selection, good to excellent results can be expected in 95% of patients, and the survival rate of a knee implant is expected to be 95% at 15 years (80). Joint replacement is an irreversible intervention and should be reserved for persons in whom other treatments have failed. However, once other options have been exhausted, joint replacement should not be delayed. If joint replacement is postponed and the patient's functional status continues to decline, surgery may not be able to restore function to the level when conservative treatment was first undertaken (81).

Under what circumstances should clinicians consider consultation with a rheumatologist or orthopedist for management?

Consider referring patients to a rheumatologist if they:

- Display atypical features and may have a different or concurrent rheumatologic disease
- Have not responded to standard therapy and may need a different combination of methods
- May require otherwise difficult-to-perform arthrocentesis
- May require an overall evaluation to address nondrug therapy needs

Consider referring patients to an orthopedic surgeon for joint replacement or other surgical procedures if medical therapy fails.

74. Scharf HP, Mansmann U, Streitberger K, et al. Acupuncture and knee osteoarthritis: a three-armed randomized trial. Ann Intern Med. 2006;145:12-20. [PMID: 16818924]
75. Moseley JB, O'Malley K, Petersen NJ, et al. A controlled trial of arthroscopic surgery for osteoarthritis of the knee. N Engl J Med. 2002;347:81-8. [PMID: 12110735]
76. Naudie D, Bourne RB, Rorabeck CH, Bourne TJ. The Install Award. Survivorship of the high tibial valgus osteotomy. A 10- to -22-year followup study. Clin Orthop Relat Res. 1999:18-27. [PMID: 10546594]
77. Stukenborg-Colsman C, Wirth CJ, Lazovic D, Wefer A. High tibial osteotomy versus unicompartmental joint replacement in unicompartmental knee joint osteoarthritis: 7-10-year follow-up prospective randomised study. Knee. 2001;8:187-94. [PMID: 11706726]
78. Brouwer RW, Jakma TS, Bierma-Zeinstra SM, Verhagen AP, Verhaar J. Osteotomy for treating knee osteoarthritis. Cochrane Database Syst Rev. 2005:CD004019. [PMID: 15674926]
79. Mancuso CA, Ranawat CS, Esdaile JM, Johanson NA, Charlson ME. Indications for total hip and total knee arthroplasties. Results of orthopaedic surveys. J Arthroplasty. 1996;11:34-46. [PMID: 8676117]
80. Callahan CM, Drake BG, Heck DA, Dittus RS. Patient outcomes following tricompartmental total knee replacement. A meta-analysis. JAMA. 1994;271:1349-57. [PMID: 8158821]
81. Fortin PR, Clarke AE, Joseph L, et al. Outcomes of total hip and knee replacement: preoperative functional status predicts outcomes at six months after surgery. Arthritis Rheum. 1999;42:1722-8. [PMID: 10446873]

Treatment... Comprehensive management includes a combination of options directed toward the common goal of alleviating pain and improving tolerance for functional activity. Primary care for OA should emphasize nonpharmacologic treatments, including weight loss, exercise, and physical therapy. Only when more conservative efforts fail to improve function should pharmaceuticals be offered. Acetaminophen remains the first-line therapy for mild pain. NSAIDs should be used with caution with due attention to their side effects. Surgery should be reserved for patients with advanced disease and intractable symptoms unresponsive to other measures.

CLINICAL BOTTOM LINE

Practice Improvement

What do professional organizations recommend regarding the care of patients with OA?

The European League Against Rheumatism (EULAR) recommendations for management of knee OA, published in 2003, were developed using an evidence-based and consensus approach. These recommendations cover many treatment options for management of hip and knee OA (39).

The OA Research Society International (OARSI) Treatment Guidelines Committee has developed updated evidence-based, consensus recommendations for the management of hip and knee OA. This committee has undertaken a critical appraisal of published guidelines, and a systematic review of more recent evidence on the effectiveness of relevant therapies has been completed. Publication is planned for late 2007.

The MOVE Consensus developed and published evidence-based recommendations on the role of exercise in the management of hip and knee OA in 2005 (40). The Consensus differentiated research-based evidence from expert opinion to guide health care practitioners caring for patients with OA. Ten propositions related to aerobic and strengthening exercise, group versus home exercise, adherence, contraindications, and predictors of response were adopted.

Are there performance measures related to the care of patients with OA?

The Centers for Medicare and Medicaid Services (CMS) initiated a Medicare pay-for-performance program, the Physicians' Quality Reporting Initiative (PQRI) in July 2007, which enables physicians to report on quality measures applicable to their practice through the claims process. To date, although many of the measures are relevant to internal medicine, none relate to OA. Expansion of the list of quality measures is expected, and given the high prevalence of OA, it is likely to include OA-related care measures in the future.

---

in the clinic
Tool Kit

Osteoarthritis

http://pier.acponline.org

Osteoarthritis module in PIER, an electronic decision support resource designed for rapid access to information at the point of care.

www.hopkins-arthritis.org/mngmnt/mngmnt.html

The role of exercise in arthritis. Complete resource on management of arthritis including weight control, nutrition, exercise, pain management, complementary and alternative therapies and rehabilitation.

www.arthritis.org/conditions/exercise/default.asp

Exercises including video on range-of-motion exercises.

www.nutrition.tufts.edu/research/growingstronger

Strength training for older adults developed by Tufts University and the Centers for Disease Control and Prevention.

www.sportsmed.org/sml/exercises.asp

Twenty specific low-impact exercises with video demonstration designed for the American Orthopaedic Society for Sports Medicine.

THINGS PEOPLE SHOULD KNOW ABOUT OSTEOARTHRITIS

Osteoarthritis causes pain, swelling, and difficulty moving, especially in the knees, hips, and hands. Exercise and keeping your weight down are as important as medication in treating osteoarthritis.

Web Sites with Good Information about Osteoarthritis

The Arthritis Foundation
www.arthritis.org

National Institute of Arthritis and Musculoskeletal and Skin Diseases
www.niams.nih.gov

Arthritis Research Campaign (UK)
ww.arc.org.uk/arthinfo/patpubs/6254/6254.asp

American College of Rheumatology
www.rheumatology.org

Arthritis Research Campaign
www.arc.org.uk/arthinfo/patpubs/6254/6254.asp

HEALTH TiPS*

Osteoarthritis makes your joints hurt and swell. It can make it hard to move around and do the things you want to do.

What You Can Do:

Keep as active as you can.

If you are too heavy, try to lose weight. Ask your doctor for help.

Do the exercises you and your doctor agree are right for you. Go to physical therapy if you need to.

Use canes, braces, and other aids to make it easier to get around.

Call your doctor if you have fever; red, hot, or swollen joints; more pain than usual; falls.

Things to Ask your Doctor:

• Which medicines are best to treat my pain?

• Are there side effects? If so, what are they?

• What do I do if my medicines stop working?

• Will shots into my joints help?

• Will I need surgery on my joints?

*HEALTH TiPS are developed by the American College of Physicians Foundation and PIER

Patient Information

Dyslipidemia

Dyslipidemia affects 1 of every 2 American adults and is a major risk factor for cardiovascular disease (CVD), cardiovascular death, and all-cause mortality. Large observational studies have found a strong, graded relationship between increasing levels of low-density lipoprotein (LDL) cholesterol or decreasing levels of high-density lipoprotein (HDL) cholesterol and increasing risk for coronary artery disease (CAD) events (1, 2). Long-term prospective epidemiologic studies have consistently shown that persons with healthier lifestyles and fewer coronary risk factors, particularly those with normal lipid profiles, have an overall lower incidence of CVD. Prevention and sensible management of dyslipidemia can markedly alter cardiovascular morbidity and mortality.

Prevention and Screening

1. Anderson KM, Castelli WP, Levy D. Cholesterol and mortality. 30 years of follow-up from the Framingham study. JAMA. 1987;257:2176-80. [PMID: 3560398]
2. Goldbourt U, Yaari S. Cholesterol and coronary heart disease mortality. A 23-year follow-up study of 9902 men in Israel. Arteriosclerosis. 1990;10:512-9. [PMID: 2369362]
3. Grundy SM, Balady GJ, Criqui MH, et al. Guide to primary prevention of cardiovascular diseases. A statement for healthcare professionals from the Task Force on Risk Reduction. American Heart Association Science Advisory and Coordinating Committee. Circulation. 1997;95:2329-31. [PMID: 9142014]
4. National Cholesterol Education Program. Detection, Evaluation, and Treatment of High Blood Cholesterol in Adults. National Institutes of Health: Bethesda, MD 2002. NIH No. 02-5215 accessed at www.nhlbi.nih.gov/guidelines/cholesterol/atp3full.pdf on 11 July 2007.
5. Screening for Lipid Disorders in Adults. U.S. Preventive Services Task Force: Rockville, MD; 2001. Accessed at www.ahrq.gov/clinic/uspstf/uspschol.htm on 11 July 2007.

What preventive lifestyle measures should clinicians recommend to reduce risk for dyslipidemia?

Lifestyle changes can favorably affect total cholesterol, HDL cholesterol, LDL cholesterol, and triglyceride levels. Clinicians should routinely encourage all patients to adopt the following habits (3, 4):

- Attain and maintain normal body weight.
- Follow a diet containing less than 25%–35% of calories from fat, less than 7% of calories from saturated fat, and fewer than 200 mg of cholesterol per day.
- Emphasize a plant-based diet (vegetables, fruits, and high-fiber foods), with the goal of consuming at least 2 grams per day of plant sterols and 10–25 grams per day of viscous (soluble) fiber.
- Exercise aerobically for at least 30 minutes on most and preferably all days of the week.
- Avoid all forms of tobacco.
- Consume no more than 1–2 alcoholic beverages per day.

Regardless of the presence of preexisting CVD, patients who adopt these habits will have healthier lipid profiles, placing them in lower risk strata for cardiovascular events. Because of their higher baseline risk, patients with preexisting disease may see the most marked alteration in risk for poor health outcomes. Ultimately, increasing healthy lifestyles should reduce population-wide lipid levels and reduce the need for drug therapy.

Who should be screened for dyslipidemia?

No direct evidence links lipid screening and subsequent treatment with reduced adverse outcomes from CVD or stroke. However, moderate-quality indirect evidence supports routine dyslipidemia screening for men older than 35 years of age and women older than 45 (5). Clinicians should also screen younger adults (men aged 20–35 years or women aged 20-45 years) who have other risk factors for CVD, whose family history suggests a heritable familial lipid disorder, or who have evidence of hyperlipidemia on physical examination. Of note, the National Cholesterol Education Program Adult Treatment Panel III (NCEP–ATP III) recommends beginning screening of all adults at age 20, regardless of cardiovascular risk profile (4). The rationale is that screening promotes healthy behaviors and increases public awareness of cholesterol, in addition to identifying very high-risk patients (6, 7). However, the incremental yield and cost-effectiveness of earlier universal screening as opposed to risk factor–based screening in young adults is unclear.

Moderate-quality evidence supports screening adults older than 65 years. Total cholesterol predicts CVD in the elderly, and persons older than 65 have a higher baseline risk for CVD, increasing their potential absolute benefit from interventions to manage dyslipidemia (8). Regardless of age, all patients with known CVD should have lipid levels measured.

How and how often should clinicians screen for dyslipidemia?

It is acceptable to screen for dyslipidemia with nonfasting serum total cholesterol and HDL cholesterol levels since these measures can identify persons at increased risk for CVD as well as other lipid measures.

A study that compared fasting and nonfasting total cholesterol values in 181 general internal medicine outpatients found no clinically important difference in fasting and nonfasting results for total and HDL cholesterol levels (9).

The NCEP–ATP III advocates initial screening with a fasting lipid profile that includes measurement of triglycerides and indirect calculation of LDL cholesterol level (4). The U.S. Preventive Services Task Force does not recommend the inclusion of triglyceride measurement as part of lipid profile evaluation (5). LDL cholesterol and triglyceride measurements are useful for guiding treatment, but do not improve risk prediction better than measurement of total and HDL cholesterol only.

When screening for dyslipidemia, clinicians should confirm abnormalities with 2 measurements at least a week apart before initiating therapy (10). The average of the 2 measures should be considered the baseline when lipid control interventions are instituted. Clinicians should measure LDL cholesterol in patients with unfavorable total and HDL cholesterol levels to guide management decisions after screening. Measurement of LDL cholesterol requires a fasting sample. Direct measurement of LDL does not require fasting, but it is not offered in all laboratories, may be expensive, and does not improve risk prediction. However, it is necessary when triglyceride levels are > 400 mg/dL.

In the absence of data to support a specific screening interval, screening every 5 years seems reasonable in low-risk patients since lipid levels do not vary greatly from year to year. Clinicians might consider more frequent screening for patients who have lipid values near treatment thresholds or who develop new cardiovascular risk factors.

Prevention and Screening... Healthy diet, regular exercise, and avoidance of tobacco can help patients avoid dyslipidemia. Evidence best supports routine screening for dyslipidemia in men aged > 35 years and women > 45 years. However, the NCEP–ATP III advocates that screening for dyslipidemia begin at age 20 as a way to increase awareness of dyslipidemia and promote healthy behaviors. Screening at earlier ages is warranted for patients with cardiovascular risk factors or a clinical history suggestive of familial hyperlipidemia. Nonfasting total and HDL cholesterol levels are sufficient for initial screening, but abnormal values should be confirmed with a second test and LDL levels are warranted for guiding treatment decisions. Some authors also advocate routine measurement of triglycerides. In the absence of good data to guide screening frequency, screening every 5 years seems reasonable unless patients are near a threshold for therapy or develop new risk factors.

CLINICAL BOTTOM LINE

6. Cleeman JI, Grundy SM. National Cholesterol Education Program recommendations for cholesterol testing in young adults. A science-based approach. Circulation. 1997;95:1646-50. [PMID: 9118536]
7. LaRosa JC, He J, Vupputuri S. Effect of statins on risk of coronary disease: a meta-analysis of randomized controlled trials. JAMA. 1999;282:2340-6. [PMID: 10612322]
8. Murray DM, Kurth C, Mullis R, et al. Cholesterol reduction through low-intensity interventions: results from the Minnesota Heart Health Program. Prev Med. 1990;19:181-9. [PMID: 259741]
9. Craig SR, Amin RV, Russell DW, Paradise NF. Blood cholesterol screening influence of fasting state on cholesterol results and management decisions. J Gen Intern Med. 2000;15:395-9. [PMID: 10886474]
10. Cooper GR, Myers GL, Smith SJ, et al. Blood lipid measurements. Variations and practical utility. JAMA. 1992;267:1652-60. [PMID: 1542176]

Diagnosis

How should clinicians interpret results of lipid screening in relation to evaluating overall cardiovascular risk?

When diagnosing dyslipidemia, clinicians should estimate a patient's cardiovascular risk. Calculation of risk using specific risk equations appears more accurate than using lipid levels alone or simply counting risk factors.

Data from the Lipid Research Clinic Prevalence and Follow-up Studies, which included 3678 men and women aged 35 to 74 years, suggest that a Framingham-based coronary risk model (area under the receiver-operating characteristic curve, 0.85) was superior to all other screening maneuvers, including lipid measures alone and algorithms based on expert guidelines (11).

Electronic tools for calculating risk are publicly available (12). Patients and clinicians can also calculate risk using Figure 1. The Framingham risk equation allows the clinician to classify patients by their respective level of risk, including the following: CAD or CAD risk equivalent (including > 20% 10-year risk for a cardiovascular event), moderate risk (10% to 20% risk), or low risk (< 10%). These assessments of risk should guide treatment strategies and goals.

What laboratory tests should clinicians obtain before starting therapy for dyslipidemia?

Epidemiologic studies have associated high levels of LDL cholesterol with particularly high absolute risk for CAD in the presence of 2 or more CAD risk factors (13). Prospective studies consistently show > 20% 10-year risk for myocardial infarction or CAD death in patients in this risk subgroup. Therefore, the clinician must first focus on identifying elevated LDL cholesterol.

In addition to obtaining 2 measures of LDL cholesterol to confirm diagnosis, it is important for clinicians to set thresholds before initiating potential lifelong therapy and to identify causes of LDL > 130 mg/dL so that they can target diet and drug therapy to the lipid transport abnormality that is elevating the LDL cholesterol (Table 1). Randomized clinical trials of various lipid-lowering drugs have found that efficacy in lowering LDL cholesterol is related to the abnormality in lipid metabolism (14).

How should clinicians measure and interpret HDL cholesterol and triglyceride levels?

HDL Cholesterol

Clinicians should pay close attention to HDL cholesterol and potential causes of levels <40 mg/dL (Table 2), which include elevated triglycerides, obesity, physical inactivity, type 2 diabetes, tobacco, very high carbohydrate intake (> 60% of calories), and certain drugs (β-blockers, anabolic steroids, progestational agents). Identification of the specific disorder of low HDL cholesterol allows institution of therapies to raise HDL cholesterol.

Triglycerides

Triglyceride levels are another secondary target for therapy. Many prospective epidemiologic studies have shown increased triglycerides to be related to increased risk for CAD (15). Meta-analyses of prospective studies indicate that elevated triglycerides are an independent risk factor for CAD (16). In men, adjustment for other risk factors (e.g., diabetes, HDL cholesterol, obesity) often removes the association. Despite evidence suggesting a stronger association of elevated triglyceride levels with CAD in women than in men (17), there are no trials examining the benefit of triglyceride lowering in

11. Grover SA, Coupal L, Hu XP. Identifying adults at increased risk of coronary disease. How well do the current cholesterol guidelines work? JAMA. 1995;274:801-6. [PMID: 7650803]

12. National Cholesterol Education Program. Risk Assessment Tool for Estimating 10-year Risk of Developing Hard CHD (Myocardial Infarction and Coronary Death). National Institutes of Health: Bethesda, MD; 2002 Accessed at http://hp2010.nhlbi-hin.net/atpiii/calculator.asp?usertype=prof on 11 July 2007.

13. Brand FN, Larson M, Friedman LM, et al. Epidemiologic assessment of angina before and after myocardial infarction: The Framingham study. Am Heart J. 1996;132:174-8. [PMID: 8701860]

Step 1: Determine the patient's Framingham point scores

Risk Factor Age	Points Men (Women)
20-34	-9 (-7)
35-39	-4 (-3)
40-44	0 (0)
45-49	3 (3)
50-54	6 (6)
55-59	8 (8)
60-64	10 (10)
65-69	11 (12)
70-74	12 (14)
75-79	13 (16)

HDL Cholesterol	Men and Women
≥60	-1
50-59	0
40-49	1
<40	2

Systolic BP (mm Hg)	Untreated Men (Women)	Treated Men (Women)
<120	0 (0)	0 (0)
120-129	0 (1)	1 (3)
130-139	1 (2)	2 (4)
140-159	1 (3)	2 (5)
≥160	2 (4)	3 (6)

Total Cholesterol	Age 20-39 Men (Women)	Age 40-49 Men (Women)	Age 50-59 Men (Women)	Age 60-69 Men (Women)	Age 70-79 Men (Women)
<160	0 (0)	0 (0)	0 (0)	0 (0)	0 (0)
160-199	4 (4)	3 (3)	2 (2)	1 (1)	0 (1)
200-239	7 (8)	5 (6)	3 (4)	1 (2)	0 (1)
240-279	9 (11)	6 (8)	4 (5)	2 (3)	1 (2)
≥280	11 (13)	8 (10)	5 (7)	3 (4)	1 (2)

Tobacco	Age 20-39 Men (Women)	Age 40-49 Men (Women)	Age 50-59 Men (Women)	Age 60-69 Men (Women)	Age 70-79 Men (Women)
Nonsmoker	0 (0)	0 (0)	0 (0)	0 (0)	0 (0)
Smoker	8 (9)	5 (7)	3 (4)	1 (2)	1 (1)

Step 2: Add points from above to estimate patient's 10-year risk of a cardiovascular event

Men		Women	
Total Points	10-Year Risk (%)	Total Points	10-Year Risk (%)
<0	<1	<9	<1
0	1	9	1
1	1	10	1
2	1	11	1
3	1	12	1
4	1	13	2
5	2	14	2
6	2	15	3
7	3	16	4
8	4	17	5
9	5	18	6
10	6	19	8
11	8	20	11
12	10	21	14
13	12	22	17
14	16	23	22
15	20	24	27
16	25	≥25	≥30
≥17	≥30		

Figure 1. Tool to estimate 10-year risk of cardiovascular event using Framingham point scores

women. The clinician should stratify patients, based on fasting triglyceride levels as follows: normal, <150 mg/dL; borderline high, 150 to 199 mg/dL; high, 200 to 499 mg/dL; and very high, > 500 mg/dL. Borderline high triglyceride levels suggest specific familial abnormalities of triglyceride-rich lipoprotein metabolism in which the liver overproduced triglyceride-rich lipoproteins. Persons with elevated triglyceride

14. Grundy SM. Statin trials and goals of cholesterol-lowering therapy [Editorial]. Circulation. 1998;97:1436-9. [PMID: 9576422]

15. Miller M. Is hypertriglyceridaemia an independent risk factor for coronary heart disease? The epidemiological evidence. Eur Heart J. 1998;19 Suppl H:H18-22. [PMID: 9717060]

16. Sarwar N, Danesh J, Eiriksdottir G, et al. Triglycerides and the risk of coronary heart disease: 10,158 incident cases among 262,525 participants in 29 Western prospective studies. Circulation. 2007;115:450-8. [PMID: 17190864]

17. Austin MA, Hokanson JE, Edwards KL. Hypertriglyceridemia as a cardiovascular risk factor. Am J Cardiol. 1998;81:7B-12B. [PMID: 9526807]

Table 1. Differential Diagnosis of Elevated LDL Cholesterol*

Disease	Characteristics	Notes
Heterozygous familial hypercholesterolemia (Frederickson-Levy type IIa)	• LDL cholesterol >220 mg/dL • Xanthomas, elevated total or LDL cholesterol in childhood confirm diagnosis • Autosomal-dominant inheritance with 1/500 prevalence in United States • First-degree relative with early-onset CAD and/or familial hypercholesterolemia	• Identifies persons with deficiency of LDL receptors best treated with HMG-CoA reductase inhibitors and/or bile acid–binding resins
Familial combined hyperlipidemia (Frederickson-Levy type IIb)	• Elevated LDL cholesterol and/or elevated triglycerides • Elevated apolipoprotein B levels • First-degree relative with early-onset CAD and/or lipid disorder • Autosomal-dominant inheritance with incomplete penetrance; gene prevalence as high as 25% in United States • Associated with the metabolic syndrome	• Identifies persons with hepatic overproduction of B-containing lipoproteins who may benefit from niacin therapy
Dysbetalipoproteinemia (Fredrickson-Levy type III)	• Elevated LDL cholesterol and triglycerides • Family history of early-onset CAD and/or hyperlipidemia • Low prevalence of xanthomas • Associated with apolipoprotein E_2 homozygosity • Prevalence of 1/1750 in patients with CAD • Associated with atherosclerotic disease, especially peripheral vascular disease	• Broad beta band on lipoprotein electrophoresis, but best confirmed by apolipoprotein E_2–E_2 genotype • Responsive to fibric acids, HMG-CoA reductase inhibitors
Polygenic hypercholesterolemia	• Elevated LDL cholesterol • Variable family history of early-onset CAD and/or hyperlipidemia • Unclear inheritance pattern	• Most common pattern in hypercholesterolemia
Secondary hypercholesterolemia	• Elevated LDL cholesterol with or without high triglycerides • Associated with signs and symptoms of the underlying condition	• Diet and drug therapies often ineffective • Correction of underlying secondary cause may normalize lipid profile

* CAD = coronary artery disease; HDL = high-density lipoprotein; LDL = low-density lipoprotein.

Coronary Artery Disease Equivalents
• Diabetes mellitus
• Aortic aneurysm
• Peripheral vascular disease (claudication, ankle–brachial index < 0.9)
• Symptomatic carotid artery disease (transient ischemic attack, stroke)
• 10-year risk for coronary artery disease > 20% using Framingham risk equation

---

levels are more likely to have the metabolic syndrome. High triglyceride levels may also be due to reduced clearance of triglyceride-rich lipoprotein or may identify persons with other metabolic problems in need of intervention (e.g., diabetes, alcoholism, chronic renal failure, and the nephrotic syndrome). Triglyceride levels > 500 mg/dL are associated with pancreatitis and warrant treatment.

What should clinicians look for in the history and physical examination of a patient with dyslipidemia?

History and physical examination should focus on identifying coronary risk factors and detection of secondary causes of dyslipidemia. Physical examination should include measurement of body mass index and blood pressure; peripheral vascular examination with measurement of ankle–brachial index and evaluation for bruits to assess cardiovascular risk; and evaluation of the liver and thyroid to identify evidence of secondary causes of dyslipidemia, skin for xanthomas, and eyes for xanthelasmas and hypertensive changes.

What are the causes of secondary dyslipidemia and how should clinicians diagnose them?

Secondary causes of dyslipidemia include hypothyroidism, obstructive

Table 2. Differential Diagnosis of Low HDL Cholesterol* (< 40 mg/dL)

Disease	Characteristics
Familial hypoalphalipoproteinemia	• HDL cholesterol levels may be very low (<10 mg/dL) • Many rare genetic defects have been identified (Tangier disease, Fisheye disease, apolipoprotein A_1 Milano) • Not all cases are high risk, but family history of early-onset atherosclerosis is associated with deleterious forms • Usually low apolipoprotein A_1 levels
Familial combined hyperlipidemia	• HDL cholesterol levels inversely related to triglyceride levels, except in cases of alcoholism and estrogen use • Part of the metabolic syndrome • May respond to weight loss and drug therapies that reduce triglyceride levels
Low HDL cholesterol in the presence of low total cholesterol	• Populations with low total cholesterol and triglyceride levels (triglyceride <150 mg/dL) may have low HDL cholesterol but normal apolipoprotein A_1 levels • Probably not related to CAD risk • Reassure patient if apolipoprotein A_1 levels are normal
Secondary hypoalphalipoproteinemia	• May be secondary to drug therapy (progestogens, anabolic steroids, and β-blockers without intrinsic sympathetic activity), chronic renal failure, cigarette smoking, or obesity

* CAD = coronary artery disease; HDL= high-density lipoprotein; LDL = low-density lipoprotein.

liver disease, the nephrotic syndrome, renal failure, uncontrolled diabetes mellitus, and tobacco or alcohol use. Various drugs can also cause dyslipidemia.

It is important to control secondary causes before starting drug therapy to modify lipids because the lipid abnormality may disappear with correction of the secondary cause and drug therapy can be ineffective in the presence of these conditions. If a drug is suspected to be the cause of the lipid abnormality, consider the benefits vs. the risks before discontinuing therapy.

When should clinicians consider specialized lipid tests or referral to a specialist?

Clinicians should consider apolipoprotein evaluation and referral to a lipid specialist when they suspect the patient might have genetic familial hypercholesterolemia. These persons may have difficulty controlling lipds and are at a high risk for early CVD. Screening first-degree relatives is warranted.

Drugs That Can Cause Dyslipidemia

Corticosteroids
Androgenic steroids
Progestrogens
Thiazide diuretics
β-blockers
Retinoic acid derivatives
Oral estrogens

Diagnosis... Clinicians should obtain 2 measures of LDL 1 week apart in patients found to have unfavorable total and HDL cholesterol levels on screening examination. LDL levels should be interpreted in light of cardiovascular risk using the Framingham risk equation. Measurement of HDL cholesterol and triglycerides can help to identify the causes of dyslipidemia and further target intervention. Focus history and physical examination on the identification of CVD, cardiovascular risk factors, and potential secondary causes of dyslipidemia. Specialized testing and specialty referral may be useful if familial hypercholesterolemia is suspected.

CLINICAL BOTTOM LINE

Treatment

18. Ernst ND, Sempos CT, Briefel RR, et al. Consistency between US dietary fat intake and serum total cholesterol concentrations: the National Health and Nutrition Examination Surveys. Am J Clin Nutr. 1997;66:965S-972S. [PMID: 9322575]

19. de Lorgeril M, Salen P, Martin JL, et al. Mediterranean diet, traditional risk factors, and the rate of cardiovascular complications after myocardial infarction: final report of the Lyon Diet Heart Study. Circulation. 1999;99:779-85. [PMID: 9989963]

20. Carleton RA, Bazzarre T, Drake J, et al. Report of the Expert Panel on Awareness and Behavior Change to the Board of Directors, American Heart Association. Circulation. 1996;93:1768-72. [PMID: 8653885]

21. Grundy SM, Pasternak R, Greenland P, et al. V. Assessment of cardiovascular risk by use of multiple-risk-factor assessment equations: a statement for healthcare professionals from the American Heart Association and the American College of Cardiology. Circulation. 1999;100:1481-92. [PMID: 10500053]

22. Shepherd J, Cobbe SM, Ford I, et al. Prevention of coronary heart disease with pravastatin in men with hypercholesterolemia. West of Scotland Coronary Prevention Study Group. N Engl J Med. 1995;333:1301-7. [PMID: 7566020]

23. West of Scotland Coronary Prevention Study Group. The effects of pravastatin on hospital admission in hypercholesterolemic middle-aged men. J Am Coll Cardiol. 1999;33:909-15. [PMID: 10091815]

24. Downs JR, Clearfield M, Weis S, et al. Primary prevention of acute coronary events with lovastatin in men and women with average cholesterol levels: results of AFCAPS/TexCAPS. Air Force/Texas Coronary Atherosclerosis Prevention Study. JAMA. 998;279:1615-22. [PMID: 9613910]

When should clinicians consider therapeutic interventions for patients with dyslipidemia?

Once dyslipidemia has been confirmed and the patient's coronary risk status has been evaluated, the NCEP–ATP III advocates intervention as summarized in the following discussion (4).

What should clinicians advise patients with dyslipidemia about lifestyle changes?

All patients with lipid disorders should be advised about the importance of therapeutic lifestyle changes. Patients should institute these changes regardless of whether drug therapy is also prescribed. Use of the NCEP–ATP III Therapeutic Lifestyle Change Diet (Table 3) can result in a 5% to 15% reduction in LDL cholesterol. According to the National Health and Nutrition Examination Survey (NHANES) III, a 15% reduction in LDL cholesterol could reduce the need for cholesterol-lowering drugs from 14% to 5%, if applied to the entire U.S. population (18). A diet rich in fruits, vegetables, nuts, and whole grains with use of monounsaturated oils (olive oil, canola oil) and low in red meat and animal fat seems to substantially reduce risk, independent of serum lipid levels (19).

Increased soy consumption can increase HDL cholesterol.

Patients with dyslipidemia should attain and maintain a normal body weight. Overweight patients should reduce their caloric intake from fat and simple carbohydrates and aim for at least 30 minutes of physical activity on most days. A structured aerobic exercise program using large muscle groups (e.g., running, walking, cycling, or swimming) will greatly enhance weight reduction programs. Studies of weight loss with or without exercise suggest that exercise facilitates optimizing lipids (20).

The clinician and patient should set goals and select treatment strategies for weight loss and risk factor control and schedule periodic weight checks and maintenance counseling. Obese patients may require more intensive interventions for weight reduction.

When should clinicians recommend drug therapy?

Decisions regarding when to add drug therapy to dietary modifications depend on underlying risk factors and the individual clinical situation. Strong evidence supports drug therapy for high-risk patients when LDL cholesterol levels are

---

Table 3. Diet for Therapeutic Lifestyle Changes

Nutrient	Recommended Intake
Saturated fat*	<7% of total calories
Polyunsaturated fat	Up to 10% of total calories
Monounsaturated fat	Up to 20% of total calories
Total fat	25%–35% of total calories
Carbohydrate (especially complex)	50%–60% of total calories
Fiber	20–30 g/d
Protein	Approximately 15% of total calories[†]
Cholesterol	<200 mg/d

*Trans fatty acids also raise low-density lipoprotein cholesterol, and intake should be kept to a minimum.

†Balance energy intake and expenditure to maintain desirable body weight.

above NCEP-ATP III LDL cholesterol goals. Low-risk patients should complete a 6-month trial of lifestyle changes before considering drugs. A lower threshold for starting drugs is reasonable when LDL cholesterol levels are > 15% above threshold. In patients with CAD or a CAD equivalent, LDL cholesterol level > 100 mg/dL is a threshold for initiation of therapy. In high-risk patients with evidence of CVD progression, some clinicians begin therapy at lower LDL cholesterol levels (> 70 mg/dL). For patients hospitalized with CAD, many experts initiate LDL cholesterol-lowering drugs before discharge if LDL cholesterol > 130 mg/dL (21). Reduction in LDL cholesterol levels will reduce the risk for clinical coronary disease and stroke in diverse settings, including primary prevention, secondary prevention, and diabetes. The recommendations on when to start therapy are based on the evidence for the effectiveness of drug therapy for reducing cardiovascular events by improving lipid levels.

In a primary prevention trial that randomly assigned 6595 men 45 to 64 years of age to pravastatin or placebo, the relative risk reduction of coronary events with pravastatin was 31% (95% CI, 17% to 43%) with no excess death from noncardiovascular causes (22). In another analysis, pravastatin therapy reduced hospital admissions for CVD without adverse effects on noncardiovascular hospitalization (23).

In a trial comparing lovastatin with placebo for primary prevention in adults with average total cholesterol and LDL cholesterol levels and below-average HDL cholesterol levels, lovastatin reduced the incidence of first acute major coronary events (relative risk, 0.63 [CI, 0 .50 to 0.79) (24).

A trial evaluated the effect of simvastatin vs. placebo on mortality and morbidity in 4444 patients with CAD and found that the relative risk for death in patients receiving simvastatin vs. those receiving placebo was 0.70 [CI, 0.58 to 0.85] (25).

In a secondary analysis of a randomized, controlled trial, pravastatin reduced the

rate of recurrent cardiovascular events in patients aged 65 to 75 years (26).

A trial compared the secondary prevention effects of pravastatin with those of a placebo over 6.1 years in 9014 patients who were 31 to 75 years of age. The study found that the relative risk reductions for pravastatin vs. placebo were 24% (CI, 12% to 35%) for CAD death and 22% (CI, 13% to 31%) for overall mortality (27).

What options are available for drug therapy?

There are various lipid-lowering agents that can be used alone or combined to achieve the patient's individual NCEP–ATP III cholesterol goals (Table 4). A good knowledge of drug actions and interactions allows the clinician to adapt drug therapy to meet the specific lipid abnormality. After LDL cholesterol goals are attained, attempt to increase HDL cholesterol to > 40 mg/dL and reduce triglycerides to < 150 mg/dL by selection or combination of drugs with effects on multiple lipoproteins.

When is combination drug therapy for dyslipidemia warranted?

Combination therapy should be considered in patients with severely elevated lipids that are unresponsive to monotherapy. In some disorders, such as familial hypercholesterolemia, up to 3 or 4 drugs may be required. It is also important to realize that specific agents are more effective when used in combination as they act synergistically to treat certain lipid abnormalities where single-drug therapy has been ineffective in normalizing the lipid profile.

Numerous randomized trials of short duration (3 to 6 months) have compared single and combination drug regimens for their effects on serum lipid levels. Combination drug regimens are often superior in their ability to lower LDL cholesterol and concomitantly lower triglyceride levels and raise HDL

Implementation of Interventions for Dyslipidemia

Patients with 0–1 cardiac risk factor:
- If LDL cholesterol ≥ 160 mg/dL, institute lifestyle changes.
- If LDL cholesterol ≥ 190 mg/dL, add drug therapy.
- If LDL cholesterol 160–189 mg/dL, consider adding drug therapy based on patient preferences.

Patients with 2 or more risk factors and 10-year risk <10%:
- If LDL cholesterol > 130 mg/dL, institute lifestyle changes.
- If LDL cholesterol > 160 mg/dL, consider adding drug therapy.

Patients with 10-year risk 10–20%:
- If LDL cholesterol >10 mg/dL, strongly consider adding drug therapy to lifestyle changes.
- If LDL cholesterol 100–129 mg/dL, consider adding drug therapy to lifestyle changes based on patient preferences.

Patients with 10-year risk > 20%, CAD, or CAD risk equivalents:
- If LDL cholesterol > 100 mg/dL, initiate drug therapy and lifestyle changes.
- If LDL cholesterol 70–100 mg/dL, initiate lifestyle changes and consider drug therapy.

25. The Scandinavian Simvastatin Survival Study Group. Randomised trial of cholesterol lowering in 4444 patients with coronary heart disease.Lancet.1994;34 4:1383-9. [PMID: 7968073]
26. Lewis SJ, Moye LA, Sacks FM, et al. Effect of pravastatin on cardiovascular events in older patients with myocardial infarction and cholesterol levels in the average range. Results of the Cholesterol and Recurrent Events (CARE) trial. Ann Intern Med. 1998;129:681-9. [PMID: 9841599]
27. The Long-Term Intervention with Pravastatin in Ischaemic Disease Study Group. Prevention of cardiovascular events and death with pravastatin in patients with coronary heart disease and a broad range of initial cholesterol levels. N Engl J Med. 998;339:1349-57. [PMID: 9841303]

Table 4. Drug Treatment for Lipid Disorders*

Drug Class	Mechanism of Action	Dosage	Benefits	Side Effects	Notes
Statins (HMG-CoA reductase inhibitors)	Partially inhibit HMG-CoA reductase, the rate-limiting step of cholesterol synthesis; this induces LDL-receptor formation and removal of LDL cholesterol from blood	Atorvastatin (10–80 mg QD) Fluvastatin (20–40 mg every night or 80 mg XL every night) Lovastatin (20–80 mg every night) Pravastatin (10–40 mg every night) Rosuvastatin (5–40 mg every night) Simvastatin (5–80 mg every night)	Well-studied for safety and efficacy in many trials	Abnormal liver function tests (less common than previously thought); myositis/myalgias (use with fibrates increases risk); rosuvastin should not be given with warfarin or gemfibrozil	Drug of choice for elevated LDL cholesterol based on efficacy and safety. The 6 statins are metabolized differently, allowing substitution if side effects occur. Used in combination with bile acid–binding resins to synergistically reduce LDL cholesterol. Use in combination with niacin and fibrates in patients with combined hyperlipidemia. Rosuvastatin is newest and not as thoroughly studied as the other statins.
Bile acid sequestrants	Interrupt bile acid reabsorption requiring bile acid synthesis from cholesterol	Colestipol (2 scoops bid or tid) Colesevelam hydrochloride (three 625-mg tablets bid [3.8 g total])	Nonabsorbed with long-term safety established; LDL cholesterol lowering 10%–15%	Taste/texture, bloating, heartburn, constipation, drug interaction (avoidable by administration of drugs 1 hour before or 4 hours after meals); triglyceride increase	First-line drug to lower LDL cholesterol in children and in women with child-bearing potential. Second-line drug with statins to synergistically induce LDL receptors. Do not use if triglycerides levels are >300 mg/dL or if the patient has a gastrointestinal motility disorder.
Fibrates	Reduce VLDL synthesis and induces lipoprotein lipase	Gemfibrozil (600 mg bid) Fenofibrate (43–200 mg/day depending on brand)	Best triglyceride-reducing drugs, lowers 50% or more in many patients; increases HDL 15%	Nausea, skin rash; use with caution if renal insufficiency or gallbladder disease	Does not reliably reduce (and may increase) LDL cholesterol. Use cautiously with statins due to myositis/myalgia. Use with repaglinide may cause severe hypoglycemia.
Ezetimibe	Selectively inhibits intestinal absorption of cholesterol and related phytosterols	10 mg once daily	Reduces LDL by 18%, triglycerides by 8%, and apolipoprotein B by 16%	Well tolerated, but contraindicated in patients with liver disease or elevated liver enzymes	Can use in combination with statins to yield further LDL reduction, increase in HDL, and triglyceride reduction. Do not combine with resins, fibrates, or cyclosporine.
Niacin	Largely unknown; reduces hepatic production of B-containing lipoproteins, increases HDL cholesterol production	Niacin (500 mg–1 g tid or 500 mg–2 g every night of extended-release niacin	Lowers LDL cholesterol and triglycerides 10%–30%; most effective drug at raising HDL cholesterol (25%–35%)	Flushing, nausea, glucose intolerance, gout, liver function test abnormalities, and elevated uric acid levels; may increase homocysteine levels	Drug of choice for combined hyperlipidemia and in patients with low HDL cholesterol. Extended-release preparations limit flushing and liver function test abnormalities. Long-acting OTC niacin preparations are not recommended, as they increase the incidence of hepatotoxicity. Lowers lipoprotein (a). Used in combination with statins or bile acid–binding resins in patients with combined hyperlipidemia.
Omega-3 polyunsaturated fatty acids	Inhibit hepatic triglyceride synthesis and augment chylomicron triglyceride clearance secondary to increased activity of lipoprotein lipase	4 g/day	Effective in controlling triglyceride levels up to 45%.; raises HDL 13%	Dyspepsia, nausea; may increase bleeding time; use cautiously in patients receiving anticoagulant therapy	Can increase LDL in some patients with increased triglycerides.
Ezetimibe and simvastatin (combination drug)	Both selectively inhibit the intestinal absorption of cholesterol and partially inhibit HMG-CoA reductase	Ezetimibe: 10 mg/ simvastatin: 10, 20, 40, or 80 mg every night	Combination therapy fosters patient adherence; synergistic benefits	Abnormal liver function tests, myositis/myalgia	Contraindicated in liver disease, pregnant or nursing women. Avoid use with fibrates, >1 g niacin, amiodarone, or verapamil due to increased risk for myopathy.

*bid = twice daily; CAD = coronary artery disease; HDL = high-density lipoprotein; LDL = low-density lipoprotein; OTC = over the counter; tid = three times daily; VLDL = very-low-density lipoprotein.

cholesterol levels—both secondary goals in lipid management (28, 29).

A community-based, randomized trial involving over 3000 patients found that LDL cholesterol levels can be significantly reduced by another 25.8% with the addition of ezetimibe (10 mg) to statin therapy (30).

When prescribing combination therapy, be vigilant for drug interactions, such as those between P-450–metabolized drugs, like statins, and fibrates; this interaction may induce rhabdomyolysis.

What are the goals of treatment?
Just like therapeutic decisions, treatment goals are individually determined according to the patient's level of risk based on the presence or absence of CAD, CAD risk equivalents, noncoronary vascular disease, and other risk factors (Table 5).

How should therapy for dyslipidemia be monitored?
Most interventions for dyslipidemia require 6 months or more to affect clinical event rates, and all treatments are usually life-long. Regular follow-up is important after initiation of drug therapy for dyslipidemia. In the absence of direct evidence to support a specific monitoring interval, it seems reasonable to schedule follow-up 6 weeks after the initiation of any new lipid-lowering agent with a fasting lipid profile. During this follow-up visit, the clinician should discuss adherence, identify side effects, and encourage lifestyle changes. The frequency of follow-up visits should depend on the patient's progress. Although some authors advocate routine monitoring of liver function tests before each follow-up visit, statin-induced hepatotoxicity seems to be less common than previously believed, and the American College of Physicians' guideline on treatment for dyslipidemia in type 2 diabetes does not advocate routine measurement of liver function tests in patients receiving statins (31, 32).

More frequent visits may be necessary to deliver counseling about therapeutic lifestyle changes, which require much support from the clinician in fostering adherence. New agents that are used as monotherapy or combination therapy should be added one drug at a time because if adverse reactions occur, the clinician will be better able to determine

---

Selection of Drugs for Lipid Control

- In patients with high LDL only, consider statins first, resins or an intestinal absorption blocker second, and niacin third.
- In patients with high LDL and low HDL, consider statins first and niacin second.
- In patients with high LDL, low HDL, and high triglycerides, consider niacin and statins first and fibrates second.
- In patients with high triglycerides, with or without low HDL, consider fibrates first, niacin second, and statins third.
- In patients with low HDL only, consider niacin first and fibrates second.

Table 5. Goals and Thresholds for Therapy according to LDL Cholesterol Levels

Risk Group	Low-Density Lipoprotein Cholesterol Goal (mg/dL)	Initiate Lifestyle Change (mg/dL)	Consider Drug Therapy (mg/dL)
High risk: CAD* or CAD risk equivalents† (10-year risk >20%)	<100 (optional goal <70)	≥100‡	≥100 (or >70)
Moderately high risk: ≥2 risk factors‡ (10-year risk 10%–20%)	<130 (optional goal <100)	≥130‡	≥130 (or 100–129)
Moderate risk: ≥2 risk factors‡ (10-year risk <10%)	<130	≥130	≥160
Lower risk: 0–1 risk factor	<160	≥160	≥190

Coronary artery disease (CAD) includes history of myocardial infarction, unstable angina, stable angina, coronary artery procedures (angioplasty or bypass surgery), or evidence of clinically significant myocardial ischemia.

† CAD risk equivalents include clinical manifestations of noncoronary forms of atherosclerosis (peripheral vascular disease, abdominal aortic aneurysm, and carotid disease; diabetes, and ≥2 risk factors with 10-year risk for CAD >20%).

‡ Any person at high risk or moderately high risk who has lifestyle-related risk factors (obesity, physical inactivity, elevated triglycerides, low HDL cholesterol, or the metabolic syndrome) is a candidate for lifestyle change to modify these risk factors regardless of LDL cholesterol level.

28. Ezetimibe Study Group. Effect of ezetimibe coadministered with atorvastatin in 628 patients with primary hypercholesterolemia: a prospective, randomized, double-blind trial. Circulation. 2003;107:2409-15. [PMID: 12719279]
29. Ezetimibe Study Group. Efficacy and safety of ezetimibe added to ongoing statin therapy for treatment of patients with primary hypercholesterolemia. Am J Cardiol. 2002;90:1084-91. [PMID: 12423708]
30. Pearson TA, Denke MA, McBride PE, et al. A community-based, randomized trial of ezetimibe added to statin therapy to attain NCEP ATP III goals for LDL cholesterol in hypercholesterolemic patients: the ezetimibe add-on to statin for effectiveness (EASE) trial. Mayo Clin Proc. 2005;80:587-95. [PMID: 15887425]

which agent is causing the effects. Consensus recommendations advocate 6-week follow-up with lipid measurement after each new agent is started.

What are the side effects of drug therapy for dyslipidemia?

Statins (HMG-CoA reductase inhibitors) can cause myalgia, myositis, and elevated liver enzymes. Fibrates can cause nausea and skin rashes and must be used cautiously with statins because the combination tends to increase the incidence myositis and myalgias. The intestinal cholesterol absorption–blocking drugs and the bile acid–binding drugs tend to cause abdominal bloating and constipation, although generally they are otherwise well-tolerated. Niacin is valuable and efficacious but is probably the least tolerated lipid lowering agent. It can cause flushing, nausea, headache, glucose intolerance, and gout. Some of these untoward effects can be minimized with proper drug administration. To minimize flushing, a nonenteric coated aspirin can be taken 1 hour before the evening dose along with a low-fat snack. Patients should also avoid hot beverages, baths, or showers around the time of a niacin dose.

A systematic review quantified the risks for musculoskeletal, renal, and hepatic complications associated with statin therapy. After examining data from 74 102 persons enrolled in 35 trials and followed for 1 to 65 months, the authors concluded that statin therapy is associated with a small excess risk for aminotransferase elevations (risk difference/1000 patients [RD, 4.2 [CI, 1.5 to 6.9]) but not for myalgias (RD, 2.7 [CI, −3.2 to 8.7]), creatine kinase elevations (RD, 0.2 [CI,−0.6 to 0.9]), rhabdomyolysis (RD, 0.4 [CI, −0.1 to 0.9], or withdrawal of therapy compared with placebo (RD, −0.5 [CI,−4.3 to 3.3]). Trial findings may differ from what occurs in practice (33).

Clinicians should be vigilant for side effects when prescribing drugs for dyslipidemia. Unfortunately, there is insufficient evidence to establish clear recommendations for the monitoring for and management of side effects. When severe side effects occur, discontinuation may be the only option. Clinicians and patients need to weigh the risks and benefits of therapy with minor side effects. Because metabolism of the various statins differ, it may be reasonable to substitute one for another when side effects occur.

What should clinicians advise patients about the use of complementary–alternative therapies for dyslipidemia?

Among commonly used alternative therapies for controlling lipids, stanol-ester–containing margarines or foods (34), flaxseed (35), and garlic (36) show some effectiveness. Other nontraditional therapies that have possible evidence of some effect on lipids are green tea extract, commiphora wighti (guggul or guggulipid), and pomegranate juice. However, these therapies should not substitute for drug therapy in high-risk patients.

When should clinicians consult a lipid specialist for help in managing patients with dyslipidemia?

The clinician should consider consulting a lipid specialist for patients with lipid disorders that are rare or resistant to treatment. These include those patients with specific rare disorders that require either special monitoring or complex regimens that are difficult to initiate in a routine practice setting. Patients considered in this category may include patients with familial hypercholesterolemia, type III dyslipoproteinemia, very low HDL cholesterol syndromes (HDL cholesterol < 20 mg/dL), and resistant hypertriglyceridemia (triglycerides > 1000 mg/dL). Also, patients who are at a very high risk for a vascular event, such as very young patients with vascular disease before the age of 45 and those with evidence of

31. American College of Physicians. Pharmacologic lipid-lowering therapy in type 2 diabetes mellitus: background paper for the American College of Physicians. Ann Intern Med. 2004;140:650-8. [PMID: 15096337]

32. Clinical Efficacy Assessment Subcommittee of the American College of Physicians. Lipid control in the management of type 2 diabetes mellitus: a clinical practice guideline from the American College of Physicians. Ann Intern Med. 2004;140:644-9. [PMID: 15096336]

33. Kashani A, Phillips CO, Foody JM, et al. Risks associated with statin therapy: a systematic overview of randomized clinical trials. Circulation. 2006;114:2788-97. [PMID: 17159064]

disease progression despite treatment, should be considered as candidates for referral to a lipid specialist. Patients at very high risk may need multiple interventions to lower their LDL cholesterol substantially below the usual goal, to raise HDL cholesterol, or to identify and treat other lipid and nonlipid risk factors. Current treatments to lower LDL cholesterol are very efficacious; however, a poor response may prompt an examination of secondary causes, such as unusual lipid and lipoprotein disorders, lack of compliance, or other causes.

Treatment... Treatment of dyslipidemia should always include modification of diet and exercise to optimize lipid levels. Clinicians should base decisions to add drug therapy on the individual patient's risk for cardiovascular events and select drugs that target the lipid abnormalities. Strong evidence supports statin therapy for high-risk patients.

CLINICAL BOTTOM LINE

Practice Improvement

What measures do U.S. stake-holders use to evaluate the quality of care for patients with dyslipidemia?

In April 2005, The Ambulatory Care Quality Alliance released a set of 26 health care quality indicators for clinicians, consumers, and health care purchasers to use in quality improvement efforts, public reporting, and pay-for-performance programs at www.aqaalliance.org. In May 2005, the Centers for Medicare & Medicaid Services endorsed the development of these indicators. Of the 26 indicators, 3 focus on dyslipidemia (Table 6). In addition, a voluntary program within Medicare, the Medicare Physicians Quality Reporting Initiative, pays physicians a bonus for reporting on quality measures that apply to their patients from 1 July through 31 December 2007 (37) and includes a measure related to lipid control in patients with diabetes.

34. Miettinen TA, Puska P, Gylling H, et al. Reduction of serum cholesterol with sitostanol-ester margarine in a mildly hypercholesterolemic population. N Engl J Med. 1995;333:1308-12. [PMID: 7566021]

35. Jenkins DJ, Kendall CW, Vidgen E, et al. Health aspects of partially defatted flaxseed, including effects on serum lipids, oxidative measures, and ex vivo androgen and progestin activity: a controlled crossover trial. Am J Clin Nutr. 1999;69:395-402. [PMID: 10075322]

36. Stevinson C, Pittler MH, Ernst E. Garlic for treating hypercholesterolemia. A meta-analysis of randomized clinical trials. Ann Intern Med. 2000;133:420-9. [PMID: 10975959]

37. American College of Physicians. Medicare Pay-for-Reporting Program: Physicians Quality Reporting Initiative (PQRI) Resources Physicians Quality Report Initiative (PQRI) Overview. Accessed at www.acponline.org/pmc/pqri.htm on 11 July 2007.

Table 6. Ambulatory Care Quality Alliance Dyslipidemia–Related Quality Indicators*

Indicator	Description	Notes
Lipid measurement	Percentage of patients with diabetes with ≥1 LDL cholesterol test or 1 all-component test	The all-component test is a lipid panel that includes LDL cholesterol, HDL cholesterol, and triglycerides separately
		Measurement interval is the past 15 mo
LDL cholesterol level measurement	Percentage of patients with diabetes with ≥1 LDL cholesterol level <100 mg/dL or <130 mg/dL	Actually 2 measures reflecting moderately successful (<130 mg/dL) and optimal (<100 mg/dL) treatment outcomes
		Measurement interval is the past 15 mo
Drug therapy for lowering LDL cholesterol	Percentage of patients with CAD who were prescribed a lipid-lowering therapy	Based on current ACC/AHA guidelines

*ACC/AHA = American College of Cardiology/American Heart Association; HbA$_{1c}$ = hemoglobin A$_{1c}$; HDL = high-density lipoprotein; LDL = low-density lipoprotein.

What do professional organizations recommend regarding the care of patients with dyslipidemia?

As noted earlier, several organizations offer recommendations about dyslipidemia screening and these recommendations differ with respect to the age at which screening should be started and which screening tests should be used (4, 5). In addition, evidence-based guidelines are available to guide clinicians in the care of patients with the disorder and include an American College of Physicains guideline on lipid control in patients with type 2 diabetes (32). A comprehensive listing of guidelines is available through the National Guideline Clearinghouse at www.guidelines.gov . However, the most widely used lipid guideline in the United States is the the National Heart Lung and Blood Institute's NCEP–ATP III document, which is available at www.nhlbi.nih.gov/guidelines/cholesterol/index.htm (4).

in the clinic
Tool Kit

Dyslipidemia

PIER Modules
http://PIER.acponline.org

Access the following PIER modules: Screening for Dyslipidemia, Lipid Disorders.

Practice Guidelines
www.ahrq.gov/clinic/uspstf/uspschol.htm

Access the U.S. Preventive Services Task Force recommendations on screening for dyslipidemia (update anticipated in late 2007).

www.nhlbi.nih.gov/guidelines/cholesterol/index.htm

Access the National Cholesterol education Program Adult Treatment Panel III recommendations on detection, evaluation, and treatment of high cholesterol.

www.annals.org/cgi/reprint/140/8/644.pdf

Access the American College of Physicians' guideline on pharmacologic treatment of dyslipidemia in patients with type 2 diabetes.

Framingham Risk Calculator
http://hp2010.nhlbihin.net/atpiii/calculator.asp?usertype=prof

Use this calculator to estimate a person's risk for cardiovascular events.

LDL Calculator
http://cpsc.acponline.org/enhancements/ldlCalc.html

Use this calculator to determine a patient's LDL from total cholesterol, HDL cholesterol and triglyceride levels.

Patient Information
www.annals/intheclinic/tools

Download a copy of the patient information sheet that appears on the following page for duplication and distribution to your patients.

www.doctorsforadults.com/images/healthpdfs/cholesterol_report.pdf

Obtain the patient information pamphlet, "Managing Your Cholesterol," developed by the American College of Physicians.

THINGS PEOPLE SHOULD KNOW ABOUT LIPIDS (CHOLESTEROL)

Lipids (cholesterol) are fatty substances in the blood. Lipids can build up inside arteries and lead to heart attack, stroke, or other forms of heart disease. There are several types of lipids that affect health.

Ideal lipid levels and the need for treatment to control lipids depend on whether a person has diabetes, high blood pressure, tobacco use, family history of heart disease, or other factors that make them high risk for heart attack and stroke. Discuss your lipid levels with your doctor.

Lipids and Their Role in Health

Lipid Type	Description	Normal and Abnormal Levels, mg/dL
LDL (low-density lipoprotein cholesterol)	"Bad" cholesterol: High levels increase buildup of lipids and blockages in arteries	Below 100 (very good) 100–129 (OK) 130–159 (borderline bad) 160–189 (bad) 190 or above (very bad)
HDL (high-density lipoprotein cholesterol)	"Good" cholesterol: High levels protect arteries from buildup of lipids and blockages in arteries	Below 40 (bad) 40–60 (OK) 60 or above (good)
Total cholesterol	Combination of different types of cholesterol	Below 200 (good) 200–239 (borderline bad) 240 or above (bad)
Triglycerides	Another type of fat in the blood; high levels can block arteries	Below 150 mg/dL (good) 150–199 (borderline bad) 200–499 (bad) 500 or above (very bad)

Things You Can Do to Control Lipids
- Keep body weight normal.
- Follow a diet containing less than 25% to 35% of calories from fat, less than 7% of calories from saturated fat, and less than 200 mg of cholesterol per day.
- Eat a diet that contains more plant-based foods (vegetables, fruits, grains) than animal-based foods (meat, dairy, eggs).
- Exercise at least 30 minutes on most days of the week.
- Avoid all forms of tobacco.
- Consume no more than 1 to 2 alcoholic beverages per day.

Web Sites with Good Information about Lipids

MedlinePLUS
www.nlm.nih.gov/medlineplus/cholesterol.html

American Heart Association
www.americanheart.org/presenter.jhtml?identifier=4488

National Heart, Lung, and Blood Institute
www.nhlbi.nih.gov/chd/why.htm

Influenza

R ecent vaccine shortages, reports of human infection caused by avian strains, and the specter of pandemic disease have kept influenza in the public eye over the past few years. Even during a typical influenza season, the impact on public health, though less heralded, is significant. Influenza and its complications cause approximately 36 000 deaths and 226 000 hospitalizations per year (1). Safe, cost-effective vaccines are available but have been underutilized by both the public and health care workers because of widespread misconceptions about both the disease and the vaccines. Antiviral prophylaxis is an effective alternative for persons in whom vaccination is contraindicated. Early treatment of infection reduces the duration of illness, but the medications are expensive. Limiting social interaction and, in institutional settings, using droplet precautions and cohorting infected patients may help to curb an outbreak.

Prevention

What kinds of influenza vaccine are available in the United States?
There are 2 vaccines available in the United States, the trivalent inactivated vaccine (TIV), which is injected, and live attenuated influenza vaccine (LAIV), which is administered by nasal spray. Both vaccines contain 3 strains of influenza: an H3N2 influenza A virus, an H1N1 influenza A virus, and an influenza B virus. In any given year, both kinds of vaccine contain antigenically equivalent strains. Vaccine composition is adjusted yearly. In the spring or early summer of each year, the pattern of prevailing strains in areas of the world where influenza is currently endemic is used to select the viruses that will be included in vaccine produced for the U.S. population. As the influenza season progresses globally, the match between vaccine strains and strains that come to be prevalent is not always perfect. However, even when the match is not exact, there is often sufficient similarity between the expected strain and the prevailing strain to provide good immunity. Both vaccines are immunogenic and well tolerated. Their properties are compared in Table 1, and each is discussed in detail below.

Who should be immunized against influenza?
Current guidelines, updated yearly by the Centers for Disease Control

and Prevention (CDC), recommend yearly immunization with TIV of all persons in the following high-risk groups: children aged 6 to 59 months; adults aged 50 years or older; children and adolescents (aged 6 months to 18 years) who receive long-term aspirin therapy and therefore are at risk for Reye syndrome after influenza infection; women who will be pregnant during the influenza season; adults or children with chronic pulmonary (including asthma), cardiovascular (excluding hypertension), renal, hepatic, hematologic, or metabolic disorders (including diabetes mellitus); immunosuppressed adults and children (including immunosuppression caused by medications and HIV); adults and children who have any condition (e.g., cognitive dysfunction, spinal cord injury, seizure disorder, or other neuromuscular disorders) that compromises respiratory function or the handling of respiratory secretions or that predisposes to aspiration; and residents of nursing homes and other long-term care facilities (Table 2).

In addition, to prevent transmission to high-risk persons, the following close contacts should be immunized: healthy household members (including children); health care workers; and other caregivers, including day care workers (1). These recommendations are aimed at

1. Advisory Committee on Immunization Practices (ACIP), Centers for Disease Control and Prevention (CDC). Prevention and control of influenza. Recommendations of the Advisory Committee on Immunization Practices (ACIP), 2007. MMWR Recomm Rep. 2007;56:1-54. [PMID: 17625497]

Table 1. Live Attenuated Influenza Vaccine (LAIV) Compared with Trivalent Inactive Vaccine (TIV)

Factor	LAIV	TIV
Route of administration	Intranasal	Intramuscular
Type of vaccine	Live virus	Killed virus
No. of included virus strains	3 (2 influenza A, 1 influenza B)	3 (2 influenza A, 1 influenza B)
Vaccine virus strains updated	Annually	Annually
Frequency of administration	Annually	Annually
Approved age and risk groups	Healthy persons aged 5–49 y	Persons aged $\geq$6 mo
Interval between 2 doses recommended for children aged 6 mo–8 y who are receiving influenza vaccine for the first time	6–10 wk	4 wk
Can be administered to family members or close contacts of immunosuppressed persons not requiring a protective environment	Yes	Yes
Can be administered to family members or close contacts of immunosuppressed persons requiring a protected environment (e.g., hematopoeitic stem cell transplant recipient)	No	Yes
Can be administered to family members or close contacts of persons at high risk but not severely immunosuppressed	Yes	Yes
Can be simultaneously administered with other vaccines	Yes*	Yes[†]
If not simultaneously administered, can be administered within 4 wk of another live vaccine	Prudent to space 4 wk apart	Yes
If not simultaneously administered, can be administered within 4 wk of inactivated vaccine	Yes	Yes

No data are available regarding effect on safety or efficacy.

† Inactivated influenza vaccine coadministration has been evaluated systematically only among adults with pneumo-coccal polysaccharide vaccine.

Fiore AE, Shay DK, Haber P, et al. Prevention and Control of Influenza. Recommendations of the Advisory Committee on Immunization Practices (ACIP) 2007. MMWR. 2007;56:1-54.

protecting persons at high risk for severe infection or complications and their close contacts. However, vaccination should be offered to anyone who wants it, provided that vaccine supplies are adequate and there are no contraindications.

Current guidelines are based on public health considerations and assessment of risk by CDC. However, several large cohort studies have shown reduced rates of hospitalization and death in high-risk persons who received vaccine compared with those who did not. These include elderly persons living in the community (2, 3) and patients with chronic medical conditions (4).

In cohorts of community-dwelling elderly persons enrolled in managed care organizations, of whom 55.5% and 59.7% were immunized during 1998–1999 and 1990–2000, respectively, vaccination against influenza was associated with a 19% reduction in hospitalization for cardiac disease during both seasons, a 16% reduction in cerebrovascular disease during 1998–1999 and 23% during 1999–2000, and a 32% reduction in pneumonia or influenza during 1998–1999 and 29% during 1999–2000. The overall reduction in risk for death from all causes was 48% during the 1998–1999 season and 50% during the 1990–2000 season (2).

Similarly, several well-designed prospective studies demonstrate benefit to high-risk patients through vaccination of close contacts, including health care workers in long-term care facilities. These

2. Nichol KL, Nordin J, Mullooly J, Lask R, Fillbrandt K, et al. Influenza vaccination and reduction in hospitalizations for cardiac disease and stroke among the elderly. N Engl J Med. 2003;348: 1322-32. [PMID: 12672859]
3. Mangtani P, Cumberland P, Hodgson CR, Roberts JA, Cutts FT, et al. A cohort study of the effectiveness of influenza vaccine in older people, performed using the United Kingdom general practice research database. J Infect Dis. 2004;190:1-10. [PMID: 15195237]
4. Hak E, Buskens E, van Essen, GA, de Bakker DH, Grobbee DE, et al. Clinical effectiveness of influenza vaccination in persons younger than 65 years with high-risk medical conditions: the PRISMA study. Arch Intern Med. 2005;165:274-80. [PMID: 15710789]

Table 2. High-Risk Groups Recommended to Receive Annual Influenza Vaccination

- All persons, including school-aged children, who want to reduce the risk for influenza or for transmitting influenza to others
- All children aged 6 to 59 mo (i.e., 6 mo to 4 y)
- All persons aged ≥ 50 y
- Children and adolescents (aged 6 mo to 18 y) receiving long-term aspirin therapy who may thus be at risk for Reye syndrome after influenza virus infection
- Women who will be pregnant during the influenza season
- Adults and children who have chronic pulmonary (including asthma); cardiovascular (except hypertension); and renal, hepatic, hematologic, or metabolic disorders (including diabetes mellitus)
- Adults and children who are immunosuppressed, including immunosuppression caused by medications or by HIV
- Adults and children who have any condition (e.g., cognitive dysfunction, spinal cord injuries, seizure disorders, or other neuromuscular disorders) that can compromise respiratory function or the handling of respiratory secretions or that can increase risk for aspiration
- Residents of nursing homes and other long-term care facilities
- Health care personnel
- Healthy household contacts (including children) and caregivers of children aged < 5 y and adults aged ≥ 50 years, with particular emphasis on vaccinating contacts of children aged < 6 mo
- Healthy household contacts (including children) and caregivers of persons with medical conditions that put them at higher risk for severe complications from influenza

Fiore AE, Shay DK, Haber P, et al. Prevention and Control of Influenza. Recommendations of the Advisory Committee on Immunization Practices (ACIP) 2007. MMWR. 2007;56:1-54.

5. Potter J, Stott DJ, Roberts MA, Elder AG, O'Donnell B, et al. Influenza vaccination of health care workers in long-term-care hospitals reduces the mortality of elderly patients. J Infect Dis. 1997;175:1-6. [PMID: 8985189]

6. Carman WF, Elder AG, Wallace LA, McAulay K, Walker A, et al. Effects of influenza vaccination of health-care workers on mortality of elderly people in long-term care: a randomised controlled trial. Lancet. 2000;355:93-7. [PMID: 10675165]

7. Hayward AC, Harling R, Wetten S, Johnson AM, Munro S, et al. Effectiveness of an influenza vaccine programme for care home staff to prevent death, morbidity, and health service use among residents: cluster randomised controlled trial. BMJ. 2006;333:1241. [PMID: 17142257]

8. Ohmit SE, Victor JC, Rotthoff JR, Teich ER, Truscon RK, et al. Prevention of antigenically drifted influenza by inactivated and live attenuated vaccines. N Engl J Med. 2006;355:2513-22. [PMID: 17167134]

9. LaMontagne JR, Noble GR, Quinnan GV, et al. Summary of clinical trials of inactivated influenza vaccine-1978. Rev Infect Dis. 1983;5:723-36. [PMID: 6353529]

10. Lo W, Whimbey E, Elting L, Couch R, Cabanillas F, et al. Antibody response to a two-dose influenza vaccine regimen in adult lymphoma patients on chemotherapy. Eur J Clin Microbiol Infect Dis. 1993;12:778-82. [PMID: 8307050]

studies show a significant reduction in hospitalization for influenza-like illness and its complications as well as in mortality (5–7).

In a cluster randomized, controlled trial carried out in 44 nursing homes, vaccination was offered to staff in 22 intervention facilities. Uptake was 48.2% in intervention homes and 5.9% in control homes in 2003–2004 and 43.2% and 3.5%, respectively, in 2004–2005. During periods of influenza activity during 2003–2004, there was a significant decrease in mortality in intervention facilities compared with control facilities (rate difference, –5.0 per 100 residents [95% CI, –7.0 to –2.0]), influenza-like illness, and physician consultations and hospitalizations for influenza-like illness. No differences were found in 2004–2005 or when there was no influenza activity in 2003–2004 (7).

A recent study showed that vaccine may confer significant benefit even when the prevailing strains have "drifted" from the vaccine strains (8).

In whom should the dose of influenza vaccine be modified?
The dose of TIV depends on the age, vaccine history, and possibly the immune status of the patient. A 2-dose schedule usually is needed to elicit antibody in immunologically unprimed persons (such as young children), but multiple doses do not improve antibody responses in older children and adults primed by previous vaccination or exposure (9). Certain immunosuppressed patients may mount greater humoral immune responses to TIV after 2 doses than after 1 dose (10–12).

There are no established recommendations for a 2-dose regimen in any patient group other than children. Not all TIV products are licensed for use in children, and no vaccine is approved for use in infants younger than 6 months of age (Table 3). The package insert should be consulted for U.S. Food and Drug Administration approval in children and for the dose, which is based on age and vaccine history.

Which patients should not receive inactivated influenza vaccine?
Inactivated vaccine should not be given to persons with a history of anaphylactic reactions to eggs or to other vaccine components. Vaccination should be postponed for moderate or severe febrile illness of any cause but can safely be given

Table 3. Approved Influenza Vaccines for Different Age Groups—United States, 2007–08 Season*

Vaccine	Trade Name	Manufacturer	Presentation	Thimerosal mercury content (µg Hg/0.5-mL dose)	Age Group	No. of Doses	Route
TIV[†]	Fluzone	Sanofi Pasteur	0.25-mL prefilled syringe	0	>6–35 mo	1 or 2[‡]	Intramuscular[§]
			0.5-mL prefilled syringe	0	≥36 mo	1 or 2[‡]	Intramuscular[§]
			0.5-mL vial	0	≥36 mo	1 or 2[‡]	Intramuscular[§]
			5.0-mL multidose vial	25	≥6 mo	1 or 2[‡]	Intramuscular[§]
TIV[†]	Fluvirin	Novartis Vaccine	5.0-mL multidose vial	24.5	≥4 y	1 or 2[‡]	Intramuscular[§]
TIV[†]	Fluarix	GlaxoSmithKline	0.5-mL prefilled syringe	<1.0	≥18 y	1	Intramuscular[§]
TIV[†]	FluLuval	GlaxoSmithKline	5.0-mL multidose vial	25	≥18 y	1	Intramuscular[§]
LAIV	FluMist‖	MedImmune	0.2-mL sprayer	0	5–49 y	1 or 2[¶]	Intranasal

*LAIV = live attenuated influenza vaccine; TIV = trivalent inactivated vaccine.

† A 0.5-mL dose contains 15 µg each of A/Solomon Islands/3/2006 (H1N1)-like, A/Wisconsin/67/2005 (H3N2)-like, and B/Malaysia/2506/2004-like antigens.

‡ Two doses administered at least 1 mo apart are recommended for children aged 6 mo–8 y who are receiving TIV for the first time, and those who only received 1 dose in their first year of vaccination should receive 2 doses in the following year.

§ For adults and older children, the recommended site of vaccination is the deltoid muscle. The preferred site for infants and young children is the anterolateral aspect of the thigh.

‖ FluMist dosage and storage requirements have changed for the 2007–08 influenza season. FluMist is now shipped to end users at 35°F to 46°F (2°C to 8°C). LAIV should be stored at 35°F to 46°F (2°C to 8°C) upon receipt and should remain at that temperature until it expires. The dose is 0.2 mL, divided equally between nostrils.

¶ Two doses administered at least 6 wk apart are recommended for children aged 5–8 y who are receiving LAIV for the first time, and those who received only 1 dose in their first year of vaccination should receive 2 doses in the following year.

Fiore AE, Shay DK, Haber P, et al. Prevention and Control of Influenza. Recommendations of the Advisory Committee on Immunization Practices (ACIP) 2007. MMWR. 2007;56:1-54.

during illness in which fever is mild or absent. A history of Guillain-Barré syndrome occurring within 6 weeks after a previous influenza vaccination is a relative contraindication, but vaccine may still be given to patients at high risk for influenza-related disease if other forms of prophylaxis are contraindicated (1).

Who should be vaccinated with intranasal live attenuated influenza vaccine?

LAIV is approved for use in healthy, nonpregnant persons aged 5 to 49 years. Its use is encouraged in this population, especially when there is a shortage of TIV. The vaccine is given by nasal spray and therefore may be acceptable to patients who decline a parenteral vaccine. It may also offer a protective advantage by eliciting respiratory mucosal as well as systemic immunity.

In a large, randomized, double-blind, placebo-controlled trial of LAIV among working adults, reductions in the immunized group compared with the placebo group were as follows: 18.8% in severe febrile illness, 23.6% in febrile upper respiratory trace illness, 22.9% in reported days of all illness, 17.9% in days of work lost for severe febrile illness, 28.4% for febrile upper respiratory illness, and 24.8% in health care provider visits for severe febrile illness and 40.9% for visits for febrile upper respiratory visits. The vaccinated group also used fewer prescription and over-the-counter medicines. Vaccinated persons had more runny nose and sore throat in the week following vaccination than those who received placebo (13).

School-based use of LAIV in children has also been used as part of a strategy to prevent the spread of the disease in the community.

In a study of 11 clusters of elementary schools, LAIV was given to 47% of students in intervention schools. As compared with households of control schools, those in the intervention schools had significantly fewer influenza symptoms during a week of predicted influenza activity. However, overall rates of hospitalization and school absenteeism did not differ between the groups (14).

11. Engelhard D, Nagler A, Hardan I, Morag A, Aker M, et al. Antibody response to a two-dose regimen of influenza vaccine in allogeneic T cell-depleted and autologous BMT recipients. Bone Marrow Transplant. 1993;11:1-5. [PMID: 8431706]
12. Soesman NM, Rimmelzwaan GF, Nieuwkoop NJ, Beyer WE, Tilanus HW, et al. Efficacy of influenza vaccination in adult liver transplant recipients. J Med Virol. 2000;61:85-93. [PMID: 10745238]
13. Nichol KL, Mendelman PM, Mallon KP, Jackson LA, Gorse GJ, et al. Effectiveness of live, attenuated intranasal influenza virus vaccine in healthy, working adults: a randomized controlled trial. JAMA. 1999;282:137-44. [PMID: 10411194]
14. King JC Jr., Stoddard JJ, Gaglani, et al. Effectiveness of school-based influenza vaccination. N Engl J Med. 2006;355:2523-32. (PMID: 17167135).

Start vaccinating patients in October or November but continue to offer vaccine through the winter, because influenza season doesn't peak until February or early March.

15. Monto AS, Robinson DP, Herlocher ML, Hinson JM Jr., Elliott MJ, et al. Zanamivir in the prevention of influenza among healthy adults: a randomized controlled trial. JAMA. 1999;282:31-5. [PMID: 10404908]

In whom is intranasal live attenuated influenza vaccine contraindicated?

LAIV is not licensed for use in patients with conditions that place them at high risk for severe influenza or complications. Because LAIV contains live (albeit attenuated) virus that may shed into the environment, family members and other close contacts (e.g., health care workers) of severely immunosuppressed persons in special care units should receive TIV rather than LAIV. Close contacts (including health care workers) of persons with less severe immune deficiency and of patients with other indications for influenza vaccination may receive LAIV. Likewise, LAIV should not be administered to anyone with severe immune deficiency, but may be administered to persons who fall into other high-risk categories (1).

Otherwise, there are few contraindications. Vaccination should be postponed in cases of severe nasal congestion that might result in poor penetration of the spray. LAIV should not be given concomitantly with antiviral medications (e.g., zanamivir and oseltamivir). It may be given 48 hours after antiviral drugs have been stopped, but antivirals should not be given for 2 weeks after LAIV has been administered. It should not be given to children or adolescents on long-term aspirin therapy or to persons with a history of Guillain-Barré syndrome or hypersensitivity to eggs.

When should vaccine be given?

Ideally, persons living in the United State should be vaccinated in October and November, but vaccine should be offered throughout the winter, because the influenza season often does not peak until February or early March. Likewise, if vaccine is available in September, it should be offered to high-risk patients who present for routine appointments or at the time of hospital discharge to avoid delayed or missed opportunities. Nursing home residents should not be immunized before October because antibody levels may not last through the influenza season. These recommendations reflect the consensus of experts, based on the usual chronology of influenza activity in the United States, the duration of antibody levels, and anticipated vaccine supplies.

How does vaccine supply influence vaccination priority and/or timing?

If difficulties in vaccine production or distribution result in shortages or delays, priority should be given to vaccinating those at high risk for severe disease or complications, and their close contacts, including health care workers. The CDC has established a Web site to guide triage efforts (www.cdc.gov/flu/professionals/vaccination/vax_priority.htm).

What is the role of antiviral agents in preventing influenza?

Antiviral drugs can be used to control outbreaks in institutions and in households and to supplement or replace vaccine if there is a shortage or if it is contraindicated. Currently, only oseltamivir and zanamivir are recommended, as there has been widespread resistance to amantadine and rimantadine among circulating strains of influenza virus in recent years. The recommended doses for prophylaxis in adults are oseltamivir 75 mg/d and zanamivir 2 inhalations daily. The dosage of oseltamivir must be adjusted in patients with renal failure. Zanamivir should be used with caution, if at all, in patients with pulmonary disease.

In a double-blind, randomized trial, healthy adults were given zanamivir or placebo at the beginning of an influenza outbreak. Symptom records and specimens were collected for viral isolation and antibody titer. Zanamivir was 67% efficacious in preventing laboratory-confirmed influenza and 84% efficacious in preventing similar illness with fever during the 4-week trial (15).

A randomized, double-blind, placebo-controlled study examined the efficacy of prophylactic oseltamivir in 415 household contacts of 163 outpatients with laboratory-confirmed influenza. The overall protective efficacy for contacts who took oseltamivir 75 mg once daily for 7 days, starting within 48 hours of symptoms in the index case, was 89% for individuals (CI, 67% to 97%; P< 0.001) and 84% for households (CI, 49% to 95%; P< 0.001), compared with household contacts administered placebo (16).

A meta-analysis has been published on the efficacy of oseltamivir and zanamivir for both prevention and treatment of influenza (17), and other studies have demonstrated the usefulness of these drugs in preventing influenza in household contacts (16, 18-20).

The use of antiviral agents to control institutional outbreaks of influenza has also been recommended, although there are few definitive studies. When an outbreak is detected, unvaccinated staff members and residents should be vaccinated if vaccine is available. Staff members vaccinated at the onset of an outbreak should be given chemoprophylaxis for 2 weeks, while the immune response is developing.

In addition, the closed environment of nursing homes, the potential for high-intensity virus exposure, and possible suboptimal immune response to vaccine by debilitated patients suggest that all residents, regardless of previous vaccination, should be given chemoprophylaxis in an outbreak. Antiviral medications should be continued in residents for at least 2 weeks and for 1 week longer than the duration of the outbreak if surveillance indicates continued new cases. Chemoprophylaxis for a similar duration should also be considered for unvaccinated staff members and for all employees in an outbreak caused by a strain that is not included in the vaccine.

Short-term prophylaxis for 10 to 14 days can also be used for persons (and their close contacts) who are at high risk and are vaccinated after the seasonal influenza epidemic has begun in the community for protection until vaccination becomes effective. Postexposure prophylaxis (e.g., in a household setting) should be considered for unimmunized high-risk persons in conjunction with vaccination if possible, and for healthy household contacts of persons with recently diagnosed influenza.

Short-term prophylaxis should be considered for travelers, especially those with high-risk conditions, if traveling in large groups or to areas with influenza activity. Influenza occurs from April through September in the southern hemisphere and throughout the year in the tropics. Outbreaks may occur when unimmunized travelers mix with others from areas currently experiencing the yearly influenza epidemic. If it is not flu season in the United States, vaccine may not be available.

Prophylaxis with antiviral medication may be provided throughout the influenza outbreak to high-risk persons and their close contacts (including health care workers) when vaccine is unavailable or contraindicated, when there is a major antigenic difference between the epidemic strain and the vaccine strains, or when severe immunosuppression makes response to the vaccine unlikely.

What measures should clinicians take to prevent influenza in health care institutions and among institutional staff?

All health care personnel should be vaccinated against influenza unless vaccine is contraindicated or unavailable. In the latter case, clinicians should consider prophylaxis with antiviral medications for themselves and other health care

The use of antiviral agents to control institutional outbreaks of influenza has also been recommended, although there are few definitive studies.

16. Welliver R, Monto AS, Carewicz O. Effectiveness of oseltamivir in preventing influenza in household contacts: a randomized controlled trial. JAMA. 2001;285:748-54. [PMID: 11176912]
17. Cooper NJ, Sutton AJ, Abrams KR, Wailoo A, Turner D, et al. Effectiveness of neuraminidase inhibitors in treatment and prevention of influenza A and B: systematic review and meta-analyses of randomized controlled trials. BMJ. 2003;326:1235. [PMID: 12791735]
18. Zanamivir Family Study Group. Inhaled zanamivir for the prevention of influenza in families. Zanamivir Family Study Group. N Engl J Med. 2000;343:1282-9. [PMID: 11058672]
19. Hayden FG, Atmar RL, Schilling M, Johnson C, Poretz D, et al. Use of the selective oral neuraminidase inhibitor oseltamivir to prevent influenza. N Engl J Med. 1999;341:1336-43. [PMID: 10536125]
20. Hayden FG, Belshe R, Villanueva C, Lanno R, Hughes C, et al. Management of influenza in households: a prospective, randomized comparison of oseltamivir treatment with or without postexposure prophylaxis. J Infect Dis. 2004;189:440-9. [PMID: 14745701]

workers, as outlined previously. The use of standing orders, which allow trained health care professionals other than physicians to identify and vaccinate high-risk patients, improves rates of immunization of hospital patients at discharge and of nursing home residents (21). Likewise, providing cost-free vaccine at convenient times and places may improve vaccine coverage among hospital and nursing home staff.

Prevention... Influenza vaccine is effective in preventing influenza and its complications, including hospitalization and death. Vaccine should be given to adults older than 50 years, children between 6 and 59 months, and immunosuppressed persons or those with chronic medical conditions. Vaccination should be encouraged in those who have close contact with high-risk persons, including health care workers. Prophylaxis with antiviral medication may serve as a substitute or an adjunct under certain circumstances. In such cases, oseltamivir and zanamivir are the drugs of choice; amantadine and rimantadine should not be used because of viral resistance.

CLINICAL BOTTOM LINE

Diagnosis

21. Fedson DS, Houck P, Bratzler D. Hospital-based influenza and pneumococcal vaccination: Sutton's law applied to prevention. Infect Control Hosp Epidemiol. 2006; 21:692-9. [MID:11089652]
22. Zambon M, Hays J, Webster A, Newman R, Keene O. Diagnosis of influenza in the community: relationship of clinical diagnosis to confirmed virological, serologic, or molecular detection of influenza. Arch Intern Med. 2001;161:2116-22. [PMID: 11570941]
23. Monto AS, Gravenstein S, Elliott M, Colopy M, Schweinle J. Clinical signs and symptoms predicting influenza infection. Arch Intern Med. 2000;160:3243-7. [PMID: 11088084]

What symptoms and signs should prompt clinicians to suspect influenza?

The symptoms of influenza frequently overlap those of a viral respiratory infection, but fever, cough, malaise, and myalgia are perhaps the most frequently described. The presentation can be more subtle in older patients and young children, who may not be able to describe their symptoms accurately. Several large prospective studies show the importance of fever and nonproductive cough in differentiating influenza from other viral respiratory symptoms, especially when influenza is known to be present in the community (22, 23).

In a retrospective pooled analysis of baseline clinical trial data from mainly unvaccinated adults and adolescents who had influenza-like symptoms, cough and fever were found to be the best multivariate predictors of influenza infection in the setting of an outbreak with a positive predictive value of 79% and a sensitivity of 64% for laboratory-documented influenza (23).

Higher temperatures and more severe symptoms are also likely to support a diagnosis of influenza during the appropriate season (22, 23). Rhinorrhea is more common in influenza, especially when associated with fever and cough (23). Although weakness, myalgia, sore throat, nausea, and headache are commonly experienced in influenza, they occur with similar frequency in other viral respiratory illnesses. In most cases, gastrointestinal symptoms suggest another diagnosis (Table 4).

In addition to fever, the physical examination may reveal nasal congestion and tracheal tenderness. The presence of rales or consolidation on chest examination may suggest viral pneumonia but should raise the possibility of other diagnoses or complications, such as bacterial pneumonia or heart failure.

When should clinicians obtain diagnostic testing, including rapid tests, to confirm the diagnosis of influenza?

Testing should be performed early in a suspected outbreak to confirm the presence of influenza in the community and whenever necessary to confirm the diagnosis in atypical cases. Testing can also be done to investigate and monitor outbreaks in hospitals and nursing homes. However, it does not need to be done in all patients who present with a typical clinical picture of influenza when the disease is prevalent in the community.

Information from a phase 3 drug study was used to assess the value of clinical signs and symptoms in the diagnosis of influenza. Viral isolation, hemagglutinin inhibition serology, and polymerase chain reaction tests were obtained in enrolled patients. In the 692 (67%) patients in whom the results of all 3 tests agreed, there was an association between greater severity of symptoms and increasing number of positive test results. In addition, an increasing number of positive tests correlated with a longer time to improvement in symptoms in the placebo group. The data suggested that influenza could be accurately diagnosed without testing in approximately 77% of adults at a time when the disease was prevalent in the community, especially when cough and fever were among the presenting symptoms (22).

Although viral cultures on nasopharyngeal specimens are most sensitive and specific, results may take 3 to 10 days or longer, which limits clinical usefulness. Rapid tests for influenza are widely available and can be helpful for individual patients when the results will contribute to diagnostic and treatment decisions. In hospitalized patients, rapid confirmation of diagnosis aids in prompt institution of appropriate infection control measures.

In a published hospital record review, rapid testing led to a reduction in antibiotic use in patients who tested positive for influenza, but studies on the impact of testing on other outcomes are lacking (24).

Testing adds cost to care and is not recommended for most outpatients. In general, CLIA-waived tests for physicians' offices are more than 70% sensitive and more than 90% specific. Sensitivity is higher in children than in adults, higher with nasal samples than with throat samples, and higher during the first few days of illness (Table 5).

Table 4. Symptoms and Signs of Laboratory-Confirmed Influenza and Influenza-like Illness from Other Causes

Symptom/Sign	Laboratory-Confirmed Influenza (%)	Influenza-like Illness from Other Causes (%)
Elevated temperature	68 to 77	40 to 73
Fever or chills	83 to 90	75 to 89
Fatigue/malaise	75 to 94	62 to 94
Cough (minimal or nonproductive)	84 to 93	72 to 80
Shortness of breath	6	6
Chest discomfort or pleuritic chest pain	35	23
Headache	84 to 91	74 to 89
Myalgia	67 to 94	73 to 94
Sore throat	64 to 84	64 to 84
Rhinorrhea	79	68
Nausea/vomiting	12	12
Abdominal pain	22	22

Adapted from Bridges CB, Fukuda K, Cox NJ, et al. Prevention and control of influenza. Recommendations of the advisory committee on immunization practices (ACIP). MMWR. 2001; 50(RR4):1-44.

Table 5. CLIA-Waived Rapid Tests for the Diagnosis of Influenza

Test	Type of Influenza Detected	Specimen
NOW Influenza A (Binax)	A	Nasal wash or aspirate; nasopharyngeal swab
NOW Influenza B (Binax)	B	Nasal wash or aspirate; nasopharyngeal swab
NOW Influenza A+B	A and B	Nasal wash or aspirate; nasopharyngeal swab
QuickVue Influenza Test (Quidel)	A and B (does not distinguish)	Nasal wash or aspirate; nasopharyngeal swab
QuickVue Influenza A+B Test (Quidel)	A and B	Nasal wash or aspirate; nasopharyngeal swab
SAS Influenza A Test	A	Nasopharyngeal wash or aspirate
SAS Influenza B Test	B	Nasopharyngeal wash or aspirate
ZstatFlu (ZymeTx)	A and B (does not distinguish)	Throat swab

Adapted from www.cdc.gov/flu/professionals/diagnosis/labprocedures.htm.

24. Falsey AR, Murata Y, Walsh EE. Impact of rapid diagnosis on management of adults hospitalized with influenza. Arch Intern Med. 2007;167:354-60. [PMID: 17242309]

A summary of information on approved diagnostic tests is available at www.cdc.gov/flu/professionals/diagnosis/labprocedures.htm.

When should clinicians suspect bacterial complications in patients initially believed to have influenza?

The possibility of bacterial complications should be considered in patients who remain ill, worsen, or have acute onset of high fever and malaise after initial improvement. Fever in adults with uncomplicated influenza generally lasts about 3 days, by which time most will show signs of improvement. Although it may take 10 to 14 days for complete recovery, failure to improve or worsening symptoms suggests either a complication or an alternative diagnosis.

Acute bronchitis is the most commonly recognized complication, but others include sinusitis, pneumonia, and noninfectious sequelae (25). Patients who remain febrile for more than 3 to 5 days, or who develop fever or other new symptoms, should be evaluated. Blood work, cultures, and imaging studies should be guided by the symptoms and clinical findings. Consultation with a specialist should be considered, especially if the patient is severely ill or immunosuppressed.

Occasionally, serious systemic bacterial infections, such as pneumonia, staphylococcal bacteremia, meningococcal disease, and inhalational anthrax can present initially with influenza-like symptoms. The differential diagnosis should be broadened in patients who deteriorate rapidly, and work-up and treatment should be adjusted accordingly. Again, consultation with a specialist might be appropriate in such cases (Table 6).

When should clinicians suspect avian influenza?

Avian influenza, caused by an H5N1 influenza A virus, should be considered in patients who have traveled to areas in which the disease is currently reported, especially if they have had close contact with birds or with a known case, or if the illness occurs outside of the usual influenza season.

25. Connolly AM, Salmon RL, Lervy B, Williams DH. What are the complications of influenza and can they be prevented? Experience from the 1989 epidemic of H3N2 influenza A in general practice. BMJ. 1993;306:1452-4. [PMID: 8518643]

Table 6. Differential Diagnosis of Influenza

Disease	Characteristics	Notes
Common cold	Upper respiratory symptoms dominated by rhinitis, usually fever absent or mild	Fever is a negative predictor of rhinovirus infection in adults
Streptococcal pharyngitis	Sore throat with accompanying nasal symptoms is typical of viral pharyngitis; presence of tender unilateral adenopathy and exudate is typical of streptococcal pharyngitis	Severe sore throat is evidence against influenza
Acute mononucleosis	Presence of elevated liver function test results, splenomegaly, and atypical lymphocytes on peripheral smear, positive monospot test	
Bacterial pneumonia	Classic association with pleuritic chest pain and productive sputum	Bacterial pneumonia may be concurrent with viral pneumonia or may occur up to 2 wk after recovery from influenza
Bacterial meningitis	Generally presents with clouded sensorium and prominent headache, but early presentation may be confused with influenza	Patients with influenza should have some improvement within 48 hours; influenza is associated with increased risk for invasive meningococcal disease
Other diseases	A large list of relatively rare conditions can present with influenza-like symptoms, such as inhalational anthrax	

Treatment

What is the role of hydration and antipyretics in treating patients with influenza?

Hydration is important to replace the large insensible water losses that occur with fever. Antipyretics, such as acetaminophen or ibuprofen can help to reduce fever and thus prevent further insensible loss. Reduction of fever can prevent other consequences of increased metabolic rate, such as tachycardia, and may relieve such symptoms as chills and myalgia. There is no convincing evidence that antipyretic therapy either prolongs or reduces the course of illness. Aspirin and aspirin-containing medicines should be avoided, particularly in adolescents and children because of their association with Reye syndrome.

When should clinicians prescribe antiviral agents for patients with influenza? Which agents should be used when?

The antiviral agents oseltamivir and zanamivir are effective in shortening the duration of illness due to influenza by 1 to 2 days and allowing a more rapid return to normal activities but only when initiated within 48 hours of symptom onset. They can be considered for treating patients with uncomplicated illness who present within that time. These neuraminidase inhibitors are approved for treatment of uncomplicated cases of influenza A and B. Oseltamivir is given as an oral 75-mg dose twice daily; zanamivir is administered as two 10-mg inhalations twice daily. The recommended course of treatment with either drug is 5 days. The dose of oseltamivir must be adjusted in patients with renal insufficiency (Table 7).

Oseltamivir has been studied in healthy nonimmunized adults in 2 large randomized, controlled trials, in which the drug reduced the duration and severity of symptoms (26, 27). Zanamivir has been studied more extensively in a broad range of patient groups and has been found to be similarly effective in the treatment of influenza and in reducing complications requiring antibiotics (28–31).

Table 7. Drug Treatment for Influenza*				
Agent	Dosage	Benefits	Side Effects	Notes
Zanamivir	2 inhalations (10 mg) BID for 5 d	1–2 d earlier resolution of symptoms; reduction in complications by about 40%	Same as placebo in controlled trials, but postmarketing reports suggest rare bronchospasm	Active against both influenza A and B viruses; approved only for persons without pulmonary or cardiovascular disease
Oseltamivir	75 mg PO BID for 5 d	1–2 d earlier resolution of symptoms; reduction in complications by about 40%	Nausea (about 10% of first dose) and vomiting (about 6%); postmarketing reports include some cases of confusion, self-injury	Active against both influenza A and B viruses; dose reduction for CrCL < 30 mL/min

BID = twice daily; CrCl = creatinine clearance; PO = orally.

26. Treanor JJ, Hayden FG, Vrooman PS, Barbarash R, Bettis R, et al. Efficacy and safety of the oral neuraminidase inhibitor oseltamivir in treating acute influenza: a randomized controlled trial. US Oral Neuraminidase Study Group. JAMA. 2000;283:1016-24. [PMID: 10697061]
27. Nicholson KG, Aoki FY, Osterhaus AD, Trottier S, Carewicz O, et al. Efficacy and safety of oseltamivir in treatment of acute influenza: a randomised controlled trial. Neuraminidase Inhibitor Flu Treatment Investigator Group. Lancet. 2000;355:1845-50. [PMID: 10866439]
28. Monto AS, Webster A, Keene O. Randomized, placebo-controlled studies of inhaled zanamivir in the treatment of influenza A and B: pooled efficacy analysis. J Antimicrob Chemother. 1999;44 Suppl B:23-9. [PMID: 10877459]
29. Lalezari J, Campion K, Keene O, Silagy C. Zanamivir for the treatment of influenza A and B infection in high-risk patients: a pooled analysis of randomized controlled trials. Arch Intern Med. 2001;161:212-7. [PMID: 11176734]
30. Hayden FG, Osterhaus AD, Treanor JJ, Fleming DM, Aoki FY, et al. Efficacy and safety of the neuraminidase inhibitor zanamivir in the treatment of influenzavirus infections. GG167 Influenza Study Group. N Engl J Med. 1997;337:874-80. [PMID: 9302301]
31. Mäkelä MJ, Pauksens K, Rostila T, Fleming DM, Man CY, et al. Clinical efficacy and safety of the orally inhaled neuraminidase inhibitor zanamivir in the treatment of influenza: a randomized, double-blind, placebo-controlled European study. J Infect. 2000;40:42-8. [PMID: 10762110]

Amantadine and rimantadine should not be used for influenza because of widespread resistance to these agents.

Meta-analyses provide good evidence that both oseltamivir and zanamivir can be used in healthy adults to reduce symptom severity and duration and allow them to return to work or school sooner and in high-risk patients to reduce the risk for more serious infectious complications.

In a meta-analysis of 7 randomized, double-blind, controlled trials, 3815 mainly healthy adolescents and adults had an influenza-like illness fewer than 2 days in duration. The diagnosis of influenza was laboratory-confirmed in 66%. The incidence of respiratory events, including mainly acute sinusitis and acute bronchitis, leading to antibiotic use was 17% in the placebo-treated patients. Inhaled zanamivir reduced the number of lower respiratory tract events (relative risk [RR], 0.60; CI, 0.42 to 0.85), but the reduction of upper respiratory tract events (RR, 0.90; CI, 0.63 to 1.27) was not significant (32).

In a meta-analysis of 17 treatment trials and 7 prevention trials involving children under 12, healthy individuals aged 12 to 65, and high-risk persons, zanamivir reduced the mean duration of symptoms by 1.0 day (CI, 0.5 to 1.5), 0.8 day (CI, 0.3 to 1.3), and 0.9 day (CI, −0.1 to 1.9), respectively. Oseltamivir reduced symptoms in the same groups for 0.9 day (CI, 0.3 to 1.5), 0.9 day (CI, 0.3 to 1.4) and 0.4 day (CI, −0.7 to 1.4), respectively. The authors concluded that both drugs were effective in treating influenza, although the evidence was limited for treatment of certain populations (17).

A retrospective pooled analysis of data exclusively from 321 high-risk patients with a clinical diagnosis of influenza showed that 154 of those patients treated with inhaled zanamavir 10 mg twice daily experienced a reduction in the length of illness by 2.5 days compared with those given placebo (P = 0.015). Treated high-risk patients returned to normal activities 3.0 days earlier (P = 0.022) and had a 43% reduction in the incidence of complications requiring antibiotics (P = 0.045) (29).

There is less information about efficacy of treatment of influenza B under field conditions than there is about treatment of influenza A. Oseltamavir is somewhat less active against influenza B neuraminidases, and some experts recommend doubling the dose of oseltamivir in adults with proven or probable influenza B. Both agents have been shown to reduce the duration and quantity of viral shedding in experimental influenza B infection in humans (33, 34).

Most of the clinical trials evaluating efficacy of the neuraminidase inhibitors have been done in outpatients with uncomplicated disease; consequently, they are approved only for use in uncomplicated cases. Little information is available on the efficacy of these agents in severe or complicated cases of influenza, and clinical judgment should be applied in such cases.

Although the adamantanes (amantadine and rimantadine) were used in the past for treatment of influenza, widespread resistance of influenza virus strains to these drugs has been reported in recent years, and their use is no longer recommended.

When should clinicians consider hospitalizing patients with influenza?
Hospitalization should be considered for patients who are severely ill because of influenza or its complications. Such conditions as dehydration, inability to maintain adequate intake, respiratory distress, or hypoxemia should prompt admission. Likewise, an uncertain clinical course or frail baseline health might prompt admission for close observation.

When should physicians obtain consultation from an infectious disease specialist or public health authorities?
Consultation should be considered for help with diagnosis or management as needed. Diagnostic consultation might be useful in seriously ill patients in whom the

32. Kaiser L, Keene ON, Hammond JM, Elliott M, Hayden FG. Impact of zanamivir on antibiotic use for respiratory events following acute influenza in adolescents and adults. Arch Intern Med. 2000;160:3234-40. [PMID: 11088083]
33. Hayden FG, Lobo M, Hussey EK, et al. Efficacy of intranasal GG167 in experimental human influenza A and B virus infection. In: Brown LE, Hampson AW, Webster RG, eds. Options for the Control of Influenza III. Amsterdam: Elsevier; 1996:718-25.
34. Hayden FG, Jennings L, Robson R, Schiff G, Jackson H, et al. Oral oseltamivir in human experimental influenza B infection. Antivir Ther. 2000;5:205-13. [PMID: 11075941]

diagnosis of influenza is suspected but unproven, in patients with an atypical presentation, when a complication is suspected, or when the differential diagnosis is unusually broad (e.g., an immunosuppressed patient with atypical pneumonia).

Consultation for management might be sought with infectious disease specialists for guidance in the use of antiviral agents and the need for antibacterial antibiotics, and with pulmonary or critical care specialists for maintaining oxygenation and obtaining specimens for testing.

Consultation from public health authorities should be sought if avian influenza is suspected. Public health officials can expedite laboratory confirmation of avian influenza, and can guide decisions on antiviral therapy based on available susceptibility data. Also, they are responsible for monitoring disease outbreaks, determining the source, evaluating possible human-to-human transmission, and instituting measures to limit spread of disease. Avian influenza is a nationally reportable disease, and public health considerations justify consultation even in suspected cases.

Treatment... Initiate treatment of influenza with hydration and antipyretics. The antiviral agents oseltamivir and zanamivir given early in the course can reduce duration of illness. Avoid amantadine and rimantadine because of viral resistance to them. Hospitalization and subspecialty consultation should be considered for severe illness, uncertain diagnosis, or complications.

CLINICAL BOTTOM LINE

Practice Improvement

What do professional organizations recommend for preventing and treating influenza?
The recommendations of most professional organizations agree with the CDC's Advisory Committee on Immunization Practices (ACIP) consensus. ACIP includes representatives from the American Academy of Family Physicians, the American Academy of Pediatrics, the American College of Obstetrics and Gynecologists, the American Medical Association, the American College of Physicians, the American Osteopathic Society, the Infectious Disease Society of America, the National Foundation for Infectious Disease, the Society for Healthcare Epidemiology of America, and numerous other organizations.

The ACIP encourages physicians and other health care providers to maximize vaccine coverage among high-risk patients by establishing systems to identify such patients within a practice and to notify and remind them of the need for vaccination. ACIP also recommends vaccination of high-risk persons at routine office visits (or hospital discharge) as soon as vaccine is available so that opportunities are not lost.

In April 2005, the Ambulatory Care Quality Alliance (AQA) released a set of 26 health care quality indicators for clinicians, consumers, and health care purchasers to use in quality improvement efforts, public reporting, and pay-for-performance programs (www.ahrq.gov/qual/aqastart.htm). In May

35. Centers for Medicare and Medicaid Services. Medicare and Medicaid Programs. Condition of participation: immunization standard for long-term care facilities. Final rule. Federal Register. 2005:70:194; 58833-52. [PMID: 16211747]
36. Finch M. Point: mandatory influenza vaccination for all heath care workers? Seven reasons to say "no". Clin Infect Dis. 2006;42:1141-3. [PMID: 16575732]
37. Backer H. Counterpoint: in favor of mandatory influenza vaccine for all healthcare workers. Clin Infect Dis. 2006;42:1144-7. [PMID: 16575733]

38. Talbot T, Bradley S, Cosgrove S, Ruef C, Siegel J, et al. Influenza Vaccination of Healthcare Workers and Vaccine Allocation for Healthcare Workers During Vaccine Shortages. Vanderbilt University Medical Center. Departments of Medicine and Preventive Medicine. Accessed at www.shea-online.org/Assets/files/HCW_Flu_Position_Paper_Final_9-28.pdf. Accessed 7/20/07.

39. Pandemic and Seasonal Influenza Principles for U.S. Action. Alexandria, Virginia: Infectious Diseases Society of America; 2007. Accessed at www.idsociety.org/Content/Navigation-Menu/News_Room1/Pandemic_and_Seasonal_Influenza?IDSA_flufinalAPPROVED1.24.07.pdf. Accessed on 7/20/07.

2005, the Centers for Medicare & Medicaid (CMS) endorsed the development of these indicators. One of the original 26 AQA measures focuses on influenza vaccine: Percentage of patients 50 to 64 years who received an influenza vaccination in the measurement year (September 1 through December).

CMS has started a Physician Quality Reporting Initiative (PQRI) program, through which clinicians can report a designated set of quality measures on claims for services provided during the period from 1 July through 31 December 2007 and earn bonus payments. At this time, however, influenza vaccination has not been included in the list of eligible measures in the PQRI program.

CMS also requires nursing homes to report efforts to vaccinate residents, and promotes standing orders to improve rates (35).

Whether to mandate vaccination for health care workers is a subject of fierce debate (36, 37). The Society for Healthcare Epidemiology of America recommends that hospitals require signatures from health care workers who decline vaccine (38). The Infectious Disease Society of America concurs with these recommendations and, in the event of a pandemic, recommends mandatory vaccination of health care workers (39). The Joint Commission on Accreditation of Health Care Organizations requires that hospitals offer influenza vaccine to employees (1).

in the clinic
Tool Kit

Influenza

www.pier.acponline.org

Influenza module with updated information on current vaccine and treatment and recommendations, designed for rapid access at point of care.

www.annals.intheclinic/tools

Download copies of the Patient Information sheet that appears on the following page for duplication and distribution to your patients.

www.cdc.gov/flu

Current information on vaccine and treatment recommendations, vaccine availability, and influenza activity. Includes information for health professionals and patients.

www.cdc.gov/flu/professionals/vaccination/vax_priority.htm

Guidelines from the CDC for the tiered use of inactivated influenza vaccine in the event of a vaccine shortage.

www.cdc.gov/flu/professionals/diagnosis/labprocedures.htm

Updated summary of CLIA waived tests for rapid diagnosis of influenza.

THINGS PEOPLE SHOULD KNOW ABOUT INFLUENZA

- Influenza (the flu) has some of the same symptoms as a cold but is caused by a different virus.
- Doctors usually can make the diagnosis without special tests, but they may need to do tests to rule out other illnesses.
- Fluids and medicines to bring down fever are helpful, and flu medicines may shorten the time you are sick.
- Older patients, very young children, and persons with other illnesses should get flu shots every fall to keep them from getting the flu. The flu shot does not cause the flu.

Web Sites with Good Information about Influenza

CDC
www.cdc.gov/flu

American Lung Association
www.lungusa.org/site/pp.asp?c=dvLUK9O0E&tb=35426

National Institute of Allergy and Infectious Diseases
www3.niaid.nih.gov/healthscience/healthtopics/Flu/aboutFlu/
DefinitionsOverview.htm

American Thoracic Society
www.thoracic.org/sections/education/patient-education/patient
-education-materials/patient-information-series/what-is-the-flu.html

---

HEALTH TiPS*   Influenza

Influenza (flu) comes in the late fall and winter and causes fever, cough, body aches, tiredness, sore throat, and runny nose. Here is what you can do to keep from getting it or to feel better if you do.

Get a flu shot every fall if you:
- Are over 50 years of age
- Have diabetes, heart or lung disease, or other health problems
- Live with or take care of an older person or someone with health problems

Wash your hands often with soap and water and try not to touch your eyes, nose, or mouth.

Stay away from people who are sick.

If you get sick, stay home from work or school.

Ask Your Doctor about getting a flu shot every year no later than October or November.

Ask Your Doctor if you get sick and don't know if it's the flu or just a cold.

Ask Your Doctor if you need medicine for the flu even if you had a flu shot.

Call Your Doctor if you have the flu and you:
- Have a high fever for more than 3 days
- Are short of breath
- Cannot eat or drink

Other things to ask your doctor about the flu:
- How serious is the flu? Why is it so important to keep from getting it?
- Are there different kinds of flu vaccines? Can I get one without getting a shot?
- Should children and other people I live with get a flu shot?
- Why do people sometimes get sick after getting a flu shot?
- How is the flu different from a cold?
- What can I do for the fever, cough, and aches of the flu?
- Are there special medicines for the flu? What do they do?
- How can I keep from giving the flu to other people?

*HEALTH TiPS are developed by the American College of Physicians Foundation and PIER

Patient Information

Migraine

M igraine headache affects 18% of women and 6% of men. Three quarters of migraine sufferers have moderate-to-severe symptoms that interfere with work, school, and other normal daily activities. Despite being a significant cause of episodic but disabling symptoms, the condition remains underrecognized, underdiagnosed, and undertreated. Migraine pain was previously believed to be largely vascular in cause, but evidence now shows that it involves genetic control of the activity of some brain cells. It is hypothesized that migraine activity begins in the brainstem and ends with distention and inflammation of meningeal vessels. These events cause an instability in brain cells that triggers surges of abnormal impulses to the periphery and releases inflammatory substances. Although migraines can be highly disruptive to daily life, effective behavioral and drug treatments can prevent attacks or relieve symptoms.

Diagnosis

What clinical features are helpful in distinguishing migraine headache from tension headache?
The International Classification of Headache Disorders (ICHD) classifies headache disorders (1), but several simpler diagnostic criteria have been validated against the ICHD. Five important features of migraine are headache that is unilateral, pulsatile, or throbbing; associated with nausea or vomiting; of sufficient intensity to interrupt usual daily activities; and usually lasting 4 to 72 hours if untreated.

Individuals with 3 of the 5 criteria listed above are likely to have migraine; those with 4 of 5 are highly likely to have migraine (2). Other diagnostic criteria perform similarly, including 1 that considers nausea, photophobia, and headache-related disability (any day in the past 3 mo); individuals who have 2 of

these 3 symptoms are highly likely to have migraine (3) (Table 1).

The presence of prodrome or aura distinguishes migraine from other types of headache. Prodrome is the occurrence of euphoria, depression, fatigue, hypomania, food cravings, dizziness, cognitive slowing, or asthenia that occurs up to 24 hours before headache. Aura are neurologic symptoms that occur within 1 hour of or during headache and last a few minutes to 1 hour. Aura includes such symptoms as visual changes, loss of vision, hallucinations, numbness, tingling, weakness, or confusion. Approximately 60% to 70% of patients with migraine report prodrome, and 15% to 20% report aura.

What clinical features suggest that the cause of headache may be more serious than migraine?

Other primary causes of headache include tension-type headache, as well as medication-overuse headache and cluster headache. Although they can be disabling, primary headache conditions are generally benign. However, clinicians should exclude secondary causes of headache.

Serious secondary causes of headache include stroke, tumor, arteritis, meningitis, acute glaucoma, and subarachnoid hemorrhage.

"POUND" (as in "a pounding headache") is one way to remember symptoms consistent with migraine headache:

Pulsatile quality of headache described
One-day duration (duration < 4 hours suggests tension-type headache)
Unilateral location
Nausea or vomiting
Disabling intensity.

1. Headache Classification Subcommittee of the International Headache Society. The International Classification of Headache Disorders: 2nd edition. Cephalalgia. 2004;24 Suppl 1:9-160. [PMID: 14979299]
2. Michel P, Dartigues JF, Henry P, et al. Validity of the International Headache Society criteria for migraine. GRIM. Groupe de Recherche Interdisciplinaire sur la Migraine. Neuroepidemiology. 1993;12:51-7. [PMID: 8327023]
3. ID Migraine validation study. A self-administered screener for migraine in primary care: The ID Migraine validation study. Neurology. 2003;61:375-82. [PMID: 12913201]

Table 1. Elements of Patient History for Clinical Diagnosis of Migraine versus Tension-Type Headache

Clinical Feature	Sensitivity, %	Specificity, %	Positive Likelihood Ratio	Negative Likelihood Ratio
Nausea or vomiting	42–60	81–93	6.0	0.62
Duration 4–72 h	74	53	1.6	0.49
Pounding or throbbing character	64–87	22–83	3.8	0.43
Unilateral head pain	65–75	60–85	4.3	0.41
Disabling for usual activities	59–87	52–76	2.5	0.54
Presence of ≥4 of the symptoms above	29	100	23.0	0.71
Presence of ≥3 of the symptoms above	80	94	13.0	0.21
Presence of ≥2 of the following 3 symptoms: nausea, photophobia, and headache-related disability (any day in the previous 3 mo)	81	75	3.25	0.25

Several historical and physical examination findings are predictive of such secondary causes (See Box). "Red flag" historical findings include changes in the intensity, frequency, or pattern of headaches; blurred vision; dizziness or lack of coordination; sudden, explosive onset of headache with rapid progression; or headache pain aggravated by coughing or movement. Red flag physical findings include fever and scalp nodules or lesions.

Patients may suffer from more than 1 type of headache, have headaches that cannot be easily described or classified, or have had a change in headache pattern over time. The history should include questions about the onset and frequency of the headache disorder; the duration of attacks; pain location, severity, and quality; precipitating and ameliorating factors; and family history. Table 2 presents the differential diagnosis of headache.

What is the role of physical examination in patients who present with migraine?

The physical examination should evaluate for features that suggest a secondary headache, such as fever, meningeal or other signs of infection, neurologic abnormalities, changes in visual acuity, increased intraocular pressure, elevated blood pressure, and mental status changes.

What is the role of diagnostic testing, including imaging studies and electroencephalography, in patients with suspected migraine?

Neuroimaging, such as magnetic resonance imaging (MRI) or computed tomography, is not usually warranted for patients with migraine symptoms and a normal

---

"Red Flag" or Alarm Features That Suggest Headache Is Due to Nonbenign, Secondary Causes

- Changes in headache pattern, frequency, or intensity
- Daily headache
- Blurred vision
- Dizziness, syncope, discoordination, or focal neurologic abnormality
- Sudden, explosive onset
- Pain worse with coughing or movement
- Change in personality or mental status
- Headache awakens person from sleep
- Onset after 50 years of age
- Fever
- Meningeal signs
- Diastolic blood pressure >120 mm Hg
- Diminished pulse or tenderness of temporal artery
- Papilledema
- Necrotic or tender scalp lesions
- Increased intraocular pressure

Table 2. Differential Diagnosis of Headache*

Disease	Characteristics
Tension-type headache	Common; duration 30 min–7 d; typically bilateral, nonpulsating pressing quality; mild to moderate in intensity without prohibiting activity; no nausea or vomiting (anorexia may occur)
Cluster headache	Uncommon; sudden onset; duration, minutes to hours; repeat over a course of weeks, then disappear for months or years; often unilateral tearing and nasal congestion; pain is severe, unilateral, and periorbital; more common in men
Frontal sinusitis	Usually worse when lying down; associated with nasal congestion; tenderness over affected sinus
Cervical spondylosis	Worse with neck movement; posterior distribution; pain is neuralgic and sometimes referred to vertex or forehead; more common in elderly patients
Greater occipital neuralgia	Occipital location; tenderness at base of skull; pain is neuralgic in character and sometimes referred to vertex or forehead; more common in elderly patients
Postconcussion syndrome	History of antecedent head trauma; vertigo (often positional), lightheadedness, or giddiness; poor concentration and memory; lack of energy; irritability and anxiety
Trigeminal neuralgia	Brief episodes of sharp, stabbing pain with trigeminal nerve distribution
TMJ dysfunction	Pain generally involves the TMJ and temporal areas and is associated with symptoms when chewing
Medication-induced headache	Chronic headache with few features of migraine; tends to occur daily; HRT and hormonal contraceptives are frequent culprits
Subarachnoid hemorrhage	Explosive onset of severe headache; 10% preceded by "sentinel" headaches
Acute or chronic subdural hematoma	History of antecedent trauma; may have subacute onset; altered level of consciousness or neurologic deficit may be present
Meningitis	Fever; meningeal signs
Encephalitis	Associated with neurologic abnormalities, confusion, altered mental state, or change in level of consciousness
Intracranial neoplasms	Worse on awakening; generally progressive; aggravated by coughing, straining, or changing position
Benign intracranial hypertension (pseudotumor cerebri)	Often abrupt onset; associated with nausea, vomiting, dizziness, blurred vision, and papilledema; may have CN VI palsy; headache aggravated by coughing, straining, or changing position
Temporal arteritis	Occurs almost exclusively in patients aged over 50; associated with tenderness of scalp or temporal artery, and jaw claudication; visual changes
Acute severe hypertension	Marked BP elevation (systolic ≥210 mm Hg or diastolic ≥120 mm Hg); may have symptoms of encephalopathy (e.g., confusion, irritability)
CO poisoning	May be insidious or associated with dyspnea; occurs more commonly in the colder months
Acute glaucoma	Associated with blurred vision, nausea, vomiting, and seeing halos around lights; ophthalmologic emergency
Carotid dissection	Cause of stroke; can be spontaneous or following minor trauma or sudden neck movement; unilateral headache or face pain; ipsilateral Horner syndrome; ophthalmologic emergency

*BP = blood pressure; CN VI = cranial nerve VI; CO = carbon monoxide; HRT = hormone replacement therapy; TMJ = temporomandibular joint.

4. Frishberg BM. The utility of neuroimaging in the evaluation of headache in patients with normal neurologic examinations. Neurology. 1994;44:1191-7. [PMID: 8035914]

5. Detsky ME, McDonald DR, Barelocher-MO, et al. Does thsi patients with a headache have migarine or need neuroimaging?JAMA. 2006;296:1274-83. [PMID: 16968852]

6. Huston KA, Hunder GG, Lie JT, et al. Temporal arteritis: a 25-year epidemiologic, clinical, and pathologic study. Ann Intern Med. 978;88:162-7. [PMID: 626444]

neurologic examination. A meta-analysis of studies of patients with migraine and a normal neurologic examination found a 0.18% rate of significant intracranial lesions (4). Clinicians should apply a lower threshold for obtaining neuro-imaging for patients with atypical headache features, substantial change in headache pattern, or symptoms or signs of neurologic abnormalities (5). For instance, MRI is indicated in patients with a long history of migraine headache who develop substantial changes in headache pattern or in any patient with headache and focal neurologic signs or symptoms.

In patients with new onset headache after 50 years of age, it is important to obtain an erythrocyte sedimentation rate (ESR) to evaluate for secondary causes of headache, particularly temporal arteritis or other vasculitides, even if symptoms are consistent with migraine. An elevated ESR (>30 mm/h) suggests temporal arteritis but lacks specificity, making a temporal artery biopsy necessary in patients in whom temporal arteritis is suspected. Headache is the predominant symptom in 65% to 80% of patients with temporal arteritis (6), and the combination of new-onset headache, jaw claudication, and abnormal (nodular or tender) arteries is highly predictive of temporal arteritis (7).

Electroencephalography (EEG) is not routinely used in evaluation of headache, and should be considered only if associated symptoms suggest a seizure disorder, such as atypical migrainous aura or episodic loss of consciousness. A systematic review found no increased prevalence of EEG abnormalities in patients with headache, no useful headache subgroups defined by EEG, and no ability of EEG to identify patients whose headaches have a structural cause (8).

Diagnosis... In patients with normal neurologic examination, evaluation of symptoms distinguishes migraine from tension or other types of headache. Migraines are typically pulsatile, are unilateral, last 4 to 72 hours, are associated with nausea or vomiting, and make it necessary for patients to alter their usual activities. Neuroimaging is not usually warranted for patients with normal neurologic examination, and EEG has not been shown to be useful. Clinicians should ask patients about features that suggest serious secondary causes of headache and conduct appropriate evaluation for these causes.

CLINICAL BOTTOM LINE

Treatment

What is the role of diet in the management of patients with migraine?

Dietary triggers for migraine are idiosyncratic and can be difficult to identify. However, some foods are known to be associated with migraines (see Box). About 20% of patients with migraine report dietary triggers (9, 10). Clinicians should encourage patients to identify and avoid dietary factors that may contribute to headaches. There is also some controversy over the role of aspartame in triggering migraine.

Researchers at the Montefiore Medical Center Headache Unit questioned 190 consecutive patients about the effect of alcohol, carbohydrates, and aspartame in triggering their headaches. Of the 171 patients who completed the survey, 49.7% reported alcohol as a precipitating factor, 8.2% reported aspartame, and 2.3% reported carbohydrates. Patients with

migraine were significantly more likely to report alcohol as a triggering factor and reported aspartame as a precipitant 3 times more often than those having other types of headache (11).

There is some evidence of a causal relationship between food and migraine through elimination diets, reintroduction, and double-blind rechallenge (12-14). In these studies, elimination diets decreased symptoms substantially in some individuals. The findings suggested that greater efforts are needed to educate patients about the possible benefits of adjusting diet to decrease headache frequency.

An investigation of the awareness and impact of dietary risk factors on patients with chronic headache found that three quarters of the 130 participants were aware of the possible link between certain foods and headache, although most did not

---

Common Dietary Triggers for Migraine

- Caffeine withdrawal
- Nitrates and nitrites in preserved meats
- Phenylethylamines, tyramines, xanthines in aged cheeses, red wine, beer, champagne, chocolate
- Monosodium glutamate in some Asian and prepared foods
- Dairy products
- Fatty foods

---

7. Rodriguez-Valverde V, Sarabia JM, et al. Risk factors and predictive models of giant cell arteritis in polymyalgia rheumatica. Am J Med. 1997;102:331-6. [PMID: 9217613]

8. Gronseth GS, Greenberg MK. The utility of the electroencephalogram in the evaluation of patients presenting with headache: a review of the literature. Neurology. 1995;45:1263-7. [PMID: 7617180]

9. Peatfield RC. Relationships between food, wine, and beer-precipitated migrainous headaches. Headache. 1995;35:355-7. [PMID: 7635722]

10. Van den Bergh V, Amery WK, Waelkens J. Trigger factors in migraine: a study conducted by the Belgian Migraine Society. Headache. 1987;27:191-6. [PMID: 3597073]

11. Lipton RB, Newman LC, Cohen JS, Solomon S. Aspartame as a dietary trigger of headache. Headache. 1989;29:90-2. [PMID: 2708042]

12. Egger J, Carter CM, Wilson J, et al. Is migraine food allergy? A double-blind controlled trial of oligoantigenic diet treatment. Lancet. 1983;2:865-9. [PMID: 6137694]

13. Mansfield LE, Vaughan TR, Waller SF, Haverly RW, Ting S. Food allergy and adult migraine: double-blind and mediator confirmation of an allergic etiology. Ann Allergy. 1985;55:126-9. [PMID: 4025956]

14. Kueper T, Martinelli D, Konetzki W, et al. Identification of problem foods using food and symptom diaries. Otolaryngol Head Neck Surg. 1995;112:415-20. [PMID: 7870442]

report hearing about this from their doctor. Notably, knowledge of the possible link did not prompt changes in food consumption practices (15).

Is behavioral therapy effective in the management of migraine?
Behavioral approaches provide headache relief for some patients with migraine. Randomized, controlled trials (RCTs) have shown that relaxation training, thermal biofeedback with relaxation training, electromyogram (EMG) biofeedback, and cognitive behavioral therapy reduce migraine frequency by 30% to 50%. These data suggest that behavioral therapies can be as effective as many pharmacologic treatments.

A meta-analysis that included 25 clinical trials involving propranolol and 35 clinical trials involving relaxation or biofeedback training showed substantial and similar 43% reductions in migraine activity following both propranolol and relaxation or biofeedback training, compared with 14% reduction from placebo and no reduction in untreated patients (16).

Data are lacking to guide selection of a specific type of behavioral therapy for specific patients. A review of randomized and quasi-randomized controlled trials comparing noninvasive physical treatments for chronic or recurrent headaches to a control found that although some noninvasive physical treatments seem to prevent chronic or recurrent headaches with little risk for adverse effects, determining the clinical effectiveness and cost-effectiveness of noninvasive physical treatments requires further research (17).

Behavioral approaches are particularly recommended for patients who prefer nondrug interventions, who tolerate drugs poorly, who have medical contraindications to drug therapy, or who have insufficient response to specific drug treatments. Behavioral therapies are also good options for patients who are pregnant, nursing, or planning to become pregnant. Patients under

significant stress or who have deficient stress-coping skills may derive benefit from nonpharmacologic interventions. Restful sleep decreases irritability in the brain and therefore may decrease the frequency and severity of migraine. However, clinicians should be aware that not all nonpharmacologic treatments are clearly beneficial. Acupuncture, spinal manipulation, and hypnosis have not been shown to be effective in relieving migraine (17,18).

When should migraine drug therapy be administered?
Treatment of migraine should begin as early as possible during the episode to increase the chances of headache relief and minimize the total amount of medication needed. Regardless of the form of migraine-specific medication used, the headache phase being treated determines the level of efficacy achieved. Treatment during prodrome or aura or within the first hour of headache is significantly more effective than treatment during later stages. Treatment efficacy decreases after headache has been present for more than 2 hours. This time-dependent nature of efficacy may be a result of central (within the brain) sensitization during migraine, which causes hypersensitivity to environmental stimuli, such as light, sound, smells, and touch (19). Once central sensitization begins, migraine treatment becomes less effective and repeated doses may be necessary to relieve symptoms.

Which drugs are indicated for patients with mild-to-moderate migraine?
When symptoms are not severe and there is no vomiting, mild over-the-counter analgesics are effective, less expensive, and less likely to cause adverse effects than migraine-specific drugs. Nonspecific therapy with acetaminophen or other nonsteroidal anti-inflammatory drugs (NSAIDs), aspirin, or combination analgesics (e.g., aspirin plus acetaminophen plus caffeine) should be

15. Guarnieri P, Radnitz CL, Blanchard EB. Assessment of dietary risk factors in chronic headache. Biofeedback Self Regul. 1990;15:15-25. [PMID: 2361144]
16. Holroyd KA, Penzien DB. Pharmacological versus non-pharmacological prophylaxis of recurrent migraine headache: a meta-analytic review of clinical trials. Pain. 1990;42:1-13. [PMID: 2146583]
17. Bronfort G, Nilsson N, Haas M, et al. Non-invasive physical treatments for chronic/recurrent headache. Cochrane Database Syst Rev. 2004; CD001878. [PMID: 15266458]
18. Goslin RE, Gray RN, McCrory DC, et al. Behavioral and physical treatments for migraine headache. Technical review 2.2. Agency for Health Care Policy and Research; 1999. AHCPR no. 290-94-2025.
19. Burstein R, Cutrer MF, Yarnitsky D. The development of cutaneous allodynia during a migraine attack clinical evidence for the sequential recruitment of spinal and supraspinal nociceptive neurons in migraine. Brain. 2000;123 (Pt 8):1703-9. [PMID: 10908199]
20. Lipton RB, Baggish JS, Stewart WF, et al. Efficacy and safety of acetaminophen in the treatment of migraine: results of a randomized, double-blind, placebo-controlled, population-based study. Arch Intern Med. 2000;160:3486-92. [PMID: 11112243]

used in patients with mild-to-moderate headache without severe nausea or vomiting. Table 3 provides information on drug therapy for acute migraine symptoms.

A randomized, double-blind, placebo-controlled study compared oral acetaminophen 1000 mg with placebo in the treatment of a single acute migraine episode . The headache response rate 2 hours after dosing was 57.8% in the acetaminophen group compared with 38.7% in the placebo group (P = 0.002). Pain-free rates at 2 hours were 22.4% in the acetaminophen group and 11.3% in the placebo group (P = 0.01) (20).

A randomized trial evaluated the efficacy of a single 1000-mg dose of aspirin in 4 09 persons for the treatment of acute moderate-to-severe migraine, with or without aura. The 2-hour headache response rate was 52% with aspirin versus 34% with placebo (P < 0.001), and significantly more participants were pain-free from the 1-hour evaluation through the 6-hour evaluation (21).

In a study that examined the benefits of acetaminophen, aspirin, and caffeine in the treatment of severe, disabling migraine attacks, there was significant improvement in functional disability, photophobia, and phonophobia with the combined analgesic compared with placebo from 2 to 6 hours after dosing (22).

Which drugs are indicated for patients with severe migraine?

Migraine-specific agents (triptans, dihydroergotamine, and ergotamines) are advised for patients with severe migraine or headaches that respond poorly to acetaminophen, NSAIDs, or over-the-counter combination analgesics (Table 3). Evidence suggests that initial selection of a migraine-specific drug leads to better outcomes than a stepped-care approach for severe symptoms (23).

Triptans

When using migraine-specific therapy, clinicians should consider triptans first because they are more effective and cause less nausea in most patients. However, triptans are contraindicated in persons with a history of coronary disease because they are associated with a low but real risk for cardiac side effects. The high cost of triptans may deter their use as first-line therapy in some patients. Triptans may be administered orally, intranasally, or by injection. Administration by injection or nasal spray may be preferred by patients who desire rapid relief, are nauseated, or develop headache rapidly. However, triptan administration by injection is associated with more side effects, including chest discomfort, nausea, dizziness, somnolence, tingling, numbness, and flushing.

One systematic review evaluated 30 studies on the effects of 6 mg subcutaneous, 100 mg oral, and 20 mg intranasal sumatriptan for treating migraine attacks. The review found that subcutaneous sumatriptan was the most efficacious and the fastest-acting form of administration. However, there were more adverse events with subcutaneous sumatriptan than with oral sumatriptan (data were limited on adverse events for intranasal sumatriptan). Intranasal sumatriptan had the same efficacy as oral sumatriptan and a quicker onset of action, but the difference in therapeutic effect was limited to the first 30 minutes after administration (24).

A systematic review of the data from 53 double-blind RCTs of oral triptans in migraine involving 24 089 patients showed that all oral triptans were effective and well tolerated. The investigators found that 10 mg rizatriptan, 80 mg eletriptan, and 12.5 mg almotriptan were most likely to be consistently successful for treating migraine (25).

Another systematic review evaluated the effects of various migraine treatments in 54 trials with 79 placebo comparisons and found that headache relief at 2 hours was best for subcutaneous sumatriptan 6 mg and that sustained relief over 24 hours was best for eletriptan 80 mg. Most migraine interventions were effective in relieving headache pain (26).

Triptans with both long (e.g., frovatriptan)and short (e.g., sumatriptan) half-lives are available. Those with a short half-life generally have a more rapid action

21. Lipton RB, Goldstein J, Baggish JS, et al. Aspirin is efficacious for the treatment of acute migraine. Headache. 2005;45:283-92. [PMID: 15836564]
22. Goldstein J, Hoffman HD, Armellino JJ, et al. Treatment of severe, disabling migraine attacks in an over-the-counter population of migraine sufferers: results from three randomized, placebo-controlled studies of the combination of acetaminophen, aspirin, and caffeine. Cephalalgia. 1999;19:684-91. [PMID: 10524663]
23. Disability in Strategies of Care Study group. Stratified care vs step care strategies for migraine: the Disability in Strategies of Care (DISC) Study: A randomized trial. JAMA. 2000;284:2599-605. [PMID: 11086366]
24. Tfelt-Hansen P. Efficacy and adverse events of subcutaneous, oral, and intranasal sumatriptan used for migraine treatment: a systematic review based on number needed to treat. Cephalalgia. 1998;18:532-8. [PMID: 9827244]
25. Ferrari MD, Roon KI, Lipton RB, et al. Oral triptans (serotonin 5-HT(1B/1D) agonists) in acute migraine treatment: a meta-analysis of 53 trials. Lancet. 2001;358:1668-75. [PMID: 11728541]
26. Oldman AD, Smith LA, McQuay HJ, et al. Pharmacological treatments for acute migraine: quantitative systematic review. Pain. 2002;97:247-57. [PMID: 12044621]

Table 3. Short-Term Drug Treatment for Migraine*

Agent (Route)	Mechanism of Action	Dosage	Notes
Migraine-specific			
Sumatriptan (subcutaneous)	Selective serotonin (5-HT1B/1D) agonist	6 mg at onset (may repeat after 1 h; maximum 12 mg/d)	Rapid onset of action; little sedation; treatment of choice for moderate-severe attacks; not effective if given during aura; contraindicated in patients with CAD, uncontrolled hypertension, or patients with strictly basilar or hemiplegic migraine; pregnancy category C
Sumatriptan (oral)	Selective serotonin (5-HT1B/1D) agonist	25–100 mg at onset (may repeat after 2 h; maximum 200 mg/d)	Well tolerated; little sedation; less rapid onset; may be used again for recurrent headache; no evidence of teratogenicity
Sumatriptan (nasal)	Selective serotonin (5-HT1B/1D) agonist	20 mg at onset (may repeat after 2 h; maximum 40 mg/d)	Well tolerated; little sedation; speed of action and effectiveness similar to oral sumatriptan; useful when non-oral route of administration needed; no evidence of teratogenicity
Almotriptan (oral)	Selective serotonin (5-HT1B/1D) agonist	6.25–12.5 mg at onset maximum 25 mg/d)	Similar efficacy to oral sumatriptan
Eletriptan (oral)	Selective serotonin (5-HT1B/1D) agonist	20–40 mg at onset (may repeat after 2 h; maximum 80 mg/d)	Highly effective oral triptan; rapid onset of action; slightly higher efficacy compared with oral sumatriptan
Frovatriptan (oral)	Selective serotonin (5-HT1B/1D) agonist	2.5 mg at onset (may repeat after 2 h; maximum 7.5 mg/d)	Well tolerated; little sedation; effective for prevention of menstrual migraine
Naratriptan (oral)	Selective serotonin (5-HT1B/1D) agonist	1.0–2.5 mg at onset (may repeat after 4 h; maximum 5 mg/d)	Possibly lower risk for headache recurrence than other oral triptans; relatively lower efficacy and incidence of side effects than other triptans
Rizatriptan (oral)	Selective serotonin (5-HT1B/1D) agonist	5–10 mg at onset (may repeat after 2 h; maximum 30 mg/d)	Available in a fast-melt preparation, which may be no faster in providing pain relief than the regular tablet; slightly higher efficacy compared with oral sumatriptan
Zolmitriptan (oral)	Selective serotonin (5-HT1B/1D) agonist	1.25–2.5 mg at onset (may repeat after 2 h; maximum 10 mg/d)	Similar efficacy to oral sumatriptan; also available in a rapidly dispersing tablet formulation
Dihydroergotamine (nasal)	Nonselective serotonin agonist	1 spray (0.5 mg) into each nostril (may repeat after 15 min; maximum 4 sprays/d, 8/wk)	No sedation; should not be used with a 5-HT1B/1D; pregnancy category X
Dihydroergotamine (all other routes)	Nonselective serotonin agonist	1 mg SC/IM/IV (may repeat after 1 h; maximum 2 mg/dose, 3 mg/attack, 6 mg/wk)	Useful in status migrainosus; contraindicated in patients with CAD; pregnancy category X
Nonspecific (good evidence for effectiveness)			
Naproxen and other NSAIDs (oral)	Inhibits cyclo-oxygenase, decreases prostaglandin synthesis	500 mg at onset (may repeat after 6–8 h)	Well tolerated; treatment of choice for mild-to-moderate attacks; may be given with antiemetic; avoid in pregnancy after 32-wk gestation; pregnancy category B
Aspirin/metoclopramide (oral)	Blocks dopamine receptors in CTZ; increases response to acetylcholine in upper GI tract	650 mg/10 mg at onset (may repeat after 3–4 h)	Antinausea effect; elderly are more likely to develop dystonic reactions than are younger adults; use lowest recommended doses initially; pregnancy category C (D in third trimester)
Butorphanol (nasal)	Opiate agonist-antagonist	1 spray in 1 nostril (may repeat after 1 h)	Well-tolerated rescue medication; risk for opiate dependence; pregnancy category C
Metoclopramide/ diphenhydramine (intravenous)	Blocks dopamine receptors in CTZ	20–25 mg over 20 min (may repeat after 1 h)	Antinausea effect; recent RCT showed equal effectiveness to sumatriptan; pregnancy category C
Nonspecific (moderate evidence for effectiveness)			
Acetaminophen (oral)	Analgesic; mechanism unknown	650–1000 mg at onset (may repeat after 4–6 h; maximum 4 g/d)	Well tolerated; little sedation; no stomach irritation; pregnancy category B
Codeine combinations: acetaminophen/codeine (oral)	Opiate agonist	Acetaminophen 300 mg/ codeine 30 mg; dosage based on codeine 1–2 tablets (30–60 mg codeine) every 4–6 h	High potential for drug-induced or "rebound" headache; risk for opiate dependence; pregnancy category C (D if prolonged or at term)

Table 3. Short–Term Drug Treatment for Migraine (continued)

Agent (Route)	Mechanism of Action	Dosage	Notes
Chlorpromazine or other phenothiazine, prochlorperazine	Selective dopamine antagonist (D$_2$)	Chlorpromazine 25 mg IM/IV (may repeat after 30 min); prochlorperazine 10 mg IM/IV or 25 mg rectally (may repeat)	Antinausea effect; rescue therapy in supervised setting; pregnancy category C
Lidocaine, 4% topical solution	Anesthetic	1–4 drops in nostril ipsilateral to head pain (may repeat after 2 min)	Rapid onset of action; uncertain effectiveness over 2–4 h
Isometheptene-containing compound (acetaminophen/ dichloral-phenazone/ isomethetene) (oral)	Weak sedative	2 capsules (2 x 325 mg/ 100 mg/65 mg) at onset (may repeat 1 capsule after 1 h; maximum 5 capsules every 12 h)	Well tolerated, but limited effectiveness; pregnancy category C
Conflicting or inconsistent evidence of effectiveness			
Ergotamine/caffeine combination tablet, ergotamine/caffeine combination suppository, ergotamine tartrate tablet	Nonselective serotonin agonist	1–2 tablets (1 mg/100 mg) orally (may repeat after 1 h); 1 suppository (2 mg/100 mg) rectally (may repeat after 1 h); 1 tablet (2 mg) sublingual (may repeat after 30 min; maximum 6 mg/d, 10 mg/wk based on ergotamine)	No sedation; contraindicated in patients with CAD or pregnancy; relatively weak evidence for effectiveness; should not be used with 5-HT1B/1D agonists, protease inhibitors, or macrolide antibiotics; a European consensus conference recommended ergotamine as the drug of choice in a limited number of persons with migraine who have infrequent or long-duration headaches; pregnancy category X
Dexamethasone or other corticosteroids (IV)	Multiple glucocorticoid and mineralocorticoid effects	6 mg	Rescue therapy for status migrainosus; relatively little evidence for effectiveness; pregnancy category C

*5-HT = 5-hydroxytryptamine; CAD = coronary artery disease; CTZ = chemoreceptor trigger zone; GI = gastrointestinal; IM = intramuscular; IV = intravenous; NSAIDs = nonsteroidal anti-inflammatory drugs; RCT = randomized, controlled trial; SC = subcutaneous.

but also have more side effects than long half-life agents, but these findings may not apply in all patients because of idiosyncratic differences among individuals. Triptans with a long half-life also may be beneficial in prophylaxis of migraine when administered during prodrome or before onset of predictable headaches, such as menstrual migraines.

Generally, the following factors should guide selection of triptans: Triptans do not have a class effect, so lack of efficacy or side effects associated with 1 triptan agent is not predictive of a patient's response to other triptans. Also, once a patient has been successfully treated with a particular triptan, recurrence of headache may indicate the need for a repeated dose, not treatment failure. Patients taking triptans should note the following factors: the stage of migraine at which medication was begun,

efficacy, side effects, and whether migraine returns. Treatment with an alternate triptan is indicated in patients who take medication during an early migraine phase but have inconsistent relief or side effects that preclude early use of that medication in the future.

Dihydroergotamine
Dihydroergotamine is the alternative to triptans for migraine-specific treatment (27, 28). Dihydroergotamine may be administered via nasal spray or injection. Intravenous dihydroergotamine is the preferred treatment for patients with status migrainosus. With training, patients may self-administer this agent via intramuscular or subcutaneous injection. As with triptans, administration of dihydroergotamine via injection is more effective than other methods but may be associated with more side effects, specifically nausea and restlessness. Compared with administration via injection, nasal

27. Winner P, Ricalde O, Le Force B, et al. A double-blind study of subcutaneous dihydroergotamine vs subcutaneous sumatriptan in the treatment of acute migraine. Arch Neurol. 1996;53:180-4. [PMID: 8639069]
28. Colman I, Brown MD, Innes GD, et al. Parenteral dihydroergotamine for acute migraine headache: a systematic review of the literature. Ann Emerg Med. 2005;45:393-401. [PMID: 15795718]
29. Bigal ME, Lipton RB, Krymchantowski AV. The medical management of migraine. Am J Ther. 2004;11:130-40. [PMID: 14999365]

dihydroergotamine has fewer side effects and an efficacy profile similar to many oral triptans (29).

Ergotamines

The effectiveness of ergotamine is less certain than for the other migraine-specific drugs (26, 30).

What therapies should clinicians consider in addition to analgesics and migraine-specific therapies?

Antiemetic agents, such as metoclopromide, may be helpful in treating the nausea and vomiting associated with migraine. In patients with mild-to-moderate nausea, using an oral or rectal antiemetic drug enables patients to take oral analgesics for migraine pain relief. Patients with severe nausea or vomiting may require a nonoral route of administration for antiemetics and migraine-specific drugs. Intravenous metoclopramide is effective for relief of both pain and nausea and thus may be considered for monotherapy (31).

What is the appropriate treatment strategy for patients who do not respond to their usual first-line migraine drugs?

Systematic reviews of controlled clinical trials have found that rescue agents are effective for reducing headache severity when acute therapy is ineffective (32). Patients should have a rescue medication and a plan for use in the event of a debilitating migraine that fails to respond to initial treatment.

Rescue medications are intended for infrequent use when a patient with migraine has no relief within 1 hour from initial acute treatment. Opiate analgesics are typically prescribed for this purpose. These agents should not be used more than a few times per year. Their use for migraine treatment is somewhat controversial because of the potential for dependence, diversion, or abuse.

Frequent use of migraine drug treatments may lead to a medication-overuse headache, a pattern of increasing headache frequency that often results in daily headaches. Some research has suggested that about one half of recurrent headache sufferers do not adhere properly to drug treatment regimens, with as many as two thirds of patients failing to make optimal use of abortive medications. A written plan can help the patient to use rescue medications properly.

When should clinicians consider preventive therapy for patients with migraine, and which drugs are useful in migraine prevention?

Taking a daily preventive medication typically reduces headache frequency by one third to one half. Preventive drug treatment may be called for in persons with frequent disabling headaches (usually at least 2/mo) or poor relief from appropriately used short-term treatments, or in those with uncommon migraine, such as basilar or hemiplegic migraine. Other appropriate candidates for preventive medications are those with a contraindication to acute therapy, failure or overuse of acute therapy, adverse effects from acute therapy, or a preference for preventive therapy.

Good symptomatic control of individual attacks, however, may make preventive medication unnecessary. Before starting preventive therapy, clinicians should ask the patient to keep a headache diary for 1 month, and they should also consider the presence of coexisting conditions and the drug's adverse effect profile. Efficacy may not be immediately clear, so patients should use a particular drug therapy for at least 2 months before declaring it to be ineffective.

Preventive drug therapies for migraine are listed in Table 4. The strength of evidence is greatest for

30. Tfelt-Hansen P, Saxena PR, Dahlöf C, et al. Ergotamine in the acute treatment of migraine: a review and European consensus. Brain. 2000;123 (Pt 1):9-18. [PMID: 10611116]
31. Colman I, Brown MD, Innes GD, et al. Parenteral metoclopramide for acute migraine: meta-analysis of randomised controlled trials. BMJ. 2004;329:1369-73. [PMID: 15550401]
35. Gray RN, McCrory DC, Eberlein K, et al. Self-administered drug treatments for acute migraine headache. Technical review 2.4. Agency for Health Care Policy and Research; 1999. ACHPR no. 290-94-2025.
32. Holroyd KA, Cordingley GE, Pingel JD, et al. Enhancing the effectiveness of abortive therapy: a controlled evaluation of self-management training. Headache. 1989;29:148-53. [PMID: 2496052]
33. Holroyd KA, Penzien DB, Cordingley GE. Propranolol in the management of recurrent migraine: a meta-analytic review. Headache. 1991;31:333-40. [PMID: 1830566]
34. Linde K, Rossnagel K. Propranolol for migraine prophylaxis. Cochrane Database Syst Rev. 2004:CD003225. [PMID: 15106196]
35. Chronicle E, Mulleners W. Anticonvulsant drugs for migraine prophylaxis. Cochrane Database Syst Rev. 2004:CD003226. [PMID: 15266476]

Table 4. Preventive Drug Treatment for Migraine*

Agent	Mechanism of Action	Dosage	Side Effects
Medium-to-High Efficacy, Good Strength of Evidence, and Mild-to-Moderate Side Effects			
Amitriptyline	SSRI; also inhibits norepinephrine	Amitriptyline, 30–150 mg PO qd	Anticholinergic effects, dry mouth, drowsiness; weight gain
Divalproex sodium, other anticonvulsants (e.g., sodium valproate, gabapentin, topiramate)	Unknown	Divalproex sodium, 250–500 mg PO bid	Bone marrow suppression, liver inflammation, alopecia, tremors, weight loss with topiramate
Propranolol, other non-ISA ß-adrenergic antagonists (e.g., timolol, atenolol, metoprolol, nadolol)	ß-adrenergic antagonists	Propranolol, 120–240 mg PO qd in divided doses	Fatigue, bradycardia, hypotension (check blood pressure and heart rate before prescribing)
Lower Efficacy than above or Limited Strength of Evidence and Mild-to-Moderate Side Effects			
Fluoxetine	SSRI	20–40 mg PO qd	Insomnia, anxiety
Verapamil, other calcium-channel blockers (e.g., nimodipine)	Vasodilator	Verapamil, 80–120 mg PO tid	Constipation, hypotension
Naproxen, other long-acting NSAIDs (e.g., naproxen sodium, ketoprofen)	Inhibits cyclo-oxygenase, reduces prostaglandin synthesis	Naproxen, 250–500 mg PO bid	Stomach irritation
Feverfew	Inhibitory effects on platelet aggregation, release of serotonin, and prostaglandin synthesis	Powdered or granulated feverfew leaves, 50–143 mg PO qd	"Post-feverfew syndrome" (i.e., rebound of migraine symptoms, anxiety, insomnia, and muscle and joint stiffness)
High-dose riboflavin (vitamin B$_2$)	Unknown, but presumably related to its necessity for conversion of tryptophan to niacin	400 mg PO qd	
Magnesium	Unknown, but presumably relates to calcium-antagonist properties	Magnesium oxide, 400 mg PO qd; Magnesium gluconate 1500 mg PO tid	Infrequent adverse effects
ACE inhibitors (e.g., lisinopril) and angiotensin II receptor blockers (e.g., candesartan)	Unknown, but presumably through reduced effect of angiotensin II	Lisinopril, 20 mg PO qd; Candesartan, 16 mg PO qd	Angioedema, hyperkalemia, hypotension, cough (ACE inhibitors only)
Medium-to-High Efficacy, Good Strength of Evidence, but with Side-Effect Concerns			
Methysergide	Selective serotonin agonist (5-HT2); constricts cranial and peripheral blood vessels	4–8 mg PO qd	Retroperitoneal fibrosis, pulmonary fibrosis, nausea, vomiting

*5-HT = 5-hydroxytryptamine; ACE = angiotensin-converting enzyme; bid = twice daily; ISA = intrinsic sympathomimetic activity; NSAIDs = nonsteroidal anti-inflammatory drugs; PO = oral; qd = once daily; RCT = randomized, controlled trial; SSRI = selective serotonin reuptake inhibitor; tid = three times daily.

ß-blockers without intrinsic sympathomimetic activity (33, 34), followed by anticonvulsants (35), antidepressants, and calcium antagonists (36). Of note, valproate is the only anticonvulsant with U.S. Food and Drug Administration approval for migraine prevention. Perimenstrual preventive therapy with a triptan may be helpful for patients with migraines associated with menstruation (37). When preventive therapy is appropriate, it should be started at a low dose and slowly increased over 1 to 2 months to minimize adverse effects. Once a therapeutic dose is achieved, the treatment should be continued for at least 2 months to assess benefit. If headaches are

36. Gray RN, Goslin RE, McCrory DC, et al. Drug treatments for the prevention of migraine headache. Technical review 2.3. Agency for Health Care Policy and Research; 1999. ACHPR no. 290-94-2025.
37. Silberstein SD, Elkind AH, Schreiber C, et al. A randomized trial of frovatriptan for the intermittent prevention of menstrual migraine. Neurology. 2004;63:261-9. [PMID: 15277618]

well controlled for 6 to 12 months, tapering and discontinuation can be considered, and the medication can be resumed if headaches recur.

Definitive data are lacking about the usefulness of injections of botulinum toxin into the scalp and face for migraine prophylaxis (38). Ongoing multicenter national trials may determine a standardized method for botulinum toxin administration for migraine.

Any preventive drug therapy may be combined with nondrug preventive treatments, such as relaxation and biofeedback, which work in different and complementary ways and may have additive effects.

A trial that studied the effects of propranolol combined with 1) thermal biofeedback plus relaxation plus cognitive behavioral therapy, 2) thermal biofeedback plus relaxation, and 3) EMG biofeedback found that concomitant propranolol therapy significantly enhanced the effectiveness of relaxation-biofeedback training when either daily headache recordings (79% vs. 54% reduction in migraine activity) or a neurologist's clinical evaluations (90% vs. 66% reduction) were used to assess treatment outcome (39).

When should clinicians consider hospitalizing patients with migraine?

Patients with prolonged, intractable migraine (status migrainosus) with associated nausea and vomiting may require hospitalization for hydration, parenteral dihydroergotamine, corticosteroids, phenothiazines, or parenteral analgesics after primary and rescue treatments have failed (40, 41). Patients with headache associated with excessive use of analgesic medications—so-called medication-overuse or rebound headache—may also require hospitalization when outpatient weaning fails.

What are the components of good follow-up care for patients with migraine?

Clinicians should monitor headache severity, frequency, and disability to assess treatment response and the need to change treatment. Because attacks vary in severity, treating at least 3 attacks of migraine is necessary before evaluating response to a specific treatment. Response to particular medications is highly individual, so a trial-and-error approach is reasonable.

Clinicians should ask patients about medication adherence and attempt to identify medication overuse, which is defined as the use of more than 10 doses per week of analgesic medications, ergotamine tartrate, or ergotamine tartrate plus caffeine. Additionally, clinicians should also periodically ask patients about lifestyle factors associated with headache symptoms. In evaluating the effectiveness of treatment, it can be helpful for patients to keep a daily record of symptoms between clinic visits. Retrospective recall of headache frequency and severity is unreliable compared with contemporaneously recorded symptoms (42).

Is it appropriate to taper or discontinue preventive treatment for migraine?

Migraine symptoms change over time, and preventive therapy may become unnecessary in patients who previously needed it. After a sustained reduction in headache frequency that lasts 6 to 12 months, a trial of medication withdrawal may allow the patient to cease preventive treatment and avoid the associated risks and costs. However, a 1999 systematic review found no published studies to evaluate systematic withdrawal of preventive medications (36), and we continue to be lack evidence

38. Göbel H. Botulinum toxin in migraine prophylaxis. J Neurol. 2004;251 Suppl 1:I8-11. [PMID: 14991336]
39. Holroyd KA, France JL, Cordingley GE, Rokicki LA, Kvaal SA, Lipchik GL, et al. Enhancing the effectiveness of relaxation-thermal biofeedback training with propranolol hydrochloride. J Consult Clin Psychol. 1995;63:327-30. [PMID: 7751496]
40. Silberstein SD, Schulman EA, Hopkins MM. Repetitive intravenous DHE in the treatment of refractory headache. Headache. 1990;30:334-9. [PMID: 2370132]
41. Gallagher RM. Emergency treatment of intractable migraine. Headache. 1986;26:74-5. [PMID: 3957657]
42. Penzien DB, Johnson CA, Seville J, et al. Interrelationships among daily and global self-report measures of headache. Headache Q. 1994;5:8-14.84

regarding the best way to withdraw preventive therapy.

Are patients with migraine at risk for cardiovascular complications?

Migraine with aura has been associated with an adverse cardiovascular risk profile, prothrombotic factors, and a possible increased risk for ischemic vascular events. A large prospective cohort study in women showed that those with migraine with aura had an increased risk for cardiovascular disease (myocardial infarction, ischemic stroke, angina, and other events), but those without aura did not have an increased risk for cardiovascular events (43). A cohort study in men did not include information on aura and showed that those with migraine had higher risk for cardiovascular events than those without migraine but found no significant association with ischemic stroke (44). Patients who have aura that persists for more than 24 hours have complicated migraine, a rare condition that can lead to infarction from sustained metabolic disturbance.

When should clinicians consider subspecialty referral for patients with migraine?

Some patients with migraine benefit from a referral to a headache specialist for specialized treatment. Referral is advised for patients with intractable migraine (status migrainosus), failure to respond to standard treatment, need for experimental or high-risk medications such as methysergide, medication-overuse headache, or analgesic dependency. Uncontrolled case series suggest potential benefits of intensive approaches, such as multidisciplinary headache clinics (45).

Treatment... Nonpharmacologic management of migraine includes modification of diet to avoid foods that trigger symptoms, sleep hygiene, and behavioral therapy. Over-the-counter analgesics are appropriate first-line therapy for mild-to-moderate symptoms. More severe symptoms require migraine-specific therapy with triptans, dihydroergotamine, or ergotamine. When symptoms are frequent, refactory to therapy, or include neurologic sequelae, preventive drug therapy is indicated. Evidence for effectiveness in prevention is greatest for β-blockers, followed by valproate, antidepressants, and then calcium antagonists. Patients should participate in the selection of therapy and have a clear plan to institute when symptoms occur.

CLINICAL BOTTOM LINE

Practice Improvement

What do professional organizations recommend about caring for patients with migraine?

In 2000, the U.S. Headache Consortium published evidence-based guidelines for migraine (46). In 2002, the American College of Physicians and the American Academy of Family Physicians with the American Headache Society developed a clinical guideline based on systematic reviews that had been part of the evidence base for the 2000 U.S. Headache Consortium guideline (47). The Figure summarizes an evidence-based strategy for the mangement of acute migraine.

43. Kurth T, Gazian JM, Cook NR, et al. Migraine and risk of cardiovascular disease in women. JAMA. 2006;296:283-91. [PMID: 16849661]

44. Kurth T, Gazian JM, Cook NR, et al. Migraine and risk of cardiovascular disease in men. Arch Intern Med. 2007;167:795-801. [PMID: 17452542]

45. Saper JR, Lake AE , Madden SF, et al. Comprehensive/Tertiary care for headache: a 6-month outcome study. Headache. 1999;39:249-63. [PMID: 15613222]

46. Silberstein SD. Practice parameter: evidence-based guidelines for migraine headache (an evidence-based review): report of the Quality Standards Subcommittee of the American Academy of Neurology. Neurology. 2000;55:754-62. [PMID: 10993991]

47. Snow V, Weiss K, Wall EM, et al. Pharmacologic management of acute attacks of migraine and prevention of migraine headache. Ann Intern Med. 2002;137:840-9. [PMID: 12435222]

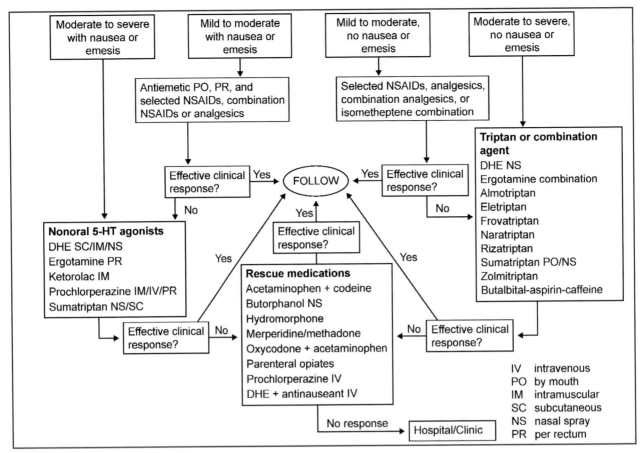

Figure. Strategy for the management of acute migraine.

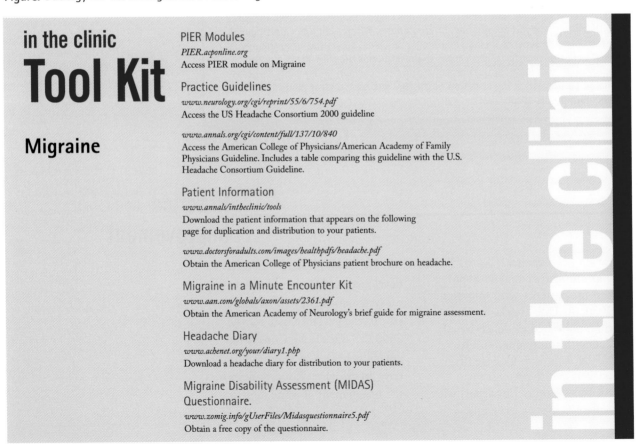

THINGS PEOPLE SHOULD KNOW
ABOUT MIGRAINE

Migraines are headaches related to changes in chemicals and blood vessels in the brain.

"POUND" (as in "a pounding headache") is one way to remember migraine symptoms:

> **P**ulsatile quality of headache described
> **O**ne-day duration (duration < 4 hours suggests tension-type headache)
> **U**nilateral location
> **N**ausea or vomiting
> **D**isabling intensity.

- Good sleep habits, avoidance of foods that trigger migraine symptoms, behavioral therapy (such as biofeedback), and drugs can all help to decrease the frequency and severity of migraine attacks. Migraine sufferers should participate in selecting treatment.
- Over-the-counter drugs, such as acetaminophen, aspirin, and ibuprofen, are usually the first drugs used to treat migraine. When these drugs do not help, prescription drugs may be necessary.
- Talk to your doctor if you think you may have migraine headaches.

Daily drugs to prevent migraine may help you if you:

- Get 2 or more migraines per month
- Are unable to use migraine treatments because of side effects
- Get no benefit from migraine treatment
- Have migraine complicated by nerve symptoms, such visual changes, numbness, or weakness

Web Sites with Good Information about Migraine

American Academy of Neurology
www.aan.com/globals/axon/assets/2346.pdf

MedlinePLUS
www.nlm.nih.gov/medlineplus/headache.html

National Institute of Neurological Disorders and Stroke
www.ninds.nih.gov/disorders/headache/headache.htm

National Headache Foundation
www.headaches.org/consumer/topicsheets/migraine.html

Heart Failure

Approximately 5 million people in the United States have heart failure, and the number is on the rise, according to the National Heart Lung and Blood Institute. Heart failure is the most frequent cause of hospitalization in U.S. patients older than 65 years, and the disease leads to about 300 000 deaths per year (1). Heart failure is a significant problem throughout the rest of the world as well, but few accurate data are available. The most common cause of heart failure in industrialized countries is ischemic cardiomyopathy, whereas other causes, such as infectious diseases, assume a larger role in underdeveloped countries. Despite recent advances in the management of patients with heart failure, morbidity and mortality rates remain high. The estimated 5-year mortality rate is 50%.

Diagnosis

What patients should clinicians consider to be at risk for heart failure?

Elderly persons are at highest risk. The overall prevalence of heart failure in persons over 80 years of age is approximately 10% compared with just 1% among persons under age 50 (2). African Americans also face an increased risk for heart failure. African Americans between 45 and 64 years of age are 2.5 times more likely to die from heart failure than Caucasians in the same age range (3). Men have a higher rate of heart failure than women, although this difference narrows as women get older.

Certain conditions and behaviors also increase the risk for heart failure, and these conditions should be treated to reduce the risk (see Box). In addition to these, epidemiologic study has linked increased risk for heart failure to physical inactivity, obesity, and lower levels of education (4).

Hypertension
Longstanding untreated hypertension is associated with the development of both systolic and diastolic heart failure as well as an independent risk for coronary artery disease (CAD). Clinical trials have shown that a reduction in systolic or diastolic blood pressure can reduce the subsequent risk for developing heart failure (5). Even modest decreases in systolic blood pressure reduce mortality and the risk for heart failure (6).

Diabetes
Diabetes markedly increases the risk for heart failure and is an independent risk factor for CAD.

The HOPE (Heart Outcomes Prevention Evalutaion) trial found that among patients at least 55 years of age with either atherosclerosis or diabetes and at least 1 other risk factor but without a history of heart failure, the angiotensin-converting enzyme (ACE) inhibitor ramipril reduced the risk for stroke, myocardial infarction (MI), and death from cardiovascular disease by 22% while also significantly reducing heart failure (6).

Cardiotoxic Substance Use
Alcohol is a direct myocardial toxin and can be the primary cause of heart failure. Abstinence from alcohol may reverse left ventricular dysfunction. Tobacco and cocaine use significantly increase the risk for CAD, which in turn can lead to heart failure. Cocaine also has direct effects on the myocardium. Chemotherapeutic agents, such as anthracycline and trastuzumab, can also exert toxic effects on the myocardium.

Common Conditions and Behaviors that Increase the Risk for Heart Failure
- Hypertension
- Diabetes
- Cardiotoxic substance use
- Hyperlipidemia
- Thyroid disorders
- Tachycardia
- Coronary artery disease

---

1. Finn P. American Heart Association—scientific sessions 2005. 13-16 November 2005, Dallas, TX, USA. IDrugs. 2006;9:13-5. [PMID: 16374724]
2. Kannel WB. Current status of the epidemiology of heart failure. Curr Cardiol Rep. 1999;1:11-9. [PMID: 10980814]
3. Centers for Disease Control and Prevention (CDC). Mortality from congestive heart failure—United States, 1980-1990. MMWR Morb Mortal Wkly Rep. 1994;43:77-81. [PMID: 8295629]
4. He J, Ogden LG, Bazzano LA, et al. Risk factors for congestive heart failure in US men and women: NHANES I epidemiologic follow-up study. Arch Intern Med. 2001;161:996-1002. [PMID: 11295963]
5. The sixth report of the Joint National Committee on prevention, detection, evaluation, and treatment of high blood pressure. Arch Intern Med. 1997;157:2413-46. [PMID: 9385294]
6. HOPE Investigators. Effects of ramipril on coronary events in high-risk persons: results of the Heart Outcomes Prevention Evaluation Study. Circulation. 2001;104:522-6. [PMID: 11479247]

Hyperlipidemia

Hyperlipidemia is strongly associated with CAD, which may ultimately lead to heart failure. Large-scale clinical trials have shown the benefit of lipid lowering for primary and secondary prevention of cardiovascular events.

The CARE (Cholesterol and Recurrent Events) trial found that pravastatin treatment significantly reduced mortality as well as subsequent cardiovascular events and reduced the incidence of heart failure (7).

Thyroid Disorders

Both hyperthyroidism and hypothyroidism are associated with heart failure, and correction to a euthyroid state can potentially return ventricular function to normal (8, 9). Hyperthyroidism is associated with atrial fibrillation and tachycardia, which may complicate or worsen heart failure.

Tachycardia

Studies have shown that rapid prolonged ventricular rates can lead to cardiomyopathy. Restoration of normal rhythm or rate control in patients with poorly controlled atrial fibrillation and other supraventricular tachycardias can improve function and potentially prevent left ventricular dysfunction (10–12).

Coronary Artery Disease

Aggressive risk-factor modification with cholesterol-lowering drugs and aspirin, ACE inhibitors, and β-blockers can significantly reduce mortality and the risk for future cardiovascular complications, including heart failure.

The CAPRICORN (Carvedilol Post-Infarct Survival Control in Left Ventricular Dysfunction) trial demonstrated that the β-blocker carvedilol significantly benefited mortality in patients with left ventricular dysfunction with or without heart failure after MI in the setting of background therapy with ACE inhibitors, revascularization, and aspirin (13).

What symptoms and signs should prompt clinicians to consider the diagnosis of heart failure?

Patients with underlying risk factors, including CAD, valvular heart disease, and longstanding hypertension, may be asymptomatic, and clinicians should not wait for symptoms to develop before evaluating and treating them for early left ventricular dysfunction. Once structural or functional heart disease affects the ability of the myocardium to fill and pump blood normally, patients may develop dyspnea, fatigue, exercise intolerance, and fluid retention manifested by pulmonary congestion and edema. Sometimes the breathing difficulties and cough of heart failure are initially misdiagnosed as bronchitis, pneumonia, or asthma, especially in young patients. Physical signs of heart failure may reflect the underlying cause, as shown by elevated blood pressure or an abnormal cardiac murmur, or the resulting fluid retention, as shown by elevated jugular venous pressure, pulmonary crackles, a third heart sound, and lower extremity edema.

What tests should clinicians consider in the evaluation of patients with suspected heart failure?

Electrocardiography

The American College of Cardiology (ACC)/American Heart Association (AHA) recommends electrocardiography (ECG) in any patient at risk for or with a history of cardiac disease, including new-onset or exacerbated heart failure. If possible, the tracing should be compared with a previous baseline tracing. Results can help document the presence of ventricular hypertrophy, atrial abnormality, arrhythmias, conduction abnormalities, prior MI, and evidence of active ischemia.

Echocardiography

Two-dimensional echocardiography with Doppler should be performed

7. Sacks FM, Pfeffer MA, Moye LA, et al. The effect of pravastatin on coronary events after myocardial infarction in patients with average cholesterol levels. Cholesterol and Recurrent Events Trial investigators. N Engl J Med. 1996;335:1001-9. [PMID: 8801446]

8. Klein I, Ojamaa K. Thyroid hormone and the cardiovascular system. N Engl J Med. 2001;344:501-9. [PMID: 11172193]

9. Fadel BM, Ellahham S, Ringel MD, et al. Hyperthyroid heart disease. Clin Cardiol. 2000;23:402-8. [PMID: 10875028]

10. Coleman HN III, Taylor RR, Pool PE, et al. Congestive heart failure following chronic tachycardia. Am Heart J. 1971;81:790-8. [PMID: 5088355]

11. Peters KG, Kienzle MG. Severe cardiomyopathy due to chronic rapidly conducted atrial fibrillation: complete recovery after restoration of sinus rhythm. Am J Med. 1988;85:242-4. [PMID: 3400701]

12. Grogan M, Smith HC, Gersh BJ, Wood DL. Left ventricular dysfunction due to atrial fibrillation in patients initially believed to have idiopathic dilated cardiomyopathy. Am J Cardiol. 1992;69:1570-3. [PMID: 1598871]

13. Dargie HJ. Effect of carvedilol on outcome after myocardial infarction in patients with left-ventricular dysfunction: the CAPRICORN randomised trial. Lancet. 2001;357:1385-90. [PMID: 11356434]

in all patients with suspected heart failure. It is a key study for determining left ventricular cavity size and function, identifying wall motion abnormalities, measuring left and right ventricular ejection fractions, documenting the presence of valvular abnormalities, and differentiating between systolic and diastolic heart failure. In diastolic heart failure, the ejection fraction is normal (>50%), and there is evidence of ventricular hypertrophy. In systolic dysfunction, the ejection fraction is <50%, and there is left ventricular dilatation. The degrees of left ventricular systolic and diastolic dysfunction are important in predicting prognosis, and the treatment of systolic and diastolic heart failure may differ.

Exercise Testing

A traditional exercise stress test or a pharmacologic stress test using dipyridamole, dobutamine, or adenosine for patients who are unable to exercise can be used to look for ischemia and quantitate functional capacity in patients with heart failure. Metabolic stress testing with respiratory gas analysis can determine the extent of disability, differentiate between cardiac or pulmonary limitation to exercise, and determine functional class in patients who are candidates for cardiac transplantation (14).

Cardiac Catheterization and Endomyocardial Biopsy

Cardiac catheterization should be considered in patients with heart failure when echocardiography is insufficient in defining severity of valvular heart disease and when known or suspected ischemic heart disease is being evaluated. Endomyocardial biopsy should not be done in most patients with suspected myocarditis unless giant cell myocarditis is being considered. Even when systemic diseases, such as hemochromatosis, sarcoidosis, or amyloidosis, are thought to be the cause of infiltrative disease in the heart, the diagnosis can usually be made without endomyocardial biopsy.

B-Type Natriuretic Peptide

B-type natriuretic peptide (BNP) is a sensitive marker of ventricular pressure and volume overload and can be useful in determining the cause of dyspnea when the clinical presentation and physical examination are equivocal in the acute setting (15). However, BNP levels can also be elevated in women, older patients, persons with renal disease, and in patients with acute MI and some noncardiac conditions.

Other Laboratory Studies

Consider obtaining serum thyroid-stimulating hormone levels in all patients with new-onset heart failure to rule out occult thyroid disease. Anemia, renal insufficiency, infection, and concurrent pulmonary disease can exacerbate heart failure, and the clinical situation should dictate the need for additional tests, including complete blood cell count, electrolytes, blood urea nitrogen, creatinine, chest X-ray, pulmonary function studies, or appropriate cultures to guide therapy.

What are the types of heart failure, and how should clinicians go about differentiating them?
There are multiple causes of heart failure, and it is sometimes useful to divide them into dilated, hypertrophic, and restrictive types (Table 1). Most causes of heart failure lead to cardiac dilatation. Hypertrophic cardiomyopathy is due to genetic abnormalities or hypertension. Restrictive heart failure is usually due to systemic infiltrative diseases.

More important is the functional distinction between systolic and diastolic heart failure. In systolic

14. Myers J, Madhavan R. Exercise testing with gas exchange analysis. Cardiol Clin. 2001;19:433-45. [PMID: 11570115]

15. Morrison LK, Harrison A, Krishnaswamy P, et al. Utility of a rapid B-natriuretic peptide assay in differentiating congestive heart failure from lung disease in patients presenting with dyspnea. J Am Coll Cardiol. 2002;39:202-9. [PMID: 11788208]

16. Owan TE, Hodge DO, Herges RM, et al. Trends in prevalence and outcome of heart failure with preserved ejection fraction. N Engl J Med. 2006;355(3):251-9. [PMID: 16855265]

heart failure, the heart is dilated with an ejection fraction below 50%, whereas in diastolic heart failure, which occurs more often in elderly patients with hypertension, there is less dilatation and a normal ejection fraction. Among patients with heart failure, those with preserved ejection fraction represent a significant proportion and have a similar survival rate to those with systolic heart failure (16, 17)

17. Bhatia RS, Tu JV, Lee DS, et al. Outcome of heart failure with preserved ejection fraction in a population-based study. N Engl J Med. 2006;355(3):260-9. [PMID: 16855266]

Table 1. Underlying Causes of Heart Failure*

Causes	Characteristics
Dilated cardiomyopathies	
Ischemic heart disease	Occurs in people with a history of MI, presence of infarction pattern on ECG, or risk factors for coronary disease.
Hypertension	Presents in people with a history of poorly controlled blood pressure, presence of an S4 on physical examination, or left ventricular hypertrophy on echocardiogram or ECG. Hypertension can also cause hypertrophic as well as dilated caridomyopathy.
Valvular heart disease	Mitral regurgitation: ejection murmur at apex, dyspnea on exertion, atrial fibrillation. Aortic stenosis: dyspnea with exertion, ejection murmur at base that radiates to carotid arteries, decreased carotid upstroke, syncope, angina.
Bacterial myocarditis	Fever, exposure to known agent, or positive blood cultures. Includes *Borrelia burgdorferi* (Lyme disease), diphtheria, rickettsia, streptococci, and staphylococci.
Parasitic myocarditis	Travel history to endemic areas, fever, or peripheral stigmata of infection. Rare in United States. Includes *Trypanosoma cruzi* (Chagas disease), leishmaniasis, and toxoplasmosis.
Giant cell myocarditis	Intractable ventricular or supraventricular arrhythmias with rapidly progressive left ventricular dysfunction: Endomyocardial biopsy specimen may be used to confirm the diagnosis. Effective immunotherapy may be available, but prognosis is poor without ventricular assist device or transplantation.
Familial dilated cardiomyopathies	Family history of heart failure or sudden cardiac death in blood relatives.
Toxic cardiomyopathies	History of exposure to toxic agents, such as alcohol, anthracycline, radiation, cocaine, or catecholamines.
Collagen vascular disease	History, positive serology results, or other stigmata of a collagen vascular disease, including systemic lupus erythematosus, polyarteritis nodosa, scleroderma, or dermatomyositis.
Granulomatous disease, such as sarcoidosis	Atrial and ventricular arrhythmias that are difficult to control, rapidly progressive left ventricular dysfunction, heart block.
Endocrinologic or metabolic disorders	Clinical history of hyperthyroidism, acromegaly, hypothyroidism, uremia, pheochromocytoma, diabetes mellitus, thiamine deficiency, selenium deficiency, carnitine deficiency, kwashiorkor, carcinoid tumor, or obesity; serum test for endocrine abnormality; long-term resident of a developing country or an area with endemic nutritional deficiency. Nutritional deficiencies are rare in the United States.
Peripartum cardiomyopathy	Heart failure symptoms with left ventricular dysfunction within 6 months of a pregnancy.
Neuromuscular disorders	Clinical history of Becker muscular dystrophy, myotonic dystrophy, Friedreich ataxia, limb-girdle muscular dystrophy, or Duchenne muscular dystrophy. Physical examination findings depend on the underlying disease.
Cardiac transplant rejection	History of cardiac transplant, medication noncompliance, shortness of breath, atrial or ventricular arrhythmias, or tachycardia, summation gallop on examination.
Hypertrophic cardiomyopathies	
Hypertrophic obstructive cardiomyopathy	History or family history of hypertrophic cardiomyopathy, echocardiographic and ECG findings of hypertrophy. Screen for outflow tract gradient by physical examination, echocardiography, or cardiac catheterization. Significant hypertrophy can also be seen in hypertension.
Restrictive cardiomyopathies	
Infiltrative diseases affecting the myocardium	History of amyloidosis, sarcoidosis, hemochromatosis, Fabry disease, glycogen storage diseases, Gaucher disease, mucopolysaccharidosis, endomyocardial fibrosis, or hypereosinophilic syndrome; thickening of the myocardium on echocardiogram, suggesting an infiltrative process; cardiac MRI showing infiltration; family history of an inborn error of metabolism or amyloidosis; presence of S_4 on examination; right-sided heart failure more severe than left-sided failure; other organs involved in underlying disease process.

*ECG = electrocardiography; MI = myocardial infarction; MRI = magnetic resonance imaging.

Treatment

New York Heart Association (NYHA) Classification System:

- NYHA class I (mild): Patient has asymptomatic left ventricular dysfunction. Normal physical activity does not cause undue fatigue, palpitation, or shortness of breath.
- NYHA class II (mild): Patient has fatigue, palpitation, or shortness of breath with normal physical activity.
- NYHA class III (moderate): Patient has shortness of breath with minimal activity, including usual activities of daily living.
- NYHA class IV (severe): Patient has shortness of breath at rest and is unable to carry out any physical activity without discomfort. Physical activity of any kind increases discomfort.

18. Sullivan MJ, Cobb FR. The anaerobic threshold in chronic heart failure. Relation to blood lactate, ventilatory basis, reproducibility, and response to exercise training. Circulation. 1990;81:II47-58. [PMID: 2295152]
19. Myers J, Gianrossi R, Schwitter J, et al. Effect of exercise training on postexercise oxygen uptake kinetics in patients with reduced ventricular function. Chest. 2001;120:1206-11. [PMID: 11591562]
20. Sullivan MJ, Cobb FR. Central hemodynamic response to exercise in patients with chronic heart failure. Chest. 1992;101:340S-346S. [PMID: 1576862]

How should clinicians evaluate functional capacity in patients with suspected heart failure to determine treatment?

Clinicians should determine functional capacity by using the New York Heart Association (NYHA) classification system (see Box). Tracking changes in clinical NYHA class at every visit may identify patients with progressive heart failure who may eventually benefit from specialized care or cardiac transplantation.

Additional functional capacity tests that can be followed over time include the 6-minute walk test (see Box) and formal exercise or pharmacologic stress testing. Measuring peak oxygen consumption (VO_2) at the time of exercise testing can be useful in determining prognosis.

How to Perform the 6-minute Walk Test

Ask the patient to walk for 6 minutes in a straight line back and forth between 2 points separated by 60 feet. Allow the patient to stop and rest or even sit, if necessary. At either end of the course, place chairs that can quickly be moved if the patient needs to sit. Note the total distance walked in 6 minutes, which correlates well with other measures of functional capacity. Gender-specific equations have been developed using age, height, and weight to calculate predicted distance for healthy adults.

What is the role of diet in the management heart failure?

Despite a paucity of definitive evidence, ACC/AHA and other guidelines recommend sodium restriction in patients with symptomatic heart failure as well as avoidance of salt-retaining medications, such as nonsteroidal anti-inflammatory drugs. Some clinicians recommend that patients with more advanced heart failure limit intake to 2 grams of sodium and 2 quarts of fluid per day to increase the effectiveness of diuretic therapy. Limitation of salt and fluid intake results in fewer hospitalizations for decompensated heart failure. Patients who have cardiovascular risk factors, such as hyperlipidemia, obesity, or diabetes, should also be encouraged to follow dietary recommendations specific to these underlying conditions.

What should clinicians advise patients about exercise? Do formal exercise programs provide benefit?

Exercise improves physical and psychological well-being. In patients with heart failure, it improves peak VO_2 (18, 19) as well as metabolic and hemodynamic indices and delays the onset of anaerobic threshold (18, 20). Clinicians should enroll patients with medically stable NYHA class II, III, and perhaps class IV heart failure in a long-term aerobic exercise program tailored to the patient's functional capacity. A structured cardiac rehabilitation program may be particularly effective because it can provide supervised exercise as well as support in making lifestyle modifications. Exercise should be stopped temporarily in patients with worsening heart failure until symptoms are stabilized. In addition, if patients show evidence of exercise-induced ischemia, exercise should be stopped until further evaluation and therapy are initiated.

When should clinicians begin first-line drug therapy with ACE inhibitors or angiotensin-receptor blockers? What are the alternatives for patients who cannot tolerate these drugs?

ACE Inhibitors

ACE inhibitors should be used by all patients with heart failure regardless of functional class except those with intolerance or a contraindication, such as angioedema. These vasodilators alter the natural history of the disease and improve survival and quality of life. Numerous randomized, placebo-controlled clinical trials have demonstrated that ACE inhibitors reduce mortality in patients with left ventricular dysfunction, even in those without symptoms.

The CONSENSUS (Cooperative North Scandinavian Enalapril Survival Study) trial evaluated 253 patients with NYHA class I to IV heart failure who were randomly assigned to enalapril or placebo in a blinded study. All patients were also receiving diuretics, and 93% received digitalis glycosides. The mortality rate was reduced by 27% (P < 0.001) in the patients receiving enalapril compared with placebo (21).

The SOLVD (Studies of Left Ventricular Dysfunction) treatment trial randomly assigned 2569 patients with NYHA class I to IV heart failure to enalapril vs. placebo. In patients with heart failure receiving enalapril compared with placebo, there was a 16% (P < 0.005) reduction in mortality rate, a 30% (P < 0.0001) reduction in heart failure hospitalizations, a 7% (P < 0.01) reduction in total hospitalizations, a 44% (P < 0.01) reduction in worsening heart failure, and a 23% (P < 0.02) reduction in MI (22).

The SOLVD prevention trial enrolled 4228 patients with NYHA class I. These patients had asymptomatic left ventricular dysfunction and were randomly assigned to enalapril vs. placebo. There was an 8% reduction in mortality rate, a 31% (P < 0.001) reduction in heart failure hospitalizations, a 50% (P < 0.01) reduction in episodes of worsening heart failure, and a 24% (P < 0.01) reduction in MI in patients receiving enalapril vs. placebo (23).

Initiate enalapril, captopril, lisinopril, or ramipril at low doses and titrate upward while monitoring blood pressure. The end point for blood pressure can be as low as 80 to 90 mm Hg systolic as long as the patient is asymptomatic. Important side effects include cough, worsening renal insufficiency, and hyperkalemia.

Angiotensin-Receptor Blockers

Clinicians should consider using angiotensin-receptor blockers (ARBs) in patients with intolerable side effects from ACE inhibitors, such as cough.

The ELITE I (Evaluation of Losartan in the Elderly) trial compared captopril with losartan in elderly patients with heart failure and showed a decrease in all-cause mortality (4.8% vs. 8.7%; risk reduction 46%, P = 0.035) in the losartan group. Admissions with heart failure were the same in both groups (5.7%), as was improvement in NYHA functional class from baseline (24). The ELITE II trial also compared captopril with losartan, but there were no significant differences in all-cause mortality (11.7% vs. 10.4% average annual mortality rate) or sudden death or resuscitated arrests (9.0% vs. 7.3%) between the groups (hazard ratios, 1.13 [95.7% CI, 0.95 to 1.35], P = 0.16, and 1.25 [CI, 0.98 to 1.60], P = 0.08) (25).

The Val-HeFT (Valsartan–Heart Failure Trial) randomly assigned patients with heart failure to valsartan or placebo in addition to standard heart failure medications. There was no difference in mortality, but the incidence of the combined end point of morbidity or mortality was 13.2% lower with valsartan than with placebo (relative risk, 0.87 [CI, 0.77 to 0.97]; P = 0.009) (26). In a subgroup analysis, those not receiving an ACE inhibitor but who were randomized to

21. The CONSENSUS Trial Study Group. Effects of enalapril on mortality in severe congestive heart failure. Results of the Cooperative North Scandinavian Enalapril Survival Study (CONSENSUS). N Engl J Med. 1987;316:1429-35. [PMID: 2883575]
22. The SOLVD Investigators. Effect of enalapril on survival in patients with reduced left ventricular ejection fractions and congestive heart failure. N Engl J Med. 1991;325:293-302. [PMID: 2057034]
23. The SOLVD Investigators. Effect of enalapril on mortality and the development of heart failure in asymptomatic patients with reduced left ventricular ejection fractions. N Engl J Med. 1992;327:685-91. [PMID: 1463530]
24. Pitt B, Segal R, Martinez FA, et al. Randomised trial of losartan versus captopril in patients over 65 with heart failure (Evaluation of Losartan in the Elderly Study, ELITE). Lancet. 1997;349:747-52. [PMID: 9074572]
25. Pitt B, Poole-Wilson PA, Segal R, et al. Effect of losartan compared with captopril on mortality in patients with symptomatic heart failure: randomised trial—the Losartan Heart Failure Survival Study ELITE II. Lancet. 2000;355:1582-7. [PMID: 10821361]
26. Cohn JN, Tognoni G. A randomized trial of the angiotensin-receptor blocker valsartan in chronic heart failure. N Engl J Med. 2001;345:1667-75. [PMID: 11759645]
27. Maggioni AP, Anand I, Gottlieb SO, et al.; Val-HeFT Investigators (Valsartan Heart Failure Trial). Effects of valsartan on morbidity and mortality in patients with heart failure not receiving angiotensin-converting enzyme inhibitors. J Am Coll Cardiol. 2002;40:1414-21. [PMID: 12392830]

28. Granger CB, McMurray JJ, Yusuf S, et al. Effects of candesartan in patients with chronic heart failure and reduced left-ventricular systolic function intolerant to angiotensin-converting-enzyme inhibitors: the CHARM-Alternative trial. Lancet. 2003;362:772-6. [PMID: 13678870]

29. Opie LH. Cellular basis for therapeutic choices in heart failure. Circulation. 2004;110(17):2559-61. [PMID: 15505109]

30. Loeb HS, Johnson G, Henrick A, et al. Effect of enalapril, hydralazine plus isosorbide dinitrate, and prazosin on hospitalization in patients with chronic congestive heart failure. The V-HeFT VA Cooperative Studies Group. Circulation. 1993;87:VI78-87. [PMID: 8500244]

31. Johnson G, Carson P, Francis GS, Cohn JN. Influence of prerandomization (baseline) variables on mortality and on the reduction of mortality by enalapril. Veterans Affairs Cooperative Study on Vasodilator Therapy of Heart Failure (V-HeFT II). V-HeFT VA Cooperative Studies Group. Circulation. 1993;87:VI32-9. [PMID: 8500237]

32. African-American Heart Failure Trial Investigators. Combination of isosorbide dinitrate and hydralazine in blacks with heart failure. N Engl J Med. 2004;351:2049-57. [PMID: 15533851]

33. Packer M, Bristow MR, Cohn JN, et al. The effect of carvedilol on morbidity and mortality in patients with chronic heart failure. U.S. Carvedilol Heart Failure Study Group. N Engl J Med. 1996;334:1349-55. [PMID: 8614419]

34. CIBIS Investigators and Committees. A randomized trial of beta-blockade in heart failure. The Cardiac Insufficiency Bisoprolol Study (CIBIS). Circulation. 1994;90:1765-73. [PMID: 7923660]

receive valsartan had a 33% reduction in all-cause mortality. This result is similar to the magnitude of mortality reduction with ACE inhibitors (27).

Evidence from the randomized, placebo-controlled CHARM-Alternative (Candesartan Cilexitil [Atacand] in Heart Failure Assessment of Reduction Mortality and Morbidity) trial showed that the ARB candesartan decreased a combined end point of death from cardiovascular causes or hospitalization due to heart failure when compared with placebo in patients with left ventricular dysfunction intolerant of ACE inhibitors (28).

There have been some studies suggesting that combining ACE inhibitors and ARBs may be beneficial in reducing left ventricular size and decreasing hospitalizations, with an equivocal effect on mortality (29).

Hydralazine and Nitrates

Patients who are intolerant of both ACE inhibitors and ARBs should receive hydralazine and long-acting nitrates. Evidence has shown that this combination improves clinical outcomes and decreases mortality in patients with heart failure and depressed ejection fraction (30, 31). However, the combination does not seem to have as much effect on mortality rates as ACE inhibitors. Hydralazine plus nitrates should also be considered in addition to standard therapy, including an ACE inhibitor or ARB, in African-American patients with symptomatic heart failure, because this combination may favorably affect myocardial remodeling and mortality in these patients.

The A-HeFT (African American Heart Failure Trial), which compared isosorbide plus hydralazine with placebo isordil in African-American patients with heart failure, showed that the addition of this therapy increased survival among those who were already taking other neurohormonal blockers, including ACE inhibitors and β-blockers (32).

When should clinicians add β-blockers, aldosterone antagonists, and loop diuretics?

β-Blockers

β-blockers should be used in all NYHA classes of heart failure if the patient is stable on ACE inhibitors or other vasodilators and are not volume overloaded. β-blockers can reduce heart failure symptoms, improve clinical outcomes, improve ejection fraction, and decrease mortality rate. Patients with less-severe heart failure have the greatest long-term benefit, including those with left ventricular dysfunction but no symptoms. Various studies testing carvedilol, bisoprolol, and long-acting metoprolol succinate have all found that β-blockers reduced hospitalizations, sudden death, and overall mortality in patients with heart failure.

The CAPRICORN trial randomized patients with left ventricular dysfunction after MI with or without heart failure to β-blockade with carvedilol. There was a significant reduction in mortality that was even more marked in the group that never had symptomatic heart failure (13).

The U.S. carvedilol trial randomly assigned 696 patients to the carvedilol group and 398 to the placebo group. Patients were classified with NYHA class I to IV heart failure. A 65% (P < 0.0001) reduction in mortality was seen in the carvedilol group. Cardiovascular hospitalizations were reduced (33).

The CIBIS (Cardiac Insufficiency Bisoprolol Study) I trial randomly assigned 320 patients to bisoprolol, 5 mg/d, or placebo. There was a statistically insignificant 20% reduction in mortality and a significant reduction in heart failure hospitalizations (34). The CIBIS II trial randomly assigned patients with NYHA class III to IV heart failure to bisoprolol, 5 mg/d, or placebo. A total of 3.6% of patients in the bisoprolol group had sudden cardiac death versus 6.3% in the placebo group (P < 0.01) (35).

The MERIT-HF (Metoprolol CR/XL Randomized Intervention Trial–Heart Failure) randomly assigned 3991 patients with NYHA class II to IV heart failure to metoprolol CR/XL (up to 200 mg/d) versus placebo.

There was a 34% reduction in all-cause mortality (P < 0.001) and a 59% reduction in sudden death (P < 0.001) for patients receiving metoprolol versus placebo (36).

The COPERNICUS (Carvedilol Prospective Randomized Cumulative Survival) trial randomly assigned patients with NYHA class IV heart failure to carvedilol or placebo. There was a 24% decrease in the combined risk for death or hospitalization with carvedilol (P < 0.001) (37).

β-blockers should be initiated at the lowest dose and slowly titrated upward every 2 to 4 weeks to the highest therapeutic dose tolerated, as limited by bradycardia, hypotension, or side effects. Instruct patients to check their body weight and watch for worsening heart failure symptoms during initiation and upward titration of β-blockade.

Aldosterone Antagonists

If patients continue to have NYHA class III to IV symptoms despite therapy with ACE inhibitors and β-blockers, consider treatment with low doses of an aldosterone antagonist. Spironolactone has been studied the most.

The RALES (Randomized Aldosterone Evaluation Study), a large, randomized, placebo-controlled trial involving 1663 patients with NYHA class III to IV heart failure on appropriate therapy with or without spironolactone, was halted 18 months early by the Data Safety Monitoring Board because there were significantly fewer deaths in the spironolactone group than in the placebo group (284 vs. 386 deaths; 35% reduction, P < 0.0001) (38).

Eplenerone is a newer, more selective aldosterone antagonist with fewer undesirable side effects and has been shown to decrease all-cause mortality in patients with an ejection fraction < 40% after acute MI (39), but it has only been approved for use in hypertension.

Higher rates of hyperkalemia have been documented in patients taking ACE inhibitors and spironolactone, necessitating careful monitoring of serum potassium levels (40). The combination of ACE inhibitors, ARBs, and spironolactone should be avoided because of a significantly increased risk for hyperkalemia.

Diuretics

Diuretics, which is the only therapy that acutely produces symptomatic benefits, can reduce pulmonary capillary wedge pressure and edema and improve exercise capacity. No clinical trials have assessed their long-term safety or impact on mortality in heart failure.

A single trial comparing furosemide with torsemide found that torsemide had the theoretical benefit of improved oral absorption, plus patients receiving torsemide were less likely to be readmitted for heart failure (41).

Loop diuretics should be used in combination with a low-sodium diet to control volume overload, maintain a stable weight, and improve the functional capacity of patients with NYHA class II to IV heart failure. Diuretics should never be used alone to treat heart failure because they do not prevent the progression of disease or maintain clinical stability over time.

For patients resistant to loop diuretics, thiazide diuretics may be added to augment diuresis. Furthermore, the use of a thiazide diuretic in combination with a loop diuretic can be part of an effective "sliding" diuretic regimen based on a patient's daily weight and symptoms. A second class of diuretic may act synergistically with the first by blocking the adaptive processes that limit diuretic effectiveness. With all diuretics, clinicians should frequently monitor patient renal function and electrolytes, especially potassium levels.

What is the role of digoxin in the treatment of heart failure?

Digoxin can alleviate symptoms and decrease hospitalizations in patients with heart failure; however, it should be reserved specifically for

35. The Cardiac Insufficiency Bisoprolol Study II (CIBIS-II): a randomised trial. Lancet. 1999;353:9-13. [PMID: 10023943]
36. Effect of metoprolol CR/XL in chronic heart failure: Metoprolol CR/XL Randomised Intervention Trial in Congestive Heart Failure (MERIT-HF). Lancet. 1999;353:2001-7. [PMID: 10376614]
37. Packer M, Coats AJ, Fowler MB, et al. Effect of carvedilol on survival in severe chronic heart failure. N Engl J Med. 2001;344:1651-8. [PMID: 11386263]
38. Pitt B, Zannad F, Remme WJ, et al. The effect of spironolactone on morbidity and mortality in patients with severe heart failure. Randomized Aldactone Evaluation Study Investigators. N Engl J Med. 1999;341:709-17. [PMID: 10471456]
39. Eplerenone Post-Acute Myocardial Infarction Heart Failure Efficacy and Survival Study Investigators. Eplerenone, a selective aldosterone blocker, in patients with left ventricular dysfunction after myocardial infarction. N Engl J Med. 2003;348:1309-21. [PMID: 12668699]
40. Juurlink DN, Mamdani MM, Lee DS, et al. Rates of hyperkalemia after publication of the Randomized Aldactone Evaluation Study. N Engl J Med. 2004;351(6):543-51. [PMID: 15295047]
41. Murray MD, Deer MM, Ferguson JA, et al. Open-label randomized trial of torsemide compared with furosemide therapy for patients with heart failure. Am J Med. 2001;111:513-20. [PMID: 11705426]

patients with symptomatic NYHA class II to IV heart failure, because research indicates that it provides no survival difference compared with placebo (42). Furthermore, digoxin does not appear to be effective in rate control for patients with atrial fibrillation, providing only rate control at rest (43).

It is important to ensure that electrolytes and renal function are stable before starting digoxin, and serum levels should be monitored, especially if renal function is changing. Some controversy exists over the appropriate serum level of digoxin. A recent study suggested that lower serum levels of digoxin were as efficacious as "therapeutic" levels, with a lower risk for side effects (44). In fact, in a post hoc subgroup analysis of 1 recent study, mortality rate was increased among women on digoxin compared with men, which may have been due to higher serum digoxin levels (45).

What drug therapy is appropriate for patients with diastolic dysfunction?

The goals of treatment of diastolic heart failure are: 1) to control heart rate to allow for adequate filling of the ventricle; 2) to maintain normal sinus rhythm, if possible; 3) to control volume status to decrease diastolic pressures; 4) to control blood pressure or other stimuli to left ventricular hypertrophy; and 5) to minimize myocardial ischemia in the setting of left ventricular hypertrophy, even in the absence of epicardial coronary disease.

There have been few randomized trials of the treatment for diastolic heart failure, and recommendations are based on investigations in small groups of patients or are based on theoretical concepts. The publication of consensus guidelines on the definition of diastolic heart failure has allowed for the design of multicenter clinical trials (46), several of which are now underway and

involve use of calcium-channel antagonists, aldosterone antagonists, ARBs, and clonidine in patients with and without hypertension.

ACC/AHA guidelines and others suggest that patients with diastolic dysfunction should be treated with diuretics, β-blockers, ACE inhibitors, ARBs, and nitrates. Calcium-channel blockers, such as verapamil and diltiazem, may also alleviate symptoms and improve exercise capacity. It is important to avoid overdiuresis, because dehydration can lead to lightheadedness and syncope in patients with diastolic dysfunction.

When should clinicians consider placement of an intracardiac device in patients with heart failure?

Patients with left ventricular dysfunction with an ejection fraction < 30% in NYHA class I, II, or III and an overall life expectancy of more than 6 months should be considered for placement of an intracardiac device (ICD) to monitor heart rate and rhythm and correct arrhythmia when it occurs. Data suggest that patients with class IV symptoms do not benefit from ICD placement, but those in class II may benefit most. Studies show a clear decrease in sudden death and overall mortality.

The DEFINITE (Defibrillators in Non-ischemic Cardiomyopathy Treatment Evaluation) trial randomized 458 patients with dilated nonischemic cardiomyopathy and left ventricular ejection fraction < 36% to standard medical therapy or standard medical therapy plus a single-chamber ICD. Over a follow-up period of 29 months, 28 deaths occurred in the ICD group compared with 40 in the standard medical therapy group. Although overall mortality was not significantly lower, there were 3 sudden deaths in the ICD group vs. 14 in the standard therapy group, P = 0.006 (47).

In the MADIT II (Multicenter Automatic Defibrillator Implantation Trial II), 1232 patients with a previous MI and an ejection fraction < 30% were randomly assigned (in

42. The Digitalis Investigation Group. The effect of digoxin on mortality and morbidity in patients with heart failure. N Engl J Med. 1997;336:525-33. [PMID: 9036306]

43. Khand AU, Rankin AC, Kaye GC, Cleland JG. Systematic review of the management of atrial fibrillation in patients with heart failure. Eur Heart J. 2000;21:614-32. [PMID: 10731399]

44. Adams KF Jr, Gheorghiade M, Uretsky BF, et al. Clinical benefits of low serum digoxin concentrations in heart failure. J Am Coll Cardiol. 2002;39:946-53. [PMID: 11897434]

45. Rathore SS, Wang Y, Krumholz HM. Sex-based differences in the effect of digoxin for the treatment of heart failure. N Engl J Med. 2002;347:1403-11. [PMID: 12409542]

46. How to diagnose diastolic heart failure. European Study Group on Diastolic Heart Failure. Eur Heart J. 1998;19:990-1003. [PMID: 9717033]

47. Kadish A, Dyer A, Daubert JP, et al. Prophylactic defibrillator implantation in patients with nonischemic dilated cardiomyopathy. N Engl J Med. 2004;350:2151-8. [PMID: 15152060]

48. Moss AJ, Zareba W, Hall WJ, et al. Prophylactic implantation of a defibrillator in patients with myocardial infarction and reduced ejection fraction. N Engl J Med. 2002;346:877-83. [PMID: 11907286]

the absence of electrophysiologic testing or other risk stratification) to ICD placement with conventional drug therapy or conventional drug therapy alone. The ICD group experienced a 28% reduction in mortality at 3 years (P = 0.007) (48).

The SCD-HeFT (Sudden Cardiac Death in Heart Failure trial) randomly assigned 2521 patients with NYHA class II or III heart failure and a left ventricular ejection fraction < 35% to conventional therapy for heart failure plus placebo; conventional therapy plus amiodarone; or conventional therapy plus a conservatively programmed, shock-only, single-lead ICD. During a median follow-up of 45.5 months, mortality was 29% in the placebo group, 28% in the amiodarone group, and 22% in the ICD group. The ICD therapy was associated with a 23% decreased risk for death (P = 0.007) compared with placebo (49).

Placement of a biventricular pacemaker can improve quality of life and decrease hospitalizations in patients with heart failure, an ejection fraction < 35%, a QRS interval > 130 msec on ECG, and symptoms despite maximal medical therapy.

In the MIRACLE-ICD (Multicenter InSync ICD Randomized Clinical Evaluation) trial, 369 patients with class III or IV heart failure, ejection fraction, and QRS interval < 130 msec received an ICD with resynchronization device. Those in whom the latter device was turned on demonstrated improved quality of life, functional status, and exercise capacity but no change in heart failure status, rates of hospitalization, or survival (50).

In the CARE-HF (Cardiac Resynchronization in Heart Failure) study, 813 patients with NYHA class III or IV heart failure due to left ventricular systolic dysfunction and cardiac dyssynchrony who were receiving standardized drug therapy were randomly assigned to receive medical therapy alone or with cardiac resynchronization. The study concluded that, in these patients, cardiac resynchronization improved symptoms and quality of life and reduced the risk for death (51).

When should clinicians use inotropic agents in patients with heart failure?

Inotropic agents, such as dobutamine and milrinone, can improve cardiac output in patients with low cardiac output and decrease afterload in patients with severe heart failure unresponsive to the traditional heart failure medications. However, all inotropic agents with the exception of digoxin have been associated with excess mortality and should be reserved for patients unresponsive to traditional oral heart failure medications. Because of the increased risk for sudden cardiac death, they should only be used in a monitored setting or for palliation of end-stage disease.

When should clinicians consider using anticoagulants in patients with heart failure?

Dilated cardiomyopathy with depressed ejection fraction below 35%, valvular lesions (especially mitral stenosis), and atrial fibrillation are all associated with embolic stroke. The incidence of thromboembolic events was about 2.7 per 100 patient-years in the 1 large trial database of patients with heart failure (52). Although many experts advocate anticoagulation to reduce the risk for stroke for patients with heart failure and significantly depressed ejection fraction who have no contraindications, anticoagulation remains controversial for patients with an ejection fraction below 35% without atrial fibrillation, documented clot, or valvular heart disease; and in another trial database, the use of warfarin in such patients was not associated with a reduction in all-cause mortality (53). Therefore, it seems most appropriate to initiate anticoagulation with warfarin in patients with documented left ventricular clot on echocardiogram or ventriculogram, atrial fibrillation, or prior embolic event and to use aspirin or clopidogrel in patients with coronary

49. Bardy GH, Lee KL, Mark DB, et al. Amiodarone or an implantable cardioverter-defibrillator for congestive heart failure. N Engl J Med. 2005;352:225-37. [PMID: 15659722]
50. Young JB, Abraham WT, Smith AL, et al. Combined cardiac resynchronization and implantable cardioversion defibrillation in advanced chronic heart failure: the MIRACLE ICD Trial. Multicenter InSync ICD Randomized Clinical Evaluation (MIRACLE ICD) Trial Investigators. JAMA. 2003;289:2685-94. [PMID: 12771115]
51. Cleland JG, Daubert JC, Erdmann E, et al. The effect of cardiac resynchronization on morbidity and mortality in heart failure. N Engl J Med. 2005;352:1539-49. [PMID: 15753115]
52. Dunkman WB, Johnson GR, Carson PE, et al. Incidence of thromboembolic events in congestive heart failure. The V-HeFT VA Cooperative Studies Group. Circulation. 1993;87:VI94-101. [PMID: 8500246]
53. Al-Khadra AS, Salem DN, Rand WM, et al. Warfarin anticoagulation and survival: a cohort analysis from the Studies of Left Ventricular Dysfunction. J Am Coll Cardiol. 1998;31:749-53. [PMID: 9525542]

Table 2. Drug Treatment for Heart Failure*

Agent, Dosage	Mechanism of Action	Benefits	Side Effects	Notes
ACE inhibitors				
Enalapril, 5–20 mg PO bid Captopril, 12.5–50.0 mg PO tid Lisinopril, 5–40 mg PO qd or 5–20 mg PO bid	Inhibits angiotensin-converting enzyme; results in decreased conversion of angiotensin I to angiotensin II and decreased metabolism of bradykinin. The latter produces prostaglandins and nitric oxide	Improves patient exercise tolerance, hemodynamic status, survival; may halt progression and cause regression of HF	Cough, angioedema, renal insufficiency, hyperkalemia	Follow BUN, creatinine, and potassium levels; withdraw or decrease dose if renal insufficiency exacerbated. For all classes of heart failure.
Angiotensin–receptor antagonists				
Losartan, 25–100 mg PO qd Valsartan, 80–320 mg PO qd Candesartan, 16–32 mg PO qd	Inhibits renin–angiotensin system at angiotensin receptor level	Improvement in hemodynamics and symptoms. Should be used in patients who cannot take ACE inhibitors. May be detrimental in patients already on ACE inhibitors and ß-blockers	Hyperkalemia, exacerbation of renal insufficiency, hypotension	Follow BUN, creatinine, and potassium levels. May use these agents in addition to ACE inhibitors in patients with severe HF.
ß-blockers				
Carvedilol, 3.125–25.0 mg PO bid (50 mg PO bid for patients weighing >85 kg) Carvedilol CR, 10–80 mg qd Metoprolol XL/CR (succinate), 50–200 mg PO qd XL Bisoprolol, 5 mg PO bid	Inhibits adrenergic nervous system; improves survival and LVEF in patients with HF; reduces sudden death risk	Improves hemodynamic status, LVEF, survival; may halt progression and cause regression of HF	Bradycardia, depression, hypotension, diabetes, exacerbation of asthma or COPD	Avoid in patients with significant asthma, or high-grade conduction system disease without pacemaker. For all classes of heart failure. Use with caution in patients with class IV heart failure.
Afterload reducers				
Hydralazine, 25–100 mg PO qid	Reduces afterload and preload	Combination with nitrates improves survival in patients with HF; survival benefit not as great as ACE inhibitors	Hypotension, lupus-like syndrome (high doses of hydralazine)	Combination with nitrates reserved for patients intolerant to ACE inhibitors and ARBs
Isosorbide dinitrate, 10–40 mg PO tid	Reduces afterload and preload	Combination with hydralazine improves survival in patients with HF; survival benefit not as great as ACE inhibitors	Headache	Combination with hydralazine reserved for patients intolerant to ACE inhibitors and ARBs
Aldosterone antagonists				
Spironolactone, 12.5–50.0 mg PO qd Eplerenone, 25–50 mg PO qd	Inhibits aldosterone, which can escape ACE inhibition and has numerous deleterious effects on cardiovascular system in patients with HF	Improves survival in patients with NYHA stages III to IV HF. Improves survival after MI with LV dysfunction.	Hyperkalemia, gynecomastia	Follow potassium level, especially in patients taking ACE inhibitors. Aldosterone antagonists alone are not an adequate substitute for a loop diuretic in patients who require diuretics. Eplerenone has fewer sex-hormone–related side effects. Avoid with combination of ACE inhibitors and ARBs.
Loop diuretics				
Furosemide, 10–160 mg PO qd bid Torsemide, 10–40 mg PO qd bid Bumetanide, 1–4 mg PO qd bid Ethacrynic acid, 25–100 mg PO qd bid	Inhibits chloride uptake in the loop of Henle; result is diuresis	Palliative in patients with congestive symptoms. No survival benefit.	Hypokalemia, hypomagnesemia, volume depletion, renal insufficiency	Follow BUN, creatinine, potassium, and magnesium levels and volume status.
Digitalis glycoside				
Digoxin, 0.125–0.25 mg PO qd	Positive inotropic agents. Increased extracellular calcium, slow heart rate through vagal effects.	Improves exercise tolerance, reduces hospitalizations. Slows heart rate. No survival benefit.	Arrhythmias, bradycardia (exacerbated by hypokalemia); visual changes. Low therapeutic index	Follow levels (aim for level <2.0). Follow potassium levels and avoid hypokalemia. Only positive inotropic agent not associated with increased mortality. Use lower dose in elderly patients and patients with renal insufficiency.
Positive inotropic agents				
Dobutamine, 2–10 µg/kg per min IV Milrinone, 0.1–0.7 µg/kg per min IV	Improves hemodynamics; arrhythmogenic	Palliative in patients with severe HF in whom oral agents have failed to improve hemodynamics	Arrhythmogenic; no survival benefit	Cardiology consultation strongly encouraged before initiation. Should be reserved for patients awaiting transplantation (ideally in monitored setting) or for palliation of patients with severe, end-stage HF who are not transplant candidates.

* ACE = angiotensin-converting enzyme; ARB = angiotensin-receptor blocker; bid = twice daily; BUN = blood urea nitrogen; HF = heart failure; COPD = chronic obstructive pulmonary disease; IV = intravenous; LV = left ventricular; LVEF = left ventricular ejection fraction; PO = oral; qid = four times daily; qd = once daily; tid = three times daily.

disease, regardless of ejection fraction.

What should clinicians advise patients to do to prevent exacerbations of heart failure?

Clinicians should advise patients to adhere to their fluid and salt restriction and medical regimen, weigh themselves daily, and to report deviations from their "dry weight" before they become symptomatic. Some patients can learn to use a sliding dose of diuretic to maintain their weight. Help from nurses, dietitians, home health staff, and physical therapists can be invaluable in helping patients prevent exacerbations. Patients should receive pneumococcal vaccine and annual influenza immunization.

Patients with established CAD should begin aggressive risk-factor modification, including attention to diet, exercise, weight control, and smoking cessation. Behavior modifications should be prescribed as well as pharmacologic therapy unless contraindicated. Multiple studies have shown that risk-factor modification with cholesterol-lowering drugs and the use of aspirin or other antiplatelet drugs, ACE inhibitors, and β-blockers can significantly reduce the risk for future cardiovascular events and reduce mortality.

When should clinicians consider consulting a cardiologist about management of patients with heart failure?

If symptoms worsen despite optimal medical therapy, consult a cardiologist for help in reviewing the need for hospitalization for parenteral inotropic drug treatment; catheterization; placement of an ICD, biventricular pacemaker, or left ventricular assist device; or cardiac transplantation. Consider obtaining pulmonary consultation when primary lung disease, such as chronic obstructive pulmonary disease or sleep apnea, is thought to be contributing to the patient's symptoms.

When should clinicians hospitalize patients with heart failure?

Patients with severe NYHA class IV heart failure, characterized by dyspnea at rest, severe fatigue, or volume overload unresponsive to oral diuretics or that requires inpatient evaluation and management should be hospitalized. This includes patients with life-threatening ventricular arrhythmias or atrial arrhythmias that worsen heart failure symptoms or cause hypotension. It also includes patients with syncope, sudden cardiac death, and atrial arrhythmias with worsening clinical signs and symptoms of heart failure who require parenteral drug treatment or device placement.

Treatment... Determine NYHA functional class to guide treatment in patients with heart failure. Limit salt and fluid intake in patients with symptomatic heart failure, and recommend regular exercise as tolerated. Begin first-line drug therapy with ACE inhibitors or ARBs (or hydralazine and nitrates if these are not tolerated) as well as β-blockers in patients who are not volume overloaded. Add loop diuretics and digoxin in patients with NYHA classes II, III, and IV heart failure and aldosterone antagonists in those with class III and IV and monitor potassium and renal function. Consult a cardiologist in patients with severe heart failure who may require hospitalization for inotropic agents; placement of ICD devices, pacemakers, or left ventricular assist devices; or cardiac transplantation. Recognize that anticoagulation for patients with depressed ejection fractions remains controversial. Teach patients to participate in their own care by encouraging them to monitor their diet, medical regimen, and weight.

CLINICAL BOTTOM LINE

54. American College of Cardiology/American Heart Association Task Force on Practice Guidelines (Committee to Revise the 1995 Guidelines for the Evaluation and Management of Heart Failure). ACC/AHA Guidelines for the Evaluation and Management of Chronic Heart Failure in the Adult: Executive Summary. Circulation. 2001;104:2996-3007. [PMID: 11739319]

55. American College of
Cardiology.
ACC/AHA 2005
Guideline Update for
the Diagnosis and
Management of
Chronic Heart Failure
in the Adult: a report
of the American Col-
lege of Cardiology/
American Heart As-
sociation Task Force
on Practice Guide-
lines (Writing Com-
mittee to Update
the 2001 Guidelines
for the Evaluation
and Management of
Heart Failure): devel-
oped in collabora-
tion with the Ameri-
can College of Chest
Physicians and the
International Society
for Heart and Lung
Transplantation: en-
dorsed by the Heart
Rhythm Society.
Circulation.
2005;112:e154-235.
[PMID: 16160202]
56. Heart Failure Society
of America. HFSA
2006 Comprehen-
sive Heart Failure
Practice Guideline. J
Card Fail. 2006;12:e1-
2. [PMID: 16500560]
57. Pharmacy Benefits
Management Strate-
gic Healthcare Group
and the Medical Ad-
visory Panel; Depart-
ment of Veterans Af-
fairs, Veterans Health
Administration. The
Pharmacologic Man-
agement of Chronic
Heart Failure. Ac-
cessed at http://www
.oqp.med.va.gov/
cpg/CHF/CHF_Base.
htm on 11 October
2007.

What do professional organizations recommend with regard to the care of patients with heart failure?

The ACC/AHA published guidelines for the Evaluation and Management of Chronic Heart Failure in the Adult in 2001 (54), and these were updated in 2005 (55). The guidelines contain extensive information on the characterization of heart failure as a clinical syndrome, initial and serial clinical assessment of patients, drug and device therapy for patients with heart failure at various stages of the disease, treatment of special populations, managing patients with heart failure and concomitant disorders, end-of-life considerations, and issues involved in implementation of the guidelines. The updated guidelines stress the importance of early diagnosis to stop or slow disease progression and changes in drug therapy based on several pivotal clinical trials.

In addition to the ACC/AHA guidelines, other significant guidelines include the Heart Failure Society of America 2006 Comprehensive Heart Failure Practice Guideline (56) and the Department of Veterans Affairs/Veterans Health Administration 2003 guidelines relating to the pharmacologic management of chronic heart failure (57).

What measures do stakeholders use to evaluate the quality of care for patients with heart failure?

The Centers for Medicare and Medicaid (CMS) has started a Physician Quality Reporting Initiative (PQRI) program, through which clinicians can report a designated set of quality measures on claims for services provided during the period from 1 July through 31 December 2007 and earn bonus payments. Among the current measures in the PQRI program, 2 relate to heart failure. The first is similar to the Ambulatory Care Quality Alliance measure relating to use of ACE inhibitors or ARBs, calling for use of these agents in patients over 18 years of age with a diagnosis of heart failure and left ventricular dysfunction. The second measures use of β-blocker therapy in the same population.

In addition, the Agency for Healthcare Research and Quality is using quality indicators to measure the hospital admission rate for heart failure, and CMS has proposed the public reporting of hospital-level 30-day mortality for patients with heart attack and heart failure.

in the clinic

Tool Kit

Heart Failure

PIER Modules

www.pier.acponline.org

Heart failure and percutaneous coronary intervention modules with updated information on current diagnosis and treatment of heart failure, designed for rapid access at the point of care.

Patient Information

www.annals.org/intheclinic

Download copies of the Patient Information sheet that appears on the following page for duplication and distribution to your patients.

Quality Improvement Tools

www.ihi.org/ihi/search/searchresults.aspx?searchterm=heart+failure+tools&searchtype=basic

Links to a variety of helpful tools for managing various aspects of heart failure, compiled by the Institute for Healthcare Improvement.

www.gericareonline.net/tools/eng/heartfailure/index.html

Download a complete heart failure toolkit covering various topics in assessment, management, and follow-up with accompanying flowsheets from the Practicing Physician in Education project, supported by the John A. Hartford Foundation.

www.cardiologyinoregon.org/information/information.html#toolkit

Resources from the Oregon Heart Failure GAP Toolkit, part of an American College of Cardiology project in 3 states to improve heart failure care.

THINGS PEOPLE SHOULD KNOW
ABOUT HEART FAILURE

- Heart failure, sometimes called congestive heart failure, is a condition in which the heart can't pump as well as it should. Because the heart has a hard time getting blood to the rest of the body, patients with heart failure can feel weak and tired.

- In some patients with heart failure, fluid (edema) builds up in the lungs and parts of the body, making it hard to breathe and causing swelling in the legs.

Heart Failure Symptoms:

Breathlessness during activity, at rest, or while sleeping

Wheezing or coughing that may be dry or may produce white or pink blood-tinged phlegm

Swelling in the feet, ankles, legs or abdomen, or unexplained weight gain

A constant lack of energy and difficulty performing everyday activities

A sense of having a full or sick stomach

A feeling like the heart is racing or pounding

A feeling the heart is skipping beats or occasionally pounding very hard

- Heart failure can result from many different conditions that directly or indirectly affect the heart. People with high blood pressure, diabetes, high cholesterol, and coronary artery disease can develop heart failure. Treating these conditions may prevent heart failure.

- Treating heart failure means working together with your doctor to control salt in your diet, watching your weight, and taking all your medications every day. It's important to keep your regular doctor appointments.

- Heart failure affects nearly 5 million adults, and 550 000 new cases are diagnosed each year. It is more common in older people but can occur at any age. Although there is no cure yet, heart failure is very treatable and millions of Americans lead a full life by managing their condition through medications and by making healthy changes in their lifestyles.

Web Sites with Good Information on Heart Failure

American College of Physicians
www.doctorsforadults.com/images/healthpdfs/heartfail.pdf

American Heart Association
www.americanheart.org/presenter.jhtml?identifier=1486

National Heart, Lung, and Blood Institute
www.nhlbi.nih.gov/health/dci/Diseases/Hf/HF_WhatIs.html

Insomnia

People with insomnia have trouble falling or staying asleep, and the result is poor-quality sleep of insufficient duration. Insomnia is common, affecting 1 in 3 adults intermittently and 1 in 10 adults chronically, and can seriously affect wellbeing. It typically causes excessive daytime sleepiness, irritability, and lack of energy. Long-term insomnia may lead to depression, inattention, learning and memory problems, and job or school underperformance. Given these substantial health consequences and the prevalence of insomnia, clinicians should be skilled in managing it.

Screening

1. National Heart Lung and Blood Institute. Who is At Risk for Insomnia? U.S. Department of Health and Human Services. National Institutes of Health. Accessed at www.nhlbi.nih.gov/health/dci/Diseases/inso/inso_whoisatrisk.html on 9 November 2007.
2. Foley DJ, Monjan AA, Brown SL, et al. Sleep complaints among elderly persons: an epidemiologic study of three communities. Sleep. 1995;18:425-32. [PMID: 7481413]
3. Maggi S, Langlois JA, Minicuci N, et al. Sleep complaints in community-dwelling older persons: prevalence, associated factors, and reported causes. J Am Geriatr Soc. 1998;46:161-8. [PMID: 9475443]
4. Gellis LA, Lichstein KL, Scarinci IC, et al. Socioeconomic status and insomnia. J Abnorm Psychol. 2005;114:111-8. [PMID: 15709817]
5. Paine SJ, Gander PH, Harris R, Reid P. Who reports insomnia? Relationships with age, sex, ethnicity, and socioeconomic deprivation. Sleep. 2004;27:1163-9. [PMID: 15532211]
6. Wingard DL, Berkman LF. Mortality risk associated with sleeping patterns among adults. Sleep. 1983;6:102-7. [PMID: 6878979]
7. Suka M, Yoshida K, Sugimori H. Persistent insomnia is a predictor of hypertension in Japanese male workers. J Occup Health. 2003;45:344-50. [PMID: 14676413]

Which patient populations have the highest prevalence of insomnia?
People especially prone to insomnia include those who are under stress, are depressed or have other emotional distress, are working at night or having frequent major shifts in their work hours, or are traveling long distances with time changes (1). Insomnia can occur at any age, but it is particularly prevalent in the elderly. One large study found that the prevalence of insomnia complaints ranged between 23% and 34% among people 65 years and older (2). Among this population, sleep complaints are commonly associated with medication use and medical problems (3). Population-based studies have found an association between lower socioeconomic status and insomnia (4, 5).

Should clinicians screen for insomnia? If so, how should they screen?
Clinicians should consider screening for insomnia as part of regular patient care given its high prevalence and potential impact on wellbeing. Insomnia puts people at increased risk for poor health, and it can also reduce work performance and quality of life (6–9).

Evidence that screening for insomnia improves patient outcomes is not available. However, screening can be accomplished in a relatively straightforward, brief manner by asking patients about trouble initiating or maintaining sleep, early morning waking, or nonrestorative sleep (10). Further evaluation can be limited to individuals with these complaints.

> Screening... Given the high prevelance of insomnia and its potential impact on health and quality of life, clinicians should consider incorporating screening for insomnia as a regular part of patient care. It can be done in a relatively straightforward way that does not take long by asking patients about difficulty initiating or maintaining sleep, early morning awakening, or nonrestorative sleep. People prone to insomnia are those who are under a lot of stress; who are depressed or have other emotional distress; and those who work nights, have frequent major shifts in their work hours, or travel long distances with time changes.
>
> **CLINICAL BOTTOM LINE**

Diagnosis

What are the components of a comprehensive sleep history?
A consensus paper from the American Academy of Sleep Medicine recommends detailed historical information, as well as medical, psychological, and psychiatric assessment to evaluate insomnia (11).

Comprehensive assessment enables clinicians to establish the cause of insomnia and to plan effective treatment.

Clinicians should ask about specific sleep complaints and duration, sleep hygiene, mood disorders, underlying medical disorders, medication use, and substance use. Patient sleep diaries can supplement history by helping to obtain a more accurate record of sleep habits than general questioning alone and to assess total sleep time. If asking patients to keep a sleep diary, clinicians should instruct them to record bedtime, sleep time, nocturnal waking, and rising time in sleep diaries daily for at least 1 to 2 weeks. Standardized sleep questionnaires are primarily used in research settings, but their utility in clinical settings is uncertain.

Which conditions should clinicians consider as potential secondary causes of insomnia?

The most common type of insomnia is secondary insomnia, meaning that it is attributable to an underlying condition, poor sleep environment, or use of medications or other substances that interfere with sleep. A longitudinal study of more than 200 general medical patients found a strong linkage between severe insomnia and chronic medical and psychiatric disorders (12). A study of 2398 community-dwelling individuals aged 65 years and older found that sleep complaints were common and associated with a range of medications and medical problems (3). The American Sleep Disorders Association released an international classification of sleep disorders manual to better define these various causes (13). Tables 1 and 2 summarize the main considerations in the differential diagnosis of potential causes of secondary insomnia.

What is the role of physical examination in the evaluation of patients with insomnia?

The physical examination can identify signs that suggest a specific disorder underlying insomnia. Underlying causes include obstructive sleep apnea syndrome (OSAS), obesity, hypertension, thyroid dysfunction, restless leg syndrome (RLS), or other cardiopulmonary or neurologic disease

When should clinicians consider laboratory testing in the evaluation of patients with insomnia?

Laboratory testing should not be used routinely in the evaluation of insomnia. However, judicious use may be indicated in some patients with clinical evidence of concomitant disease that may be associated with insomnia (10).

Polysomnography

The American Academy of Sleep Medicine report recommends using polysomnography (overnight sleep test) or a multiple sleep latency test (MSLT), or both, to evaluate patients with sleep-disordered breathing; specific sleep disorders, such as narcolepsy and periodic limb movements; or insomnia resistant to initial therapeutic measures (14).

Multiple Sleep Latency Test (MLST)

The MSLT is a standard nap test that takes place in a sleep laboratory after an overnight sleep study. This test is a series of four 20-minute naps designed to objectively measure

---

Things to Ask about When Taking a Comprehensive Sleep History

- Problems of sleep initiation, sleep maintenance, early morning waking, or nonrestorative sleep
- Ascertain if the patient has acute, short-term, or chronic insomnia
- Stability or progression of symptoms—that is, if the insomnia is stable, worsening, or improving
- Precipitating causes of insomnia
- Bedtime, wake time, length of sleep time
- Caffeine and alcohol use
- Any current or previous behavioral therapies used to treat insomnia
- Previous over-the-counter or prescription sedative-hypnotic use
- Shifting work and irregular sleep schedule
- Potential acute stressors, such as:
  ○ Medical or psychiatric illness
  ○ Medication use, both prescribed and illicit
  ○ Acute stress at home or work
  ○ Circadian rhythm stressors, such as jet lag

8. Studio Morfeo Committee. Studio Morfeo: insomnia in primary care, a survey conducted on the Italian population. Sleep Med. 2004;5:67-75. [PMID: 14725829]
9. Ohayon MM, Roth T. Place of chronic insomnia in the course of depressive and anxiety disorders. J Psychiatr Res. 2003;37:9-15. [PMID: 12482465]
10. Chesson A Jr, Hartse K, Anderson WM, et al. Practice parameters for the evaluation of chronic insomnia. An American Academy of Sleep Medicine report. Standards of Practice Committee of the American Academy of Sleep Medicine. Sleep. 2000;23:237-41. [PMID: 10737341]
11. Sateia MJ, Doghramji K, Hauri PJ, Morin CM. Evaluation of chronic insomnia. An American Academy of Sleep Medicine review. Sleep. 2000;23:243-308. [PMID: 10737342]
12. Hohagen F, Rink K, Käppler C, et al. Prevalence and treatment of insomnia in general practice. A longitudinal study. Eur Arch Psychiatry Clin Neurosci. 1993;242:329-36. [PMID: 8323982]
13. American Sleep Disorders Association. International classification of sleep disorders, revised: Diagnostic and coding manual. Westchester, IL: American Academy of Sleep Medicine; 1997.
14. Reite M, Buysse D, Reynolds C, Mendelson W. The use of polysomnography in the evaluation of insomnia. Sleep. 1995;18:58-70. [PMID: 7761745]

Table 1. Differential Diagnosis of Underlying Causes of Insomnia*

Disease	Characteristics	Notes
Psychophysiologic insomnia	Disturbed sleep from conditioned arousal, usually to the bedroom	Look for a history of sleep improvement when away from the bedroom; patients may have an inordinate concern over sleep.
RLS	An uncomfortable or restless feeling in legs most prominent at night and at rest; alleviated by movement	Look for a family history of RLS, history of caffeine abuse, iron deficiency, renal disease, pregnancy, ADHD, and, less likely, vitamin B12 or folate deficiency. RLS may also be present with colon adenocarcinoma. Approximately 80% of patients with RLS have PLMS on polysomnography. Occurs in 11% of general population.
Periodic limb movement disorder	Repetitive stereotypic leg movement during sleep	Look for a history of repetitive leg movements during sleep that leads to disturbed sleep. Polysomnography is necessary for diagnosis.
Sleep-state misperception	Objectively normal sleep in the face of the patient's complaint of insufficient sleep	Polysomnography will document normal sleep. The factor(s) that generate the complaint are unclear. Patients have no obvious psychopathology.
Idiopathic insomnia	Lifelong sleep problems with suspected neurologic abnormality of sleep-wake system	Look for lifelong persistent insomnia.
Central sleep apnea syndrome	Repetitive pauses in breathing during sleep without upper airway occlusion	Look for associated history of congestive heart failure or central nervous system disease. Polysomnography is necessary for diagnosis.
OSAS	Upper airway obstruction during inspiration in sleep	Look for a history of snoring, respiratory pauses, and daytime sleepiness. Polysomnography is needed for diagnosis. OSAS occurs in about 2% of middle-aged females and 4% of middle-aged males.
Extrinsic sleep disorders		
Inadequate sleep hygiene	Disturbed sleep associated with caffeine, tobacco, alcohol use, or irregular sleep habits	Comprehensive sleep history will facilitate the diagnosis. Believed to be a common factor in insomnia.
Environmental sleep disorder	Disturbed sleep associated with environmental elements	Comprehensive sleep history will facilitate the diagnosis.
Altitude insomnia	Disturbed sleep associated with altitude	Look for a history of ascent to high altitudes. Can begin as low as 2000 m for persons from sea level and is common above 4000 m. Characterized by periodic breathing and central apnea events.
Hypnotic-dependent sleep disorder	Disturbed sleep associated with tolerance to or withdrawal from hypnotic drugs	Ask for positive history of sustained hypnotic use with development of tolerance leading to increased dose.
Stimulant-dependent sleep disorder	Disturbed sleep associated with stimulant drug use	Comprehensive sleep history will facilitate the diagnosis.
Alcohol-dependent sleep disorder	Alcohol used to initiate sleep; sleep that follows is fragmented	Ask for patient's history of alcohol use to facilitate sleep for at least the last 30 days. May be preceded by other sleep-disturbing factors.
Toxin-induced sleep disorder	Disturbed sleep associated with arsenic, copper, lead, or mercury ingestion	The clinician must be alert to chronic or acute ingestion. Diagnosed with tests for heavy metals, CBC, hepatic, and renal testing.
Circadian rhythm sleep disorders		
Shift-work sleep disorder	Sleep occurs at times that are counter to normal circadian rhythm and environmental factors	Look for a history of insomnia associated with shift work. Remember that shift work includes those patients working a permanent night shift. Occurs in approximately 2% to 5% of population.
Delayed sleep-phase syndrome	A circadian rhythm disorder in which the major sleep phase is delayed relative to clock time	Look for a history of sleep-onset insomnia and difficulty awakening at the desired time. Patients have no difficulty maintaining sleep once asleep. Most common in adolescents.
Advanced sleep-phase syndrome	A circadian rhythm disorder in which the major sleep phase is advanced relative to clock time	Look for a history of inability to stay awake until desired bedtime and early morning awakening. Occurs most commonly in the elderly.
Time zone change syndrome (jet lag)	Travel leads to complaints of poor sleep, daytime sleepiness, or both. Physical complaints may ensue (e.g., GI upset)	Look for a history of recent travel across multiple time zones.

*ADHD = attention deficit hyperactivity disorder; CBC = complete blood count; COPD = chronic obstructive pulmonary disorder; OSAS = obstructive sleep apnea syndrome; PLMS = periodic leg movements in sleep; RLS = restless leg syndrome.

Table 2. Other Medical Disorders that Can Be Underlying Causes of Insomnia

Disease	Characteristics	Notes
Nocturnal leg cramps	Pain in calf or foot, resulting in sleep awakening	Look for a history of painful cramps awakening the patient from sleep. Predisposing factors include diabetes, exercise, pregnancy, and metabolic and endocrine abnormalities. May occur with Parkinson disease and arthritis.
Anxiety and depressive disorders	May trigger sleep initiation or sleep maintenance problem	Look for a history of anxiety or depression. Most patients with anxiety and insomnia will present with anxiety first or concomitant with insomnia. In contrast, depression tends to follow the complaint of insomnia
Cerebral degenerative or traumatic disorders	Insomnia associated with a cerebral degenerative disorder	Look for the presence of abnormal body movements, reduced sleep efficiency, and increased awakenings. Objective testing (multiple sleep latency test or maintenance of wakefulness test) shows daytime sleepiness. Insomnia complaints frequently complicate traumatic brain injury.
Dementia	Insomnia associated with dementia; manifested by wandering, aggressive behavior, verbalization, and delirium in early evening hours	Look for these symptoms in a patient with a progressive dementing illness. Note that other sleep disorders, such as sleep apnea, may exacerbate this disorder.
Parkinsonism	Insomnia is commonly associated with Parkinson disease	Look for sleep-onset and maintenance problems. A number of potential causes to insomnia in Parkinson disease exist, including depression and anti-Parkinson drugs.
Fatal familial insomnia	Prion-related thalamic degeneration, resulting in progressive insomnia	Look for a progressive problem initiating sleep associated with a number of other symptoms, such as fever, excessive salivation, and sweating. Death occurs in 7 to 13 months.
Sleep-related epilepsy	Sleep-related epilepsy is defined as when 75% of the events occur during sleep	This condition affects about 25% of patients with epilepsy. Seizure-related complaints include sudden awakenings, urinary incontinence, and unusual but stereotypic movements at night. Patients with nocturnal epilepsy do not commonly complain of insomnia.
Sleep-related headaches	A number of classes of headache are closely tied to sleep, including migraine, cluster headache, and paroxysmal nocturnal hemicrania	Look for a history of headache arising during sleep or noted on first awakening. Paroxysmal nocturnal hemicrania may respond to indomethacin.
Asthma/COPD	Nighttime attacks of lower airway obstruction may occur in asthma. Cough, sputum production, wheeze, or shortness of breath may interrupt sleep in COPD	Look for a history of nocturnal awakenings due to cough, wheeze, or shortness of breath. Note that asthma may present with symptoms at night as an initial manifestation of suboptimal control.
Gastroesophageal reflux disease	Symptoms or histologic changes in the esophagus due to the reflux of gastric contents into the esophagus	Look for a history of sleep-related heartburn, nocturnal cough, and chest pain.
Fibromyalgia syndrome	Chronic generalized musculoskeletal pain, nonrefreshing sleep, fatigue associated with trigger points	Look for muscle tenderness and trigger points. Laboratory testing for inflammatory arthritis is normal.

daytime sleepiness and the onset of REM sleep. A latency of less than 8 minutes to stage 1 sleep suggests pathologic hypersomnolence.

Sleep Actigraphy

In this noninvasive test, the patient wears a small, watch-like electronic device around the wrist of the nondominant arm for an extended period of time. Although actigraphy provides an accurate recording of sleep patterns, it may underestimate severity in patients with sleep-onset insomnia. Sleep actigraphs can provide a reliable measurement of sleep patterns and circadian rhythms (15)

and are most often used in research settings.

Other Tests to Evaluate for Underlying Comorbidity

Various other tests may be needed to check for underlying cardiac, pulmonary, gastrointestinal, or neurologic disorders contributing to or causing the insomnia.

Complete blood count and serum ferritin levels can identify anemia, which is associated with RLS. A blood urea nitrogen test and serum creatinine test can check for renal disease, which is also associated with RLS. Thyroid function tests

15. Ancoli-Israel S, Cole R, Alessi C, et al. The role of actigraphy in the study of sleep and circadian rhythms. Sleep. 2003;26:342-92. [PMID: 12749557]

can reveal hypothyroidism or hyperthyroidism, conditions that are associated with sleep problems. Urine drug screening may also be useful, because stimulant medication and benzodiazepine hypnotic medications may alter sleep.

Clinicians should consider electrocardiography and echocardiography if there is a concern about congestive heart failure, which can interfere with sleep. A chest X-ray may be used to identify heart failure or chronic obstructive pulmonary disease. In patients with respiratory symptoms, pulmonary function testing may identify upper and lower airway obstruction. Barium swallow and 24-hour pH probe may be helpful in the evaluation of patients in whom symptoms suggest that gastroesophageal reflux may be contributing to insomnia.

Diagnosis... Insomnia is most often due to underlying medical or psychological conditions, medications or other substances that interfere with sleep, or poor sleep environment. A detailed history and physical evaluation is necessary in the evaluation of insomnia. This might include the use of sleep diaries, sleep questionnaires, and laboratory testing to evaluate for underlying conditions.

CLINICAL BOTTOM LINE

Treatment

What is sleep hygiene and what is its role in the treatment of patients with insomnia?
Sleep hygiene is the practice of following simple guidelines (see Box) to promote sound sleep and daytime alertness.

Poor sleep hygiene can contribute to sleep fragmentation, circadian rhythm disturbance, discomfort, and overstimulation. Clinicians should review and correct poor sleep hygiene in all patients complaining of insomnia, customizing the application of sleep hygiene rules to specific patient needs, such as the need to work night shifts.

Stimulus control consists of advising patients to associate the bed and bedroom with sleepiness. It can be an effective treatment for insomnia when conditioned arousal to the sleeping environment is a problem and perhaps even in the absence of obvious evidence of conditioning. Patients should spend no more than 20 minutes awake in bed and leave the bedroom to engage in nonstimulating activity until tired before returning to bed. Keeping set bedtimes and rising times is important, even if patients are awake during the night. Research has shown that such practices can improve time to onset of sleep and total sleep time (16).

Good sleep hygiene behaviors:
- Maintain stable bed times and rising times
- Spend no more than 8 hours in bed
- Experience regular daytime light exposure
- Maintain a quiet, dark bedroom
- Maintain adequate nutrition
- Avoid sleep-fragmenting substances, such as caffeine, nicotine, and alcohol
- Avoid clock-watching
- Maintain regular exercise
- Avoid heavy exercise within 2 hours of bedtime
- Avoid bright light before bedtime
- Maintain a 30-minute relaxation period before bedtime
- Avoid using alcohol to initiate sleep

16. Morin CM, Mimeault V, Gagné A. Nonpharmacological treatment of late-life insomnia. J Psychosom Res. 1999;46:103-16. [PMID: 10098820]
17. McDowell JA, Mion LC, Lydon TJ, Inouye SK. A nonpharmacologic sleep protocol for hospitalized older patients. J Am Geriatr Soc. 1998;46:700-5. [PMID: 9625184]
18. Edinger JD, Wohlgemuth WK, Radtke RA, et al. Does cognitive-behavioral insomnia therapy alter dysfunctional beliefs about sleep? Sleep. 2001;24:591-9. [PMID: 11480656]

Is sleep restriction or other behavioral therapy useful in the treatment of patients with insomnia?

Behavioral treatments may reduce insomnia significantly in many patients. In patients with chronic insomnia, behavioral therapy should be tried before instituting drug treatment. Several studies suggest that nondrug therapies may be more effective if not used in conjunction with drugs. However, behavioral therapy may also be combined with drug therapy to reduce the need for sleeping pills (17). A sleep disorders specialist or knowledgeable therapist should be consulted when considering behavioral therapies for insomnia.

Sleep Restriction

Sleep restriction is a behavioral intervention that limits, then slowly increases, the time for sleep. Patients keep a sleep diary for 1 to 2 weeks, and then alter their sleep schedule so that their time in bed is equal to their average total sleep time, which is calculated based on the sleep diary. Note, however, that sleep restriction should be no less than 5 hours in bed, and daily rising time should be the same every day. Using this method, patients gradually increase the amount of time they spend in bed. Patients make bedtime earlier by 15-minute increments as long as sleep efficiency (total sleep time divided by total time in bed) is 90% or better as documented by the sleep log.

Sleep restriction may be initiated in patients with insomnia associated with no underlying medical or psychological disorder and in whom sleep hygiene maneuvers have been unsuccessful. Clinicians should caution patients that sleep restriction therapy may lead to excessive daytime sleepiness and that they should be careful performing potentially dangerous activities, such as driving.

Cognitive Behavioral Therapy

Cognitive behavioral therapy (CBT) is used to correct misconceptions about sleep. In CBT, the practitioner reviews normal sleep needs, specifically by reinforcing the idea that patients require 7 to 8 hours of sleep per night; discussing changes in sleep with aging, such as increased light sleep and decreased deep sleep; and alleviating exaggerated patient concerns about the impact and consequences of insomnia. Studies have shown that CBT reduces dysfunctional beliefs about sleep and alleviates insomnia, outperforming placebo and relaxation procedures, and providing elements not found in other behavioral techniques (18, 19).

A small, single-blind study found that one half of participants experienced a 50% reduction in their time awake after sleep onset using an abbreviated 2-session CBT intervention (20).

Behavioral techniques were more effective than drug therapy or placebo in the long-term in a randomized, placebo-controlled study of 78 older patients with chronic insomnia (21).

A randomized, placebo-controlled trial of 63 middle-aged and young adults found that CBT was superior to drug therapy in the treatment of insomnia characterized by difficulty with sleep initiation (22).

Biofeedback and Progressive Muscle Relaxation

Biofeedback and progressive muscle relaxation techniques also have potential usefulness in the management of insomnia. The literature indicates that physiologic, muscular, and cognitive arousal can interfere with sleep, and that relaxation can help. However, any intervention that increases the expectation of falling asleep more quickly, including placebo, might be equally effective (23). In these interventions, patients practice ways to reduce high levels of arousal by using specific

19. Edinger JD, Wohlgemuth WK, Radtke RA, et al. Cognitive behavioral therapy for treatment of chronic primary insomnia: a randomized controlled trial. JAMA. 2001;285:1856-64. [PMID: 11308399]
20. Edinger JD, Sampson WS. A primary care "friendly" cognitive behavioral insomnia therapy. Sleep. 2003;26:177-82. [PMID: 12683477]
21. Morin CM, Colecchi C, Stone J, et al. Behavioral and pharmacological therapies for late-life insomnia: a randomized controlled trial. JAMA. 1999;281:991-9. [PMID: 10086433]
22. Jacobs GD, Pace-Schott EF, Stickgold R, Otto MW. Cognitive behavior therapy and pharmacotherapy for insomnia: a randomized controlled trial and direct comparison. Arch Intern Med. 2004;164:1888-96. [PMID: 15451764]

Things to Consider when Prescribing Drugs to Treat Insomnia

- Use a GABA agonist over other sedative-hypnotics for treatment of acute or short-term insomnia.
- Use the minimal effective dose.
- Avoid long half-life medications, including long half-life metabolites.
- Be aware of potential interactions between drugs, including over-the-counter drugs.
- Caution patients on these medications about interaction with alcohol.
- Review potential side effects—in particular, daytime sleepiness.
- Look for rebound insomnia after discontinuation.
- Confer with the patient to determine an appropriate period of use.
- Consider intermittent or long-term use of hypnotic medications, depending on the clinical situation.
- Consider consultation with sleep specialists before starting long-term therapy with hypnotic medication.
- Recognize that concomitant use of hypnotics and behavior therapy may mitigate the efficacy of the behavioral measures.

---

23. Nicassio PM, Boylan MB, McCabe TG. Progressive relaxation, EMG biofeedback and biofeedback placebo in the treatment of sleep-onset insomnia. Br J Med Psychol. 1982;55:159-66. [PMID: 7104246]

24. Weiler JM, Bloomfield JR, Woodworth GG, et al. Effects of fexofenadine, diphenhydramine, and alcohol on driving performance: a randomized, placebo-controlled trial in the Iowa Driving Simulator. Ann Intern Med. 2000;132:354-63.

25. Basu R, Dodge H, Stoehr GP, Ganguli M. Sedative-hypnotic use of diphenhydramine in a rural, older adult, community-based cohort: effects on cognition. Am J Geriatr Psychiatry. 2003;11:205-13. [PMID: 12611750]

26. Balter MB, Uhlenhuth EH. The beneficial and adverse effects of hypnotics. J Clin Psychiatry. 1991;52 Suppl:16-23. [PMID: 2071567]

techniques of tensing and relaxing different muscle groups or using visual or auditory feedback that focuses on a specific physiologic measure. Although biofeedback may be effective, it requires special equipment and training, and it may only be effective in subgroups of patients with insomnia. For instance, research indicates that younger patients respond better to relaxation techniques than older patients (16).

How should clinicians advise patients about the use of nonprescription agents in the treatment of insomnia?

Antihistamines

Products containing the antihistamines diphenhydramine or doxylamine may induce sedation. Combinations of an antihistamine plus a nonsteroidal anti-inflammatory drug target minor pain-related insomnia. Although over-the-counter products containing antihistamines are marketed as sleep aids and are commonly used, they are associated with adverse events, including strong anticholinergic side effects, daytime sedation, and cognitive impairment. Consequently, patients may not feel rested even if insomnia is improved. Few data support a favorable risk-benefit ratio for antihistamines in the treatment of insomnia.

A cross-over study examined patient's automobile driving performance when operating a driving simulator after ingesting 50 mg diphenhydramine, 60 mg fexofenadine (a second-generation antihistamine), 50 mg alcohol, or placebo. Driving performance was poorest after participants took diphenhydramine, indicating that it negatively influenced driving performance more than alcohol (24).

A study of more than 1600 subjects showed that extended use of over-the-counter diphenhydramine in an older rural population was associated with impairment on the Mini Mental Status Examination (25).

In addition, a large telephone survey found that, although users of prescription hypnotics felt favorably about them and reported few

adverse effects, those taking over-the-counter sleep medications felt that they were less effective and caused more side effects (26).

Alternative Therapies

Other nonprescription agents include natural remedies, such as melatonin, valerian, kava, or St. John's wort. The efficacy and safety of these agents is not clear and has not been well-studied, and their use is generally discouraged. Melatonin may be useful for short-term adaptation to jet lag or other circadian rhythm sleep disorders. However, effectiveness for chronic insomnia is less clear, and optimal dose and long-term adverse effects also are not known.

A small, randomized, cross-over study in 10 patients with primary insomnia did not show that melatonin produced any sleep benefit measured by sleep electroencephalography, sleep duration, or subjective sleep quality (27).

When should clinicians consider prescription drug therapy for patients with insomnia?

When other approaches prove inadequate, prescription drug therapy tailored to the underlying cause of insomnia may be warranted. Although drug therapy in the short-term is as effective as behavioral interventions, concomitant use of hypnotics and behavior therapy may mitigate the efficacy of the behavioral measures.

Prescription treatment options include either benzodiazepines, such as clorazepate, diazepam, lorazepam, oxazepam, temazepam, and triazolam, or nonbenzodiazepine hypnotics, such as zolpidem, zaleplon, and eszopiclone (Table 3). The nonbenzodiazepines are preferred because they do not alter sleep architecture and have a more favorable side-effect profile.

Benzodiazepines

Benzodiazepines exert their effects through enhancement of the gamma-aminobutyric acid (GABA)

Table 3. Drag Treatment for Insomnia*

Agent, Dosage	Mechanism of Action	Benefits	Side Effects	Notes
Benzodiazepines Estazolam, 1–2 mg Flurazepam, 15–30 mg Quazepam, 7.5–30 mg Temazepam, 7.5–30 mg Triazolam, 0.125–0.5 mg	GABA agonist	Shorten sleep latency and reduce unscheduled waking	Daytime sedation, anterograde amnesia, falls, rebound insomnia	Temazepam is water-soluble instead of lipid-soluble and has a longer onset of action (about 1 hour). Flurazepam and quazepam have long half-life active metabolites.
Nonbenzodiazepine -sedative hypnotic agents Zolpidem, 5–10 mg Zaleplon, 5–10 mg	GABA agonist	Shorten sleep latency and reduce unscheduled waking	Daytime sedation, anterograde amnesia, falls, rebound insomnia	Zaleplon has the shortest half-life (about 1 hour).
Dopaminergic agents Pramipexole, 0.125–1.5 mg in 2–3 doses Levodopa and carbidopa, up to 100–200 mg in divided doses Ropinirole, 0.25–3 mg in 2–3 divided doses Pergolide, 0.025–0.5 mg in 2–3 divided doses	Increased dopaminergic activity via dopamine agonist activity (pramipexole, ropinirole, pergolide) or dopamine precursor (levodopa)	Elimination of evening and nighttime RLS symptoms	Nausea/vomiting, nasal congestion, swelling, bloating, and chest pain.	Evening/nighttime dose may push RLS symptoms later into the night and perhaps into the day. Therefore, dose should be taken 2 to 3 hours before bedtime.
Antidepressants Tricyclic antidepressants Amitriptyline, 10–50 mg Doxepin, 10–50 mg Trimipramine, 25–50 mg	α_1 blockade	Shorten sleep latency and reduce unscheduled waking	Daytime sedation, anterograde amnesia, rebound insomnia, anticholinergic side effects	Do not use in the absence of underlying depression. Trimipramine does not suppress REM sleep, as shown in a placebo/lormetazepam-controlled study of 55 patients.
Mirtazapine, 15 mg	Antagonizes α_2 and 5-HT$_2$ receptors	Shorten sleep latency and reduce unscheduled waking	Daytime sedation, flu-like symptoms, tremor, abnormal dreams	Do not use in the absence of underlying depression. Improves sleep and does not suppress REM sleep.
Trazodone, 50–100 mg	α_1 blockade	Shorten sleep latency and reduce unscheduled waking	Priapism, syncope	Do not use in the absence of underlying depression. Evidence suggests that trazodone may increase deep sleep.
Antihistamines Diphenhydramine, 25 mg Doxtlamine, 25mg	Ethanolamine H$_1$ receptor antagonists	Shorten sleep latency and reduce unscheduled waking	Anticholinergic activity, sedation, dizziness	Morning hangover effects may be greater than those of GABA agonists.

*GABA = γ-aminobutyric acid; REM = rapid eye movement; RLS = restless legs syndrome.

benzodiazepine receptor complex. GABA is an inhibitory neurotransmitter, which exerts its effect at GABA-A, -B, and -C receptor subtypes, all of which are affected by benzodiazepines. Benzodiazepines are effective for increasing sleep duration; however, potential tolerance and dependence limit their use to short-term insomnia. The therapy in the short-term is as effective as behavioral interventions, but clinical efficacy tends to decline when patients take benzodiazepines for longer than 30 days.

Adverse effects from benzodiazepines include residual daytime cognitive impairment, hangover effects, psychomotor impairment, and anterograde amnesia. At discontinuation, tapering withdrawal

27. Almeida Montes LG, Ontiveros Uribe MP, Cortés Sotres J, Heinze Martin G. Treatment of primary insomnia with melatonin: a double-blind, placebo-controlled, crossover study. J Psychiatry Neurosci. 2003;28:191-6. [PMID: 12790159]

28. Krystal AD, Walsh JK, Laska E, et al. Sustained efficacy of eszopiclone over 6 months of nightly treatment: results of a randomized, double-blind, placebo-controlled study in adults with chronic insomnia. Sleep. 2003;26:793-9. [PMID: 14655910]

29. Maarek L, Cramer P, Attali P, et al. The safety and efficacy of zolpidem in insomniac patients: a long-term open study in general practice. J Int Med Res. 1992;20:162-70. [PMID: 1521672]

30. Walsh JK, Roth T, Randazzo A, et al. Eight weeks of non-nightly use of zolpidem for primary insomnia. Sleep. 2000;23:1087-96. [PMID: 11145323]

31. The U.S. Food and Drug Administration. FDA Requests Label Change for All Sleep Disorder Drug Products. Accessed at www.fda.gov/bbs/topics/NEWS/2007/NEW01587.html on 9 November 2007.

32. Balter MB, Uhlenhuth EH. New epidemiologic findings about insomnia and its treatment. J Clin Psychiatry. 1992;53 Suppl:34-9; discussion 40-2. [PMID: 1487478]

mitigates rebound insomnia, irritability, and anxiety. The minimal effective dose is advised to decrease the likelihood of rebound insomnia.

Nonbenzodiazepine GABA Agonists
Nonbenzodiazepines are selective GABA agonists that result in fewer side effects than benzodiazepines and other sedative-hypnotics. Additionally, half-lives of 1 to 5 hours allow for more selective treatment. The 1-hour half-life of zaleplon, for example, makes it potentially helpful for patients who have problems with sleep induction. Studies of intermittent nonbenzodiazepine dosing that examined patients' self-regulating dosing and taking 3 to 5 doses weekly report improved and sustained outcomes in some cases, similar to daily dosing.

One trial randomly assigned patients aged 21 to 69 with primary insomnia to eszopiclone 3 mg (n = 593) or placebo (n = 195) nightly for 6 months. Compared with placebo, patients in the eszopiclone group reported improvements in sleep latency, total sleep time, awakenings, wake time after sleep onset, quality of sleep, and daytime alertness. Adverse effects included headache and unpleasant taste (28).

Following an open-label study of zolpidem over 180 days in 96 patients, 49 patients continued zolpidem for another 180 days and 47 discontinued the drug. Of the 47 patients who discontinued the drug, 21 showed no rebound insomnia or withdrawal signs during follow-up, but data were not reported for the other discontinuers. About 90% of patients who continued the drug for a total of 360 days continued to report improved sleep (29).

In a randomized trial, 163 adults with primary insomnia received either placebo or as-needed zolpidem 10 mg 3 to 5 times weekly for 8 weeks. Patients who took intermittent zolpidem reported better subjective sleep outcomes compared with those who took placebo. No evidence of rebound insomnia was observed on nights that zolpidem was not taken (30).

Adverse reactions associated with nonbenzodizepine hypnotic agents include nausea, vertigo, general malaise, residual sedation,

disorientation, nightmares, agitation, antagonistic morning mood, amnesia, headache, and visual distortion. Clinicians should also warn patients that zolpidem can lead to sleep driving, which is driving an automobile while not fully awake after ingestion of a sedative-hypnotic product with no recollection of the event. Sleepwalking and sleep eating have been reported; however, these cases seem to occur when the drug is taken at a high dosage or mixed with alcohol or antidepressants.

In March 2007, the Food and Drug Administration (FDA) required new, stronger warnings for 13 sleep-inducing pharmaceutical products: zolpidem (Ambien/Ambien CR®), butabarbital (Butisol®), pentobarbital and carbromal (Carbrital®), flurazepam (Dalmane®), quazepam (Doral®), triazolam (Halcion®), eszopiclone (Lunesta®), ethchorvynol (Placidyl®), estazolam (Prosom®), temezepam (Restoril®), ramelteon (Rozerem®), secobarbital (Seconal®), and Zaleplon (Sonata®). These warnings describe potential risks, including severe allergic reactions, such as anaphylaxis and angioedema, and complex sleep-related behaviors, such as sleep driving. The agency also recommended that manufacturers develop patient handouts and conduct clinical studies to investigate the frequency of adverse effects in association with individual drugs (31).

Nonbenzodiazepine abuse can occur, especially among patients with comorbid substance abuse and psychiatric illness. However, in general, GABA agonists are preferred over other sedating agents because of their safety profile. A number of other sedative-hypnotic medications may have lethal effects with overdose. These include sedating tricyclic antidepressants that affect cardiac conduction; barbiturates that suppress respiration; and others, such as chloral hydrate, that also suppress respiration.

Drug Therapy for Insomnia Secondary to Restless Leg Syndrome

In the absence of increased caffeine intake or iron deficiency in patients with RLS, a low bedtime dose of a dopaminergic agonist agent, such as pramipexole or ropinirole, may be helpful. If dopaminergic agents are ineffective, poorly tolerated, or contraindicated, consider using a benzodiazepine, such as clonazepam; an opiate, such as propoxyphene, hydrocodone, or oxycodone; or an antiepileptic drug, such as gabapentin.

What is the appropriate duration of prescription drug therapy for insomnia?

Some literature, consensus opinion, and the FDA recommend that use should be limited to 1 month, and medications with a long half-life, including long half-life metabolites, should be avoided. Although most sleep specialists do not recommend long-term use of hypnotic agents, clinical practice suggests that patients who are using hypnotics long-term to good effect and without side effects may continue to do so. One study estimated that 10% to 15% of individuals who use hypnotics do so for longer than 1 year (32). Data supporting long-term use are derived from a small number of uncontrolled studies (33).

Clinicians and patients should look for rebound insomnia after discontinuation. Tapering rather than abrupt discontinuation may result in less rebound insomnia; however, not all studies have found significant rebound.

One randomized, double-blind study comparing zolpidem, triazolam, and placebo in 99 patients showed that zolpidem did not manifest rebound insomnia, and triazolam did so only on the first night of discontinuation (34).

An analysis of 75 sleep laboratory studies of short-acting sedative-hypnotic agents published from 1966 to 1997 showed initial efficacy for all 5 drugs studied. Tolerance with intermediate and long-term use occurred with triazolam, was marginally present with midazolam and zolpidem, and could not be estimated for brotizolam or zopiclone because of insufficient data. The studies suggested severe rebound insomnia on the first withdrawal night with triazolam, mild rebound with zolpidem, and data were insufficient for brotizolam, midazolam, and zopiclone. The review concluded that differences among the rapidly eliminated hypnotics with respect to tolerance and rebound insomnia suggest that, in addition to short elimination half-life, other pharmacologic properties contribute to these side effects (35).

Agents aimed at the treatment of insomnia characterized by nocturnal awakenings are under study, but not yet approved by the FDA at the time of this writing (36).

When should clinicians consider antidepressants in the treatment of patients with insomnia?

Antidepressants are often used for insomnia not specifically related to depression. However, expert consensus is that antidepressants should be reserved for treating underlying depression rather than for treatment of insomnia itself (37). Compared with GABA agonists, the side-effect profile of antidepressants, which includes cardiac dysrhythmia and orthostatic hypotension, tends to be more severe and has limited evidence of greater efficacy. Furthermore, some antidepressants, such as fluoxetine, can exacerbate insomnia.

Limited data have documented the ability of some antidepressants to increase sleep time, sleep efficiency, and deep sleep. If sedating antidepressants are required, consider using trazodone, doxepin, trimipramine, or mirtazapine (Table 3). In persons with a history of drug or alcohol abuse, antidepressants may have less potential for abuse than benzodiazepines (38).

33. Kramer M. Hypnotic medication in the treatment of chronic insomnia: non nocere! Doesn't anyone care? Sleep Med Rev. 2000;4:529-541. [PMID: 12531035]
34. Ware JC, Walsh JK, Scharf MB, et al. Minimal rebound insomnia after treatment with 10-mg zolpidem. Clin Neuropharmacol. 1997;20:116-25. [PMID: 9099463]
35. Soldatos CR, Dikeos DG, Whitehead A. Tolerance and rebound insomnia with rapidly eliminated hypnotics: a meta-analysis of sleep laboratory studies. Int Clin Psychopharmacol. 1999;14:287-303. [PMID: 10529072]
36. Roth T, Zammit GK, Scharf MB, et al. Efficacy and safety of as-needed, post bedtime dosing with indiplon in insomnia patients with chronic difficulty maintaining sleep. Sleep. 2007;30:1731-38.
37. Sharpley AL, Cowen PJ. Effect of pharmacologic treatments on the sleep of depressed patients. Biol Psychiatry. 1995;37:85-98. [PMID: 7718684]
38. Rush CR, Baker RW, Wright K. Acute behavioral effects and abuse potential of trazodone, zolpidem and triazolam in humans. Psychopharmacology (Berl). 1999;144:220-33. [PMID: 10435388]

What are the contraindications to drug therapy in the treatment of patients with insomnia?

In general, H_1-blocker antihistamines are not recommended for patients with angina, heart disease, glaucoma, pulmonary disease, or problems with urinating, as well as patients taking some medications. Likewise, natural remedies, such as St. John's wort, may interact adversely with prescribed medications.

Patients taking sedative-hypnotic agents should restrict alcohol intake, or avoid alcohol all together. They must use particular care when driving or using hazardous equipment.

Patients who are pregnant or breastfeeding should avoid hypnotics. Patients with underlying disorders, such as OSAS, in which hypnotic use can be counterproductive should also avoid them.

Benzodiazepines are commonly abused, and they should not be used by patients with a current alcohol or drug abuse problem or by patients in recovery. Although intentional or accidental overdose of benzodiazepines alone rarely results in death or serious illness, they are frequently taken with either alcohol or other medications, which can be dangerous.

What is the evidence for the comparative effectiveness of behavioral versus drug therapy and among the various drug therapies for insomnia?

Several studies suggest that non-drug therapies may be more effective if not used in conjunction with drugs, especially in long-term treatment. Behavioral interventions are certainly also less likely than pharmacotherapy to cause side effects. Evidence comparing nonbenzodiazepine sedative-hypnotics with one another is lacking.

Behavioral techniques were more effective than drug therapy or placebo in the long-term in a randomized, placebo-controlled study of 78 older patients with chronic insomnia (21).

In a randomized, placebo-controlled trial of 63 middle-aged and young adults, CBT was found to be superior to drug therapy in the treatment of chronic sleep-onset insomnia (22).

A meta-analysis of 21 studies including a total of 470 patients showed that both drug therapy and behavioral therapy had similar magnitudes of effect (39).

One prospective open study of as-needed zolpidem use in 2690 subjects noted that behavioral therapy on nights not using zolpidem led to improved sleep with reduced sleep latency and increased total sleep time as well as a 30% reduction in use of zolpidem (40).

A randomized, controlled trial of 26 subjects with insomnia showed that behavioral therapy at 10 months was more effective than the combination of behavioral therapy and hypnotics (41).

A randomized, controlled trial of both medicated and nonmedicated patients with insomnia (n = 41) showed that stimulus control therapy was less effective in patients taking hypnotics (42).

Clinical consequences of short half-life hypnotics may include early morning insomnia and tolerance or rebound with benzodiazepines. Clinical consequences of long half-life hypnotics may include daytime sedation, motor incoordination, amnesia, diminished responsiveness, and performance decrements and accidents.

When should clinicians consider specialty referral for patients with insomnia?

Clinicians should consider referring patients with insomnia to a sleep specialist if diagnosis remains unclear after evaluation, if daytime functioning is impaired, or if the patient requests consultation. Consultation may also be helpful if 1 of the following conditions is suspected: sleep apnea, parasomnias, RLS, narcolepsy, circadian rhythm disturbances, and psychophysiologic insomnia. Referral to a sleep

39. Smith MT, Perlis ML, Park A, et al. Comparative meta-analysis of pharmacotherapy and behavior therapy for persistent insomnia. Am J Psychiatry. 2002;159:5-11. [PMID: 11772681]
40. Hajak G, Bandelow B, Zulley J, Pittrow D. "As needed" pharmacotherapy combined with stimulus control treatment in chronic insomnia—assessment of a novel intervention strategy in a primary care setting. Ann Clin Psychiatry. 2002;14:1-7. [PMID: 12046635]
41. Hauri PJ. Can we mix behavioral therapy with hypnotics when treating insomniacs? Sleep. 1997;20:1111-8. [PMID: 9493920]
42. Riedel B, Lichstein K, Peterson BA, et al. A comparison of the efficacy of stimulus control for medicated and nonmedicated insomniacs. Behav Modif. 1998;22:3-28. [PMID: 9567734]

specialist offers an opportunity for a comprehensive assessment of the multiple causes of insomnia and, when necessary, performance of polysomnography.

Referral to a psychiatrist for diagnostic evaluation can be helpful when it is unclear whether a concurrent psychiatric disorder, such as depression, is present. Psychiatric conditions are prevalent in persons with chronic insomnia but may prove difficult to identify (43). An untreated chronic psychiatric condition may lead to a worse outcome. Referral is also warranted when the patient history elicits chronic use of moderate-to-large doses of hypnotic medications with continuing complaint of insomnia, because there is no evidence to indicate that moderate-to-large doses of hypnotic medications are necessary to treat insomnia in the absence of psychiatric conditions, such as stress and anxiety disorders. Psychiatric consultation may be warranted for tapering patients from long-term use of hypnotics.

Consider referral to other specialists depending on the nature of the underlying disorder. Consider referral to a pulmonologist for patients with sleep apnea syndromes. An otolaryngologist, oral surgeon, or dentist may be consulted for surgical procedures on the airway or mandibular positioning or stabilization in patients with sleep apnea. A neurologist may be considered for management of complex neurologic diseases, such as Parkinson disease, cerebrovascular disease, or dementia.

How should clinicians manage insomnia in hospitalized patients?
In hospitalized patients, the most common causes of acute insomnia are the effects of illness, environmental sleep disruption, medication, anxiety, and depression (44). Treatment should focus on correcting the underlying medical disorders; reducing environmental sleep disruptions; and lowering anxiety with psychological interventions, medication, and relaxation training. Special clinical problems include chronic pain, delirium, and insomnia in the elderly.

Nondrug treatment can often be effective in hospitalized patients. When sedative-hypnotic medications are needed, consideration of pharmacokinetic profile is important, and long half-life hypnotics should be avoided. Intermediate-acting benzodiazepines, such as lorazepam or temazepam, are advised. Zaleplon and zolpidem are also attractive hypnotic agents; however, they are typically reserved for second-line therapy because of cost (45).

What type of follow-up care should clinicians provide for patients with insomnia?
Treatment of insomnia is most often long-term and always includes supportive follow-up. Clinicians should follow up patients with chronic insomnia until it is resolved or alleviated. Follow-up visits are used to monitor response to therapy, adjust therapy, provide education about sleep hygiene and behavioral techniques, and to address other potential underlying causes. One-month follow-up is needed in patients on hypnotic therapy to assess side effects, efficacy, and the need for continuing treatment. If a particular hypnotic is ineffective, review the initial diagnosis and consider alternative treatments, such as behavior therapy. In patients on dopaminergics for RLS, follow up at 1 month and at least annually thereafter. Follow-up frequency should be determined on a case-by-case basis in patients on antidepressants for mood disorder and insomnia to determine if the insomnia and depression are resolving. Frequent visits may be helpful for patients with psychophysiologic insomnia in order to ensure that they understand and are carrying out behavioral recommendations.

43. Ford DE, Kamerow DB. Epidemiologic study of sleep disturbances and psychiatric disorders. An opportunity for prevention? JAMA. 1989;262:1479-84. [PMID: 2769898]
44. Berlin RM. Management of insomnia in hospitalized patients. Ann Intern Med. 1984;100:398-404. [PMID: 6141753]
45. Lenhart SE, Buysse DJ. Treatment of insomnia in hospitalized patients. Ann Pharmacother. 2001;35:1449-57. [PMID: 11724098]

Practice Improvement

Important Components of Patient Education About Insomnia

- Insomnia has multiple causes.
- Insomnia may precede or be a cause of depression or other mood disorders.
- It is necessary to address all contributing factors to insomnia.
- Patients should actively engage in behavioral treatments, including making changes in sleep hygiene.
- Behavioral treatments have longer-lasting benefit than drug therapy alone.
- Progress often takes 1 to 2 months.
- Behavioral recommendations must be continued even after insomnia improves.

Are there professional organization guidelines for insomnia?

Experts urge primary-care physicians to use American Academy of Sleep Medicine practice parameters for the recognition of insomnia (10). This consensus-based document supports screening for insomnia (because many patients are unaware of the impact of insomnia on functioning), discusses the identification of underlying causes of insomnia, and considers the role of sleep testing in the evaluation of insomnia.

What is the role of patient education in the management of insomnia?

Patient education plays an important role in insomnia management (see Box) and clinicians should provide patients with information about insomnia and its treatment.

in the clinic

Tool Kit

Insomnia

PIER Modules

PIER.acponline.org
Access the following PIER module: Insomnia. Provides updated information designed for rapid access at the point of care.

Patient Information

www.annals.org/intheclinic
Download a copy of the patient information page that appears on the following page for duplication and distribution to your patients.

www.acponline.org/atpro/timssnet/catalog/books/restful_sleep.htm
Order copies of the ACP's Guide to a Restful Sleep, a 30-minute patient education DVD and accompanying guidebook.

ACP Observer Article

www.acponline.org/journals/news/july06/special.pdf
View a copy of a July-August 2006 ACP Observer special focus article on insomnia.

Sleep Diary

pier.acponline.org/physicians/diseases/d166/figures/d166-figures.html

Web Sites

National Heart Lung and Blood Institute
www.nhlbi.nih.gov/health/dci/Diseases/inso/
American Academy of Sleep Medicine
www.aasmnet.org/

THINGS PEOPLE SHOULD KNOW
ABOUT INSOMNIA

People with insomnia have trouble falling asleep or staying asleep. People with insomnia may feel sleepy during the day, depressed, moody, or have trouble concentrating.

People do not always know why they have insomnia, but some common causes are:

Stress

Caffeine

Alcohol

Depression (insomnia can cause depression, and depression can cause insomnia)

Changes in work schedules

Pain or other symptoms from health conditions

Sometimes changing sleep habits is enough to make insomnia better. When other treatments are needed, behavioral treatments are usually better than taking medicines. Behavioral therapies may take 1 to 2 months to help insomnia and need to be kept up even after the insomnia gets better.

If you have trouble sleeping, try these things:

- Do not use caffeine, alcohol, and stimulant medications (including some cold and allergy medicines)
- Try to go to sleep around the same time each night and wake up around the same time each morning
- Follow a bedtime routine that helps you relax before bed (reading, listening to music, or taking a bath)
- Do not exercise or eat big meals shortly before bedtime
- Make your bedroom comfortable, quiet, dark, and do not turn on the television or computer

Your doctor may want you to fill out a sleep diary. The diary will help you keep track of when you go to bed, how long you lie in bed before falling asleep, how often you wake during the night, when you get up in the morning, and how well you sleep.

Sleeping pills may only help for a short time, have side effects, and can be unsafe in some people. Sleeping pills should not be used for longer than a few days. Using them regularly can make insomnia worse.

If you have insomnia, see your doctor for help.

Web Sites with Good Information about Insomnia

National Heart Lung and Blood Institute
www.nhlbi.nih.gov/health/dci/Diseases/inso/

American Academy of Sleep Medicine
www.sleepeducation.com

Consumer Reports Best Buy Drugs
www.crbestbuydrugs.org/drugreport_DR_sleepingpills.shtml

Colorectal Cancer Screening

Colorectal cancer is the fourth most common type of cancer and the second leading cause of cancer death in the United States (1). Outside the United States, the impact of colorectal cancer is also immense. In terms of global incidence, it ranks third among cancers affecting women and fourth for men (2). Assuming no improvement in cancer control strategies, colorectal cancer prevalence rates will increase more rapidly than U.S. population growth during the years 2000 to 2020, largely because of population aging (3). Fortunately, ample evidence shows that screening for colorectal cancer with any of several available strategies significantly decreases colorectal cancer mortality. Because most colorectal cancer arises from adenomatous polyps, detection and removal of polyps can substantially decrease the incidence of this cancer. However, many people who would benefit from colorectal cancer screening do not receive it.

1. Jemal A, Siegel R, Ward E, et al. Cancer statistics, 2007. CA Cancer J Clin. 2007;57:43-66. [PMID: 17237035]
2. Parkin DM, Bray F, Ferlay J, et al. Global cancer statistics, 2002. CA Cancer J Clin. 2005;55:74-108. [PMID: 15761078]
3. Mariotto AB, Yabroff KR, Feuer EJ, et al. Projecting the number of patients with colorectal carcinoma by phases of care in the US: 2000-2020. Cancer Causes Control. 2006;17:1215-26. [PMID: 17111252]
4. Regula J, Rupinski M, Kraszewska E, et al. Colonoscopy in colorectal-cancer screening for detection of advanced neoplasia. N Engl J Med. 2006;355:1863-72. [PMID: 17079760]
5. Theuer CP, Wagner JL, Taylor TH, et al. Racial and ethnic colorectal cancer patterns affect the cost-effectiveness of colorectal cancer screening in the United States. Gastroenterology. 2001;120:848-56. [PMID: 11231939]
6. Losi L, Di Gregorio C, Pedroni M, et al. Molecular genetic alterations and clinical features in early-onset colorectal carcinomas and their role for the recognition of hereditary cancer syndromes. Am J Gastroenterol. 2005;100:2280-7. [PMID: 16181381]
7. Winawer SJ, Zauber AG, Gerdes H, et al. Risk of colorectal cancer in the families of patients with adenomatous polyps. National Polyp Study Workgroup. N Engl J Med. 1996;334:82-7. [PMID: 8531963]

Risk Factors

Who is at risk for colorectal cancer?

The lifetime risk for colorectal cancer in both men and women in the United States is approximately 6%. About 93% of diagnoses are made in patients older than 50 years, with the remaining 7% in patients 40 to 50 years of age. Colorectal cancer is rare before age 40 years. Some data suggest different relationships between age and disease incidence by sex and ethnic group, but these differences are not large (4, 5).

What factors put individuals at higher risk for colorectal cancer?

About 10% of adults in the United States have a first-degree relative with colorectal cancer. People with 1 or more first-degree relatives with the disease have a lifetime risk for colorectal cancer that is 2 to 4 times higher than that for the average population. Individual risk is increased the younger the affected relative.

A first-degree relative with adenomatous polyps also increases an individual's risk for colorectal cancer. This risk is more pronounced if the affected family member is younger than 60 at the time of polyp detection (7). Clinicians should ask about colon polyps when collecting family history data.

Colon cancer syndromes (hereditary nonpolyposis colorectal cancer [HNPCC] and familial adenomatous polyposis [FAP]) in aggregate account for about 5% of all cases of colon cancer. Colon cancer risk in these settings exceeds 80% absent any preventive measures. Concern about such a syndrome is usually prompted by the presence of multiple cases of colorectal cancer in a family; onset of cancer before 50 years of age; and the early onset of some types of extracolonic cancer, particularly gynecologic malignancies and cancer of the stomach, biliary tree, or urinary tract (6).

A 2001 systematic review to assess familial risk for colorectal cancer showed a nearly 2-fold increase in risk in individuals with a first-degree relative with adenomatous polyps, a more than 2-fold increase in risk in individuals with colorectal cancer, and a more than 4-fold increase in risk in individuals with more than 1 first-degree relative with colorectal cancer. The relative risk was higher for individuals with relatives diagnosed with colorectal cancer before age 60 years (relative risk [RR], 2.25) than for those with relatives diagnosed at or after age 60 years (RR, 1.82) (8).

Others common clinical situations associated with elevated risk include a history of inflammatory bowel disease or of advanced polyp formation (>3 adenomas, adenoma with a villous component or high-grade dysplasia, adenoma larger than 1 cm, or previous colorectal cancer).

Risk Factors... The lifetime risk for colorectal cancer is 6% in both men and women. The great majority of colorectal cancer diagnoses occur in people age 50 years and older, and the condition is rare before age 40. Risk increases with increasing age. Having 1 or more first-degree relatives with colorectal cancer increases a person's risk for the disease 2 to 4 times over average population risk. A family history of adenomatous polyps, particularly polyps detected before age 60 years, also increases risk. A history of advanced adenoma, inflammatory bowel disease, or previous colorectal cancer also increases colorectal cancer risk.

CLINICAL BOTTOM LINE

Prevention

Can patients reduce their risk for colorectal cancer by modifying their health behaviors or using certain drugs?

Epidemiologic studies show associations between some health behaviors and colorectal cancer, so clinicians should advise patients about the potential benefits of such behaviors in lowering colorectal cancer risk (see Box). These healthy behaviors have been associated with up to 0.5- to 2.0-fold risk reductions. However, evidence is mixed for some behaviors, including modification of fat, fruit, and vegetable intake. Individuals who are non-adherent with colorectal cancer screening are also more likely than adherent individuals to have other behavior-related risk factors for colorectal cancer (9).

Several other micronutrients have been associated with a decreased risk for colorectal cancer, but further study is necessary before supplemental intake of these specific items should be routinely recommended. These micronutrients include calcium; vitamins A, D, and E; folate; and selenium.

In addition, there is evidence that postmenopausal estrogen, aspirin, and other nonsteroidal anti-inflammatory drugs (NSAIDs) can decrease the risk for colorectal cancer and adenomatous polyps, but the balance of benefits and harms does not favor their use for primary prevention. Prospective trials have shown that aspirin and other NSAIDs decrease recurrent polyps, but the U.S. Preventive Services Task Force recommends against the routine use of these drugs for colorectal cancer or polyp prevention in average-risk individuals (10).

Postmenopausal estrogen supplements have also been shown to reduce colorectal cancer risk, but as with aspirin and NSAIDs, the balance of benefits and harms led the U.S. Preventive Services Task Force to recommend against the use of postmenopausal estrogen for the primary prevention of colorectal cancer (11–13).

Health Behaviors Possibly Associated with a Reduced Risk for Colorectal Cancer

- Moderate intake of red meat and fat (both saturated and unsaturated)
- Regular physical activity
- Maintenance of normal body weight
- Avoidance of alcohol and tobacco
- Consumption of 5 to 7 daily servings of fresh fruits and vegetables
- Adequate calcium and vitamin D intake

---

8. Johns LE, Houlston RS. A systematic review and meta-analysis of familial colorectal cancer risk. Am J Gastroenterol. 2001;96:2992-3003. [PMID: 11693338]
9. Coups EJ, Manne SL, Meropol NJ, et al. Multiple behavioral risk factors for colorectal cancer and colorectal cancer screening status. Cancer Epidemiol Biomarkers Prev. 2007;16:510-6. [PMID: 17372246]
10. Dubé C, Rostom A, Lewin G, et al.; U.S. Preventive Services Task Force. The use of aspirin for primary prevention of colorectal cancer: a systematic review prepared for the U.S. Preventive Services Task Force. Ann Intern Med. 2007;146:365-75. [PMID: 17339622]
11. Rossouw JE, Anderson GL, Prentice RL, et al.; Writing Group for the Women's Health Initiative Investigators. Risks and benefits of estrogen plus progestin in healthy postmenopausal women: principal results from the Women's Health Initiative randomized controlled trial. JAMA. 2002;288:321-33. [PMID: 12117397]
12. Hulley S, Furberg C, Barrett-Connor E, et al.; HERS Research Group. Noncardiovascular disease outcomes during 6.8 years of hormone therapy: Heart and Estrogen/progestin Replacement Study follow-up (HERS II). JAMA. 2002;288:58-66. [PMID: 12090863]
13. U.S. Preventive Services Task Force. Postmenopausal hormone replacement therapy for primary prevention of chronic conditions: recommendations and rationale. Ann Intern Med. 2002;137:834-9. [PMID: 12435221]

Screening

Does the early detection of colorectal neoplasm improve patient outcomes?

Colorectal cancer survival is closely related to the clinical and pathologic stage at diagnosis. High-quality evidence shows that survival is improved when colorectal cancer is treated at earlier stages. The 5-year survival rate for colorectal cancer is 80% to 90% when cancer is limited to the bowel wall, 60% when lymph nodes are involved, and less than 10% if metastasis has occurred at the time of diagnosis (14). Colorectal cancer detected before lymph node involvement can often be effectively treated without radiation or chemotherapy.

In addition, colorectal cancer screening not only reduces disease-associated morbidity and mortality, it can also prevent cancer occurrence by removal of precancerous polyps (15).

What modalities are effective in screening for colorectal cancer?

Available evidence supports the use of a number of different modalities as screening tests for colorectal cancer (Table 1). These include fecal occult blood testing (FOBT), flexible sigmoidoscopy, double-contrast barium enema (DCBE), and colonoscopy. However, direct evidence from randomized screening trials is available only for FOBT. Evidence for barium enema, flexible sigmoidoscopy alone, and colonoscopy is ample, but largely from observational studies rather than from trials. Newer modalities, such as DNA-based stool tests and virtual colonoscopy, show promise, but definitive evidence for their effectiveness in colorectal cancer screening is not yet available.

Fecal Occult Blood Testing

Screening average-risk individuals over the age of 50 with annual or biennial FOBT has been shown in multiple randomized trials to reduce colorectal cancer incidence and mortality rates. Annual screening results in greater reduction in mortality rate than biennial screening.

A large, long-duration trial in the United States randomly assigned 46 551 volunteers aged 50 to 80 years to 5 years of screening with either annual FOBT with a guaiac-based test, biennial FOBT, or usual care. The cumulative 13-year colorectal cancer mortality rate was 33% lower in the annual group than in the control group, whereas the biennial group had a 21% lower colorectal cancer mortality rate than the control group (16, 17).

A Danish trial randomly assigned 61 933 people aged 45 to 75 years to usual care or screening with an initial nonrehydrated, guaiac-based FOBT followed by biennial FOBT for 7 rounds of screening over 13 years. At 13 years, the colorectal cancer mortality rate was 18% lower in those screened than among controls (mortality rate ratio, 0.82 [95% CI, 0.69 to 0.97]) (18).

A population-based trial in the United Kingdom randomly assigned 152 850 people aged 45 to 74 years to either control or

14. American Cancer Society. Cancer facts and figures 2007. Atlanta: American Cancer Society; 2007.

15. Winawer SJ, Zauber AG, Ho MN, et al. Prevention of colorectal cancer by colonoscopic polypectomy. The National Polyp Study Workgroup. N Engl J Med. 1993;329:1977-81. [PMID: 8247072]

16. Mandel JS, Bond JH, Church TR, et al. Reducing mortality from colorectal cancer by screening for fecal occult blood. Minnesota Colon Cancer Control Study. N Engl J Med. 1993;328:1365-71. [PMID: 8474513]

17. Mandel JS, Church TR, Ederer F, et al. Colorectal cancer mortality: effectiveness of biennial screening for fecal occult blood. J Natl Cancer Inst. 1999;91:434-7. [PMID: 10070942]

Table 1. Advantages and Disadvantages of Available Colorectal Cancer Screening Techniques*

Test	Frequency	Advantages	Disadvantages
FOBT	Annual	No referral required; inexpensive; RCTs show effectiveness in decreasing colorectal cancer mortality; noninvasive	Positive tests require follow-up colonoscopy; many false positives will require follow-up endoscopy
Flexible sigmoidoscopy	Every 5 years	Quicker and less expensive than colonoscopy; less intense preparation; no sedation, so patient can go home without assistance	Does not visualize the entire colon; uncomfortable for some patients (no sedation); positive test requires follow-up colonoscopy; requires referral in some settings
Double-contrast barium enema	Every 5 years	Inexpensive; no sedation, so patient can go home without assistance	Less sensitive for polyp and cancer detection than colonoscopy; uncomfortable for many patients; positive test requires follow-up colonoscopy; requires referral
Colonoscopy	Every 10 years	Visualization of entire colon and rectum; allows for biopsy and polypectomy, so screening is a 1-step process; seems cost-effective	Invasive with low but definite risks of adverse events; bowel preparation is unpleasant, but sedation makes actual test comfortable for most patients; patients cannot go home independently after test; requires referral
CT colonography	Unknown	Shorter test than colonoscopy; noninvasive; allows visualization of entire colon and rectum	Uncomfortable for many patients because of air insufflation during procedure; requires bowel preparation; performance is operator-dependent; not presently endorsed for screening; requires referral

CT = computed tomography; FOBT = fecal occult blood test; RCT = randomized, controlled trial.

FOBT at entry and then 3 to 6 rounds of screening every 2 years. There were 360 colorectal cancer deaths in the screened group compared with 420 in the control group (odds ratio [OR], 0.85 [CI, 0.74 to 0.98]) (19).

A population-based trial in Sweden randomly assigned 68308 people aged 60 to 64 years to control or 2 rounds of FOBT screening at baseline and then at 16 to 24 months. Mortality data have not been published, but were made available for a meta-analysis of the 4 FOBT trials, which showed a 16% reduction in colorectal cancer death (RR, 0.84 [CI, 0.77 to 0.93]) in the screening group. In an analysis of participants who adhered to screening, the risk reduction was 23% (20).

When using FOBT to screen for colorectal cancer, it is imperative that the test is used correctly, with specimens obtained at home by the patient from each of 3 consecutive bowel movements (see Box). A single test performed during a digital

---

How to Use Fecal Occult Blood Testing to Screen for Colorectal Cancer

- Instruct patient to avoid red meat and more than 1 aspirin or NSAID for 3 days before and during testing
- Instruct patient to collect 2 stool samples from each of 3 consecutive bowel movements and apply to 3 cards, then return slides for development by trained personnel
- Positive FOBT is defined as 1 or more of 6 slides positive
- All positive tests should be followed by colonoscopy (not by repeat FOBT testing, even in the absence of recommended dietary restriction)
- When using a combination of FOBT and sigmoidoscopy for screening, FOBT should be done first because a positive result would lead to colonoscopy instead of flexible sigmoidoscopy
- A single FOBT during rectal examination is inadequate

---

18. Jørgensen OD, Kronborg O, Fenger C. A randomised study of screening for colorectal cancer using faecal occult blood testing: results after 13 years and seven biennial screening rounds. Gut. 2002;50:29-32. [PMID: 11772963]
19. Hardcastle JD, Chamberlain JO, Robinson MH, et al. Randomised controlled trial of faecal-occult-blood screening for colorectal cancer. Lancet. 1996;348:1472-7. [PMID: 8942775]
20. Towler BP, Irwig L, Glasziou P, et al. Screening for colorectal cancer using the faecal occult blood test, hemoccult. Cochrane Database Syst Rev. 2000:CD001216. [PMID: 10796760]

21. Collins JF, Lieberman DA, Durbin TE, et al.; Veterans Affairs Cooperative Study #380 Group. Accuracy of screening for fecal occult blood on a single stool sample obtained by digital rectal examination: a comparison with recommended sampling practice. Ann Intern Med. 2005;142:81-5. [PMID: 15657155]

22. Nadel MR, Shapiro JA, Klabunde CN, et al. A national survey of primary care physicians' methods for screening for fecal occult blood. Ann Intern Med. 2005;142:86-94. [PMID: 15657156]

23. Levi Z, Rozen P, Hazazi R, et al. A quantitative immunochemical fecal occult blood test for colorectal neoplasia. Ann Intern Med. 2007;146:244-55. [PMID: 17310048]

24. Selby JV, Friedman GD, Quesenberry CP Jr, et al. A case-control study of screening sigmoidoscopy and mortality from colorectal cancer. N Engl J Med. 1992;326:653-7. [PMID: 1736103]

25. Newcomb PA, Norfleet RG, Storer BE, et al. Screening sigmoidoscopy and colorectal cancer mortality. J Natl Cancer Inst. 1992;84:1572-5. [PMID: 1404450]

26. Müller AD, Sonnenberg A. Prevention of colorectal cancer by flexible endoscopy and polypectomy. A case-control study of 32,702 veterans. Ann Intern Med. 1995;123:904-10. [PMID: 7486484]

27. Winawer SJ, Flehinger BJ, Schottenfeld D, et al. Screening for colorectal cancer with fecal occult blood testing and sigmoidoscopy. J Natl Cancer Inst. 1993;85:1311-8. [PMID: 8340943]

28. Berry DP, Clarke P, Hardcastle JD, et al. Randomized trial of the addition of flexible sigmoidoscopy to faecal occult blood testing for colorectal neoplasia population screening. Br J Surg. 1997;84:1274-6. [PMID: 9313712]

rectal examination in the office is not adequate for screening (21). Any FOBT test with 1 or more positive slides is considered positive and warrants follow-up colonoscopy. Inadequate follow-up is frequently reported in primary care settings (22).

There is increasing evidence that immunochemical, as opposed to guaiac-based, FOBT may offer improved performance characteristics for screening. This newer technology is used like other FOBTs and does not have a substantial impact on cost (23).

Flexible Sigmoidoscopy
3 case–control studies show that screening with sigmoidoscopy every 5 years is associated with reduced colorectal cancer mortality. More definitive data are awaited from 3 ongoing trials.

A case–control study nested within a randomized trial of a health check-up that included sigmoidoscopy compared case-patients that had died of colorectal cancer with control participants who had not. For cancer within the reach of the sigmoidoscope, 8.8% of case-patients and 24.4% of control participants had a rigid sigmoidoscopy within the previous 10 years (OR for colorectal cancer, 0.41 [CI, 0.25 to 0.69]). Cancer rates were similar among case-patients and control participants for cancer beyond the reach of the sigmoidoscope (24).

Another case–control study matched 74 patients who died of colorectal cancer to 206 controls. Previous sigmoidoscopy had occurred in 10% of case-patients and 30% of control participants (OR for colorectal cancer, 0.21 [CI, 0.08 to 0.52]). The effect was limited to distal cancers (25).

In a case–control study that matched 8722 case-patients with colon cancer and 7629 case-patients with rectal cancer to control participants, case-patients with cancer were less likely to have undergone a previous endoscopic procedure (mostly flexible sigmoidoscopy) than control participants (OR for colon cancer, 0.51 [CI, 0.44

to 0.58], OR for rectal cancer, 0.55 [CI, 0.47 to 0.64]) (26).

Combined Fecal Occult Blood Testing and Flexible Sigmoidoscopy
Clinicians should consider using both FOBT and flexible sigmoidoscopy in combination, as several studies suggest that using the tests in combination may detect more cases of cancer and reduce colorectal cancer mortality rates more than either modality alone (27–29).

In a study in the Veteran's Administration system, FOBT detected 23.9% of patients with advanced neoplasia, flexible sigmoidoscopy detected 70.3%, and the tests combined detected 75.8% (30).

Double-Contrast Barium Enema
The effectiveness of DCBE as a screening test to prevent colorectal cancer mortality has been extrapolated from observational data. However, the use of DCBE has become less common, particularly in settings where endoscopic screening is available, because many patients find DCBE uncomfortable. Any abnormal DCBE result must be followed by endoscopy, leading to a multistep screening process.

In a study comparing results of colonoscopy with DCBE in the surveillance of 580 individuals with previous polyps, DCBE detected polyps in only one third of individuals found to have 1 or more adenomas on colonoscopy, indicating that DCBE cannot be considered a substitute for colonoscopy (31).

Colonoscopy
Colonoscopy permits visual examination of the entire colon and detects most cases of early-stage cancer and at least twice as many polyps as flexible sigmoidoscopy (32). A number of studies have shown increased detection of adenomas and carcinomas with colonoscopy compared with FOBT or flexible sigmoidoscopy (33–35). However, to date there are no randomized, controlled trials evaluating

the efficacy of screening colonoscopy in the primary prevention of colorectal cancer. Cohort studies suggest that colonoscopy with polypectomy reduces the incidence of colorectal cancer by 76% to 90% (15, 36–38). Because of these observational data, colonoscopy is among the recommended screening modalities for colorectal cancer.

Advantages of colonoscopy include visual examination of the entire colon and rectum and biopsy and removal of lesions at the time of screening rather than requiring referral for a second test. In addition to allowing polypectomy, colonoscopy allows for biopsy of other lesions and other interventions, such as cautery of bleeding lesions, dilatation of strictures, or injection of dye, to localize a tumor for subsequent surgical removal.

Disadvantages of colonoscopy include the need for colonic preparation, patient sedation, specialty referral, and the invasive nature of the procedure. Although the risks of colonoscopy and polypectomy are small, the procedure may result in bleeding, perforation, or other complications.

A prospective study of 502 asymptomatic patients who had colonoscopy for screening, surveillance, or follow-up of another positive screening test found that although 34% of patients reported mild complications (bloating and pain), only 6 had unexpected hospitalizations or emergency department visits within 30 days following colonoscopy. 94% of patients lost 2 or fewer days from normal activities because of the preparation for colonoscopy and recovery (39).

Virtual Colonoscopy
There is limited evidence available evaluating virtual colonoscopy (computerized tomographic [CT] colonography) as a screening tool for colorectal cancer. Numerous studies have included over 100 patients undergoing both CT

colonography and colonoscopy, but have not been performed in screening populations. As compared with colonoscopy, sensitivity for detection of polyps >10 mm ranged from 70% to 96% and specificity ranged from 72% to 96% (40–44). A study involving highly trained radio-logists showed that virtual colonoscopy was nearly as effective as colonoscopy in detecting polyps larger than 5 mm (45), but a subsequent community-based study showed worse performance (46).

A study compared the detection of advanced neoplasia from virtual colonoscopy in 3120 adults to conventional colonoscopy in 3163 adults and found 123 and 121 advanced neoplasms, respectively. Of patients who received virtual colonoscopy, 7.9% were referred for conventional colonoscopy for polypectomy of lesions 6 mm or larger. The total numbers of polyps removed were 561 in the virtual colonoscopy and 2434 in the conventional colonoscopy groups. Seven colonic perforations occurred in the conventional group compared with none in the virtual colonoscopy group (47).

Although evidence supports the effectiveness of virtual colonoscopy in detecting colonic neoplasms, there are no studies of the effectiveness of CT colonography as a screening test in reducing mortality from colorectal cancer, and it is not yet among the tests recommended for colorectal cancer screening. Advantages are that it is non-invasive and can examine the entire colon. However, colonic preparation is required, and some patients find the procedure uncomfortable when air must be injected to distend the colon. Abnormal findings require referral for traditional colonoscopy. In addition, approximately 11% of patients will have new extracolonic abnormalities identified during virtual colonoscopy, and these may require investigation or intervention (48). Early studies regarding patient preference between virtual and

Risks Associated with Colonoscopy
- Perforation
- Bleeding
- Adverse reaction to sedation
- Fever with localized pain due to postpolypectomy coagulation syndrome
- Cardiovascular event
- Electrolyte, renal, or volume abnormalities secondary to bowel preparation

29. Rasmussen M, Kronborg O, Fenger C, et al. Possible advantages and drawbacks of adding flexible sigmoidoscopy to hemoccult-II in screening for colorectal cancer. A randomized study. Scand J Gastroenterol. 1999;34:73-8. [PMID: 10048736]

30. Lieberman DA, Weiss DG; Veterans Affairs Cooperative Study Group 380. One-time screening for colorectal cancer with combined fecal occult-blood testing and examination of the distal colon. N Engl J Med. 2001; 345:555-60. [PMID: 11529208]

31. Winawer SJ, Stewart ET, Zauber AG, et al. A comparison of colonoscopy and double-contrast barium enema for surveillance after polypectomy. National Polyp Study Work Group. N Engl J Med. 2000;342: 1766-72. [PMID: 10852998]

32. Atkin WS, Hart A, Edwards R, et al. Uptake, yield of neoplasia, and adverse effects of flexible sigmoidoscopy screening. Gut. 1998;42:560-5. [PMID: 9616321]

33. Reilly JM, Ballantyne GH, Fleming FX, et al. Evaluation of the occult blood test in screening for colorectal neoplasms. A prospective study using flexible endoscopy. Am Surg. 1990;56:119-23. [PMID: 2316930]

34. Johnson DA, Gurney MS, Volpe RJ, et al. A prospective study of the prevalence of colonic neoplasms in asymptomatic patients with an age-related risk. Am J Gastroenterol. 1990;85:969-74. [PMID: 2375325]

35. Lieberman DA, Weiss DG, Bond JH, et al. Use of colonoscopy to screen asymptomatic adults for colorectal cancer. Veterans Affairs Cooperative Study Group 380. N Engl J Med. 2000;343:162-8. [PMID: 10900274]

36. Thiis-Evensen E, Hoff GS, Sauar J, et al. Population-based surveillance by colonoscopy: effect on the incidence of colorectal cancer. Telemark Polyp Study I. Scand J Gastroenterol. 1999; 34:414-20. [PMID: 10365903]

37. Citarda F, Tomaselli G, Capocaccia R, et al.; Italian Multicentre Study Group. Efficacy in standard clinical practice of colonoscopic polypectomy in reducing colorectal cancer incidence. Gut. 2001;48:812-5. [PMID: 11358901]

38. Lang CA, Ransohoff DF. Fecal occult blood screening for colorectal cancer. Is mortality reduced by chance selection for screening colonoscopy? JAMA. 1994;271:1011-3. [PMID: 8139058]

39. Ko CW, Riffle S, Shapiro JA, et al. Incidence of minor complications and time lost from normal activities after screening or surveillance colonoscopy. Gastrointest Endosc. 2007;65:648-56. [PMID: 17173914]

40. Fenlon HM, Nunes DP, Schroy PC 3rd, et al. A comparison of virtual and conventional colonoscopy for the detection of colorectal polyps. N Engl J Med. 1999;341:1496-503. [PMID: 10559450]

41. Fletcher JG, Johnson CD, Welch TJ, et al. Optimization of CT colonography technique: prospective trial in 180 patients. Radiology. 2000;216:704-11. [PMID: 10966698]

42. Miao YM, Amin Z, Healy J, et al. A prospective single centre study comparing computed tomography pneumocolon against colonoscopy in the detection of colorectal neoplasms. Gut. 2000;47:832-7. [PMID: 11076883]

optical colonoscopy have demonstrated mixed results.

Emerging Colorectal Cancer Screening Techniques

Emerging technologies not recommended for general screening at present include fecal DNA testing and enhanced endoscopic technologies, such as high-magnification chromoendoscopy, spectroscopy, and optical coherence tomography (49). Carcinoembryonic antigen measurement is not appropriate for colorectal cancer screening.

How should clinicians and patients choose from the different screening modalities?

Because there is no clear evidence that one screening modality outperforms the others, clinicians and patients can choose either annual FOBT testing, sigmoidoscopy with or without FOBT every 5 years, DCBE every 5 years, or colonoscopy every 10 years. Doctors and patients should weigh

cost, convenience, availability, and patient preference when choosing a test. Table 2 summarizes the performance characteristics of screening modalities.

Is colorectal cancer screening cost-effective, and is one strategy for screening more cost-effective than others?

Screening for colorectal cancer has a cost per life-year saved that is similar to other nationally recommended screening programs. Available costing and cost-effectiveness analyses find some form of colorectal cancer screening to be cost-effective even without perfect adherence.

A 2002 systematic review of 7 cost-effectiveness analyses found that the cost-effectiveness of the commonly used screening modalities cost between $10 000 to $25 000 per year of life saved compared with no colorectal cancer screening. This review found that no single strategy consistently had the best cost-effectiveness ratio (50).

Table 2. Operating Characteristics for Colorectal Cancer Screening Tests*

Test	Sensitivity, %	Specificity, %	Notes
Fecal occult blood test	~50	>90	The 50% sensitivity figure is for a 1-time test, but the test is 90% sensitive when used as part of an annual screening program
Flexible sigmoidoscopy with biopsy	88–98 for large, distal adenomas or cancer	92–94 for large, distal adenomas and 92–96 for distal cancers	Only evaluates distal colon and rectum, should not be used alone to evaluate symptoms or signs, especially if a patient is over age 40
Colonoscopy with biopsy	90–97	>98	Preferred evaluation for positive screening tests and suggestive symptoms or signs, colonoscopy is considered the "gold standard" for both screening and evaluation of the colon
Double-contrast barium enema	~85	~80	Can be used if colonoscopy is not available or contraindicated
Virtual colonoscopy (CT colonography)	lesions ≤ 5 mm: 4 lesions 6–9 mm: 33 lesions ≥ 10 mm: 82	90	Awaits further study before clinical application can be generally recommended

CT = computed tomography.

What are the risks for individuals with a false-positive screening test result?

False-positive FOBT tests expose patients to the risk for colonoscopy. Clinicians and patients should understand that many noncancerous conditions and polyps that were not destined to progress will be discovered and treated, exposing patients to the potential adverse effects of further evaluation or therapy. These adverse effects include complications of colonoscopy and polypectomy, which apply regardless of the initial screening strategy because all positive screening tests require follow-up with colonoscopy. Factors that increase the risk for complications during colonoscopy include advanced age, strictures, severe colitis, significant dehydration, poor bowel preparation, and pelvic adhesions.

At what age should patients begin colorectal cancer screening?

Table 3 summarizes the recommended ages for initiation of colorectal cancer screening based on the patient's personal and family history. Persons with average risk should initiate screening at age 50 years. Of note, the American College of Gastroenterology suggests that colonoscopic screening for African Americans begin at age 45, because of epidemiologic data suggesting earlier onset and more proximal distribution of colorectal cancer (51). Recommendations about screening frequency in high-risk patients depend on the degree of increased risk and are generally based on consensus rather than direct evidence.

At what age should patients cease colorectal cancer screening?

The age at which to stop colorectal cancer screening is not known with certainty, but depends on life expectancy and the anticipated benefit of screening. Clinicians and patients should temper enthusiasm for screening the elderly with knowledge of average life expectancy in the United States. At age 75, the average woman can expect to live another 12.1 years and the average man can expect to live another 10.2 years. At age 85, life expectancy is 6.7 and 5.6 years, respectively. Because the benefits of early detection of colorectal cancer accrue over time, limited life expectancy reduces the potential benefits of screening. Clinicians and patients should consider the benefits and harms of screening for any individual elderly patient.

A cross-sectional study evaluated 1244 patients who underwent screening colonoscopy and found neoplasia in 13.8% of 50- to 54-year-old patients, 26.5% of 55- to 79-year-old patients, and 28.6% of 80-year-old patients. However, this study estimated that the mean extension of life expectancy among patients above 80 years of age was only 15% of that for those aged 50 to 54 years (52).

How frequently should patients repeat colorectal cancer screening?

According to available evidence and consensus, screening with FOBT should be repeated every year and DCBE or flexible sigmoidoscopy every 5 years if index examination reveals no abnormality that necessitates colonoscopic examination. If no high-risk polyps are detected during index colonoscopy, an average-risk person should have a repeated examination at 10-year intervals. There is no specific consensus regarding appropriate follow-up intervals for some common clinical situations, such as larger polyps removed in multiple

---

Characteristics of High-Risk Polyps

- Larger than 1 cm
- Villous lesion or high-grade dysplasia on histological examination
- 3 or more in number

---

43. Mendelson RM, Foster NM, Edwards JT, et al. Virtual colonoscopy compared with conventional colonoscopy: a developing technology. Med J Aust. 2000;173:472-5. [PMID: 11149303]
44. Yee J, Akerkar GA, Hung RK, et al. Colorectal neoplasia: performance characteristics of CT colonography for detection in 300 patients. Radiology. 2001;219:685-92. [PMID: 11376255]
45. Pickhardt PJ, Choi JR, Hwang I, et al. Computed tomographic virtual colonoscopy to screen for colorectal neoplasia in asymptomatic adults. N Engl J Med. 2003;349:2191-200. [PMID: 14657426]
46. Cotton PB, Durkalski VL, Pineau BC, et al. Computed tomographic colonography (virtual colonoscopy): a multicenter comparison with standard colonoscopy for detection of colorectal neoplasia. JAMA. 2004;291:1713-9. [PMID: 15082698]
47. Kim DH, Pickhardt PJ, Taylor AJ, et al. CT colonography versus colonoscopy for the detection of advanced neoplasia. N Engl J Med. 2007;357:1403-12. [PMID: 17914041]
48. Edwards JT, Wood CJ, Mendelson RM, et al. Extracolonic findings at virtual colonoscopy: implications for screening programs. Am J Gastroenterol. 2001;96:3009-12. [PMID: 11693340]
49. Regueiro CR; AGA Future Trends Committee. AGA Future Trends Committee report: Colorectal cancer: a qualitative review of emerging screening and diagnostic technologies. Gastroenterology. 2005;129:1083-103. [PMID: 16143145]
50. Pignone M, Saha S, Hoerger T, et al. Cost-effectiveness analyses of colorectal cancer screening: a systematic review for the U.S. Preventive Services Task Force. Ann Intern Med. 2002;137:96-104. [PMID: 12118964]

51. Agrawal S, Bhupinderjit A, Bhutani MS, et al.; Committee of Minority Affairs and Cultural Diversity, American College of Gastroenterology. Colorectal cancer in African Americans. Am J Gastroenterol. 2005;100:515-23; discussion 514. [PMID: 15743345]

52. Lin OS, Kozarek RA, Schembre DB, et al. Screening colonoscopy in very elderly patients: prevalence of neoplasia and estimated impact on life expectancy. JAMA. 2006;295:2357-65. [PMID: 16720821]

53. Itzkowitz SH, Present DH; Crohn's and Colitis Foundation of America Colon Cancer in IBD Study Group. Consensus conference: Colorectal cancer screening and surveillance in inflammatory bowel disease. Inflamm Bowel Dis. 2005;11:314-21. [PMID: 15735438]

54. Bodmer WF, Bailey CJ, Bodmer J, et al. Localization of the gene for familial adenomatous polyposis on chromosome 5. Nature. 1987;328:614-6. [PMID: 3039373]

55. Mills SJ, Chapman PD, Burn J, et al. Endoscopic screening and surgery for familial adenomatous polyposis: dangerous delays. Br J Surg. 1997;84:74-7. [PMID: 9043460]

56. Syngal S. Hereditary nonpolyposis colorectal cancer: a call for attention [Editorial]. J Clin Oncol. 2000;18:2189-92. [PMID: 10829037]

pieces or following colonoscopy with less-than-optimal laxative preparation. In these settings, shorter screening intervals are usually recommended.

In patients who have had 1 or more adenomatous polyps, colonoscopy is the recommended test for further surveillance. The histologic type, number, and size of the polyps should guide frequency of follow-up. Consensus recommendations advocate repeated colonoscopy in 5 years for patients with only 1 or 2 small (<1 cm) tubular adenomas (in the absence of more significant history); 3 years in patients with 3 to 10 adenomas or advanced lesions (>1 cm diameter, villous histologic component, or high-grade dysplasia); and sooner than 3 years depending on the completeness of the initial examination, certainty of complete polyp removal, and whether there are more than 10 polyps. Referral to a specialist is recommended if a hereditary syndrome is suspected.

Should clinicians screen people with higher-than-average risk for colorectal cancer differently from those at average-risk?

Table 3 describes risks for colorectal cancer and the corresponding screening recommendations. Some gastroenterologists screen patients with a family history of sporadic colorectal cancer in first-degree relatives every 3 years rather than every 5 years. Any family history confers some increase in risk, but the closer the relative, the higher the risk. Having 2 second-degree relatives with colon cancer is thought to confer a level of risk similar to having 1 first-degree relative with colon cancer. Individuals with 1 second- or third-degree relative with colon cancer and no personal history generally should be screened according to average-risk guidelines.

More aggressive screening strategies are recommended for very-high-risk individuals, including those with ulcerative colitis, FAP, or HNPCC. In ulcerative colitis, patients should begin surveillance colonoscopy after 8 to 10 years of disease. The objective of surveillance is to look for dysplasia or carcinoma. Once dysplasia is present, colectomy is recommended. Although the data are less robust, similar recommendations are appropriate for patients with Crohn colitis (53).

Adenomatous polyps occur throughout the bowel in FAP and precede the development of colorectal cancer. Clinicians should encourage individuals and families at risk for FAP to undergo genetic counseling and testing. Flexible sigmoidoscopy should begin at puberty in high-risk persons; once polyps are identified, colectomy is indicated, because further screening is ineffective at reducing the risk for cancer. Mutations of the APC gene on chromosome 5 can be identified in 70% of affected families. In a family where a specific mutation has been identified, family members who test negative have the same colorectal cancer risk as the general population (54,55).

The age to begin screening and the frequency of colonoscopy in HNPCC kindreds are unknown, but individuals at high risk for HNPCC should be referred for genetic counseling and potential testing. Mutations in DNA mismatch repair genes can be identified in 50% of families suspected of having HNPCC. In such a family, an individual with a negative test result has a risk for colorectal cancer similar to that of the general population (56). If the individual is mutation-positive, regular colonoscopy screening is warranted.

If genetic testing cannot be done or is noninformative, individuals at high clinical risk for colon cancer are currently treated as if they are mutation-positive.

Table 3. Risk for Colorectal Cancer and Screening Recommendations*

Clinical Scenario	Approximate Lifetime Risk for Colorectal Cancer	Screening Recommendation
General population risk in the United States	6%	Begin screening at age 50; the American College of Gastroenterology advocates initiation of screening at age 45 for African Americans because of epidemiologic data that shows earlier onset and more proximal disease in this population.
One first-degree relative with an adenomatous polyp diagnosed at age ≥60 years[†]	1.5- to 2-fold increased	Begin screening at age 50 or 10 years earlier than age at which adenomas were identified, whichever is earliest.
One first-degree relative with colon cancer diagnosed at age <60 years[†]	2- to 3-fold increased	Begin screening at age 40 years. If normal, repeat in 5 years.
Two or more first-degree relatives with colorectal cancer[†]	3- to 4-fold increased	Colonoscopy every 5 years, beginning at age 40 or 10 years younger than the earliest family diagnosis (whichever comes first).
First-degree relative with colon cancer or adenomatous polyps diagnosed at ≤50 years[†]	3- to 4-fold increased	Colonoscopy every 5 years beginning at age 40 or 10 years younger than the earliest family diagnosis (whichever comes first).
Personal history of ulcerative colitis, Crohn colitis	0.5% risk/year beginning 8 to 10 years after diagnosis	Begin surveillance colonoscopy every 1–2 years, starting 8–10 years after disease onset. Once dysplasia is detected, physicians should proceed to operative management.
Suspected FAP or HNPCC	In mutation-positive individuals without intervention, risk is 80% to 100% by age 60 years	For FAP, flexible sigmoidoscopy/colonoscopy at puberty. Refer to specialist for risk assessment, possible genetic testing, and follow-up or surveillance. For HNPCC, colonoscopy beginning at age 20. Repeat every 1–2 years. Refer to specialist for risk assessment, possible genetic testing, and follow-up or surveillance.
Personal history of an adenomatous polyp	Cancer risk increased, but magnitude not well-defined	Obtain colonoscopy 3 years after complete removal of high-risk polyp(s) (adenomatous polyp ≥1 cm, multiple adenomas, high-grade dysplasia, or villous features); If the initial adenoma is a single lesion <1 cm, obtain initial follow-up colonoscopy in 5 years; If first follow-up colonoscopy is negative, repeat in 5 years.
Personal history of hyperplastic polyp(s)	No increase in risk	Obtain next colonoscopy in 10 years

*Recommendations for individuals at higher-than-average risk are based largely on consensus from the organizations in the U.S. Multi-Society Task Force on Colorectal Cancer (Table 4).

† First-degree relatives include parents, siblings, and children. Second-degree relatives include grandparents, aunts, and uncles. Third-degree relatives include great-grandparents and cousins.

‡ FAP = familial adenomatous polyposis; HNPCC = hereditary nonpolyposis colon cancer.

Screening… Patients at average risk for colorectal cancer should begin screening at age 50 with either annual FOBT, flexible sigmoidoscopy every 5 years, DCBE every 5 years, or colonoscopy every 10 years. Some advocate beginning screening at age 45 in African Americans, but data are lacking to directly support a benefit of earlier screening in this population. Evidence is also lacking to identify any strategy as optimal, so clinicians should discuss the advantages and disadvantages of the various screening techniques with patients. Virtual colonoscopy and fecal-based DNA tests are promising technologies, but not yet recommended for routine colorectal cancer screening. Patients with a family history of colorectal cancer or adenomas or a personal history of high-risk polyps or inflammatory bowel disease should begin screening earlier. Life expectancy, rather than age alone, should guide decisions about when to stop colorectal cancer screening.

CLINICAL BOTTOM LINE

Practice Improvement

57. U.S. Preventive Services Task Force. Screening for colorectal cancer: recommendation and rationale. Ann Intern Med. 2002;137:129-31. [PMID: 12118971]

58. American Academy of Family Physicians. Clinical Preventive Services. Accessed at www.aafp.org/online/en/home/clinical/exam.html on 12 December 2007.

59. Winawer S, Fletcher R, Rex D, et al.; Gastrointestinal Consortium Panel. Colorectal cancer screening and surveillance: clinical guidelines and rationale-Update based on new evidence. Gastroenterology. 2003;124:544-60. [PMID: 12557158]

60. American Cancer Society. Accessed at www.cancer.org on 12 December 2007.

61. American College of Gastroenterology. Clinical Updates. Accessed at www.acg.gi.org/physicians/clinical updates.asp#guidelines on 12 December 2007.

62. Davila RE, Rajan E, Baron TH, et al.; Standards of Practice Committee, American Society for Gastrointestinal Endoscopy. ASGE guideline: colorectal cancer screening and surveillance. Gastrointest Endosc. 2006;63:546-57. [PMID: 16564851]

63. Meissner HI, Breen N, Klabunde CN, et al. Patterns of colorectal cancer screening uptake among men and women in the United States. Cancer Epidemiol Biomarkers Prev. 2006;15:389-94. [PMID: 16492934]

64. Nichols S, Koch E, Lallemand RC, et al. Randomised trial of compliance with screening for colorectal cancer. Br Med J (Clin Res Ed). 1986;293:107-10. [PMID: 3089411]

65. Zapka JG, Lemon SC, Puleo E, et al. Patient education for colon cancer screening: a randomized trial of a video mailed before a physical examination. Ann Intern Med. 2004;141:683-92. [PMID: 15520425]

What measures do U.S. stakeholders use to evaluate the quality of colorectal cancer screening?

The Centers for Medicare and Medicaid Services has issued specifications for measures that make up the 2008 Physician Quality Reporting Initiative. Of these measures, 1 relates to colorectal cancer. This measure evaluates the percentage of adults 50 to 80 years of age who are under the care of the physician and underwent appropriate screening for colorectal cancer with either FOBT testing in the measurement year, flexible sigmoidoscopy or barium enema within the measurement year or the previous 4 years, or colonoscopy during the measurement year or the previous 9 years (see Box).

What do professional organizations recommend regarding colorectal cancer screening?

National organizations, such as the American Cancer Society, and most major medical and surgical societies have advocated colorectal cancer screening of the asymptomatic, average-risk population with a variety of screening tests starting at age 50. Table 4 summarizes the recommendations of various groups.

In 2002, the U.S. Preventive Services Task Force strongly recommended screening with 1 of several tests for all adults over age 50 years (57), and the American Academy of Family Practice endorses these same recommendations (58). Similar recommendations were advocated in 2003 by the U.S. Multi-Society Task Force on Colorectal Cancer (59) and in 2006 by the American Cancer Society (60). The American College of Gastroenterology advocates colonoscopy as the preferred screening modality and screening for African American patients to begin at age 45 instead of age 50 (61). The American Society of Gastrointestinal Endoscopy also advocates colonoscopy as the preferred screening modality (62).

Are there ways to improve adherence to colorectal cancer screening?

Many people who would benefit from colorectal cancer screening do not receive it (63). People are generally poorly informed about colorectal cancer screening and patient–physician interactions during routine visits.

A variety of strategies has been studied to increase colorectal cancer screening, including reminder systems, educational videos, and educational pamphlets, and these have had varying results (64–66). However, it appears that patients who receive a clear recommendation for cancer screening from a primary care physician are more likely to follow through with screening than

---

National Committee for Quality Assurance Colorectal Cancer Screening Performance Measure

The percentage of adults who had an appropriate screening for colorectal cancer

Numerator: Number of adult patients 50 to 80 years of age who had 1 or more screenings for colorectal cancer as defined by any 1 of the 4 following criteria:

• FOBT during the measurement year
• Flexible sigmoidoscopy during the reporting period or the previous 4 years
• Barium enema (double or air contrast) during the reporting period or the previous 4 years
• Colonoscopy during the reporting period or the previous 9 years

Denominator: Patients 50 to 80 years of age during the reporting period

---

Table 4. Guidelines for Screening Average–Risk Individuals for Colorectal Cancer*

Organization and Date	Summary of Recommendation(s)	Basis of Recommendation(s)	Notes
U.S. Preventive Services Task Force 2002	Strongly recommends that clinicians screen all adults ≥50 years with FOBT, FSIG alone or with FOBT, DCBE, or colonoscopy.	Based on systematic review of the literature, Grade A recommendation based on fair-to-good-quality evidence	Insufficient data to determine which screening strategy is best in terms of the balance of benefits and harms or cost-effectiveness
U.S. Multi-Society Task Force on Colorectal Cancer† 2003	Recommends screening adults ≥50 years by offering options for different screening strategies: annual FOBT, FSIG every 5 years, annual FOBT plus FSIG every 5 years, colonoscopy every 10 years, DCBE every 5 years	Based on an update of evidence published after 1997 AHCPR guideline	Follow up positive tests with diagnostic colonoscopy; no rehydration for FOBT
American Cancer Society 2006	Beginning at age 50, both men and women should follow one of these 5 screening options: annual FOBT or FIT every year, FSIG every 5 years, annual FOBT or FIT and FSIG every 5 years, DCBE every 5 years, colonoscopy every 10 years	Based on research evidence and align with the U.S. Preventive Services Task Force guidelines	FOBT or FIT test should be done at home following manufacturer's recommendations and not in the doctor's office; combined testing preferred over either annual FOBT or FIT, or FSIG every 5 years, alone. No justification for repeating FOBT in response to an initial positive finding
American College of Gastroenterology 2000, 2005 update	Screen average risk individuals beginning at age 50 with colonoscopy every 10 years as the preferred screening strategy	American College of Gastroenterology panel with expertise in colorectal cancer screening considered new data to update 1997 AHCPR guideline	Alternate strategies: flexible sigmoidoscopy every 5 years with annual FOBT, DCBE every 5 years
	Screen African Americans aged 45 years and older with colonoscopy (2005)	Based on expert consensus because of high incidence of colorectal cancer and a greater prevalence of proximal lesions	
American Academy of Family Practice 2006	Strongly recommends screening men and women 50 years of age or older for colorectal cancer.	Based on 2002 U.S. Preventive Services Task Force recommendations	
American Society of Gastrointestinal Endoscopy 2006	Screen adults 50 years and older with one of the following: Annual FOBT, FSIG every 5 years, annual FOBT plus FSIG every 5 years, colonoscopy every 10 years		Advocates colonoscopy as the preferred screening strategy

* AHCPR = Agency for Health Care Policy and Research; DCBE = double-contrast barium enema; FIT = fecal immunochemical test; FOBT = fecal occult blood test; FSIG = flexible sigmoidoscopy.

† Multi-Society Task Force included American College of Gastroenterology, American College of Physicians, American Gastroenterology Association, American Society of Gastrointestinal Endoscopy.

patients who do not receive such a message.

What information should clinicians include in discussions with patients about colorectal cancer screening?

When discussing colorectal cancer screening with patients, clinicians should inform patients that colorectal cancer is common and that screening reduces both colorectal cancer incidence, through the removal of polyps, and mortality, by identifying cancer at earlier, more treatable stages. Patients should be informed about the advantages and

66. Denberg TD, Coombes JM, Byers TE, et al. Effect of a mailed brochure on appointment-keeping for screening colonoscopy: a randomized trial. Ann Intern Med. 2006;145:895-900. [PMID: 17179058]

disadvantages of the recommended screening modalities before selecting which to use.

If colonoscopy is chosen, the clinician should inform the patient about the risks of the procedure and give careful instructions regarding the preparation so they understand that their activity on the day before the procedure will be limited by the diarrhea resulting from the preparation. Most medications, including blood pressure medications, may be taken on the day of the procedure, preferably before whatever preparation is required on that day. In general, aspirin and other NSAIDs do not need to be discontinued in the absence of a preexisting bleeding disorder However, oral iron- and bismuth-containing medications should be discontinued for several days before the procedure because they may impair visualization. Insulin and anticoagulation will require individualized adjustment. Patients should not eat or drink for a few hours before the procedure to reduce the risk for aspiration. Patients should know that they will receive sedation and will need a ride home after the procedure, but can expect to return to their usual activities the following day.

Practice Improvement... The measurement of appropriate colorectal cancer screening rates for patients 50 to 80 years of age is among the measures that the Centers for Medicare and Medicaid Services are using to evaluate the quality of care that physicians provide. Several professional organizations advocate colorectal cancer screening beginning at age 50 years and acknowledge a variety of screening modalities as adequate, although a few subspecialty societies advocate for colonoscopy as the preferred screening intervention. Despite consensus about the value of colorectal cancer screening, many patients do not receive screening. A clear message about the importance of colorectal cancer screening to patients from their physicians can increase patients' participation.

CLINICAL BOTTOM LINE

---

in the clinic
Tool Kit

Colorectal Cancer Screening

PIER Modules

www.pier.acponline.org
Access PIER modules on colorectal cancer, screening for colorectal cancer, and colonoscopy.

Quality Measures

pier.acponline.org/qualitym/prv.html
Access the PIER Quality Measure Tool, designed to link newly developed quality measures issued by the Ambulatory Quality Alliance and the Physician Quality Improvement QA Alliance and CMS's Physician Quality Reporting Initiative program to administrative criteria for each measure and readily available clinical guidance to help improve care.
www.cms.hhs.gov/PQRI
Access information on the Centers for Medicare and Medicaid Services 2008 Quality Reporting Initiative.

Patient Information

www.annals.org/intheclinic/tools
Download copies of the Patient Information sheet that appears on the following page for duplication and distribution to your patients.

Educational Slide Presentation

media.acponline.org/acponline/handouts2007/mtp028.pdf
View slides from a presentation on colorectal cancer screening delivered at ACP's Internal Medicine 2007 meeting.

WHAT YOU SHOULD KNOW ABOUT COLORECTAL CANCER SCREENING

Colorectal cancer is cancer of the colon (large intestine) or rectum (end of the large intestine). It is one of the most common types of cancer in both men and women.

Surgery can cure colorectal cancer if it is found early. Cancers found later may not be curable.

Screening checks for cancer in people who have no cancer symptoms. Colorectal cancer screening helps patients by:

1) finding and removing noncancer growths (polyps) before they become cancer

2) finding cancer early, when it can be cured.

Adults should begin colorectal cancer screening at age 50 years. People with family members with colorectal cancer should ask their doctors if they should be screened before age 50.

Tests used to screen for colorectal cancer

Test (Frequency)	What is it?	Advantages	Disadvantages
Fecal occult blood test (every year)	Uses a chemical to test for blood in stool	Inexpensive; Samples taken at home, then sent to laboratory	Many things besides colorectal cancer cause blood in stool; Any positive test needs follow-up colonoscopy
Barium enema (every 5 years)	X-rays of the abdomen after an enema that contains barium	No sedation	Any positive test needs follow-up colonoscopy; Can cause discomfort
Flexible sigmoidoscopy (every 5 years)	Doctor looks into the rectum and lower colon through a short, flexible tube-shaped instrument	No sedation; Does not need to be done by a specialist	Only looks at the lower one third of the colon, can miss cancers higher up; Any positive test needs follow-up colonoscopy; Requires a laxative to clean out the colon
Colonoscopy (every 10 years)	Doctor looks into the entire rectum and colon through a long, flexible tube-shaped instrument	Can take samples of the colon (biopsies) and remove polyps during the procedure; Examines the entire colon	Requires patient to see a specialist; Sedation needed; Complications rare, but can be serious; Requires a laxative to clean out the colon before test
Virtual colonoscopy (best frequency unknown)	Computerized X-rays of the colon	Examines whole colon; Sedation not needed	Cannot take samples during this test; Any positive test needs follow-up colonoscopy; Requires a laxative to clean out the colon before the test

Web Sites with Good Information about Colorectal Cancer Screening

American Cancer Society
www.cancer.org/docroot/LRN/LRN_0.asp?dt=10

Centers for Disease Control
www.cdc.gov/cancer/colorectal/sfl/

National Cancer Institute
www.cancer.gov/cancertopics/factsheet/Detection/colorectal-screening

Chronic Obstructive Pulmonary Disease

Chronic obstructive pulmonary disease (COPD) is a common cause of morbidity and mortality worldwide. Unlike the sharp reduction in death from heart disease, there has been an almost 100% increase in age-adjusted mortality between 1970 and 2002 due to COPD. It is currently the fourth leading cause of mortality and is projected to continue increasing for the foreseeable future. In 2000, the number of deaths in women was equal to that in men (1).

Screening

What is COPD, and which patient populations are at risk?
COPD is a treatable and preventable, but incurable, disease characterized by progressive airflow obstruction associated with an abnormal inflammatory response of the lungs to noxious particles or gases (2–4). Patients with COPD may meet the spirometry criteria for the diagnosis but remain asymptomatic. On the other hand, they may present with a variety of respiratory symptoms, including those of chronic bronchitis, or signs of emphysema on physical examination or imaging studies.

Patients younger than 35 years rarely get COPD, because susceptible individuals develop COPD only after inhalational exposure of sufficient intensity and duration to causative agents. It is estimated that about 80% to 90% of COPD is due to tobacco smoke (whether from smoking or exposure to "second-hand" smoke). The prevalence of COPD among cigarette smokers depends on the number of pack-years, the age of the patient, and the genetic predisposition. A risk of 15% for clinically significant COPD among cigarette smokers is commonly quoted, but this may be an underestimate (5).

Between 10% and 20% of COPD is caused by occupational or other exposure to chemical vapors, irritants, and fumes. More information is needed to determine the role of other possible inhaled irritants, such as those found in outdoor air pollution.

Although genetic factors remain largely unknown, the most clearly documented genetic risk for the development of COPD is serum α_1-antitrypsin deficiency.

Should clinicians screen asymptomatic patients for COPD?
There are no clear-cut data to support screening of asymptomatic patients for COPD with spirometry. Therefore, the United States Preventive Services Task Force recommends against screening for COPD in the general population (6). On the other hand, epidemiologic evidence suggests that one half of the current population with COPD has not been identified (7), and patients who smoke or have other risk factors may have COPD despite being asymptomatic.

A potential benefit of early detection is that it is an opportunity to further encourage patients to stop smoking. However, data on the effectiveness of COPD screening in motivating smoking cessation conflict (8). Screening may detect patients who consider themselves to be asymptomatic but in fact have adapted their lifestyle to accommodate a reduced level of activity. However, there are also few data to support this as a rationale for screening asymptomatic patients (9).

Other professional organizations recommend a case-finding approach in patients who present with risk factors or possible symptoms. For example, the updated 2007 guidelines from the Global Initiative for Chronic Obstructive Lung Disease suggest that

1. Global Initiative for Chronic Obstructive Lung Disease. Accessed at www.goldcopd.org on 17 January 2008.
2. American Thoracic Society. COPD Guidelines. Accessed at www.thoracic.org/copd on 17 January 2008.
3. Department of Veterans Affairs and Department of Defense. COPD Guidelines. Accessed at www.oqp.med.va.gov/cpg/COPD/COPD_base.htm on 17 January 2008.
4. National Institute of Clinical Excellence. Management of chronic obstructive pulmonary disease in adults in primary and secondary care. Accessed at www.nice.org.uk/nicemedia/pdf/CG012_niceguideline.pdf on 17 January 2008.
5. Rennard SI, Vestbo J. COPD: the dangerous underestimate of 15%. Lancet. 2006;367:1216-9. [PMID: 16631861]
6. U.S. Preventive Services Task Force. Screening for Chronic Obstructive Pulmonary Disease Using Spirometry: U.S. Preventive Services Task Force Recommendation Statement. Ann Intern Med. 2008. In press.
7. Mannino DM, Buist AS. Global burden of COPD: risk factors, prevalence, and future trends. Lancet. 2007;370:765-73. [PMID: 17765526]

clinicians doing spirometry look for COPD in patients with symptoms, such as chronic cough and sputum or shortness of breath (1). The American Thoracic Society/ European Respiratory Society recommends spirometry in people exposed to tobacco smoke and those with a family history of COPD (2).

Screening... The major risk factors for COPD are inhalational exposure to tobacco smoke, including second-hand smoke, and occupational or other exposure to dusts, chemical vapors, irritants, and fumes. α_1-Antitrypsin deficiency is the most clearly documented genetic risk factor that clinicians should consider, especially when patients develop COPD before age 50 years. Screening for COPD in the asymptomatic general population is not recommended. Some professional organizations recommend spirometry in specific patient groups as a case-finding measure and to encourage patients to stop smoking.

CLINICAL BOTTOM LINE

Diagnosis

When should clinicians consider a diagnosis of COPD?

Patients with COPD exhibit a broad spectrum of clinical findings, which are more specific than sensitive. When present, symptoms include cough, sputum production, dyspnea, and decreased exercise tolerance. Examination may reveal evidence of hyperinflation, such as hyperresonance and distant breath sounds. However, whereas chronic bronchitis (defined as at least 90 days of cough and sputum production for 2 consecutive years) and emphysema (a pathologic diagnosis suggested by hyperinflation on examination and imaging studies) are commonly associated with COPD, neither is required to make the diagnosis.

What is the role of pulmonary function testing in the diagnosis of COPD?

Spirometry is the essential component of pulmonary function testing required for diagnosis and classification of COPD. The spirometric criterion for the diagnosis of COPD is a postbronchodilator FEV_1/FVC ratio less than 0.70. The FEV_1 percentage predicted can be measured to classify COPD as mild (>80%), moderate (50%–80%), severe (30%–50%), or very severe (<30%) (1–3).

The other components of pulmonary function testing, including lung volumes, diffusing capacity, and arterial blood gases and pulse oximetry, are not required for diagnosis. These tests may be helpful in further determining severity of COPD; suggesting the presence of emphysema; excluding other lung diseases, such as restrictive lung disease; and determining if a patient is a candidate for long-term oxygen therapy or if chronic hypercapnia is present. Moreover, the degree of reversibility of airflow limitation (for example, degree of improvement in FEV_1 after bronchodilator or other intervention) is not recommended for diagnosis, differential diagnosis with asthma, or prediction of response to long-term treatment with bronchodilators or glucocorticosteroids (1).

Spirometric data can also be used in calculating the BODE index (Table 1) (10), which stands for **B**ody mass index; **O**bstruction, as measured by FEV_1; **D**yspnea, as measured by the Modified Medical Research Council dyspnea questionnaire (11); and **E**xercise, as determined by a 6-minute walk

8. Wilt TJ, Niewoehner D, Kim C, et al. Use of spirometry for case finding, diagnosis, and management of chronic obstructive pulmonary disease (COPD). Evid Rep Technol Assess (Summ). 2005:1-7. [PMID: 16238364]

9. Wilt TJ, Niewoehner D, MacDonald R, et al. Management of stable chronic obstructive pulmonary disease: a systematic review for a clinical practice guideline. Ann Intern Med. 2007;147:639-53. [PMID: 17975187]

10. Celli BR, Cote CG, Marin JM, et al. The body-mass index, airflow obstruction, dyspnea, and exercise capacity index in chronic obstructive pulmonary disease. N Engl J Med. 2004;350:1005-12. [PMID: 14999112]

11. Bestall JC, Paul EA, Garrod R, et al. Usefulness of the Medical Research Council (MRC) dyspnoea scale as a measure of disability in patients with chronic obstructive pulmonary disease. Thorax. 1999;54:581-6. [PMID: 10377201]

Table 1. The MMRC Dyspnea Severity Scale* for Calculation of the BODE Index

Severity	Score	Degree of Breathlessness Related to Activities
None	0	Not troubled with breathlessness except with strenuous exercise
Mild	1	Troubled by shortness of breath when hurrying or walking up a slight hill
Moderate	2	Walks slower than people of the same age due to breathlessness or has to stop for breath when walking at own pace on level ground
Severe	3	Stops for breath after walking approximately 100 meters or after a few minutes on level ground
Very severe	4	Too breathless to leave the house or breathless when dressing or undressing

Variable	Points on BODE Index[†]			
	0	1	2	3
FEV$_1$ (percentage predicted)	≥65	50–64	36–49	≤35
Distance walked in 6 min, *m*	≥350	250–349	150–249	≤149
MMRC dyspnea scale score	0–1	2	3	4
Body mass index	>21	≤21		

Adapted from Veterans' Affairs and Department of Defense guidelines (3). BODE = Body mass index, Obstruction, Dyspnea, and Exercise; COPD = chronic obstructive pulmonary disease; MMRC = Modified Medical Research Council.

† Points for each variable are summed with a possible range from 0 to 10. Higher numbers indicate worse prognosis. Adapted from (10).

test. The BODE index is beneficial in estimating risk for hospitalization and determining prognosis and is recommended in evaluating patients for lung transplantation (12).

The BODE index was validated prospectively in 625 patients with COPD. The average FEV$_1$ percentage predicted varied from 39% to 47%. For each 1-point increase in the BODE index, there was a 1.34 increase in the hazard ratio for subsequent death from any cause and a 1.62 increase for death from respiratory failure (10).

What other laboratory tests should clinicians order when evaluating patients with COPD?

Apart from the specific pulmonary function tests described previously, no other tests are routinely recommended in diagnosing COPD, classifying its severity, or helping to determine prognosis. However, chest X-rays show flattened diaphragms and hyperlucency and computed tomography (CT) scanning shows destruction of pulmonary parenchyma (in patients with emphysema).

Clinicians should consider obtaining an α_1-antitrypsin level in patients who have documented COPD with onset as early as the

fifth decade of life or in the absence of a recognized risk factor, such as smoking and occupational dust exposure. It should also be considered in patients with a family history of emphysema or α_1-antitrypsin deficiency, bronchiectasis, liver disease, or panniculitis.

Exercise testing may also be useful in the differential diagnosis of patients with dyspnea when it is unclear whether symptoms are pulmonary or cardiac in origin.

What other disorders should clinicians consider in patients with suspected COPD?

Clinicians should consider any condition that produces airflow obstruction, such as asthma; bronchiectasis; cystic fibrosis; bronchiolitis; and upper airway obstruction due to tumors of the trachea, tracheal stenosis, tracheomalacia, and vocal cord dysfunction. Clinicians should also consider other conditions that cause dyspnea, such as interstitial lung disease. Patients with dyspnea and cardiac disease are a frequent challenge and often require specific cardiologic studies to determine the cause of their symptoms.

12. Pulmonary Scientific Council of the International Society for Heart and Lung Transplantation. International guidelines for the selection of lung transplant candidates: 2006 update—a consensus report from the Pulmonary Scientific Council of the International Society for Heart and Lung Transplantation. J Heart Lung Transplant. 2006; 25:745-55. [PMID: 16818116]
13. Anthonisen NR, Connett JE, Kiley JP, et al. Effects of smoking intervention and the use of an inhaled anticholinergic bronchodilator on the rate of decline of FEV1. The Lung Health Study. JAMA. 1994;272:1497-505. [PMID: 7966841]

How should clinicians distinguish between patients with COPD and those with asthma?

Because spirometric obstruction, cough, wheeze, and dyspnea are common to both COPD and asthma, it is sometimes difficult to distinguish between the disorders. In general, patients with asthma develop symptoms at a younger age, are less likely to be smokers, and experience symptoms intermittently and with more variability. Those with COPD tend to have onset of disease later in life; commonly have chronic productive cough; have more persistent dyspnea; and may have a less consistent response to drugs, such as inhaled corticosteroids.

Diagnosis... Clinicians should suspect COPD in patients with a smoking history or occupational exposure to inhaled irritants; those with chronic cough, sputum, or dyspnea; and those with a family history of respiratory disease. Confirm the diagnosis by spirometry with a FEV_1/FVC ratio of less than 0.70 measured after administration of a bronchodilator. Use clinical data to determine disease severity and to exclude other disorders. Consider ordering an α_1-antrypsin level test in patients who present with early-onset COPD or in those with a compatible family history.

CLINICAL BOTTOM LINE

Treatment

What is the evidence that smoking cessation benefits patients even after COPD is present, and what smoking cessation interventions are most effective in patients with COPD?

Clinicians should urge all patients with COPD who smoke to quit and enroll in a smoking cessation program. There is excellent evidence that patients with COPD who stop smoking have a reduced rate of decline in pulmonary function (13).

In a multicenter, randomized, controlled trial (RCT) of an intensive smoking cessation program that included behavioral modification and nicotine gum versus placebo, middle-aged smokers in the intervention group had a smaller decline in FEV_1 of 34 mL/y than those in the placebo group, who declined 63 mL/y, over a 5-year period (13).

Smoking cessation therapies range from brief interventions in physicians' offices to more structured programs, which typically include 2 to 3 longer advice sessions and medications, such as nicotine preparations, burpropion, or varenicline. These programs are effective in up to 30% of patients at 1 year.

However, it is unclear that any particular medication is more effective than another in patients with COPD (14). For more information, see our issue on Smoking Cessation (15).

How should clinicians approach drug therapy in patients with COPD?

Inhaled medications—including β_2-agonists, anticholinergics, and corticosteroids—form the cornerstone of pharmacotherapy for COPD and should be considered as part of an overall treatment strategy that includes smoking cessation, education, and pulmonary rehabilitation. None of these therapies significantly alter the course of the disease in reducing the rate of decline in pulmonary function or decreasing mortality. The goal of treatment should be symptom relief, particularly dyspnea; prevention of exacerbations; and improvement in respiratory health status.

Before therapy is initiated, it is important to assess pulmonary function and severity, including history of exacerbations, both through clinical assessment and use

14. Wu P, Wilson K, Dimoulas P, et al. Effectiveness of smoking cessation therapies: a systematic review and meta-analysis. BMC Public Health. 2006;6:300. [PMID: 17156479]
15. Wilson JF. In the Clinic Smoking Cessation Toolkit. Accessed at www.annals.org/intheclinic/toolkit-smoking-cessation.html?itcab out on 17 January 2008.

16. Clinical Efficacy Assessment Subcommittee of the American College of Physicians. Diagnosis and management of stable chronic obstructive pulmonary disease: a clinical practice guideline from the American College of Physicians. Ann Intern Med. 2007;147:633-8. [PMID: 17975186]

17. Calverley PM, Anderson JA, Celli B, et al.; TORCH investigators. Salmeterol and fluticasone propionate and survival in chronic obstructive pulmonary disease. N Engl J Med. 2007; 356:775-89. [PMID: 17314337]

18. van Noord JA, Aumann JL, Janssens E, et al. Comparison of tiotropium once daily, formoterol twice daily and both combined once daily in patients with COPD. Eur Respir J. 2005;26:214-22. [PMID: 16055868]

19. van Noord JA, Aumann JL, Janssens E, et al. Effects of tiotropium with and without formoterol on airflow obstruction and resting hyperinflation in patients with COPD. Chest. 2006;129:509-17. [PMID: 16537846]

20. van Noord JA, de Munck DR, Bantje TA, et al. Long-term treatment of chronic obstructive pulmonary disease with salmeterol and the additive effect of ipratropium. Eur Respir J. 2000;15:878-85. [PMID: 10853852]

21. COMBIVENT Inhalation Aerosol Study Group. In chronic obstructive pulmonary disease, a combination of ipratropium and albuterol is more effective than either agent alone. An 85-day multicenter trial. COMBIVENT Inhalation Aerosol Study Group. Chest. 1994; 105:1411-9. [PMID: 8181328]

of validated instruments, such as the Modified Medical Research Council scale of dyspnea (Table 1), and to reassess periodically as the disease progresses. Symptoms do not necessarily correlate with the level of FEV_1, and dyspnea may respond to drug therapy at any level. However, most studies of the effectiveness of drug therapy with end points of health status and frequency of COPD exacerbations have been performed in symptomatic patients with an FEV_1 less than 60% predicted. In view of this, the American College of Physicians (ACP) recommends that long-acting bronchodilator and inhaled corticosteroid treatment for stable COPD be reserved for patients who have respiratory symptoms and FEV_1 less than 60% predicted (16).

How should clinicians use inhaled bronchodilators?

There are no data to recommend initial use of any particular bronchodilator over another, and the choice should be based on patient preference, potential toxicity, and cost. Clinicians should begin with single bronchodilator therapy and step up to combination bronchodilator therapy if additional symptomatic relief is required. Inhaled corticosteroids are then added as needed, again usually when the FEV_1 is less than 60% (9). The Figure, which is from the American Thoracic Society/European Respiratory Society guidelines (2), outlines an approach to step therapy.

Clinicians should choose short-acting bronchodilators with durations of action of 3 to 6 hours in patients with mild COPD, patients who need treatment of intermittent symptoms, or those on regular medication regimens who need rescue treatment for breakthrough symptoms. These include β_2-agonists or the anticholinergic agent ipratropium (Table 2). Ipratropium is also short-acting (albeit with slower onset of action) and can be used for rescue as monotherapy or

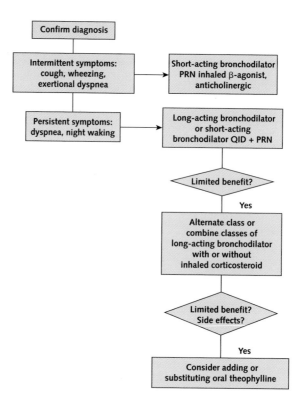

Figure. Step therapy for patients with COPD (from the ATS/ERS guidelines)

Table 2. Drug Treatment for COPD*

Agent	Dosage	Side Effects	Notes
Bronchodilator agents			
Inhaled short-acting β_2-agonist: albuterol levalbuterol metaproterenol pirbuterol	2 inhalations as needed, up to 12 inhalations per day	Sympathomimetic symptoms, such as tremor and tachycardia	Generally used as needed
Inhaled short-acting anticholinergic: ipratropium	2 inhalations qid, increase as tolerated	Dry mouth, mydriasis on contact with eye	Use as maintenance therapy. Not to be used with tiotropium
Inhaled long-acting anticholinergic: tiotropium	18 µg/d	Dry mouth, mydriasis on contact with eye	Use as maintenance therapy. Not to be used with ipratropium
Inhaled long-acting β_2-agonist: salmeterol formoterol aformoterol	Salmeterol, 42 µg bid by MDI and 50 µg bid by DPI; formoterol, 12 µg bid by DPI and 20 µg by nebulized solution; aformoterol, 15 µg bid by nebulized solution	Sympathomimetic symptoms, such as tremor and tachycardia	Use as maintenance therapy. Overdosage can be fatal. No change for exacerbations
Oral theophylline aminophylline: generic and brand name sustained and short acting	Aim for serum levels between 5 and 14 µg/mL	Tachycardia, nausea, vomiting, disturbed pulmonary function, and sleep. Overdose can be fatal with seizures and arrhythmias	Use as maintenance therapy. Use intravenously in emergency departments. May also improve respiratory muscle function.
Oral β_2-agonists: albuterol metaproterenol terbutaline	Albuterol, 4 mg bid; metaproterenol, 5 to 10 mg tid to qid; terbutaline, 2.5 to 5 mg tid	Sympathomimetic symptoms, such as tremor and tachycardia	Use as maintenance therapy. Rarely used because of side effects but may be beneficial to patients who cannot use inhalers.
Anti-inflammatory agents			
Inhaled corticosteroids: fluticasone budesonide triamcinolone	Fluticasone, 880 µg/d; budesonide, 800 µg/d; triamcinolone, 1200 µg/d; all in divided doses.	Skin bruising, oral candidiasis, rarely adrenal suppression possibly glaucoma, decreased bone density, diabetes systemic hypertension, and cataracts	Can be used as maintenance therapy. In patients with a history of frequent exacerbations, high doses are best studied. Pulmonary function improved in 10%–20% of patients, but symptoms and exacerbations reduced in a larger percentage. No effect on decline in pulmonary function. Not approved by the FDA for treatment of COPD.
Oral corticosteroids: prednisone prednisolone	Varying doses	Skin bruising, adrenal suppression, glaucoma, osteoporosis	Avoid use, if possible, in stable COPD. Pulmonary function improved in 10%–20% of patients. Reduce to lowest effective dose, including transition to inhaled corticosteroids, alternate day oral corticosteroids, or both. Intravenous or oral corticosteroids are standard therapy and are effective for acute exacerbations.
Combination agents			
Combined inhaled long-acting β_2-agonist and inhaled corticosteroid: fluticasone salmeterol	Fluticasone, 250 µg bid, and salmeterol, 50 µg bid, single inhaler; combination of comparable doses of inhaled corticosteroids and long-acting β_2-agonists in separate inhalers	See long-acting β_2 agonist and inhaled corticosteroid	The single inhaler combination is approved by the FDA for maintenance treatment of airflow obstruction in COPD associated with chronic bronchitis. Other combinations have not been approved by the FDA. Combinations are not to be used for treatment of acute bronchospasm. Overdosage of combination can be fatal because of long-acting β_2-agonist.

COPD = chronic obstructive pulmonary disease; DPI = dry-powder inhaler; FDA = Food and Drug Administration; MDI = metered-dose inhaler; qid = four times daily; tid = three times daily.

22. Aaron SD, Vandemheen KL, Fergusson D et al.; Canadian Thoracic Society/Canadian Respiratory Clinical Research Consortium. Tiotropium in combination with placebo, salmeterol, or fluticasone-salmeterol for treatment of chronic obstructive pulmonary disease: a randomized trial. Ann Intern Med. 2007;146:545-55. [PMID: 17310045]

23. ZuWallack RL, Mahler DA, Reilly D, et al. Salmeterol plus theophylline combination therapy in the treatment of COPD. Chest. 2001; 119:1661-70. [PMID: 11399688]

24. Molfino NA, Zhang P. A meta-analysis on the efficacy of oral theophylline in patients with stable COPD. Int J Chron Obstruct Pulmon Dis. 2006;1:261-6. [PMID: 18046863]

25. Ram FS, Jardin JR, Atallah A, et al. Efficacy of theophylline in people with stable chronic obstructive pulmonary disease: a systematic review and meta-analysis. Respir Med. 2005; 99:135-44. [PMID: 15715180]

26. Rossi A, Kristufek P, Levine BE, et al.; Formoterol in Chronic Obstructive Pulmonary Disease (FICOPD) II Study Group. Comparison of the efficacy, tolerability, and safety of formoterol dry powder and oral, slow-release theophylline in the treatment of COPD. Chest. 2002; 121:1058-69. [PMID: 11948033]

27. Prevention and control of influenza: recommendations of the Advisory Committee on Immunization Practices (ACIP). MMWR Recomm Rep. 1997;46:1-25. [PMID: 9148134]

28. Poole PJ, Chacko E, Wood-Baker RW, et al. Influenza vaccine for patients with chronic obstructive pulmonary disease. Cochrane Database Syst Rev. 2006: CD002733. [PMID: 16437444]

in combination with albulterol. Metered-dose inhalers, dry-powder inhalers, and nebulizers are all equally efficacious, although all require appropriate patient education regarding proper technique to ensure adequate drug delivery.

Monotherapy with long-acting bronchodilators reduces exacerbations and slightly improves overall respiratory health status but does not significantly reduce hospitalizations or mortality (17). Approved long-acting β_2-agonists include salmeterol, formoterol, and aformoterol, all of which require twice daily dosing. The only long-acting anticholinergic agent is tiopropium, which is given once daily. Salmeterol and tiopropium have a slow onset of action, whereas formoterol and aformoterol have a rapid onset of action. Long-acting bronchodilators should never be used as rescue therapy or in doses greater than those indicated on package inserts.

Oral β_2-agonists have not been well studied in COPD. They may be effective but are slower in onset, have more side effects (1), and are generally avoided.

If monotherapy is insufficient, clinicians should consider using inhaled combination therapy with a β_2-agonist and an anticholinergic agent. Most studies show that such combinations may improve levels of FEV_1 (18–21), but there are few data suggesting that combination therapy is significantly better than monotherapy in alleviating clinical symptoms, such as relieving shortness of breath, improving exercise tolerance, and reducing COPD exacerbations. A recent study suggests that combination therapy with tiotropium and salmeterol improves disease-specific quality of life (22).

When should clinicians prescribe corticosteroids in patients with COPD?

Clinicians should consider adding inhaled corticosteroids to regimens of inhaled long-acting bronchodilators in patients with moderate-to-severe COPD, usually with FEV_1 less than 60% predicted, who remain symptomatic or have had repeated exacerbations. When paired with a long-acting β_2-agonist, inhaled corticosteroids afford even greater improvement in pulmonary function and clinical outcomes than either agent alone (17).

Data also indicate that combining the long-acting anticholinergic tiotropium with the long-acting β_2-agonist salmeterol plus an inhaled corticosteroid improves quality of life compared with monotherapy with a long-acting anticholinergic (22).

A randomized, double-blind trial compared inhaled salmeterol plus fluticasone with placebo, salmeterol alone, or fluticasone alone for a period of 3 years in 6112 patients with an FEV_1 less than 60% predicted. The combination of salmeterol and fluticasone decreased the annual rate of moderate-to-severe exacerbations. A statistically significant effect on mortality was not seen (17).

Oral steroids should be reserved for acute exacerbations of COPD and should be avoided in patients with stable disease.

When should clinicians consider adding oral theophylline to inhaled drug therapy for COPD?

Methylxanthines, such as aminophylline or theophylline, can be considered in patients with COPD who remain symptomatic despite use of other bronchodilators with or without inhaled corticosteroids and who do not have potential risk factors for toxicity, such as seizures and tachydysrhythmias. In such patients, theophylline can be started at a low dose and titrated to effect. A therapeutic blood level is generally between 5 and 14 μg/mL (2, 3). Theophylline should be discontinued if there is no improvement after several weeks, and it should not be used in treating acute exacerbations of COPD. Several RCTs have demonstrated oral theophylline to be a relatively weak bronchodilator (23–26). The narrow therapeutic window, multiple interactions with other medications, and potential toxicity necessitate frequent monitoring of serum theophylline levels.

What immunizations should clinicians administer to patients with COPD?

The Advisory Committee on Immunization Practices recommends influenza and pneumococcal vaccinations for persons who have chronic disorders of the pulmonary or cardiovascular systems, including COPD (27). Influenza vaccination should be administered yearly to all patients with COPD. This is supported by 3 meta-analyses (28–30).

In a Cochrane review of 11 RCTs, 6 of which were performed in patients with COPD, use of inactivated vaccine resulted in a significant reduction in the total number of exacerbations per vaccinated subject compared with those who received placebo (weighted mean difference, −0.37 [95% CI, −0.64 to −0.11]; P= 0.006) (28).

Pneumococcal vaccination should be given once before age 65 and again after age 65 if the previous vaccination was given more than 5 years earlier (27). If the patient was not vaccinated before age 65, then a 1-time vaccination is recommended.

How should clinicians manage patients with acute exacerbations of COPD?

Although there is no single definition of a COPD exacerbation, a frequently used approach is to apply the criteria shown in the Box on this page. Acute exacerbations of COPD frequently develop following an upper respiratory

---

Criteria and Classification of Acute COPD Exacerbation

Major criteria
- Increase in sputum volume
- Increase in sputum purulence (generally yellow or green)
- Worsening dyspnea

Additional criteria
- Upper respiratory infection in the past 5 days
- Fever of no apparent cause
- Increase in wheezing and cough
- Increase in respiratory rate or heart rate 20% above baseline

Mild exacerbation = 1 major criterion plus 1 or more additional criteria
Moderate exacerbation = 2 major criteria
Severe exacerbation = all 3 major criteria
(Adapted from ref. 31)

---

infection. Management includes prompt recognition of the exacerbation, adjustment of bronchodilator and steroid therapy, initiation of antibiotics, and assessment of the need for hospitalization.

Clinicians should strongly consider prescribing antibiotics for patients who meet the criteria for a moderate or severe exacerbation. Although some exacerbations are due to viral infection or inhaled irritants, the most common bacterial causes are *Haemophilus influenza*, *Streptococcus pneumoniae*, and *Moraxella catarrhalis* (32, 33). Antibiotic coverage should generally be directed toward these bacteria, taking into account local bacterial resistance patterns. To date, there are insufficient clinical data to recommend any single antimicrobial agent over another. However, there is consensus that the severity of the exacerbation, the degree of pulmonary function impairment, the history of exacerbations, and the response to previous treatment should be used to help guide therapy. For patients with moderate or severe exacerbations, a β-lactam/β-lactamase

29. Vu T, Farish S, Jenkins M, et al. A meta-analysis of effectiveness of influenza vaccine in persons aged 65 years and over living in the community. Vaccine. 2002; 20:1831-6. [PMID: 11906772]
30. Jefferson T, Rivetti D, Rivetti A, et al. Efficacy and effectiveness of influenza vaccines in elderly people: a systematic review. Lancet. 2005;366: 1165-74. [PMID: 16198765]
31. Anthonisen NR, Manfreda J, Warren CP, et al. Antibiotic therapy in exacerbations of chronic obstructive pulmonary disease. Ann Intern Med. 1987;106:196-204. [PMID: 3492164]
32. Sethi S, Evans N, Grant BJ, et al. New strains of bacteria and exacerbations of chronic obstructive pulmonary disease. N Engl J Med. 2002; 347:465-71. [PMID: 12181400]
33. Sethi S. Infectious exacerbations of chronic bronchitis: diagnosis and management. J Antimicrob Chemother. 1999;43 Suppl A: 97-105. [PMID: 10225579]
34. Ram FS, Rodriguez-Roisin R, Granados-Navarrete A, et al. Antibiotics for exacerbations of chronic obstructive pulmonary disease. Cochrane Database Syst Rev. 2006: CD004403. [PMID: 16625602]
35. Saint S, Bent S, Vittinghoff E, et al. Antibiotics in chronic obstructive pulmonary disease exacerbations. A meta-analysis. JAMA. 1995;273:957-60. [PMID: 7884956]
36. McCrory DC, Brown C, Gelfand SE, et al. Management of acute exacerbations of COPD: a summary and appraisal of published evidence. Chest. 2001;119: 1190-209. [PMID: 11296189]

37. Snow V, Lascher S, Mottur-Pilson C; Joint Expert Panel on COPD of the American College of Chest Physicians and the American College of Physicians-Amercian Society of Internal Medicine. The evidence base for management of acute exacerbations of COPD: clinical practice guideline, part 1. Chest. 2001;119:1185-9. [PMID: 11296188]
38. Sachs AP, Koëter GH, Groenier KH, et al. Changes in symptoms, peak expiratory flow, and sputum flora during treatment with antibiotics of exacerbations in patients with chronic obstructive pulmonary disease in general practice. Thorax. 1995;50:758-63. [PMID: 7570411]
39. Wood-Baker RR, Gibson PG, Hannay M, et al. Systemic corticosteroids for acute exacerbations of chronic obstructive pulmonary disease. Cochrane Database Syst Rev. 2005: CD001288. [PMID: 15674875]
40. Niewoehner DE, Erbland ML, Deupree RH, et al. Effect of systemic glucocorticoids on exacerbations of chronic obstructive pulmonary disease. Department of Veterans Affairs Cooperative Study Group. N Engl J Med. 1999;340: 1941-7. [PMID: 10379017]

inhibitor, an extended-spectrum macrolide, a second- or third-generation cephalosporin, or a fluoroquinolone can be used. Those with a mild exacerbation can be treated with tetracycline or trimethoprim–sulfamethoxazole. In any case, always consider antibiotics in patients with 1 major criterion and an abnormal chest X-ray or an FEV_1 less than 35% predicted. It is not necessary to routinely obtain sputum Gram stain and culture in patients with an exacerbation.

Previous meta-analyses and systematic reviews have provided support for the efficacy of antibiotics in patients with exacerbations of COPD (34–38). Specifically, antibiotics improve peak flow, reduce mortality, and reduce treatment failure. This effect appears to be most pronounced in patients with more severe exacerbations (36).

A Cochrane review of 11 RCTs included 917 patients with COPD. Of these, 10 trials used increased cough, sputum volume, and purulence as diagnostic criteria for a COPD exacerbation. Antibiotic therapy, regardless of antibiotic choice, significantly reduced mortality, treatment failure, and sputum purulence, with a number needed to treat of 8. There was a small increase in risk for diarrhea with antibiotics (relative risk, 2.86 [CI, 1.06 to 7.76]) (35).

Oral corticosteroids should be considered in patients with moderate-to-severe acute exacerbations of COPD. Although the appropriate dose is not well defined, 30 to 60 mg/d for up to 2 weeks is commonly used (39). There is good evidence to suggest that a 6-week course of systemic steroids is no more beneficial than a 2-week course and that the longer course increases the risk for adverse effects (40).

Tailoring therapy to prevent future exacerbations is difficult because there is no sufficiently accurate way to predict which subset of patients with COPD is at greatest risk. Most studies suggest that a history

of previous exacerbations, a baseline FEV_1 less than 50% predicted, and perhaps age may be the most useful predictors (41–43).

It is important to recognize patients in whom outpatient management of a COPD exacerbation is insufficient and hospitalization with possible intubation and mechanical ventilation may be necessary (see Box). Venous thromboembolism should be considered in patients with COPD exacerbations of unknown cause who do not have evidence of infection (44).

When should clinicians recommend pulmonary rehabilitation for patients with COPD?

Pulmonary rehabilitation is a multidisciplinary program of care that comprises a variety of interventions grouped into categories, including exercise training, education, and psychological and nutritional counseling. Although the individual components have benefits, the most effective approach is a comprehensive, integrated program (3). A team of health care practitioners usually provides pulmonary rehabilitation in a structured program administered to groups of patients with COPD.

Clinicians should recommend pulmonary rehabilitation for all symptomatic patients with COPD as part of their overall treatment plan as they are optimizing drug treatment. Patients who are most likely to benefit are those with impaired quality of life from COPD, who experience breathlessness and anxiety that limit activity, and who are willing to undertake an intensive education and exercise program (1–3).

Most studies involve patients with more severe disease, but patients with mild-to-moderate COPD may also benefit. More recent data suggest that pulmonary rehabilitation may be helpful in patients after an acute exacerbation (45).

In a meta-analysis of 20 RCTs of 979 patients, including studies to the year 2000, it was concluded that pulmonary rehabilitation increased exercise ability and health-related quality of life and reduced dyspnea. Inspiratory muscle training, by itself, was not effective. Patients with severe COPD required a program lasting at least 6 months to achieve benefit. Patients with mild-to-moderate COPD could benefit from shorter programs (46).

What other adjunctive measures should clinicians consider in managing patients with COPD?
There are several other commonly used adjunctive therapies. Chest physiotherapy, percussion and vibration, and postural drainage are used to enhance clearance of sputum and alleviate shortness of breath. Relaxation techniques may reduce anxiety due to shortness of breath. Pursed-lip breathing and diaphragmatic breathing are used to reduce shortness of breath. Nutritional interventions aim to achieve ideal body weight and improve ability to perform daily activities and exercise (1, 3, 4). However, data to support the effectiveness of these measures are lacking.

When should clinicians prescribe oxygen therapy for patients with COPD?
Patients with moderate-to-severe COPD should be periodically evaluated for the need for supplemental oxygen. The Box lists criteria for initiation of long-term oxygen therapy. Measurement of PaO_2 after 30 minutes of breathing room air is the most accurate clinical standard for initiating therapy. Pulse oximetry can be used to qualify patients for long-term oxygen therapy. Oximetry can also be used to adjust oxygen delivery (for example, oxygen flow rates) after initial diagnosis and over time.

When long-term oxygen therapy is indicated, continuous oxygen

---

> **Criteria for Initiation of Long-Term Oxygen Therapy**
> - Room air PaO_2 no greater than 55 mm Hg or between 55 and 60 mm Hg with cor pulmonale; signs of tissue hypoxia, such as polycythemia; or an SaO_2 no greater than 88% or 89% with signs of tissue hypoxia, OR
> - Nocturnal hypoxemia with an SaO_2 no greater than 88% (use oxygen only at night), OR
> - Exercise hypoxemia with a PaO_2 55 mm Hg or less or an SaO_2 88% of less (use oxygen only with exertion).

should be used for a minimum of 15 hours and ideally for 24 hours a day. Patients should have an initial follow-up within at least 3 months and yearly thereafter to guide subsequent oxygen therapy (47). However, the criteria of the Centers for Medicare & Medicaid Services do not generally require follow-up assessment if the qualifying PaO_2 was 55 mm Hg or less or the qualifying SaO_2 was 88% or less (48).

Long-term oxygen therapy can be used during exercise in persons with exertional desaturation to improve symptoms (49, 50) and during sleep in those who desaturate at night (51).

In a Cochrane review, meta-analysis of 6 RCTs showed that home long-term oxygen therapy improved survival in a select group of patients with COPD and severe hypoxemia (arterial PaO_2 less than 55 mm Hg [8.0 kPa]). Home oxygen therapy did not improve survival in patients with mild-to-moderate hypoxemia or in those with only arterial desaturation at night (50).

When should clinicians refer patients to a pulmonologist?
Clinicians should consider referring patients with COPD to a pulmonologist when there is diagnostic uncertainty or when patients are not responding well to treatment. Table 3 lists recommendations for referral adapted from guidelines.

Clinicians should consider pulmonary consultation in patients with COPD and severe disease undergoing surgery, those being

41. van der Valk P, Monninkhof E, van der Palen J, et al. Effect of discontinuation of inhaled corticosteroids in patients with chronic obstructive pulmonary disease: the COPE study. Am J Respir Crit Care Med. 2002;166:1358-63. [PMID: 12406823]
42. Jones PW, Willits LR, Burge PS, et al.; Inhaled Steroids in Obstructive Lung Disease in Europe study investigators. Disease severity and the effect of fluticasone propionate on chronic obstructive pulmonary disease exacerbations. Eur Respir J. 2003;21:68-73. [PMID: 12570111]
43. Niewoehner DE, Lokhnygina Y, Rice K, et al. Risk indexes for exacerbations and hospitalizations due to COPD. Chest. 2007;131:20-8. [PMID: 17218552]
44. Tillie-Leblond I, Marquette CH, Perez T, et al. Pulmonary embolism in patients with unexplained exacerbation of chronic obstructive pulmonary disease: prevalence and risk factors. Ann Intern Med. 2006;144:390-6. [PMID: 16549851]
45. Puhan MA, Scharplatz M, Troosters T, et al. Respiratory rehabilitation after acute exacerbation of COPD may reduce risk for readmission and mortality—a systematic review. Respir Res. 2005;6:54. [PMID: 15943867]
46. Salman GF, Mosier MC, Beasley BW, et al. Rehabilitation for patients with chronic obstructive pulmonary disease: meta-analysis of randomized controlled trials. J Gen Intern Med. 2003;18:213-21. [PMID: 12648254]
47. Guyatt GH, Nonoyama M, Lacchetti C, et al. A randomized trial of strategies for assessing eligibility for long-term domiciliary oxygen therapy. Am J Respir Crit Care Med. 2005;172:573-80. [PMID: 15901604]
48. Centers for Medicare & Medicaid Services. Evidence of medical necessity oxygen claims. Accessed at www.cms.hhs.gov/transmittals/downloads/r1742B3.pdf on 17 January 2008.

49. Bradley JM, O'Neill B. Short-term ambulatory oxygen for chronic obstructive pulmonary disease. Cochrane Database Syst Rev. 2005: CD004356. [PMID: 16235359]

50. Cranston JM, Crockett AJ, Moss JR, et al. Domiciliary oxygen for chronic obstructive pulmonary disease. Cochrane Database Syst Rev. 2005: CD001744. [PMID: 16235285]

51. Fletcher EC, Luckett RA, Goodnight-White S, et al. A double-blind trial of nocturnal supplemental oxygen for sleep desaturation in patients with chronic obstructive pulmonary disease and a daytime PaO2 above 60 mm Hg. Am Rev Respir Dis. 1992;145:1070-6. [PMID: 1586049]

52. American College of Physicians. Preoperative pulmonary risk stratification for noncardiothoracic surgery: systematic review for the American College of Physicians. Ann Intern Med. 2006;144:581-95. [PMID: 16618956]

53. Trayner E Jr, Celli BR. Postoperative pulmonary complications. Med Clin North Am. 2001;85:1129-39. [PMID: 11565490]

54. Ferreira IM, Brooks D, Lacasse Y, et al. Nutritional supplementation for stable chronic obstructive pulmonary disease. Cochrane Database Syst Rev. 2005: CD000998. [PMID: 15846608]

55. Fishman A, Martinez F, Naunheim K, et al. A randomized trial comparing lung-volume-reduction surgery with medical therapy for severe emphysema. N Engl J Med. 2003;348: 2059-73. [PMID: 12759479]

56. Hillerdal G, Löfdahl CG, Ström K, et al. Comparison of lung volume reduction surgery and physical training on health status and physiologic outcomes: a randomized controlled clinical trial. Chest. 2005;128: 3489-99. [PMID: 16304304]

Table 3. When to Consider Referral to a Pulmonary Specialist*

Disease onset before 40 years of age

Frequent exacerbations (2 or more per year) despite adequate treatment

Rapidly progressive course of disease (decline in FEV_1, progressive dyspnea, decreased exercise tolerance, unintentional weight loss)

Severe COPD (FEV_1 <50% predicted) despite optimal treatment

Need for oxygen therapy

Onset of comorbid condition (osteoporosis, heart failure, bronchiectasis, lung cancer)

Diagnostic uncertainty (for example, coexisting COPD and asthma)

Symptoms disproportionate to the severity of the airflow obstruction

Confirmed or suspected α_1-antitrypsin deficiency

Patient requests a second opinion

Patient is a potential candidate for lung transplantation or lung-volume reduction surgery

Patient has very severe disease and requires elective surgery that may impair respiratory function

*Adapted and modified from American Thoracic Society/European Respiratory Society and Veterans' Affairs/Department of Defense guidelines (2, 3). COPD = chronic obstructive pulmonary disease.

considered for lung-volume reduction surgery, and those who might be candidates for lung transplantation.

Preoperative Assessment

Patients with COPD have a 2.7- to 4.7-fold increase in the risk for postoperative pulmonary complications depending on the severity of COPD and the type, location, and urgency of the surgical procedure (52, 53). With COPD, patients undergoing thoracic and upper abdominal procedures are at greater risk. Patient-related risk factors include age, American Society of Anesthesiologists class, and cigarette smoking (52, 53).

A systematic review of interventions to reduce postoperative pulmonary complications after noncardiothoracic surgery found that a few are clearly effective. Effective measures include early ambulation; lung expansion maneuvers, such as incentive spirometry; deep breathing exercises; and continuous positive airway pressure to reduce pulmonary complications, such as atelectasis, pneumonia, and respiratory failure. Teaching patients about lung expansion maneuvers increases efficacy. Data that favor use of nasogastric tubes, epidural anesthesia and analgesia, laparoscopic operations, and enteral nutrition interventions are less clear-cut (52–54).

When should clinicians consider surgical therapies for COPD?

Lung-Volume Reduction Surgery

Lung-volume reduction surgery involves resection of up to 30% of diseased or nonfunctioning parenchyma to allow remaining lung to function more efficiently. It may be considered in patients with COPD who have completed a pulmonary rehabilitation program and meet the following criteria: 1) evidence of bilateral emphysema on CT scan; 2) postbronchodilator total lung capacity and residual volume greater than 150% and 100% predicted, respectively; 3) maximum FEV_1 no greater than 45% predicted; and 4) room air $PaCO_2$ no more than 60 mm Hg and a PaO_2 of at least 45 mm Hg. Patients with an FEV_1 no greater than 20% predicted and either homogeneous emphysema on CT scan or a carbon monoxide diffusing capacity of no more than 20% predicted should not be considered for lung-volume reduction surgery (55).

In patients with COPD who meet specific clinical criteria, lung-volume reduction surgery increases the chance for improved exercise capacity, lung function, dyspnea, and quality of life but does not improve overall survival compared with medical therapy alone. In a subgroup of patients with upper lobe emphysema and low exercise capacity, lung-volume reduction surgery may improve survival, but definitive long-term data are not yet available (55–57).

Lung Transplantation

COPD disease-specific guidelines for candidate selection for lung transplantation include patient with a BODE index of 7 to 10 and at least 1 of the following (12): 1) history of hospitalization for exacerbation associated with acute hypercapnia (partial pressure of carbon dioxide greater than 50 mm Hg); 2) pulmonary hypertension, cor pulmonale, or both despite oxygen therapy; and 3) FEV_1 less than 20% predicted and either carbon monoxide diffusion in the lungs less than 20% or homogeneous distribution of emphysema. There are also a number of relative and absolute contraindications to lung transplantation that are beyond the scope of this review (12).

Lung transplantation results in improved pulmonary function; exercise capacity; quality of life; and in highly selected patients, possibly survival (2). Average actuarial survival following single lung transplantation for patients with COPD is 82.9%, 59.7%, and 43.3% at 1, 3, and 5 years, respectively. Double lung transplantation survival is similar or slightly higher (58). By 5 years after lung transplantation, the prevalence of chronic allograft rejection (obliterative bronchiolitis), the leading cause of long-term morbidity and mortality, is as high as 50% to 70% among survivors (59).

Treatment... All patients with COPD who smoke should be urged to stop and to enter a smoking cessation program. Patients who have symptoms, such as dyspnea, can be treated with inhaled β_2-agonists or anticholinergic agents alone or in combination. The greatest benefit from treatment with long-acting bronchodilators is achieved in patients with an FEV_1 less than 60% predicted with an improvement in health status and a reduction in COPD exacerbations. These benefits may be enhanced with the addition of an inhaled corticosteroid. Acute exacerbations should be treated by optimizing bronchodilator therapy and adding systemic corticosteroids or antibiotics when clinically indicated. All patients should be encouraged to exercise. Pulmonary rehabilitation should be offered to patients with moderate-to-severe COPD to improve dyspnea and health status. Continuous long-term oxygen therapy is recommended for patients with severe disease and hypoxemia. Eligible patients should be evaluated for lung-volume reduction surgery or lung transplantation.

CLINICAL BOTTOM LINE

Practice Improvement

What do professional organizations recommend with regard to prevention, screening, diagnosis, and treatment of COPD?

Guidelines from professional organizations include those from the Global Initiative for Chronic Obstructive Lung Disease, updated in 2007 (1); the American Thoracic Society/European Respiratory Society, updated in 2005 (2); the Veterans' Affairs and Department of Defense, updated in 2007 (3); the National Institute of Clinical Excellence, published in 2004 (4); and the American College of Physicians (ACP), published in 2007 (16). The first 4 present a comprehensive approach to the diagnosis and management of COPD and draw information and evidence from a variety of sources, including RCTs; cohort studies; case–control studies; recommendations from public policy organizations, such as the Advisory Committee on Immunization

57. Ramsey SD, Shroyer AL, Sullivan SD, et al. Updated evaluation of the cost-effectiveness of lung volume reduction surgery. Chest. 2007;131:823-32. [PMID: 17356099]
58. United Network for Organ Sharing. The organ procurement and transplantation network. Accessed at www.optn.org/latestData/rptStrat.asp on 14 January 2008.

Practices; and expert opinion. The ACP guidelines are based almost solely on RCTs (9, 16). Although most guidelines suggest treating patients with COPD when they become symptomatic, the contribution of the ACP meta-analysis and guideline is to emphasize that the evidence indicates that inhaled drug therapy is most effective in patients in whom FEV_1 is less than 60% predicted.

What measures do stakeholders use to evaluate the quality of care for patients with COPD?
The Centers for Medicare & Medicaid Services has issued specifications for measures for the 2008 Physicians Quality Reporting Initiative. Of these measures, 2 relate to COPD. The first measure evaluates the percentage of patients age 18 years or older with a diagnosis of COPD who had spirometry evaluation documented in the measurement year. The second measure evaluates the percentage of patients age 18 years or older who had a diagnosis of COPD; an FEV_1/FVC ratio less than 0.70; symptoms, such as dyspnea, cough, sputum, or wheezing; and who were prescribed an inhaled bronchodilator.

What is the role of patient education in optimizing care of patients with COPD?
It is important that patients with COPD participate in the management of their disease by understanding the cause, treatment, course, and prognosis of COPD. They should be instructed in proper inhaler techniques, recognition of signs of deterioration, proper use of medications and exercise, smoking cessation, and precautions to take when traveling by air. Some of this education is available in multidisciplinary rehabilitation programs. Although some studies have shown that patient education programs have decreased hospitalizations and related measures, systematic reviews have documented less marked benefits (16).

According to the ACP guidelines on COPD, as of January 2005, the evidence shows that disease management and patient education efforts have not been effective in decreasing deaths, exacerbations, all-cause readmissions, lengths of stay, or number of visits to physicians or increasing improvements on health questionnaires, patient satisfactions, adherence to treatment, or self-management skills (16, 60).

59. Heng D, Sharples LD, McNeil K, et al. Bronchiolitis obliterans syndrome: incidence, natural history, prognosis, and risk factors. J Heart Lung Transplant. 1998;17:1255-63. [PMID: 9883768]
60. Monninkhof EM, van der Valk PD, van der Palen J, et al. Self-management education for chronic obstructive pulmonary disease. Cochrane Database Syst Rev. 2003;1:CD002990. [PMID: 12535447]

in the clinic
Tool Kit

Chronic Obstructive Pulmonary Disease

PIER Module
pier.acponline.org/physicians/diseases/d153/pdf/d153.pdf
Access PIER module on COPD.

COPD Pocket Card
www.oqp.med.va.gov/cpg/COPD/G/COPD_Pock.pdf
Download pocket card version of Veterans Administration/Department of Defense COPD Guidelines.

National Lung Health Education Project
www.nlhep.org/resources-medical.html
Pocket cards, wallet cards, posters, spirometry review materials, and other resources for physicians.

International COPD Coalition
www.internationalcopd.org/materials/professionals/default.aspx
COPD guidelines and patient information materials.

Joint Commission on Accreditation of Healthcare Organizations
www.jointcommission.org/CertificationPrograms/COPD
COPD certification program that lists a number of areas that should be in place for disease-specific care.

in the clinic

WHAT YOU SHOULD KNOW ABOUT CHRONIC OBSTRUCTIVE PULMONARY DISEASE

What is COPD?

- Chronic obstructive pulmonary disease (COPD) damages the lungs and the tubes that carry air from the nose and mouth to the lungs.
- COPD makes you cough and bring up mucus. It makes it hard to breathe and do the things you want to do.

How can you prevent COPD?

- Cigarette smoke is the most common cause of COPD. Stopping smoking can keep you from getting COPD.
- If you already have COPD, stopping smoking can keep it from getting worse.

How is COPD treated?

- Some people with COPD need medicines to open the airways. Most medicines are given by inhalers that deliver the medicine to the lungs in spray form.
- Sometimes antibiotics are needed to fight infections that make COPD worse.
- It is important to exercise and keep active.
- Some people need extra oxygen when COPD keeps them from getting enough.

How to Use an Inhaler

1. Take off the cap and shake the inhaler hard.
2. Breathe out all the way.
3. Hold the inhaler about 2 fingerwidths from your mouth.
4. Start to breath in slowly through your mouth as you press down on the inhaler once and keep breathing in slowly until you can't breathe in any more.
5. Hold your breath and count to 10 slowly.
6. Repeat steps 1 to 5 if your doctor has prescribed more than 1 puff of medicine, wait about 1 minute between puffs.

Web Sites with Good Information about COPD

MedlinePLUS
www.nlm.nih.gov/medlineplus/copdchronicobstructivepulmonarydisease.html#cat1

American Lung Association
www.lungusa.org/site/pp.asp?c=dvLUK9OOEEtb=23050

International COPD Coalition
www.internationalcopd.org/materials/professionals/default.asp

Patient Information

Dementia

1. Brookmeyer R, Gray S, Kawas C. Projections of Alzheimer's disease in the United States and the public health impact of delaying disease onset. Am J Public Health. 1998;88:1337-42. [PMID: 9736873]

2. Mitchell SL, Teno JM, Miller SC, et al. A national study of the location of death for older persons with dementia. J Am Geriatr Soc. 2005;53:299-305. [PMID: 15673356]

3. Launer LJ, Ross GW, Petrovitch H, et al. Midlife blood pressure and dementia: the Honolulu-Asia aging study. Neurobiol Aging. 2000;21:49-55. [PMID: 10794848]

4. Forette F, Seux ML, Staessen JA, et al. Prevention of dementia in randomised double-blind placebo-controlled Systolic Hypertension in Europe (Syst-Eur) trial. Lancet. 1998;352:1347-51. [PMID: 9802273]

5. PROGRESS Collaborative Group. Effects of blood pressure lowering with perindopril and indapamide therapy on dementia and cognitive decline in patients with cerebrovascular disease. Arch Intern Med. 2003;163:1069-75. [PMID: 12742805]

6. Notkola IL, Sulkava R, Pekkanen J, et al. Serum total cholesterol, apolipoprotein E epsilon 4 allele, and Alzheimer's disease. Neuroepidemiology. 1998;17:14-20. [PMID: 9549720]

7. Jick H, Zornberg GL, Jick SS, et al. Statins and the risk of dementia. Lancet. 2000;356:1627-31. [PMID: 11089820]

8. Curb JD, Rodriguez BL, Abbott RD, et al. Longitudinal association of vascular and Alzheimer's dementias, diabetes, and glucose tolerance. Neurology. 1999;52:971-5. [PMID: 10102414]

9. Meyer JS, McClintic KL, Rogers RL, et al. Aetiological considerations and risk factors for multi-infarct dementia. J Neurol Neurosurg Psychiatry. 1988;51:1489-97. [PMID: 3221215]

Dementia is defined as a decline in cognitive function from baseline. It is a syndrome caused by a variety of disorders, the most common of which are Alzheimer disease, vascular dementia, Lewy body dementia, and frontotemporal dementia. The incidence and prevalence of dementia increase with age. It is estimated that by the year 2047, more than 9 million Americans will have some form of it (1). Institutionalization is ultimately required for many patients with dementia, and 67% die in nursing homes (2). Although there is currently no cure for most forms of dementia, research findings and accumulated clinical experience support a set of practices that serve to maximize the function and overall well-being of patients with dementia and their caregivers.

Prevention

What medical interventions or health behaviors can help patients prevent dementia?

Although there are several risk factors for different types of dementia, data supporting the effectiveness of specific preventive measures are limited.

Hypertension

Untreated hypertension in mid-life and later is a proven risk factor for both Alzheimer disease and vascular dementia (3). A number of randomized, controlled trials (RCTs) have shown that treating hypertension reduces the risk for dementia.

A large, placebo-controlled RCT with 2418 participants demonstrated that treating systolic hypertension in patients over the age of 60 years reduced the incidence of dementia by 50%, from 7.7 cases to 3.8 cases per 1000 patient-years (4).

Another placebo-controlled RCT with 6106 participants showed that treating hypertension with the angiotensin-converting enzyme inhibitor perindopril with or without the thiazide diuretic indapamide reduced the incidence of recurrent stroke with dementia by 34% and of recurrent stroke with any cognitive decline by 45% in patients with past stroke or transient ischemic attack (5).

Hypercholesterolemia and Diabetes Mellitus

Hypercholesterolemia, particularly in mid-life, is associated with an increased incidence of both Alzheimer disease and vascular dementia, (6), and case–control studies have shown an association between use of cholesterol-lowering medications and reduced incidence of dementia (7). Diabetes has been shown in both longitudinal cohort and case–control studies to be an independent risk factor for vascular dementia (8, 9). However, as with hypercholesterolemia, there are no trials that demonstrate that treating diabetes prevents dementia.

Lifestyle Modifications

Cigarette smoking is associated with an increased risk for stroke, although the evidence for an association with Alzheimer disease is mixed (10). Head injury earlier in life has been shown in a number of epidemiologic studies to be associated with dementia later in life (11). Finally, physical inactivity, both in mid-life and later, has been associated with an increased risk for dementia in both retrospective and prospective studies (12, 13). Thus, counseling patients to quit smoking; engage in behaviors to reduce the risk for head injury, such as wearing seat belts and bike helmets; and be physically active may reduce the risk for dementia.

Medications

Clinicians should regularly review the medication regimens of elderly patients and minimize use of medications that can cause cognitive impairment, such as benzodiazepines, anticholinergics, barbiturates, and other sedative-hypnotics. A number of studies have shown that elderly patients taking benzodiazepines or other sedative-hypnotics perform more poorly on cognitive tests than those not taking these medications (14).

Because inflammation is present in the brains of patients with Alzheimer disease and epidemiologic evidence links use of non-steroidal anti-inflammatory drugs (NSAIDs) earlier in life to a lower risk for Alzheimer disease (15), some have questioned whether NSAIDs might prevent dementia. However, prospective studies to date have not shown a protective effect of NSAIDs, and they are not recommended for prevention of dementia (16).

Significant epidemiologic evidence links mid-life estrogen use to a lower incidence of dementia later in life (17). However, in prospective prevention trials, including the large Women's Health Initiative Memory Study, use of estrogen plus progestin for prevention of dementia was associated with an increased incidence of dementia, as well as other medical complications (18).

Prevention... Although there are few data to support specific measures to prevent dementia, clinicians should treat cardiovascular risk factors, such as hypertension, hypercholesterolemia, and diabetes, and encourage smoking cessation and regular exercise. They should also counsel patients about avoiding head injury and avoid prescribing medications that can alter cognitive function. Neither NSAIDs nor estrogen should be recommended for prevention of dementia.

CLINICAL BOTTOM LINE

Screening

Should clinicians screen for dementia?
The U.S. Preventive Services Task Force concluded that there is insufficient evidence to recommend for or against widespread screening for dementia in elderly patients (19). However, many patients with dementia in the primary care setting, even those in more advanced stages of the disease, remain undiagnosed despite having routine general medical care (20).

Moreover, patients referred to dementia specialists after "screening" have been diagnosed at an earlier stage of illness than those referred from physicians or families (21). Therefore, given the high prevalence of dementia and its associated morbidity, the clinician should consider secondary case-finding measures for dementia in elderly patients with unexplained functional decline, deterioration in hygiene, questionable adherence to medication regimens, or new-onset psychiatric symptoms.

What methods should clinicians use when looking for dementia?
When looking for dementia in elderly patients, clinicians should use a standardized screening instrument together with a brief history from the patient and a knowledgeable informant. The screening instrument should be easy to use, demonstrate high sensitivity, be widely available, and be supported by normative population data relevant to the patient. Two examples of such instruments are the Mini-Mental Status Examination (22) and the Mini-Cog (23).

10. Lee PN. Smoking and Alzheimer's disease: a review of the epidemiological evidence. Neuroepidemiology. 1994;13:131-44. [PMID: 8090255]

11. Mortimer JA, van Duijn CM, Chandra V, et al. Head trauma as a risk factor for Alzheimer's disease: a collaborative reanalysis of case-control studies. EURODEM Risk Factors Research Group. Int J Epidemiol. 1991;20 Suppl 2:S28-35. [PMID: 1833351]

12. Broe GA, Henderson AS, Creasey H, et al. A case-control study of Alzheimer's disease in Australia. Neurology. 1990;40:1698-707. [PMID: 2146525]

13. Yoshitake T, Kiyohara Y, Kato I, et al. Incidence and risk factors of vascular dementia and Alzheimer's disease in a defined elderly Japanese population: the Hisayama Study. Neurology. 1995;45:1161-8. [PMID: 7783883]

14. Larson EB, Kukull WA, Buchner D, et al. Adverse drug reactions associated with global cognitive impairment in elderly persons. Ann Intern Med. 1987;107:169-73. [PMID: 2886086]

15. Etminan M, Gill S, Samii A. Effect of non-steroidal anti-inflammatory drugs on risk of Alzheimer's disease: systematic review and meta-analysis of observational studies. BMJ. 2003;327:128. [PMID: 12869452]

16. ADAPT Research Group. Cardiovascular and cerebrovascular events in the randomized, controlled Alzheimer's Disease Anti-Inflammatory Prevention Trial (ADAPT). PLoS Clin Trials. 2006;1:e33. [PMID: 17111043]

17. Cache County Memory Study Investigators. Hormone replacement therapy and incidence of Alzheimer disease in older women: the Cache County Study. JAMA. 2002;288:2123-9. [PMID: 12413371]

Diagnosis

Clinical Diagnosis of Alzheimer Disease (AD)

Definite AD:
• Clinical criteria for probable AD plus histopathology confirmation

Probable AD:
• Dementia by clinical examination and standardized instrument (e.g., Mini-Mental State Examination)
• Deficits in >2 areas of cognition
• Progressive cognitive decline
• Normal levels of consciousness
• Onset between age 40 and 90 years
• No other cause
• Supportive factors, including positive family history, cerebral atrophy on neuroimagining, normal electroencephalogram and lumbar puncture

18. WHIMS Investigators. Estrogen plus progestin and the incidence of dementia and mild cognitive impairment in postmenopausal women: the Women's Health Initiative Memory Study: a randomized controlled trial. JAMA. 2003;289: 2651-62. [PMID: 12771112]
19. U.S. Preventive Services Task Force. Screening for dementia and other diseases. Guide to clinical preventive services. 2nd ed. Baltimore: Williams & Wilkins; 1996: 531-40. Accessed at www.guideline.gov/summary/summary.aspx?doc_id=3690 on 7 February 2008.
20. Valcour VG, Masaki KH, Curb JD, et al. The detection of dementia in the primary care setting. Arch Intern Med. 2000;160:2964-8. [PMID: 11041904]

What elements of the history are most important in evaluating patients with suspected dementia? Clinicians should use the patient's history to characterize the cognitive deficits, generate a differential diagnosis, and attempt to determine the cause of the dementia. This is best accomplished by identifying medical, neurologic, and psychiatric symptoms that may be clues to the cause of the cognitive problems and detailing their order of appearance, severity, and associated features. In the case of cognitive difficulties, it is mandatory to try to obtain collateral information from a knowledgeable informant, because cognitive dysfunction can impair the patient's ability to serve as an accurate reporter. It is often easier to collect this information, as well as information about psychiatric symptoms, without the patient present.

In taking the history, it is critical for clinicians to be knowledgeable about the differential diagnosis and natural history of the most common types of dementia (Table 1). For example, in classic Alzheimer disease, early symptoms are dominated by difficulties with short-term memory, subtle language and visuospatial perception difficulties, and changes in executive function with significant reductions in efficiency and organizational abilities of which the patient may or may not be aware. Symptoms begin insidiously and are slowly progressive. Overall level of alertness remains unimpaired. Patients or families may not label these difficulties as memory problems per se but may instead report multiple repetitions of questions or conversations with no recollection of previous discussions, increased forgetfulness manifested by losing objects or becoming confused while shopping, or simply overall increased disorganization and decreased efficiency. Symptoms are often first noticed or reported at the time of a life change, such as the death of a spouse or a move into a new residence. See the Box for clinical diagnostic criteria for definite and probable Alzheimer disease (24).

Many elderly patients report minor cognitive problems, such as mild forgetfulness, difficulty remembering names, and mildly reduced concentration. In patients without dementia, these symptoms are typically sporadic, do not worsen significantly over time, are easily compensated for, and do not affect function. In contrast, in early dementia, the symptoms insidiously become established as a pattern, worsen over time, are difficult to compensate for, and eventually affect speech fluency and hamper the performance of routine activities, such as meal preparation, bill paying, and financial planning. Patients with memory problems should be screened for dementia as described previously, but a complete dementia evaluation should be reserved for those with the clinical syndrome of dementia.

Table 1. Differential Diagnosis of Cognitive Difficulties*

Disease	Characteristics	Notes
Alzheimer disease	Early symptoms include gradual memory loss, preserved level of consciousness, impaired IADL performance, subtle language errors, and worsened visual–spatial perception. Middle-stage symptoms include apraxia, disorientation, and impaired judgment. As the illness progresses, aphasia, apraxia, agnosia, inattention, and left–right confusion develop. In the final stages patients are dependent for IADL care, and lose the ability to ambulate and even swallow	The presenting problem to the physician may not relate to cognition. Earliest presenting symptoms may be paranoid delusions or depression, which are only later appreciated as part of a dementia. Dementia may initially become manifest with a major life change. Neurologic signs, such as falls, tremor, weakness, or reflex abnormalities, are not typical early in the disease. Seizures occur frequently in advanced disease; their presence earlier suggests a diagnosis other than Alzheimer disease.
Vascular dementia	Ideally, loss of function should be correlated temporally with cerebrovascular events. "Stepwise" deterioration may be seen. Level of consciousness should be normal. May be present in patients with "silent" strokes, multiple small strokes, or severe diffuse cerebrovascular disease.	Should be suspected in any patient with cerebrovascular risk factors, even if a neurologic examination does not suggest a stroke.
Lewy body dementia	Mild parkinsonism; unexplained falls; hallucinations and delusions early in the illness; extreme sensitivity to extrapyramidal side effects of antipsychotic medications; gait difficulties and falls; and fluctuating cognition.	May account for up to 20% of total dementia cases. Should be suspected in patients with nonvascular dementia but abnormal neurologic examination.
Frontotemporal dementia	Onset often before age 60 years. Language difficulties are common. Memory often preserved early on. Prominent personality changes, often with behavioral disturbances, such as hyperphagia, worsened impulsivity or aggression, or prominent apathy.	Includes such disorders as progressive supranuclear palsy, primary progressive aphasia, semantic dementia, amyotrophic lateral sclerosis with dementia, and corticobasal degeneration. Functional neuroimaging often demonstrates diminished function in frontal or temporal lobes.
Delirium	Altered and fluctuating level of alertness and attention, often with globally impaired cognition. May have abrupt onset. Patients may have psychomotor retardation and mental status abnormalities of depressed or elevated mood, hallucinations, delusions, and agitated behavior.	Must be excluded in order to diagnose dementia. Diagnosis is critical because delirium may reflect serious systemic disturbance, such as metabolic abnormalities, medication effects, or infection.
Major depression	Low mood; anhedonia; diminished sense of self-worth; hopelessness; altered appetite, libido, and sleep; increased somatic complaints; irritability; and wishes for death.	Cognitive impairment may result solely from major depression. Major depression may also be the initial presentation of dementia.
Medications	Common offenders include benzodiazepines, barbiturates, anticholinergics, and other sedative-hypnotics.	Cognitive impairment of patients with dementia may be exacerbated by medications.
Mild cognitive impairment	Evidence of memory impairment in the absence of other cognitive deficits or functional decline.	Many progress to dementia at a rate of about 12%–15% per year.
Subdural hematoma	May or may not occur in setting of falls or head injury. Nonspecific headache. Level of consciousness may wax and wane.	Classic presentation is the exception rather than the rule. Neurologic deficits may be minor.
Traumatic brain injury	Clinical features may vary according to site of injury. Personality and mood changes are common.	The postconcussion syndrome may include inattention.
Normal-pressure hydrocephalus	Dementia, gait abnormality (slow, broad-based, impaired turning), and urinary incontinence. Dementia is often associated with psychomotor slowing and apathy.	If suspicion is high, lumbar puncture with pre- and post-tap gait monitoring is performed. Ventriculoperitoneal shunting can be curative in some patients.
Brain tumor (primary or metastatic)	Frontal or corpus callosum tumors result in memory impairment with global intellectual decline. Parietal lobe tumors may produce apraxia, aphasia, agnosia, agraphesthesia, astereognosia, and neglect.	Neuroimaging rules the diagnosis in or out.
Vitamin B_{12} deficiency	Insidious onset. May be associated with depression. Neurologic examination may reveal diminished proprioception and vibratory sense, ataxia, and positive Babinski sign.	If serum B_{12} is in the low-normal range, elevated serum methylmalonic acid and homocysteine levels indicate low intracellular vitamin B_{12}. Anemia may be absent.
Thyroid disease	Both hypo- and hyperthyroidism can lead to cognitive difficulties.	Thyroid-stimulating hormone should be checked at the beginning of the dementia work-up.
Chronic alcohol use	Chronic alcohol use appears to lead to a mild-to-moderate dementia, which may reverse after a period of abstinence.	This is distinct from the Korsakoff syndrome, an isolated loss of short-term memory without global dementia.
Toxins	Aromatic hydrocarbons, solvents, heavy metals, marijuana, opiates, and sedative-hypnotics.	Urine or serum toxicology and heavy metal screens are useful.
Parkinson disease	Features of subcortical dementia, cortical dementia, or both. Free recall may be impaired with preservation of recognition memory. May have impaired visual–spatial function.	In contrast to Lewy body dementia, patients with Parkinson disease and dementia typically have motor symptoms of Parkinson disease long before dementia, and do not have prominent psychotic symptoms or fluctuating consciousness.
Other causes	Multiple sclerosis, CNS vasculitis, neurosarcoidosis, systemic lupus erythematosus, advanced liver or renal disease, Wilson disease, chronic CNS infection, electrolyte abnormalities, neurosyphilis, HIV-associated dementia, Huntington disease, and Creutzfeldt–Jacob disease.	

*CNS = central nervous system; IADL = instrumental activities of daily living.

21. Barker WW, Luis C,
    Harwood D, et al.
    The effect of a mem-
    ory screening pro-
    gram on the early
    diagnosis of
    Alzheimer disease.
    Alzheimer Dis Assoc
    Disord. 2005;19:1-7.
    [PMID: 15764864]
22. Folstein MF, Folstein
    SE, McHugh PR.
    "Mini-mental state".
    A practical method
    for grading the cog-
    nitive state of
    patients for the clini-
    cian. J Psychiatr Res.
    1975;12:189-98.
    [PMID: 1202204]
23. Borson S, Scanlan J,
    Brush M, et al. The
    mini-cog: a cogni-
    tive 'vital signs'
    measure for demen-
    tia screening in
    multi-lingual elderly.
    Int J Geriatr Psychia-
    try. 2000;15:1021-7.
    [PMID: 11113982]
24. McKhann G, Drach-
    man D, Folstein M, et
    al. Clinical diagnosis
    of Alzheimer's dis-
    ease: report of the
    NINCDS-ADRDA
    Work Group under
    the auspices of
    Department of
    Health and Human
    Services Task Force
    on Alzheimer's Dis-
    ease. Neurology.
    1984;34:939-44.
    [PMID: 6610841]

How can clinicians distinguish dementia from delirium?

Clinicians evaluating a patient with a change in cognition or overall function must consider delirium. Delirium is global impairment of cognition with characteristic worsening of alertness and attention. Onset may be abrupt or gradual, often with notable fluctuations in the level of impairment. Although some patients may be agitated and manifest psychotic symptoms, others are slowed, drowsy, and appear mildly depressed or withdrawn. Prompt diagnosis of delirium is critical, because it usually reflects an underlying systemic condition, such as infection, metabolic derangement, medication effect, or malignancy.

How should clinicians evaluate patients with suspected dementia?

Clinicians should use the general physical examination to look for signs of conditions that can cause or worsen cognitive decline (Table 1). A complete mental status examination begins with an evaluation of alertness, general appearance, and cooperation. Speech should be evaluated both for its content (grammatical or semantic errors) and form (rate, fluency, volume). The patient's mood and affect should be assessed for evidence of depression, anxiety or mania, and suicidality, and thought content and perception are examined for the presence of delusions or hallucinations, as well as obsessions or compulsions.

The cognitive examination should include a standard instrument, such as the MMSE, which can be performed in about 5 minutes and provides an overview of orientation, immediate recall, concentration, naming, language function, praxis, and visual–spatial perception. The MMSE should be augmented by testing delayed recall by asking the patient to repeat 3 words from the MMSE 20 to 30 minutes after their initial presentation. Naming

and praxis can be further tested by asking the patient to name a series of common and uncommon objects and by asking them to demonstrate tasks, such as brushing hair or teeth or slicing bread. Abstract reasoning and judgment should be tested by asking for solutions to real-life problems, such as what to do if one smells smoke in the house, or for interpretation of proverbs or similes. Drawing a clock (spontaneously, or copying from an already drawn figure in the event of difficulty) is a quick test of visual–spatial perception, praxis, and planning ability. Corticosensory deficits, such as neglect or left–right confusion, can be quickly tested for as well.

What laboratory tests are helpful in the evaluation of patients with cognitive dysfunction?

According to guidelines from the American Psychiatric Association and American Academy of Neurology, patients who are being evaluated for cognitive problems should have a laboratory evaluation for common medical disorders, with selected additional studies depending on the specific clinical situation (see Box on opposite page).

In general, patients with cognitive difficulties less than 3 years in duration should undergo a neuroimaging study (computed tomography [CT] or magnetic resonance imaging [MRI] scanning of the head) to exclude cerebrovascular disease, hemorrhage, tumor, or hydrocephalus as the cause of the cognitive dysfunction. Studies show that, in patients with cognitive problems, neuroimaging detects significant cerebrovascular disease even in patients in whom it was not suspected clinically (25). The yield is higher in patients with early age of onset, rapid progression, focal neurologic deficits, cerebrovascular disease risk factors, recent falls, central nervous system (CNS) infection, unexplained fluctuating level of consciousness, or symptoms atypical of Alzheimer disease. The routine use of single-photon emission CT (SPECT) or positron emission tomography (PET) scanning is not recommended, although these tests may be useful in specific instances, such as in differentiating Alzheimer disease from frontotemporal dementia (26).

Genetic studies are not routinely indicated in the evaluation of dementia unless there is a specific concern about Huntington disease. There is evidence that testing for the *ApoE4* allele does not add substantially to the diagnosis (27). Testing for 1 of the 3 autosomal dominant gene mutations found in patients with familial Alzheimer disease is occasionally pursued when multiple family members are affected.

Other tests should be reserved for specific situations. Electroencephalography may be useful when there is a question of delirium, seizures, or encephalitis. Lumbar puncture may be indicated in patients under age 55 years and in those with rapidly progressive dementia, a positive rapid plasma reagin, suspicion of acute or chronic CNS infection or malignancy, or immunosuppression. Neuropsychological testing provides the most comprehensive assessment of cognitive function and is particularly useful when the diagnosis of dementia is unclear or it is necessary to precisely characterize the patient's cognitive impairment.

> **Laboratory Studies for Patients Being Evaluated for Cognitive Problems**
> - Comprehensive metabolic profile
> - Complete blood count
> - Thyroid-stimulating hormone level
> - Vitamin B_{12} level
> - Rapid plasma reagin or fluorescent treponemal antibody
>
> Selected patients may need to undergo additional tests, including:
> - HIV
> - Toxicology screen
> - Erythrocyte sedimentation rate
> - Heavy metal screen
> - Folate
> - Chest X-ray
> - Urinalysis

> Diagnosis... Clinicians should evaluate patients who present with cognitive and functional decline with a detailed history of medical, neurologic, and psychiatric symptoms from the patient and a knowledgeable informant and with a thorough physical, mental status, and cognitive examination. Basic laboratory studies include a comprehensive metabolic panel, complete blood count, thyroid-stimulating hormone level, and vitamin B_{12} level. Selected patients may require additional laboratory tests. Clinicians should consider CT or MRI scanning of the head in patients with cognitive difficulties with a duration less than 3 years and in those with early age of onset, rapid progression, focal neurologic deficits, cerebrovascular disease risk factors, or atypical symptoms.
>
> **CLINICAL BOTTOM LINE**

Treatment

What should clinicians advise patients (and their caregivers) about their general health and hygiene?

Even in the early stages of dementia, patients may have difficulty comprehending the details of their medical care requirements; organizing their care; and keeping track of appointments, medications, or other recommendations. The clinician should be alert to these limitations and help prepare a care plan that compensates for them. Later in the illness, patients may be unable to identify physical signals, such as constipation, dysuria, tooth pain, or diminished visual or auditory acuity, and the clinician should proactively look for these problems.

It is important to attend to general medical and preventive care as conscientiously as in patients without dementia. A major stroke or heart attack due to uncontrolled hypertension is likely to impair a patient's function and quality of life as much as the dementia itself, at least in the early and middle stages of the disease. For patients with more advanced dementia, ongoing attention to nutritional needs, skin care (particularly perineal), toileting

25. Massoud F, Devi G, Moroney JT, et al. The role of routine laboratory studies and neuroimaging in the diagnosis of dementia: a clinico-pathological study. J Am Geriatr Soc. 2000;48:1204-10. [PMID: 11037005]
26. Foster NL, Heidebrink JL, Clark CM, et al. FDG-PET improves accuracy in distinguishing frontotemporal dementia and Alzheimer's disease. Brain. 2007;130:2616-35. [PMID: 17704526]
27. van der Cammen TJ, Croes EA, Dermaut B, et al. Genetic testing has no place as a routine diagnostic test in sporadic and familial cases of Alzheimer's disease. J Am Geriatr Soc. 2004;52:2110-3. [PMID: 15571552]

schedules, and dental and denture care become more important.

What should clinicians advise about safety issues and other activities that may require supervision?

All patients with progressive dementia ultimately lose the ability to drive, but predicting when it is unsafe for an individual patient to continue to drive is difficult. Nonetheless, it is imperative to address the issue, as numerous studies have demonstrated that driving ability becomes impaired in early stages of the disease.

In a prospective, case–control study using the Washington University Road Test (with off-road and on-road components), 19% of patients with very mild Alzheimer disease failed the test, 41% with mild Alzheimer disease failed, and only 3% of controls failed (P < 0.001). Driving experience did not protect against this deterioration (28).

The clinician should inquire about recent motor vehicle accidents, near misses, or changes in the patient's driving ability. These inquiries should be made in a setting that facilitates an open exchange of information and may necessitate meeting with an informant without the patient present. Patients with early dementia who have deteriorating driving skills should be instructed to stop driving immediately. Patients with early dementia without any history of driving problems should undergo a driving evaluation through the local Motor Vehicle Administration (MVA) or an occupational therapy program at a local hospital. These evaluations should be repeated every 6 months to promptly detect deterioration.

State laws differ in regard to reporting patients with a diagnosis of dementia to local MVAs, and the clinician should be familiar with the applicable regulations. The overall approach to assessment of driving in patients with dementia is outlined in detail in the American Academy of Neurology Evidence-Based Practice Parameter (29).

Clinicians should assess other safety issues with the patient and family on an ongoing basis. Medication administration, cooking, use of power tools and lawnmowers, and handling of firearms eventually become unsafe for all patients to perform independently. Occupational therapy home-safety assessments can be useful in determining which activities can be performed safely and which need to be limited or supervised. An activity can often be modified to allow ongoing participation in a safe fashion, such as cooking or gardening together with a family member or friend. Wandering away from home, a fairly common occurrence, presents significant safety concerns and must be addressed regularly.

What should clinicians advise about nonpharmacologic approaches to sleep problems, behavioral problems, and psychiatric manifestations of dementia?

Psychiatric symptoms, such as depression, anxiety, sleep problems, agitation, hallucinations, and delusions are common in patients with dementia and often require intervention (30). When symptoms are mild or do not pose immediate danger, nonpharmacologic management may be sufficient. Such approaches emphasize that many emotional and behavioral disturbances can be "decoded" or understood in terms of internal or environmental triggers. Clinicians and caregivers should consider the time of day, location, antecedent factors, people present or absent, proximity to eating or other activities, and the consequences of the behavior. If patterns are noted, targeted interventions can be developed, implemented, and refined. Approaching behavioral disturbances this way can often forestall the use of

28. Hunt LA, Murphy CF, Carr D, et al. Reliability of the Washington University Road Test. A performance-based assessment for drivers with dementia of the Alzheimer type. Arch Neurol. 1997;54:707-12. [PMID: 9193205]

29. Dubinsky RM, Stein AC, Lyons K. Practice parameter: risk of driving and Alzheimer's disease (an evidence-based review): report of the quality standards subcommittee of the American Academy of Neurology. Neurology. 2000;54: 2205-11. [PMID: 10881240]

30. Lyketsos CG, Steinberg M, Tschanz JT, et al. Mental and behavioral disturbances in dementia: findings from the Cache County Study on Memory in Aging. Am J Psychiatry. 2000;157:708-14. [PMID: 10784462]

31. Qaseem A, Snow V, Cross JT Jr, et al. Current Pharmacologic Treatment of Dementia: A Clinical Practice Guideline from the American Academy of Family Physicians and the American College of Physicians. Ann Intern Med. 2008;148:370-8.

32. Raina P, Santaguida P, Ismaila A, et al. Effectiveness of Cholinesterase Inhibitors and Memantine for Treating Dementia: Evidence Review for a Clinical Practice Guideline. Ann Intern Med. 2008;148:379-97.

psychotropic medications or physical restraints.

When should clinicians prescribe acetylcholinesterase inhibitors and memantine to slow cognitive decline?

Clinicians should consider prescribing acetylcholinesterase inhibitors, such as donepezil, galantamine, or rivastigmine, to delay cognitive decline in patients with mild, moderate, or advanced Alzheimer disease. These drugs are better tolerated if they are slowly titrated to reach the target dose. The appropriate duration of treatment has not been defined. Although there are no placebo-controlled trials beyond 2 years, and most trials only last 6 months, clinicians often continue these medications for much longer when they feel the patient is benefiting from them. When the benefit is unclear, clinicians can consider stopping the drug and resuming it if an acute cognitive deterioration occurs. The neuropeptide-modifying agent memantine is approved for use in moderate-to-advanced Alzheimer disease and can be used in conjunction with acetylcholinesterase inhibitors. Table 2 lists specific recommendations for their use. Tacrine has more side effects and is no longer recommended.

Patients and families should be educated about realistic expectations from these agents. All of them have shown statistically significant improvement in scores on standardized tests in patients with dementia in clinical trials as well as improvement on global assessment, but the benefits have been modest and difficult to extrapolate to the clinical practice setting. Side effects of anticholinesterase inhibitors include dizziness, nausea, vomiting, and diarrhea and anorexia.

Table 2. Pharmacologic Therapy for Dementia*

Agent	Mechanism of Action	Dosage	Benefits	Side Effects	Notes
Donepezil	Acetylcholinesterase inhibition	Begin 5 mg/d. If tolerated, increase to target dose of 10 mg/day after 1 month.	Delayed symptom progression in mild, moderate, and advanced Alzheimer disease	Nausea, vomiting, diarrhea, anorexia	Routine liver function testing is unnecessary. The higher end of the dosing range may be harder for patients to tolerate.
Galantamine	Acetylcholinesterase inhibition	Start 4 mg twice daily. Target dose 24 mg total per day. Increase by 4 mg twice daily every 1 month until in target range.	Delayed symptom progression in mild, moderate, and advanced Alzheimer disease	Nausea, vomiting, diarrhea, anorexia	Routine liver function testing is unnecessary. The higher end of the dosing range may be harder for patients to tolerate.
		Begin extended-release (once daily) galantamine at 8 mg/d. Increase by 8 mg/d every 1 month to the target dose of 24 mg/d.	Improvement in caregiver-rated quality of life was observed.		
Rivastigmine	Acetylcholinesterase inhibition	Start 1.5 mg twice daily. Target range is 6 to 12 mg/d. Increase by 1.5 mg twice daily every 1 month until in target range.	Delayed symptom progression in mild, moderate, and advanced Alzheimer disease	Nausea, vomiting, diarrhea, anorexia	Routine liver function testing is unnecessary. The higher end of the dosing range may be harder for patients to tolerate. Also available in a transdermal patch.
Memantine	NMDA-receptor antagonism	Begin 5 mg/d. Increase by 5 mg/d every 1 month until reaching target of 10 mg twice daily.	Less functional decline, improved cognition, and reduced demands on caregivers in moderate-to-advanced Alzheimer disease	Dizziness, confusion, headache, constipation	Available in tablets or solution. Avoid concomitant use with amantadine.

*NMDA = N-methyl-D-aspartic acid.

33. Emre M, Aarsland D, Albanese A, et al. Rivastigmine for dementia associated with Parkinson's disease. N Engl J Med. 2004; 351:2509-18. [PMID: 15590953]

34. McKeith I, Del Ser T, Spano P, et al. Efficacy of rivastigmine in dementia with Lewy bodies: a randomised, double-blind, placebo-controlled international study. Lancet. 2000; 356:2031-6. [PMID: 11145488]

35. Beversdorf DQ, Warner JL, Davis RA, et al. Donepezil in the treatment of dementia with lewy bodies [Letter]. Am J Geriatr Psychiatry. 2004;12:542-4. [PMID: 15353396]

36. Sano M, Ernesto C, Thomas RG, et al. A controlled trial of selegiline, alpha-tocopherol, or both as treatment for Alzheimer's disease. The Alzheimer's Disease Cooperative Study. N Engl J Med. 1997;336: 1216-22. [PMID: 9110909]

37. Miller ER III, Pastor-Barriuso R, Dalal D, Riemersma RA, Appel LJ, Guallar E. Meta-analysis: high-dosage vitamin E supplementation may increase all-cause mortality. Ann Intern Med. 2005; 142:37-46. [PMID: 15537682]

38. Schneider LS, DeKosky ST, Farlow MR, et al. A randomized, double-blind, placebo-controlled trial of two doses of Ginkgo biloba extract in dementia of the Alzheimer's type. Curr Alzheimer Res. 2005;2:541-51. [PMID: 16375657]

39. Zubenko GS, Zubenko WN, McPherson S, et al. A collaborative study of the emergence and clinical features of the major depressive syndrome of Alzheimer's disease. Am J Psychiatry. 2003;160:857-66. [PMID: 12727688]

40. Olin JT, Schneider LS, Katz IR, et al. Provisional diagnostic criteria for depression of Alzheimer disease. Am J Geriatr Psychiatry. 2002; 10:125-8. [PMID: 11925273]

Memantine can cause dizziness, confusion, headache, and constipation. Neither class of agent should be used in patients with uncontrolled asthma, closed-angle glaucoma, the sick sinus syndrome, or left bundle-branch block. The American College of Physicians has issued new guidelines on pharmacologic treatment of dementia, recommending that clinicians base the decision to initiate therapy with these agents on individualized assessment and choose among them on the basis of tolerability, side effect profile, ease of use, and cost (31).

A systematic review of 59 studies of cholinesterase inhibitors and memantine found that all agents had consistent but modest effects on cognition and global assessment. Behavior and quality of life were assessed less frequently and showed less-consistent effects. The duration of most studies averaged only 6 months, and there were only 3 head-to-head comparative trials (32).

Which other pharmacologic agents may be helpful in treating less-common types of dementia?
The acetylcholinesterase inhibitor rivastigmine has been shown to be effective in improving cognitive performance in patients with mild-to-moderate Parkinson disease in doses similar to those used in Alzheimer disease, and it is believed that this benefit will be seen with the other acetylcholinesterase inhibitors (33). A number of trials have also demonstrated the benefits of acetylcholinesterase inhibitor treatment for cognition in dementia with Lewy bodies (34, 35).

Which pharmacologic agents are ineffective in treating dementia and should be avoided?
Vitamin E is no longer recommended for routine use in Alzheimer disease, because its use is associated with a possibile increase in mortality and because of a lack of adequate evidence of efficacy (36, 37). The effectiveness of the herbal supplement *Ginkgo biloba* is not supported by sufficient data to recommend its general use in patients with dementia (38). Similarly, NSAIDs, estrogen, and ergoid mesylates should not be prescribed for the treatment of cognitive decline.

When should clinicians prescribe antidepressants in patients with dementia?
Clinicians should consider prescribing antidepressants in patients with dementia who have coexisting depression. Major depression is highly prevalent among patients with dementia, with nearly one third of patients developing an episode of major depression following the onset of dementia (39). Certain symptoms of major depression may overlap with those of dementia, such as weight loss and disturbed sleep, and this sometimes complicates the diagnosis (40).

A number of RCTs have established the efficacy of antidepressant medications in the treatment of major depression in patients with dementia (41–43), although there have been a number of negative clinical trials as well. In general, the selective serotonin reuptake inhibitors are better tolerated than tricyclic agents, but tricyclic agents may be used in select patients. These agents may cause mild gastrointestinal upset at the start of treatment or when doses are changed and increase risk for falls, agitation, delirium, or parkinsonism. Tricyclic agents can also cause orthostatic hypotension, dry mouth, sedation, urinary retention, and constipation and can worsen narrow-angle glaucoma. Medications with greater anticholinergic properties, such as amitriptyline, should generally be avoided.

When should clinicians consider prescribing antipsychotic agents to treat behavioral disturbances or psychotic symptoms?

Psychotic symptoms, such as hallucinations, delusions, and agitated behavior, that are mild or infrequent can often be managed with supportive care. However, when symptoms cause significant distress or danger to the patient or others, pharmacotherapy is indicated. Second-generation antipsychotic agents are usually recommended because of a lower risk for tardive dyskinesia than first-generation agents, such as haloperidol, but first-generation agents may be used as well in certain patients. Overall, the efficacy of these agents is modest. Although the efficacy of risperidone and olanzapine is best supported in the literature, quetiapine and aripiprazole are often used. They should be prescribed at the lowest possible dose and for the shortest possible time once prescribed; use should be regularly monitored. They should not be used routinely as sleep agents alone, because of side effects, which include sedation, orthostatic hypotension, delirium, ataxia, dry mouth, urinary retention, constipation, and stroke. First-generation agents are more likely to cause tardive dyskinesia and neuroleptic malignant syndrome.

In a meta-analysis of all RCTs of second-generation antipsychotics for behavioral disturbance in patients with dementia, there was a relative risk of 1.54 (95% CI, 1.06 to 2.23) for mortality compared with placebo-treated patients (45).

In reports released by the manufacturers, rates of cerebrovascular events were 4% for risperidone-treated patients (compared with 2% for placebo-treated), 1.3% for olanzapine (0.4% for placebo), and 1.3% for aripiprazole (0.6% for placebo). There was no evidence of increased risk for stroke with quetiapine use (44).

Evidence of increased mortality and cardiovascular events in patients treated with second-generation antipsychotics prompted the U.S. Food and Drug Administration to place a black-box warning on the label of these agents (44–47). Treatment with antipsychotic medications is also associated with the metabolic syndrome, as well as weight gain, hyperlipidemia, and diabetes mellitus. Clinicians must weigh the risks and benefits of these agents when prescribing them.

Which drugs should clinicians use to treat sleep problems in patients with dementia?

Clinicians should try nonpharmacologic methods to treat sleep problems before using medications in patients with insomnia because of the potential risks associated with sedative-hypnotic use in this population. Careful attention should be paid to sleep environment, caffeine consumption, daytime sleeping, afternoon and evening medications, and other elements of basic sleep hygiene. If necessary, trazodone 25 to 50 mg, zolpidem 5 to 10 mg, or a similar agent can be used cautiously (48).

What other steps should clinicians take to maximize quality of life in patients with dementia?

Clinicians should proactively address issues that have the potential to significantly affect quality of life. Examples include attending to the working order of sensory aides, such as glasses and hearing aides, to ensure proper function; dental care; levels of noise, lighting, and temperature; presence of sufficient social and cognitive stimuli; cleanliness; pain levels; and constipation.

When should clinicians consult a neurologist or psychiatrist and other professionals in patients with dementia?

Clinicians should consider consulting a geriatric psychiatrist, neurologist, geriatrician, or dementia specialist regarding the diagnosis of dementia in patients with

41. Lyketsos CG, Del-Campo L, Steinberg M, et al. Treating depression in Alzheimer disease: efficacy and safety of sertraline therapy, and the benefits of depression reduction: the DIADS. Arch Gen Psychiatry. 2003;60:737-46. [PMID: 12860778]
42. Nyth AL, Gottfries CG, Lyby K, et al. A controlled multicenter clinical study of citalopram and placebo in elderly depressed patients with and without concomitant dementia. Acta Psychiatr Scand. 1992;86:138-45. [PMID: 1529737]
43. Petracca GM, Chemerinski E, Starkstein SE. A double-blind, placebo-controlled study of fluoxetine in depressed patients with Alzheimer's disease. Int Psychogeriatr. 2001;13:233-40. [PMID: 11495397]
44. Gill SS, Bronskill SE, Normand SL, et al. Antipsychotic drug use and mortality in older adults with dementia. Ann Intern Med. 2007;146:775-86. [PMID: 17548409]
45. Schneider LS, Dagerman KS, Insel P. Risk of death with atypical antipsychotic drug treatment for dementia: meta-analysis of randomized placebo-controlled trials. JAMA. 2005;294:1934-43. [PMID: 16234500]
46. Schneider LS, Dagerman K, Insel PS. Efficacy and adverse effects of atypical antipsychotics for dementia: meta-analysis of randomized, placebo-controlled trials. Am J Geriatr Psychiatry. 2006;14:191-210. [PMID: 16505124]
47. Wang PS, Schneeweiss S, Avorn J, et al. Risk of death in elderly users of conventional vs. atypical antipsychotic medications. N Engl J Med. 2005;353:2335-41. [PMID: 16319382]
48. Shaw SH, Curson H, Coquelin JP. A double-blind, comparative study of zolpidem and placebo in the treatment of insomnia in elderly psychiatric in-patients. J Int Med Res. 1992;20:150-61. [PMID: 1521671]

49. Chan DC, Kasper JD, Black BS, et al. Presence of behavioral and psychological symptoms predicts nursing home placement in community-dwelling elders with cognitive impairment in univariate but not multivariate analysis. J Gerontol A Biol Sci Med Sci. 2003;58:548-54. [PMID: 12807927]

50. Yaffe K, Fox P, Newcomer R, et al. Patient and caregiver characteristics and nursing home placement in patients with dementia. JAMA. 2002;287:2090-7. [PMID: 11966383]

51. Mittelman MS, Ferris SH, Shulman E, et al. A family intervention to delay nursing home placement of patients with Alzheimer disease. A randomized controlled trial. JAMA. 1996;276:1725-31. [PMID: 8940320]

52. Teri L, Logsdon RG, Uomoto J, et al. Behavioral treatment of depression in dementia patients: a controlled clinical trial. J Gerontol B Psychol Sci Soc Sci. 1997;52:P159-66. [PMID: 9224439]

53. Haupt M, Karger A, Jänner M. Improvement of agitation and anxiety in demented patients after psychoeducative group intervention with their caregivers. Int J Geriatr Psychiatry. 2000; 15:1125-9. [PMID: 11180469]

54. Rabins PV, Blacker D, Rover BW, et al. Practice Guideline for the treatment of patients with Alzheimer's disease and other dementias. Supp Am J Psych. 2007;164: 25-7.

55. Knopman DS, DeKosky ST, Cummings JL, et al. Practice parameter: diagnosis of dementia (an evidence-based review). Report of the Quality Standards Subcommittee of the American Academy of Neurology. Neurology. 2001;56:1143-53. [PMID: 11342678]

atypical features, such as early onset, presence of early neurologic symptoms, rapid progression, early personality changes, or unusual symptom patterns.

Consultation with a geriatric psychiatrist or dementia specialist should also be considered for the evaluation or management of difficult-to-treat psychiatric symptoms, such as depression, psychosis, or behavioral disturbances, because these symptoms cause significant suffering, can sometimes create dangerous situations for the patient and others, and reduce quality of life.

Treatment of dementia ideally incorporates elements of many treatment modalities, including preventive medicine, psychoeducation, behavioral therapy, and pharmacotherapy. For optimum care, it is often necessary to interface with a broad range of professionals, including occupational therapists, social workers, physical therapists, and speech and language pathologists.

When should clinicians recommend hospitalization for patients with dementia?

During the assessment of cognitive impairment, hospitalization should be considered for patients who cannot be evaluated safely or comprehensively as an outpatient because of dangerous behavior, unsafe living conditions, compromised nutrition, neglected medical conditions, or inability to cooperate.

Psychiatric hospitalization is sometimes required because of the severity of psychiatric symptoms. For example, hospitalization should be seriously considered for depressed patients who exhibit suicidality, significantly decreased food and fluid intake, delusional depression, immobility, inability to attend to other medical conditions, and a need for electroconvulsive therapy.

Patients with behavioral disturbances who are dangerous to themselves or others, or who cannot be treated safely or successfully as an outpatient, may need hospitalization. Examples of such disturbances include wandering, violence, calling out, hyperphagia, and severely disordered sleep–wake cycle. Patients with hallucinations and delusions may also require hospitalization if the symptoms do not respond to outpatient treatment, require the addition of multiple medications, cause patient distress and behavioral disturbances, or present a danger to others. Involuntary commitment may be required.

How can clinicians help families make decisions about long-term care?

Generally, a move into an assisted-living facility or nursing home is prompted by physical limitations that cannot be managed at home, such as the need for full assistance with transferring, ambulation, toileting, or feeding. Other patients have to move because of unmanageable psychiatric symptoms or caregivers' inability to provide necessary care at home (49).

Families with ample financial resources may be able to provide many services at home that usually are provided in a facility. Periods of respite care may help families delay placement. Families should be supported and guided through the difficult and painful decision-making process. Clinicians should encourage families to investigate facilities in their region early in the course of dementia to avoid hurried decision-making should placement in a long-term care facility become necessary.

What specific caregiver needs should be addressed by the clinician?

Caregiving for a patient with dementia is physically and

emotionally taxing, and inquiring about caregiver wellbeing is a critical component of longitudinal dementia care. Common caregiver symptoms include guilt, anger, grief, fatigue, loneliness, demoralization, and depression. Untreated caregiver burden can also worsen the patient's emotional well-being and lead to nursing home placement earlier than may otherwise be necessary (50). Patient's symptoms and the consequent demands on the caregiver change over time, and therefore monitoring of caregiver well-being must be conducted at every visit. Caregivers should be informed about local respite programs, and long-term planning should be supported.

Caregivers should also receive information about local educational programs and support groups. A number of large, well-conducted trials have shown that psychoeducational and support groups with a focus on problem-solving, communication, management of behavioral disturbances, and emotional support are effective in delaying nursing home placement for up to 1 year, and in diminishing caregiver and patient depression and patient agitation and anxiety (51–53).

Treatment... Clinicians should adopt a broad treatment approach that incorporates attention to quality of life, cognitive enhancement, management of behavioral and psychiatric symptoms, and caregiver well-being. In considering pharmacologic therapy for dementia, clinicians should base the decision to initiate an anti-cholinesterase inhibitor or memantine on individual assessment, taking into account tolerability, ease of use, and side-effect profile. It is important to identify and treat psychiatric symptoms, such as depression, psychosis, anxiety, and behavioral disturbances, with both behavioral and pharmacologic treatment to maximize treatment of cerebrovascular disease risk factors, and to treat any general medical conditions that could be negatively affecting cognition. Clinicians should attend to safety issues on an ongoing basis. It is important to attend to caregiver burden and consider referral to support groups and other psychoeducational activities.

CLINICAL BOTTOM LINE

Practice Improvement

What do professional organizations recommend with regard to screening, diagnosis, and treatment of dementia?
Guidelines from professional organizations include those from the American Psychiatric Association, published in their second edition in 2007 (54), the American Academy of Neurology, published in 2001 (55), and the U.S. Preventive Services Task Force, published in 2003 (19). The U.S. Preventive Services Task Force document states that there is insufficient evidence to recommend general population screening for cognitive impairment. The American Academy of Neurology guideline covers detection, diagnosis, and management of dementia, and the American Psychiatric Association guideline also provides comprehensive recommendations on overall care. The American College of Physicians has just issued new guidelines on

56. Assessing Care of Vulnerable Elders (ACOVE). ACOVE Quality Indicator Library. Accessed at www.acove.com/QI/Acove.hta on 12 February 2008.

the treatment of dementia (31) based on the results of a systematic review (32). This guideline and review emphasize the modest effect of current drug therapy for dementia and the importance of individual patient assessment.

What measures do stakeholders use to evaluate the quality of care for patients with dementia?
The Center for Medicare & Medicaid Serviecs has issued specifications for measures for its 2008 Physicians Quality Reporting Initiative. Despite lack of evidence for screening asymptomatic patients for dementia, one of these measures relates to dementia and evaluates the percentage of patients age 65 years or older who have documentation of screening for cognitive impairment using a standardized tool. Another measure relates to advance care planning. The Assessing Care of Vulnerable Elders (ACOVE) quality-of-care measurement program includes specific quality measures on dementia (56).

What is the role of patient education in optimizing care of patients with dementia?
In speaking with patients about their memory problems and the necessity to make lifestyle changes, clinicians should consult with caregivers about appropriate disclosure of the diagnosis and presentation of information. It is important to determine what the patient already knows about their condition and what else he or she wants to know. Clinicians should address safety concerns directly with patients and caregivers and eventually approach long-term issues, such as management of finances, medical decision-making, and possible placement, when appropriate.

It is essential to attend to the needs of the caregiver and to educate them about the course of dementia and the challenges they face. Referral to psychoeducational programs may be helpful in managing caregiver grief, anger, guilt, demoralization, and fatigue. Local respite programs should also be considered.

in the clinic
Tool Kit

Dementia

PIER Modules
pier.acponline.org/physicians/diseases/d224/d224.html
pier.acponline.org/physicians/screening S375/S375.html
Access PIER modules on dementia and screening for dementia

Patient Information Page
www.annals.org/intheclinic
Download copies of the Patient Information sheet that appears on the following page for duplication and distribution to your patients

Washington University: Alzheimer Diseases Research Center
www.biostat.wustl.edu/adrc
Global clinical dementia rating

ACOVE Quality Indicator Library
www.acove.com/QI/Acove.hta
Evidence-based quality indicators to improve health care in older adults

American Academy of Neurology
www.aan.com/professionals/practice/pdfs/dementia_guideline.pdf
Detection, diagnosis, and management of dementia

WHAT YOU SHOULD KNOW ABOUT DEMENTIA

People with dementia get forgetful and can later have problems doing everyday things, such as eating and getting dressed.

Medicines may help some people with dementia think better and keep from getting worse for a while.

Keeping active with family and friends also helps people with dementia

There is no cure for dementia. It usually gets worse over time.

When this happens, it is important to plan for the future.

Caring for People with Dementia

- Learn what to expect from the patient you help care for and find out what help he or she needs.

- Keep the patient busy with family and friends and ask about day programs that keep him or her active.

- Ask the doctor if and when medicines may help and which medicines may make things worse.

- Call the doctor if there are big changes in how the person is acting or thinking and have a plan for emergencies.

- Try to keep the patient from falling, getting lost, or getting hurt.

- Get a safe-return bracelet in case the patient gets lost. You can get one from the Alzheimer Association Safe Return Program at P.O. Box 9307, St. Louis, MO 63117-0307; 888-572-8566

- Be sure to take care of yourself by asking for help with caretaking; going to joint support groups; making time for yourself; staying healthy; and talking to your doctor if you feel very tired, sad, stressed, guilty, or burned out.

- Make a plan in case you can no longer care for the person at home.

Web Sites with Good Information about Dementia

Alzheimer Association
www.alz.org/alzheimers_disease_what_is_alzheimers.asp

ACP Foundation HealthTips
foundation.acponline.org/files/ht/dem_en.pdf

Family Caregiver Alliance
www.caregiver.org/caregiver/jsp/content_node.jsp?nodeid=569

National Institute on Aging
www.niapublications.org/agepages/forgetfulness.asp

Low Back Pain

Low back pain has a lifetime prevalence of nearly 80% and is the fifth most common reason for physician visits in the United States (1). It is also costly, accounting for a large and increasing proportion of health care expenditures without evidence of corresponding improvements in outcomes (2). Most low back pain is due to nonspecific musculoskeletal strain, and episodes generally resolve within days to a few weeks with self-care. Up to one third of patients, however, reports persistent back pain of at least moderate intensity 1 year after an acute episode, and 1 in 5 report substantial limitations in activity (3). Because low back pain is common, chronic, and can lead to substantial disability, it is important that physicians be proficient with its evaluation and management.

Prevention

1. Deyo RA, Mirza SK, Martin BI. Back pain prevalence and visit rates: estimates from U.S. national surveys, 2002. Spine. 2006; 31:2724-7. [PMID: 17077742]
2. Martin BI, Deyo RA, Mirza SK, et al. Expenditures and health status among adults with back and neck problems. JAMA. 2008;299:656-64. [PMID: 18270354]
3. Von Korff M, Saunders K. The course of back pain in primary care. Spine. 1996; 21:2833-7; discussion 2838-9. [PMID: 9112707]
4. U.S. Preventive Services Task Force. Primary care interventions to prevent low back pain in adults: recommendation statement. Am Fam Physician. 2005; 71:2337-8. [PMID: 15999872]
5. Daltroy LH, Iversen MD, Larson MG, et al. A controlled trial of an educational program to prevent low back injuries. N Engl J Med. 1997; 337:322-8. [PMID: 9233870]

What factors are associated with the development of low back pain?

Factors associated with the development of low back pain include obesity, physical inactivity, occupational factors, and depression and other psychological conditions. Such strategies as maintenance of normal body weight and physical fitness and avoidance of activities that can injure the back should decrease the risk for low back pain, but direct evidence documenting the value of such interventions is not available.

It is important to keep in mind that back pain (the symptom), a health care visit for back pain, and work loss or disability due to back pain are not necessarily different aspects of the same construct. Symptom severity does not correlate well with utilization or functional outcome.

Should clinicians advise patients about preventing low back pain?

In 2005, the U.S. Preventive Services Task Force concluded that the evidence was insufficient to recommend for or against the routine use of interventions in primary care settings to prevent low back pain in healthy adults (4). The Task Force noted that, although exercise has not been shown to prevent low back pain, regular physical activity has other proven health benefits.

Are specific preventive measures effective in preventing low back pain at work?

People whose jobs require heavy lifting and other physical work are thought to be at greater risk for low back pain than people in less physically demanding occupations. Low back pain is a common cause of days lost from work and the need for workers' compensation. Studied approaches to prevent low back pain in the workplace include educational interventions and mechanical supports. Results regarding their effectiveness in the primary and secondary prevention of low back pain have generally not shown large benefits. A large randomized, controlled trial (RCT) of an educational program to prevent low back pain among mail carriers who did or did not have previous low back pain did not report any benefits (5). Similarly, a large trial in workers in physically demanding jobs did not report any benefits of a work-site prevention program (6), and another trial using education and lumbar supports also showed no reduction in low back pain compared with usual care (7). Furthermore, evidence is lacking that external back support, such as with a back brace or belt, provides benefit (8).

A recent randomized trial compared use of a patient-selected lumbar support with no support for home care workers with a history of low back pain. Although patients in the support groups reported fewer days with low back pain, work absenteeism rates were high and statistically similar in both the intervention and control groups (9).

Diagnosis

What elements of history and physical examination should clinicians incorporate into the evaluation of low back pain?
History and physical examination should aim to place the patient into 1 of 3 categories: nonspecific low back pain, back pain potentially associated with radiculopathy or spinal stenosis, or back pain potentially associated with another specific systemic or spinal cause. Table 1 shows the history and physical examination findings for different types of back pain.

When evaluating a patient with low back pain, clinicians should identify features that indicate a serious underlying cause, or radiculopathy, and psychosocial factors that could delay recovery. Key elements of the physical examination include checking for sensory loss, muscle weakness, or limited range

Table 1. Common History and Physical Examination Features for Different Back Pain Causes

Disease	History	Physical Examination	Notes
Degenerative joint disease	Nonspecific	Nonspecific	Common radiological abnormalities that may or may not be related to symptoms
Degenerative disk disease with herniation	Sciatic pain	Impaired ankle or patella reflex; positive ipsilateral or crossed straight-leg–raise test; great toe, ankle, or quadriceps weakness; lower extremity sensory loss	Common cause of nerve root impingement and radicular symptoms
Spinal stenosis	Severe leg pain; pseudoclaudication; no pain when seated	Wide-based gait; abnormal Romberg test results; thigh pain after 30 seconds of lumbar extension	More common with advancing age, uncommon before age 50 y
Ankylosing spondylitis	Gradual onset; morning stiffness; improves with exercise; pain > 3 mo; pain not relieved when supine	Decreased spinal range of motion	Usual onset before age 40 y
Osteomyelitis or spinal abscess	Source of infection, such as urinary tract infection, skin infection, or history of intravenous drug abuse	Fever and localized tenderness	Can cause cord compression
Malignancy in the spine or surrounding structures	Weight loss or other symptoms of malignancy; known past or current cancer diagnosis; failure to improve after 4 wk; no relief with bed rest	Localized tenderness	Metastatic disease. Commonly from prostate, breast, and lung cancer; can cause cord compression; more common in patients > 50 y
Intra-abdominal visceral disease	Depends on affected viscera	Depends on affected viscera	Peptic ulcer, pancreatitis, nephrolithiasis, pyelonephritis, prostatitis, pelvic infection or tumor, and aortic dissection can cause back pain
Metabolic bone disease with or without compression fracture	Nonspecific pain; osteoporosis or osteoporosis risk factors; trauma; corticosteroid use	Localized tenderness if vertebral fracture	Best example is osteoporosis with compression fracture
Herpes zoster	Unilateral pain in distribution of dermatome	Unilateral dermatomal rash	Most common in elderly or immune-compromised patients
Psychosocial distress	Symptoms do not follow a clear clinical or anatomical pattern; psychological and emotional distress	Physical examination findings that do not follow a clear clinical or anatomical pattern	Patients with psychosocial distress and low back pain are at high risk for poor outcomes

6. IJzelenberg H,
Meerding WJ, Bur-
dorf A. Effectiveness
of a back pain pre-
vention program: a
cluster randomized
controlled trial in an
occupational setting.
Spine. 2007;32:711-9.
[PMID: 17414902]
7. van Poppel MN,
Koes BW, van der
Ploeg T, et al. Lum-
bar supports and
education for the
prevention of low
back pain in indus-
try: a randomized
controlled trial.
JAMA. 1998;
279:1789-94.
[PMID: 9628709]
8. Jellema P, van Tulder
MW, van Poppel MN,
et al. Lumbar sup-
ports for prevention
and treatment of
low back pain: a sys-
tematic review
within the frame-
work of the
Cochrane Back
Review Group.
Spine. 2001;26:377-
86. [PMID: 11224885]
9. Roelofs PD, Bierma-
Zeinstra SM, van
Poppel MN, et al.
Lumbar supports to
prevent recurrent
low back pain
among home care
workers: a random-
ized trial. Ann Intern
Med. 2007;147:685-
92. [PMID: 18025444]
10. Deyo RA, Rainville J,
Kent DL. What can
the history and
physical examina-
tion tell us about
low back pain?
JAMA. 1992;268:760-
5. [PMID: 1386391]
11. Fairbank JC, Couper
J, Davies JB, et al. The
Oswestry low back
pain disability ques-
tionnaire. Physio-
therapy. 1980;
66:271-3. [PMID:
6450426]
12. Roland M, Morris R.
A study of the natu-
ral history of back
pain. Part I: develop-
ment of a reliable
and sensitive meas-
ure of disability in
low-back pain.
Spine. 1983;8:141-4.
[PMID: 6222486]

of motion in the legs and feet and characterizing the pain level.

What serious underlying systemic conditions should clinicians consider as possible causes of low back pain?

Underlying systemic disease that causes back pain is rare but must be considered. Prevalence is 4% for compression fracture, less than 1% for nonskin cancer, 0.3% for ankylosing spondylitis, and 0.01% for infection (10).

Factors associated with cancer include history of cancer, unexplained weight loss, no relief with bed rest, pain lasting more than 1 month, and increased age.

Osteomyelitis should be considered if there is a history of intravenous drug use, urinary tract infection, or fever. Increased age, white race, trauma, or prolonged corticosteroid use are associated with compression fractures.

Patients with at least 4 of the following characteristics require further evaluation for ankylosing spondylitis: morning stiffness, decreased discomfort with exercise, onset of back pain before age 40, slow onset of symptoms, and pain persisting for more than 3 months. However, because of the low prevalence of ankylosing spondylitis, the positive predictive value of any of these characteristics is still very low.

The absence of any of these worrisome features is highly sensitive but not very specific for excluding patients with systemic illness. The presence of these features may indicate the need for further evaluation.

Is the classification of low back pain by duration of symptoms clinically useful?

Classifying patients according to duration of low back pain (acute, subacute, or chronic) is useful because evidence does suggest different effectiveness of some

therapies on the basis of symptom duration.

Although there is no strong evidence-based method for classifying duration of acute back pain, it is generally defined as back pain lasting less than 4 weeks. Usually the result of trauma or arthritis, acute low back pain is the most common type of low back pain. Most acute back pain resolves within 4 weeks with self care. Subacute low back pain lasts between 4 to 12 weeks and may require clinical intervention. Chronic back pain is defined as pain that lasts longer than 12 weeks. It is often progressive, and identifying a specific cause is often difficult. People with low back pain usually have at least 1 episode of recurrence and can develop "acute-on-chronic" symptoms.

Is there a role for standardized low back pain assessment instruments in the evaluation of patients with low back pain?

Quantitative scales that gauge pain and function provide objective measures for judging response to therapy. Questions addressing pain, back-specific function, general health status, work disability, psychological status, and patient satisfaction can be used to assess the extent of work disability as a result of low back pain. Commonly used quantitative measures include the Roland–Morris modification of the Sickness Impact Profile and the Oswestry Disability Questionnaire (11, 12). Although a meaningful change is not precisely defined, a 2- to 3-point change on these instruments is a commonly proposed threshold (13, 14). These quantitative measures have been validated and are often used in research settings, but there are no data that their use in clinical settings improves patient outcomes.

What factors should lead clinicians to suspect nerve root involvement?

When patients present with back and leg pain, nerve root involvement must be considered. Nerve root involvement can cause neurologic compromise at the level of the nerve root (common causes include lumbar disk herniation in patients under age 50 years and spinal stenosis in older patients) or the upper motor neuron (causes include tumor or central-disk herniation).

When upper motor neurons are involved, urgent specialist consultation is required (10). Signs and symptoms that suggest upper motor neuron involvement include bowel or bladder dysfunction, diminished perineal sensation, sciatica, sensory motor deficits, and severe or progressive motor deficits.

Patients with leg pain that is worse than back pain, a positive straight-leg–raising test, and unilateral neurologic symptoms in the foot are very likely to have a herniated disk with nerve root compression as the source. The most common sites for lumbar disk herniation are at L4–5 or L5–S1. Pain that radiates from the back through the buttocks to the legs (sciatica) is common, and the more distal the pain radiation, the more specific the symptom is for nerve root involvement. Other common symptoms of disk herniation include weakness of the ankle and great toe dorsiflexors, loss of ankle reflex, and sensory loss in the feet.

Symptoms of vascular claudication can be difficult to distinguish from spinal stenosis, and clinicians should consider vascular disease in patients with risk factors for cardiovascular disease before attributing symptoms to spinal stenosis.

What psychosocial issues are important for clinicians to consider in evaluating patients with low back pain?

An important factor predicting the course of low back pain is the presence of psychosocial distress. Psychosocial distress is more common in patients with chronic low back pain, and attention to this distress may be beneficial to recovery. Clinicians should consider the following factors associated with poor outcomes in patients with low back pain: job dissatisfaction, depression, substance abuse, and desire for disability compensation.

A cross-sectional study of workers in the general population concluded that such individual psychological factors as distress and such work place factors as work load were highly related to the development of back pain (15).

A cohort study of patients presenting to primary care providers with first-onset low back pain found that psychological factors were strongly associated with persisting symptoms at 3 months (16).

When should clinicians consider imaging studies for patients with low back pain?

Radiographic examinations are usually of limited use in patients with low back pain unless the history or physical examination suggests a specific underlying cause. X-ray findings correlate poorly with low back symptoms (17). Spinal imaging studies in asymptomatic individuals commonly reveal anatomical findings, such as bulging or herniated disks, spinal stenosis, annular tears, and disk degeneration, which may not be clinically relevant and can reduce the specificity of imaging tests (18). Thus, the demonstration of an anatomical abnormality should not automatically lead the clinician to assume that it is the cause of the pain.

Imaging is important, however, for detecting some causes of low back pain. The American College of Radiology has developed appropriateness

---

Physical Examination Maneuvers that Suggest Herniated Disk
Straight-leg–raising test: Passive lifting of the affected leg by the examiner to an angle less than 60 degrees reproduces pain radiating distal to the knee.
Crossed straight-leg–raising test: Passive lifting of the unaffected leg by the examiner reproduces pain in the affected (opposite) leg.

13. Childs JD, Piva SR, Fritz JM. Responsiveness of the numeric pain rating scale in patients with low back pain. Spine. 2005;30:1331-4. [PMID: 15928561]
14. Ostelo RW, de Vet HC. Clinically important outcomes in low back pain. Best Pract Res Clin Rheumatol. 2005; 19:593-607. [PMID: 15949778]
15. Linton SJ. Do psychological factors increase the risk for back pain in the general population in both a cross-sectional and prospective analysis? Eur J Pain. 2005;9:355-61. [PMID: 15979015]
16. Grotle M, Brox JI, Veierød MB, et al. Clinical course and prognostic factors in acute low back pain: patients consulting primary care for the first time. Spine. 2005;30:976-82. [PMID: 15834343]
17. Bigos SJ. Acute Low Back Problems in Adults. Clinical Practice Guideline no. 14. Rockville, MD: U.S. Department of Health and Human Services; 1994;(14):iii-iv, 1-25. AHCPR publication no. 95-0642 [PMID: 7987418]
18. Jarvik JG, Deyo RA. Diagnostic evaluation of low back pain with emphasis on imaging. Ann Intern Med. 2002; 137:586-97. [PMID: 12353946]

criteria for radiographic procedures in the evaluation of patients with low back pain, where were last updated in 2005 (Table 2) (19). These criteria are meant to guide clinicians' decision-making depending on careful consideration of each patient's clinical circumstances.

A 2007 guideline developed by the American College of Physicians and the American Pain Society recommends that clinicians not routinely obtain imaging or other diagnostic tests in patients with nonspecific low back pain; that clinicians perform diagnostic imaging and testing for patients with low back pain when severe or progressive neurologic deficits are present or when serious underlying conditions are suspected; and that they evaluate patients with persistent low back pain and signs or symptoms of radiculopathy or spinal stenosis with magnetic resonance imaging (preferred) or computed tomography only if they are potential candidates for surgery or epidural steroid injection (for suspected radiculopathy). The guideline developers rated these recommendations as strong and based on moderate-quality evidence (20).

In summary, imaging is most useful when the pretest probability of underlying serious disease requiring surgical intervention is high. There is no consensus on when a negative result on plain radiographs should be followed by an advanced imaging study or when the physician should go directly to an advanced study. A negative plain film does not definitively exclude cancer or infection in someone at high risk for these conditions. For such persons, early advanced imaging may be appropriate. Of note, patients with low back pain often expect radiographic procedures.

An RCT of routine radiography for patients with low back pain of at least 6 weeks in duration reported more patient satisfaction with their health care but worse pain and function scores (21).

Under what circumstances should clinicians consider electromyography and other laboratory tests?
Clinicians should reserve electromyography and nerve conduction tests for patients in whom there is diagnostic uncertainty about the relationship of leg symptoms to anatomical findings on advanced imaging. Electrophysiologic tests

Table 2. American College of Radiology Appropriateness Criteria for Lumbar Spine Radiographic Procedures in Patients with Low Back Pain*

Radiographic Procedure	Clinical Scenario					
	Uncomplicated LBP	Low-Velocity Trauma, Osteoporosis, or age >70 y	Suspicion of Cancer or Immunosupression	Radiculopathy	Past Lumbar Surgery	Cauda Equina Syndrome
X-ray	2	6	5	3	5	3
CT without contrast	2	6	4	5	6	4[†]
MRI without contrast	2	8	8	8	6	9
MRI with and without contrast	2	3	7	5	8	8
Nuclear bone scan, targeted	2	4	5	2	5	2
X-ray myelography	2	1	2	2	2	2
CT myelography	2	1	2	5	5	6

*How to use this table: If you are considering radiologic procedures for a patient with one of the clinical scenarios displayed in the table, choose the test or tests with the highest numeric appropriateness rating. If all tests have low appropriateness ratings, consider whether a radiologic procedure is likely to inform decision-making before proceeding with testing. Rating scale: 1 = least appropriate; 9 = most appropriate. CT = computed tomography; LBP = low back pain; MRI = magnetic resonance imaging.

† With and without contrast.

can assess suspected myelopathy, radiculopathy, neuropathy, and myopathy. With radiculopathy or neuropathy, electromyography results might be unreliable in limb muscles until a patient has significant limb symptoms for more than 3 to 4 weeks, so testing should not be done in patients with a duration of symptoms less than 4 weeks.

Diagnosis... Clinical evaluation of patients with low back pain should focus on identification of features that indicate a potential serious underlying condition, radiculopathy, and psychosocial factors. Clinicians should classify low back pain as acute, subacute, or chronic because treatment options can differ with duration. Most patients with acute symptoms will not require imaging tests, which should be reserved for patients with a high pretest probability of serious underlying systemic illness, fracture, cord compression, or spinal stenosis or if surgery is being considered.

CLINICAL BOTTOM LINE

Treatment

What are reasonable goals for clinicians and patients for treatment of low back pain?

Most acute, nonspecific pain resolves over time without treatment. Controlling pain and maintaining function while symptoms diminish on their own is the goal for most individuals with acute low back pain. Clinicians should inform patients that back pain is common, that the spontaneous recovery rate is more than 50% to 75% at 4 weeks and more than 90% at 6 weeks, and that most people do not need surgery even with herniated disks.

Subacute or chronic low back pain can be difficult to treat, and exacerbations can recur over time. Patients should understand that the goal of therapy is to maintain function and manage psychosocial distress, even if it is not possible to achieve complete resolution of pain. The patient should be encouraged to take personal responsibility for the continued management and prevention of further exacerbations and chronicity. Functional outcome depends more on patient behavior than on medical treatments.

What psychosocial factors influence recovery in patients with low back pain?

Psychosocial factors and emotional distress are stronger predictors of low back pain outcomes than either physical examination findings or severity and duration of pain (22–24). Assessment of psychosocial factors, such as depression, unemployment, job dissatisfaction, somatization disorder, or psychological distress, identifies patients who may have delayed recovery and could help target behavioral interventions, such as intensive multidisciplinary rehabilitation.

What should clinicians advise patients regarding level of activity and exercise?

A wealth of evidence suggests that prolonged bed rest or inactivity is associated with worse outcomes for patients with acute, subacute, or chronic low back pain. Clinicians should encourage patients to maintain activity levels as near to normal as possible but advise against back-specific exercises while in acute pain. Although work might need to be modified on a short-term basis to accommodate patient recovery, most patients with nonspecific occupational low back pain can

19. ACR Appropriateness Criteria. Reston, VA: American College of Radiology; 2005. Accessed at www.acr.org/SecondaryMainMenuCategories/quality_safety/app_criteria.aspx on 17 March 2008.
20. Chou R, Qaseem A, Snow V, et al. Clinical Efficacy Assessment Subcommittee of the American College of Physicians. Diagnosis and treatment of low back pain: a joint clinical practice guideline from the American College of Physicians and the American Pain Society. Ann Intern Med. 2007; 147:478-91. [PMID: 17909209]
21. Kendrick D, Fielding K, Bentley E, et al. Radiography of the lumbar spine in primary care patients with low back pain: randomised controlled trial. BMJ. 2001;322:400-5. [PMID: 11179160]
22. Pengel LH, Herbert RD, Maher CG, et al. Acute low back pain: systematic review of its prognosis. BMJ. 2003;327:323. [PMID: 12907487]
23. Fayad F, Lefevre-Colau MM, Poiraudeau S, et al. [Chronicity, recurrence, and return to work in low back pain: common prognostic factors]. Ann Readapt Med Phys. 2004;47:179-89. [PMID: 15130717]
24. Pincus T, Burton AK, Vogel S, et al. A systematic review of psychological factors as predictors of chronicity/disability in prospective cohorts of low back pain. Spine. 2002; 27:E109-20. [PMID: 11880847]

25. Malmivaara A, Häkkinen U, Aro T, et al. The treatment of acute low back pain—bed rest, exercises, or ordinary activity? N Engl J Med. 1995;332:351-5. [PMID: 7823996]

26. Hagen KB, Jamtvedt G, Hilde G, et al. The updated cochrane review of bed rest for low back pain and sciatica. Spine. 2005;30:542-6. [PMID: 15738787]

27. Liddle SD, Baxter GD, Gracey JH. Exercise and chronic low back pain: what works? Pain. 2004;107:176-90. [PMID: 14715404]

28. Hayden JA, van Tulder MW, Tomlinson G. Systematic review: strategies for using exercise therapy to improve outcomes in chronic low back pain. Ann Intern Med. 2005; 142:776-85. [PMID: 15867410]

29. Hayden JA, van Tulder MW, Malmivaara AV, et al. Meta-analysis: exercise therapy for nonspecific low back pain. Ann Intern Med. 2005; 142:765-75. [PMID: 15867409]

30. Sherman KJ, Cherkin DC, Erro J, et al. Comparing yoga, exercise, and a self-care book for chronic low back pain: a randomized, controlled trial. Ann Intern Med. 2005; 143:849-56. [PMID: 16365466]

31. van Tulder MW, Koes BW, Bouter LM. Conservative treatment of acute and chronic nonspecific low back pain. A systematic review of randomized controlled trials of the most common interventions. Spine. 1997;22:2128-56. [PMID: 9322325]

32. Bronfort G, Haas M, Evans RL, et al. Efficacy of spinal manipulation and mobilization for low back pain and neck pain: a systematic review and best evidence synthesis. Spine J. 2004;4:335-56. [PMID: 15125860]

33. Assendelft WJ, Morton SC, Yu EI, et al. Spinal manipulative therapy for low back pain. A meta-analysis of effectiveness relative to other therapies. Ann Intern Med. 2003;138:871-81. [PMID: 12779297]

return to work quickly. Lacking any warning signs of serious underlying pathologic conditions, clinicians should encourage patients to minimize bed rest, to be as active as possible, and to return to work as soon as possible even if not entirely pain-free.

A randomized trial that enrolled 186 employees of the city of Helsinki, Finland, who presented to an occupational health center with acute, nonspecific low back pain found that patients assigned to continue usual activities had better recovery at 3 and 12 weeks than those assigned to bed rest for 2 days or back-mobilizing exercises. Recovery was slowest among patients assigned to bed rest (25).

A 2005 systematic review of RCTs investigating bed rest for patients with acute low back pain concluded that people with low back pain without sciatica who receive advice for bed rest have more pain and worse functional recovery than those advised to continue normal activities. Pain and functional outcomes were similar for patients with sciatica whether they followed bed rest or remained active (26).

Another systematic review of 39 randomized trials that involved 7347 patients with acute, subacute, or chronic symptoms concluded that advice to stay active was sufficient for acute low back pain. Advice delivered as part of an educational program ("back school") seemed effective for patients with subacute symptoms, but the quality of the evidence for subacute low back pain was limited and of poor quality. For chronic low back pain, there is strong evidence to support advice to remain active in addition to specific advice about exercise and self-management (27).

Various back-specific exercise programs have been advocated beginning when acute symptoms subside, but there is little evidence to support any specific exercise therapy. Clinicians should advise patients that attainment and maintenance of general physical fitness may help to prevent recurrences of low back pain.

A meta-analysis of 61 RCTs that included 6390 patients with acute (11 trials), subacute (6 trials), chronic (43 trials), or uncertain-duration (1 trial) low back pain concluded

that exercise offers slight benefits in pain and function in adults with chronic low back pain, especially in health care rather than occupational settings. In patients with subacute pain, some evidence supported the effectiveness of graded exercise programs in improving work absenteeism, but the evidence was inconclusive for other outcomes. For patients with acute low back pain, exercise therapy was as effective as no therapy or other conservative treatments (28).

A review of 43 trials that included 72 exercise treatment groups and 31 comparison groups found that exercise therapy delivered under supervision and consisting of individually tailored programs that include stretching or strengthening may improve pain and function for patients with chronic, nonspecific low back pain. Available trials were heterogeneous and of variable quality, so the authors were unable to make definitive conclusions about the relationship of outcomes with patient characteristics or exercise type (29).

An RCT compared 12-week sessions of yoga, conventional exercise, or a self-care book in 101 adults with chronic low back pain. Patients in the yoga group had the best outcomes with respect to pain and function, followed by exercise then self-care (30).

What other physical interventions are effective in the treatment of low back pain?

Physical interventions for treatment of low back pain include physical therapy and complementary–alternative medicine approaches, such as spinal manipulation and massage. There is limited evidence that physical treatments help to prevent recurrent back pain, and their use is associated with increased cost. Nevertheless, physical treatments may be helpful in improving function and reducing pain in symptomatic acute and subacute low back pain (31–33). Clinicians should consider physical interventions for patients with acute symptoms that persist after 1 to 2 weeks. It is possible that prescribed physical therapy can help reduce disability by encouraging patients to be active in a safe, supervised setting.

A 2007 systematic review of nonpharma-cologic therapies for acute and chronic low back pain considered the benefits and harms of acupuncture, back schools, psychological therapies, exercise therapy, functional restoration, interdisciplinary therapy, massage, physical therapies (inferential therapy, low-level laser therapy, lumbar supports, short-wave diathermy, superficial heat, traction, transcutaneous electrical nerve stimulation, and ultrasonography), spinal manipulation, and yoga. According to these authors, there is good evidence of moderate efficacy in chronic or subacute low back pain for cognitive behavioral therapy, exercise, spinal manipulation, and interdisciplinary rehabilitation. For acute low back pain, the only therapy with good evidence of efficacy was superficial heat (34).

When should drug therapies be considered for the treatment of low back pain and which drugs are effective?

Various drug therapies are used for low back pain (Table 3). Evidence is insufficient to identify one medication as offering a clear overall advantage because of complex trade-offs between benefits and harms, but acetaminophen or non-steroidal anti-inflammatory drugs (NSAIDs) should be used as first-line drug therapy. The latter have been shown to reduce low back pain compared with placebo in systematic reviews of clinical trials (35, 36). Although no randomized trials of acetaminophen in low back pain are available, it is reasonable to recommend it as appropriate therapy because of its known effectiveness and safety as an analgesic.

Short courses of muscle relaxants or opiates should be considered as adjunctive therapy only when needed for patients who do not respond to first-line analgesics. Muscle relaxants are more effective than placebo in reducing pain and relieving symptoms. However, studies have not shown them to be more effective than NSAIDs, and the muscle relaxants have more side effects, including adverse central nervous system effects (37, 38).

Although opiates are commonly prescribed for acute, subacute, and chronic low back pain, they have not been shown to be more effective than acetaminophen or NSAIDs and are associated with more side effects, including the potential for addiction (37, 39).

A systematic review of studies of opioids for the treatment of chronic back pain in non-pregnant adults found that opioid prescription rates in 11 studies varied widely (3% to 66%). In 4 short-term, randomized trials that compared opioids with placebo or nonopioid analgesics, opioids did not provide better pain relief. In poor-quality, heterogeneous studies, the prevalence of current substance abuse disorders in patients taking long-term opioids for back pain was as high as 43%. Aberrant medication-taking behaviors varied from 5% to 24% (40).

The role of antidepressants in treating chronic low back pain in patients without depression is uncertain. Antidepressants that inhibit norepinephrine reuptake (for example, tricyclic and tetracyclic antidepressants) may improve symptoms in patients with chronic low back pain, but antidepressants lacking inhibition of norepinephrine reuptake (for example, selective serotonin reuptake inhibitors) have not shown benefit in pain relief or functional status (41). A review of 9 RCTs found that tricyclic antidepressants were more effective than placebo in reducing the severity of pain but not in improving functional status in chronic back pain (42). Antidepressants are not appropriate therapy for acute low back pain.

Anticonvulsants, such as carbemaza-pine or gabapentin, are sometimes used to treat chronic low back pain and have demonstrated efficacy in treating sciatica, but evidence is lacking about their effectiveness in the management of low back pain. Similarly, limited evidence supports the use of tramadol. There is good evidence that systemic

34. Chou R, Huffman LH. American Pain Society. Nonpharmacologic therapies for acute and chronic low back pain: a review of the evidence for an American Pain Society/American College of Physicians clinical practice guideline. Ann Intern Med. 2007; 147:492-504. [PMID: 17909210]

35. Schnitzer TJ, Ferraro A, Hunsche E, et al. A comprehensive review of clinical trials on the efficacy and safety of drugs for the treatment of low back pain. J Pain Symptom Manage. 2004;28:72-95. [PMID: 15223086]

36. van Tulder MW, Scholten RJ, Koes BW, et al. Nonsteroidal anti-inflammatory drugs for low back pain: a systematic review within the framework of the Cochrane Collaboration Back Review Group. Spine. 2000;25:2501-13. [PMID: 11013503]

37. Chou R, Huffman LH. American Pain Society. Medications for acute and chronic low back pain: a review of the evidence for an American Pain Society/American College of Physicians clinical practice guideline. Ann Intern Med. 2007;147:505-14. [PMID: 17909211]

38. van Tulder MW, Touray T, Furlan AD, et al. Cochrane Back Review Group. Muscle relaxants for non-specific low back pain: a systematic review within the framework of the cochrane collaboration. Spine. 2003;28:1978-92. [PMID: 12973146]

39. Deshpande A, Furlan A, Mailis-Gagnon A, et al. Opioids for chronic low-back pain. Cochrane Database Syst Rev. 2007:CD004959. [PMID: 17636781]

40. Martell BA, O'Connor PG, Kerns RD, et al. Systematic review: opioid treatment for chronic back pain: prevalence, efficacy, and association with addiction. Ann Intern Med. 2007; 146:116-27. [PMID: 17227935]

Table 3. Drug Treatment for Low Back Pain*

Agent	Mechanism of Action	Side Effects	Notes
Acetaminophen, 500–1000 mg q 4–6 h (max daily dose 4 g)	Inhibition of prostaglandin synthesis in the CNS.	Antipyretic effect may mask fever. Hepatotoxicity at high doses.	First-line analgesic therapy for low back pain. Avoid dosing >4 g/d, especially in patients who use combination products. Inexpensive.
Salicylates/NSAIDs, Aspirin, 500–1000 mg q4–6h (max daily dose, 4 g) Ibuprofen, 400–800 mg, q 6–8 h (max daily dose, 2400 mg) Naproxen, 250–275 mg, q 8–12 h (max daily dose, 1250 mg)	Decrease prostaglandins produced by the arachidonic acid cascade in response to noxious stimuli, thereby decreasing the number of pain impulses received by the CNS.	Gastrointestinal upset or ulceration. Decreased renal blood flow. Inhibition of platelet aggregation. Antipyretic effect may mask fever in patients in whom fever would be an important clinical clue. COX-2–selective agents, and potentially NSAIDs, are associated with increased cardiovascular risk.	First-line analgesic therapy for low back pain. Generic agents are inexpensive. No evidence that COX-2–selective agents are more effective than nonselective agents. Anecdotal reports indicate benefit in patients with bone-related pain.
Short-acting opioids, Codeine (alone, or in acetaminophen with codeine), 30–60 mg, q 4 h Hydrocodone (alone or with acetaminophen, aspirin, or ibuprofen), 5–10 mg, q 4 h Oxycodone (alone or with acetaminophen), 5–10 mg, q 4 h	Activate endogenous pain modulating systems and produce analgesia by mimicking the action of endogenous opioid compounds.	Constipation, nausea, and sedation are common side effects. Dry mouth, pruritus, mental confusion, biliary spasm, urinary retention, and myoclonus or respiratory depression (at high doses) are less-common side effects. Addiction potential.	Short courses can be considered as adjunctive therapy only when needed for patients who do not respond to first-line analgesics. Should not be used long-term to treat chronic low back pain. Use equianalgesic conversion to convert between different opioids and different routes. Evidence lacking to show greater efficacy than first-line analgesic agents.
Muscle relaxants, Baclofen, start with 5 mg PO tid, increase slowly, max daily dose 80 mg given in 3–4 divided doses Cyclobenzaprine, 5 mg tid	Reduce muscle spasm that may be contributing to symptoms.	CNS effects.	Short courses can be used as adjunctive therapy for patients who do not respond to first-line analgesics. More effective than placebo in reducing pain and relieving symptoms, but no more effective than first-line analgesics. Insufficient evidence to recommend one over another.
Antidepressants, Amitriptyline, doses of 10–150 mg/d PO can be used. Start at low doses and gradually increase as needed.	Affects pathways that lead to neuropathic pain.	Drowsiness, dry mouth, dizziness, and constipation are common. Trials not designed to assess serious adverse events, such as overdose, suicidality, or arrhythmias.	Most evidence of effectiveness for tricyclic antidepressants. Paroxetine and trazadone did not show effectiveness. Insufficient evidence to judge relative effectiveness of tricyclic antidepressants versus selective serotonin reuptake inhibitors. Should not be used for acute low back pain. More effective than placebo for pain relief, but had no clear benefit on function.
Anticonvulsants, Gabapentin, 300–900 mg tid (start 300 mg, qhs, and titrate quickly to max daily dose 3600 mg) Carbamazepine, 200–600 mg bid	Affect pathways that lead to neuropathic pain.	Sedation. Need to adjust gabapentin dose on the basis of renal function.	Limited evidence or effectiveness. Can be expensive. Other, newer agents being evaluated for use in neuropathic pain include lamotrigine and topiramate.
Tramadol, 100 mg PO daily of the extended-release tablets. Titrate in 100-mg increments every 5 days, if needed, up to max daily dose 300 mg. Concomitant use of the extended-release tablets with other tramadol products is not recommended.	Centrally acting analgesic with a dual mechanism of action. It is a μ-opioid receptor agonist and a weak inhibitor of norepinephrine and serotonin reuptake.	Flushing, insomnia, orthostatic hypotension, weakness, rigors, and anorexia. Other side effects include dizziness, vertigo, dry mouth, gastrointestinal symptoms diaphoresis, and CNS effects.	More effective than placebo for short-term improvement in pain and function. No trials available that compare tramadol with first-line analgesics.

* bid = twice daily; CNS = central nervous system; COX-2 = cyclooxygenase 2; GI = gastrointestinal; NSAID = nonsteroidal anti-inflammatory drug; PO = orally; qd = once daily; qhs = every night; qid = four times daily; tid = three times daily.

corticosteroids do not improve chronic low back pain (37).

Are complementary–alternative medicine therapies effective in the treatment of low back pain?

Complementary–alternative medicine therapies are commonly used for back pain. Among the interventions that probably have some benefit are spinal manipulation, massage, and acupuncture. Some evidence supports the use of willow bark extract, also known as salicin, and devil's claw. There is only limited research on homeopathic remedies, acupressure, and chondroitin sulfate. Treatments with unknown effectiveness include glucosamine, balneotherapy or spa therapy, and pilates. Alternative therapies that are probably ineffective include bipolar magnets, the Feldenkrais Method, and reflexology.

A Cochrane review of massage concluded that for subacute and early, chronic low back pain, moderate evidence suggests that massage improves pain intensity and pain quality, compared with sham treatment. However, these effects were similar to the effects for exercise and manipulation (43).

A systematic evidence review concluded that spinal manipulation is efficacious compared with placebo in the short term for both acute and chronic low back pain, but evidence does not support it as being more effective than other standard treatments (33).

The most recent Cochrane review of acupuncture and dry-needling for low back pain included 35 RCTs. It noted evidence of pain relief and functional improvement for chronic low back pain (immediately after therapy or on short-term follow-up). Although the effects are small, acupuncture used as an adjunct to conventional therapies appears to relieve pain and improve function in chronic low back pain more than the conventional therapies alone. Only 3 of the studies looked at acute low back pain, so the authors were unable to draw conclusions about efficacy of acupuncture for acute symptoms (44).

A Cochrane review concluded that there is some evidence that taking 240 mg of willow bark extract (salicin) per day provides short-term benefit for acute exacerbations of chronic, nonspecific low back pain (45).

A Cochrane review concluded that there is strong evidence that taking devil's claw containing 50 to 100 mg of harpagoside per day was better than placebo for short-term improvement of acute or chronic back pain. There is no evidence to support long-term use of devil's claw, and safety has not been carefully studied (45).

What are the indications for surgical intervention for low back pain?

Most cases of low back pain do not require surgery. However, patients with suspected cord or cauda equina compression or spinal infection require urgent surgical referral for possible decompression or debridement to prevent loss of neurologic function. Nonurgent surgical evaluation is also appropriate in patients with worsening suspected spinal stenosis, neurologic deficits, or intractable pain that is resistant to conservative treatment. Standard surgery for spinal stenosis is posterior decompressive laminectomy.

In a study that enrolled patients with imaging-confirmed lumbar spinal stenosis without spondylolisthesis and at least 12 weeks of symptoms in either a randomized cohort (n = 289) or an observational cohort (n = 365), 67% of patients randomly assigned to surgery and 43% of those randomly assigned to nonsurgical care had surgery. In the randomized cohort, pain but not functional outcomes were better among those assigned to surgery than among those assigned to nonsurgical care. In an analysis of both cohorts, patients who had surgery had better pain and functional outcomes at 3 months and at 2 years than those who did not have surgery (46).

A prospective cohort study of patients with disk herniations treated at 13 U.S. spine centers found that patients with sciatica who chose operative intervention reported greater improvements than those who chose nonsurgical care (47).

41. Staiger TO, Gaster B, Sullivan MD, et al. Systematic review of antidepressants in the treatment of chronic low back pain. Spine. 2003; 28:2540-5. [PMID: 14624092]

42. Salerno SM, Browning R, Jackson JL. The effect of antidepressant treatment on chronic back pain: a meta-analysis. Arch Intern Med. 2002;162:19-24. [PMID: 11784215]

43. Furlan AD, Brosseau L, Imamura M, et al. Massage for low-back pain: a systematic review within the framework of the Cochrane Collaboration Back Review Group. Spine. 2002;27: 1896-910. [PMID: 12221356]

44. Furlan AD, van Tulder MW, Cherkin DC, et al. Acupuncture and dry-needling for low back pain. Cochrane Database Syst Rev. 2005: CD001351. [PMID: 15674876]

45. Gagnier JJ, van Tulder MW, Berman B, et al. Herbal medicine for low back pain: a Cochrane review. Spine. 2007;32:82-92. [PMID: 17202897]

46. Weinstein JN, Tosteson TD, Lurie JD, et al. SPORT Investigators. Surgical versus nonsurgical therapy for lumbar spinal stenosis. N Engl J Med. 2008;358:794-810. [PMID: 18287602]

47. Weinstein JN, Lurie JD, Tosteson TD, et al. Surgical vs nonoperative treatment for lumbar disk herniation: the Spine Patient Outcomes Research Trial (SPORT) observational cohort. JAMA. 2006;296:2451-9. [PMID: 17119141]

Signs that urgent surgical intervention may be necessary include bowel- or bladder-sphincter dysfunction, particularly urinary retention or incontinence; diminished perineal sensation, sciatica, or sensory motor deficits; and bilateral or unilateral motor deficits that are severe and progressive. Signs that nonurgent surgical intervention may be necessary include weakness of the ankle and great toe dorsiflexors, loss of ankle reflex, sensory loss in the feet as manifestations of the most common disk herniations, neurogenic claudication or "pseudoclaudication," and leg pain in addition to and more severe than back pain.

Although definitive evidence on the effectiveness of facet joint injections or nerve blocks is not available, such procedures are often done in patients who do not respond to conservative care.

How should clinicians follow patients with low back pain?
Follow-up, based on the suspected cause and course of disease in patients with low back pain, is an important component of treatment. On the basis of consensus, clinicians should consider scheduling an office visit or a telephone call after 2 to 4 weeks of treatment to assess progress in patients with acute low back pain. The follow-up history should address patient response to treatment, resolution of symptoms, and development of complications. It is important to assess the probability of a transition to the subacute or chronic phase of back pain. Patients with acute back pain who are still moderately symptomatic at 4 weeks are more likely to develop chronic symptoms than those who report improved symptoms. If recovery is delayed, consider reevaluation for possible underlying causes of back pain. Development of symptoms of neurologic dysfunction or systemic disease should prompt additional evaluation.

Reinforcement of healthy lifestyle messages and patient education is an important part of management and prevention of recurrence. This should include advice on treatment, prognosis, and recommendations on general exercise and fitness. In particular, patients with low back pain should be encouraged to continue normal activities. For patients with chronic low back pain, the addition of individually specific advice about the most appropriate exercise and functional activities is required. Regular follow-up contact is also thought to reinforce efforts and to develop ways to overcome barriers to regular physical activity.

48. U.S. Preventive Services Task Force. Primary Care Interventions to Prevent Low Back Pain: Brief Evidence Update. Rockville, MD: Agency for Healthcare Research and Quality; 2004. Accessed at www.ahrq.gov/clinic/3rduspstf/lowback/lowbackup.htm on 17 March 2008.

Treatment... Most acute nonspecific pain will resolve over days to weeks even without medical intervention. Clinicians should discourage bed rest and encourage all patients to maintain normal activities as much as possible. When symptoms persist, clinicians should consider nondrug, physical interventions, such as physical therapy, exercise, spinal manipulation, and massage. When analgesia is necessary, acetaminophen or NSAIDs should be used as first-line therapy. Short courses of muscle relaxants or opiates should be used cautiously, and antidepressants may be helpful in some patients with chronic symptoms. Psychosocial factors are strong predictors of low back pain outcomes, but good evidence is lacking to support specific strategies for addressing them. Urgent surgical referral is indicated when infection, cancer, acute nerve compression, or the cauda equina syndrome is suspected. Nonurgent surgical referral may be appropriate for patients with persistent back pain and signs of nonacute nerve compression or spinal stenosis.

CLINICAL BOTTOM LINE

What do professional organizations recommend regarding the management of patients with low back pain?
In 2007, the American College of Physicians and American Pain Society released guidelines on the diagnosis and treatment of low back pain (20). The guidelines included 7 key recommendations for guiding diagnosis and treatment (see Box).

Several other low back pain guidelines are available. In 1994, the Agency for Health Care Policy and Research published practice guidelines for the assessment and treatment of acute low back problems in adults (17). Topics covered include the initial assessment, identification of signs that suggest esrious underlying disease, management, and diagnostic considerations. An update published in 2004 reported new evidence that back schools and back belts (lumbar supports) are ineffective in preventing low back pain (48).

In 2005, the American College of Sports Medicine released guidelines for exercise testing and prescription in healthy persons and individuals with disease, including guidance for low back pain (49).

A 2001 study of guidelines on low back pain compared clinical guidelines from 11 countries and found that their content was similar regarding diagnostic classification and the use of diagnostic and therapeutic interventions (50) but noted discrepancies for recommendations regarding exercise

---

Recommendations from the Joint Clinical Practice Guideline from the American College of Physicians and the American Pain Society (20):

Recommendation 1: Clinicians should conduct a focused history and physical examination to help place patients with low back pain into 1 of 3 broad categories: nonspecific low back pain, back pain potentially associated with radiculopathy or spinal stenosis, or back pain potentially associated with another specific spinal cause. The history should include assessment of psychosocial risk factors, which predict risk for chronic disabling back pain (strong recommendation, moderate-quality evidence).

Recommendation 2: Clinicians should not routinely obtain imaging or other diagnostic tests in patients with nonspecific low back pain (strong recommendation, moderate-quality evidence).

Recommendation 3: Clinicians should perform diagnostic imaging and testing for patients with low back pain when severe or progressive neurologic deficits are present or when serious underlying conditions are suspected on the basis of history and physical examination (strong recommendation, moderate-quality evidence).

Recommendation 4: Clinicians should evaluate patients with persistent low back pain and signs or symptoms of radiculopathy or spinal stenosis with magnetic resonance imaging (preferred) or computed tomography only if they are potential candidates for surgery or epidural steroid injection (for suspected radiculopathy) (strong recommendation, moderate-quality evidence).

Recommendation 5: Clinicians should provide patients with evidence-based information on low back pain with regard to their expected course, advise patients to remain active, and provide information about effective self-care options (strong recommendation, moderate-quality evidence).

Recommendation 6: For patients with low back pain, clinicians should consider the use of medications with proven benefits in conjunction with back care information and self-care. Clinicians should assess severity of baseline pain and functional deficits, potential benefits, risks, and relative lack of long-term efficacy and safety data before initiating therapy (strong recommendation, moderate-quality evidence). For most patients, first-line medication options are acetaminophen or NSAIDs.

Recommendation 7: For patients who do not improve with self-care options, clinicians should consider the addition of nonpharmacologic therapy with proven benefits—for acute low back pain, spinal manipulation; for chronic or subacute low back pain, intensive interdisciplinary rehabilitation, exercise therapy, acupuncture, massage therapy, spinal manipulation, yoga, cognitive-behavioral therapy, or progressive relaxation (weak recommendation, moderate-quality evidence).

---

49. American College of Sports Medicine. ACSM's Guidelines for Exercise Testing and Prescription. 7th ed. Philadelphia: Lippincott Williams & Wilkins; 2005.
50. Koes BW, van Tulder MW, Ostelo R, et al. Clinical guidelines for the management of low back pain in primary care: an international comparison. Spine. 2001;26:2504-13; discussion 2513-4. [PMID: 11707719]

therapy, spinal manipulation, muscle relaxants, and patient information. In 2004, a systematic review of 17 available guidelines for acute low back pain concluded that the overall quality of the evidence suppporting recommendations was disappointing (51), but the diagnostic and therapeutic recommendations of the guidelines were largely similar.

What is the role of patient education in the management of low back pain?
Patient education is important in the overall management of low back pain, and all patients should receive information about the treatment of back pain and its prognosis. Information and advice given to patients about the management of back pain needs to be individually specific and relevant. Patient education about low back pain should inform patients that back pain is common, that the spontaneous recovery rate is more than 50% to 75% at 4 weeks and more than 90% at 6 months, and that most people do not need surgery even with herniated disks. Clinicians should advise patients to remain active and encourage weight control and should counsel patients about the role of psychosocial distress.

A randomized trial in 162 patients with back pain compared patients' use of a booklet entitled "The Back Book" to more traditional educational materials. Patients who received the experimental booklet showed an improvement in beliefs about back pain and some improvement in disability measures (52).

51. van Tulder MW, Tuut M, Pennick V, et al. Quality of primary care guidelines for acute low back pain. Spine. 2004;29:E357-62. [PMID: 15534397]
52. Burton AK, Waddell G, Tillotson KM, et al. Information and advice to patients with back pain can have a positive effect. Spine. 1999;24:2481-91. [PMID: 10626311]

in the clinic
Tool Kit

Low Back Pain

PIER Modules

www.pier.acponline.org
Access the following PIER Modules: Low Back Pain, Back Pain (Complementary/Alternative Medicine). PIER modules provide evidence-based guidance for clinical decisions at the point-of-care.

Patient Education Resources

www.annals.org/intheclinic/toolkit
Access the patient information material that appears on the following page for duplication and distribution to patients.
www.annals.org/cgi/content/summary/147/7/478
Access a "Summary for Patients" of the American College of Physicians/American Pain Society guidelines on the diagnosis and treatment of low back pain for duplication and distribution to patients.

Clinical Guidelines

American College of Physicians/American Pain Society
www.annals.org/cgi/reprint/147/7/478.pdf
Access the 2008 American College of Physicians/American Pain Society guidelines on the diagnosis and treatment of low back pain.
www.annals.org/cgi/content/full/147/7/478/DC1
Access an audio summary of the American College of Physicians/American Pain Society guidelines.

Agency for Healthcare Research and Quality
www.ahrq.gov/clinic/3rduspstf/lowback/lowbackrs.htm
Access the US Preventive services Task Force recommendations on primary care interventions to prevent low back pain in adults.

American College of Radiology
www.acr.org/SecondaryMainMenuCategories/quality_safety/app_criteria/pdf/ExpertPanelonNeurologicImaging/LowBackPainDoc7.aspx
Access the American College of Radiology Appropriateness Criteria for radiographic procedures in patients with low back pain.

What you should know about
Low Back Pain

Many people have low back pain at some time in their lives. Back pain is rarely caused by a serious health condition. It often gets better within a few days or weeks. Low back pain can become chronic, meaning that it comes and goes over months to years.

If you have low back pain:

- Do not lift heavy things or do strenuous activity
- Try to keep doing everyday activities and walking, even if it hurts
- Do not stay in bed longer than 1 to 2 days, because it can make your recovery slower

To help you feel better, try some of these things at home:

- Medicines from the drug store to reduce pain, (acetaminophen, ibuprofen—read the labels)
- Heating pads or hot showers
- Massage

See a doctor if:

- Pain runs down the leg below the knee
- The leg, foot, groin, or rectal area feels numb
- Fever, nausea or vomiting, stomachache, weakness, or sweating occurs
- Bowel or bladder control is lost
- Pain was caused by an injury
- Pain is so bad you can't move around
- Pain doesn't seem to be getting better after 2 to 3 weeks

The American College of Physicians and the American Pain Society published guidelines on the diagnosis and treatment of low back pain in December 2007. For a "Summary for Patients" of these guidelines go to **www.annals.org/ cgi/reprint/147/7/478.pdf**

For More Information

MedlinePlus
http://www.nlm.nih.gov/medlineplus/backpain.html

The Arthritis Foundation
http://ww2.arthritis.org/conditions/DiseaseCenter/back_pain.asp
National Institutes of Neurological Disorders and Stroke
http://www.ninds.nih.gov/disorders/backpain/backpain.htm

**American Academy of Family Physicians
(information available in English and Spanish)**

http://familydoctor.org/online/famdoces/home/common/
pain/treatment/117.html

ACP

AMERICAN COLLEGE OF PHYSICIANS
INTERNAL MEDICINE | *Doctors for Adults*®

Patient Information

Hepatitis C

1. Armstrong GL, Wasley A, Simard EP, et al. The prevalence of hepatitis C virus infection in the United States, 1999 through 2002. Ann Intern Med. 2006;144:705-14. [PMID: 16702586]

2. Bialek SR, Terrault NA. The changing epidemiology and natural history of hepatitis C virus infection. Clin Liver Dis. 2006; 10:697-715. [PMID: 17164113]

3. National Institutes of Health. National Institutes of Health Consensus Development Conference Statement: Management of hepatitis C: 2002—June 10-12, 2002. Hepatology. 2002;36:S3-20. [PMID: 12407572]

4. El-Serag HB, Davila JA, Petersen NJ, et al. The continuing increase in the incidence of hepatocellular carcinoma in the United States: an update. Ann Intern Med. 2003;139:817-23. [PMID: 14623619]

5. Hwang LY, Kramer JR, Troisi C, et al. Relationship of cosmetic procedures and drug use to hepatitis C and hepatitis B virus infections in a low-risk population. Hepatology. 2006;44:341-51. [PMID: 16871571]

6. Lanphear BP, Linnemann CC Jr, Cannon CG, et al. Hepatitis C virus infection in healthcare workers: risk of exposure and infection. Infect Control Hosp Epidemiol. 1994;15:745-50. [PMID: 7534324]

7. Fabrizi F, Poordad FF, Martin P. Hepatitis C infection and the patient with end-stage renal disease. Hepatology. 2002;36:3-10. [PMID: 12085342]

8. Macedo de Oliveira A, White KL, Leschinsky DP, et al. An outbreak of hepatitis C virus infections among outpatients at a hematology/oncology clinic. Ann Intern Med. 2005;142:898-902. [PMID: 15941696]

9. Terrault NA. Sexual activity as a risk factor for hepatitis C. Hepatology. 2002;36:S99-105. [PMID: 12407582]

Chronic hepatitis C virus (HCV) infection is the most common blood-borne infection in the United States, with an estimated overall prevalence of 3.2 million persons (1.3%) and prevalence peaks between age 40 to 49 years (1). The worldwide prevalence of HCV infection is even higher at 2.0%, corresponding to 140 million persons (2).

In terms of complications, cirrhosis due to HCV disease is the most frequent indication for liver transplantation in the United States (3), and the overall incidence of hepatocellular carcinoma, a complication of HCV cirrhosis, continues to increase at alarming rates. In an evaluation of population-based registries of the Surveillance, Epidemiology, and End Results (SEER) program in the United States, the overall age-adjusted incidence rates of hepatocellular carcinoma increased from 1.4 per 100 000 in 1975 to 1977 to 3.0 per 100 000 in 1996 to 1998 (4).

Prevention

What factors increase the risk for hepatitis C virus (HCV) infection?
The predominant risk factor for the transmission of HCV is percutaneous exposure to infected blood, which most commonly takes place through remote or chronic injection drug use. Transmission of HCV historically occurred with transfusion of blood products before screening of the blood supply in the United States before 1992. There seems to be no increased risk for HCV transmission through cosmetic procedures, such as tattooing and piercings, unless infection control measures are not followed (5).

Transmission of HCV in health care workers after a needle-stick exposure occurs in up to 10% of cases (6). Additionally, the prevalence of HCV infection in hemodialysis patients is approximately 8.9% in the United States, with higher rates in developing countries (7). Nosocomial outbreaks have also been reported to be related to failures in infection control, such as reuse of needles and syringes as well as multidose vials and saline bags to make flushes (8).

Sexual intercourse is another mode of HCV transmission, but persons in long-term monogamous partnerships have a lower risk (0% to 0.6% per year) than persons with multiple partners or those at risk for sexually transmitted infections (0.4% to 1.8%

per year) (9). Mother-to-child transmission in the presence of HCV viremia in the mother is approximately 4% to 7%. However, the risk for HCV transmission to the neonate increases up to 4- to 5-fold when the mother has both HCV and HIV infection (10).

How can individuals, including those who live with an infected individual, reduce their risk for HCV infection?
Avoidance of high-risk behaviors is the mainstay of risk reduction in HCV. Treatment programs or needle-exchange programs should be considered if available for persons injecting drugs. These programs have demonstrated reductions in high-risk practices, such as sharing needles, but the evidence has been less convincing for reductions in HCV transmission (11).

A recent study of a Dutch cohort of 714 injection drug users found that the combination of a methadone program and a needle-exchange program led to a decreased risk for HIV seroconversion (incidence rate ratio, 0.43 [95% CI, 0.21 to 0.87]) and HCV (incidence rate ratio, 0.36 [CI, 0.13 to 1.03]) when compared with no treatment (12).

Individuals infected with HCV who have multiple sexual partners should be advised to use condoms to prevent transmission of HCV and other sexually transmitted infections (3) (Monogamous couples should also be advised that condoms may reduce the risk for transmission, but they are not routinely recommended because of the low risk for sexual transmission in this situation). The exact risk for horizontal transmission of HCV to household contacts of individuals with active HCV infection remains unclear, but avoiding sharing razors, toothbrushes, and nail clippers with an individual with chronic HCV infection is recommended. Although this advice was initially based on general recommendations for preventing transmission of blood-borne infections (13), samples from toothbrushes from infected individuals have been shown to contain HCV RNA (14), and sharing of razors has been found to be an independent risk factor for HCV infection (15).

How can risk for HCV infection be reduced in the health care setting?

Health care workers and volunteers should follow appropriate infection control practices to decrease their personal risk for infection and to reduce the risk for spreading HCV from one patient to another. For example, health care workers should never reuse a needle or syringe from another patient to withdraw medicine from a vial or bag of intravenous fluids. Medicines in multidose vials may present a particular risk, and a new needle and clean syringe should always be used to access the medication from such containers (16).

Risk Factors for HCV Infection

- Injection drug use (past or present)
- Receipt of clotting factor concentrates produced before 1987
- Long-term hemodialysis treatment
- Repeatedly elevated (or unexplained intermittently elevated) serum alanine aminotransferase levels
- Receipt of blood or blood components (for example, red cells, platelets, fresh-frozen plasma) or solid-organ transplants before July 1992
- Receipt of blood from an HCV-positive donor
- Specific high-risk exposure to known HCV-positive blood in health care workers, (e.g., needle-sticks or other sharp exposure or mucosal exposure [splash accidents])
- HIV infection
- Being the child of HCV-positive woman
- History of multiple sex partners or sexually transmitted infections
- Sharing razors

Prevention... The most significant risk factor for acquiring HCV infection is percutaneous exposure, historically through transfusion of blood products and now most commonly through injection drug use. Although sexual transmission risk is low and condom use is not routinely recommended for monogamous couples, it is recommended for HCV-positive patients with multiple sex partners. Sharing razors, toothbrushes, and nail clippers should be avoided. Infection control practices are critical to reduce the risk to health care workers and among patients in health care settings.

CLINICAL BOTTOM LINE

Screening

Should clinicians screen patients for hepatitis C infection?

In 2004, the U.S. Preventive Services Task Force concluded that there were inadequate data to recommend screening healthy asymptomatic adults for hepatitis C infection. The report highlighted the lack of published trials of screening for HCV infection and the absence of data that treatment improved long-term outcomes (17).

This recommendation was strongly challenged by members of the national societies of gastroenterology and hepatology, who felt that, because of the long natural history of HCV infection, it would be inappropriate to wait several decades to be able to prove the benefit of screening. They emphasized that treatment must be provided before the onset of complications of cirrhosis and recommended continued screening of persons with risk factors for HCV infection (Box) (18).

What test should clinicians use when screening for hepatitis C infection?

The test of choice to screen for HCV infection is the antibody to HCV by enzyme-linked immunosorbent assay (ELISA). Performed with second- or third-generation assays, the ELISA has a sensitivity of 98.9% to 100% and a specificity of 99.3% to 100% (19).

10. Roberts EA, Yeung L. Maternal-infant transmission of hepatitis C virus infection. Hepatology. 2002;36:S106-13. [PMID: 12407583]
11. Hagan H, Thiede H. Changes in injection risk behavior associated with participation in the Seattle needle-exchange program. J Urban Health. 2000;77:369-82. [PMID: 10976611]
12. Amsterdam Cohort. Full participation in harm reduction programmes is associated with decreased risk for human immunodeficiency virus and hepatitis C virus: evidence from the Amsterdam Cohort Studies among drug users. Addiction. 2007;102:1454-62. [PMID: 17697278]
13. Shapiro CN. Transmission of hepatitis viruses [Editorial]. Ann Intern Med. 1994;120:82-4. [PMID: 8250462]
14. Lock G, Dirscherl M, Obermeier F, et al. Hepatitis C - contamination of toothbrushes: myth or reality? J Viral Hepat. 2006;13:571-3. [PMID: 16907842]

Diagnosis

Extrahepatic Manifestations of HCV Infection

- Arthritis
- Porphyria cutanea tarda
- Leukocytoclastic vasculitis
- Lichen planus
- Raynaud phenomenon
- The sicca syndrome
- Idiopathic thrombocytopenic purpura
- Membranoproliferative glomerulonephritis
- Membranous nephropathy
- Hypo/hyperthyroidism
- Diabetes mellitus
- Essential mixed cryoglobulinemia
- Monoclonal gammopathy
- Non-Hodgkin lymphoma

Prevalence of Genotypes in Different Areas

1a: Northern Europe, United States
1b: Global, Southern Europe
2: Europe, North Africa
3: Southeast Asia
4: Middle East
5: South Africa
6: Asia

What is the clinical spectrum of hepatitis C infection?

At the time of acute infection with HCV, most individuals are asymptomatic. Among symptomatic patients with acute infection, jaundice may occur, but the presentation is more commonly nonspecific with fatigue, nausea, abdominal pain, or flu-like symptoms. Acute liver failure due to HCV infection is very uncommon. Chronic infection develops in 74% to 86% of exposed patients over time, during which patients usually remain asymptomatic. Most patients with chronic HCV infection present with abnormal liver tests, although many may have normal alanine aminotransferase levels and up to 20% of those with normal levels may have significant fibrosis on liver biopsy (20).

Cirrhosis develops in 15% to 20% of chronically infected patients, although natural history data are limited given the prolonged course of disease and the small number of prospective cohort studies. Patients with cirrhosis may then progress to develop the complications of portal hypertension. The risk for hepatocellular carcinoma is up to 3% per year among patients with cirrhosis (3). Those with advanced disease have fatigue, jaundice, lower extremity edema, ascites, altered mental status due to hepatic encephalopathy, or gastrointestinal bleeding from varices or portal gastropathy. Additional findings of chronic liver disease, such as splenomegaly, spider angiomata, caput medusae, and gynecomastia, may be seen. An abdominal mass in a patient with anorexia and weight loss suggests HCV-related hepatocellular carcinoma.

Patients with HCV infection may present with manifestations of other related disorders (Box).

In a series of 321 patients, 38% had at least 1 extrahepatic manifestation of HCV infection, including arthralgia, skin manifestations, xerostomia, xerophthalmia, and sensory neuropathy. Mixed cryoglobulins were found in 56% of patients, and at least 1 autoantibody was found in 70% (21).

What laboratory tests should clinicians use to diagnose hepatitis C infection?

A positive antibody to HCV by ELISA should prompt measurement of HCV RNA by polymerase chain reaction to confirm chronic infection. Quantitative HCV RNA viral load should be obtained to serve as a baseline, although there is poor correlation between viral load and hepatic histology. For those with detectable viral loads, HCV genotype should be obtained in any patient being considered for therapy, because genotype affects likelihood of treatment response and duration of therapy (22). Specific genotypes are more prevalent in different areas of the world (Box). Most other liver function studies lack specificity, and other laboratory tests should be reserved for patients with evidence of cirr-hosis or extrahepatic manifestations of HCV infection (Table 1).

When should clinicians consider liver biopsy?

Once HCV infection has been confirmed with HCV RNA testing,

Table 1. Laboratory Tests and Other Studies for Hepatitis C*

Test	Notes
HCV Ab ELISA (first-line assay)	Sensitivity and specificity of 93% to 99%; positive results do not distinguish between acute, chronic, or resolved infection; may be falsely negative in immunosuppressed patients or patients on hemodialysis
HCV RNA	Use to assess for chronic HCV infection if the HCV Ab ELISA is positive; positive result is associated with chronic infection
ALT and AST levels	ALT levels are the most common abnormality in HCV infection; usually <10 times the upper reference level; underestimates infection and lacks specificity for HCV
Other liver function tests	Prothrombin time and levels of total bilirubin, total protein, albumin, and alkaline phosphatase are usually normal until end-stage liver disease is present
CBC with platelet counts	Low platelets can suggest the presence of cirrhosis; low sensitivity
Serum ferritin level	Elevated levels of ferritin are found in many patients with chronic hepatitis C
ANA and anti-smooth muscle antibodies	Antibody testing has low sensitivity and specificity; low levels are often present in chronic hepatitis C but have no clinical relevance
HIV antibody by ELISA	Risk factors for HIV and HCV are similar; all patients with HCV infection should be screened for HIV infection
HBV serologies	All patients with HCV infection should be screened for HBV infection
HCV genotyping	Only assess when HCV RNA is present; high sensitivity and specificity; useful in determining treatment-response rates and duration of treatment
Imaging studies (ultrasonography, CT, or MRI of the liver)	Usually reserved for the patients with a likely diagnosis of cirrhosis
Special tests (cryoglobulin level, urinary porphyrin level)	Testing for cryoglobulins is appropriate in patients with evidence of vasculitis or glomerulonephritis; testing for urinary porphyrins is appropriate when porphyria cutanea tarda is suspected

*ALT = alanine aminotransferase; ANA = antinuclear antibody; AST = aspartate aminotransferase; CBC = complete blood count; CT = computed tomography; MRI = magnetic resonance imaging; ELISA = enzyme-linked immunosorbent assay; Ab = antibody; HBV = hepatitis B virus; HCV = hepatitis C virus; HIV = human immunodeficiency virus; RNA = ribonucleic acid.

clinicians should consider the potential value of additional information afforded by liver biopsy. Given the significant side effects and modest response rates in genotypes 1 and 4 associated with drug treatment, clinicians may decide to recommend biopsy to help identify patients at greatest risk for disease progression. In this case, patients with moderate-to-severe fibrosis on liver biopsy should be considered for treatment, whereas patients with minimal or no fibrosis on liver biopsy may defer treatment given the slow natural history of HCV infection and the minimal risk for complications in the early stages of disease. However, even in patients with normal alanine aminotransferase levels, liver biopsy may demonstrate the presence of significant fibrosis, a finding that would lead to consideration of therapy (24). Biopsy can also help clinicians assess the risk versus benefit of treatment in patients with relative contraindications to therapy. Liver biopsy may thus be a helpful tool in making treatment decisions, and repeated determination of

hepatic histology over time is useful to decrease sampling error and estimate rate of progression. However, liver biopsy should not be an absolute requirement in the evaluation process for patients who desire treatment regardless of biopsy findings (3). Moreover, some have suggested that liver biopsy is not necessary in genotype 2 or 3 infection given the higher response rates to treatment.

What other hepatic conditions have clinical presentations similar to hepatitis C infection?

Because the symptoms and laboratory abnormalities associated with HCV infection are nonspecific, and infected individuals are most often asymptomatic, the differential diagnosis of HCV-related liver disease is particularly broad. Any liver disease causing mild-to-moderate elevations in levels of transaminases or cirrhosis should be considered (Table 2). In addition, HCV infection can occur in patients with other liver diseases; therefore, additional testing may be warranted.

15. Sawayama Y, Hayashi J, Kakuda K, et al. Hepatitis C virus infection in institutionalized psychiatric patients: possible role of transmission by razor sharing. Dig Dis Sci. 2000;45:351-6. [PMID: 10711450]

16. Siegel JD, Rhinehart E, Jackson, M, et al., and the Healthcare Infection Control Practices Advisory Committee. Guideline for Isolation Precautions: Preventing Transmission of Infectious Agents in Healthcare Settings 2007, June 2007. Accessed at www.cdc.gov/ncidod/dhqp/pdf/guidelines/Isolation2007.pdf on 14 April 2008.

17. U.S. Preventive Services Task Force. Screening for hepatitis C virus infection: a review of the evidence for the U.S. Preventive Services Task Force. Ann Intern Med. 2004; 140:465-79. [PMID: 15023713]

18. Alter MJ, Seeff LB, Bacon BR, Thomas DL, Rigsby MO, Di Bisceglie AM. Testing for hepatitis C virus infection should be routine for persons at increased risk for infection. Ann Intern Med. 2004;141:715-7. [PMID: 15520428]

Table 2. Differential Diagnosis of Hepatitis C*

Disease	Characteristics	Laboratory Work–Up
Chronic hepatitis B and D	Epidemiologic features resemble those of chronic hepatitis C	Test for HBsAg and anti-HBc; if positive, testing for anti-HDV is appropriate
Autoimmune hepatitis	Largely affects women, other autoimmune disorders may be present, including autoimmune thyroiditis; Sjogren syndrome; and celiac sprue	Test for ANA and serum immunoglobulin levels
Drug-induced chronic hepatitis	History of drug use and improvement on discontinuation of drug	Liver biopsy sometimes used in diagnosis but usually not needed, as discontinuation of the offending agent is necessary in management
Metabolic and genetic disorders (e.g., hemachromatosis, Wilson disease, α_1-antitrypsin deficiency)	Iron overload is not usually clinically evident until mid-life; Wilson disease is rarely diagnosed after age 40	Testing for iron overload (serum iron level, transferrin saturation, genetic testing, and if necessary, hepatic iron index based on quantitative measurement of iron in liver biopsy sample); testing for Wilson disease (serum ceruloplasmin level, serum and urinary copper levels in patients <40 years, and if necessary, measurement of hepatic copper concentration in liver biopsy sample); test for α_1-antitrypsin deficiency (serum level and phenotype); obtain stain of liver biopsy tissue, if available, for PAS–positive diastase-resistant globules
Alcoholic hepatitis	AST level exceeds ALT level in 90% of cases; history of excessive alcohol consumption and improvement on discontinuation	Liver biopsy demonstrates histologic features of alcoholic hepatitis although liver biopsy often not necessary for diagnosis
Nonalcoholic steatohepatitis	Associated with diabetes mellitus, obesity, and other disorders; requires the absence of history of alcohol consumption	Steatohepatitis is confirmed by liver biopsy

* ALT = alanine aminotransferase; ANA = antinuclear antibody; anti-HBc = anti–hepatitis B core antigen; AST = aspartate aminotransferase; HBsAg = hepatitis B surface antigen; HDV = hepatitis D virus; PAS = periodic acid-Schiff.

Diagnosis... Chronic HCV infection is usually asymptomatic, and most patients present with abnormal liver function tests. The diagnosis may also be suggested by extrahepatic manifestations or signs and symptoms of portal hypertension or hepatocellular carcinoma. Diagnosis is suggested with the antibody to HCV by ELISA and confirmed with the HCV RNA by polymerase chain reaction. Clinicians should consider liver biopsy to evaluate the degree of fibrosis and guide treatment decisions.

CLINICAL BOTTOM LINE

19. Vrielink H, Reesink HW, van den Burg PJ, et al. Performance of three generations of anti-hepatitis C virus enzyme-linked immunosorbent assays in donors and patients. Transfusion. 1997;37:845-9. [PMID: 9280331]
20. Alberti A. Towards more individualised management of hepatitis C virus patients with initially or persistently normal alanineaminotransferase levels. J Hepatol. 2005;42:266. [PMID: 15664254]
21. Cacoub P, Renou C, Rosenthal E, et al. Extrahepatic manifestations associated with hepatitis C virus infection. A prospective multicenter study of 321 patients. The GERMIVIC. Groupe d'Etude et de Recherche en Medecine Interne et Maladies Infectieuses sur le Virus de l'Hepatite C. Medicine (Baltimore). 2000;79:47-56. [PMID: 10670409]

Treatment

Are dietary and other lifestyle interventions helpful in the management of hepatitis C infection?

Alcoholic liver disease often complicates HCV-related liver disease. The presence of cirrhosis has been shown to be hastened by increased alcohol consumption in HCV-infected individuals, and abstinence from alcohol is therefore recommended (25).

Hepatotoxic drugs should clearly be avoided in patients with any liver disease. Use of acetaminophen in normal doses is not contraindicated, but clinicians and patients should be aware of the danger of intentional or accidental overdose through heavy use of multiple analgesics containing acetaminophen (26). Similar care should be taken with non-steroidal anti-inflammatory drugs, which are particularly risky in patients with cirrhosis.

A low-sodium diet is recommended for patients with cirrhosis and ascites complicating HCV infection, but no specific dietary interventions are necessary at earlier stages of disease. Protein restriction should be avoided in patients with cirrhosis.

Are complementary-alternative therapies useful in the treatment of patients with hepatitis C infection?

According to the evidence, herbal remedies, such as milk thistle, do not improve the outlook for HCV infection.

A systematic review of randomized clinical trials in patients with alcoholic liver disease, hepatitis B infection, and HCV determined that the overall methodological quality of trials was low. Although milk thistle was not associated with a statistically significantly increased risk for adverse events (RR, 0.83; CI, 0.46 to 1.50), it had no statistically significant effect on mortality (RR, 0.78; CI, 0.53 to 1.15), complications of liver disease (RR, 0.95; CI, 0.83 to 1.09), or liver histology (27).

In the case of milk thistle, no significant harm has been observed in studies to date (27). However, a number of herbal remedies, such as chaparral, leaf germander, jin bu huan, kava kombucha mushroom, margosa oil, mistletoe, pennyroyal, pyrrolizidine alkaloids, and traditional Chinese herbs, are known to be hepatotoxic (28). Patients with HCV infection should avoid using these remedies.

When should clinicians consider drug therapy for hepatitis C infection?

Clinicians should consider antiviral therapy in any patient who has no absolute contraindications (Box) for treatment, compensated liver disease (absence of ascites and encephalopathy), and detectable serum HCV RNA, especially if they have clinical or histologic signs of progression. Treatment for HCV is safe in patients with compensated cirrhosis; however, the presence of advanced fibrosis or cirrhosis is associated with decreased treatment response.

An alternative strategy is to perform periodic liver biopsies to assess progression of liver disease. Although there are no data to indicate the appropriate interval between liver biopsies, pending better evidence the consensus of opinion is that every 3 to 5 years is reasonable.

Although the effects of the 2 strategies (biopsy versus empirical treatment) have not been compared in randomized trials, both have merit given the substantial side effects of drug treatment for HCV disease and the modest response rates. Each individual patient therefore requires thorough evaluation and discussion of the risks and benefits of treatment (3).

What are the contraindications to drug therapy for hepatitis C infection?

Contraindications to HCV therapy are listed in the Box. Ribavirin is contraindicated in pregnancy because of its teratogenicity. Ribavirin is cleared by the kidney, and its side effects, including hemolysis, can be severe in patients with renal insufficiency or those on hemodialysis. Treatment with interferon-α compounds has been associated with severe neuropsychiatric side effects, including suicide. Therefore, patients with a history of depression should be considered for HCV treatment only with close monitoring for exacerbation of psychiatric symptoms during treatment (3).

The most recent National Institutes of Health Consensus Conference Statement did not include active alcohol and illicit drug use as contraindications, and this remains an area of controversy. Alcohol use is associated with a decreased response rate to therapy, and cessation of alcohol use before initiation of drug therapy for hepatitis C infection should thus be encouraged. Formal alcohol treatment programs should be considered in patients who abuse alcohol.

Contraindications to Antiviral Therapy with Pegylated Interferon-α and Ribavirin

- Uncontrolled major depression, particularly with past suicide attempts
- Autoimmune hepatitis or other autoimmune disorders, including thyroid disease
- Bone marrow, lung, heart, or kidney transplantation
- Severe hypertension, coronary heart disease, congestive heart failure, cerebral vascular disease, or other serious nonliver disorders likely to reduce life expectancy
- Renal insufficiency
- Noncompliance with office visits or medications
- Decompensated cirrhosis or hepatocellular carcinoma
- Pregnancy or inability to practice birth control methods
- Severe anemia, thrombocytopenia, or granulocytopenia

22. Recommendations for prevention and control of hepatitis C virus (HCV) infection and HCV-related chronic disease. Centers for Disease Control and Prevention. MMWR Recomm Rep. 1998;47:1-39. [PMID: 9790221]
23. Simmonds P. Viral heterogeneity of the hepatitis C virus. J Hepatol. 1999;31 Suppl 1:54-60. [PMID: 10622561]
24. Marcellin P. Hepatitis C: the clinical spectrum of the disease. J Hepatol. 1999;31 Suppl 1:9-16. [PMID: 10622554]
25. Wiley TE, McCarthy M, Breidi L, et al. Impact of alcohol on the histological and clinical progression of hepatitis C infection. Hepatology. 1998;28:805-9. [PMID: 9731576]
26. Benson GD, Koff RS, Tolman KG. The therapeutic use of acetaminophen in patients with liver disease. Am J Ther. 2005;12:133-41. [PMID: 15767831]

27. Rambaldi A, Jacobs BP, Iaquinto G, et al. Milk thistle for alcoholic and/or hepatitis B or C liver diseases—a systematic cochrane hepato-biliary group review with meta-analyses of randomized clinical trials. Am J Gastroenterol. 2005;100:2583-91. [PMID: 16279916]

28. Verma S, Thuluvath PJ. Complementary and alternative medicine in hepatology: review of the evidence of efficacy. Clin Gastroenterol Hepatol. 2007;5:408-16. [PMID: 17222587]

29. Singal AK, Anand BS. Mechanisms of synergy between alcohol and hepatitis C virus. J Clin Gastroenterol. 2007;41: 761-72. [PMID: 17700425]

30. Bica I, McGovern B, Dhar R, et al. Increasing mortality due to end-stage liver disease in patients with human immunodeficiency virus infection. Clin Infect Dis. 2001;32:492-7. [PMID: 11170959]

31. ANRS HCO2 RIBAVIC Study Team. Pegylated interferon alfa-2b vs standard interferon alfa-2b, plus ribavirin, for chronic hepatitis C in HIV-infected patients: a randomized controlled trial. JAMA. 2004;292:2839-48. [PMID: 15598915]

32. Kim AI, Dorn A, Bouajram R, et al. The treatment of chronic hepatitis C in HIV-infected patients: a meta-analysis. HIV Med. 2007;8:312-21. [PMID: 17561878]

33. Lauer GM, Walker BD. Hepatitis C virus infection. N Engl J Med. 2001;345:41-52. [PMID: 11439948]

34. PEGASYS International Study Group. Peginterferon-alpha2a and ribavirin combination therapy in chronic hepatitis C: a randomized study of treatment duration and ribavirin dose. Ann Intern Med. 2004; 140:346-55. [PMID: 14996676]

35. Fried MW, Shiffman ML, Reddy KR, et al. Peginterferon alfa-2a plus ribavirin for chronic hepatitis C virus infection. N Engl J Med. 2002; 347:975-82. [PMID: 12324553]

A systematic review indicates that patients with HCV infection who abuse alcohol develop more severe fibrosis, cirrhosis, and hepatocellular cancer than nondrinkers. They have a lower rate of response to drug treatment with interferon as a result of nonadherence (29).

Small studies have demonstrated the feasibility and effectiveness of HCV treatment in patients in methadone programs and in those using illicit injection drugs. Patients actively using drugs should therefore be considered on a case-by-case basis by HCV infection treatment programs with appropriate multidisciplinary resources (3).

Clinicians should strongly consider antiviral therapy in patients with both HIV and HCV infection. With improved survival in HIV-infected patients in the past decade, complications of chronic liver disease have become more common among these patients (30). Although increased rates of acute pancreatitis and lactic acidosis were initially reported in patients treated with highly active antiretroviral treatment regimens containing didanosine along with ribavirin (31), a meta-analysis of recent studies of pegylated interferon-α and ribavirin report sustained virologic response rates of 26% to 44% overall and 14% to 38% in patients with genotype 1 with low incidence of pancreatitis and lactic acidosis (32). Pegylated interferon-α-2α combined with ribavirin is approved by the U.S. Food and Drug Administration for treatment of patients coinfected with HIV and HCV.

Which drugs are effective in the treatment of hepatitis C infection, and how should clinicians choose from among available treatment regimens?

The optimal treatment in previously untreated patients with hepatitis C infection is combination therapy with pegylated interferon-α and ribavirin (Table 3). Pegylated interferon-α is traditional

interferon-α attached to a polyethylene glycol chain, which functions to decrease renal clearance, increase stability, and prolong action. The 2 currently commercially available preparations are pegylated interferon-α-2a and pegylated interferon-α-2b. A large prospective head-to-head trial comparing the 2 pegylated interferon-α preparations has recently been completed, and results are expected soon, but to date there is no compelling evidence of the superiority of one over the other. Subcutaneous injections of pegylated interferon-α are administered once weekly, and ribavirin is given by mouth in divided doses twice daily.

Genotype should determine the treatment duration and likelihood of response. Genotype 1 infection is most common in the United States and requires 48 weeks of therapy; genotypes 2 and 3 require 24 weeks of therapy and have much higher response rates (33). The standard dose of ribavirin for HCV genotype 1 is weight-based (800 to 1400 mg/d); however, the dose is fixed and lower (800 mg/d) for genotypes 2 and 3 (34) (Table 3). Both available pegylated interferons have been shown to be more effective than unmodified interferon-α in large, randomized trials.

In a prospective, randomized, controlled trial (RCT), 1121 patients with chronic HCV infection received 1 of 3 regimens: pegylated interferon-α-2a 180 µg weekly plus daily ribavirin (1000 or 1200 mg, depending on body weight); pegylated interferon-α-2a plus daily placebo; or 3 million units of unmodified interferon-α-2b 3 times weekly plus daily ribavirin. Sustained virologic response (defined as the absence of detectable HCV RNA 24 weeks after cessation of therapy) was higher in patients receiving pegylated interferon-α-2a and ribavirin than among those who received unmodified interferon-α-2b plus ribavirin (56% vs. 44%; P < 0.001) or pegylated interferon-α-2a alone (56% vs. 29%; P < 0.001). Among patients with genotype 1 infection, the highest sustained virologic response

Table 3. Drug Treatment for Hepatitis C with Pegylated Interferon Regimens*

Agent	Mechanism of Action	Dosage	Benefits	Side Effects	Notes
Pegylated interferon-α-2a, and α-2b monotherapy	Antiviral, immunomodulatory	For interferon-α-2a, 180 µg sc weekly. For interferon α-2b, 1.0 µg/kg sc weekly	Sustained virologic response rate of 25% to 39%	Flulike illness, fatigue, depression or severe mental illness, cytopenias, rashes, and thyroid dysfunction; teratogen	Contraindicated in the presence of severe depression, cytopenias, or pregnancy
Pegylated interferon-α-2a plus ribavirin	Antiviral, immunomodulatory	For interferon-α-2a, 180 µg sc weekly, plus ribavirin, 800 mg daily for genotypes 2 and 3 1000 to 1200 mg daily for genotype 1 depending on weight[†]	Sustained virologic response rate of 54%; genotype 1, 42%; genotypes 2 or 3, 82%	As above with pegylated interferon-α monotherapy plus hemolytic anemia	Contraindicated as with pegylated interferon-α-2a and 2b (see above) and in the presence of renal failure, anemia, and significant or unstable CAD
Pegylated interferon-α-2b plus ribavirin	Antiviral, immunomodulatory	For interferon-α-2b, 1.5 µg/kg sc weekly plus ribavirin 800 mg po daily for genotypes 2 and 3 and 800 to 1400 mg daily for genotype 1, depending on weight[†]	Sustained virologic genotype 1, 42%; genotypes 2 and 3, 82%	As above with pegylated interferon-α monotherapy plus hemolytic anemia	Contraindicated as with pegylated interferon-α-2a and 2b (see above) and in the presence of renal failure, anemia, and significant or unstable CAD

* CAD = coronary artery disease; HCV = hepatitis C virus; po = oral; RNA = ribonucleic acid; sc = subcutaneous.
† Duration of therapy is typically 12 months. Six months is adequate for genotypes 2 and 3, but cirrhotic patients are often treated for 12 months. Testing for HCV RNA after 12 weeks of treatment is useful in deciding whether to continue therapy (if HCV RNA is negative or there is a >2-log decrease in viral load) for an additional 9 months in genotype 1.

(46%) occurred in the pegylated interferon-α-2a and ribavirin group (35).

In another prospective RCT, 1530 patients with chronic HCV infection received 1 of 3 regimens: high-dose pegylated interferon-α-2b (1.5 µg per kilogram body weight), lower-dose pegylated interferon-α-2b (1.0 µg per kilogram body weight) with ribavirin, and unmodified interferon-α-2b with ribavirin. In all genotypes, high-dose pegylated interferon-α with ribavirin led to an increased sustained virologic response (54%) compared with lower-dose pegylated interferon-α (47%) or unmodified interferon (47%) in combination with ribavirin. The sustained virologic response rate in patients with genotype 1 was 42% with higher-dose pegylated interferon-α-2b with ribavirin in contrast to those with genotype 2 or 3, in which the sustained virologic response rate was approximately 80% (36).

Factors associated with a higher sustained virologic response in these studies included genotypes other than 1, lower baseline HCV RNA, minimum fibrosis, lower body weight, and ethnicity (not African-American). Multiple studies have now shown that African-Americans have a reduced response rate to HCV treatment, but approximately 25% of African-American patients will respond (37).

Which vaccinations should patients with hepatitis C infection receive?

Clinicians should question patients with HCV infection about previous vaccinations or exposure to hepatitis A (HAV) and hepatitis B (HBV). If exposure or vaccination or disease cannot be documented, anti-HBs should be measured, and if negative, the patient should receive the HBV vaccination series. The cost–benefit ratio may favor empirical HAV vaccination rather than measurement of antibody followed by vaccine if antibody is absent (38). All patients with HCV infection should receive the influenza vaccine annually (39), and patients

36. Manns MP, McHutchison JG, Gordon SC, et al. Peginterferon alfa-2b plus ribavirin compared with interferon alfa-2b plus ribavirin for initial treatment of chronic hepatitis C: a randomised trial. Lancet. 2001;358: 958-65. [PMID: 11583749]
37. Virahep-C Study Group. Peginterferon and ribavirin treatment in African American and Caucasian American patients with hepatitis C genotype 1. Gastroenterology. 2006;131:470-7. [PMID: 16890601]
38. Jakiche R, Borrego ME, Raisch DW, et al. The cost-effectiveness of two strategies for vaccinating US veterans with hepatitis C virus infection against hepatitis A and hepatitis B viruses. Am J Med Sci. 2007;333: 26-34. [PMID: 17220691]

with cirrhosis should also receive the pneumococcal vaccine (40). These vaccines should be administered regardless of whether the patient receives drug treatment for HCV infection.

What is the appropriate clinical management for patients who do not respond to hepatitis C therapy or who relapse after an initial response?

There are 2 main categories of suboptimal response to hepatitis C treatment: nonresponse and relapse. Nonresponders demonstrate little or no response to treatment, whereas relapsers have undetectable HCV RNA at the end of treatment but detectable levels in follow-up monitoring.

Currently, there are no approved treatments for patients who do not initially respond to pegylated interferon-α and ribavirin. When evaluating patients with previous relapse or nonresponse to therapy, it is critical to evaluate the previous course of therapy. If patients relapsed after standard interferon monotherapy or combination interferon- α with ribavirin, they may benefit from treatment with pegylated interferon-α and ribavirin. If patients were nonresponders, it is important to determine whether any deficiencies in the first treatment could be improved with the second course. If a patient was nonadherent during the first course of treatment, a second course might be considered if it is believed that the patient may be more adherent on repeat treatment. If the previous dosing of medicine was incorrect or if inappropriate dose reductions occurred, treatment could be considered again. Merely repeating the same course of therapy is very unlikely to benefit the patient unless there is a realistic possibility of improving on the previous treatment experience. Treatment decisions in nonresponders can be aided greatly by examination of liver histology.

For patients who do not respond or who relapse after standard treatment, referral to a hepatologist for consideration of alternative approaches to standard therapy or enrollment in clinical trials should be considered. One recent strategy in clinical trials has been long-term maintenance therapy to theoretically reduce the risk for cirrhosis and portal hypertension. Early results from these studies have demonstrated conflicting findings, and there is insufficient evidence at this point to support this approach (41). Direct antiviral therapies, such as protease and polymerase inhibitors, are in the early phases of clinical trials and thus are not approved for treatment of HCV disease (42). In view of early data suggesting viral resistance to these agents used as monotherapy, these medications are being administered in combination with pegylated interferon-α and ribavirin, and results from these trials are expected over the next several years.

What are the side effects of hepatitis C drugs and how should clinicians manage patients who develop side effects?

Therapy for HCV puts patients at risk for substantial side effects and requires diligent monitoring. The most common side effects are listed in Table 4. Although practitioners often tolerate lower neutrophil counts because the risk for infection is low (43), the current labels for pegylated interferon-α recommend dose reduction when neutrophil counts are less than 750 cells/mL and consideration of discontinuation for counts less than 500 cells/mL. Doses should be reduced when patients develop thrombocytopenia and when hemoglobin levels are less than 10 g/dL. Efforts should be made to avoid dose reductions and interruptions in treatment because retrospective analyses have suggested that these events for both pegylated interferon-α and ribavirin are

39. Immunization of health-care workers: recommendations of the Advisory Committee on Immunization Practices (ACIP) and the Hospital Infection Control Practices Advisory Committee (HICPAC). MMWR Recomm Rep. 1997; 46:1-42. [PMID: 9427216]

40. Prevention of pneumococcal disease: recommendations of the Advisory Committee on Immunization Practices (ACIP). MMWR Recomm Rep. 1997;46:1-24. [PMID: 9132580]

41. Kelleher TB, Afdhal N. Maintenance therapy for chronic hepatitis C. Curr Gastroenterol Rep. 2005;7:50-3. [PMID: 15701299]

42. Forestier N, Reesink HW, Weegink CJ, et al. Antiviral activity of telaprevir (VX-950) and peginterferon alfa-2a in patients with hepatitis C. Hepatology. 2007;46:640-8. [PMID: 17879366]

Table 4. Side Effects of Drugs Used in the Treatment of Hepatitis C

Common Interferon-α Side Effects
   Fatigue
   Flulike symptoms
   Nausea and vomiting
   Headaches
   Low-grade fever
   Weight loss
   Irritability
   Depression
   Hair thinning
   Bone marrow suppression
   Irritation at the injection site
Common Ribavirin Side Effects
   Hemolytic anemia
   Fatigue
   Pruritus
   Rashes
   Cough, bronchospasm, dyspnea
Uncommon Interferon-α Monotherapy and Combination Therapy Side Effects
   Autoimmune thyroiditis
   Seizures
   Suicidal ideation or attempts
   Retinopathy
   Sepsis
   Myocardial infarction
   Pulmonary fibrosis

associated with lower treatment response (3).

Erythropoietin and granulocyte colony-stimulating factor therapies have been used to correct cytopenias associated with therapy. Erythropoietin has been associated with improved quality of life and ability to maintain higher ribavirin doses on treatment; however, no data can adequately demonstrate the clinical benefit on virologic response compared with the risk of this approach (44). In 2007, the U.S. Food and Drug Administration issued a Public Safety Advisory on the potential dangers of erythropoiesis-stimulating agents, and a black box warning was added to the labels of these drugs noting serious cardiovascular and arterial and venous thromboembolic events (45). In regard to the management of thrombocytopenia, therapy with thrombopoietin-receptor agonists is an exciting advance in the treatment of liver disease, especially in patients with portal hypertension and hypersplenism.

Further studies regarding their use are needed (46).

How should clinicians evaluate the response to hepatitis C drug therapy?
Assessing HCV RNA titers is the mainstay of monitoring response to antiviral treatment. The goal of treatment is sustained virologic response, which means that the patient has undetectable HCV RNA for 6 months after cessation of therapy. A baseline viral load should be drawn at or just before initiation of therapy. In order to prevent patients from receiving long courses of therapy with little chance of response, retrospective analyses of randomized trials of patients with genotype 1 infection have suggested determining viral load at week 12 for early virologic response, defined as at least a 2-log reduction in HCV RNA compared with baseline. As a result, patients who do not achieve early virologic response should discontinue treatment. If patients achieve early virologic response, their next landmark is week 24, and HCV RNA should be

43. Soza A, Everhart JE, Ghany MG, et al. Neutropenia during combination therapy of interferon alfa and ribavirin for chronic hepatitis C. Hepatology. 2002;36:1273-9. [PMID: 12395340]
44. PROACTIVE Study Group. Epoetin alfa improves quality of life in anemic HCV-infected patients receiving combination therapy. Hepatology. 2004;40:1450-8. [PMID: 15565613]
45. U.S. Food and Drug Administration. FDA Public Health Advisory: Erythropoiesis-Stimulating Agents (ESAs). Accessed at www.fda.gov/cder/drug/advisory/RHE2007.htm on 14 April 2008.
46. TPL102357 Study Group. Eltrombopag for thrombocytopenia in patients with cirrhosis associated with hepatitis C. N Engl J Med. 2007;357:2227-36. [PMID: 18046027]

undetectable by this time point, or treatment should be halted.

In a retrospective analysis of a large clinical trial database, 131 of 511 patients receiving pegylated interferon-α-2b and ribavirin did not achieve early virologic response, and none of these patients went on to achieve sustained virologic response. Between 69% and 76% of patients did achieve this threshold, depending on the treatment regimen, and 67% to 80% achieved sustained virologic response (47).

More recently, there has been interest in measuring the viral load at 4 weeks to determine whether an individual has had a rapid virologic response, defined as an undetectable viral load at that time point. Whereas early virologic response assessment at 12 weeks has been studied and used in patients with genotype 1 infection, patients with genotype 1, 2, and 3 have been studied in clinical trials to determine whether treatment should be shortened or prolonged depending on the response at 4 weeks (48). These promising early studies require confirmation before changes are made in standard recommendations for monitoring.

Are there other drug regimens with documented effectiveness in the treatment of hepatitis C?
Unmodified interferon with or without ribavirin was previously used to treat HCV before pegylated interferon-α was introduced. Now the standard of care involves combination regimens that include pegylated interferon-α. However, monotherapy with pegylated interferon-α is used when there are contraindications to treatment with ribavirin, including renal insufficiency, hemoglobinopathies, and coronary or cerebral artery disease (49).

Is it possible to cure hepatitis C infection?
Hepatitis C infection is felt to be initially cured after achievement of a sustained virologic response. Although it is possible to have a relapse after a sustained virologic response, the likelihood is quite low. If sustained virologic response is achieved, at least 98% of patients maintain an undetectable viral load indefinitely, and maintenance of sustained virologic response for 2 years is synonymous with a cure of HCV infection (49). It should be emphasized, however, that antibody is not protective, and patients can be reinfected after successful therapy.

When is liver transplantation indicated for patients with hepatitis C infection?
Clinicians should refer patients with cirrhosis due to HCV infection for liver transplantation evaluation when their Model for End-Stage Liver Disease (MELD) score is 10 or greater following their first major complication of portal hypertension (for example, ascites, hepatic encephalopathy, or variceal bleeding). The MELD score is a logarithmic calculation derived from the patient's serum creatinine level, serum bilirubin level, and prothrombin time or international normalized ratio. The MELD score predicts survival in the next 3 months and leads to scores ranging from 6 (less ill) to 40 (gravely ill). The current organ allocation system for liver transplantation is based on the MELD score (50). Hepatocellular carcinoma is also an important indication for referral for liver transplantation.

What is the risk for hepatocellular carcinoma in patients with hepatitis C infection and should they undergo routine screening for this cancer?
Hepatocellular carcinoma complicating HCV infection typically develops in the setting of cirrhosis. The rate of occurrence is estimated at up to 3% per year after the development of cirrhosis (3). Practice guidelines recommend screening with ultrasonography

47. Davis GL, Wong JB, McHutchison JG, et al. Early virologic response to treatment with peginterferon alfa-2b plus ribavirin in patients with chronic hepatitis C. Hepatology. 2003;38:645-52. [PMID: 12939591]
48. Poordad F, Reddy KR, Martin P. Rapid virologic response: a new milestone in the management of chronic hepatitis C. Clin Infect Dis. 2008;46:78-84. [PMID: 18171217]
49. Dienstag JL, McHutchison JG. American Gastroenterological Association technical review on the management of hepatitis C. Gastroenterology. 2006;130:231-64; quiz 214-7. [PMID: 16401486]
50. AASLD. AASLD practice guidelines: Evaluation of the patient for liver transplantation. Hepatology. 2005;41:1407-32. [PMID: 15880505]
51. Zhang BH, Yang BH, Tang ZY. Randomized controlled trial of screening for hepatocellular carcinoma. J Cancer Res Clin Oncol. 2004;130:417-22. [PMID: 15042359]

every 6 to 12 months, although some of the data come from screening trials involving patients with chronic HBV disease (51).

In an RCT of 18 816 patients with HBV infection or history of chronic hepatitis in China, biannual screening with ultrasonography and α-fetoprotein was compared with no screening over a 20-year period. In the screened group, 32 people died from hepatocellular carcinoma compared with 54 in the control group, yielding rates of 83.2 per 100 000 and 131.5 per 100 000, respectively. The rate ratio for mortality was 0.63 (CI, 0.41 to 0.98) (51).

Serum α-fetoprotein has limited utility as a screening test but should be used if imaging is not available. Area under the receiver-operating curve analysis suggests that the optimal cutoff value is 20 ng/mL, but this level yields a sensitivity of only 60% (52).

When is specialty consultation indicated for patients with hepatitis C infection?

Referral to a hepatologist or infectious disease specialist is indicated if there are questions or concerns regarding the diagnosis or management of HCV infection. Distinguishing HCV infection from other or coexisting liver diseases, determining the need for liver biopsy, choosing the next steps in patients who did not respond to pegylated interferon-α and ribavirin, or
evaluating for liver transplantation should also prompt referral.

Treatment... Clinicians should individualize decisions on treatment of hepatitis C infection on the basis of stage of disease, clinical and laboratory evaluation, and patient preference. Standard treatment for HCV infection consists of pegylated interferon-α and ribavirin with dose and duration determined by genotype. Treatment success is sustained virologic response, defined as undetectable HCV RNA levels 6 months after cessation of therapy. Treatment requires close monitoring for side effects and evaluation of virologic response to determine whether to discontinue treatment early in patients who are not responding. Patients who do not respond to standard treatment should consider consultation for evaluation and consideration of other treatment strategies. Patients with cirrhosis and MELD scores of 10 or greater and those with hepatocellular carcinoma should be referred for liver transplantation evaluation. All patients should be considered for vaccination for hepatitis A, hepatitis B, and influenza; patients with cirrhosis should receive the pneumoccal vaccination.

CLINICAL BOTTOM LINE

Practice Improvement

What do professional organizations recommend with respect to hepatitis C infection?

The American Association for the Study of Liver Diseases Guidelines of the Diagnosis, Management and Treatment of HCV, published in 2004, provide recommendations on laboratory testing and counseling for hepatitis C as well as initial treatment of various patient groups, including children and
those with HIV co-infection, renal disease, or decompensated cirrhosis and those undergoing solid organ transplantation. Management of patients with acute HCV infection and those who are active drug users is also covered (53).

The American Gastroenterological Association Technical Review covers screening, natural history, and treatment of HCV in adults and

52. Practice Guidelines Committee, American Association for the Study of Liver Diseases. Management of hepatocellular carcinoma. Hepatology. 2005;42:1208-36. [PMID: 16250051]
53. American Association for the Study of Liver Diseases. Diagnosis, management, and treatment of hepatitis C. Hepatology. 2004;39:1147-71. [PMID: 15057920]

children as well as patients with renal disease and HIV co-infection, those actively using injection drugs, and recipients of liver transplants. Other treatment groups requiring particular consideration are patients with extrahepatic disease, African-Americans, and those with hematologic disorders (49).

The National Institutes of Health has released a Health Consensus Development Conference Statement on the management of hepatitis C covering its natural history, prevention, diagnosis, and areas for future research (3).

The U.S. Department for Veterans Affairs has issued guidelines covering epidemiology, prevention, testing, and counseling, as well as management of HIV/HCV co-infection and complications of HCV infection (54).

The United States Preventive Services Task Force issued guidelines in 2004 indicating that there were insufficient data to recommend screening for HCV infection in healthy individuals (17).

What measures do stakeholders use to evaluate the quality of care for patients with hepatitis C infection?

The Center for Medicare & Medicaid Services has issued specifications for performance measures for its 2008 Physicians Quality Reporting Initiative (PQRI). These include 5 measures applicable to patients with hepatitis C. Two involve HCV RNA as part of initial evaluation in all patients 18 years and older with the diagnosis and again within 6 months before initiating treatment. A third measure mandates HCV genotype testing before starting treatment. Two additional measures deal with treatment. The first involves consideration of drug treatment with pegylated interferon and ribavirin, and the second with HCV RNA testing at 12 weeks from initiation of antiviral treatment.

54. U.S. Department of Veterans Affairs. The United States Department for Veterans Affairs Hepatitis C Testing and Prevention Counseling Guidelines for VA Health Care Practitioners. Accessed at www.hepatitis.va.gov on 14 April 2008

in the clinic
Tool Kit
Hepatitis C Infection

PIER Module

pier.acponline.org/physicians/diseases/d163/d163.html
Access the PIER module on hepatitis C

Patient Information

www.annals/org/intheclinc/tools
Download copies of the Patient Information sheet that appears on the following page for duplication and distribution to your patients.

Centers for Disease Control and Prevention

www.cdc.gov
Patient handouts on HCV infection in English and other languages

National Institute for Diabetes and Digestive Diseases and Kidney Diseases of the National Institutes of Health (NIDDK)

digestive.niddk.nih.gov
Information for patients entitled "What I need to know about Hepatitis C."

American Liver Foundation

www.liverfoundation.org/
Patient information in question and answer format.

U.S. Veterans Affairs National Hepatitis C Program

www.hepatitis.va.gov/
Information about hepatitis C for patients and the public.

MELD Calculator

www.unos.org/resources/MeldPeldCalculator.asp?index-98
MELD Calculator for adult and pediatric patients.

Hepatitis C

What is Hepatitis C?

- Hepatitis C virus can cause liver disease.

- People can get hepatitis C virus if they share or have ever shared needles or have other contact with blood from someone with hepatitis C. People can also get hepatitis C if they have sex with many people.

- Most people don't know they have hepatitis C virus until they have blood tests that show it.

- If you have hepatitis C, you may get a liver biopsy. Biopsy takes a small piece of the liver to look at under a microscope to find out how bad the liver disease is.

Treatment

- There are medicines that can help hepatitis C disease. Ask your doctor whether these medicines might be right for you.

- Sometimes people with hepatitis C need to take medicines for many months.

- Be sure to take the medicines the way your doctor tells you and report any side effects.

- The medicines can cure hepatitis in some people but not in everyone.

- If you have hepatitis C, do not drink alcohol and check with your doctor before taking any drugs because some might hurt the liver.

Other Problems from Hepatitis C

- A few people who have hepatitis C for a long time can get scarring in the liver (cirrhosis) or liver cancer.

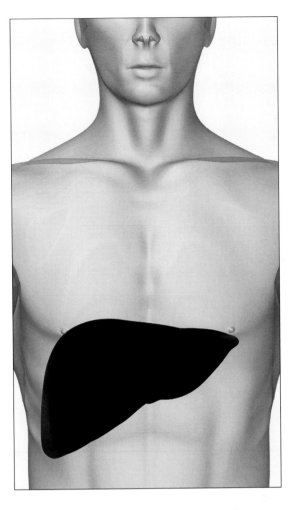

- People with cirrhosis need to see their doctor often to check for liver cancer.

- Sometimes people with cirrhosis or liver cancer have surgery to get a new liver (liver transplantation).

For More Information

Centers for Disease Control and Prevention (CDC)
Hepatitis C Prevention
www.cdc.gov/ncidod/diseases/hepatitis/c/hepcprev.htm
Viral Hepatitis C
www.cdc.gov/ncidod/diseases/hepatitis/c/index.htm

National Institute of Diabetes and Digestive and Kidney Diseases (NIDDK)
Chronic Hepatitis C: Current Disease Management
digestive.niddk.nih.gov/ddiseases/pubs/chronichepc/index.htm
What I Need to Know about Hepatitis C
digestive.niddk.nih.gov/ddiseases/pubs/hepc_ez/index.htm (English)
digestive.niddk.nih.gov/spanish/pubs/hepc_ez/index.htm (Spanish)

AMERICAN COLLEGE OF PHYSICIANS
INTERNAL MEDICINE | *Doctors for Adults*®

Patient Information

Acne

A cne (also known as acne vulgaris, true acne, or teenage acne) affects 85% of U.S. adolescents but also occurs in up to 78% of preadolescents, 12% of adult women, and 3% of adult men. In addition to cosmetic effects, which can include permanent scarring, acne can have detrimental effects on self-image and social interactions. The annual cost of acne care in the United States, including over-the-counter products, outpatient visits, and prescription drugs, exceeds $2.2 billion. Despite its ubiquity, acne is poorly understood and often suboptimally treated.

Prevention

Who is at risk for acne?

Those at greatest risk for acne are adolescents whose first-degree relatives have been affected. Acne in girls tends to linger beyond the teen years, but boys tend to have more severe acne and an elevated risk for developing nodular acne.

Can acne be prevented?

Acne is not altogether preventable, as it is an inherited condition that usually accompanies pubertal maturation.

Although some observers hypothesize that low-glycemic diets prevent acne (1), there is no clear evidence that dietary changes prevent acne (2).

More than 30 years ago, a crossover, single-blinded study of 65 patients showed equal acne occurrence with the daily ingestion for 1 month of 2 concentrated chocolate bars versus chocolate-free bars (3).

A retrospective survey of 47355 nurses found no association between severe teenage acne and dietary intake of common foods, including pizza, sweets, and French fries (4).

In a prospective cohort study of 49 acne patients and 42 healthy control participants, researchers measured levels of serum glucose, insulin, insulin-like growth factor (ILGF)-I, ILGF-binding protein 3, and leptin. In addition, a self-completed questionnaire about food consumption was used to calculate overall glycemic index and dietary glycemic load. There were no differences between the groups in levels of serum glucose, insulin, leptin, glycemic index, or dietary glycemic load, suggesting that these are not involved in acne pathogenesis (5).

Although dietary measures do not prevent acne, sensible hygiene may help delay acne onset and lessen its severity. Cleansing twice a day appears to be superior to once or three times a day (6). Mild soaps and liquid cleansers that are either nonmedicated or contain salicylic acid are recommended. Alkaline soaps and frequent or too-vigorous scrubbing may increase the tendency to develop acne.

Although there are no high-quality studies that directly show that using noncomedogenic (non–pore-clogging) skin care products prevents acne, it seems prudent to advise patients concerned about acne to look for skin care, hair care, and cosmetic products labeled as noncomedogenic, non–pore-clogging, or oil-free.

1. Cordain L, Lindeberg S, Hurtado M, et al. Acne vulgaris: a disease of Western civilization. Arch Dermatol. 2002;138:1584-90. [PMID: 12472346]
2. Rasmussen JE. Diet and acne. Int J Dermatol. 1977;16:488-92. [PMID: 142748]
3. Fulton JE Jr, Plewig G, Kligman AM. Effect of chocolate on acne vulgaris. JAMA. 1969;210:2071-4. [PMID: 4243053]
4. Adebamowo CA, Spiegelman D, Danby FW, et al. High school dietary dairy intake and teenage acne. J Am Acad Dermatol. 2005;52:207-14. [PMID: 15692464]
5. Kaymak Y, Adisen E, Ilter N, et al. Dietary glycemic index and glucose, insulin, insulin-like growth factor-I, insulin-like growth factor binding protein 3, and leptin levels in patients with acne. J Am Acad Dermatol. 2007;57:819-23. [PMID: 17655968]
6. Choi JM, Lew VK, Kimball AB. A single-blinded, randomized, controlled clinical trial evaluating the effect of face washing on acne vulgaris. Pediatr Dermatol. 2006;23:421-7. [PMID: 17014635]
7. Stoll S, Shalita AR, Webster GF, et al. The effect of the menstrual cycle on acne. J Am Acad Dermatol. 2001;45:957-60. [PMID: 11712049]
8. Kaidbey KH, Kligman AM. The pathogenesis of topical steroid acne. J Invest Dermatol. 1974;62:31-6. [PMID: 4271838]
9. White GM. Recent findings in the epidemiologic evidence, classification, and subtypes of acne vulgaris. J Am Acad Dermatol. 1998;39:S34-7.[PMID: 9703121]

Prevention... Because hereditary factors seem to play a large role in the development of acne, most primary prevention strategies have not been shown to be effective. Moderate-quality evidence does not support the theory that acne can be prevented by adhering to a low-glycemic diet or other dietary restrictions. However, some evidence suggests that sensible hygiene, including washing acne-prone areas twice a day and using noncomedogenic skin-care products, might delay acne onset or ameliorate its course.

CLINICAL BOTTOM LINE

How should clinicians diagnose acne?

In most cases, the diagnosis of acne is obvious on initial examination. However, some elements of the history provide the basis for confirming the diagnosis of true acne and ruling out other acneiform disorders.

What elements of the history should clinicians focus on in evaluating patients with acne?

History should aim to identify risk factors for acne and potential drug-related adverse events that may occur during acne treatment (see Box).

Clinicians should gather information on age at onset, duration, and chronicity or intermittent nature of symptoms. In most cases, true acne develops between the ages of 10 and 17 years and tends to wax and wane, particularly in relation to menstrual cycles in women. In female patients, 40% note premenstrual acne exacerbation (7). The acute onset of an acneiform eruption is unusual and may signify an endocrine disorder or be a clue to bacterial folliculitis or a drug-induced acneiform eruption.

Clinicians should ask patients about medications and topically applied products, such as moisturizers; cosmetics; hair products; over-the-counter and prescription acne treatments; and other topical drugs, particularly corticosteroid preparations. Both topical and systemic corticosteroids can cause acneiform eruptions that are unresponsive to standard therapy unless the causative agent is stopped (8). Hormonal therapies and anabolic steroids can also trigger acne.

The female patient's history is not complete without discussing sexual activity, menstrual history, and contraception, because few acne drugs are approved for use during pregnancy. It is also essential to discuss issues that could be clues to hyperandrogenism or the polycystic ovary syndrome, such as irregular menses, infertility, hirsutism, loss of scalp hair, and midsection weight gain.

How should clinicians carry out a systematic skin examination in patients with acne?

Physical examination for acne requires careful inspection of acne-prone skin sites—face, neck, chest, upper back, and shoulders—with the naked eye, using a high-quality examination light. To make a diagnosis of acne, there must be typical comedones in one or more of these locations. It is helpful but not necessary to see inflammatory lesions, which include erythematous papules, pustules, and nodules (cysts) (see Box).

Clinicians should also be alert for evidence of systemic disease that might masquerade as or contribute to acne, especially hirsutism or central obesity that might indicate the polycystic ovary syndrome.

How should clinicians classify acne type?

Acne is generally classified as either noninflammatory or inflammatory (9). Noninflammatory acne involves mainly comedones with little or no redness, whereas inflammatory acne involves erythematous papules, pustules, and sometimes nodules. Acne sequelae, such as crusts, post-inflammatory redness, and scars, are seen only in the inflammatory type but are not always present. Inflammatory acne includes papulopustular and nodular acne. There are 2 rare subtypes known as acne conglobata and acne fulminans. Acne conglobata is characterized by draining abscesses and sinus tracts and possible oligoarthritis. In acne fulminans, granulation tissue, prominent scarring, and possible fevers or arthralgias occur.

How should clinicians classify the severity of acne?

There is no universally accepted grading system for acne severity,

---

Factors to Address When Taking a History of a Patient with Acne

- Dermatologic: Ask about sensitive skin, atopic eczema.
- Hepatic and renal: Ask about diseases that may affect drug metabolism or excretion.
- Allergies: Ask about previous drug reactions.
- Musculoskeletal: Ask about body building, anabolic steroid abuse.
- Psychiatric: Ask about mood disorders, depression, suicidal ideation.
- Female endocrine and reproductive: Ask about contraceptive use, irregular menses, current or past pregnancies, breast feeding, weight gain, diabetes, infertility, hirsutism, loss of scalp hair.

Acne Lesions: Medical Terms (Common Names)

- Open comedo (blackhead): a visible plug consisting of keratin (epidermal debris) and sebum (oil from the sebaceous gland) located in the follicular orifice at the skin surface.
- Closed comedo (whitehead): a smooth whitish bump, 1 to 3 mm in size, without redness, located in the follicular duct just below the skin surface.
- Papule (pimple, zit, blemish): a tender erythematous bump <5 mm.
- Pustule (pimple, zit, blemish): a tender erythematous bump <5 mm containing visible purulent material.
- Nodule (cyst): a tender erythematous bump ≥5 mm.

but experts agree that severity grading should guide management (10). Acne severity is usually graded with simple descriptions, such as mild (slightly noticeable), moderate (easily seen), severe (very obvious), and very severe (disfiguring). For the purpose of grading acne severity, other factors besides appearance are often considered, such as the impact on a patient's economic and psychosocial circumstances and the presence or absence of prolonged erythema, scarring, or keloid formation.

What other skin disorders should clinicians consider in patients with suspected acne?

Typical acne is not a diagnostic challenge, but when the history or physical examination are unusual, other conditions that can mimic acne should be considered in the differential diagnosis. Disorders that can mimic true acne include rosacea, drug-induced acne, folliculitis, and *acne excoriée des jeunes filles*.

Rosacea, formerly called acne rosacea, is characterized by onset after age 20 years, erythema, telengiectases, and inflammatory lesions localized to the central face.

Drug-induced acneiform eruptions, most commonly from topical or systemic corticosteroids, are usually acute and rapidly progressive. Corticosteroid acne lacks comedones and consists of a monomorphic eruption of papules or pustules. In contrast, acne induced by anabolic steroid use is true acne with prominent comedones. Clinicians should be alert for anabolic steroid use when the onset of acne occurs during the late teens or early twenties in athletes or bodybuilders (11).

When patients are treated with prolonged antibiotic therapy, gram-negative folliculitis may occur, particularly in young men. This disorder is characterized by the appearance of closely grouped pustules, mainly around the nose and beard area. Bacterial folliculitis caused by *Staphylococcus aureus* may appear acne-like but usually presents on the thighs and buttocks, and each pustule surrounds a visible hair shaft.

Acne excoriée des jeunes filles, seen almost exclusively in female patients, is a treatment-resistant condition wherein mainly excoriations, crusting, and scarring are seen. Primary acne lesions are scarce or absent. It respresents an anxiety disorder in which patients pick at their skin but usually deny doing so.

Certain granulomatous and neoplastic disorders, such as facial sarcoidosis, tuberous sclerosis, and multiple trichoepitheliomas may mimic acne. However, comedones are usually absent in these conditions, and lesions tend to be sessile in contrast with the constantly evolving nature of acne lesions.

What laboratory studies should clinicians obtain in patients with acne?

Laboratory tests are rarely needed to diagnose acne unless the history and physical examination suggest atypical acneiform eruptions. Bacterial culture can be helpful to diagnose bacterial folliculitis, and skin biopsy will confirm or rule out granulomatous and neoplastic conditions. When signs of androgen excess are present in female patients, measurement of levels of total and free testosterone, dehydro-epiandrosterone sulfate, leutinizing hormone, and follicle-stimulating hormone may be helpful. If the polycystic ovary syndrome is suspected, fasting glucose and insulin levels and pelvic ultrasonography can assist in confirming the diagnosis.

When should clinicians consult a dermatologist for diagnostic help?

Unusual acneiform eruptions may require dermatologic consultation, especially when skin biopsy is being considered.

10. American Academy of Dermatology/ American Academy of Dermatology Association. Guidelines of care for acne vulgaris management. J Am Acad Dermatol. 2007; 56:651-63. [PMID: 17276540]
11. Melnik B, Jansen T, Grabbe S. Abuse of anabolic-androgenic steroids and body-building acne: an underestimated health problem. J Dtsch Dermatol Ges. 2007;5:110-7. [PMID: 17274777]

Treatment

What should clinicians advise patients about diet, nutritional supplements, and herbal therapies for acne?

Numerous studies show no link between acne and such foods as chocolate, sweets, French fries, and pizza. The American Academy of Dermatology states that evidence does not support dietary intervention as acne treatment (10). However, some researchers hypothesize that high-glycemic diets cause acne. Advocates of this theory believe that eating low-glycemic carbohydrates instead of foods containing refined sugars and starches can successfully treat acne (1), but evidence does not support this theory (5).

Forty-three male acne patients were instructed to follow either a low-glycemic diet or a diet in which refined carbohydrates were encouraged. After 12 weeks, acne improved in both groups, suggesting that a placebo effect or observer bias may account for anecdotal observations that associate a high glycemic diet with acne (12).

However, because a low-glycemic diet may lead to other health benefits, it is not unreasonable to recommend that acne patients avoid refined sugars and starches, provided that traditional evidence-based therapy is not withheld.

Currently, no scientific evidence supports the use of herbs, nutritional supplements, or any other form of alternative medicine for acne treatment, aside from a single clinical trial showing a modest effect of topical tea tree oil (13). Furthermore, safety data for most herbal products are limited (14).

How should clinicians choose between topical and systemic acne therapies?

As a general rule, mild acne does not warrant systemic therapy. Moderate-to-severe acne often requires both topical and oral therapy, such as antibiotics and hormonal agents (see Figure on page 14).

What should clinicians consider in choosing topical therapy for patients with mild acne?

Table 1 shows drugs used to treat acne, and the Figure summarizes how clinicians should select from available treatments on the basis of acne severity and response. Every acne medication is aimed at 1 or more of the 4 principal mechanisms of acne pathogenesis: hyperkeratinization (excess accumulation of epidermal debris), which leads to occlusion of the pilosebaceous follicle; high sebum production due to increased androgenic hormone levels; skin colonization with *Propionibacterium acnes*; and inflammation that develops as a result of sebum breakdown into pro-inflammatory byproducts.

The choice of topical treatment depends on whether the acne is noninflammatory (comedonal) or inflammatory (papulopustular).

Noninflammatory acne

The predominant lesions of non-inflammatory acne are open and closed comedones. The most useful topical agents are those that promote comedolysis (dissolution of pore impactions) or keratolysis (peeling away the horny layer at the pore opening). The most powerful

12. Smith RN, Mann NJ, Braue A, et al. A low-glycemic-load diet improves symptoms in acne vulgaris patients: a randomized controlled trial. Am J Clin Nutr. 2007;86:107-15. [PMID: 17616769]
13. Enshaieh S, Jooya A, Siadat AH, et al. The efficacy of 5% topical tea tree oil gel in mild to moderate acne vulgaris: a randomized, double-blind placebo-controlled study. Indian J Dermatol Venereol Leprol. 2007;73:22-5. [PMID: 17314442]
14. Bedi MK, Shenefelt PD. Herbal therapy in dermatology. Arch Dermatol. 2002;138:232-42. [PMID: 11843645]

Table 1. Drug Treatment for Acne

Agent (class)	Mechanism of Action	Dosage	Notes
Single-agent topical formulations			
Tretinoin (topical retinoid)	Comedolysis, induction of orthokeratosis, and inhibition of inflammation	Apply qhs; gel: 0.025%; cream: 0.025%, 0.05%, 0.1%; microsponge gel: 0.04%, 0.1%	First-line treatment for all acne. Retinoids as a class are known to cause local skin irritation. Acne exacerbation may occur in the early weeks of treatment. Pregnancy Category C.
Adapalene (topical retinoid)	Comedolysis, induction of orthokeratosis, and inhibition of inflammation	Apply qhs; gel: 0.1% or 0.3%; cream: 0.1%	Alternative first-line treatment for all acne. Retinoids as a class are known to cause local skin irritation. Acne exacerbation may occur in the early weeks of treatment. Pregnancy Category C.
Tazarotene (topical retinoid)	Comedolysis, induction of orthokeratosis, and inhibition of inflammation	Apply qhs; gel: 0.1%, cream: 0.1%, off-label 0.05% formulations	Second-line treatment for all types of acne because of greater expense, irritation, and lab animal teratogenicity compared with tretinoin and adapalene. Retinoids as a class are known to cause local skin irritation. Acne exacerbation may occur in the early weeks of treatment. Pregnancy Category X.
Salicylic acid (β-hydroxy acid)	Keratolysis, mild comedolysis	Apply qd to bid; OTC cleanser: 2%; solutions: 0.5%–2%	Nonprescription products useful for mild comedonal acne, adult acne, and keratosis pilaris, mainly in patients with retinoid-intolerant skin. May cause mild local skin irritation. Not recommended for use during pregnancy.
Benzoyl peroxide (topical antibacterial)	Potent bactericidal against *Propionibacterium acnes*, keratolysis, and comedolysis	Apply qd to bid; gels, creams, cleansers (OTC and by prescription): 2.5%–10%	First-line topical therapy for all acne, reduces comedones and inflammatory lesions, no known resistant bacteria. May cause local skin irritation (5%); contact sensitization (1%–2.5%); bleaching of skin, hair, fabrics, and carpeting; tumor promotion in lab animals. Use lower concentrations (2.5%–4%) for sensitive skin. Pregnancy Category C.
Clindamycin phosphate (topical antibiotic)	Antibacterial against *P. acnes*, indirect suppression of inflammation	Apply qd to bid; solution: 1%; pledgets: 1%; gel: 1%; lotion: 1%	Short-to-intermediate–term therapy for mild-to-moderate inflammatory acne. May cause local skin irritation, promotion of antibiotic-resistant bacteria; pseudomembranous enterocolitis has been reported rarely. Pregnancy Category B.
Erythromycin (topical antibiotic)	Antibacterial against *P. acnes*, indirect suppression of inflammation	Apply qd to bid; solution: 2%; pledgets: 2%; gel: 2%	Short-to-intermediate–term therapy for mild-to-moderate inflammatory acne. May cause local skin irritation, promotion of antibiotic-resistant bacteria. Pregnancy Category B.
Dapsone (topical antibiotic)	Antibacterial against *P. acnes*, indirect suppression of inflammation	Apply qd to bid; gel: 5%	Short-to-intermediate–term therapy for mild-to-moderate inflammatory acne. May cause local skin irritation, possible hemolytic anemia in G6PD-deficient patients; prescreening for G6PD level may be warranted. Pregnancy Category C.
Sulfur, sulfacetamide sodium (topical antibiotics)	Antibacterial against *P. acnes*, indirect suppression of inflammation. Sulfur is a mild keratolytic agent.	Apply qd to bid; various OTC and prescription lotions and cleansers: 2%–10%	Adjunctive therapy for mild-to-moderate teenage and adult acne. May cause local skin irritation and contact reactions in sulfonamide-sensitive patients; has unpleasant odor. Pregnancy Category C.
Azelaic acid (topical antibiotic, mild anticomedonal drug)	Modest antibacterial activity against *P. acnes*, modulates keratin formation	Apply bid; cream: 20%; gel: 15%	Adjunctive therapy for mild-to-moderate acne, especially when hyperpigmentation is present, because of ability to cause hypopigmentation as a side effect. May cause local skin irritation, mainly burning and stinging. Pregnancy Category B.
Fixed-combination topical formulations			
Clindamycin-benzoyl peroxide (topical antibacterial)	Potent bactericidal effect against *P. acnes*, mild keratolytic agent	Apply qd to bid; gel with clindamycin: 1%; benzoyl peroxide: 5%	More effective than individual components alone, benzoyl peroxide prevents bacterial resistance to clindamycin. See side effects of individual agents above. Pregnancy Category C.
Erythromycin-benzoyl peroxide (topical antibacterial)	Potent bactericidal effect against *P. acnes*, mild keratolytic agent	Apply qd to bid; gel with erythromycin: 3%; benzoyl peroxide: 5%	Topical antibacterial and keratolytic combination for all acne–more effective than individual components alone, and benzoyl peroxide prevents bacterial resistance to erythromycin. See side effects of individual agents above. Pregnancy Category C.
Oral antibiotic drugs			
Tetracycline (oral antibiotic)	Antibacterial against *P. acnes*, indirect suppression of inflammation	250 mg PO qid, 500 mg PO bid	First-line oral therapy for moderate-to-severe inflammatory acne. May cause phototoxicity, vaginal yeast infection, dyspepsia, rare liver toxicity, staining of teeth in fetuses and children, reduced efficacy of oral contraceptives. Requires empty stomach, cannot be taken with dairy products. Pregnancy Category D; not for acne treatment in children under age 12.

Table 1. Drug Treatment for Acne (continued)

Agent (class)	Mechanism of Action	Dosage	Notes
Oral antibiotic drugs (continued)			
Doxycycline (oral antibiotic)	Antibacterial against *P. acnes*, indirect suppression of inflammation	20, 40, 50, 75, or 100 mg PO bid; 75–100 mg PO qd	Modestly priced alternative to tetracycline. May cause dose-related phototoxicity (requires sun protection), vaginal yeast infection, dyspepsia. May be taken with food. Pregnancy Category D. Not for acne treatment in children under age 12.
Minocycline (oral antibiotic)	Antibacterial against *P. acnes*, indirect suppression of inflammation	50, 75, or 100 mg PO bid; or extended-release form 45, 90, or 135 mg qd	Second-line alternative to tetracycline because of higher cost. May cause dizziness, vertigo, discolored teeth, blue-gray skin staining, rare hepatotoxicity and lupus-like syndrome, mild phototoxicity. May be taken with food. Extended-release form is most expensive. Pregnancy Category D. Not for acne treatment in children under age 12.
Erythromycin (oral antibiotic)	Antibacterial against *P. acnes*, indirect suppression of inflammation	1–1.2 gm/d PO in divided doses	Alternative to tetracycline for moderate-to-severe inflammatory acne. Often causes gastric upset or diarrhea. Useful in pediatric age group. Pregnancy Category B.
Azithromycin (oral antibiotic)	Antibacterial against *P. acnes*, indirect suppression of inflammation	500 mg PO on day 1; 250 mg/d PO on days 2–5	Second-line therapy for moderate-to-severe inflammatory acne because of higher cost. May cause gastric upset or diarrhea, rare cholestatic jaundice and angioedema. Useful in pediatric age group. Pregnancy Category B.
Sulfamethoxazole-trimethoprim (oral antibiotic)	Antibacterial against *P. acnes*, indirect suppression of inflammation	1 DS tablet bid	Second-line therapy for severe inflammatory acne. May cause gastric distress, skin rashes, rare Stevens–Johnson syndrome. Useful when isotretinoin is contraindicated. Pregnancy Category C. Pediatric use approved after age 2 months.
Oral contraceptive drugs and hormonal therapy			
Norethindrone acetate-ethinyl estradiol (oral contraceptive)	Regulation of androgens by preventing cyclical progesterone surge	1 pill PO qd for 21 d, skip 7 d, then repeat cycle	First-line treatment of moderate-to-severe acne in women with laboratory evidence of hyperandrogenism. May cause skin rashes, nausea, vomiting, migraine headaches, mood disorders, hypertension, menstrual irregularities, venous thrombosis, jaundice. Not for use in children or women who are pregnant or lactating.
Norgestimate-ethinyl estradiol (oral contraceptive)	Regulation of androgens by preventing cyclical progesterone surge	1 pill PO qd for 21 d, skip or take null pill for 7 d, repeat cycle	First-line treatment of moderate-to-severe acne in women with laboratory evidence of hyperandrogenism. May cause skin rashes, nausea, vomiting, migraine headaches, mood disorders, hypertension, menstrual irregularities, venous thrombosis, jaundice. Not for use in children or women who are pregnant or lactating.
Spironolactone (oral antiandrogen)	Antagonism of endogenous androgenic hormones	50–100 mg PO bid	Off-label use for moderate-to-severe acne in women with laboratory evidence of hyperandrogenism. May cause breast tenderness, frequent menses, hypotension, hyperkalemia, feminization of male fetuses. Pregnancy Category C.
Prednisone (oral corticosteroid)	Anti-inflammatory, suppression of adrenal androgen production	High dose: 40 mg PO qd, tapering to zero over 2–4 weeks; Low dose: 5 mg PO qd	High dose: useful for temporary control of severe nodular acne, acne conglobata, and acne fulminans. Low dose: useful for longer-term adrenal suppression in rare cases. May cause gastric distress, fluid retention, increased blood glucose, hypertension, impaired wound healing, mood swings, growth disturbances, cataracts, glaucoma. Pregnancy Category C.
Oral retinoid drug			
Isotretinoin (oral retinoid)	Modulation of epidermal proliferation, induction of orthokeratosis, comedolysis, inhibition of inflammation, and inhibition of sebum secretion	0.5–2 mg/kg per day, qd or divided bid, for 20-wk total course	Treatment of choice for severe recalcitrant nodular acne; prolonged remissions (1–3 y) are seen in about 80% of cases. Side effects include dry skin; chapped lips; dry eyes; nosebleeds; hair loss; major birth defects; hyperlipidemias; transient liver enzyme elevations; musculoskeletal pain; hyperostosis; decreased bone mineral density; diminution of night vision; psychiatric effects (controversial), including mood swings, depression, suicide risk, and aggressive or violent behavior. Pregnancy Category X. All prescribers, patients, wholesalers, and dispensing pharmacies must be registered in the FDA-approved iPLEDGE program (www.ipledgeprogram.com).

bid = twice daily; DS = double strength; G6PD = glucose 6-phosphate dehydrogenase; OTC = over-the-counter; PO = orally; qd = once daily; qhs = every night; qid = four times daily.

comedolytic drugs are the topical retinoids: tretinoin, adapalene, and tazarotene (15). A fourth drug in this class, topical isotretinoin, is not available in the United States. These drugs are called retinoids because they have the ability to bind to vitamin A receptors in the skin. The retinoid antiacne agents function as potent vitamin A agonists: they modulate epidermal proliferation, prevent hyper-keratosis, dissolve comedones by disrupting desmosomal bridges, and inhibit inflammation.

Benzoyl peroxide and salicylic acid possess mild keratolytic properties and have the advantages of less skin irritation, lower cost, and over-the-counter availability (10). In addition, benzoyl peroxide is available as both wash-off cleansers and gels that can remain on the skin for 12 hours or more. In a head-to-head trial, benzoyl peroxide and tretinoin reduced comedones with equal efficacy, but benzoyl peroxide caused less peeling (16).

Azelaic acid has mild activity against comedones, but most experts believe it is not as effective as retinoids or benzoyl peroxide (10).

Inflammatory acne
In inflammatory acne, erythematous lesions predominate. All grades of inflammatory acne, including mild cases, require an antibacterial agent effective against *P. acnes*, in addition to a comedolytic or keratolytic agent. Benzoyl peroxide is a powerful bactericidal agent and does not cause bacterial resistance, a problem that occurs with prolonged use of the commonly prescribed topical antibiotics, clindamycin and erythromycin.

A 10-year surveillance study of bacteriologic samples from the skin of 4274 treated acne patients found that the proportion of patients carrying strains of P. acnes that were resistant to at least 1 of the commonly used antiacne antibiotics rose from 34.5% in 1991 to 64% in 1997. Erythromycin

resistance was most common, followed by resistance to clindamycin. Tetracycline resistance was relatively uncommon and did not increase substantially over 10 years (17).

Experts agree that combination therapy for inflammatory acne is the best treatment because its efficacy is superior to treatment with a single agent (18, 19). When a 2-agent regimen is prescribed, it is traditional to recommend one in the morning and the other at bedtime, unless they are known to be compatible. Examples of compatibility include benzoyl peroxide with clindamycin and benzoyl peroxide with erythromycin. These can be obtained as fixed-combination products. A combination product containing adapalene 0.1% and benzoyl peroxide 2.5% was recently reported to be faster-acting and more effective for reducing total lesion counts than either ingredient alone (20), but is not yet available on the market.

When topical agents are selected, it is important to consider possible side effects. The retinoid medications frequently cause local skin reactions, such as dryness, redness, itching, and peeling. Treatment with these agents is usually initiated at the lowest concentrations. Cream formulations are less irritating to the skin than gels and solutions. Adapalene has been shown to be better tolerated than tretinoin or tazarotene.

Thirty-five healthy participants were randomly assigned to 3 groups, each applying combination therapy with a clindamycin–benzoyl peroxide fixed-combination product once daily and 1 of 3 topical retinoids once daily. The 3 retinoid preparations were tretinoin gel 0.04%, adapalene gel 0.1%, and tazarotene cream 0.05%. The mean irritancy index of adapalene was statistically significantly lower than that of tretinoin or tazarotene, which did not differ significantly from each other. Fewer participants in the adapalene group dropped out of the study because of skin irritation (21).

15. Cunliffe WJ, Poncet M, Loesche C, et al. A comparison of the efficacy and tolerability of adapalene 0.1% gel versus tretinoin 0.025% gel in patients with acne vulgaris: a meta-analysis of five randomized trials. Br J Dermatol. 1998;139 Suppl 52:48-56. [PMID: 9990421]

16. Belknap BS. Treatment of acne with 5% benzoyl peroxide gel or 0.05% retinoic acid cream. Cutis. 1979;23:856-9. [PMID: 157264]

17. Coates P, Vyakrnam S, Eady EA, et al. Prevalence of antibiotic-resistant propionibacteria on the skin of acne patients: 10-year surveillance data and snapshot distribution study. Br J Dermatol. 2002;146:840-8. [PMID: 12000382]

18. Thiboutot DM, Gollnick HP. Treatment considerations for inflammatory acne: clinical evidence for adapalene 0.1% in combination therapies. J Drugs Dermatol. 2006;5:785-94. [PMID: 16989194]

19. Leyden JJ, Berger RS, Dunlap FE, et al. Comparison of the efficacy and safety of a combination topical gel formulation of benzoyl peroxide and clindamycin with benzoyl peroxide, clindamycin and vehicle gel in the treatments of acne vulgaris. Am J Clin Dermatol. 2001;2:33-9. [PMID: 11702619]

20. Adapalene-BPO Study Group. Adapalene-benzoyl peroxide, a fixed-dose combination for the treatment of acne vulgaris: results of a multicenter, randomized double-blind, controlled study. J Am Acad Dermatol. 2007;57:791-9. [PMID: 17655969]

For patients with very dry or sensitive skin, nonretinoid medications, such as salicylic acid and azelaic acid, are sometimes better tolerated. Of all the commonly used topical prescription medications, only azelaic acid and erythromycin have been established by the U.S. Food and Drug Administration (FDA) as safe for patients under age 12. When treating girls and women of childbearing potential, prescribers must be mindful of drug Pregnancy Categories (see Table 1). In such patients, tazarotene use is strictly prohibited in the absence of reliable contraception.

Expense is also a consideration in selecting acne therapy. There is about a 5-fold difference in cost among topical retinoid products, with generic tretinoin being the least expensive. Third-party payment for topical retinoids is highly variable; in most cases, many insurers currently require preauthorization or deny reimbursement for brand-name tretinoin and all forms of tazarotene. Furthermore, these costly retinoid formulas may be 10 to 20 times more expensive than nonprescription benzoyl peroxide. The often-prescribed topical antibiotics, clindamycin and erythromycin, are found in moderately priced generic products that are usually covered by prescription plans.

What should clinicians consider in choosing topical and oral therapy, including antibiotics and hormonal therapies, for patients with moderate-to-severe acne?

Topical therapy and oral antibiotics
First-line treatment for moderate acne begins with the same combination of topical drugs used for mild acne. In order to hasten improvement and prevent scarring, dermatologists often add an oral antibiotic drug to treat all male patients and those female patients with normal hormone profiles. The most commonly prescribed oral agents are tetracycline and its relatives, doxycycline and minocycline (22-24). Although some experts believe that the latter are more effective than the former, evidence from head-to-head trials is lacking. The next most-frequently prescribed agents are the macrolides, erythromycin and azithromycin (25, 26). Trimethoprim with and without sulfamethoxazole has also been used successfully (10).

Meta-analysis of 27 randomized, controlled trials showed that minocycline for acne has been compared with placebo (2 trials), oxytetracycline (1 trial), tetracycline (6 trials), doxycycline (7 trials), lymecycline (2 trials), topical drugs (5 trials), oral contraceptives (1 trial), and oral isotretinoin (2 trials). Results showed that the trials were mostly small and of low quality. Minocycline was demonstrated to be an effective treatment, but only 2 studies found it superior to less-expensive drugs in the class, and these studies were methodologically flawed. The authors concluded that there is not enough evidence to justify first-line use of minocycline for acne (24).

When oral antibiotic therapy is considered, the risk for antibiotic resistance must be taken into account, and for this reason the current recommendation favors short-term courses instead of traditional prolonged therapy (10). Notable adverse events caused by tetracycline-class agents include vaginal candidiasis; phototoxicity, which is most likely to occur from doxycycline; and vertigo and tooth-staining from minocycline. Minocycline has also been associated with very rare but serious lupus-like reactions. The macrolides are well known to cause gastric upset and diarrhea. Trimethoprim–sulfamethoxazole may cause drug eruptions and rarely the Stevens–Johnson syndrome.

There is about a 5-fold difference in cost among topical retinoid products, with generic tretinoin being the least expensive.

21. Dosik JS, Gilbert RD, Arsonnaud S. Cumulative irritancy comparison of topical retinoid and antimicrobial combination therapies. Skinmed. 2006;5:219-23. [PMID: 16957432]
22. Lane P, Williamson DM. Treatment of acne vulgaris with tetracycline hydrochloride: a double-blind trial with 51 patients. Br Med J. 1969;2:76-9. [PMID: 4237796]
23. Plewig G, Petrozzi JW, Berendes U. Double-blind study of doxycycline in acne vulgaris. Arch Dermatol. 1970;101:435-8. [PMID: 4245454]
24. Garner SE, Eady EA, Popescu C, et al. Minocycline for acne vulgaris: efficacy and safety. Cochrane Database Syst Rev. 2003:CD002086. [PMID: 12535427]
25. Gammon WR, Meyer C, Lantis S, et al. Comparative efficacy of oral erythromycin versus oral tetracycline in the treatment of acne vulgaris. A double-blind study. J Am Acad Dermatol. 1986;14:183-6. [PMID: 2936772]
26. Parsad D, Pandhi R, Nagpal R, et al. Azithromycin monthly pulse vs daily doxycycline in the treatment of acne vulgaris. J Dermatol. 2001;28:1-4. [PMID: 11280457]

27. Leyden J, Shalita A, Hordinsky M, et al. Efficacy of a low-dose oral contraceptive containing 20 microg of ethinyl estradiol and 100 microg of levonorgestrel for the treatment of moderate acne: A randomized, placebo-controlled trial. J Am Acad Dermatol. 2002;47:399-409. [PMID: 12196750]

28. van Vloten WA, van Haselen CW, van Zuuren EJ, et al. The effect of 2 combined oral contraceptives containing either drospirenone or cyproterone acetate on acne and seborrhea. Cutis. 2002;69:2-15. [PMID 12096825]

29. Shaw JC. Low-dose adjunctive spironolactone in the treatment of acne in women: a retrospective analysis of 85 consecutively treated patients. J Am Acad Dermatol. 2000;43:498-502. [PMID: 10954662]

30. Strauss JS, Leyden JJ, Lucky AW, et al. A randomized trial of the efficacy of a new micronized formulation versus a standard formulation of isotretinoin in patients with severe recalcitrant nodular acne. J Am Acad Dermatol. 2001; 45:187-95. [PMID: 11464179]

31. Lammer EJ, Chen DT, Hoar RM, et al. Retinoic acid embryopathy. N Engl J Med. 1985;313:837-41. [PMID: 3162101]

Hormonal therapy

Treatment with oral contraceptive agents, in addition to topical acne therapy, is the regimen of choice for female patients whose laboratory results show androgen excess, and also for those who desire a hormonal method of pregnancy prevention. Theoretically, oral antibiotics given concurrently with birth control agents can lead to contraceptive failure. Evidence supports the use of several agents in this class (27). The FDA has approved 2 agents, norethindrone acetate-ethinyl estradiol and norgestimate-ethinyl estradiol, specifically for acne treatment (Table 1). Acne trials have not been conducted with hormone patches, implants, or injections. Patience is required when treating acne with oral contraceptive agents. Clinical trials showed that 5 cycles produce gradual improvements averaging 50% to 60% diminution in acne lesions. The side effects of this class of drugs include skin rashes, migraine headaches, nausea, and rare but serious venous thrombosis. An oral contraceptive that contains drospirenone, an androgen antagonist, has been shown to be effective in improving acne (28).

The androgen antagonist spironolactone has shown some effectiveness in treating acne but is not currently FDA-approved for this indication (29). When spironolactone is being used for treatment, concurrent hormonal contraception is routinely prescribed to prevent pregnancy. Feminization of male fetuses has been reported with spironolactone.

Oral corticosteroids can be used in either of 2 methods to reduce severe inflammatory acne when other treatments are ineffective. The first method is a short course, starting with a high dose and gradually tapering off completely within 2 to 4 weeks. This regimen is occasionally used to suppress acute acne flare-ups, as may occur in acne fulminans. The second method is the long-term use of low-dose corticosteroids for suppression of adrenal activity. Oral corticosteroid therapy is fraught with side effects and was used more frequently in the era predating oral contraceptives and isotretinoin therapy (10).

When should clinicians consider systemic isotretinoin therapy for acne, and what special requirements should they be aware of?

Isotretinoin, an isomer of vitamin A, is the drug of choice in suitable patients with severe nodular acne that is unresponsive to oral antibiotic therapy (10). Physicians and patients must be aware that isotretinoin is associated with a high risk for major birth defects if taken during pregnancy.

A randomized, controlled trial of a 20-week course of isotretinoin without any concomitant topical drugs in patients with severe recalcitrant nodular acne documented prolonged remissions in about 80% of patients (30).

Researchers investigated the outcomes of 154 cases of human pregnancies during the early experience with isotretinoin. The outcomes included 95 elective terminations, 12 spontaneous abortions, 21 malformed infants, and 26 normal births. Among the 21 malformed infants, there was a characteristic pattern of multiple major defects involving the craniofacial, cardiac, and central nervous systems. The most frequently reported anomalies were small or absent ears in 15 infants and aortic-arch abnormalities in 7 infants (31).

The U.S. government requires all patients taking isotretinoin, prescribing physicians, dispensing pharmacies, wholesalers, and manufacturers to register with iPLEDGE, a risk-management program designed to prevent pregnancy. More information is available on the official Web site (www.ipledgeprogram.com).

Besides causing birth defects, isotretinoin is associated with numerous mucocutaneous adverse effects, including chapped lips, dry eyes and mucous membranes, nose bleeds, and hair shedding. Possible systemic sequelae include musculoskeletal effects, such as hyperostosis and premature closure of the epiphyses—these have been reported with long-term use for other disorders but not during acne therapy—and neuropsychiatric effects, such as headaches and mood changes including reports of depression, suicidal ideation, and suicide. Depression has not been shown to occur more frequently in patients taking isotretinoin than in the age-matched population at large, but there are anecdotal reports of improvement after drug withdrawal and relapse on reintroduction (32). Patients and the parents or legal guardians of minors must be made aware of the risks for mood disorders, even though a causal relationship between the drug and depression has not been proven.

During isotretinoin therapy, regular monitoring of levels of cholesterol, triglycerides, and transaminases can detect isotretinoin-induced hyperlipidemias and transient elevations in liver enzymes (33). For sexually active female patients, the iPLEDGE program requires baseline and monthly pregnancy tests within a short window of time before filling prescriptions.

When should clinicians refer patients with acne to a dermatologist?

Very severe acne and cases that resist standard treatment should be considered for dermatologic consultation. Any physician not wishing to participate in iPLEDGE must refer patients in need of isotretinoin to a registered prescriber.

Is there a role for surgical treatment in acne?

Acne surgery is the physical intervention of removing impacted blackheads and whiteheads with a specially designed instrument called a comedo extractor. Closed comedones are first gently lanced with a no. 11 surgical blade. The extractor is used to exert even pressure around the periphery of the lesion. Although some experts believe that acne surgery produces a rapid improvement in appearance, clinical trials have not been conducted to document that results are superior to drug therapy alone (10).

What is the role of newer technologies, such as blue-light phototherapy, certain laser treatments, nonablative radiofrequency, and photodynamic therapy, in the management of acne?

Although studies demonstrate that light-based, laser, and radiofrequency technologies can be safe and reasonably effective treatments for acne (34-36), their use is limited by high cost, insufficient third-party reimbursement, and almost inevitable acne relapse within 3 to 6 months. Expert opinion generally favors reserving these modalities for recalcitrant acne when isotretinoin is contraindicated. The American Academy of Dermatology Acne Task Force has deferred making a recommendation on these modalities (10).

What psychosocial factors influence management of patients with acne?

Psychosocial factors are interconnected with acne management in several ways. A large survey of adolescents showed that seeking treatment is often delayed by 1 year or more, even though 96% of patients reported that acne had a negative impact on self-image (37). These findings suggest that physicians can perform a valuable service by identifying and treating acne during visits for other reasons. It is reasonable

32. Wysowski DK, Pitts M, Beitz J. An analysis of reports of depression and suicide in patients treated with isotretinoin. J Am Acad Dermatol. 2001;45:515-9. [PMID: 11568740]

33. Bershad S, Rubinstein A, Paterniti JR, et al. Changes in plasma lipids and lipoproteins during isotretinoin therapy for acne. N Engl J Med. 1985;313:981-5. [PMID: 2931603]

34. Goldman MP, Boyce SM. A single-center study of aminolevulinic acid and 417 NM photodynamic therapy in the treatment of moderate to severe acne vulgaris. J Drugs Dermatol. 2003;2:393-6. [PMID: 12884461]

35. Ruiz-Esparza J, Gomez JB. Nonablative radiofrequency for active acne vulgaris: the use of deep dermal heat in the treatment of moderate to severe active acne vulgaris (thermotherapy): a report of 22 patients. Dermatol Surg. 2003;29:333-9; discussion 339. [PMID: 12656809]

36. Patel N, Clement M. Selective nonablative treatment of acne scarring with 585 nm flashlamp pulsed dye laser. Dermatol Surg. 2002;28:942-5; discussion 945. [PMID: 12410680]

37. Tan JK, Vasey K, Fung KY. Beliefs and perceptions of patients with acne. J Am Acad Dermatol. 2001;44:439-45. [PMID: 11209112]

to treat acne more aggressively when it has a particular impact on a patient's socioeconomic circumstances (for example, a professional model or actor) or when the disorder causes psychological distress. Finally, for patients with evidence of severe depression, past suicide attempts, or suicidal ideation, isotretinoin should be avoided because of its possible association with mood disorders.

How should clinicians follow patients with acne?

There is no high-quality evidence establishing the optimal interval for follow-up visits. Visits can be useful for evaluating progress,

adjusting therapy, and reinforcing patient compliance. The iPLEDGE program mandates monthly visits during isotretinoin therapy.

The acne follow-up visit should include an assessment of patient satisfaction with the efficacy and tolerability of the regimen, an update of female patients' contraceptive history and pregnancy status, a physical examination to grade acne severity and course, an adjustment of therapy for cases of inadequate response after a sufficient duration of therapy (see Box), and advice about good hygiene and adherence to therapy

Treatment... The standard of care for mild, noninflammatory acne is topical therapy with a comedolytic or keratolytic agent (usually benzoyl peroxide or a retinoid agent). For mild, inflammatory acne, optimal treatment consists of combination therapy with a comedolytic agent and a topical antibacterial agent. A limited course of an oral antibiotic is indicated for moderate-to-severe acne. Female patients may respond to hormonal therapy, especially when there is evidence of androgen excess. Patients with severe nodular acne who do not improve on oral antibiotic treatment are candidates for oral isotretinoin, requiring the prescriber and the patient to enroll in the iPLEDGE Program to prevent birth defects.

CLINICAL BOTTOM LINE

Practice Improvement

38. Zaenglein AL, Thiboutot DM. Expert committee recommendations for acne management. Pediatrics. 2006;118: 1188-99. [PMID: 16951015]

How do U.S. stakeholders evaluate the quality of care for patients with acne?

Current national measures of quality of care do not include measures related to acne care. The American Academy of Dermatology Clinical Guidelines Task Force established guidelines for acne care in 2007 but did not recommend using a validated instrument to ensure a standard of care (10).

What do professional organizations recommend regarding the management of patients with acne?

The American Academy of Dermatology has developed guidelines of care for acne management (10),

which are reflected in the guidance provided in this review.

The Global Alliance to Improve Outcomes in Acne, an international committee of acne physicians and researchers, met in 2003 to develop consensus guidelines of care for acne by using evidence-based standards and expert opinion (38). Compared with the American Academy of Dermatology guidelines, this group makes a stronger case for topical retinoids being the foundation of treatment in most patients. Their recommendations agree with the American Academy of Dermatology guidelines that combination therapy is optimal. This group recommends reserving oral antibiotics for severe cases and discontinuing these agents within 8 to 12 weeks.

What is the role of patient education in the management of acne?

Patient education is essential to provide reasonable expectations, to explain proper medication use, and to encourage compliance with the therapeutic regimen. A published survey demonstrated that a majority of acne patients have unrealistic beliefs and expectations (37). Clinicians should explain to patients that acne is not curable, but that it is manageable with ongoing therapy until it eventually resolves around age 20 years. It is important to stress that improvement will probably be gradual over 2 to 3 months. In the case of oral

contraceptives, acne response could require 5 cycles or more.

Familiarity with how to apply medications is crucial to success. Topical preparations are applied to acne-prone areas, not to individual lesions, because the main purpose of acne medications is to prevent new lesions, not to heal existing ones. The thinner the coating of topical agent, the lower the risk for local skin irritation. The average dose of a topical cream or gel to treat the entire face is a small, pea-sized amount. It is important to follow the treatment schedule very closely. Skipping doses, whether because of forgetfulness or because acne has improved, will lead to treatment failure in the long run. Inconsistent use of oral or topical antibiotics has the added risk for promoting drug-resistant bacteria.

in the clinic
Tool Kit
Acne

PIER Module

www.pier.acponline.org
Access the following PIER Module: Acne. PIER modules provide evidence-based guidance for clinical decisions at the point-of-care.

Acne Management Algorithm

www.annals.org/intheclinic/toolkit
Download and print copies of the treatment algorithm that appears on the following page.

Patient Education Resources

www.annals.org/intheclinic/toolkit
Access the Patient Information material that appears on page 15 for duplication and distribution to patients.

www.aad.org/media/background/factsheets/fact_acne.html
Access a fact sheet about acne prepared by the American Academy of Dermatology.

www.aad.org/public/publications/pamphlets/common_acne.html?media=print
Access a free pamphlet about acne from the American Academy of Dermatology.

www.nlm.nih.gov/medlineplus/tutorials/acne/htm/index.htm
An interactive audiovisual acne tutorial for patients from the National Library of Medicine and the National Institutes of Health's MedLine Plus program.

iPLEDGE

https://www.ipledgeprogram.com/
Read about and register for the FDA iPLEDGE program if you are interested in becoming a registered prescriber of systemic isoretoin therapy.

Other Reliable Sources of Acne Information

AcneNet (FAQ from the American Academy of Dermatology)
www.skincarephysicians.com/acnenet/FAQ.html

American Academy of Family Physicians
familydoctor.org/online/famdocen/home/common/skin/disorders/001.html

National Institute of Arthritis and Musculoskeletal and Skin Diseases
www.niams.nih.gov/Health_Info/Acne/default.asp

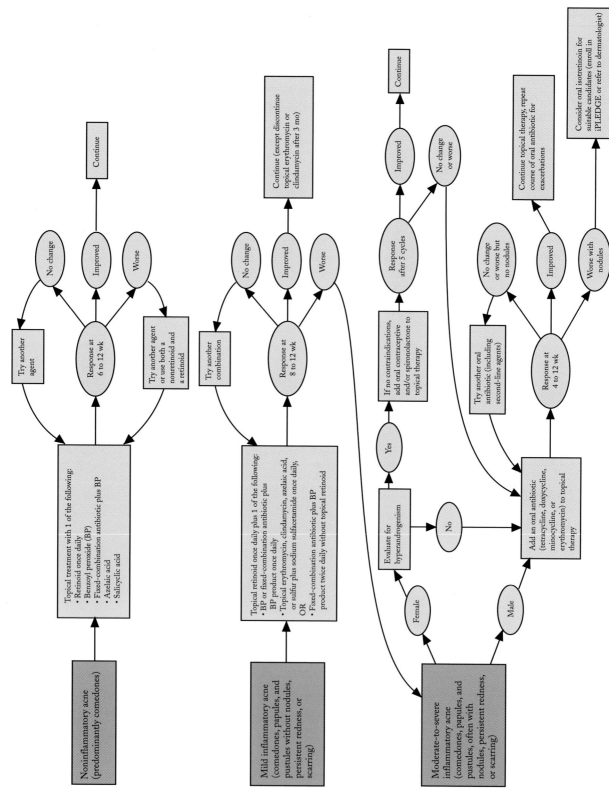

Figure. Pharmacologic management of acne in patients who are not pregnant or lactating.

WHAT YOU SHOULD KNOW ABOUT ACNE

What is acne?

- Acne occurs when skin pores get plugged up and swell. These are called pimples or zits. You can have acne on the face, neck, chest, back, and shoulders.

- Acne usually occurs in teenagers and clears up at around age 20 years, but adults can also have acne.

- The exact cause of acne is not known, but you are more likely to have acne if it runs in your family.

- Teenage hormones, oily skin, and certain bacteria on the skin can make acne worse.

- Acne is not caused by foods. But if you think that some foods make you break out, then do not eat them.

What can I do on my own to keep from getting acne or to make it better?

- Wash your face with a gentle soap 2 times per day.

- Check the label on skin-care products for the words "noncomedogenic," "non-pore-clogging," or "oil-free."

- You can get many acne medicines at the drugstore. If your acne is mild, try a product that contains benzoyl peroxide or salicylic acid.

- If you have acne that is very bad, leaves scars, or does not get better with non-prescription medicine, see your doctor.

What will my doctor do for acne?

- Your doctor may give you lotions, gels, creams, or pills. Often, these pills are antibiotics or birth-control pills.

- A very strong acne medicine is called isotretinoin (trade names: Accutane, Amnesteem, Claravis, Sotret). It is for very bad acne that does not get better with other medicines.

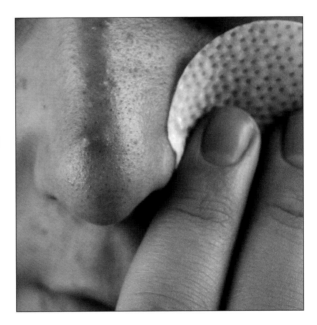

For More Information

American Academy of Dermatology
www.skincarephysicians.com/acnenet/FAQ.html
www.aad.org/public/publications/pamphlets/common_acne.html?media=print

Medline Plus
www.nlm.nih.gov/medlineplus/tutorials/acne/htm/index.htm

National Institute of Arthritis and Musculoskeletal and Skin Diseases
www.niams.nih.gov/Health_Info/Acne/default.asp

ACP
AMERICAN COLLEGE OF PHYSICIANS
INTERNAL MEDICINE | *Doctors for Adults*®

Patient Information

Gastroesophageal Reflux Disease

G astroesophageal reflux disease (GERD) is one of the most common gastrointestinal disorders in Western industrialized countries. Men and women develop GERD with equal frequency, but complicated GERD occurs more frequently in men and with advanced age. It is typically the result of prolonged exposure of the esophagus to gastric acid due to impaired esophageal motility, defects in the lower esophageal sphincter, and impairments in the antireflux barrier at the gastroesophageal junction. The acid exposure can damage the esophageal mucosa, potentially leading to Barrett's esophagus and esophageal cancer. GERD is a chronic disease, and many patients require lifelong therapy. Treatment helps to reduce symptoms, promote esophageal healing, and reduce the risk for cancer.

Diagnosis

Consider GERD in Patients with the Following Symptoms
- Heartburn or regurgitation
- Wheezing or dyspnea
- Chronic cough
- Chronic hoarseness or sore throat
- Globus
- Throat clearing
- Chest pain
- Halitosis

What symptoms and signs should prompt clinicians to consider GERD?

Typical GERD symptoms include chest discomfort (heartburn) and regurgitation. Symptoms occur most often after meals, especially fatty meals. Lying down, bending, or physical exertion often aggravate symptoms, and antacids provide relief. Patients with classic symptoms rarely require testing to confirm the diagnosis because of the high positive predictive value of classic symptoms (1). When heartburn (89% specificity, 81% positive predictive value) and regurgitation (95% specificity, 57% positive predictive value) occur together, a physician can diagnose GERD with greater than 90% accuracy (2).

GERD can also cause extraesophageal symptoms, including wheezing, chronic cough, shortness of breath, hoarseness, unexplained chest pain, globus (choking sensation), halitosis, and sore throat or a sense of needing to clear one's throat. Up to 80% of patients have at least one extraesophageal symptom. It is worth noting that although these symptoms are associated with GERD, establishing a definitive causal relationship between GERD and extraesophageal symptoms is difficult because GERD may be one of many causes of these symptoms.

When should clinicians consider an empirical therapeutic trial of acid-suppression therapy to support a preliminary diagnosis of GERD?

Performing diagnostic tests for all patients presenting with symptoms that might indicate GERD would be costly and is not necessary to arrive at a sufficiently accurate diagnosis. Response to an empirical trial of acid-suppression therapy is considered a sufficiently sensitive and specific method for establishing a GERD diagnosis among patients with classic symptoms of heartburn or regurgitation. Although proton pump inhibitors (PPIs) are more expensive than H_2-receptor blockers, PPIs are considered the drug of choice for an empirical therapeutic trial because they block acid more effectively than H_2-receptor blockers. An empirical trial typically consists of a double-dose of a PPI (such as omeprazole 20 to 40 mg twice daily) for 1 week or a standard-dose PPI (such as omeprazole 20 to 40 mg once daily) for 2 weeks.

A study that compared 24-hour pH monitoring with a 2-week course of high-dose omeprazole in 35 patients with erosive esophagitis found that the omeprazole test was at least as sensitive as 24-hour pH monitoring in diagnosing GERD (3).

A study randomly assigned 85 patients who had ambulatory pH monitoring and grade 0 or 1 esophagitis by upper endoscopy to either omeprazole 40 mg/d or placebo for 14 days and concluded that a symptomatic response to omeprazole had a sensitivity

1. DeVault KR, Castell DO. Updated guidelines for the diagnosis and treatment of gastroesophageal reflux disease. Am J Gastroenterol. 2005; 100:190-200. [PMID: 15654800]
2. Klauser AG, Schindlbeck NE, Müller-Lissner SA. Symptoms in gastro-oesophageal reflux disease. Lancet. 1990;335:205-8. [PMID: 1967675]
3. Fass R, Ofman JJ, Sampliner RE, et al. The omeprazole test is as sensitive as 24-h oesophageal pH monitoring in diagnosing gastro-oesophageal reflux disease in symptomatic patients with erosive oesophagitis. Aliment Pharmacol Ther. 2000;14:389-96. [PMID: 10759617]
4. Schenk BE, Kuipers EJ, Klinkenberg-Knol EC, et al. Omeprazole as a diagnostic tool in gastroesophageal reflux disease. Am J Gastroenterol. 1997;92:1997-2000. [PMID: 9362179]

and specificity similar to ambulatory 24-hour pH monitoring (4).

According to one meta-analysis of 15 studies that compared the clinical response to PPI with objective measures, such as 24-hour pH monitoring, endoscopy, and symptom questionnaires, testing may be necessary to definitively diagnose GERD in some patients even though many patients with uncomplicated GERD respond to empirical PPI therapy (5).

When should clinicians consider upper endoscopy in evaluating patients with possible GERD?

If patients respond to empirical therapy, endoscopy is not necessary to confirm the diagnosis. Although the specificity of esophagitis on endoscopy is 90% to 100%, approximately 50% to 70% of patients with classic GERD symptoms have no esophagitis on endoscopy (6). If endoscopy is done, then histologic evaluation of seemingly normal squamous mucosa has little power to detect pathologic acid reflux (7). However, the American College of Gastroenterology recommends that clinicians consider upper endoscopy to rule out Barrett's esophagus in patients with chronic symptoms; to evaluate patients who do not respond to empirical therapy; and to investigate symptoms, such as dysphagia or weight loss, that suggest stricture, ulceration, or malignancy (1).

What other diagnoses should clinicians consider in patients with suspected GERD and atypical symptoms?

Clinicians should be aware that, in some patients, the cause of GERD-like symptoms or endoscopic esophagitis is not reflux but rather infection, pill-induced injury, or radiation. In patients who have atypical symptoms of GERD or in those who have not responded to empirical therapy, clinicians should consider alternative gastrointestinal or biliary disease processes (Table 1).

When patients present with chest pain, clinicians should always consider coronary artery disease before concluding that GERD is the cause of the chest pain. Symptoms can be unreliable for differentiating GERD from a cardiac source of chest pain (1). GERD is present in approximately 50% of unexplained chest pain cases after coronary artery disease has been excluded, and although classic symptoms are present in many cases where GERD is the cause of chest pain, they are not always present (8, 9).

Which other laboratory tests should clinicians consider in evaluating patients when the diagnosis of GERD is uncertain?

When patients present with atypical symptoms, testing with esophageal manometry, pH monitoring, and barium swallow may help to differentiate GERD from other diagnoses.

Ambulatory pH monitoring

Ambulatory pH monitoring detects the presence or absence of reflux of acidic gastric contents and is the best way to measure the actual amount of time reflux is present and to correlate symptoms with reflux episodes. However, up to 25% of patients with documented esophagitis may have normal results on pH monitoring (10). Traditionally, pH monitoring is performed with catheter-based probes. A wireless pH capsule probe is a new technique that may be more tolerable and may allow for longer assessment of esophageal pH. Impedence-pH monitoring is another emerging technique that evaluates intraluminal

---

Warning Symptoms for Stricture, Ulceration, or Malignancy

- Dysphagia or odynophagia
- Bleeding
- Weight loss
- Early satiety
- Choking (coughing, shortness of breath, or hoarseness caused by acid)
- Anorexia
- Frequent vomiting

---

5. Numans ME, Lau J, de Wit NJ, Bonis PA. Short-term treatment with proton-pump inhibitors as a test for gastro-esophageal reflux disease: a meta-analysis of diagnostic test characteristics. Ann Intern Med. 2004;140:518-27. [PMID: 15068979]

6. Tefera L, Fein M, Ritter MP, et al. Can the combination of symptoms and endoscopy confirm the presence of gastroesophageal reflux disease? Am Surg. 1997;63:933-6. [PMID: 9322676]

7. Schindlbeck NE, Wiebecke B, Klauser AG, et al. Diagnostic value of histology in non-erosive gastro-oesophageal reflux disease. Gut. 1996;39:151-4. [PMID: 8977332]

8. Hewson EG, Sinclair JW, Dalton CB, Richter JE. Twenty-four-hour esophageal pH monitoring: the most useful test for evaluating noncardiac chest pain. Am J Med. 1991;90:576-83. [PMID: 2029015]

9. Davies HA, Jones DB, Rhodes J, Newcombe RG. Angina-like esophageal pain: differentiation from cardiac pain by history. J Clin Gastroenterol. 1985;7:477-81. [PMID: 4086742]

10. Martinez SD, Malagon IB, Garewal HS, et al. Non-erosive reflux disease (NERD)—acid reflux and symptom patterns. Aliment Pharmacol Ther. 2003; 17:537-45. [PMID: 12622762]

Table 1. Differential Diagnosis of GERD

Disease	Characteristics	Notes
Pill esophagitis	Presents with dysphagia or odynophagia	History of ingestion of the offending pill (e.g., potassium chloride, quinidine, tetracycline, doxycycline, NSAIDs, alendronate)
Infectious esophagitis	Presents with dysphagia or odynophagia	Often in immunocompromised patients with candidal, cytomegalovirus, or herpes simplex virus esophagitis
Esophageal motor disorders: achalasia, diffuse esophageal spasm, hypertensive or spastic motility disorders (e.g., nutcracker esophagus)	Dysphagia for liquids and solids; also may be associated with chest pain	Nutcracker esophagus may be coincident with GERD; heartburn or chest pain in achalasia not due to reflux but to fermentation of retained esophageal contents or esophageal muscle spasm
Nonulcer dyspepsia	Functional disorder, discomfort in midline of upper abdomen with fullness, bloating, or nausea	Usually does not respond to acid suppression
Eosinophilic esophagitis	Allergic esophagitis; vomiting and abdominal pain that improve with removal of offending food	Eosinophilis seen on esophageal biopsy
Esophageal cancer	Presents with dysphagia and weight loss, often in patients with longstanding GERD	Usually incurable by the time of clinical presentation
Coronary artery disease	Chest pain that may be clinically indistinguishable from chest pain associated with GERD	In patients at high risk for cardiac disease, should rule out cardiac disease before evaluating for GERD
Conditions Associated with GERD		
Pregnancy	Symptoms are experienced by 25%–50% of pregnant women	The frequency and severity of symptoms increase throughout gestation
Hypersecretory states (e.g., the Zollinger-Ellison syndrome)	43% of patients with the Zollinger-Ellison syndrome have endoscopic esophagitis	Patients also may have associated peptic ulceration or diarrhea
Connective tissue disorders (e.g., scleroderma)	Esophagus is involved in up to 90% of patients with scleroderma; often results in severe esophagitis and stricture formation	Characterized by low or absent LES pressure and poor esophageal motor function

GERD = gastroesophageal reflux disease; LES = lower esophageal sphincter; NSAIDs = nonsteroidal anti-inflammatory drugs.

11. Sharma N, Agrawal A, Freeman J, et al. An analysis of persistent symptoms in acid-suppressed patients undergoing impedendance-ph monitoring. Clin Gastroenterol Hepatol. 2008; 6: 521-4. [PMID: 18356117]

12. Johnston BT, Troshinsky MB, Castell JA, et al. Comparison of barium radiology with esophageal pH monitoring in the diagnosis of gastroesophageal reflux disease. Am J Gastroenterol. 1996;91: 1181-5. [PMID: 8651167]

13. O'Connor HJ. Review article: Helicobacter pylori and gastrooesophageal reflux disease-clinical implications and management. Aliment Pharmacol Ther. 1999;13:117-27. [PMID: 10102940]

14. Goldblum JR, Vicari JJ, Falk GW, et al. Inflammation and intestinal metaplasia of the gastric cardia: the role of gastroesophageal reflux and H. pylori infection. Gastroenterology. 1998;114:633-9. [PMID: 9516382]

resistance and pH, so it can be helpful to distinguish nonacid from acid reflux (11). These tests may be helpful in evaluating patients with symptoms that are atypical or refractory to empirical therapy with PPIs.

Barium radiography
Barium radiography, the most sensitive test for detecting esophageal strictures, may be useful for evaluating patients who present with dysphagia. Barium radiography has limited usefulness in most patients, however, and should not be used in routine diagnosis (1). Reflux of barium during radiographic examination is positive in only 25% to 75% of patients with known GERD and is falsely positive in up to 20% of control participants (12).

Esophageal manometry
Esophageal manometry measures muscle pressure in the lower esophagus and has a very limited role in GERD diagnosis. Use of this technique is generally limited to

research protocols or to evaluate esophageal function before antireflux surgery. There are no specific manometric findings sensitive and specific for the clinical diagnosis of GERD.

Is there any connection between GERD and *Helicobacter pylori* infection?
There is controversy over the role of *Helicobacter pylori* in GERD (13). Concomitant *H. pylori* gastric infection and GERD may reduce the effects of GERD by causing gastric atrophy and decreased gastric acid production, so eradication of *H. pylori* may worsen GERD by increasing gastric acid production. Furthermore, ammonia produced by *H. pylori* infection could buffer the gastric fluid refluxing into the esophagus, an effect that would be lost after *H. pylori* eradication (14). Conversely, one prospective study demonstrated that eradication of *H. pylori* actually improved the endoscopic appearance of reflux

esophagitis in patients with duodenal ulcer (15).

In theory, patients who are receiving prolonged PPI therapy and who are also infected with *H. pylori* may be at risk for atrophic gastritis, but studies have found no evidence of accelerated development of atrophic gastritis in patients with *H. pylori* who are on long-term omeprazole (16, 17). Currently, *H. pylori* eradication in GERD patients who require long-term PPI therapy is not considered necessary to prevent the development of atrophic gastritis.

Finally, some research suggests that the type of *H. pylori* strain infecting a patient might be relevant to GERD. One study found that patients carrying cagA-positive strains of *H. pylori* may be protected against the complications of GERD, especially Barrett's esophagus and its associated dysplasia and adenocarcinoma (18).

When should clinicians consider gastroenterology consultation during the evaluation of GERD?
Consultation may be helpful when a patient does not respond to an empirical 4- to 8-week trial of acid suppression with a standard-dose PPI. It is also indicated when a patient has pulmonary or otolaryngeal symptoms, such as wheezing, shortness of breath, chronic cough or hoarseness, unexplained chest pain, globus, choking, halitosis, and sore throat, that do not respond to an empirical therapy of at least double-dose PPI for 2 to 3 months. The presence of certain warning signs also warrants further diagnostic evaluation because these symptoms may signal a complication, such as cancer, stricture, or ulceration (1).

15. Ishiki K, Mizuno M, Take S, et al. Helicobacter pylori eradication improves pre-existing reflux esophagitis in patients with duodenal ulcer disease. Clin Gastroenterol Hepatol. 2004;2:474-9. [PMID: 15181615]
16. Lundell L, Miettinen P, Myrvold HE, et al. Lack of effect of acid suppression therapy on gastric atrophy. Nordic Gerd Study Group. Gastroenterology. 1999;117:319-26. [PMID: 10419912]
17. Gillen D, Wirz AA, Neithercut WD, et al. Helicobacter pylori infection potentiates the inhibition of gastric acid secretion by omeprazole. Gut. 1999;44:468-75. [PMID: 10075952]
18. Vaezi MF, Falk GW, Peek RM, et al. CagA-positive strains of Helicobacter pylori may protect against Barrett's esophagus. Am J Gastroenterol. 2000;95:2206-11. [PMID: 11007219]

Diagnosis... Common symptoms of GERD include heartburn and regurgitation, especially when the patient is lying down. Other symptoms include dysphagia, chronic cough or hoarseness, shortness of breath or wheezing, sore throat, throat clearing, globus, and halitosis. Always consider and exclude coronary artery disease in patients with chest pain even when it is suspected to be a symptom of GERD. In most uncomplicated cases, clinicians can accurately diagnose GERD on the basis of symptoms. Relief of classic symptoms with high-dose acid suppression is sufficiently sensitive and specific to confirm the diagnosis. In patients with atypical symptoms or who are unresponsive to empirical therapy, consider alternative disease processes. Upper endoscopy is usually reserved for patients with atypical symptoms or to evaluate for Barrett's esophagus in patients with chronic GERD.

CLINICAL BOTTOM LINE

Treatment

What is the role of dietary modification in the treatment of GERD?
Dietary modifications may reduce GERD symptoms, but they have not been rigorously tested in clinical trials and their benefits are modest at best. In particular, patients may benefit from avoiding certain foods that decrease lower esophageal sphincter (LES) pressure, delay gastric emptying, or provoke reflux symptoms. Counsel patients to avoid large, fatty meals and foods and beverages that contribute to GERD symptoms (see Box).

Dietary modifications that lead to weight loss might also reduce GERD symptoms and complications. However, various studies that examined a possible link between obesity and GERD had inconclusive findings. There is some observational evidence that obesity is associated with an elevated risk for

Foods and Beverages That May Contribute to GERD Symptoms
- Chocolate
- Peppermint
- Onions
- Garlic
- Alcohol
- Carbonated beverages
- Citrus juices
- Tomato products
- Large, fatty meals

19. Corley DA, Kubo A,
    Zhao W. Abdominal
    obesity, ethnicity
    and gastro-
    oesophageal reflux
    symptoms. Gut.
    2007;56:756-62.
    [PMID: 17047097]
20. Lagergren J,
    Bergström R, Nyrén
    O. No relation
    between body mass
    and gastro-
    oesophageal reflux
    symptoms in a
    Swedish population
    based study. Gut.
    2000;47:26-9. [PMID:
    10861260]
21. Australian Cancer
    Study. Combined
    effects of obesity,
    acid reflux and
    smoking on the risk
    of adenocarcinomas
    of the oesophagus.
    Gut. 2008;57:173-80.
    [PMID: 17932103]
22. Lagergren J,
    Bergström R, Adami
    HO, Nyrén O. Associ-
    ation between med-
    ications that relax
    the lower
    esophageal sphincter
    and risk for
    esophageal adeno-
    carcinoma. Ann
    Intern Med. 2000;
    133:165-75. [PMID:
    10906830]
23. Behar J, Sheahan
    DG, Biancani P, et al.
    Medical and surgical
    management of
    reflux esophagitis. A
    38-month report of
    a prospective clinical
    trial. N Engl J Med.
    1975;293:263-8.
    [PMID: 237234]
24. Lieberman DA. Med-
    ical therapy for
    chronic reflux
    esophagitis. Long-
    term follow-up. Arch
    Intern Med.
    1987;147:1717-20.
    [PMID: 3116959]
25. Simon TJ, Berlin RG,
    Gardner AH, et al.
    Self-Directed Treat-
    ment of Intermittent
    Heartburn: A Ran-
    domized, Multicen-
    ter, Double-Blind,
    Placebo-Controlled
    Evaluation of
    Antacid and Low
    Doses of an H(2)-
    Receptor Antagonist
    (Famotidine). Am J
    Ther. 1995;2:304-313.
    [PMID: 11850668]

adenocarcinoma of the esophagus in patients with GERD.

A cross-sectional study based on data from 80110 members of the Kaiser Permanente multiphasic health check-up cohort found the presence of reflux-type symptoms in 11% of the population, with an association between obesity and an increase in GERD-like symptoms in white male patients but not in other ethnic groups (19).

A population-based study of 820 middle-aged or elderly persons in Sweden in 1995 to 1997 found no association between normal body mass index versus >25 kg/mL and GERD symptoms (odds ratio, 0.99 [95% CI, 0.66 to 1.100]) (20).

A recent Australian study compared almost 800 patients with adenocarcinoma of the esophagus with 1580 adults without cancer and found that obesity in combination with ongoing GERD symptoms increased the risk for adenocarcinoma of the lower esophagus to nearly 17 times the risk in nonobese adults without GERD symptoms (21).

Are behavioral interventions effective in the treatment of GERD?

Behavioral modifications, such as not lying down immediately after eating or elevating the head of the bed can help decrease symptoms of reflux and distal acid exposure (see Box). Although observations suggest that these lifestyle changes decrease reflux symptoms and esophageal acid exposure, the true efficacy of these maneuvers in patients has not been rigorously tested in clinical trials. Alcohol and tobacco use can also aggravate GERD and should be avoided to reduce symptoms.

Which medications cause or exacerbate GERD, and how should clinicians counsel patients regarding the use of these medications?

Certain medications may cause or exacerbate GERD by decreasing LES pressure or decreasing esophageal acid clearance (see Box) (22).

Patients with GERD-related strictures may also need to avoid pills that could lodge proximal to strictures and result in esophagitis, ulcers, and recurrent or refractory strictures. Nonsteroidal anti-inflammatory drugs, alendronate, potassium preparations, quinidine, iron supplements, and multiple antibiotics have been implicated in pill-induced esophagitis.

Which nonprescription medications are effective in the management of GERD?

The goals of drug therapy are elimination of symptoms, healing of existing esophagitis, prevention of complications, and maintenance of remission. Many patients with mild GERD have adequate relief of symptoms with antacids and over-the-counter H_2-receptor antagonists or PPIs. Two older studies that predate availability of over-the-counter H_2-receptor antagonists and PPIs in the United States suggest that effective symptom relief occurs in 20% of patients using over-the-counter agents (Table 2) (23, 24).

Antacids
Antacids are commonly used to temporarily relieve heartburn. They work within the esophageal lumen to rapidly elevate esophageal pH and neutralize esophageal acid within 15 to 30 minutes, typically producing modest relief lasting up to 90 minutes. Although inexpensive and fast-working for relief of individual heartburn episodes, drawbacks of antacids are a relatively brief duration of action and

Table 2. Drug Treatment for GERD

Agent	Mechanism of Action	Benefits	Side Effects	Notes
Antacids	Buffer gastric acid	20% efficacy rate	Diarrhea, constipation	Chewable forms increase saliva, which helps neutralize acid; faster onset of action than an OTC H_2-RA
Alginic acids	Create foamy raft on surface of gastric pool	20% efficacy rate	Diarrhea, constipation	Often combined with antacid
OTC H_2-RAs Ranitidine 75 mg bid, cimetidine 200 mg bid, famotidine 10 mg bid, nizatidine 75 mg bid,	Decrease gastric acid secretion by binding to histamine receptor on parietall cell	Less efficacy than prescription doses	Similar to prescription doses	OTC doses are one half the standard prescription dose
OTC PPIs Omeprazole 20 mg bid	Block gastric acid secretion by binding to proton pump on parietal cell	80%–100% efficacy rate	Similar to prescription doses	Indicated for patients with symptoms at least 2 d/wk. May take 1–4 d before achieving full effect
Prescription H_2-RA Ranitidine 150–300 mg bid, cimetidine 400 mg bid to tid, famotidine 20–40 mg bid, nizatidibe 150–300 mg bid	Decrease gastric acid secretion by binding to histamine receptor on parietal cell	50%–60% efficacy rate	Drug interactions with cimetidine, theophylline, phenytoin, and warfarin	No difference in clinical efficacy among agents when using standard doses; much less effective when erosive esophagitis is present; indicated in mild-to-moderate GERD; full doses needed to provide effective maintenance
Prescription prokinetic agents Metoclopramide 10–20 mg 30 min qac and qhs	Increase LES pressure and improve gastric emptying	Mild symptomatic improvement without improvement in histologic, endoscopic, or pH testing	Drowsiness, tremors, depression, irritability, extrapyramidal side effects (20%–50% incidence)	High incidence of side effects and questionable efficacy limit usefulness; may provide benefit in patients with impaired gastric emptying
Prescription PPIs Omeprazole 20–40 mg qd, esomeprazole 40 mg qd, lansoprazole 30–60 mg qd, pantoprazole 40–80 mg qd, rabeprazole 20–40 mg qd	Block gastric acid secretion by binding to the proton pump in parietal cells	80%–100% efficacy rate	Long-term use associated with increase in serum gastrin, atrophic gastritis in *Helicobacter pylori*–infected patients, decreased vitamin B_{12} absorption	Indicated in moderate-to-severe GERD; should be given before meals for maximum pharmacologic effect. No substantial complications from long-term therapy reported; no clear difference in clinical efficacy among agents when standard doses are used.

bid = twice daily; GERD = gastroesophageal reflux disease; H_2-RA = histamine-2–receptor antagonist; LES = lower esophageal sphincter; OTC = over-the-counter; PPI = proton pump inhibitor; qd = once daily; qac = before every meal; qhs = every night; tid = three times daily.

inadequacy as heartburn prophylaxis. Antacids may be combined with alginic acid, which acts as a barrier on top of stomach acids, preventing contact between the acids and the esophagus and helping to prevent symptoms. Few well-designed clinical trials with antacids exist.

A study that randomly assigned 565 patients with heartburn to as-needed treatment with famotidine 10 mg, famotidine 20 mg, antacid, or placebo demonstrated that as-needed antacids up to twice daily were superior to placebo for relief of spontaneous heartburn (25).

A small study compared various antacid formulations in 20 patients with postprandial heartburn and found that chewable tablets and effervescent bicarbonate had longer durations of action than swallowed tablets (26).

26. Robinson M, Rodriguez-Stanley S, Miner PB, et al. Effects of antacid formulation on post-prandial oesophageal acidity in patients with a history of episodic heartburn. Aliment Pharmacol Ther. 2002;16:435-43. [PMID: 11876696]

27. Euler AR, Murdock RH Jr, Wilson TH, et al. Ranitidine is effective therapy for erosive esophagitis. Am J Gastroenterol. 1993;88:520-4. [PMID: 8470632]

28. Kahrilas PJ, Fennerty MB, Joelsson B. High- versus standard-dose ranitidine for control of heartburn in poorly responsive acid reflux disease: a prospective, controlled trial. Am J Gastroenterol. 1999;94:92-7. [PMID: 9934737]

29. Inadomi JM, Jamal R, Murata GH, et al. Step-down management of gastroesophageal reflux disease. Gastroenterology. 2001;121:1095-100. [PMID: 11677201]

30. Dean BB, Gano AD Jr, Knight K, et al. Effectiveness of proton pump inhibitors in nonerosive reflux disease. Clin Gastroenterol Hepatol. 2004;2:656-64. [PMID: 15290657]

31. Lind T, Havelund T, Carlsson R, et al. Heartburn without oesophagitis: efficacy of omeprazole therapy and features determining therapeutic response. Scand J Gastroenterol. 1997;32:974-9. [PMID: 9361168]

32. Richter JE, Peura D, Benjamin SB, et al. Efficacy of omeprazole for the treatment of symptomatic acid reflux disease without esophagitis. Arch Intern Med. 2000;160:1810-6. [PMID: 10871975]

33. Gardner JD, Ciociola AA, Robinson M, et al. Determination of the time of onset of action of ranitidine and famotidine on intra-gastric acidity. Aliment Pharmacol Ther. 2002;16:1317-26. [PMID: 12144582]

H_2-receptor antagonists

H_2-receptor antagonists, which bind to H_2 receptors on gastric parietal cells to reduce gastric acid secretion, are a first-line therapy for uncomplicated GERD with mild or intermittent symptoms. They start reducing gastric acid within 1 to 2 hours of dosing, and effects last up to 9 hours. Drawbacks of H_2-receptor antagonists are the delay in effect and the fact that tolerance may develop. Given in a standard dose, H_2-receptor antagonists provide adequate symptom relief in 50% to 60% of patients with mild-to-moderate GERD and heal endoscopic esophagitis in 48% (1).

One study randomly assigned 328 patients with erosive esophagitis to either ranitidine 300 mg 4 times daily, ranitidine 150 mg 4 times daily, or placebo for up to 12 weeks. Symptom relief and healing of esophagitis was better in both ranitidine groups than with placebo (27).

Another trial in 481 patients found no difference in efficacy between ranitidine 150 mg and 300 mg twice daily in relief of heartburn symptom. This study also found that 59% of patients still had some symptoms after 6 weeks of ranitidine therapy (28).

Proton pump inhibitors

PPIs, which block gastric acid secretion by binding to the proton pump in parietal cells, are advised for patients with GERD symptoms at least twice a week. Typical first-line therapy is a 14-day course of over-the-counter omeprazole, the only PPI with U.S. Food and Drug Administration (FDA) approval for over-the-counter use. PPIs are more effective than H_2-receptor antagonists for acute treatment of severe or erosive esophagitis. H_2-receptor antagonists are ineffective for long-term maintenance of these conditions. PPIs may take up to 4 days to relieve symptoms, but patients do not seem to develop tolerance to PPIs as they can with H_2-receptor antagonists.

When should clinicians consider prescription medications, and which medications are available?

Various PPIs and H_2-receptor antagonists are available by prescription, and some are available over the counter (Table 2). There is debate about whether initial treatment should use a step-down or a step-up approach (Figure 1). The step-down approach involves starting with once- or twice-daily PPI therapy and decreasing to the least potent acid-suppression therapy that controls symptoms. The step-up approach involves initiating therapy with standard or even non-prescription doses of an H_2-receptor antagonist and titrating up to the most potent acid-suppression therapy that controls symptoms. Efficacy studies and cost-effectiveness models have not shown superiority of either approach.

One study involving patients on long-term PPI therapy found that more than one half were able to step down from PPI therapy without increasing symptoms or limiting quality of life. Forty-one of 71 (58%) were asymptomatic 1 year after going off PPI therapy. Twenty-four of 71 (34%) required H_2-receptor antagonists, 5 of 71 (7%) required prokinetic agents, 1 of 71 (1%) required both, and 11 of 71 (15%) remained asymptomatic without medication (29).

Symptomatic medical treatment of reflux esophagitis has improved dramatically since PPIs became available in 1989. PPIs provide rapid symptomatic relief and healing of esophagitis in the highest percentage of patients.

A systematic review of 7 trials that evaluated PPIs in patients with nonerosive reflux disease found that the therapeutic gain of PPIs over placebo for sufficient heartburn control was 30% to 35% (30).

A trial in 509 patients with no esophagitis on endoscopy compared omeprazole 20 mg daily, omeprazole 10 mg daily, and placebo. At 4 weeks, the proportion of patients with complete resolution of heartburn in each group was 46%, 31%, and 13%, respectively (31).

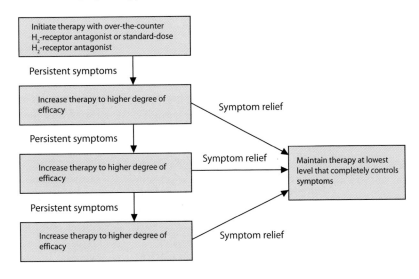

Step-up Therapy

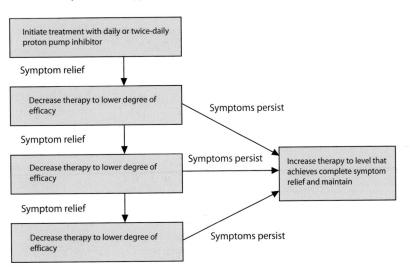

Step-down Therapy

Figure 1. Step-up vs. step-down drug therapy for gastroesophageal relux disease.

A randomized trial in 355 patients with GERD symptoms found that omeprazole 20 mg daily provided superior relief compared with omeprazole 10 mg daily and with placebo (32).

How should clinicians select from among available antireflux medications?

In general, the various H_2-receptor antagonists are equally efficacious in equipotent doses and carry similar adverse effect profiles. However, a few comparative studies of nonprescription H_2-receptor antagonists have indicated that famotidine and ranitidine may have higher potency than cimetidine, and cimetidine and ranitidine may have faster onset of effect on gastric pH than famotidine (33). Research generally also indicates that the various PPIs are equally efficacious in equipotent doses and carry similar adverse effect profiles. For patients with the uncommon form of GERD with

34. Castell DO, Kahrilas PJ, Richter JE, et al. Esomeprazole (40 mg) compared with lansoprazole (30 mg) in the treatment of erosive esophagitis. Am J Gastroenterol. 2002;97:575-83. [PMID: 11922549]

35. Schindlbeck NE, Klauser AG, Berghammer G, et al. Three year follow up of patients with gastrooesophageal reflux disease. Gut. 1992;33:1016-9. [PMID: 1356887]

36. Hetzel DJ, Dent J, Reed WD, et al. Healing and relapse of severe peptic esophagitis after treatment with omeprazole. Gastroenterology. 1988;95:903-12. [PMID: 3044912]

37. Carlsson R, Dent J, Watts R, et al. Gastro-oesophageal reflux disease in primary care: an international study of different treatment strategies with omeprazole. International GORD Study Group. Eur J Gastroenterol Hepatol. 1998;10:119-24. [PMID: 9581986]

38. Vigneri S, Termini R, Leandro G, et al. A comparison of five maintenance therapies for reflux esophagitis. N Engl J Med. 1995;333:1106-10. [PMID: 7565948]

39. Yang YX, Hennessy S, Propert K, et al. Chronic proton pump inhibitor therapy and the risk of colorectal cancer. Gastroenterology. 2007;133:748-54. [PMID: 17678926]

40. Robertson DJ, Larsson H, Friis S, et al. Proton pump inhibitor use and risk of colorectal cancer: a population-based, case-control study. Gastroenterology. 2007;133:755-60. [PMID: 17678921]

41. Yang YX, Lewis JD, Epstein S, Metz DC. Long-term proton pump inhibitor therapy and risk of hip fracture. JAMA. 2006;296:2947-53. [PMID: 17190895]

severe esophagitis, however, esomeprazole may be somewhat more effective than other PPIs (34).

When ordering GERD medications for a patient, clinicians should choose the least-expensive product that is effective for managing symptoms and preventing complications and should prescribe the lowest effective dose for the minimum duration needed.

How long should patients continue pharmacologic therapy for GERD?

Reflux symptoms disappear in only a minority of patients (35), but about 20% of patients with GERD have adequate symptom control with intermittent, nonprescription therapy and lifestyle modification. Although many patients need to remain on long-term GERD therapy to control symptoms, others may be able to reduce dosage or cease treatment once symptoms are controlled and the esophagus has healed. Clinicians may periodically consider trying step-down therapy to a lower-dose PPI or switching from a PPI to an H_2-receptor antagonist.

About 50% to 80% of patients with esophagitis have recurrence after 6 to 12 months of follow-up, regardless of the agent used to achieve healing or symptom control (36, 37). Patients with severe GERD need long-term PPI maintenance therapy to control symptoms and prevent complications. Standard or even high doses of H_2-receptor antagonists are not generally appropriate maintenance therapy for severe GERD (38).

What are the adverse effects of long-term acid-suppression therapy?

Short-term adverse effects with PPIs are uncommon and typically limited to headaches, nausea, constipation, diarrhea, and pruritus. Yet despite evidence from careful

follow-up studies, there is ongoing worry that long-term use might cause other adverse effects.

There has been concern about the potential for PPIs to increase the risk for colorectal cancer because the drugs elevate serum gastrin levels, and in vitro studies show that high gastrin levels are associated with increased growth and proliferation of colon cancer cells. However, two reports that examined the potential link between PPIs and increased colorectal cancer risk found no statistically significant overall association between long-term PPI use and colorectal cancer (39, 40).

Research has found possible associations between long-term use of PPIs and bone health, risk for gastroenteritis and other infection, and vitamin B_{12} deficiency.

In an observational study, more than 1 year of PPI therapy was associated with a 44% increased risk for hip fracture among people older than 50 years. The strength of the association with hip fractures increased with both the dosage and the duration of PPI therapy (41).

A nested case–control study performed in 364683 patients on acid-suppressive drugs found higher rates of community-acquired pneumonia among these patients than among those who did not use this type of therapy (2.45 compared with 0.6 per 100 person-years) (42).

An observational study found that current use of PPIs, but not use of H_2-receptor antagonists, was associated with an increased risk for bacterial gastroenteritis (RR, 2.9 [CI, 2.5 to 3.5]) (43).

Another observational study found that the adjusted rate ratio of Clostridium difficile–associated disease with current use of PPIs was 2.9 (CI, 2.4 to 3.4) and with use of H_2-receptor antagonists was 2.0 (CI, 1.6 to 2.7) (44).

A study that investigated whether long-term treatment with omeprazole or H_2-receptor antagonists alters vitamin B_{12} levels in patients with the Zollinger–Ellison syndrome found that B_{12} levels, but not serum folate levels, were substantially lower in patients treated with omeprazole, suggesting that serum vitamin B_{12} levels should be monitored in patients with the Zollinger–Ellison syndrome treated with PPIs (45).

When should clinicians consider surgical therapy for GERD?

Nissen fundoplication is the most common surgical intervention for GERD. This procedure aims to restore the physiology and anatomy of the gastroesophageal junction by wrapping the gastric fundus around the distal esophagus. The FDA has also approved several endoscopic procedures for treatment of GERD, including endoscopic suturing and radiofrequency ablation of the lower esophageal sphincter.

Antireflux surgery is an option for patients who have responded well to PPI therapy but who are concerned about the costs and other consequences of taking daily medication on a long-term basis. Preoperative evaluation before surgery should include documentation of GERD with pH monitoring and esophageal manometry. Patients who have not responded to medical therapy may have symptoms not caused by GERD.

Although surgical therapy is efficacious, a review comparing the efficacy, prevention of complications, safety profile, convenience, and costs of medical or surgical fundoplication therapy for GERD suggested that antireflux surgery had no clear advantage compared with medical therapy, and that medical therapy may be safer and more cost-effective (46). Fundoplication reduces costs associated with PPI use in the short term, but it does not reduce total costs because many patients subsequently return to long-term use of PPIs (47). In a follow-up study conducted 11 to 13 years after antireflux surgery, approximately 60% of the patients were again receiving medical therapy (48).

Postsurgical side effects, such as bloating, flatulence, diarrhea, and dysphagia, may be long-lasting. More serious complications, including esophageal perforation and death, have been reported. Laparoscopic antireflux surgery seems to be equal in effectiveness to open surgery, with greatly decreased morbidity.

Is it necessary to evaluate for Barrett's esophagus periodically?

Barrett's esophagus is premalignant intestinal metaplasia of the mucosa of the lower esophagus that occurs in response to chronic exposure to acidic stomach contents. Barrett's esophagus significantly increases the risk for esophageal adenocarcinoma. The risk for adenocarcinoma from Barrett's esophagus is 30 to 40 times that of the general population, or approximately 0.5% to 1.0% per year (49).

Barrett's esophagus is detected in 8% to 20% of patients with chronic GERD. White race, male gender, chronic duration of reflux symptoms, and positive family history are risk factors for Barrett's esophagus. Older age; white race; male gender; obesity; smoking; use of LES-relaxing drugs; increased frequency, greater severity, and longer duration of reflux symptoms; hiatal hernia; and duration of Barrett's esophagus are risk factors for esophageal adenocarcinoma in a patient with known Barrett's esophagus. Clinical severity of symptoms

---

> **Consider surgery as an option for patients with well-documented GERD who require long-term PPI maintenance therapy but show satisfactory relief of symptoms and who:**
>
> - Are older than 50 years
> - Consider long-term medication a financial burden
> - Are noncompliant with drug therapy
> - Prefer a single surgical intervention to long-term drug treatment
> - Experience prominent symptoms of regurgitation, even with medical control of heartburn symptoms

42. Laheij RJ, Sturkenboom MC, Hassing RJ, et al. Risk of community-acquired pneumonia and use of gastric acid-suppressive drugs. JAMA. 2004;292: 1955-60. [PMID: 15507580]
43. García Rodríguez LA, Ruigómez A, Panés J. Use of acid-suppressing drugs and the risk of bacterial gastroenteritis. Clin Gastroenterol Hepatol. 2007;5:1418-23. [PMID: 18054750]
44. Dial S, Delaney JA, Barkun AN, Suissa S. Use of gastric acid-suppressive agents and the risk of community-acquired Clostridium difficile-associated disease. JAMA. 2005;294: 2989-95. [PMID: 16414946]
45. Termanini B, Gibril F, Sutliff VE, et al. Effect of long-term gastric acid suppressive therapy on serum vitamin B12 levels in patients with Zollinger-Ellison syndrome. Am J Med. 1998;104:422-30. [PMID: 9626024]
46. Spechler SJ. Medical or invasive therapy for GERD: an acidulous analysis. Clin Gastroenterol Hepatol. 2003;1:81-8. [PMID: 15017499]
47. Dire CA, Jones MP, Rulyak SJ, Kahrilas PJ. The economics of laparoscopic Nissen fundoplication. Clin Gastroenterol Hepatol. 2003;1:328-32. [PMID: 15017676]
48. Spechler SJ, Lee E, Ahnen D, et al. Long-term outcome of medical and surgical therapies for gastroesophageal reflux disease: follow-up of a randomized controlled trial. JAMA. 2001;285: 2331-8. [PMID: 11343480]
49. Hogan WJ. Spectrum of supra-esophageal complications of gastroesophageal reflux disease. Am J Med. 1997;103:77S-83S. [PMID: 9422629]

50. Lieberman DA, Oehlke M, Helfand M. Risk factors for Barrett's esophagus in community-based practice. GORGE consortium. Gastroenterology Outcomes Research Group in Endoscopy. Am J Gastroenterol. 1997;92:1293-7. [PMID: 9260792]

51. Streitz JM Jr, Andrews CW Jr, Ellis FH Jr. Endoscopic surveillance of Barrett's esophagus. Does it help? J Thorac Cardiovasc Surg. 1993;105:383-7; discussion 387-8. [PMID: 8445916]

52. Peters JH, Clark GW, Ireland AP, et al. Outcome of adenocarcinoma arising in Barrett's esophagus in endoscopically surveyed and nonsurveyed patients. J Thorac Cardiovasc Surg. 1994;108:813-21; discussion 821-2. [PMID: 7967662]

alone is unreliable in distinguishing patients with Barrett's esophagus from those with GERD alone.

One study of 2641 patients undergoing endoscopy found that the risk for Barrett's esophagus in patients with symptoms lasting more than 5 years was 5 times that of patients with symptoms of less than 1 year (50).

Although strong evidence is not available to support a screening recommendation or to define the appropriate timing and interval of screening, consensus is that upper endoscopy should be done in patients with chronic GERD to screen for Barrett's esophagus, dysplastic changes, and early esophageal cancer. At least two studies suggest that endoscopic surveillance of patients with Barrett's esophagus detects carcinoma at an early stage and can improve long-term survival rates (51, 52).

However, the American College of Gastroenterology practice guidelines notes the lack of clear evidence that screening reduces esophageal adenocarcinoma mortality and states that screening in high-risk patients should be individualized (53). The guidelines note that the yield of screening is highest in white men older than 50 years with longstanding heartburn but do not define the specific duration of symptoms after which screening is indicated. Most experts suggest that patients with chronic GERD have endoscopy at least once during their lifetime to screen for Barrett's esophagus, regardless of whether symptoms are controlled. A case-control study found that GERD symptoms lasting longer than 13 years were associated with Barrett's esophagus (54).

How should clinicians manage patients once Barrett's esophagus is present?

Once Barrett's esophagus has been detected, surveillance endoscopy with biopsy should be performed at

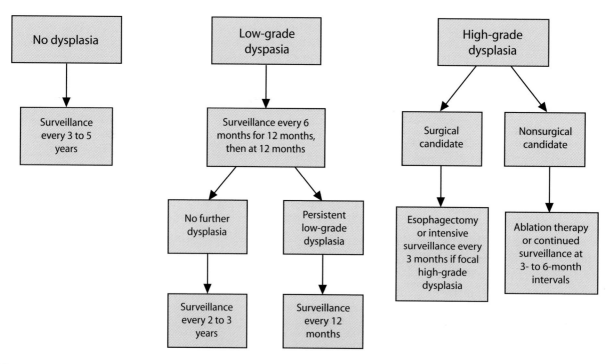

Figure 2. Proposed surveillance and management algorithm for patients with Barrett's esophagus based on grade of dysplasia detected by endoscopic biopsy.

least every 3 years (depending on the grade of dysplasia) to detect neoplastic transformation (53). Because active inflammation can be misinterpreted as dysplasia, mucosal healing should be achieved before biopsies are obtained. Diagnosis of high-grade dysplasia requires repeated endoscopy to exclude concomitant cancer (Figure 2).

Among patients with Barrett's esophagus, acid suppression is especially important because it may play a role in retarding progression of dysplasia (55). Barrett's esophagus alone is not an indication for surgical therapy for GERD (56).

How frequently should clinicians see patients with GERD and what are the components of good follow-up?

GERD is a chronic condition that usually requires ongoing follow-up and maintenance therapy to prevent complications. Clinicians should monitor for symptoms that suggest complications of cancer, stricture, or ulceration; screen for Barrett's esophagus when appropriate; and ensure that medical therapy controls symptoms in the most cost-effective manner.

When should clinicians consider gastroenterology referral for the treatment of a patient with GERD?

Consider consultation with a specialist if patients are refractory to therapy or if atypical symptoms or complications develop. Because most patients' symptoms are controlled with PPI therapy, symptoms that do not respond to PPI therapy may not be caused by GERD. Referral is also advised when evaluating for Barrett's esophagus or for possible surgical intervention for GERD.

53. Wang KK, Sampliner RE. Updated guidelines 2008 for the diagnosis, surveillance, and therapy of Barrett's esophagus. Am J Gastroenterol. 2002; 103: 788-797. [PMID: 12190150]
54. Conio M, Filiberti R, Blanchi S, et al. Risk factors for Barrett's esophagus: a case-control study. Int J Cancer 2002; 97: 225-229.
55. El-Serag HB, Aguirre T, Kuebeler M, Sampliner RE. The length of newly diagnosed Barrett's oesophagus and prior use of acid suppressive therapy. Aliment Pharmacol Ther. 2004;19:1255-60. [PMID: 15191506]
56. Csendes A, Braghetto I, Korn O, Cortés C. Late subjective and objective evaluations of antireflux surgery in patients with reflux esophagitis: analysis of 215 patients. Surgery. 1989;105: 374-82. [PMID: 2784232]

Treatment... Dietary and behavioral modifications may be effective in treatment of GERD. Many patients with mild GERD have adequate relief of symptoms with antacids and over-the-counter H_2-receptor antagonists and PPIs. Prescription medications, particularly PPIs, are indicated for moderate-to-severe GERD. There is ongoing debate about whether initial treatment should use a step-down or a step-up approach. Many patients with moderate-to-severe GERD require indefinite maintenance therapy to control symptoms and prevent complications. There is no clear evidence of serious adverse effects from long-term PPI use. Consider anti-reflux surgery in patients who have responded well to PPI therapy and who are not interested in long-term medical therapy. Clinicians should provide follow-up to monitor for complications and to ensure that medical maintenance therapy controls symptoms in the most cost-effective manner. Patients with chronic GERD should have endoscopy at least once to screen for Barrett's esophagus.

CLINICAL BOTTOM LINE

Practice Improvement

How do U.S. stakeholders evaluate the quality of care for patients with GERD?

The Center for Medicare & Medicaid Services (CMS) has developed 119 measures of quality of care to use in the 2008 Physician Quality Reporting Initiative (PQRI), an initiative that will financially reward participating physicians who

57. Canadian Association of Gastroenterology GERD Consensus Group. Canadian Consensus Conference on the management of gastroesophageal reflux disease in adults - update 2004. Can J Gastroenterol. 2005;19:15-35. [PMID: 15685294]
58. Falk GW, Fennerty MB, Rothstein RI. AGA Institute medical position statement on the use of endoscopic therapy for gastroesophageal reflux disease. Gastroenterology. 2006;131: 1313-4. [PMID: 17030198]
59. Practice Parameters Committee of the American College of Gastroenterology. ACG practice guidelines: esophageal reflux testing. Am J Gastroenterol. 2007;102:668-85. [PMID: 17335450]
60. Society of American Gastrointestinal and Endoscopic Surgeons. Guidelines for Surgical Treatment of Gastroesophageal Reflux Disease (GERD). 2001. Accessed at www.sages.org/ publications/ publication.php?id= 22 on 10 June 2008.

meet defined quality standards. Of these measures, one involves GERD (see Box). The rationale for this measure is that many patients with GERD remain on medication for years, and experts suspect that not all patients have regular reassessment to determine whether medication is still needed. Research indicates that patients on long-term GERD therapy may be able to have their medications modified on the basis of the presence or absence of symptoms.

What do professional organizations recommend regarding the management of patients with GERD?
In 2005, the American College of Gastroenterology published updated guidelines on diagnosis and treatment of GERD (1). The guidance in this article generally reflects the recommendations in those guidelines. Other GERD treatment guidelines include a 2005 Canadian Association of Gastroenterology consensus conference on the management of GERD in adults (57); a 2006 American Gastrointestinal Association Institute Medical Position Statement on the use of endoscopic therapy for

GERD (58); 2007 American College of Gastroenterology practice guidelines on esophageal reflux testing (59); 2001 Society of American Gastrointestinal and Endoscopic Surgeons consensus guidelines on the surgical treatment of GERD (60); and 2008 American College of Gastroenterology guidelines on the diagnosis, surveillance, and management of Barrett's esophagus (53).

Centers for Medicare & Medicaid Services: 2008 Physician Quality Reporting Initiative

Measure #77: Assessment of GERD Symptoms in Patients Receiving Chronic Medication for GERD

Description: Percentage of patients ≥18 years with the diagnosis of GERD who have been prescribed continuous PPI or H_2-receptor antagonist therapy who received an annual assessment of their GERD symptoms after 12 months of therapy.

Numerator: Patients who had an annual assessment of their GERD symptoms after 12 months of therapy.

Denominator: All patients ≥18 years with a diagnosis of GERD who have been prescribed ≥12 months of continuous PPI or H_2-receptor antagonist therapy.

---

in the clinic
Tool Kit
Gastroesophageal Reflux Disease

PIER Modules
pier.acponline.org
Access the following PIER modules: GERD, Barrett's Esophagus, and Upper Gastro-intestinal Endoscopy. PIER modules provide evidence-based, updated information on current diagnosis, treatment, and management, in an electronic format designed for rapid access at the point of care.

Patient Education Resources
www.annals.org/intheclinic/
Access the Patient Information material that appears on the following page for duplication and distribution to patients.
www.acponline.org/patients_families/pdfs/health/heartburn_report.pdf
Access American College of Physicians: ACP Special Report: Understanding and Treating Heartburn

Quality Improvement Tools
pier.acponline.org/qualitym/t004.html
Access the CMS PQRI quality measure for GERD with administrative criteria and background material.

Practice Guidelines
http://www.acg.gi.org/physicians/clinicalupdates.asp#guidelines
Access American College of Gastroenterology practice guidelines

WHAT YOU SHOULD KNOW ABOUT GASTROESOPAHAGEAL REFLUX DISEASE (GERD)

In gastroesophageal reflux disease (GERD), stomach acid washes up into the esophagus. The esophagus is the tube that carries food from the mouth to the stomach. GERD can harm the lining of the esophagus and cause what many people call "heartburn" or "acid indigestion." Some people with GERD may also have a cough, a sore throat, breathing problems, trouble swallowing, or bad breath.

Things that can cause GERD or make it worse:

- Pregnancy
- Smoking
- Alcohol
- Being overweight
- Some foods (fatty or fried foods, chocolate, mint, garlic, onions, citrus fruits or juices, carbonated beverages)
- Lying down after eating

How will the doctor know if problems are caused by GERD?

- Your doctor may give you medicine to make you have less stomach acid. If the medicine helps, your problems were probably from GERD and you probably won't need any tests.

- Sometimes you may need a test to measure acid or pressure or to look at the esophagus lining.

Is there a treatment?

- GERD can be treated by stopping the things that make it worse.
- Taking medicines that block stomach acid can also help.

Is GERD dangerous?

- If GERD is not treated, it can cause bleeding or scars that block the esophagus.
- GERD may make changes in the lining of the esophagus called "Barrett's esophagus." Barrett's esophagus can turn into cancer.
- People who have GERD for many years should get checked for Barrett's esophagus.
- Tell your doctor if you have trouble swallowing, weight loss, vomiting, bleeding, loss of appetite, or chest pain.
- In a few cases, an operation may be needed.

For More Information

Web Sites with Good Information on GERD

American College of Physicians: ACP Special Report: Understanding and Treating Heartburn
http://www.acponline.org/patients_families/pdfs/health/heartburn_report.pdf
National Digestive Diseases Information Clearinghouse: Heartburn, Hiatal Hernia, and GERD
http://digestive.niddk.nih.gov/ddiseases/pubs/gerd/index.htm

ACP
AMERICAN COLLEGE OF PHYSICIANS
INTERNAL MEDICINE | *Doctors for Adults*®

Patient Information

Deep Venous Thrombosis

1. White RH. The epidemiology of venous thromboembolism. Circulation. 2003;107:I4-8. [PMID: 12814979]
2. Douketis JD, Kearon C, Bates S, et al. Risk of fatal pulmonary embolism in patients with treated venous thromboembolism. JAMA. 1998;279:458-62. [PMID: 9466640]
3. Anderson FA Jr, Spencer FA. Risk factors for venous thromboembolism. Circulation. 2003;107:I9-16. [PMID: 12814980]
4. Heit JA, Silverstein MD, Mohr DN, et al. Risk factors for deep vein thrombosis and pulmonary embolism: a population-based case-control study. Arch Intern Med. 2000;160:809-15. [PMID: 10737280]
5. Rogers SO Jr, Kilaru RK, Hosokawa P, et al. Multivariable predictors of postoperative venous thromboembolic events after general and vascular surgery: results from the patient safety in surgery study. J Am Coll Surg. 2007;204:1211-21. [PMID: 17544079]
6. Ageno W, Becattini C, Brighton T, et al. Cardiovascular risk factors and venous thromboembolism: a meta-analysis. Circulation. 2008;117: 93-102. [PMID: 18086925]
7. Schwarz T, Siegert G, Oettler W, et al. Venous thrombosis after long-haul flights. Arch Intern Med. 2003;163:2759-64. [PMID: 14662630]
8. Philbrick JT, Shumate R, Siadaty MS, et al. Air travel and venous thromboembolism: a systematic review. J Gen Intern Med. 2007;22:107-14. [PMID: 17351849]
9. Geerts WH, Bergqvist D, Pineo GF, et al. Prevention of venous thromboembolism: American College of Chest Physicians Evidence-based Clinical Practice Guidelines (8th Edition). Chest 2008;133:381S-453S
10. Kearon C, Ginsberg JS, Hirsh J. The role of venous ultrasonography in the diagnosis of suspected deep venous thrombosis and pulmonary embolism. Ann Intern Med. 1998;129:1044-9. [PMID: 9867760]

Venous thromboembolism (VTE) is a relatively common and potentially life-threatening condition that affects approximately 100 persons per 100 000 per year in the United States (1). About one third of patients with VTE present with features of pulmonary embolism (PE), and two thirds present with features of deep venous thrombosis (DVT). Treated DVT has an excellent prognosis. The probability of fatal PE is 0.4% and the probability of nonfatal thromboembolism is 3.8% over a 3- to 6-month treatment period (2).

Prevention

What factors increase the risk for DVT?

The main risk factors for VTE are recent surgery (especially major general surgery, hip or knee replacement, or knee arthroscopy), trauma (especially major trauma, spinal injury, or fracture of the hip or leg), congestive heart or respiratory failure, a malignant condition, pregnancy, hormone replacement or oral contraceptive therapy, previous VTE, hereditary thrombophilia, increasing age, and immobility (3).

Hospitalization is independently associated with an 8-fold increase in the relative risk for VTE (4). Among surgical patients, a number of patient-related factors predict the risk for postoperative VTE. These include female sex, higher American Society of Anesthesiologists class, ventilator dependence, preoperative dyspnea, disseminated cancer, chemotherapy within 30 days, >4 U packed erythrocyte transfusion in the 72 hours before surgery, albumin <3.5 mg/dL, bilirubin >1.0 mg/dL, sodium >145 mmol/L, hematocrit <38%, type of surgical procedure, emergency surgery, complexity of the procedure, and infected or contaminated wounds (5). In general, cardiovascular risk factors also increase the risk for VTE.

A meta-analysis of case–control and cohort studies with a total of 63 552 patients showed that relative risk for VTE was 2.33 for obesity (95% CI, 1.68 to 3.24), 1.51 for hypertension (CI, 1.23 to 1.85), 1.42 for diabetes mellitus (CI, 1.12 to 1.77), 1.18 for smoking (CI, 0.95 to 1.46), and 1.16 for hypercholesterolemia (CI, 0.67 to 2.02) (6).

Air flights longer than 6 to 8 hours are also associated with an increased risk for DVT (7, 8).

Should clinicians screen specific types of patients for DVT?

Guidelines from the American College of Chest Physicians recommend against routinely screening asymptomatic patients for DVT, even those at increased risk (9). Ultrasound imaging, plethysmography, and D-dimer measurement all have low sensitivity for detecting asymptomatic DVT in such patients (10).

If patients are at high risk for DVT, primary prophylaxis with heparin (and warfarin if the risk is ongoing) should be initiated instead of screening. However, in high-risk patients in whom anticoagulation is contraindicated, ultrasound imaging can be considered as an alternative to prophylactic treatment to determine the need for placement of an inferior vena cava filter.

What modalities should clinicians use to prevent DVT in hospitalized medical patients?

Prophylaxis with subcutaneous heparin (unfractionated heparin 5000 U 2 or 3 times daily or low-molecular-weight heparin [LMWH], such as enoxaparin 40 mg daily), can prevent DVT in at-risk hospitalized medical patients.

A meta-analysis of prophylactic anticoagulation in at-risk medical patients showed significant reductions in any PE (relative risk, 0.43 [CI, 0.26 to 0.71]) and fatal PE (relative risk, 0.38 [CI, 0.21 to 0.69]), a nonsignificant reduction in symptomatic DVT (relative risk, 0.47 [CI, 0.22 to 1.00]), a nonsignificant increase in major bleeding (relative risk, 1.32 [CI, 0.73 to 2.37]), but no effect on all-cause mortality (relative risk, 0.97 [CI, 0.79 to 1.19]) (11).

LMWH has some advantages over unfractionated heparin as prophylaxis for hospitalized medical patients because it is associated with a lower risk for DVT and PE (12).

Guidelines recommend graduated compression stockings for hospitalized medical patients with a contraindication to anticoagulant prophylaxis (13), but this is based on limited evidence (14, 15).

What modalities should clinicians use to prevent DVT in hospitalized surgical patients?

Clinicians should consider prophylaxis with subcutaneous heparin (unfractionated heparin 5000 U 2 or 3 times daily or LMWH, such as enoxaparin 40 mg daily) to prevent DVT in hospitalized surgical patients. Low-dose unfractionated heparin reduces the risk for fatal postoperative PE from 0.7% to 0.1% (16) and is associated with a relatively low rate of major or minor bleeding complications, ranging from <0.1% for retroperitoneal bleeding to 6.9% for injection-site bruising (17).

Although twice-daily heparin dosing causes fewer major bleeding episodes, thrice-daily dosing offers somewhat better efficacy in preventing clinically relevant thrombotic events.

A meta-analysis comparing twice-daily with thrice-daily administration of subcutaneous unfractionated heparin showed that there was no difference in the overall rate (per 1000 patient-days) of VTE (5.4 for twice-daily vs. 3.5 for thrice-daily; P = 0.87). However, thrice-daily heparin showed a trend toward a decrease in PE (1.5 for twice daily vs. 0.5 for thrice daily; P = 0.09) and in proximal DVT and PE (2.3 for twice daily vs. 0.9 for thrice daily; P = 0.05). The risk for major bleeding was significantly increased with thrice-daily heparin

(0.35 for twice daily vs. 0.96 for thrice daily; P < 0.001) (18).

Unless there is a contraindication, LMWH or unfractionated heparin is used for prophylaxis in most cases. LMWH is preferred in patients undergoing hip or knee replacement or neurosurgery, patients older than 40 years undergoing general surgery for malignant conditions, and patients with an inhibitor deficiency state. Warfarin may be used in those undergoing hip and knee replacement or other hip surgery. Randomized trials and meta-analysis show superior efficacy of LMWH over unfractionated heparin in high-risk orthopedic patients (19).

In the absence of a clear contraindication, such as severe peripheral arterial disease, fragile skin, or severe edema, graduated compression stockings or intermittent pneumatic compression should be used in primary prophylaxis against postoperative DVT. Mechanical compression can be used as monotherapy in patients for whom the risks of anticoagulation outweigh the benefits.

What modalities should clinicians use to prevent DVT in pregnant patients?

Clinicians should ask pregnant women about personal or family history of VTE at their first prenatal visit. In general, women with previous idiopathic VTE, VTE related to pregnancy or estrogen therapy, or thrombophilia are at higher risk than those with previous VTE related to a temporary risk factor. Clinicians should therefore consider prenatal and postnatal prophylaxis with LMWH for those at higher risk and only postnatal prophylaxis with LMWH for those with previous VTE related to a temporary risk factor.

Recommendations for women with no history of DVT but thrombophilia identified by screening

11. Dentali F, Douketis JD, Gianni M, et al. Meta-analysis: anticoagulant prophylaxis to prevent symptomatic venous thromboembolism in hospitalized medical patients. Ann Intern Med. 2007;146:278-88. [PMID: 17310052]

12. Wein L, Wein S, Haas SJ, et al. Pharmacological venous thromboembolism prophylaxis in hospitalized medical patients: a meta-analysis of randomized controlled trials. Arch Intern Med. 2007;167:1476-86. [PMID: 17646601]

13. Geerts WH, Pineo GF, Heit JA, et al. Prevention of venous thromboembolism: The Seventh ACCP Conference on Antithrombotic and Thrombolytic Therapy. Chest 2004;126;3 (suppl):338S-400S

14. Kierkegaard A, Norgren L. Graduated compression stockings in the prevention of deep vein thrombosis in patients with acute myocardial infarction. Eur Heart J. 1993;14:1365-8. [PMID: 8262083]

15. Muir KW, Watt A, Baxter G, et al. Randomized trial of graded compression stockings for prevention of deep-vein thrombosis after acute stroke. QJM. 2000;93:359-64. [PMID: 10873185]

16. Prevention of fatal postoperative pulmonary embolism by low doses of heparin. An international multicentre trial. Lancet. 1975;2:45-51. [PMID: 49649]

17. Leonardi MJ, McGory ML, Ko CY. The rate of bleeding complications after pharmacologic deep venous thrombosis prophylaxis: a systematic review of 33 randomized controlled trials. Arch Surg. 2006;141:790-7; discussion 797-9. [PMID: 16924087]

18. King CS, Holley AB, Jackson JL, et al. Twice vs three times daily heparin dosing for thromboembolism prophylaxis in the general medical population: A metaanalysis. Chest. 2007;131:507-16. [PMID: 17296655]

19. Nurmohamed MT, Rosendaal FR, Büller HR, et al. Low-molecular-weight heparin versus standard heparin in general and orthopaedic surgery: a meta-analysis. Lancet. 1992;340:152-6. [PMID: 1352573]
20. Greer IA. Prevention of venous thromboembolism in pregnancy. Best Pract Res Clin Haematol. 2003;16:261-78. [PMID: 12763491]
21. Scottish Intercollegiate Guidelines Network. Prophylaxis of Venous Thromboembolism: A National Guideline. Edinburgh, Scotland: Scottish Intercollegiate Guidelines Network; 2002.
22. The Thrombosis: Risk and Economic Assessment of Thrombophilia Screening (TREATS) Study. Screening for thrombophilia in high-risk situations: a meta-analysis and cost-effectiveness analysis. Br J Haematol. 2005;131:80-90. [PMID: 16173967]
23. Bockenstedt PL. Management of hereditary hypercoagulable disorders. Hematology Am Soc Hematol Educ Program. 2006:444-9. [PMID: 17124097]
24. Clarke M, Hopewell S, Juszczak E, et al. Compression stockings for preventing deep vein thrombosis in airline passengers. Cochrane Database Syst Rev. 2006:CD004002. [PMID: 16625594]
25. Goodacre S, Sutton AJ, Sampson FC. Meta-analysis: The value of clinical assessment in the diagnosis of deep venous thrombosis. Ann Intern Med. 2005;143:129-39. [PMID: 16027455]
26. Wells PS, Hirsh J, Anderson DR, et al. Accuracy of clinical assessment of deep-vein thrombosis. Lancet. 1995;345:1326-30. [PMID: 7752753]

depend on the risk associated with the specific thrombophilic disorder. In general, these women do not require prenatal prophylaxis but should be offered postnatal prophylaxis.

Graduated compression stockings have not been widely evaluated in pregnancy as an addition or alternative to prophylaxis with anticoagulants but have been recommended by expert opinion for all pregnant women at risk for VTE unless there are specific contraindications (20).

Some guidelines recommend that persons with a personal or family history of VTE should be screened for thrombophilia (21) because of the increased risk for VTE associated with thrombophilic disorders (hazard ratio, 0.74 to 34.40), depending on the specific disorder (22).

However, given these data and the baseline risk for VTE in pregnancy of approximately 1 in 1000, the greatest absolute risk for VTE in pregnant women with thrombophilia is about 3.4%. The low risk plus the scant evidence supporting the benefit of thromboprophylaxis once a thrombophilic disorder has been identified makes the role of screening pregnant women for thrombophilia uncertain.

What modalities should clinicians use to prevent DVT in nonpregnant patients with thrombophilia?

The thrombophilias or hypercoagulability disorders include a variety of different syndromes with differing risk for VTE (see Box). Lifelong anticoagulation may be appropriate in some patients, but the lack of long-terms studies of VTE thromboprophylaxis for patients with hypercoagulability disorders means that recommendations are based on expert opinion (23).

Hypercoagulability disorders are usually identified as a result of

screening after apparently idiopathic VTE, and recommendations for secondary prevention of VTE usually relate to duration of anticoagulation after the initial VTE (see Treatment section). Recommendations for prevention of DVT in patients with thrombophilia but no previous VTE are limited by lack of long-term studies. Because the incidence of VTE in the general population is low, even if some thrombophilias are associated with a substantial relative risk for VTE, the absolute risk is small. Management involves individualized risk–benefit analysis, taking into account interactions of acquired and hereditary factors that determine the risk for VTE. Consultation with a specialist is recommended.

How should physicians counsel patients about DVT prevention during prolonged immobility associated with travel?

Individuals without specific risk factors should consider below-knee compression stockings starting 2 to 3 hours before flights longer than 6 to 8 hours. Individuals at high risk for DVT because of previous VTE or superficial venous thrombosis, coagulation disorders, severe obesity or limited mobility, neoplastic disease within the past 2 years, cardiovascular disease, and large varicose veins should consider a single dose of subcutaneous LMWH 2 to 4 hours before long-haul travel in addition to compression stockings.

A meta-analysis showed that wearing compression stockings reduced the risk for asymptomatic DVT (odds ratio, 0.10 [CI, 0.04 to 0.25]) associated with long air

---

Types of Thrombophilia
- Antiphospholipid antibodies
- Antithrombin III deficiency
- Protein S deficiency
- Factor V Leiden
- Prothrombin 20210A
- Hyperhomocysteinuria

flights, but their effect on symptomatic DVT, PE, and death could not be determined because no such events occurred during the trials (24).

Diagnosis

What signs and symptoms should lead clinicians to suspect DVT?
DVT should be suspected in patients with lower limb pain or swelling. Factors that increase the likelihood of DVT include malignant conditions, history of DVT, recent surgery, immobilization, and increased calf diameter >3 cm in the symptomatic leg. Other clinical features, such as warmth, erythema, and Homan sign, have limited diagnostic value (25).

The most extensively evaluated clinical score for DVT is the Wells score, which stratifies patients to high (likelihood ratio, 5.2), intermediate, and low (likelihood ratio, 0.25) risk for proximal DVT (26) (Table 1). Three other scores have been developed that use fewer items than the 9-item Wells score, and another score combines clinical evaluation with D-dimer results to determine the need for ultrasound testing (27–30). Although these scores may be simpler to use than the Wells score, they have yet to be as widely validated.

The Wells score does not accurately stratify risk for distal DVT, has not been validated in certain groups (such as intravenous drug abusers), and does not perform as well in excluding DVT in primary care settings as in hospital settings (31).

27. Kahn SR, Joseph L, Abenhaim L, et al. Clinical prediction of deep vein thrombosis in patients with leg symptoms. Thromb Haemost. 1999;81:353-7. [PMID: 10102459]
28. Constans J, Nelzy ML, Salmi LR, et al. Clinical prediction of lower limb deep vein thrombosis in symptomatic hospitalized patients. Thromb Haemost. 2001;86:985-90. [PMID: 11686356]
29. Constans J, Boutinet C, Salmi LR, et al. Comparison of four clinical prediction scores for the diagnosis of lower limb deep venous thrombosis in outpatients. Am J Med. 2003;115:436-40. [PMID: 14563499]
30. The Amsterdam Maastricht Utrecht Study on thromboEmbolism Investigators. Safely Ruling out Deep Venous Thrombosis in Primary Care. Ann Intern Med. In Press.
31. Oudega R, Hoes AW, Moons KG. The Wells rule does not adequately rule out deep venous thrombosis in primary care patients. Ann Intern Med. 2005;143:100-7. [PMID: 16027451]

Table 1. Modified Wells Clinical Score*

Clinical Characteristic	Score
Active cancer (treatment ongoing, within 6 mo, or palliative)	1
Paralysis, paresis, or recent plaster immobilization of the lower extremities	1
Recently bedridden >3 d or major surgery within 12 wk requiring general or regional anesthesia	1
Localized tenderness along the distribution of the deep venous system	1
Entire leg swollen	1
Calf swelling 3 cm larger than asymptomatic side (measured 10 cm below the tibial tuberosity)	1
Pitting edema confined to the symptomatic leg	1
Collateral superficial veins (nonvaricose)	1
Previously documented DVT	1
Alternative diagnosis at least as likely as DVT	–2

DVT = deep venous thrombosis.

* The score is obtained by summing the scores for each positive item. The original Wells score (26) categorized patients into low (score ≤0), intermediate (1–2), or high (≥3) risk for DVT. More recent use of the score (33) dichotomizes patients into DVT unlikely (≤1) or DVT likely (≥2).

What is the role of D-dimer testing in diagnosing DVT?

D-dimer testing can be used to effectively rule out DVT in patients with a low or intermediate clinical risk for DVT.

A meta-analysis showed that the 3-month incidence of VTE was 0.4% (CI, 0.04% to 1.1%) among patients with low or intermediate clinical probability of DVT and a normal highly sensitive D-dimer assay concentration and 0.5% (CI, 0.07% to 1.1%) among patients with a low clinical probability of DVT and a normal D-dimer concentration (32).

D-dimer assays generally have good sensitivity but poor specificity for proximal DVT at conventionally set thresholds that define positive results (33). However, specificity varies with pretest clinical probability of DVT and is lower among patients with a high clinical probability of DVT (34). These characteristics mean that D-dimer assay has better diagnostic accuracy and greater clinical utility in patients with a low clinical probability of DVT.

Diagnostic characteristics vary among D-dimer assays. In general, enzyme-linked immunoassay tests have higher sensitivity and lower specificity, whereas whole-blood agglutination assays have lower sensitivity and higher specificity (33). The SimpliRED D-dimer assay is a widely used point-of-care whole-blood agglutination assay. It is not as sensitive as laboratory-based enzyme-linked immunosorbent assay or latex assays, but because it can be used at the point of care, it can rule out DVT in the emergency department or in outpatient practice.

D-dimer sensitivity may be lower in pregnant patients, anticoagulated patients, and those with prolonged clinical symptoms of DVT. D-dimer specificity may be lower in patients with malignant conditions, pregnant patients, anticoagulated patients, and those with a history of DVT (34).

What is the role of venous ultrasonography in diagnosing DVT and what alternate testing modalities are available?

Clinicians should use venous ultrasound to diagnose or exclude DVT in patients with a high clinical probability of DVT or a positive D-dimer result (Figure). If D-dimer testing is unavailable or unreliable, ultrasound should be used in all patients with suspected DVT.

A meta-analysis of 100 cohort studies showed that venous ultrasound has 94% sensitivity for detecting proximal venous thrombosis, 63% sensitivity for distal DVT, and 94% specificity for both (35).

If proximal DVT is detected on ultrasonography, the patient should be treated with anticoagulants without further investigation. Negative ultrasonography results effectively rules out proximal DVT but not distal DVT.

About 1% to 2% of patients with a normal initial ultrasound have calf venous thrombosis that is destined to extend into the proximal veins, generally within 5 to 8 days (36). For this reason, ultrasound is often repeated 1 week later if initial investigation is negative. Repeated ultrasound for all patients may not be a cost-effective use of health care resources, so selection on the basis of D-dimer result may be an appropriate compromise. Because D-dimer testing has higher sensitivity for distal DVT than ultrasound, a patient with a positive D-dimer and initially negative ultrasound has a significant risk for distal DVT, thus meriting repeated ultrasonography.

Duplex ultrasonography using compression ultrasound and color-flow Doppler has higher sensitivity for detecting distal DVT but slightly lower specificity than ultrasound alone (35). The use of repeated scanning after 1 week may therefore also depend on the technique used. If compression ultrasound alone is used, then repeated

32. Fancher TL, White RH, Kravitz RL. Combined use of rapid D-dimer testing and estimation of clinical probability in the diagnosis of deep vein thrombosis: systematic review. BMJ. 2004;329:821. [PMID: 15383452]
33. Stein PD, Hull RD, Patel KC, et al. D-dimer for the exclusion of acute venous thrombosis and pulmonary embolism: a systematic review. Ann Intern Med. 2004;140:589-602. [PMID: 15096330]
34. Goodacre S, Sampson FC, Sutton AJ, et al. Variation in the diagnostic performance of D-dimer for suspected deep vein thrombosis. QJM. 2005;98:513-27. [PMID: 15955795]
35. Goodacre S, Sampson F, Thomas S, et al. Systematic review and meta-analysis of the diagnostic accuracy of ultrasonography for deep vein thrombosis. BMC Med Imaging. 2005;5:6. [PMID: 16202135]

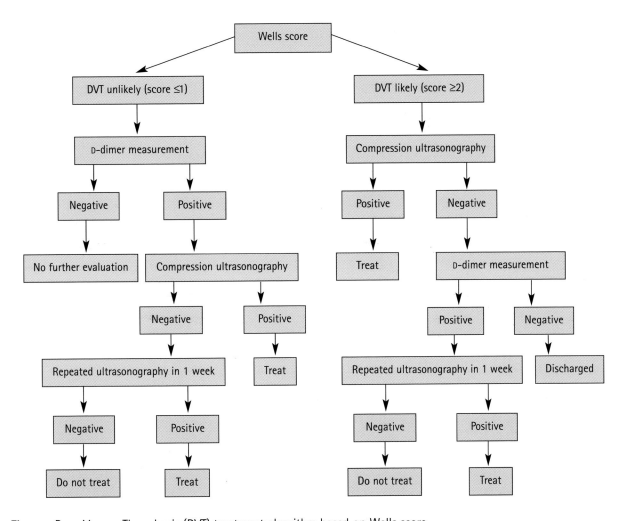

Figure. Deep Venous Thrombosis (DVT) treatment algorithm based on Wells score

scanning is likely to have greater value.

Magnetic resonance venography is an alternative to ultrasound and has equivalent accuracy (37). Impedance and strain-gauge plethysmography are alternatives that have lower accuracy and are now considered obsolete.

What other diagnoses should clinicians consider in patients with suspected DVT?

The differential diagnosis of suspected DVT is extensive. Table 2 outlines the main alternative considerations. Some of these, such as Baker cyst or superficial thrombophlebitis can be diagnosed by an experienced sonographer while investigating for DVT. Differentiation of DVT from muscle trauma

often requires ultrasound because muscle trauma may lead to elevated D-dimer levels, and DVT may complicate muscle trauma that results in immobilization. The patient with worsening pain or swelling after initially improving symptoms from muscle injury should be suspected of having DVT.

What underlying conditions and diagnostic studies should clinicians consider in patients with DVT who have no obvious inciting factor?

A number of acquired and hereditary hypercoagulability disorders can precipitate DVT in patients who are not immobilized and have no other obvious inciting factor. These include malignant conditions and thrombophilic disorders.

36. Goodacre S, Sampson F, Stevenson M, et al. Measurement of the clinical and cost-effectiveness of non-invasive diagnostic testing strategies for deep vein thrombosis. Health Technol Assess. 2006;10:1-168, iii-iv. [PMID: 16707072]
37. Sampson FC, Goodacre SW, Thomas SM, et al. The accuracy of MRI in diagnosis of suspected deep vein thrombosis: systematic review and meta-analysis. Eur Radiol. 2007;17:175-81. [PMID: 16628439]
38. Federman DG, Kirsner RS. An update on hypercoagulable disorders. Arch Intern Med. 2001;161:1051-6. [PMID: 11322838]

Table 2. Differential Diagnosis of DVT

Disease	Characteristics	Notes
Venous insufficiency (venous reflux)	Usually due to venous hypertension from such causes as venous reflux or obesity	Obtain ultrasonography of venous reflux
Superficial thrombophlebitis	Firm, tender, varicose vein	Superficial thrombosis is rarely associated with DVT
Muscle strain, tear, or trauma	Pain occurring with a range of motion more characteristic of orthopedic problem due to trauma; usually a history of leg injury	Order appropriate radiologic studies to evaluate for orthopedic problem
Leg swelling in a paralyzed limb	History of paraplegia	Patients with a paralyzed limb may develop edema without DVT
Baker cyst	Frequent pain localized to popliteal region of leg	Seen on ultrasonography
Cellulitis	Skin erythema and warmth	Consider antibiotic treatment
Lymphedema	Toe edema is more characteristic of lymphedema than of venous edema.	Lymphedema can occur in 1 or both legs

DVT = deep venous thrombosis.

Screening patients with a first episode of idiopathic DVT for thrombophilia is controversial. Testing is usually undertaken in patients who develop VTE before age 45 to 50 years, have a family history of VTE, have recurrent VTE thrombosis in an unusual site, or have life-threatening VTE (38).

Weight loss, general ill health, or specific symptoms might suggest a malignant condition. Clinicians should obtain a baseline complete blood cell count, including platelets, prothrombin time and activated partial thromboplastin time, and a serum creatinine level in all patients with DVT before starting treatment. Choice of other investigations should be guided by clinical assessment. It is important that patients with unexplained DVT undergo age-appropriate cancer screening, even if the clinical picture does not suggest underlying malignant conditions.

Diagnosis... Clinicians should consider using such instruments as the Wells clinical probability score to stratify the risk for proximal DVT and guide further investigation. Patients with a low clinical probability score and negative D-dimer levels are unlikely to benefit from further investigation. Patients with high clinical probability or positive D-dimer levels should be investigated with ultrasonography. Patients with positive D-dimer levels and negative ultrasonography should undergo repeated ultrasonography investigation after 1 week to identify proximal propagation of possible distal DVT. Testing for underlying predisposing conditions in patients with idiopathic VTE should be done on the basis of clinical assessment.

CLINICAL BOTTOM LINE

Treatment

39. Segal JB, Streiff MB, Hofmann LV, et al. Management of venous thromboembolism: a systematic review for a practice guideline. Ann Intern Med. 2007;146:211-22. [PMID: 17261856]

What criteria should clinicians use to decide whether to provide outpatient or hospital treatment for a patient with DVT?
Most patients with DVT can be safely treated as outpatients with LMWH unless they have suspected PE. Patients with suspected PE usually receive hospital treatment, although outpatient management is currently being investigated.

A systematic review comparing patients with VTE treated with LMWH administered at home with those treated with unfractionated heparin in the hospital found no difference in outcomes. Nine of 10 studies reporting treatment costs suggested cost savings with outpatient therapy when compared with inpatient therapy (39).

Patients with bilateral DVT, renal insufficiency, body weight below 70 kg, recent immobility, chronic heart failure, and cancer have an increased risk for adverse outcomes, such as symptomatic PE, recurrent DVT, major bleeding, or death and may benefit from hospital admission (40).

What local measures should clinicians recommend in patients with symptomatic DVT?

Clinicians should recommend compression stockings within 1 month of diagnosis of symptomatic proximal DVT to prevent the postthrombotic syndrome and continued use for a minimum of 1 year. Graduated compression stockings provide venous support and reduce sequelae of the postthrombotic syndrome, such as debilitating edema.

Two randomized trials in which patients used compression stockings within 1 month (41) or 1 week (42) of diagnosis both showed significant reductions of about 50% in the postthrombotic syndrome compared with control participants. However, another trial that compared use of compression stockings with placebo showed no difference in incidence of the postphlebitic syndrome after 1 year (43).

What anticoagulant regimens should clinicians use to treat patients with DVT?

Table 3 outlines anticoagulant regimens that can be used for DVT. LMWH has largely replaced unfractionated heparin as initial treatment for DVT, but unfractionated heparin may be used in patients with severe renal impairment or to achieve rapid anticoagulation in massive DVT.

Of 11 systematic reviews of trials comparing LMWH with unfractionated heparin, all but 1 showed that LMWH significantly reduced mortality during the 3 to 6 months of follow-up compared with unfractionated heparin. None of the 11 showed unfractionated heparin to be superior in preventing recurrent DVT. Patients treated with LMWH had fewer episodes of major bleeding than those treated with unfractionated heparin (39).

40. RIETE Investigators. Predicting adverse outcome in outpatients with acute deep vein thrombosis. findings from the RIETE Registry. J Vasc Surg. 2006;44:789-93. [PMID: 16926081]
41. Brandjes DP, Büller HR, Heijboer H, et al. Randomised trial of effect of compression stockings in patients with symptomatic proximal-vein thrombosis. Lancet. 1997;349:759-62. [PMID: 9074574]
42. Prandoni P, Lensing AW, Prins MH, et al. Below-knee elastic compression stockings to prevent the post-thrombotic syndrome: a randomized, controlled trial. Ann Intern Med. 2004;141:249-56. [PMID: 15313740]
43. Ginsberg JS, Hirsh J, Julian J, et al. Prevention and treatment of postphlebitic syndrome: results of a 3-part study. Arch Intern Med. 2001;161:2105-9. [PMID: 11570939]

Table 3. Drug Treatment for DVT

Agent, Dosage	Mechanism of Action	Side Effects
LMWH 　Dalteparin, 200 IU/kg SC once daily 　Enoxaparin, 1 mg/kg SC every 12 h or 1.5 mg/kg SC every 24 h 　Tinzaparin, 175 IU/kg SC once daily	Inhibits thrombin generation by acting on factor Xa; also acts on antithrombin to inhibit factor IIa activity	Bleeding, thrombocytopenia, hypersensitivity, osteoporosis, HIT
Unfractionated heparin, IV infusion or intermittent SC doses to keep aPTT ≥1.5 times control value	Enhances antithrombin activity, thereby inhibiting thrombin activity	Bleeding, thrombocytopenia, hypersensitivity, HIT, osteoporosis, elevation of liver enzymes, and hyperkalemia
Direct thrombin inhibitors 　Lepirudin, 0.1 mg/kg per h 　Bivalirudin, 0.75 mg/kg IV loading; then 1.75 mg/kg per h 　Argatroban, 2 µg/kg per min	Directly inhibits thrombin activity	Bleeding, hypersensitivity reactions, and injection-site reactions
Fondaparinux, 7.5 mg SC daily	Inhibits activated factor X	Bleeding, purpura, anemia
Coumarin derivatives (warfarin), give initial dose of 10 mg/d on day 1 of heparin, overlap for 4–5 d until INR becomes therapeutic for 2 consecutive days; adjust dose to keep INR between 2.0 and 3.0	Inhibits hepatic γ-carboxylation of glutamic acid residues of vitamin K–dependent coagulation factors II, VII, IX, and X. Inhibits production of antithrombotic proteins C and S	Hypercoagulability during first 24–36 h of therapy; bleeding; hypersensitivity; teratogenicity; many drug interactions; skin necrosis associated with malignancy and protein C and S deficiency; bleeding associated with malignancy

aPTT = activated partial thromboplastin time; DVT = deep venous thrombosis; HIT = heparin-induced thrombocytopenia; INR = international normalized ratio; IV = intravenous; LMWH = low–molecular-weight heparin; SC = subcutaneous.

44. Matisse Investigators. Fondaparinux or enoxaparin for the initial treatment of symptomatic deep venous thrombosis: a randomized trial. Ann Intern Med. 2004;140:867-73. [PMID: 15172900]
45. Sunderji R, Gin K, Shalansky K, et al. A randomized trial of patient self-managed versus physician-managed oral anticoagulation. Can J Cardiol. 2004;20:1117-23. [PMID: 15457308]
46. Gardiner C, Williams K, Longair I, et al. A randomised control trial of patient self-management of oral anticoagulation compared with patient self-testing. Br J Haematol. 2006;132:598-603. [PMID: 16445833]
47. Fitzmaurice DA, Murray ET, McCahon D, et al. Self management of oral anticoagulation: randomised trial. BMJ. 2005;331:1057. [PMID: 16216821]

Warfarin should be started at the same time as heparin. Heparin should be continued concomitantly with warfarin until the therapeutic potential of warfarin is achieved. Although more expensive, long-term treatment with LMWH is a safe and effective alternative for patients in whom oral anticoagulation is not appropriate because of difficulty in titrating dose, poor patient adherence to monitoring, or adverse effects.

Fondaparinux at a subcutaneous dose of 7.5 mg subcutaneously daily seems to be as effective as LMWH for acute treatment of DVT.

A randomized trial comparing fondaparinux with enoxaparin in 2205 patients with acute symptomatic DVT found that 43 (3.9%) of 1098 patients receiving fondaparinux had recurrent thromboembolic events compared with 45 (4.1%) of 1107 patients receiving enoxaparin (absolute difference, −0.15% [CI, −1.8% to 1.5%]). Major bleeding occurred in 1.1% of patients receiving fondaparinux and 1.2% of patients receiving enoxaparin. Mortality rates were 3.8% and 3.0%, respectively (44).

Direct thrombin inhibitors (lepirudin, bivalirudin, and argatroban) are generally only used to treat DVT in patients with known heparin hypersensitivity or heparin-induced thrombocytopenia.

How should clinicians monitor patients on anticoagulation for DVT?
Clinicians should use the activated partial thromboplastin time to adjust the dose of unfractionated heparin, but it is not necessary to do so in patients treated with LMWH. They should monitor the international normalized ratio (INR) every 4 weeks for the duration of warfarin therapy once the level of anticoagulation is stable, aiming for an INR target between 2 and 3.

Randomized trials have shown that home monitoring of anticoagulation is safe and feasible for selected patients. The quality of

anticoagulant control seems to be equivalent and possibly superior to conventional management in an anticoagulation clinic (45–48).

What important drug and food interactions should clinicians consider in treating patients with warfarin?
Drugs and food may interact with warfarin in a number of ways to enhance or inhibit warfarin activity (see Box). Drugs that decrease warfarin absorption or enhance warfarin clearance may necessitate an increase in warfarin dose to avoid subtherapeutic INR levels, whereas those that potentiate warfarin action or inhibit warfarin metabolism may require a decrease in dose to avoid supratherapeutic levels. However, these effects are not always predictable. For example, cholestyramine and phenytoin can both enhance and reduce the effect of warfarin.

Foods with large amounts of vitamins A, E, K, and C can decrease the INR level in patients on warfarin. Green leafy vegetables contain the most vitamin K. Other examples include green and herbal teas, which can also alter the prothrombin time. Proteolytic enzymes, such as papain in fried or boiled onions, increase fibrinolytic activity.

What factors should clinicians consider in determining the duration of anticoagulation therapy for DVT?
Clinicians should consider inciting events and underlying conditions in determining the duration of anticoagulation therapy for DVT (Table 4). Patients with a major transient risk factor for DVT, such as major surgery, significant medical illness, or leg casting, are usually treated for 3 months. This may be extended if exposure to the risk factor is prolonged. Patients with persistent major risk factors, such as malignant conditions, may require long-term anticoagulation. Examples of minor risk factors

Table 4. Recommendations for the Duration of Anticoagulant Therapy for Patients with DVT

Characteristics of Patient	Risk for Recurrence in the Year After Discontinuation, %	Duration of Therapy
Major transient risk factor	3	3 mo
Minor risk factor; no thrombophilia:		
Risk factor avoided	<10 if risk factor avoided	6 mo
Risk factor persistent	>10 if risk factor persistent	Until factor resolves
Idiopathic event; no thrombophilia or low-risk thrombophilia	<10	6 mo
Idiopathic event; high-risk thrombophilia	>10	Indefinite
More than 1 idiopathic event	>10	Indefinite
Cancer; other ongoing risk factor	>10	Indefinite

Reprinted from (49) with permission. Data from (50–52).

include the use of an oral contraceptive and hormone-replacement therapy. Hormone therapy is contraindicated in patients who experience DVT and should be replaced by nonhormonal alternatives. When such a risk factor can be withdrawn, anticoagulation for 6 months is appropriate.

Patients without an identifiable risk factor are more likely to develop recurrent VTE and should be treated for a minimum of 6 months with oral anticoagulation. The duration of therapy may be influenced by detection of high- or low-risk thrombophilias. Examples of low-risk thrombophilias are heterozygosity for the factor V Leiden and G20210A prothrombin-gene mutations. Examples of high-risk thrombophilia are antithrombin, protein C, and protein S deficiencies; homozygosity for the factor V Leiden or prothrombin-gene mutation or heterozygosity for both; and the presence of antiphospholipid antibodies.

Determining the exact duration of therapy also involves weighing the risks of recurrent VTE against the risks of anticoagulant-related bleeding.

A meta-analysis showed a consistent reduction in the relative risk for recurrent events during prolonged treatment (odds ratio, 0.18 [CI, 0.13 to 0.26]) that was independent of the period elapsed since the *index event and a substantial increase in bleeding complications during the entire period after randomization (odds ratio, 2.62 [CI, 1.48 to 4.61]) (53).*

D-dimer measurement may be helpful in determining treatment duration. One study showed that patients with an abnormal D-dimer level 1 month after the discontinuation of anticoagulation for idiopathic thromboembolism have a significant incidence of recurrent thromboembolism, which is reduced by the resumption of anticoagulation (54).

What are the treatment options for patients who have contraindications to anticoagulation?

Inferior vena cava (IVC) filters may be used when anticoagulation is contraindicated in patients at high risk for proximal extension of DVT or embolization, such as those with bilateral or massive DVT, immobility, chronic heart failure, or cancer. However, IVC filters may not decrease the long-term incidence of recurrent proximal DVT.

IVC filters are often placed in patients with no contraindication to anticoagulation who experience recurrent VTE while on the drug, and anticoagulants are continued to prevent further recurrence. However, the efficacy of anticoagulants to do so is questionable.

A systematic review and meta-analysis of patients who received an IVC filter showed

48. Menéndez-Jándula B, Souto JC, Oliver A, et al. Comparing self-management of oral anticoagulant therapy with clinic management: a randomized trial. Ann Intern Med. 2005;142:1-10. [PMID: 15630104]
49. Bates SM, Ginsberg JS. Clinical practice. Treatment of deep-vein thrombosis. N Engl J Med. 2004;351:268-77. [PMID: 15254285]
50. Hirsh J, Hoak J. Management of deep vein thrombosis and pulmonary embolism. A statement for healthcare professionals. Council on Thrombosis (in consultation with the Council on Cardiovascular Radiology), American Heart Association. Circulation. 1996;93:2212-45. [PMID: 8925592]
51. Hyers TM, Agnelli G, Hull RD, et al. Antithrombotic therapy for venous thromboembolic disease. Chest. 1998;114:561S-578S. [PMID: 9822063]
52. Kearon C. Duration of anticoagulation for venous thromboembolism. J Thromb Thrombolysis. 2001;12:59-65. [PMID: 11711690]
53. Hutten BA, Prins MH. Duration of treatment with vitamin K antagonists in symptomatic venous thromboembolism. Cochrane Database Syst Rev. 2006: CD001367. [PMID: 16437432]

that anticoagulation did not significantly reduce the risk for recurrent VTE (odds ratio, 0.639 [CI, 0.35 to 1.16]) (55).

What are the complications of anticoagulation?

Clinicians should make patients aware that anticoagulation carries a small but important risk for bleeding.

A meta-analysis of patients taking anticoagulant therapy for VTE estimated that over the 3- to 6-month treatment period, there was a 0.34% probability of fatal bleeding, a 0.12% probability of nonfatal intracranial bleeding, and a 2.1% probability of other nonfatal major bleeding (56).

Other complications of heparin therapy include heparin-induced thrombocytopenia (HIT), hypersensitivity reactions, osteoporosis after long-term use, and elevation of liver enzymes. Hypersensitivity reactions include urticaria, angioedema, and anaphylaxis. Other complications of warfarin therapy include hypercoagulability during the first 24 to 36 hours of therapy, hypersensitivity reactions, teratogenicity, drug interactions, and skin necrosis associated with malignant conditions and protein C and S deficiency (51).

How should clinicians manage patients who develop HIT during DVT treatment?

HIT is an immune-mediated reaction that does not usually occur until 5 to 10 days after initiating treatment and is characterized by a 50% or greater reduction in platelet count. It may be associated with thrombosis but is more often detected in the process of monitoring the platelet count. When HIT is suspected, clinicians should avoid using all heparins, including LMWH, as well as warfarin, which can paradoxically worsen the thrombosis associated with HIT and cause venous limb gangrene and skin necrosis. Two alternative anticoagulants that can be used in HIT are the direct

thrombin inhibitors, argatroban (a synthetic molecule derived from L-arginine) and lepirudin (a recombinant protein derived from leech hirudin) (57, 58).

An analysis of 3 multicenter trials in patients with HIT showed that treatment with lepirudin was associated with a reduction in a combined end point of limb amputation, thromboembolic complications, and death when compared with control participants (19.8% vs. 29.9%; P = 0.03), primarily because of a reduction in new thromboembolic complications (4.4% vs. 14.9%; P = 0.02), and was not associated with any significant difference in major bleeding episodes (14.3% vs. 8.5%; P = 0.54) (57).

When should clinicians consider intravenous or catheter-directed thrombolysis to treat DVT?

Because severe postthrombotic syndrome is probably more common in patients with iliofemoral venous thrombosis, clinicians should consider intravenous or catheter-directed thrombolytic drug therapy in such patients in an attempt to reduce the risk for the postthrombotic syndrome. The potential benefit should be weighed against the risk for bleeding.

A randomized trial in 35 patients with iliofemoral DVT compared catheter-directed thrombolysis followed by anticoagulation with anticoagulation alone. At 6 months, the patency rate was higher (13 of 18 [72%] vs. 2 of 17 [12%]; P < 0.001) and venous reflux was lower (2 patients [11%] vs. 7 [41%]; P = 0.04) in patients treated with thrombolysis (59).

What modifications in treatment should clinicians consider in specific patient groups?

DVT during pregnancy requires special treatment and monitoring. Warfarin should not be given because of its teratogenic potential. Unfractionated heparin or LMWH therapy should be used instead throughout pregnancy. Heparin should be stopped before delivery, typically at induction of labor.

54. PROLONG Investigators. D-dimer testing to determine the duration of anticoagulation therapy. N Engl J Med. 2006;355:1780-9. [PMID: 17065639]
55. Ray CE Jr, Prochazka A. The need for anticoagulation following inferior vena cava filter placement: systematic review. Cardiovasc Intervent Radiol. 2008;31:316-24. [PMID: 18080710]
56. Linkins LA, Choi PT, Douketis JD. Clinical impact of bleeding in patients taking oral anticoagulant therapy for venous thromboembolism: a meta-analysis. Ann Intern Med. 2003;139:893-900. [PMID: 14644891]

All patients with thrombophilia, both pregnant and nonpregnant, may have an increased risk for recurrent DVT and may require prolonged or even lifetime anticoagulation (38). The benefit of prolonged anticoagulation is likely to be determined by the increased risk for VTE associated with the specific thrombophilia and the number of thrombophilias identified. Thus, patients with antithrombin III deficiency, homozygous thrombophilic defect, or heterozygosity for 2 or more prothrombotic defects are most likely to benefit from lifelong anticoagulation, whereas 6 to 12 months of anticoagulation are probably appropriate for patients with a single thrombophilic defect, such as heterozygous factor V Leiden or PT G20210A (23). Clinicians should use warfarin for anticoagulation in nonpregnant patients unless contraindicated.

How should clinicians treat patients with the postthrombotic syndrome?

The postthrombotic syndrome is characterized by symptoms of recurrent pain and swelling and signs of stasis skin changes and ulceration. Clinicians should advise patients with the syndrome to elevate their feet whenever possible and should prescribe graduated compression stockings with pressures ranging from 20 to 40 mm Hg, depending on severity of edema. Patients should be instructed to replace their stockings after 6 months of repeated use because the stockings lose the elasticity needed to maintain adequate pressure. Outpatient pneumatic compression is usually reserved for patients who do not respond to foot elevation and stockings. Recurrent DVT should also be considered in patients developing symptoms and signs of the postthrombotic syndrome.

When should clinicians consult a specialist for advice in treating patients with DVT?

Clinicians should consider consulting a specialist with expertise in vascular medicine and coagulation disorders for patients with recurrent idiopathic DVT or patients with suspected or proven hypercoagulability, for complications necessitating alternatives to anticoagulation, and for management of DVT in pregnant patients.

Treatment... Clinicians should initiate LMWH as first-line treatment for proximal DVT together with warfarin for ongoing anticoagulation. The INR should be monitored at least every 4 weeks for the duration of warfarin therapy. Once the level of anticoagulation is stable, aim for an INR target of between 2 and 3. Home monitoring may be used as an alternative to anticoagulant clinic monitoring for selected patients. Compression stockings should be used within 1 month of diagnosis of proximal DVT and continued for a minimum of 1 year. The duration of anticoagulation depends on identification of transient or persistent risk factors and weighing the risks for recurrent VTE against the risks for bleeding in each individual patient. IVC filters may be used when anticoagulation is contraindicated in patients at high risk for proximal DVT extension or embolization. An intravenous or catheter-directed thrombolytic drug may reduce the postthrombotic syndrome and should be considered for patients with iliofemoral DVT.

CLINICAL BOTTOM LINE

57. Lubenow N, Eichler P, Lietz T, et al. Lepirudin for prophylaxis of thrombosis in patients with acute isolated heparin-induced thrombocytopenia: an analysis of 3 prospective studies. Blood. 2004;104: 3072-7. [PMID: 15280202]
58. Argatroban-915 Investigators. Argatroban anticoagulation in patients with heparin-induced thrombocytopenia. Arch Intern Med. 2003;163:1849-56. [PMID: 12912723]
59. Elsharawy M, Elzayat E. Early results of thrombolysis vs anticoagulation in iliofemoral venous thrombosis. A randomised clinical trial. Eur J Vasc Endovasc Surg. 2002;24:209-14. [PMID: 12217281]

Practice Improvement

60. American College of Physicians. Management of venous thromboembolism: a clinical practice guideline from the American College of Physicians and the American Academy of Family Physicians. Ann Intern Med. 2007;146:204-10. [PMID: 17261857]

61. American Society of Clinical Oncology. American Society of Clinical Oncology guideline: recommendations for venous thromboembolism prophylaxis and treatment in patients with cancer. J Clin Oncol. 2007;25:5490-505. [PMID: 17968019]

62. Khorana AA. The NCCN Clinical Practice Guidelines on Venous Thromboembolic Disease: strategies for improving VTE prophylaxis in hospitalized cancer patients. Oncologist. 2007;12:1361-70. [PMID: 18055857]

63. Kearon C, Kahn SR, Agnelli G, et al. Antithrombotic therapy for venous thromboembolic disease: American College of Chest Physicians Evidence-based Clinical Practice Guidelines (8th Edition). Chest 2008;133:454S-545S.

Do U.S. stakeholders consider management of patients with DVT when evaluating the quality of care physicians deliver?

The Center for Medicare & Medicaid Services (CMS) has developed 119 measure of quality of care to use in the 2008 Physician Quality Reporting Initiative (PQRI), an initiative that will financially reward participating physicians who meet defined quality standards. Of these measures, one involves prophylaxis for VTE in surgical patients and relates to the percentage of patients age 18 years or older undergoing procedures for which VTE prophylaxis is indicated and who had an order for LMWH, low-dose unfractionated heparin, adjusted-dose warfarin, fondaparinux, or mechanical prophylaxis to be given within 24 hours before incision time or within 24 hours after surgery end time.

What do professional organizations recommend with regard to the management of patients with DVT?

The American College of Physicians and the American Academy of Family Physicians published a clinical practice guideline for the management of VTE in 2007 specifically addressing use of LMWH and patient measurement, use of compression stockings, and duration of anticoagulations (60).

Recommendations issued by the American Society of Clinical Oncology VTE Guideline Panel in 2007 cover details of VTE thromboprophylaxis and preference for LMWH in treatment of cancer patients (61).

The National Comprehensive Cancer Network (NCCN) published clinical practice guidelines on venous thromboembolic disease in 2007, which outline strategies for improving VTE prophylaxis in hospitalized cancer patients (62).

In 2008, the American College of Chest Physicians (ACCP) issued its latest evidence-based clinical practice guidelines relating to a number of issues in VTE prevention and treatment. These include prevention of VTE (9), treatment of VTE (63), and treatment of HIT (64).

---

in the clinic

Tool Kit

Deep Venous Thrombosis

PIER Modules

pier.acponline.org
Access the following PIER modules: Deep Vein Thrombosis, Pulmonary Embolism, Venous Thromboembolism Prophylaxis in the Surgical Patient. PIER modules provide evidence-based, updated information on prevention, diagnosis, and treatment in an electronic format designed for rapid access of the point of care.

Patient Information

National Heart, Lung and Blood Institute
www.nhlbi.nih.gov/health/dci/Diseases/Dvt/DVT_WhatIs.html
Access "What is Deep Venous Thrombosis?", which provides information on all aspects of venous thromboembolic disease.

Other Useful Resources for Clinicians

www.annals.org/cgi/content/full/146/6/454
www.annals.org/cgi/content/full/146/3/204
Most recent evidence-based guidelines on diagnosis and treatment of VTE from ACP.

individual.utoronto.ca/mgreiver/dvt.htm
Wells score for deep venous thrombosis

www.acponline.org/running_practice/quality_improvement/projects/cfpi/doc_anticoag.pdf
Downloadable anticoagulation flow sheet from ACP.

WHAT YOU SHOULD KNOW ABOUT DEEP VENOUS THROMBOSIS

Deep venous thrombosis (DVT) is a blood clot in the veins deep in the leg. It may cause pain and swelling in the leg. It is important to treat DVT so the clot does not get worse or move to the lungs. If it does, it can cause serious lung problems and even death.

What causes DVT?
DVT can happen:

- If you don't move your legs after an injury
- In the hospital, when you are in bed for a long time
- After an operation
- During a long airplane trip
- In some people with cancer
- In people with blood that clots more easily
- For no clear reason

How can DVT be prevented?
- Keep moving your legs when you are laid up or on a long airplane trip.
- Take small doses of a blood thinner when in the hospital or after an operation.

How does your doctor diagnose DVT?
- When it is hard to tell if there is a clot in the leg, your doctor may order blood tests.
- An ultrasound scan using sound waves may help the doctor see a clot in the veins of the leg.
- Sometimes more tests are needed to look for the cause of the DVT.

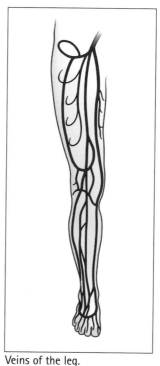

Veins of the leg.

How is DVT treated?
- Most patients with DVT do not need to be in the hospital.
- Blood thinners are given to prevent more clots in the leg and to keep a clot from going to the lungs.
- People with DVT need to take blood thinners for many months and sometimes need to keep taking them.
- Special stockings can keep the leg from swelling while the clot is being treated.

What do patients need to know?
- Too much blood thinner can cause bleeding, and too little can cause another clot.
- It is important to get regular blood tests to be sure the dose of blood thinner is right.
- Some foods and other medicines can change how much blood thinner you need. It is important to tell your doctor what you eat and about changes in your medicines.

ACP

AMERICAN COLLEGE OF PHYSICIANS
INTERNAL MEDICINE | *Doctors for Adults*®

Patient Information

Obesity

More than 30% of U.S. adults are obese (1). Generally defined as a body mass index (BMI) greater than 30 kg/m², obesity is a serious chronic problem that is difficult to treat. Obesity is associated with increased all-cause mortality and increased risk for serious medical conditions, including type 2 diabetes, dyslipidemia, hypertension, and sleep apnea. People who are obese may also experience social stigmatization. Although weight loss is difficult to achieve and maintain, several approaches are available for losing weight. Even a loss of 5% body weight can substantially reduce the risks associated with obesity.

Health Consequences

1. Ogden CL, Carroll MD, Curtin LR, et al. Prevalence of overweight and obesity in the United States, 1999-2004. JAMA. 2006;295:1549-55. [PMID: 16595758]
2. McTigue K, Larson JC, Valoski A, et al. Mortality and cardiac and vascular outcomes in extremely obese women. JAMA. 2006;296:79-86. [PMID: 16820550]
3. Freedman DM, Ron E, Ballard-Barbash R, et al. Body mass index and all-cause mortality in a nationwide US cohort. Int J Obes (Lond). 2006;30:822-9. [PMID: 16404410]
4. Diabetes Prevention Program Research Group. Reduction in the incidence of type 2 diabetes with lifestyle intervention or metformin. N Engl J Med. 2002;346:393-403. [PMID: 11832527]

What health problems are associated with being overweight?
Excess body fat, particularly visceral fat, increases the risk for numerous diseases. The increased risk results from either the metabolic consequence of the enlarged fat cells or from the increased mass of fat (Table 1).

The increased risk from the diseases associated with obesity substantially increases the risk for mortality. In essentially all studies, mortality and BMI have a J-shaped relationship.

Among more than 90 000 women in the Women's Health Initiative, there was a graded increase in the risk for death as BMI increased from normal levels to greater than 40 kg/m² (2).

Another U.S. cohort of more than 80 000 men and women was monitored for more than 14.7 years with more than 1.23 million person-years of follow-up. Excluding deaths

in the first 5 years, risk for death in patients younger than 55 years of age was directly related to BMI in both men and women, beginning at a BMI of 21 kg/m² in women and 23 kg/m² in men. In those older than 55 years of age, the increase in mortality occurred at a higher BMI, beginning at 25 kg/m² in women and 30 kg/m² in men (3).

What is the evidence that weight loss improves health outcomes?
There is good evidence that obese patients who lose weight reduce their risk for comorbid diseases, including diabetes, hypertension, sleep apnea, and cardiovascular disease, and experience improved overall quality of life. Even modest reductions in weight lead to improvement in health outcomes.

Of 3234 study participants with impaired glucose tolerance randomly assigned to either intensive lifestyle modification (n = 1079), metformin (n = 1073), or placebo (n = 1062), those in the intensive lifestyle

Table 1. Obesity–Associated Health Problems

Resulting from the metabolic effects of enlarged fat cells and visceral fat

Type 2 diabetes

HypertensionaDyslipidemia (low HDL-cholesterol levels and high triglyceride levels)

Cardiovascular disease (coronary artery disease, stroke, heart failure, and atrial fibrillation)

Cancer (in men: liver, stomach, pancreas, esophagus, multiple myeloma, rectum, and gall bladder; in women: uterus, kidney, cervix, pancreas, esophagus, gallbladder, breast, liver, ovary, colon, and rectum)

Gastrointestinal disease (GERD, erosive gastritis, gall bladder disease, gall stones, cholecystectomy, and nonalcoholic steatohepatatitis)

Kidney disease (kidney stones, chronic renal disease, and end-stage renal disease)

Endocrine changes (hyperinsulinemia and insulin resistance, disturbed menstrual cycles, and altered cortisol metabolism)

Infertility (the polycystic ovarian syndrome)

Obstetrical risks (Caesarean section, hypertension, stillbirth, and neonatal mortality)

Resulting from increased body mass

Bone and joint diseases (osteoarthritis and hospitalization for back disorders)

Pulmonary disease (sleep apnea, pulmonary embolism, and sleep-disordered breathing)

Social stigmatization

GERD = gastroesophageal reflux disease; HDL = high-density lipoprotein.

modification group experienced the best outcome, losing 7% or more of their body weight at 24 weeks, and 38% had a weight loss of 7% at average follow-up of 2.8 years. They had a 58% reduction in the risk for diabetes compared with patients in the placebo group (95% CI, 48% to 66%) (4).

In the Framingham study, a modest weight loss of 6.8 kg or more led to a 28% reduction in the risk for hypertension among middle-age adults and a 37% reduction among older adults (5).

In a clinical trial using lifestyle interventions to lower blood pressure (TOPH II), the risk for hypertension decreased by 65% in those who maintained their weight loss of 4.5 kg for 30 months (6).

In a systematic review of long-term weight-loss studies in obese adults, both dietary and lifestyle approaches and pharmacologic interventions improved markers of cardiovascular disease, particularly in patients with cardiovascular risk factors at the beginning of the study (7).

Health Consequences... Obesity increases the risk for numerous diseases, including type 2 diabetes, cardiovascular disease, pulmonary disease, and cancer. It also increases the risk for mortality, with risk increasing linearly with BMI. Even limited weight loss can substantially lower these risks.

CLINICAL BOTTOM LINE

Screening and Prevention

Should clinicians routinely screen patients for overweight or obesity?

The U.S. Preventive Services Task Force recommends that clinicians screen all adult patients for obesity and offer intensive counseling and behavioral interventions to promote sustained weight loss for obese adults (8). The National Heart, Lung, and Blood Institute also recommends determining both height and weight in order to calculate BMI in all patients (see Box).

The accepted definition of obesity is a BMI greater than 30 kg/m^2, and overweight is defined as a BMI from 25.0 to 25.9 kg/m^2 (9).

Which health behaviors reduce the risk for becoming overweight?

Certain health behaviors at different stages of life can reduce the risk for becoming overweight. Even during infancy and early childhood, risk factors for obesity may be present, and some of them are modifiable.

Women can make certain efforts to lower the risk that their children will become overweight, including maintaining normal weight gain during pregnancy, not smoking, and extending duration of breast feeding (10, 11).

Key factors predicting weight gain in children include high parental BMI, excessive weight gain in the first year, and a rise in BMI before ages 4 to 6 years (12). In addition to avoiding weight gain themselves, parents can encourage certain healthy habits in their children by making sure that they eat breakfast, limiting their intake of high sugar foods (including soft drinks and fruit drinks), reducing their time spent in such sedentary activities as watching television, and encouraging adequate sleep (13–16).

In people of all ages, monitored food intake and increased levels of activity, particularly walking and other forms of exercise, are associated with less future weight gain and should be encouraged (17).

Some drugs are associated with weight gain (see Box), and clinicians may be able to substitute a medication that produces less weight gain to help patients avoid becoming overweight.

Body Mass Index = kilograms of body weight divided by the square of the height in meters (kg/m^2)

Drugs that Produce Weight Gain

- Thioridazine
- Olanzepine
- Quetiapine
- Resperidone
- Clozapine
- Amitriptyline
- Nortriptyline
- Imipramine
- Mirtazapine
- Paroxetine
- Valproate
- Carbamazepine
- Gabapentin
- Insulin
- Sulfonylureas
- Thiazolidinediones
- Pizotifen
- Cyproheptadine
- Propranolol
- Terazosin
- Contraceptives
- Glucocorticoids
- Progestational steroids

5. Moore LL, Visioni AJ, Qureshi MM, et al. Weight loss in overweight adults and the long-term risk of hypertension: the Framingham study. Arch Intern Med. 2005;165:1298-303. [PMID: 15956011]

6. Trials for the Hypertension Prevention Research Group. Long-term weight loss and changes in blood pressure: results of the Trials of Hypertension Prevention, phase II. Ann Intern Med. 2001;134:1-11. [PMID: 11187414]

7. Douketis JD, Macie C, Thabane L, Williamson DF. Systematic review of long-term weight loss studies in obese adults: clinical significance and applicability to clinical practice. Int J Obes (Lond). 2005;29: 1153-67. [PMID: 15997250]

8. U.S. Preventive Services Task Force. Screening for obesity in adults: recommendations and rationale. Ann Intern Med. 2003;139:930-2. [PMID: 14644896]

9. Clinical Guidelines on the Identification, Evaluation, and Treatment of Overweight and Obesity in Adults—The Evidence Report. National Institutes of Health. Obes Res. 1998;6 Suppl 2:51S-209S. [PMID: 9813653]

10. Lawlor DA, Smith GD, O'Callaghan M, et al. Epidemiologic evidence for the fetal overnutrition hypothesis: findings from the mater-university study of pregnancy and its outcomes. Am J Epidemiol. 2007;165: 418-24. [PMID: 17158475]

11. Toschke AM, Montgomery SM, Pfeiffer U, von Kries R. Early intrauterine exposure to tobacco-inhaled products and obesity. Am J Epidemiol. 2003;158: 1068-74. [PMID: 14630602]

12. Avon Longitudinal Study of Parents and Children Study Team. Early life risk factors for obesity in childhood: cohort study. BMJ. 2005;330:1357. [PMID: 15908441]

Diagnosis

How does one make the diagnosis of overweight and obesity?
Clinicians should calculate the patient's BMI and follow it over time because BMI is easy to determine, very reliable, closely correlated with body fat, and linked with the broadest range of health outcomes (8, 18). The National Heart, Lung, and Blood Institute and the World Health Organization have adopted BMI as the criterion for defining overweight and obesity (9, 19). Both groups define a BMI of 18.5 to 24.9 kg/m^2 as normal weight, a BMI of 25 to 29.9 kg/m^2 as overweight, and a BMI greater than 30 kg/m^2 as obesity. The Asia-Oceania Criteria differ slightly: Normal weight is 18.5 to 22.9 kg/m^2, overweight is 23 to 24.9 kg/m^2, and obesity is greater than 25 kg/m^2 (20). At the same BMI, body fat is about 12% higher in women than in men (21).

In what types of patients might BMI measurement be misleading?
BMI may not be the best predictor of weight-related health problems in certain ethnic groups, such as African Americans and Hispanic-American women, who may have more fat-free mass in bone and muscle compared with Caucasians and thus misleadingly high BMI measurements. BMI may also be misleading in children, elderly patients, and athletes because of differences in height and proportions of fat and fat-free mass. In children, height–weight relationships are continually changing. During the first 5 to 7 years of life, BMI declines, reaches a nadir, and then begins to rise toward adult levels. BMI can be confusing in elderly individuals who have lost height, which makes the BMI seem higher than it really is. Because of decreased muscle mass in some older people, BMI may underestimate body fat. However, the effect of loss of height is more substantial. Similarly, athletes who have increased muscle mass and reduced fat mass may seem to have a high BMI but have little risk for obesity-associated diseases, such as cardiovascular disease or diabetes.

When should clinicians measure waist circumference or waist-to-hip ratio in evaluating overweight and obese patients?
Clinicians should consider measuring waist circumference and waist-to-hip ratio in most, if not all, overweight patients. Waist circumference may be a better measure of central adiposity, a correlate of visceral adiposity that is related to cardiovascular risk (although waist circumference does not improve prediction of cardiovascular risk in patients with a BMI of 35 or greater). Waist circumference is also a component of the metabolic syndrome as defined by the Adult Treatment Panel III of the National Cholesterol Education Program (22, 23). Table 2 shows criteria for the upper limits of normal waist circumference.

For individuals older than 75 years, the waist-to-hip ratio (waist circumference divided by hip circumference) may be a better predictor of death than either body mass

Table 2. Criteria for Central Adiposity

Organization	Waist Circumference Cut-Points*	
	Men	*Women*
National Heart, Lung and Blood Institute (United States)	102 cm (40 in)	88 cm (35 in)
International Diabetes Federation (Europe)	94 cm (37 in)	80 cm (31 in)
International Diabetes Federation (South Asia, China, and Japan)	90 cm (33 in)	80 cm (31 in)

*Values above these levels are considered abnormal (22, 25).

index or waist circumference alone (24). Waist-to-hip ratios greater than 0.95 in men and 0.85 in women are considered elevated.

Other measurements of fat mass, such as sagittal diameter and skin-fold thickness, can be made at the time of physical examination but are impractical in everyday clinical practice.

What other factors and conditions should clinicians consider when evaluating overweight and obese patients?

It is important to determine the patient's ethnicity and social situation; if the patient's parents were overweight; if there has been a recent life event that may affect weight, such as pregnancy, recent surgery, or disability; the level of physical activity; and medication history.

On physical examination, clinicians should look for evidence of conditions associated with increased weight, including hypertension, evidence of endocrinopathies (such as hypercortisolism or hypothyroidism), reproductive disorders (such as the polycystic ovary syndrome), and phenotypic abnormalities suggestive of uncommon genetic disorders associated with obesity.

Genetic syndromes associated with obesity include the Prader–Willi syndrome, which results from a paternal chromosomal abnormality, and the Bardet–Biedl syndrome, the Ahlstrom syndrome, the Carpenter syndrome, and the Cohen syndrome, all of which result from

autosomal recessive abnormalities. Other genetic causes of obesity include melanocortin-4 receptor defects and leptin deficiency or leptin receptor deficiency (26).

Which laboratory tests should clinicians consider in overweight and obese patients?

Clinicians should use laboratory testing to evaluate overweight and obese patients who may be at high risk for cardiovascular disease, diabetes, and thyroid disease. Some pertinent tests to consider are fasting plasma glucose or 2-hour postprandial glucose levels and serum lipid levels. Thyroid-stimulating hormone may be helpful in excluding hypothyroidism, particularly in older women. Urinary free cortisol can be obtained if hypercortisolism is suspected.

Other tests to consider depend on clinical assessment and include ultrasound for hepatic steatosis, gallstones, and the polycystic ovary syndrome; electrocardiography in patients at high risk for cardiovascular disease; polysomnography for patients with possible sleep apnea; and head computed tomography or magnetic resonance imaging when pituitary or hypothalamic disorders are suspected. Genetic testing is needed to confirm the diagnosis in patients with rare genetic disorders.

Although there are a variety of more-sophisticated laboratory techniques for gathering additional information about body fat and fat distribution, including bioelectrical impedance, dual-energy X-ray absorptiometry, and total body water determination, none of these

13. Bazzano LA, Song Y, Bubes V, et al. Dietary intake of whole and refined grain breakfast cereals and weight gain in men. Obes Res. 2005;13:1952-60. [PMID: 16339127]
14. Vartanian LR, Schwartz MB, Brownell KD. Effects of soft drink consumption on nutrition and health: a systematic review and meta-analysis. Am J Public Health. 2007;97:667-75. [PMID: 17329656]
15. Gable S, Chang Y, Krull JL. Television watching and frequency of family meals are predictive of overweight onset and persistence in a national sample of school-aged children. J Am Diet Assoc. 2007;107:53-61. [PMID: 17197271]
16. Sekine M, Yamagami T, Handa K, et al. A dose-response relationship between short sleeping hours and childhood obesity: results of the Toyama Birth Cohort Study. Child Care Health Dev. 2002;28:163-70. [PMID: 11952652]
17. Williamson DF, Madans J, Anda RF, et al. Recreational physical activity and ten-year weight change in a US national cohort. Int J Obes Relat Metab Disord. 1993;17:279-86. [PMID: 8389337]
18. Whitlock EP, Williams SB, Gold R, et al. Screening and interventions for childhood overweight: a summary of evidence for the US Preventive Services Task Force. Pediatrics. 2005;116:e125-44. [PMID: 15995013]
19. Obesity: preventing and managing the global epidemic. Report of a WHO consultation. World Health Organ Tech Rep Ser. 2000;894:i-xii, 1-253. [PMID: 11234459]

techniques is recommended for general clinical evaluation. The gold standard test for measuring central and visceral fat is with abdominal computed tomography or magnetic resonance imaging with cross-sectional cuts at L-4/L-5, but both are costly.

Diagnosis... Although BMI is used to define overweight (25 to 29.9 kg/m²) and obesity (BMI >30 kg/m²), it may not be the best predictor of weight-related health problems in children, older people, and athletes. Waist circumference and the waist-to-hip ratio may correlate better with increased cardiovascular risk. Laboratory testing should be based on clinical evaluation and used to assess risk for diseases associated with obesity. Clinicians should consider the possible role of endocrine, neuroendocrine, or genetic disorders as causes of obesity.

CLINICAL BOTTOM LINE

20. Li G, Chen X, Jang Y, et al. Obesity, coronary heart disease risk factors and diabetes in Chinese: an approach to the criteria of obesity in the Chinese population. Obes Rev. 2002;3:167-72. [PMID: 12164468]
21. Gallagher D, Heymsfield SB, Heo M, et al. Healthy percentage body fat ranges: an approach for developing guidelines based on body mass index. Am J Clin Nutr. 2000;72:694-701. [PMID: 10966886]
22. Expert Panel on Detection, Evaluation, and Treatment of High Blood Cholesterol in Adults. Executive Summary of The Third Report of The National Cholesterol Education Program (NCEP) Expert Panel on Detection, Evaluation, And Treatment of High Blood Cholesterol In Adults (Adult Treatment Panel III). JAMA. 2001;285:2486-97. [PMID: 11368702]
23. American Heart Association. Diagnosis and management of the metabolic syndrome: an American Heart Association/National Heart, Lung, and Blood Institute Scientific Statement. Circulation. 2005;112:2735-52. [PMID: 16157765]
24. Price GM, Uauy R, Breeze E, et al. Weight, shape, and mortality risk in older persons: elevated waist-hip ratio, not high body mass index, is associated with a greater risk of death. Am J Clin Nutr. 2006;84:449-60. [PMID: 16895897]
25. IDF Worldwide Definition of Metabolic Syndrome: Website of the International Diabetes Foundation. Accessed at www.idf.org/metabolic_syndrome on 13 August 2008.
26. Farooqi IS, O'Rahilly S. Genetic factors in human obesity. Obes Rev. 2007;8 Suppl 1:37-40. [PMID: 17316299]

Treatment

What counseling should clinicians provide patients about losing weight?

Clinicians should assess whether the patient is ready to make lifestyle changes and encourage attainable weight-loss goals. Patients often have a "dream weight" that involves a weight loss of nearly 30% of their initial body weight. However, weight losses of 5% to 10% are more realistically attainable and are still associated with proven health benefits. For instance, several studies have demonstrated that a weight reduction of 5% or more in "at-risk" individuals can reduce the risk for diabetes (4, 7, 27). Although additional weight loss further reduces risk (28), setting reasonable goals with the patient is one of the initial key steps in treatment (Figure).

Why is it difficult for many people to lose weight?

Body weight is controlled through a carefully regulated feedback system designed to maintain homeostasis and resist change. Even after people lose an initial amount of weight, they reach a "plateau" and stop losing any more weight, regardless of weight-loss program or treatment. Further weight loss is difficult to achieve and initial weight loss difficult to sustain. Only a small minority of people who lose weight are able to maintain their full weight loss at 3 years.

Lack of adherence to diet is another major reason for difficulty in losing weight and maintaining it. Hunger may increase over time with reduced body weight, serving as a mechanism to signal loss of energy stores and thwart efforts to lose more weight. A drop in circulating leptin may be another factor in maintaining the plateau in body weight.

What behavioral modifications are used in the treatment of obesity?

Behavior therapy is one of the cornerstones of treatment for obesity. People who are successful in losing weight and maintaining weight loss tend to monitor their behavior, eat less, increase their physical activity, and practice positive self-thinking and techniques to reduce stress (29).

Behavior modification strategies include keeping a food diary, which helps patients learn to monitor their eating behavior by recording what is eaten, determining the setting in which they eat, and identifying the situations that trigger eating. With this information, the health-care provider can help patients change their eating habits and adopt a defined eating plan.

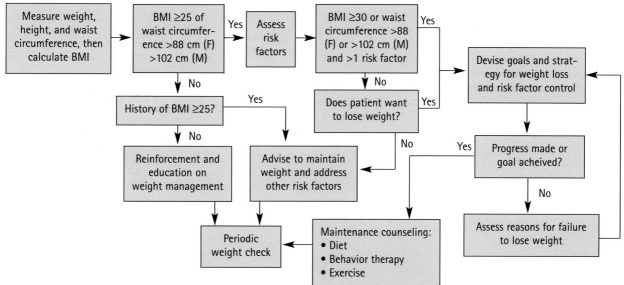

Figure. Treatment algorithm. Adapted from (9).

Exercise offers a strategy for balancing energy intake and expenditure, whether as a primary treatment for weight loss or for preventing patients from regaining weight. Generally, people who are trying to lose weight should increase their walking or other comparable activities to 30 to 60 minutes 5 or more days a week.

One study found that moderate-to-vigorous exercise for 60 minutes per day, 6 days per week, produced weight loss of 1.4 kg in women and 1.8 kg in men compared with nonexercisers over 12 months (30).

Exercise alone, however, is often inadequate as a primary treatment for weight loss. A meta-analysis of weight loss trials found that exercise alone resulted in a 3-kg weight loss compared with an 11-kg loss with diet (31). This is because it takes a lot of exercise to lose weight. A person who wishes to lose 1 pound per week through exercise needs to walk approximately 5 miles per day 7 days per week in order to achieve a deficit of 3500 kcal. For individuals wanting to monitor their exercise, inexpensive pedometers can be worn on the belt. A mile is about 2000 steps.

Counseling may help people lose weight, and simple dietary advice given by the physicians in the office may be as effective as formal nutrition counseling.

A meta-analysis of 46 studies of dietary counseling showed a maximum net treatment effect of −1.9 (CI, −2.3 to −1.5) BMI units (approximately 6% weight loss over 12 months). There was a decrease of about 0.1 BMI unit per month for the 12 months of active treatment and an increase of about 0.02 to 0.03 BMI units per month during subsequent phases. Different strategies were used in the various studies, and there was no clear basis for selecting one over the other (32).

What dietary modifications are used in the treatment of obesity?

To lose weight, a person must consume fewer calories by eating less food than the body needs for resting metabolic rate and daily activities. The amount and rate of weight loss depends on an individual's degree of adherence to a diet. Many diet plans are available for overweight individuals. These can be grouped into those that are low in fat; those that are low in carbohydrate; those that restrict most nutrients (so-called balanced deficit diets); those that highlight one particular type of food, such as the low-glycemic-index diet; and those

27. Finnish Diabetes Prevention Study Group. Prevention of type 2 diabetes mellitus by changes in lifestyle among subjects with impaired glucose tolerance. N Engl J Med. 2001;344:1343-50. [PMID: 11333990]
28. Sjöström CD, Lissner L, Sjöström L. Relationships between changes in body composition and changes in cardiovascular risk factors: the SOS Intervention Study. Swedish Obese Subjects. Obes Res. 1997;5:519-30. [PMID: 9449135]
29. Klem ML, Wing RR, McGuire MT, et al. A descriptive study of individuals successful at long-term maintenance of substantial weight loss. Am J Clin Nutr. 1997;66:239-46. [PMID: 9250100]
30. McTiernan A, Sorensen B, Irwin ML, et al. Exercise effect on weight and body fat in men and women. Obesity (Silver Spring). 2007;15:1496-512. [PMID: 17557987]
31. Miller WC, Koceja DM, Hamilton EJ. A meta-analysis of the past 25 years of weight loss research using diet, exercise or diet plus exercise intervention. Int J Obes Relat Metab Disord. 1997;21:941-7. [PMID: 9347414]
32. Dansinger ML, Tatsioni A, Wong JB, et al. Meta-analysis: the effect of dietary counseling for weight loss. Ann Intern Med. 2007;147:41-50. [PMID: 17606960]

33. Pirozzo S, Summerbell C, Cameron C, Glasziou P. Should we recommend low-fat diets for obesity? Obes Rev. 2003;4:83-90. [PMID: 12760443]

34. Ornish D, Scherwitz LW, Billings JH, et al. Intensive lifestyle changes for reversal of coronary heart disease. JAMA. 1998;280:2001-7. [PMID: 9863851]

35. Howard BV, Manson JE, Stefanick ML, et al. Low-fat dietary pattern and weight change over 7 years: the Women's Health Initiative Dietary Modification Trial. JAMA. 2006;295:39-49. [PMID: 16391215]

36. Astrup A, Grunwald GK, Melanson EL, et al. The role of low-fat diets in body weight control: a meta-analysis of ad libitum dietary intervention studies. Int J Obes Relat Metab Disord. 2000;24:1545-52. [PMID: 11126204]

37. Bell EA, Castellanos VH, Pelkman CL, et al. Energy density of foods affects energy intake in normal-weight women. Am J Clin Nutr. 1998;67:412-20. [PMID: 9497184]

38. Kral TV, Roe LS, Rolls BJ. Combined effects of energy density and portion size on energy intake in women. Am J Clin Nutr. 2004;79:962-8. [PMID: 15159224]

39. Boden G, Sargrad K, Homko C, et al. Effect of a low-carbohydrate diet on appetite, blood glucose levels, and insulin resistance in obese patients with type 2 diabetes. Ann Intern Med. 2005;142:403-11. [PMID: 15767618]

40. Foster GD, Wyatt HR, Hill JO, et al. A randomized trial of a low-carbohydrate diet for obesity. N Engl J Med. 2003;348:2082-90. [PMID: 12761365]]

41. Dansinger ML, Gleason JA, Griffith JL, et al. Comparison of the Atkins, Ornish, Weight Watchers, and Zone diets for weight loss and heart disease risk reduction: a randomized trial. JAMA. 2005;293:43-53. [PMID: 15632335]

that highlight specific foods, such as the "grapefruit diet".

However, diet composition is generally less important than total calories consumed. The standard initial weight loss diet is a balanced low-calorie diet, and use of other types of diets should be based on patient preference. For example, some patients find that diets high in protein and fiber enhance satiety. Patients with dyslipidemia may benefit from low fat diets. Portion-controlled meals provide an easy way to count calories and avoid meal preparation. Whatever diet type, eating at regular intervals throughout the day is important.

Low-Fat Diets

Low-fat diets are effective in helping patients lose weight but are probably not more effective than other types of diets (33). One advantage of very-low fat intake is slowing or reversal of coronary artery atherosclerosis (34).

A large randomized clinical trial of low-fat versus control diets randomly assigned 48835 women to low-fat or control diets and found that weight loss was 2.2 kg below baseline at 1 year and 0.6 kg below baseline at a mean of 7.5 years, and at both times was significantly greater in those on the low-fat diet. There was a clear relationship between the decrease in percent fat and weight loss (P < 0.001 for trend) (35).

In a meta-analysis of 19 studies, low-fat diets produced a mean reduction of 10.2% in dietary fat and a weight loss of 3.2 kg more than in the control group. A 1-kg greater prediet weight was associated with an additional 2-kg weight loss in those on low-fat diets (36).

Low-Energy-Density Diets

The rationale for recommending low-energy-density diets is based on the theory that filling the stomach with low-fat, high-fiber foods—low-energy-density foods—will reduce hunger and produce satiety. People eat larger amounts of food in experimental settings when it is more energy dense with more calories per unit weight (37, 38).

Low-Carbohydrate Diets

The most popular diets today are the low-carbohydrate, high-protein, high-fat diets. Carbohydrate content in some of these diets is as low as 13 g/d. When carbohydrate intake is less than 50 g/d, ketosis develops. In short-term metabolic ward studies, patients do not increase the intake of other foods to compensate for the lower calories in a very-low-carbohydrate diet (39). Several randomized clinical trials have reported greater weight loss in patients on low-carbohydrate diets at 6 months, but it is unclear whether differences can be sustained in the long-term (40).

Two recent clinical trials compared a range of low-carbohydrate diets.

In a trial that randomly assigned 160 participants to 1 of 4 popular diets, there were no significant differences in weight loss at 1 year. Weight loss was 3.9 ± 6 kg (CI, 8.58 ± 13.2 lb) with the Atkins Diet, 4.9 ± 6.9 kg (CI, 10.78 ± 15.18 lb) with the Zone Diet, 4.6 ± 5.4 kg (10.12 ± 11.88 lb) with the Weight Watchers Diet, and 6.6 ± 9.3 kg (CI, 14.52 ± 20.46 lb) with the Ornish Diet. The principal determinant of weight loss was the degree of adherence to the diet and not the diet itself (41).

In the other 1-year trial, 311 premenopausal women were randomly assigned to 1 of 4 diets. The Atkins diet produced more weight loss at 12 months (4.7 kg) compared with the other 3 diets (Zone, 1.6 kg; LEARN, 2.6 kg; Ornish, 2.2 kg). Differences in weight loss among the Zone, LEARN, and Ornish diets were not statistically significant (42).

Commercial Weight-Loss Programs

Several commercial and self-help programs, including Overeaters Anonymous, TOPS (Take Off Pounds Sensibly), Weight Watchers, Jenny Craig, Herbalife, OPTIFAST, LA Health, and e-Diets, are available. These generally combine diet with self-help programs, some of which are available on the

Internet. Only a few studies have demonstrated their effectiveness.

In a review of studies of these programs, those that included very-low-calorie diets were associated with high costs, high attrition rates, and a high probability of regaining 50% or more of lost weight in 1 to 2 years, and interventions available over the Internet and organized self-help programs produced minimal weight loss (43).

A 2-year trial involving 423 participants showed that those in the intervention group who attended the Weight Watchers meetings (n = 211) experienced a mean weight loss of 5.3% at 1 year and 3.2% at 2 years, compared with 1.5% at 1 year and 0% at 2 years in those in the control group who received a self-help intervention with 2 visits to a dietitian (44).

When should clinicians consider prescribing very-low-calorie diets?

Clinicians may consider the use of very-low-calorie diets, such as those with energy intake below 800 kcal/d, if needed for rapid weight loss before a major surgical procedure. In other settings, however, the rebound in weight that usually occurs at the end of such programs does not make them worth the extra cost.

A meta-analysis of 29 studies of very-low-calorie diets found that those on diets for at least 2 years lost substantially more weight than those eating hypoenergetic balanced diets (45).

Today, very-low-calorie diets have been largely replaced by portion-controlled diets in which calories are provided from beverages, bars, or frozen meals for use at breakfast or lunch and are fixed by the manufacturer.

In a study of such a diet compared with a 1200- to 1500-kcal control diet in 100 patients, weight loss was substantially greater at 3 months in patients on the diet with meal and snack replacements than in those on the control diet. Thereafter, patients in both groups were given meal replacements and maintained weight losses of 5% or greater at 4 years (46).

Are alternative natural or herbal therapies marketed for weight loss effective and safe?

Many different natural and herbal products are available and purported to facilitate weight loss (see Box) (47). Whether they are safe and effective is unknown in many cases. Clinicians should question patients about use of such products and caution them about uncertainties regarding effectiveness and safety.

When should clinicians consider pharmacological therapy for overweight and obese patients?

Clinicians should consider drug treatment for obesity in patients with a BMI greater than 30 kg/m^2 and no associated diseases or with a BMI greater than 27 kg/m^2 if there are associated health problems, such as diabetes, osteoarthritis, hypertension, dyslipidemia, or cardiovascular disease. Because obesity is a long-term problem, current medications should be used as part of a complete program including diet, lifestyle change, and regular physical activity. Guidelines from the American College of Physicians emphasize that pharmacologic therapy should be recommended only when patients fail to meet individualized goals with counseling on lifestyle and behavior modifications, and that physicians should discuss the limitations and adverse effects of available drugs (48).

What pharmacologic therapies are effective in the treatment of overweight and obese patients?

The U.S. Food and Drug Administration (FDA) has approved several drugs for treatment of obesity (Table 3) (49). Two of them, sibutramine and orlistat, are approved for induction and ongoing maintenance of weight loss whereas the others are approved for up to approximately 12 weeks of use.

Metabolic and Herbal Dietary Supplements Marketed to Facilitate Weight Loss

- Chromium picolinate
- Hydroxymethyl butyrate
- Pyruvate
- Conjugated linoleic acid
- Calcium
- Ephedra
- Green tea extract
- Garcinia cambogia
- Yohimbine
- Hoodia
- Bitter orange
- Chitosan
- Glucomannan
- Guar gum
- Psyllium

---

42. Gardner CD, Kiazand A, Alhassan S, et al. Comparison of the Atkins, Zone, Ornish, and LEARN diets for change in weight and related risk factors among overweight premenopausal women: the A TO Z Weight Loss Study: a randomized trial. JAMA. 2007;297:969-77. [PMID: 17341711]
43. Tsai AG, Wadden TA. Systematic review: an evaluation of major commercial weight loss programs in the United States. Ann Intern Med. 2005;142:56-66. [PMID: 15630109]
44. Heshka S, Anderson JW, Atkinson RL, et al. Weight loss with self-help compared with a structured commercial program: a randomized trial. JAMA. 2003;289:1792-8. [PMID: 12684357]
45. Anderson JW, Konz EC, Frederich RC, Wood CL. Long-term weight-loss maintenance: a meta-analysis of US studies. Am J Clin Nutr. 2001;74:579-84. [PMID: 11684524]
46. Flechtner-Mors M, Ditschuneit HH, Johnson TD, et al. Metabolic and weight loss effects of long-term dietary intervention in obese patients: four-year results. Obes Res. 2000;8:399-402. [PMID: 10968732]

Table 3. Drug Treatments for Obesity

Agent	Mechanism of Action	Dosage	Side Effects	Notes
Diethylpropion	Sympathomimetic	25 mg tid with meals or 75 mg controlled release in a.m.	Dry mouth, constipation, insomnia, asthenia	FDA schedule IV; approved for short-term use
Phentermine HCl	Sympathomimetic	18.7 to 37.5 mg before meals	Dry mouth, constipation, insomnia, asthenia	FDA schedule IV; approved for short-term use
Phentermine resin	Sympathomimetic	15 to 30 mg in a.m.	Dry mouth, constipation, insomnia, asthenia	FDA schedule IV; approved for short-term use
Sibutramine	Sympathomimetic; seritonergic	5 to 15 mg	Dry mouth, constipation, insomnia, asthenia, increase in blood pressure	FDA schedule IV; approved for long-term use and maintenance
Benzphetamine	Sympathomimetic	25 or 50 mg before breakfast	Dry mouth, constipation, insomnia, asthenia	FDA schedule III; approved for short-term use
Phendimetrazine	Sympathomimetic	35 mg before meals or 105 mg sustained release in a.m.	Dry mouth, constipation, insomnia, asthenia	FDA schedule III; approved for short-term use
Orlistat	Lipase inhibitor	120 mg tid	Bloating; decreased fat-soluble vitamin levels	Nonscheduled; FDA-approved for long-term use and maintenance

FDA = Food and Drug Administration; tid = three times daily.

47. Pittler MH, Ernst E. Complementary therapies for reducing body weight: a systematic review. Int J Obes (Lond). 2005;29:1030-8. [PMID: 15925954]

48. Clinical Efficacy Assessment Subcommittee of the American College of Physicians. Pharmacologic and surgical management of obesity in primary care: a clinical practice guideline from the American College of Physicians. Ann Intern Med. 2005;142:525-31. [PMID: 15809464]

49. Bray GA, Greenway FL. Pharmacological treatment of the overweight patient. Pharmacol Rev. 2007;59:151-84. [PMID: 17540905]

50. James WP, Astrup A, Finer N, et al. Effect of sibutramine on weight maintenance after weight loss: a randomised trial. STORM Study Group. Sibutramine Trial of Obesity Reduction and Maintenance. Lancet. 2000;356:2119-25. [PMID: 11191537]

Sibutramine

Sibutramine primarily promotes satiety but may also increase energy expenditure by blocking the reduction in metabolic rate that accompanies weight loss. Sibutramine is also effective in weight maintenance.

The STORM (Sibutramine Trial of Obesity Reduction and Maintenance) study, which began with a 6-month open-label phase to induce weight loss by using diet and sibutramine (10 mg/d), then randomly assigned patients with greater than 5% weight loss to sibutramine (10 mg/d, increased up to 20 mg/d if weight was regained) or placebo for a further 18 months. Of those who completed the trial, 43% of the sibutramine group and 16% of the placebo group maintained 80% or greater of their weight loss (odds ratio, 4.64; P < 0.001) (50).

A meta-analysis of clinical trials on the long-term effect of anti-obesity drugs found that sibutramine produced a weighted mean weight loss of 6.35 ± 6.47 kg (13.9 lb) compared with 2.18 ± 5.23 kg (4.8 lb) in the placebo group, giving a net effect—what is often called the placebo-subtracted weight loss—of 4.16 kg (CI, 4.73 to 3.59) (51).

Sibutramine, like other sympathomimetic drugs, produces a small increase in mean heart rate and blood pressure level, which accounted for inability to tolerate the drug in about 5% of patients in clinical trials. Other side effects include dry mouth, insomnia, and asthenia and are similar to those of other noradrenergic drugs. Sibutramine is not associated with valvular heart disease, primary pulmonary hypertension, or substance abuse. Sibutramine should be used with caution in patients with cardiovascular disease and in individuals taking selective serotonin reuptake inhibitors. It should not be used within 2 weeks of taking monoamine oxidase inhibitors and should not be used with other noradrenergic agents.

Orlistat

Orlistat inhibits the enzymatic action of pancreatic lipase and thereby reduces fat absorption in the small intestine.

In a 3-year study, patients who lost 5% or more of their body weight after 8 weeks on a diet were randomly assigned to lifestyle advice or lifestyle advice plus orlistat. Weight loss continued to decline for 3 months and remained below randomization levels at 12 months in the orlistat group but increased above randomization levels by 6 months in the lifestyle control group. At the end of 3 years, those on orlistat were still 2.4 kg lighter (52).

A meta-analysis of clinical trials on the long-term effect of anti-obesity drugs found that orlistat produced a weighted mean weight loss of 5.70 ± 7.28 kg (12.6 lb) compared with 2.40 ± 6.99 kg (5.3 lb) in the placebo group, giving a net—or placebo-subtracted weighted mean weight loss—of 2.87 kg (CI, 3.21 to 2.53) (6.4 lb) (51).

Generally, clinical trials of orlistat have shown that about 70% of patients achieve greater than 5% weight loss, and 70% of them maintain it at 2 years. Orlistat use has been documented for up to 4 years. One advantage of the drug is its beneficial effect on levels of low-density-lipoprotein cholesterol. Because it blocks fat absorption, the reduction in low-density-lipoprotein cholesterol is about twice that seen with weight loss alone.

Orlistat is poorly absorbed, and all of its side effects are those expected from inhibition of lipase in the intestine. It can produce fecal incontinence, anal leakage, bloating, and borborygmi, but these tend to occur early in treatment and deter very few patients. It can also lower levels of fat-soluble vitamins. A multivitamin taken at a time other than when orlistat is taken can prevent the reduction in vitamin levels.

Sympathomimetic Amines

The FDA has approved 4 sympathomimetic drugs for weight loss. Two of them—phentermine and diethylpropion—are schedule IV drugs, and the other 2—benzphetamine and phendimetrazine—are schedule III drugs. All 4 are approved only for a "few weeks" of use, usually interpreted as up to 12 weeks. These drugs are less expensive than sibutramine and orlistat. Clinicians should obtain written informed consent if phentermine is prescribed for longer than 12 weeks because data on long-term use are

insufficient. Phentermine is not available in Europe.

Off-Label Drugs for Weight Loss and Medications under Evaluation

Several other drugs have been used off-label for the treatment of overweight and obese patients, including fluoxetine, bupropion, topiramate, zonisamide, exenatide, and pramlintide. These should be used with caution, and informed consent from the patient should be obtained before they are prescribed.

New drugs for the treatment of obesity are currently under evaluation and in advanced stages of clinical trials. Four are combinations of single drugs already approved for weight loss. Two are new chemical entities: lorcaserin, (a serotonin-2C agonist) and tesofensine (a combined multi-amine reuptake inhibitor).

Rimonabant, a specific antagonist of the cannabinoid receptor, is approved and marketed in Europe for treatment of obesity but was not approved by the FDA because of increased incidence of psychiatric side-effects, such as depression and anxiety. Cannabinoid receptors respond to endogenous endocannabinoids and are distributed throughout the brain in the areas related to feeding as well as in fat cells and the gastrointestinal tract. Blocking these receptors decreases hunger and leads to weight loss similar to that seen with sibutramine and orlistat.

When should clinicians consider surgical treatment for overweight patients, and what types of surgical interventions are effective in weight reduction?
Clinicians should consider surgical treatment for adult patients if they have a BMI greater than 40 kg/m² or a BMI greater than 35 kg/m² with serious comorbid conditions, such as sleep apnea, diabetes mellitus, or joint disease (53). Guideline

51. Rucker D, Padwal R, Li SK, et al. Long term pharmacotherapy for obesity and overweight: updated meta-analysis. BMJ. 2007;335:1194-9. [PMID: 18006966]
52. Richelsen B, Tonstad S, Rössner S, et al. Effect of orlistat on weight regain and cardiovascular risk factors following a very-low-energy diet in abdominally obese patients: a 3-year randomized, placebo-controlled study. Diabetes Care. 2007;30:27-32. [PMID: 17192328]
53. NIH conference. Gastrointestinal surgery for severe obesity. Consensus Development Conference Panel. Ann Intern Med. 1991;115:956-61. [PMID: 1952493]

from the American College of Physicians set the threshold higher, suggesting that surgery be considered in patients with a BMI greater than 40 kg/m² who have associated disorders (48). Potential candidates must have tried and failed nonsurgical weight-loss treatment, must understand the procedure and its complications, and must be an acceptable surgical risk.

Several surgical procedures have been used to treat obesity, and all of them can be performed laparoscopically (see Box). Gastric bypass was one of the first, and it produces among the largest weight loss. It involves making a small pouch of stomach just below the esophagus that empties into a loop of jejunum. Gastroplasty provides elongation of the stomach with a staple line paralleling the lesser curvature and a ring at the end of this narrowing to delay entry of food into the stomach. Pancreaticobiliary bypass involves forming 2 parallel intestinal limbs, one of which empties the stomach and the other the pancreatic and biliary secretions, which are then brought together near the ileocecal valve. The least invasive is the laparoscopically-placed band around the stomach, which is similar to the gastroplasty in that it narrows the opening between the upper and lower stomach.

Only a few good-quality clinical trials have been performed to evaluate the effect of bariatric surgery on development or remission of diabetes and mortality (54).

In a randomized, controlled trial, 60 patients with diabetes and a BMI between 30 and 40 kg/m² were randomly assigned to either the lap-band operation or a lifestyle program. At 2 years, patients in the lap-band group had lost 20.0% of their body weight compared with 1.4% body weight in patients in the lifestyle group. Remission of diabetes occurred in 73% of those in the surgical group but only 13% of those in the diet-treated group. The relative

risk for remission from diabetes was 5.5 (CI, 2.2 to 14.0) and was related to weight loss (55).

The Swedish Obese Subjects Study found that patients who had bariatric surgery had greater improvements in cardiovascular risk factors than those in the control group during the first 2 years after surgery. Increased weight loss was associated with a decreased incidence of new cases of diabetes at 2 and 10 years. In the patients who lost more than 12% of their body weight and maintained it, there were no new cases of diabetes at 2 years (56). A follow-up study demonstrated a 29% reduction in mortality after 10.9 years in the surgery group compared with the control group (adjusted hazard ratio, 0.71; P = 0.01) (57).

Another study compared long-term mortality over an 8-year period among 9949 patients who had undergone gastric bypass surgery with 9628 severely obese control participants. There was a 40% adjusted reduction in long-term all-cause mortality in the surgery group compared with those in the control group (37.6 vs. 57.1 deaths per 10 000 person-years; P < 0.001) (58).

Liposuction has sometimes been used as a surgical procedure to treat obesity. It was originally developed as a plastic surgical procedure for contouring body fat stores, but with current techniques, several kilograms of fat can be removed. However, rapid removal of too much fat has been associated with fatality. Furthermore, in 1 study in which patients were compared before and after extensive liposuction, there were no significant improvements in metabolic or cardiac risk factors, suggesting that even more than subcutaneous fat must be removed in order to realize metabolic benefits (59).

What are the adverse effects of surgical interventions for obesity?
Clinicians and patients should be aware of the various adverse effects associated with surgical interventions for obesity (Table 4). Patients who undergo bariatric surgery may also develop deficiencies in levels of iron, vitamin B_{12}, folate, and calcium,

54. Maggard MA, Shugarman LR, Suttorp M, et al. Meta-analysis: surgical treatment of obesity. Ann Intern Med. 2005;142:547-59. [PMID: 15809466]

55. Dixon JB, O'Brien PE. Changes in comorbidities and improvements in quality of life after LAP-BAND placement. Am J Surg. 2002;184:51S-54S. [PMID: 12527352]

56. Swedish Obese Subjects Study Scientific Group. Lifestyle, diabetes, and cardiovascular risk factors 10 years after bariatric surgery. N Engl J Med. 2004;351:2683-93. [PMID: 15616203]

57. Swedish Obese Subjects Study. Effects of bariatric surgery on mortality in Swedish obese subjects. N Engl J Med. 2007;357:741-52. [PMID: 17715408]

58. Adams TD, Gress RE, Smith SC, et al. Long-term mortality after gastric bypass surgery. N Engl J Med. 2007;357:753-61. [PMID: 17715409]

Table 4. Adverse Effects Associated with Surgical Interventions for Obesity

Complication	Gastric Bypass	Gastroplasty	Laparoscopic Gastric Bands
Mortality	0%–1%	0%–1%	0%–0.1%
DVT and pulmonary embolus	0%–3%	0%–3%	0%–3%
Anastamotic leak or staple line disruption	0%–5.1%	27%–31%	–
Stomal stenosis or obstruction	6%–20%	20%–33%	2%
Marginal ulcer or band erosion	0.6%–13%	1%–7%	0%–3%
Ventral incisional hernia with reflux	0%–1.8%	8%–21%	–
Revisional surgery	–	–	Up to 40%
Dilatation of GI tract	–	–	Up to 10%
Infection at port site	–	–	0%–9%

DVT = deep venous thrombosis; GI = gastrointestinal. Adapted from (60).

and they should be evaluated for such deficiencies and receive appropriate treatment. Successful pregnancy has been documented after all of these procedures. In general, the infants tend to be smaller than infants born to the same mother before the bariatric operation, but there is no increase in adverse perinatal outcomes.

When should clinicians consider specialty referral for overweight patients?

Clinicians should consider specialist consultation primarily for complications of obesity. Patients with suspected obstructive sleep apnea may require referral for polysomnography and advice on treatment. Those with complicated diabetes mellitus may benefit from consultation with an endocrinologist. Overweight children may benefit from consulting a pediatric endocrinologist, especially if an inherited syndrome is suspected. Patients contemplating a very-low-calorie diet should be followed in a clinic specializing in this treatment. Finally, patients who are candidates for bariatric surgery need referral to a bariatric surgeon, preferably at an institution where these procedures are performed frequently.

What are the best strategies for maintaining weight loss?

Exercise is an important strategy for maintaining weight loss over an extended period of time (60).

In the Nurses' Health Study, women who maintained vigorous levels of physical activity had smaller weight gains over 6 years of follow-up than those who did not (61).

Another important factor for maintaining weight loss is self-monitoring of eating patterns, which can be encouraged by lifestyle-modification advice either by the primary care physician or in a more formal setting (62).

Although all calorie-restricted diets are effective in helping patients lose weight, a particular diet may be easier to follow for a particular patient. It is important for clinicians and patients to discuss the options and consider changing diets if a specific one is not effective.

Smoking may have an effect on weight, and cessation of smoking may increase weight. However, smoking carries its own substantial risks. In the Framingham study, obese female smokers lost 13.3 years of life and obese male smokers lost 13.7 years compared with 7.1 years in nonsmoking women and 5.8 years in nonsmoking men (63). Weight loss should not serve as a rationale for withholding advice about smoking cessation.

Clinicians should always be aware of medications that can cause weight gain and avoid them when possible.

59. Klein S, Fontana L, Young VL, et al. Absence of an effect of liposuction on insulin action and risk factors for coronary heart disease. N Engl J Med. 2004;350:2549-57. [PMID: 15201411]

60. Bray GA. Metabolic Syndrome and Obesity. Totawa, NJ: Humana Press; 2007.

61. Field AE, Wing RR, Manson JE, et al. Relationship of a large weight loss to long-term weight change among young and middle-aged US women. Int J Obes Relat Metab Disord. 2001;25:1113-21. [PMID: 11477495]

62. Wing RR, Phelan S. Long-term weight loss maintenance. Am J Clin Nutr. 2005;82:222S-225S. [PMID: 16002825]

63. Peeters A, Barendregt JJ, Willekens F, et al. Obesity in adulthood and its consequences for life expectancy: a life-table analysis. Ann Intern Med. 2003;138:24-32. [PMID: 12513041]

Practice Improvement

What do professional organizations recommend with regard to the management of overweight patients?

In 2003, the U.S. Preventive Services Task Force issued a guideline on screening for obesity in adults. It recommended that clinicians screen adults for obesity and offer counseling and behavioral interventions to promote weight loss in obese patients but stated that evidence was insufficient to recommend these measures to promote sustained weight loss in obese and overweight patients (8).

The American College of Physicians published guidelines on pharmacologic and surgical management of obesity in 2005. It recommended counseling for all obese patients on lifestyle and behavior modifications, such as diet and exercise, to meet their individualized goals; pharmacologic therapy with specific drugs for those who fail to meet those goals, with discussion of the limitations and adverse effects of available drugs; and bariatric surgery in experienced centers for those with a BMI greater than 40 kg/m^2 who have not maintained weight loss with other measures and present with comorbid conditions related to obesity (48).

In 1998, the National Heart, Lung, and Blood Institute issued extensive guidelines on management of patients with obesity, including detailed evidence tables on diet, physical activity, and combined interventions; behavioral therapy; and pharmacotherapy (9).

---

in the clinic

Tool Kit

Obesity

PIER modules

pier.acponline.org

Access the PIER module on obesity. PIER modules provide evidence-based, updated information on current diagnosis and treatment in an electronic format designed for rapid access at the point of care.

Body Mass Index Table and Calculator from the National Heart, Lung and Blood Institute at the NIH

Table: www.nhlbi.nih.gov/guidelines/obesity/bmi_tbl.htm

Calculator: www.nhlbisupport.com/bmi/bmicalc.htm

Easy-to-use tools to facilitate rapid determination of BMI.

Patient Education Resources

www.annals.org/intheclinic

Access the Patient Information material that appears on the following page for duplication and distribution to patients.

www.acponline.org/patients_families/pdfs/health/obesity.pdf

American College of Physicians: 100 Million Adult Americans Are Overweight and at Risk of Serious Disease

www.cdc.gov/nccdphp/dnpa/bmi/index.htm

Centers for Disease Control and Prevention: Healthy Weight: Assessing your Weight

www.cdc.gov/nccdphp/dnpa/obesity/faq.htm

Centers for Disease Control and Prevention: Overweight and Obesity: Frequently Asked Questions (FAQs)

WHAT YOU SHOULD KNOW ABOUT OBESITY

Being overweight means that you weigh more than is healthy. Overweight people have medical problems, such as high cholesterol, diabetes, heart disease, arthritis, and breathing problems, as well as shorter lives. Losing weight can be hard, but losing even a little can make you healthier.

How do you know if you are overweight?

Body mass index (BMI) measures how tall you are in meters (m) and how much you weigh in kilograms (kg) to tell you if you weigh too much.

- Normal BMI is under 25 kg/m². You are overweight if your BMI is between 25 kg/m² and 30 kg/m². You are obese if it is over 30 kg/m².

What the best ways to lose weight?

- To lose weight, you have to eat less and exercise more. Some diets are easier than others for some people.

- Sometimes getting advice or joining self-help groups makes it easier to stay on a diet.

- If diet and exercise are not enough, your doctor may give you medicine to lose weight.

- If you are very obese and have serious medical problems, your doctor may consider surgery on your stomach so that you eat less and lose weight.

Why is losing weight so hard?

- It is hard for your body to change. When you go on a diet, you lose some weight and then stop for a while.

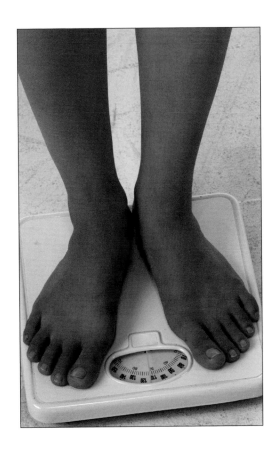

- Set a goal for your new weight that you can reach. Even a few pounds makes a difference.

Web Sites with Good Information on Losing Weight

National Heart, Lung, and Blood Institute: Aim for a Healthy Weight! www.nhlbi.nih.gov/health/public/heart/obesity/lose_wt/index.htm

American Heart Association: Healthy Lifestyle www.americanheart.org/presenter.jhtml?identifier=1200009

Centers for Disease Control and Prevention: Overweight and Obesity www.cdc.gov/nccdphp/dnpa/obesity/index.htm

Surgeon General: Physical activity and health: A report of the Surgeon General www.cdc.gov/nccdphp/sgr/sgr.htm

AMERICAN COLLEGE OF PHYSICIANS
INTERNAL MEDICINE | *Doctors for Adults®*

Atrial Fibrillation

A trial fibrillation, the most common clinically significant arrhythmia, occurs when a diffuse and chaotic pattern of electrical activity in the atria replaces the normal sinus mechanism, leading to deterioration of mechanical function. Atrial fibrillation is a major cause of morbidity, mortality, and health care expenditures, with a current prevalence of 2.3 million cases in the United States and an estimated increase in prevalence to 15.9 million by the year 2050 (1). Atrial fibrillation is associated with a 5-fold increased risk for stroke and is estimated to cause 15% of all strokes (2). Independent of coexisting diseases, the presence of atrial fibrillation confers a 2-fold increased risk for all-cause mortality (3).

Diagnosis

Who is at risk for atrial fibrillation?
Atrial fibrillation occurs in less than 1% of individuals age 60 to 65 years, but in 8% to 10% of those older than 80 years. Prevalence is higher in men than in women and higher in whites than in blacks. The risk for atrial fibrillation increases with the presence and severity of underlying heart failure and valvular disease.

What symptoms and signs should cause clinicians to suspect atrial fibrillation?
Many patients, particularly the elderly, are asymptomatic during atrial fibrillation. Other patients may have prominent symptoms, including palpitations, shortness of breath, exercise intolerance, or malaise. When present, symptoms are generally greatest at disease onset, when episodes are typically paroxysmal, and tend to diminish over time or when the pattern becomes persistent. Symptoms during atrial fibrillation result from elevation of ventricular rate (at rest and exaggerated with exercise), the irregular nature of the ventricular rate, and the loss of atrial contribution to cardiac output. Even patients with severe symptoms during atrial fibrillation episodes often have episodes of silent atrial fibrillation as well (4), which has important implications for therapeutic strategies, especially anticoagulation.

On physical examination, the signs of atrial fibrillation include a faster-than-expected heart rate (which is quite variable from patient to patient), an irregularly (irregular in timing) irregular (in terms of the amplitude of the pulse) peripheral pulse, as well as irregular heart sounds on auscultation.

Is a single electrocardiogram (ECG) sufficient to diagnose or exclude atrial fibrillation?
Figure 1 is an example of an ECG showing atrial fibrillation. A single ECG is sufficient to diagnose atrial fibrillation if it is recorded during an arrhythmia episode. However, atrial fibrillation is often paroxysmal, so a single ECG showing normal rhythm does not exclude the diagnosis. Longer-term monitoring can be helpful when atrial fibrillation is suspected but the ECG is normal. In patients with daily paroxysmal symptoms, 24- or 48-hour continuous Holter monitoring is usually sufficient to make the diagnosis. In patients with less-frequent symptoms, monitoring during longer periods with electrocardiographic loop recorders may be necessary for diagnosis. However, even monitoring for periods as long as a month can be nondiagnostic in patients with very infrequent episodes. In addition, because patients trigger loop recorders to record when symptoms occur, these recorders are not helpful in detecting episodes of asymptomatic arrhythmia. In some cases, a diagnosis of atrial fibrillation occurs only after several years of symptoms because of the nonspecific nature of symptoms

1. Miyasaka Y, Barnes ME, Gersh BJ, et al. Secular trends in incidence of atrial fibrillation in Olmsted County, Minnesota, 1980 to 2000, and implications on the projections for future prevalence. Circulation. 2006;114:119-25. [PMID: 16818816]
2. Hart RG, Benavente O, McBride R, Pearce LA. Antithrombotic therapy to prevent stroke in patients with atrial fibrillation: a meta-analysis. Ann Intern Med. 1999;131:492-501. [PMID: 10507957]

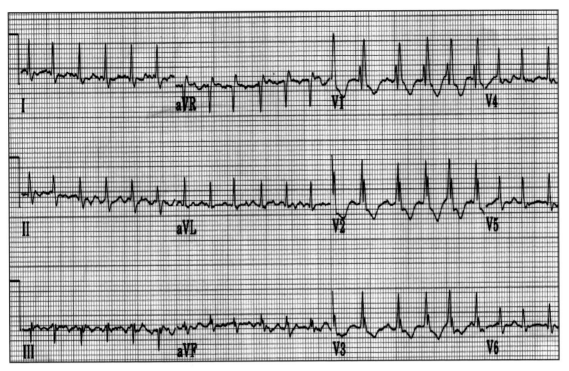

Figure 1. Electrocardiogram showing atrial fibrillation with rapid ventricular rate.

and the occasionally long periods between episodes in some patients at the beginning of the disease process.

What is the role of history and physical examination in patients with atrial fibrillation?

History and physical examination can help to determine the duration of symptoms and potential underlying causes. Clinicians should document history and physical examination evidence of hypertension, heart failure, murmurs indicating structural heart disease, or recent cardiac surgery. In addition, clinicians should look for signs and symptoms of noncardiac causes of atrial fibrillation, including pulmonary disease; hyperthyroidism; use of caffeine or other stimulants; or use of adrenergic drugs (such as those

3. Benjamin EJ, Wolf PA, D'Agostino RB, et al. Impact of atrial fibrillation on the risk of death: the Framingham Heart Study. Circulation. 1998;98:946-52. [PMID: 9737513]
4. Page RL, Wilkinson WE, Clair WK, et al. Asymptomatic arrhythmias in patients with symptomatic paroxysmal atrial fibrillation and paroxysmal supraventricular tachycardia. Circulation. 1994;89:224-7. [PMID: 8281651]

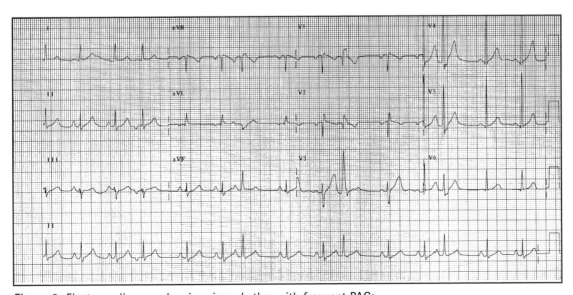

Figure 2. Electrocardiogram showing sinus rhythm with frequent PACs.

5. American College of Cardiology/American Heart Association Task Force on Practice Guidelines. ACC/AHA/ESC 2006 Guidelines for the Management of Patients with Atrial Fibrillation: a report of the American College of Cardiology/American Heart Association Task Force on Practice Guidelines and the European Society of Cardiology Committee for Practice Guidelines (Writing Committee to Revise the 2001 Guidelines for the Management of Patients With Atrial Fibrillation): developed in collaboration with the European Heart Rhythm Association and the Heart Rhythm Society. Circulation. 2006;114:e257-354. [PMID: 16908781]

used to treat pulmonary disease) or alcohol.

What other electrocardiographic arrhythmias might clinicians confuse with atrial fibrillation?

Other arrhythmias that are commonly confused with atrial fibrillation include sinus rhythm with frequent premature atrial contractions (PACs), atrial tachycardia, and atrial flutter. The key electrocardiographic components of atrial fibrillation are the absence of discernable P waves and an irregular ventricular response without any pattern. When the diagnosis of atrial fibrillation is unclear, clinicians should obtain long rhythm strips with multiple lead combinations to evaluate for irregular rhythms and P waves. Clinicians should look for deformed T waves or ST segments for evidence of P waves.

Sinus rhythm with frequent PACs is an irregular rhythm, but P waves are present (Figure 2). Atrial tachycardia and atrial flutter have evident atrial activation, but may be conducted to the ventricles in an irregular matter; even in this circumstance, there is a pattern to the irregular conduction (Figure 3). This is an important distinction because catheter ablation is first-line therapy in many patients with atrial tachycardia and atrial flutter.

How should clinicians classify atrial fibrillation according to duration and frequency?

Although there is a great deal of confusion regarding this question, the convention is to describe atrial fibrillation by the qualifiers paroxysmal, persistent, or permanent (5). "Paroxysmal" means that atrial fibrillation episodes terminate without intervention within 7 days but often in less than 24 hours. "Persistent" means that episodes last longer than 7 days or require intervention (such as cardioversion) to restore sinus rhythm. "Permanent" means that interventions to restore sinus rhythm have either failed or have not been attempted. These qualifiers are not necessarily mutually exclusive in a given patient, so clinicians should characterize the current or most-usual pattern.

Traditionally, these distinctions have been used to predict response to therapy. The response

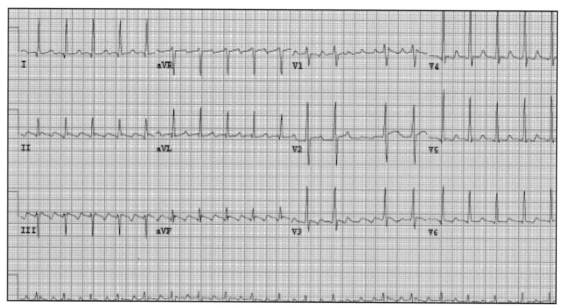

Figure 3. Atrial flutter. Classic "saw-tooth" flutter waves are seen in all 12 leads, and the ventricular response is mostly regular. (There is a transient change from 2:1 to 4:1 atrioventricular conduction following the 12th QRS complex.)

to antiarrhythmic drug therapy is less favorable as the pattern goes from paroxysmal to persistent to permanent. There is no difference in the need for anticoagulation on the basis of the pattern of atrial fibrillation.

What laboratory studies should clinicians obtain in patients with atrial fibrillation?

On initial presentation of atrial fibrillation, clinicians should measure sensitive thyroid-stimulating hormone to exclude hyperthyroidism, serum electrolytes, and renal and hepatic function to evaluate risk for toxicity to specific drugs. Transthoracic ECG is generally helpful to evaluate the presence of structural heart disease, but is specifically able to evaluate left atrial size, valvular heart disease, pericardial disease, and left ventricular hypertrophy, which are associated with responsiveness to antiarrhythmic therapy. Transesophageal ECG is indicated to exclude atrial clot when transthoracic images are inadequate or when cardioversion is planned in a patient who has been anticoagulated for less than 3 weeks. In selected patients, tests to evaluate specific disease processes that may be causative in acute episodes of atrial fibrillation, such as pulmonary embolism, acute myocardial infarction, or acute heart failure, may also be appropriate. Clinicians should test stool for occult blood before initiation of anticoagulation.

What underlying cardiac and noncardiac conditions should clinicians look for in patients with atrial fibrillation?

Of patients with atrial fibrillation, 80% have some component of structural heart disease, particularly hypertensive heart disease, but also coronary disease, valvular heart disease, or cardiomyopathies of any cause. Because the incidence of atrial fibrillation is markedly affected by aging, age-related atrial

fibrosis is considered central to the arrhythmia's pathogenesis. Some patients have atrial fibrillation in the absence of identifiable heart disease, which is referred to as lone atrial fibrillation, but the usefulness of this designation is a matter of some debate. Some experts believe that the designation "lone atrial fibrillation" should be resitricted to patients older than 60 years of age because it is difficult to exclude structural heart disease in older patients.

In 30 years of follow-up of 5209 participants in the Framingham Study, 193 men and 183 women developed atrial fibrillation. Of these, 32 men and 11 women had no evidence of underlying heart disease. Matched comparisons between patients with lone atrial fibrillation and control participants showed that individuals with atrial fibrillation had similar cardiac risk factors but significantly higher rates of preexisting nonspecific T- or ST-wave abnormalities, intraventricular block, and stroke (6).

In a population-based, longitudinal study of risk factors for coronary artery disease and stroke in 5201 men and women age ≥65 years, 4.8% of women and 6.2% of men had atrial fibrillation at baseline. Prevalence was 9.1% in patients with clinical cardiovascular disease, 4.6% in patients with evidence of subclinical but no clinical cardiovascular disease, and only 1.6% in patients with neither clinical nor subclinical cardiovascular disease. The low prevalence of atrial fibrillation in the absence of clinical and subclinical cardiovascular disease calls into question the clinical usefulness of the designation "lone atrial fibrillation," particularly in the elderly (7).

Acute illnesses that may be associated with new-onset atrial fibrillation include acute myocardial infarction, pulmonary embolism, and thyrotoxicosis. Atrial fibrillation is common after cardiac or thoracic surgery, but may also occur in reaction to another major surgery or severe illness. Atrial fibrillation has an increased incidence in sleep apnea and obesity; however, treatment of these conditions does not seem to affect the subsequent progression of arrhythmia.

6. Brand FN, Abbott RD, Kannel WB, Wolf PA. Characteristics and prognosis of lone atrial fibrillation. 30-year follow-up in the Framingham Study. JAMA. 1985;254:3449-53. [PMID: 4068186]
7. Furberg CD, Psaty BM, Manolio TA, et al. Prevalence of atrial fibrillation in elderly subjects (the Cardiovascular Health Study). Am J Cardiol. 1994;74:236-41. [PMID: 8037127]

Vagal forms of atrial fibrillation usually occur in men age 40 to 50 years who have no structural heart disease. Symptoms often occur at night, at rest, or after alcohol use. Adrenergic forms of atrial fibrillation occur during waking hours preceded by emotional stress or exercise. The mechanism of alcohol-precipitated atrial fibrillation is unclear, but may be related to increases in circulating catecholamines, changes in conduction time and refractory periods in the myocardium, and increases in vagal tone.

Diagnosis... Atrial fibrillation is the most common clinically significant arrhythmia, and prevalence increases with advancing age. Typical symptoms include palpitations, shortness of breath, and exercise intolerance. However, some patients report only general malaise, and many patients are asymptomatic. Electrocardiogram recordings during episodes are the only way to confirm the diagnosis. If the diagnosis is suspected and ECG is normal, longer-term monitoring with a Holter monitor or loop recorder can be helpful. Initial assessment should include laboratory tests (electrolytes, thyroid-stimulating hormone, and renal and hepatic function) to rule out underlying disorders or contraindications to therapies, and ECG to look for structural heart disease.

CLINICAL BOTTOM LINE

Treatment

8. Naito M, David D, Michelson EL, et al. The hemodynamic consequences of cardiac arrhythmias: evaluation of the relative roles of abnormal atrioventricular sequencing, irregularity of ventricular rhythm and atrial fibrillation in a canine model. Am Heart J. 1983;106:284-91. [PMID: 6869209]
9. Risk factors for stroke and efficacy of antithrombotic therapy in atrial fibrillation. Analysis of pooled data from five randomized controlled trials. Arch Intern Med. 1994;154:1449-57. [PMID: 8018000]
10. Hart RG, Sherman DG, Easton JD, Cairns JA. Prevention of stroke in patients with nonvalvular atrial fibrillation. Neurology. 1998;51:674-81. [PMID: 9748009]
11. Redfield MM, Kay GN, Jenkins LS, et al. Tachycardia-related cardiomyopathy: a common cause of ventricular dysfunction in patients with atrial fibrillation referred for atrioventricular ablation. Mayo Clin Proc. 2000;75:790-5. [PMID: 10943231]
12. Atrial Fibrillation Follow-up Investigation of Rhythm Management (AFFIRM) Investigators. A comparison of rate control and rhythm control in patients with atrial fibrillation. N Engl J Med. 2002;347:1825-33. [PMID: 12466506]

What are the complications of atrial fibrillation and how can therapy decrease the risk for these events?

There are 3 reasons to prescribe therapy for atrial fibrillation: to reduce symptoms, to prevent thromboembolism, and to reduce the risk for tachycardia-related myocardiopathy.

Although atrial fibrillation is not always symptomatic, when present it can be disabling for some patients. Symptoms are usually caused by inappropriately rapid ventricular rates or the irregularity of the ventricular response during atrial fibrillation (8). Rhythm control (restoring and maintaining sinus rhythm) and rate control (controlling heart rate response without attempts to restore and maintain sinus rhythm) can both help to reduce symptoms.

The average annual risk for arterial thromboembolism is 5% in patients with nonvalvular atrial fibrillation, and the risk for stroke is higher in patients older than age 75 (9). Both established risk factors for thromboembolism and specific features of atrial fibrillation modulate stroke risk (6). Left-atrial thrombi cause 75% of strokes in patients with atrial fibrillation (10). Antithrombotic therapy reduces stroke risk.

The other pathologic consequence of atrial fibrillation is tachycardia-related cardiomyopathy (11). Drug therapy to control rate or rhythm can reduce the risk for this complication.

What are the relative benefits of rate control versus rhythm control in patients with atrial fibrillation?
High-quality clinical trials suggest that rhythm control does not improve mortality, stroke rates, hospitalization rates, or quality of life compared with rate control for most patients with atrial fibrillation (12–14). Rate control is easier to accomplish and prevents exposure to potentially harmful antiarrhythmic agents. On the other hand, rhythm control may be useful in selected patients with severe atrial

fibrillation symptoms (before or after failure of rate control) or in younger patients without structural heart disease.

The AFFIRM (Atrial Fibrillation Follow-up Investigation of Rhythm Management) trial included 4060 patients with atrial fibrillation who had at least 1 risk factor for stroke. The mean age was 69 years, and structural heart disease, aside from hypertension, was unusual. All-cause mortality at 5 years was 25.9% in the rate-control group and 26.7% in the rhythm-control group (P = 0.080). Important observations from the trial are that patients with apparently successful rhythm control still need to continue anticoagulation because of persistent stroke risk, and that patients who were able to maintain sinus rhythm had a survival advantage that was almost balanced by the disadvantage imposed by antiarrhythmic drug therapy (15).

A more recent trial extended these observations to outpatients with severe heart failure by randomly assigning 1376 patients with atrial fibrillation, left ventricular ejection fraction of ≤35%, and heart failure symptoms to rate control versus rhythm control. Over 37 months, 27% of the rhythm-control group and 25% of the rate-control group died from cardiovascular causes (P = 0.6). There was no improvement in all-cause mortality, stroke, heart failure, or need for hospitalization in the rhythm-control group (16).

What drugs should clinicians consider for rate control in patients with rapid atrial fibrillation?

Clinicians should consider drug therapy to control ventricular rate in all patients with atrial fibrillation. Criteria for rate control vary with patient age, but clinicians should generally target therapy to achieve target heart rates of 60 to 80 beats per minute at rest and between 90 to 115 beats per minute during moderate exercise (17). Agents that affect atrioventricular nodal conduction and are recommended as first-line therapy in this setting include β-blockers and nondihydropyridine calcium-channel antagonists (Table 1). Amiodarone and digoxin also block the atrioventricular node, but are not recommended as first-line

monotherapy for rate control (17). Digitalis is not helpful in reducing heart rate with exercise. Additionally, monotherapy with digitalis is unlikely to control rate in patients with heart failure and high sympathetic activity.

Amiodarone is occasionally used to reduce ventricular response during continued atrial fibrillation if other agents have failed. This practice is more difficult to justify because of toxicities associated with amiodarone and the trial evidence that rhythm control is no better than rate control.

When should clinicians consider antiarrhythmic drugs in the treatment of atrial fibrillation?

Rhythm-control therapy is no longer the preferred strategy in most patients with atrial fibrillation. However, the major trials comparing rate control with rhythm control did not include younger patients or patients with highly symptomatic atrial fibrillation. Consequently, it is reasonable to consider rhythm control in these patient subgroups, either primarily or when symptoms persist despite rate control. Rhythm control is often favored for the first episode of symptomatic atrial fibrillation, particularly in young patients because many maintain sinus rhythm for a period after pharmacologic cardioversion without continued antiarrhythmic drug treatment. Antiarrhythmic drugs have been shown to have modest effects compared with placebo in prolonging time to recurrent atrial fibrillation (Table 1), but rather than the complete absence of atrial fibrillation episodes, antiarrhythmic drug therapy is generally judged to be effective if it reduces episodes and symptoms.

The Canadian Trial of Atrial Fibrillation randomly assigned 403 patients to amiodarone, sotalol, or propafenone and found that after mean follow-up of 16 months, recurrence of atrial fibrillation was 35% during amiodarone and 63% during sotalol or propafenone therapy (18).

13. STAF Investigators. Randomized trial of rate-control versus rhythm-control in persistent atrial fibrillation: the Strategies of Treatment of Atrial Fibrillation (STAF) study. J Am Coll Cardiol. 2003;41:1690-6. [PMID: 12767648]
14. Hohnloser SH, Kuck KH, Lilienthal J. Rhythm or rate control in atrial fibrillation——Pharmacological Intervention in Atrial Fibrillation (PIAF): a randomised trial. Lancet. 2000;356:1789-94. [PMID: 11117910]
15. AFFIRM Investigators. Relationships between sinus rhythm, treatment, and survival in the Atrial Fibrillation Follow-Up Investigation of Rhythm Management (AFFIRM) Study. Circulation. 2004;109:1509-13. [PMID: 15007003]
16. Atrial Fibrillation and Congestive Heart Failure Investigators. Rhythm control versus rate control for atrial fibrillation and heart failure. N Engl J Med. 2008;358:2667-77. [PMID: 18565859]
17. American College of Cardiology/American Heart Association Task Force on Practice Guidelines. ACC/AHA/ESC 2006 Guidelines for the Management of Patients with Atrial Fibrillation. Circulation. 2006; 114:e257-354. [PMID: 16908781]
18. Roy D, Talajic M, Dorian P, et al. Amiodarone to prevent recurrence of atrial fibrillation. Canadian Trial of Atrial Fibrillation Investigators. N Engl J Med. 2000;342:913-20. [PMID: 10738049]

Table 1. Drug Therapy for Rate and Rhythm Control in Atrial Fibrillation

Agent	Mechanism of Action	Dosage	Benefits	Side Effects	Notes
Rate-Controlling Agents					
β-Blockers					
Metoprolol	Selective β$_1$-adrenergic–receptor blocking agent	5 mg IV every 5 min, up to 15 mg 50–100 mg PO twice daily	Convenient IV administration in NPO patients, rapid onset of action, dependable AV nodal blockade	Bradycardia, hypotension, heart block, bronchospasm (less frequently than nonselective β-blockers), worsening of CHF	
Propranolol	Nonselective β-adrenergic–receptor blocking agent	1–8 mg IV (1 mg every 2 min). 10–120 mg PO 3 times daily; long-acting preparation: 80–320 mg PO once daily	Inexpensive, commonly available	Bradycardia, hypotension, heart block, bronchospasm, worsening of CHF	
Esmolol	Short-acting IV β$_1$ selective adrenergic receptor-blocking agent	0.05–0.2 mg/kg per min IV	Short-acting, titratable on or off with very rapid half-life	Bradycardia, hypotension, heart block, bronchospasm (less frequent)	Occasionally inconsistent effect in high-catecholamine states
Pindolol	Nonselective β-adrenergic–receptor blocking agent with intrinsic sympatho-mimetic activity	2.5–20 mg PO 2 to 3 times daily	Less bradycardia, less bronchospasm	Bradycardia, hypotension, heart block	Less propensity for heart block than other β-blockers
Atenolol	Selective β$_1$-adrenergic–receptor blocking agent	5 mg IV over 5 min, repeat in 10 min. 25–100 mg PO once daily	Does not cross blood–brain barrier, fewer CNS side effects	Bradycardia, hypotension, heart block	
Nadolol	Nonselective β-adrenergic–receptor blocking agent	20–120 mg once daily	Lower incidence of crossing of blood–brain barrier, fewer CNS side effects	Bradycardia, hypotension, heart block	Oral form only
Calcium-channel blockers					
Verapamil	Calcium-channel blocking agent	5–20 mg in 5-mg increments IV every 30 min, or 0.005 mg/kg per min infusion. 120–360 mg PO daily, in divided doses or in the slow-release form	Consistent AV nodal blockade	Hypotension, heart block, direct myocardial depression	Do not use in the Wolff–Parkinson–White syndrome
Diltiazem	Calcium-channel blocking agent	0.25–0.35 mg/kg IV followed by 5–15 mg/h. 120–360 mg PO daily as slow release	Consistent AV nodal blockade	Hypotension, heart block, less myocardial depression	Do not use in the Wolff–Parkinson–White syndrome
Cardiac glycoside					
Digoxin	Na+-K+ pump inhibitor, increases intracellular calcium	0.75–1.5 mg PO or IV in 3–4 divided doses over 12–24 h. Maintenance dose: 0.125 mg PO or IV to 0.5 mg daily	Particularly useful for rate control in CHF.	Heart block, digoxin-associated arrhythmias; dosage adjustment required in renal impairment	First-line therapy only in patients with decreased left-ventricular systolic function. Not useful for rate control with exercise. Not useful for conversion of AF or aflutter to NSR.
Antiarrhythmic agents					
Class Ia					
Procainamide	Prolongs conduction and slows repolarization by blocking inward Na+ flux	1–2 g q 12 h (shorter-acting oral preparations are no longer available)	Convenient IV dosing available with maintenance infusion, and conversion to PO tablets, very effective at converting AF to NSR	Not recommended because of frequent side effects, including hypotension, nausea, vomiting, lupus-like syndrome, QT prolongation, and arrhythmia	Need to follow drug levels and QT interval for toxicity, adjust dose in patients with renal insufficiency, Not for use in patients with severe LV dysfunction.
Quinidine gluconate	Prolongs conduction and slows repolarization. Blocks fast inward Na+ channel.	324–648 mg PO every 8–12 h	Relatively effective in converting AF to NSR but may take several days to achieve NSR because of PO dosing	Proarrhythmia, nausea, vomiting, diarrhea, QT prolongation	Not recommended because of frequent side effects. Follow drug levels and QT interval for toxicity. Adjust dose in patients with renal insufficiency. Oral agent only

Table 1. Drug Therapy for Rate and Rhythm Control in Atrial Fibrillation (continued)

Agent	Mechanism of Action	Dosage	Benefits	Side Effects	Notes
Disopyramide	Similar electrophysiologic properties to procainamide and quinidine	150 mg PO every 6–8 h, or 150–300 mg twice a day	Can be useful in patients with hypertension and normal LV function	QT prolongation (not PR or QRS), torsades de pointes, heart block	Rarely used in current era of antiarrhythmic therapy. Oral agent only, negative inotropic properties.
Class Ic					
Flecainide	Blocks Na+ channels (and fast Na+ current)	2 mg/kg, IV*. 50–150 mg PO every 12 h. Also, single loading doses of 300 mg are efficacious in conversion of recent onset AF.	Efficacy in paroxysmal AF with structurally normal hearts	Aflutter or atrial tachycardia with rapid ventricular response but not with acute single loading doses. VT and VF in diseased hearts	Not for use in patients with structurally abnormal hearts
Propafenone	Blocks myocardial Na+ channels	2 mg/kg, IV*. 150–300 mg PO every 8 h. Also, single loading doses of 600 mg are efficacious in conversion of recent onset AF.	Efficacy in paroxysmal and sustained AF	Aflutter or atrial tachycardia with rapid ventricular response, but not with acute single loading doses	Antiarrhythmic and weak calcium channel and ß-blocking properties. Not for use with structural heart disease.
C. Class III					
Ibutilide	Prolongs action potential duration (and atrial and ventricular refractoriness) by blocking rapid component of delayed rectifier potassium current	1 mg IV over 10 min. May be repeated once if necessary.	Efficacy in acute and rapid conversion of AF to NSR	Polymorphic VT (torsades de pointes) occurred in 8.3% of patients in a clinical trial (most with LV dysfunction), QT prolongation	In some centers, only used in the electrophysiology laboratory. May also be used to facilitate unsuccessful direct-current cardioversion.
Amiodarone	Blocks Na+ channels (affinity for inactivated channels). Noncompetitive ß- and ß-receptor inhibitor.	5–7 mg/kg IV up to 1500 mg per 24 h. 400–800 mg PO daily, for 3–4 wk, followed by 100–400 mg PO daily	Safest agent for use in patients with structural heart disease, good efficacy in maintaining NSR chronically	Bradycardia, QT prolongation, hyperthyroidism, lung toxicity, argyria (blue discoloration of skin) with chronic use	Can be used in the Wolff–Parkinson–White syndrome.
Sotalol	Nonselective β_1- and β_2-blocking agent, prolongs action potential duration	80–240 mg PO every 12 h	Similar efficacy to quinidine, but fewer adverse effects. Better rate control because of ß-blocking properties.	Fatigue, depression, bradycardia, torsades de pointes, CHF	ß-blocking properties, but some positive inotropic activity. Lethal arrhythmias possible. Adjust dose in patients with renal insufficiency. Initiate on telemetry.
Dofetilide	Blocks rapid component of the delayed rectifier potassium current (I_{Kr}), prolonging refractoriness without slowing conduction	500 µg twice daily	More effective than quinidine in conversion to and maintenance of NSR.	QT prolongation, torsades de pointes (2%–4% risk).	Must be strictly dosed according to renal function, body size, and age. Contra-indicated in patients with creatinine clearance <20 mL/min. Initiate on telemetry.

AF = atrial fibrillation; AV = atrioventricular; CHF = congestive heart failure; CNS = central nervous system; IV = intraventricular; LV = left ventricular; NPO = nil per os; NSR = normal sinus rhythm; PO = orally; VF = ventricular fibrillation; VT = ventricular tachycardia.

Antiarrhythmic drugs other than amiodarone are generally have equal efficacy, so susceptibility to side effects should guide choice from among them (Table 1). Drugs that block cardiac sodium channels (class I effect), such as flecainide and propafenone, are useful in patients without coronary heart disease or advanced left-ventricular dysfunction. Trial data do not support their use in patients with heart disease because of an increase in mortality (19). In patients without heart disease, the side effects are due to unwanted sodium-channel blockade in other organ systems, such as the gastrointestinal tract (resulting in anorexia or esophageal reflux) and the central nervous system. Other class I drugs, such as quinidine and procainamide, are no longer used because of their frequent noncardiac side effects.

19. The Cardiac Arrhythmia Suppression Trial (CAST) Investigators. Preliminary report: effect of encainide and flecainide on mortality in a randomized trial of arrhythmia suppression after myocardial infarction. N Engl J Med. 1989;321:406-12. [PMID: 2473403]

20. CHARM Investigators. Prevention of atrial fibrillation in patients with symptomatic chronic heart failure by candesartan in the Candesartan in Heart failure: Assessment of Reduction in Mortality and morbidity (CHARM) program. Am Heart J. 2006;152:86-92. [PMID: 16838426]
21. Maisel WH, Kuntz KM, Reimold SC, et al. Risk of initiating antiarrhythmic drug therapy for atrial fibrillation in patients admitted to a university hospital. Ann Intern Med. 1997;127:281-4. [PMID: 9265427]
22. Stroke Prevention in Atrial Fibrillation Study. Final results. Circulation. 1991;84:527-39. [PMID: 1860198]
23. Petersen P, Boysen G, Godtfredsen J, et al. Placebo-controlled, randomised trial of warfarin and aspirin for prevention of thromboembolic complications in chronic atrial fibrillation. The Copenhagen AFASAK study. Lancet. 1989;1:175-9. [PMID: 2563096]
24. Connolly SJ, Laupacis A, Gent M, et al. Canadian Atrial Fibrillation Anticoagulation (CAFA) Study. J Am Coll Cardiol. 1991;18:349-55. [PMID: 1856403]
25. Ezekowitz MD, Bridgers SL, James KE, et al. Warfarin in the prevention of stroke associated with nonrheumatic atrial fibrillation. Veterans Affairs Stroke Prevention in Nonrheumatic Atrial Fibrillation Investigators. N Engl J Med. 1992;327:1406-12. [PMID: 1406859]
26. The Boston Area Anticoagulation Trial for Atrial Fibrillation Investigators. The effect of low-dose warfarin on the risk of stroke in patients with nonrheumatic atrial fibrillation. N Engl J Med. 1990;323:1505-11. [PMID: 2233931]
27. Stroke Prevention in Atrial Fibrillation Investigators. Lessons from the Stroke Prevention in Atrial Fibrillation trials. Ann Intern Med. 2003;138:831-8. [PMID: 12755555]

Drugs that block potassium channels (class III effects), such as sotalol and dofetilide, have a potential to prolong the QT interval and cause torsades de pointes.

Amiodarone can be used in patients with advanced structural heart disease. However, amiodarone can cause permanent end organ toxicity (liver, lungs) that is dose- and duration-dependent. Other side effects include thyroid dysfunction (hypothyroidism, hyperthyroidism), sun sensitivity, and ocular symptoms.

Some nonantiarrhythmic drugs, such as angiotensin-converting enzyme inhibitors and statins, have been demonstrated (albeit primarily in patients with heart failure) to reduce the incidence of atrial fibrillation, presumably because of antifibrotic effects (20).

Before pharmacologic cardioversion of atrial fibrillation present for more than 48 hours, patients should first receive adequate therapy for rate control and anticoagulation. In addition, serum potassium level should be greater than 4.0 mmol/L, serum magnesium level should be greater than 1.0 mmol/L, and ionized calcium levels should be greater than 0.5 mmol/L [2.0 mg/dL]. In most cases, pharmacologic cardioversion should be performed in a monitored hospital setting to permit adequate assessment of the degree of rate control, bradycardia, proarrhythmic affects of antiarrhythmic agents, and other adverse effects (21).

When is anticoagulation indicated for patients with atrial fibrillation?

A meta-analysis (9) of 5 high-quality randomized trials (22–26) supports the use of antithrombotic therapy for appropriate patients with nonvalvular atrial fibrillation.

Anticoagulation is indicated for patients with atrial fibrillation when the risk for thromboembolism exceeds the risk for anticoagulation-associated bleeding (17). About one third of patients with atrial fibrillation have a low risk for thromboembolism, one third have a high risk, and one third have a moderate risk (27).

In addition to established risk factors for thromboembolism, specific features of atrial fibrillation and underlying disease also modulate thromboembolism risk. Patients with reversible causes of atrial fibrillation and those with structurally normal hearts are less likely to have persistent or recurrent episodes and may be at a lower risk for thromboembolism than patients without these features. However, clinicians should keep in mind that the rate of stroke in patients with nonvalvular atrial fibrillation and at least 1 risk factor exceeds that of hemorrhage from chronic anticoagulation.

Risk factors for thromboembolism have been identified in the Stroke Prevention in Atrial Fibrillation trial (9). Patients younger than age 65 years with nonvalvular atrial fibrillation and no risk factors have an annual stroke risk of about 0.5%, whereas patients older than 65 years with no risk factors have a risk of about 1%. This latter figure approximates the risk for major bleeding while on warfarin with an international normalized ratio (INR) of 2.0 to 3.0 (28, 29). The mean annual rate of major bleeding in the major anticoagulation trials on warfarin therapy was 1.2%.

Because of the delicate balance between risk and benefit, indices have been developed to assess which patients with atrial fibrillation are at sufficient risk for stroke to warrant anticoagulation therapy. The most popular of these is the $CHADS_2$ score (30, 31) (Table 2). Table 3 presents recommendations for therapy based on this score.

A 2007 meta-analysis of 29 trials including 28 044 participants characterized the efficacy and safety of antithrombotic agents for stroke prevention in patients who have atrial fibrillation. Compared with control participants, adjusted-dose warfarin (6 trials, 2900 participants) and antiplatelet agents (8 trials, 4876 participants) reduced stroke by 64% (95% CI, 49% to 74%) and 22% (CI, 6% to 35%), respectively. Adjusted-dose warfarin was substantially more efficacious than antiplatelet therapy (relative risk reduction, 39% [CI, 22% to 52%]) (12 trials, 12 963 participants). Absolute increases in major extracranial hemorrhage were small (0.3% per year) (32).

Some data indicate that risk factor–adjusted incidence of ischemic stroke and major bleeding is currently considerably less than that reflected in the previously described trials. The consensus is that this is related to improved therapy for hypertension (33). Less-encouraging recent data have indicated that the rate of major bleeding is high in the elderly (34).

What regimens should clinicians use to anticoagulate patients with atrial fibrillation?

Adjusted-dose warfarin to an INR of 2.0 to 3.0 is the first choice for anticoagulation of patients with atrial fibrillation. Certain patients with prosthetic valves in addition to atrial fibrillation should have warfarin titrated to an INR of 2.5 to 3.5. In patients without additional stroke risk factors (previous stroke or transient ischemic attack, age >75 years, hypertension, diabetes, heart failure) or who have contraindications to full anticoagulation, aspirin 325 mg/d can be used as alternative thromboembolism prophylaxis.

The effect of aspirin is controversial, but is probably present and less dramatic than that of warfarin (35). A recent trial demonstrated that aspirin plus clopidogrel was

Table 2. Stroke Risk in Patients with Nonvalvular Atrial Fibrillation Not Treated with Anticoagulation According to CHADS$_2$ Index*

CHADS$_2$ Risk Criteria	Score
Past stroke or TIA	2
Age >75 y	1
Hypertension	1
Diabetes mellitus	1
Heart failure	1

Patients (n= 1733)	Adjusted Stroke Rate (%/y)† (95% CI)	CHADS$_2$ Score
120	1.9 (1.2 to 2.0)	0
463	2.8 (2.0 to 3.8)	1
523	4.0 (3.1 to 5.1)	2
337	5.9 (4.6 to 7.3)	3
220	8.5 (6.3 to 11.1)	4
65	12.5 (8.2 to 17.5)	5
5	18.2 (10.5 to 27.4)	6

CHADS$_2$ = Cardiac Failure, Hypertension, Age, Diabetes, and Stroke (Doubled); TIA = transient ischemic attack.
* Reproduced from reference 5 with permission from the American Heart Association.
† The adjusted stroke rate was derived from multivariate analysis assuming no aspirin usage. Data from from references 30, 31.

Table 3. Antithrombotic Therapy for Patients with Atrial Fibrillation*

Risk Category	Recommended Therapy
No risk factors	Aspirin, 81–325 mg daily
1 moderate risk factor	Aspirin, 81–325 mg daily or warfarin (INR, 2.0–3.0, target 2.5)
Any high risk factor or more than 1 moderate risk factor	Warfarin (INR, 2.0–3.0, target 2.5)*

Less-Validated or Weaker Risk Factors	Moderate Risk Factors	High Risk Factors
Female sex	Age ≥75 y	Previous stroke, TIA, or embolism
Age 65–74 y	Hypertension	Mitral stenosis
Coronary artery disease	Heart failure	Prosthetic heart valve†
Thyrotoxicosis	LV ejection fraction 35% or less, diabetes mellitus	

INR = international normalized ratio; LV = left ventricular; TIA = transient ischemic attack.
* Reproduced from reference 5 with permission from the American Heart Association.
† If mechanical valve, target INR >2.5.

28. Jung F, DiMarco JP. Treatment strategies for atrial fibrillation. Am J Med. 1998;104:272-86. [PMID: 9552091]
29. Zabalgoitia M, Halperin JL, Pearce LA, et al. Transesophageal echocardiographic correlates of clinical risk of thromboembolism in nonvalvular atrial fibrillation. Stroke Prevention in Atrial Fibrillation III Investigators. J Am Coll Cardiol. 1998;31:1622-6. [PMID: 9626843]
30. Gage BF, Waterman AD, Shannon W, et al. Validation of clinical classification schemes for predicting stroke: results from the National Registry of Atrial Fibrillation. JAMA. 2001;285:2864-70. [PMID: 11401607]
31. van Walraven C, Hart RG, Wells GA, et al. A clinical prediction rule to identify patients with atrial fibrillation and a low risk for stroke while taking aspirin. Arch Intern Med. 2003;163:936-43. [PMID: 12719203]
32. Hart RG, Pearce LA, Aguilar MI. Meta-analysis: antithrombotic therapy to prevent stroke in patients who have nonvalvular atrial fibrillation. Ann Intern Med. 2007;146:857-67. [PMID: 17577005]

clearly inferior to adjusted-dose warfarin (36).

Institution of warfarin without loading doses or concurrent heparin is sufficient in lower-risk patients, whereas patients at high risk for thromboembolism should be hospitalized for immediate anticoagulation with unfractionated heparin before target levels of oral anticoagulation are reached. There are limited data on the use of low-molecular-weight heparin in this setting.

Patients with atrial fibrillation lasting more than 48 hours or those with intracardiac thrombus should receive anticoagulation with warfarin before cardioversion and for at least 4 weeks afterward.

Clinicians should consider chronic anticoagulation in patients who are at high risk for recurrent atrial fibrillation, have asymptomatic atrial fibrillation, have evidence of intracardiac thrombus, or have known risk factors for thromboembolism (age >65 years, recent heart failure, left-ventricular dysfunction on ECG, past thromboembolism, diabetes mellitus, hypertension, or left atrial enlargement).

Warfarin has a narrow therapeutic window, and its metabolism is affected by many drug and dietary interactions, requiring frequent INR monitoring and dosage adjustment. These limitations of warfarin have prompted a search for alternative anticoagulants. A trial showed ximelagatran not to be a suitable alternative to warfarin (37). Investigational studies to develop other oral anticoagulants (direct thrombin inhibitors, factor Xa inhibitors) are in progress, but there are no current alternatives to warfarin.

When should clinicians consider immediate cardioversion in patients with atrial fibrillation?
Prompt cardioversion should be considered for new-onset atrial

fibrillation when it is clear that the duration of the arrhythmia is less than 48 hours (as might be the case when atrial fibrillation onset occurs in a hospitalized patient on cardiac monitoring) and the patient is not at high risk for stroke. Immediate cardioversion, if successful, could obviate the need for anticoagulation.

Most patients with atrial fibrillation do not require immediate pharmacologic or electrical cardioversion, but it may be appropriate in selected patients with decompensated heart failure, severe angina or acute infarction, hypotension, or high risk for acute stroke. Patients with atrial fibrillation and the Wolff–Parkinson–White syndrome can have extremely rapid atrioventricular conduction during atrial fibrillation mediated by the accessory pathway, which is a potentially life-threatening condition that requires urgent cardioversion.

When should clinicians consider atrioventricular nodal catheter ablation, device therapy, or surgical techniques in patients with atrial fibrillation?
Nonpharmacologic therapy for atrial fibrillation should be considered after failure or intolerance to rate-control or rhythm-control therapy. Nonpharmacologic therapeutic options include catheter or surgical atrioventricular nodal ablation and pacing.

Atrioventricular nodal catheter ablation is used in situations where pharmacologic rate control cannot be achieved, usually because of intolerance to medications. This occurs most frequently in patients with advanced heart failure or obstructive pulmonary disease (limiting β-blocker usage) or elderly patients. Atrioventricular nodal ablation is highly effective (38) but requires pacemaker insertion, which introduces the risk for producing progressive left ventricular dysfunction secondary to

33. Hart RG, Tonarelli SB, Pearce LA. Avoiding central nervous system bleeding during antithrombotic therapy: recent data and ideas. Stroke. 2005;36:1588-93. [PMID: 15947271]
34. Hylek EM, Evans-Molina C, Shea C, et al. Major hemorrhage and tolerability of warfarin in the first year of therapy among elderly patients with atrial fibrillation. Circulation. 2007;115:2689-96. [PMID: 17515465]
35. The SPAF III Writing Committee for the Stroke Prevention in Atrial Fibrillation Investigators. Patients with nonvalvular atrial fibrillation at low risk of stroke during treatment with aspirin: Stroke Prevention in Atrial Fibrillation III Study. JAMA. 1998;279:1273-7. [PMID: 9565007]
36. ACTIVE Writing Group of the ACTIVE Investigators. Clopidogrel plus aspirin versus oral anticoagulation for atrial fibrillation in the Atrial fibrillation Clopidogrel Trial with Irbesartan for prevention of Vascular Events (ACTIVE W): a randomised controlled trial. Lancet. 2006;367:1903-12. [PMID: 16765759]

pacing. Catheter ablation of atrial fibrillation has been shown to be effective in preventing recurrent symptomatic atrial fibrillation in highly selected patients (39). Recent guideline statements have acknowledged that it may be reasonable to provide this therapy for highly symptomatic patients with paroxysmal atrial fibrillation in whom an attempt at antiarrhythmic drug therapy has failed. This relatively aggressive approach may prevent progressive atrial fibrillation–related morbidity (residual risk for stroke, risk for medication side effects), but the impact of this therapeutic strategy on mortality has not been demonstrated. Innovative minimally invasive surgical ablation of atrial fibrillation is also available at highly specialized centers.

Pacing therapy without atrioventricular nodal ablation has very little effect on atrial fibrillation burden, but may be helpful in patients with paroxysmal atrial fibrillation who have symptomatic bradycardia (often caused by side effects of atrial fibrillation pharmacologic therapy).

How should clinicians monitor patients with atrial fibrillation?

Although there are few studies to inform the appropriate frequency of follow-up for patients with atrial fibrillation, clinical consensus is that patients with atrial fibrillation should have regular follow-up to assess symptoms and clinical effectiveness of therapy. For many patients, anticoagulation monitoring drives the frequency of follow-up. Clinicians should assess rate control by asking about such symptoms as palpitations, easy fatigability, and dyspnea on exertion. Examination should assess resting and exercise heart rates for targets of 60 to 80 beats per minute and 90 to 115 beats per minute, respectively. Patients in whom rhythm control is chosen should be monitored for symptoms suggestive of atrial fibrillation. Sporadic asymptomatic episodes of atrial fibrillation on therapy are not important and do not need to be monitored for. However, patients who do not improve on rhythm-control drugs should be changed to less-toxic rate-control agents. Routine blood tests to evaluate for side effects of antiarrhythmic therapy are not essential, except in the case of amiodarone, which requires liver and thyroid function studies every 6 months and chest radiography every year.

Which patients with newly diagnosed atrial fibrillation should clinicians consider hospitalizing?

Although atrial fibrillation is usually managed in outpatient settings, clinicians should consider hospitalizing patients with atrial fibrillation when management requires close monitoring for safety (see Box).

Situations in Which Patients with Atrial Fibrillation May Require Hospitalization

- Uncertain or unstable underlying arrhythmia
- Acute myocardial infarction, altered mental status, decompensated heart failure, or hypotension
- Intolerable symptoms despite hemodynamic stability
- Elective cardioversion (if monitored outpatient setting is not available)
- Acute anticoagulation if very-high risk for stroke
- Telemetry monitoring during initiation of certain drugs
- Procedures such as cardiac catheterization, electrophysiologic studies, pacemakers, implantable defibrillators, or catheter or surgical ablation

---

Treatment... Treatment goals for atrial fibrillation include preventing stroke, reducing symptoms, and preventing tachycardia-related cardiomyopathy. The use of anticoagulants (aspirin or warfarin) is guided by risk classifications, such as the CHADS$_2$ score. Several randomized trials have demonstrated no general advantage to rhythm control over rate control. Rate control with calcium-channel antagonists or β-blockers to keep heart rate at 60 to 80 beats per minute at rest and 90 to 115 beats per minute during exercise should be the first-line therapy. Rhythm control, which has greater adverse effects than rate control, may be reasonable in individual patients who do not respond to rate control. Atrial and atrioventricular nodal ablation therapy may be appropriate for selected patients with highly symptomatic atrial fibrillation despite pharmacologic therapy.

CLINICAL BOTTOM LINE

37. Kaul S, Diamond GA, Weintraub WS. Trials and tribulations of non-inferiority: the ximelagatran experience. J Am Coll Cardiol. 2005;46:1986-95. [PMID: 16325029]
38. Wood MA, Brown-Mahoney C, Kay GN, Ellenbogen KA. Clinical outcomes after ablation and pacing therapy for atrial fibrillation : a meta-analysis. Circulation. 2000;101:1138-44. [PMID: 10715260]
39. Packer DL, Asirvatham S, Munger TM. Progress in non-pharmacologic therapy of atrial fibrillation. J Cardiovasc Electrophysiol. 2003;14:S296-309. [PMID: 15005218]

Do U.S. stakeholders consider management of patients with atrial fibrillation when evaluating the quality of care physicians deliver?
The Centers for Medicare & Medicaid Services (CMS) has issued specifications for 74 measures that make up the 2008 Physician Quality Reporting Initiative (PQRI). Of these 74 measures, none directly measures the quality of atrial fibrillation therapy. However, one of the stroke measures does relate to atrial fibrillation. This measure examines the percentage of patients age 18 years or older with a diagnosis of ischemic stroke or transient ischemic attack and documented permanent, persistent, or paroxysmal atrial fibrillation who were prescribed an anticoagulant at discharge.

What do professional organizations recommend with regard to the management of patients with atrial fibrillation?
The material presented in this review is consistent with the 2006 guidelines developed by a consensus panel of the American Heart Association, American College of Cardiology, and the European Society of Cardiology (17). In 2003, the American College of Physicians and the American Academy of Family Physicians released a guideline on atrial fibrillation management (40). Both guideline statements stress anticoagulation in appropriately selected patients and the nonsuperiority of the rhythm-control strategy. The AHA/ACC/ESC guideline emphasizes the cardiology perspective, whereas the ACP/AAFP focuses on the primary care perspective.

40. Snow V, Weiss KB, LeFevre M, et al. Management of newly detected atrial fibrillation: a clinical practice guideline from the American Academy of Family Physicians and the American College of Physicians. Ann Intern Med. 2003;139:1009-17. [PMID: 14678921]

in the clinic
Tool Kit
Atrial Fibrillation

PIER Modules
www.pier.acponline.org
Access PIER module on atrial fibrillation for updated, evidence-based information designed for rapid access at the point of care.

Quality Measures
pier.acponline.org/qualitym/prv.html
Access the PIER Quality Measure Tool, which links newly developed quality measures issued by the Ambulatory Quality Alliance and the Physician Quality Improvement QA Alliance and CMS's Physician Quality Reporting Initiative program to administrative criteria for each measure and provides clinical guidance to help implement the measures and improve quality of care.

Patient Information
www.annals.intheclinic/tools
Download copies of the Patient Information sheet that appears on the following page for duplication and distribution to your patients.

Anticoagulation Flow Sheet
www.acponline.org/running_practice/quality_improvement/projects/cfpi/doc_anticoag.pdf
Download a copy of a flow sheet to help manage patients on warfarin.

Guidelines
www.americanheart.org/downloadable/heart/222_ja20017993p_1.pdf
Access the American Heart Association, American College of Cardiology, and European Society of Cardiology joint 2006 guidelines for the management of patients with atrial fibrillation.
www.annals.org/cgi/reprint/139/12/1009.pdf
Access the American College of Physicians/American Academy of Family Physicians 2003 guidelines for the management of newly detected atrial fibrillation.

WHAT YOU SHOULD KNOW ABOUT ATRIAL FIBRILLATION

Atrial fibrillation is an irregular and sometimes very fast heart beat. Atrial fibrillation can come and go or be constant. It is more common in older people than in younger people and in people with heart conditions.

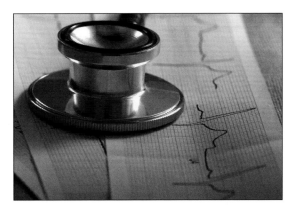

Atrial fibrillation can lead to 3 bad health outcomes:

- Symptoms that can make a person unable to do their usual activities.
- Over the long term, a very fast heart beat can damage heart muscle.
- Atrial fibrillation can cause stroke when blood clots form in the heart and travel to the brain.

How would I know if I have atrial fibrillation?

- Many people with atrial fibrillation have no symptoms and don't know that they have it.
- When people have symptoms, they include palpitations (pounding in the chest), shortness of breath, or tiredness.
- Your doctor may see atrial fibrillation on an electrocardiogram (ECG) if an episode occurs during the test.
- If you have symptoms that could be atrial fibrillation but your ECG is normal, your doctor may send you for a test that records your heartbeat while you go about your usual activities.
- If you have atrial fibrillation, your doctor may do an echocardiogram to look for heart problems. Echocardiograms use sound waves to take pictures of the heart.

What is the treatment?

- Many patients with atrial fibrillation need to be on drugs to prevent stroke. Some people need only aspirin. Others need to take the blood thinner warfarin.
- Treatment also sometimes includes drugs to slow the heart rate down or make it more regular.
- Less often, treatment with catheters, surgery, and pacemakers is needed.
- Atrial fibrillation treatment can have dangerous side effects. It is important to follow instructions and see your doctor regularly.

Web Sites with Good Information

MedlinePlus: www.nlm.nih.gov/
medlineplus/tutorials/atrialfibrillation/
htm/_no_50_no_0.htm

Heart Rhythm Society:
www.hrspatients.org/patients/heart
_disorders/atrial_fibrillation/default.asp

American Heart Association:
circ.ahajournals.org/cgi/content/full/
117/20/e340

Hypertension

Hypertension affects more than 65 million people in the United States, with about 2 million new cases diagnosed annually (1, 2). Most patients have primary or essential hypertension and are likely to remain hypertensive for life. Risk factors for hypertension include a family history of hypertension, African-American ethnicity, obesity, a high sodium or alcohol intake, and a sedentary lifestyle. Treatment to control blood pressure level reduces the risk for cardiovascular, cerebrovascular, and renal outcomes of hypertension. Unfortunately, many people with hypertension do not receive optimal therapy.

Screening and Prevention

1. Ong KL, Cheung BM, Man YB, et al. Prevalence, awareness, treatment, and control of hypertension among United States adults 1999-2004. Hypertension. 2007;49:69-75. [PMID: 17159087]
2. Chobanian AV, Bakris GL, Black HR, et al. National Heart, Lung, and Blood Institute. Seventh report of the Joint National Committee on Prevention, Detection, Evaluation, and Treatment of High Blood Pressure. Hypertension. 2003;42:1206-52. [PMID: 14656957]
3. U.S. Preventive Services Task Force. Screening for high blood pressure: U.S. Preventive Services Task Force reaffirmation recommendation statement. Ann Intern Med. 2007;147:783-6. [PMID: 18056662]
4. Julius S, Nesbitt SD, Egan BM, et al. Feasibility of treating prehypertension with an angiotensin-receptor blocker. N Engl J Med. 2006;354:1685-97. [PMID: 16537662]
5. Cook NR, Cutler JA, Obarzanek E, et al. Long term effects of dietary sodium reduction on cardiovascular disease outcomes: observational follow-up of the trials of hypertension prevention (TOHP). BMJ. 2007;334(7599):885.

What long-term health risks are associated with hypertension?
The relationship between blood pressure level and cardiovascular disease is linear, continuous, and independent of and additive to other risk factors. For persons age 40 to 70 years, each increment of either 20 mm Hg in systolic blood pressure level or 10 mm Hg in diastolic blood pressure level doubles the risk for cardiovascular disease (CVD) across the range of blood pressure levels from 115/75 mm Hg to 185/115 mm Hg (2). When other cardiovascular risk factors, such as diabetes or chronic kidney disease, are present, the CVD risk associated with hypertension is even higher. Complications of hypertension include retinopathy, cerebrovascular disease, ischemic heart disease, atrial fibrillation, heart failure, chronic kidney disease, and peripheral vascular disease.

Should clinicians screen for hypertension?
The U.S. Preventive Services Task Force recommends screening the adult general population for hypertension. It does not recommend a specific screening interval because of lack of evidence to support one (3). The Joint National Committee on Prevention, Detection, Evaluation, and Treatment of High Blood Pressure (JNC 7) recommends screening every 2 years if blood pressure level is less than 120/80 mm Hg and annually if blood pressure level is 120/80 to 139/89 mm Hg (2).

What is prehypertension and what is its proper management?
Prehypertension is a category that first appeared in the seventh JNC report. Prehypertension is defined as a blood pressure level of 120/80 to 139/89 mm Hg (2). Patients with prehypertension are at increased risk for developing overt hypertension and CVD. These patients should restrict dietary sodium, lose weight, reduce alcohol intake, and increase aerobic exercise. Several trials have evaluated drug treatment for prehypertension. At present, drug therapy is not recommended for prehypertension.

The Trial of Preventing Hypertension randomly assigned participants with prehypertension to active treatment with candesartan (an angiotensin-receptor blocker [ARB]) or placebo for 2 years and followed them for 4 years. Active treatment delayed onset of hypertension but did not prevent it (4).

Trials of Hypertension Prevention (TOHP) 1 and 2 examined the benefits of reductions in weight, sodium intake, and stress and supplementation with potassium, magnesium, fish oil, and calcium in persons with diastolic blood pressure levels of 80 to 90 mm Hg. TOHP 1 suggested that weight loss (3/2–mm Hg reduction) and sodium restriction (2/1–mm Hg reduction) were effective. TOHP 2 confirmed that weight loss and sodium restriction delay hypertension (5, 6).

Diagnosis

How should clinicians diagnose and stage hypertension?

The steps in diagnosing hypertension are simple but often not followed. The most common errors (failure to have the patient sit quietly for 5 minutes before a reading is taken, failure to support the limb used to measure blood pressure, use of a too-small cuff, and too-rapid cuff deflation) lead to falsely increased readings. The best position for patients is sitting, because the studies that established the value of treating hypertension used this position to measure the blood pressures that diagnosed hypertension and guided dose adjustment [7]. See Table 1 and the Box for instructions on blood pressure measurement.

A person's blood pressure can vary widely. A single accurate measurement is a good start but not enough: Measure blood pressure twice and take the average. The running average is more important than individual readings. Hypertension is diagnosed if the average of at least 2 readings per visit obtained at 3 separate visits each 2 to 4 weeks apart is 140 mm Hg or greater systolic and 90 mm Hg or greater diastolic. According to the JNC 7, a normal blood pressure level is 120/80 mm Hg or less [2]. Prehypertension is a blood pressure level of 120/80 to 139/89 mm Hg. Stage 1 hypertension is a systolic blood pressure level of 140 to 159 mm Hg or a diastolic blood pressure level of 90 to 99 mm Hg. Stage 2 hypertension is a systolic blood pressure level greater than or equal to 160 mm Hg or a diastolic blood pressure level greater than or equal to 100 mm Hg. The JNC 7 classification combines the stage 2 and 3 categories of older classifications [2]. In persons older than 50 years, systolic blood pressure levels greater than 140 mm Hg are a more important CVD risk factor than diastolic hypertension.

Pseudohypertension can occur in patients with stiff, incompressible arteries. To detect it, inflate the blood pressure cuff to at least 30 mm Hg above the palpable systolic pressure and then try to "roll" the brachial or radial artery underneath your fingertips ("Osler's

---

Instructions for Taking Blood Pressure

- Have patient relax, sitting (feet on floor, back supported) for ≥5 min before taking the blood pressure.
- Support patient's arm (for example, resting on a desk) for the measurement.
- Use the stethoscope bell, not the diaphragm, for auscultation.
- Check blood pressure first in both arms with the patient sitting. Note which arm gives the higher reading and use this arm for all other (standing, lying down) and future readings.
- Measure blood pressure in sitting, standing, and lying positions. All measurements should be separated by 2 min.
- Use the correct cuff size and note if a larger- or smaller-than-normal cuff size is needed (Table 1).
- Record systolic (onset of first sound) and diastolic (disappearance of sound) pressures.
- Record exact results to nearest even number.

Table 1. Blood Pressure Cuff Size Criteria

Arm Circumference	Weight Female	Male	Cuff Size to Use
24–32 cm	<150	<200	Regular
33–42 cm*	>150	>200	Large
38–50 cm*	–	–	Thigh

Either cuff is acceptable for the overlap circumferences.

6. Batey DM, Kaufmann PG, Raczynski JM, et al. Stress management intervention for primary prevention of hypertension: detailed results from Phase I of Trials of Hypertension Prevention (TOHP-I). Ann Epidemiol. 2000;10(1):45-58.

maneuver") (8). Healthy arteries should not be palpable when empty. If you feel a stiff, tube-like structure, the patient may have pseudohypertension.

What is white coat hypertension?

White coat hypertension is defined as an elevated office blood pressure with lower blood pressure readings measured at home or with a 24-hour ambulatory blood pressure monitor (9). The prevalence of white coat hypertension is 10% to 20% (10). These patients are at elevated risk for overt hypertension and CVD (11). Current guidelines do not recommend pharmacologic treatment for these patients but do recommend lifestyle modifications and regular follow-up.

When is ambulatory blood pressure monitoring indicated?

The ambulatory blood pressure monitor is a 24-hour portable device that the patient wears during their regular activities. It measures blood pressure every 15 to 20 minutes during the day and every 30 to 60 minutes at night. Ambulatory blood pressure monitoring provides the most accurate assessment of blood pressure (10). Most patients with hypertension do not need it, and the Center for Medicare & Medicaid Services pays for only 1

indication: diagnosing white coat hypertension. The Box lists the other potential situations in which ambulatory monitoring may be helpful.

Ambulatory blood pressure monitoring may also be useful in identifying high-risk blood pressure patterns that are associated with increased cardiovascular events in patients with hypertension. One is loss of "dipping status," which is associated with worse cardiovascular outcomes of hypertension. Blood pressure of patients with loss of dipping status falls less than 10% at night relative to daytime blood pressure, in contrast to the blood pressure of patients with dipper status, which falls at least 10% at night (12). The other high-risk pattern is blood pressure surges in the early morning hours (13), which is associated with increased cerebrovascular disease risk. A surge is generally defined as a greater than 55–mm Hg difference in systolic pressure level between sleeping and early hour waking. In these patients, physicians may wish to target treatment at the high morning systolic values.

What are the key elements of the history for patients with hypertension?

Assess the duration, rapidity of onset, and severity of the hypertension. Ask about cardiovascular risk factors, concomitant medical conditions, symptoms of target organ damage, past treatment and its effects, and lifestyle (dietary habits, alcohol consumption, tobacco use, and level of physical activity). Note any family history of hypertension, renal disease, cardiovascular problems, stroke, and diabetes mellitus. Ask about increased stress, physical inactivity, and dietary salt intake.

Sudden onset of severe hypertension with previously normal blood pressure levels suggests a secondary form of hypertension. Ask about symptoms that suggest secondary hypertension. Palpitations, tachycardia, paroxysmal

7. Pickering TG, Hall JE, Appel LJ, et al. Recommendations for blood pressure measurement in humans and experimental animals: part 1. Circulation. 2005;111:697-716. [PMID: 15699287]

8. Messerli FH. Osler's maneuver, pseudohypertension, and true hypertension in the elderly. Am J Med. 1986;80:906-10. [PMID: 2939716]

9. Pickering TG, Shimbo D, Haas D. Ambulatory blood-pressure monitoring. N Engl J Med. 2006;354:2368-74. [PMID: 16738273]

10. Angeli F, Verdecchia P, Gattobigio R, et al. White-coat hypertension in adults. Blood Press Monit. 2005;10:301-5. [PMID: 16496443]

11. Eguchi K, Hoshide S, Ishikawa J, et al. Cardiovascular prognosis of sustained and white-coat hypertension in patients with type 2 diabetes mellitus. Blood Press Monit. 2008;13:15-20. [PMID: 18199919]

Potential Indications for Use of Ambulatory Blood Pressure Monitoring

- Unusual variability of blood pressure level
- Possible white coat hypertension
- Evaluation of nocturnal hypertension
- Evaluation of drug-resistant hypertension
- Determining the efficacy of drug treatment over 24 hours
- Diagnosis and treatment of hypertension in pregnancy
- Evaluation of symptomatic hypotension on various medications, suggesting that the patient may be normotensive
- Evaluation of episodic hypertension or autonomic dysfunction

---

headache, and sweating suggest pheochromocytoma. Muscle weakness and polyuria suggest hypokalemia from excess aldosterone. Snoring and daytime sleepiness can indicate sleep apnea, and heat intolerance and weight loss suggest hyperthyroidism.

Review current medications, including over-the-counter drugs. Ask about oral contraceptives, corticosteroids, licorice, sympathomimetics, which can increase blood pressure level, and antimigraine drugs. Nonaspirin nonsteroidal anti-inflammatory drugs can decrease the efficacy of antihypertensive drugs (14).

What are the essential elements of the physical examination of patients with hypertension?
The physical examination should look for signs of secondary causes of hypertension and end organ damage related to hypertension. Table 2 outlines key components of the examination of the patient with hypertension.

Which laboratory tests should clinicians perform in patients with newly diagnosed hypertension?
Newly diagnosed patients should have measurement of hemoglobin or

hematocrit, serum electrolytes, serum creatinine, serum glucose, and fasting lipid levels and a urinalysis with microscopic examination and a 12-lead electrocardiogram (ECG). Additional testing may be indicated by clinical factors, suspicion of secondary causes of hypertension, and anticipated treatment.

Table 3 summarizes tests that may be useful in evaluation of possible secondary hypertension. Echocardiography is more sensitive than ECG for left-ventricular hypertrophy, which would tip the scales towards drug treatment rather than just a trial of lifestyle changes or towards true hypertension rather than white coat hypertension. If a patient has gout, check serum uric acid levels before prescribing diuretics. The presence of microalbuminuria may help to guide selection of therapy in patients with diabetes.

Which patients should be evaluated for secondary hypertension and how should they be evaluated?
The Box lists symptoms and signs that suggest secondary hypertension. Table 3 outlines suggested tests for secondary hypertension.

Symptoms and Signs that Suggest Secondary Hypertension

- New-onset hypertension at age <25 or >55 years
- Drug-resistant hypertension (requires 3 or more drugs at maximal doses)
- Spontaneous hypokalemia
- Palpitations, headaches, and sweating
- Severe vascular disease, including coronary artery disease (CAD), carotid disease, and peripheral vascular disease
- Epigastric bruit
- Radial-femoral pulse delay, especially with an interscapular murmur.

Table 2. Physical Examination and Key Findings in the Patient with Hypertension

Item	Routine Evaluation
General appearance, height, weight, BMI, waist circumference, skin lesions	Look for signs of metabolic syndrome (overweight, abdominal obesity), skin changes can indicate rare causes of secondary hypertension (striae in Cushing syndrome, mucosal fibromas can indicate MEN II)
Funduscopy	Retinal changes reflect severity of hypertension: arteriolar narrowing (grade 1), arteriovenous compression (grade 2), hemorrhages or exudates (grade 3), and papilledema (grade 4)
Examination of neck	Assess for thyroid enlargement, carotid bruits
Cardiopulmonary examination	Rales and gallops may indicate heart failure, interscapular murmur during auscultation of the back can indicate renal arterial disease
Abdominal examination	Palpable kidneys suggest polycystic kidney disease; midepigastric bruits can indicate renal arterial disease
Neurologic examination	Look for evidence of previous stroke, evaluate cognition (hypertension is a risk factor for loss of cognition).
Peripheral pulses	Reduced leg pulses can indicate coarctation of the aorta or systemic atherosclerosis

MEN = multiple endocrine neoplasia.

12. Cicconetti P, Morelli S, De Serra C, et al. Left ventricular mass in dippers and nondippers with newly diagnosed hypertension. Angiology. 2003;54:661-9. [PMID: 14666954]
13. Kario K, Pickering TG, Umeda Y, et al. Morning surge in blood pressure as a predictor of silent and clinical cerebrovascular disease in elderly hypertensives: a prospective study. Circulation. 2003;107:1401-6. [PMID: 12642361]
14. Fierro-Carrion GA, Ram CV. Nonsteroidal anti-inflammatory drugs (NSAIDs) and blood pressure [Editorial]. Am J Cardiol. 1997;80:775-6. [PMID: 9315588]

Table 3. Work-Up to Pursue Possible Secondary Hypertension

Secondary cause	Evaluation (findings)
Coarctation of aorta	Chest film (rib notching; reverse "3" sign), 2-dimensional echocardiogram, aortogram (coarctation directly seen), MRI
The Cushing syndrome	Dexamethasone suppression test (failure to suppress cortisol), 24-h urinary-free cortisol (elevated), CT (adrenomegaly)
Primary aldosteronism	Plasma aldosterone-renin ratio (increased), aldosterone excretion rate during salt loading (increased), adrenal CT (adenoma with low Hounsfield units)
Pheochromocytoma	Plasma catecholamines or metanephrines (increased), urine catecholamines or metanephrines (increased), clonidine suppression test (failure to suppress plasma norepinephrine after clonidine administration), adrenal CT, MRI (adrenal tumor; T2-weighted MRI has characteristic appearance), iodine[131]-metaiodobenzylguanidine scan (significant adrenal or extra-adrenal tumor uptake)
Renal vascular disease	Captopril renography (some limitations), renal duplex sonography (requires good operators; increased renal artery compared with aorta velocities suggests stenosis), MRA (renal vessel narrowing), CTA (renal vessel narrowing), angiography (gold standard; renal vessel narrowing), renal vein renin ratio (not commonly done)
Renal parenchymal disease	24-h urine protein and creatinine levels, renal ultrasound (small kidney size, unusual architecture), glomerular filtration rate (low), renal biopsy (usually done to determine type of glomerular disease)
Parathyroid disorders	Calcium and phosphorus levels (increased and decreased, respectively), serum parathyroid hormone level (increased), serum calcitonin level (when MEN is suspected)
Thyroid disease	Serum thyroid hormone level (increased in hyperthyroidism), thyrotropin level (suppressed in hyperthyroidism)

CT = computed tomography; CTA = computed tomographic angiography; MEN = multiple endocrine neoplasia; MRA = magnetic resonance angiography; MRI = magnetic resonance imaging

---

Diagnosis... Diagnosis of hypertension requires careful measurement of blood pressure levels on several occasions. Systolic blood pressure levels 140 mm Hg or greater or diastolic blood pressure levels 90 mm Hg or greater, based on the average of 3 sets of 2 or more readings obtained 2 to 4 weeks apart establishes the diagnosis of hypertension. The goals of the diagnostic evaluation are to search for a secondary cause, to detect other CVD risk factors, and to detect damage to target organs. In addition, the history should focus on past treatment, current medications, and contributing lifestyle factors. The focal points of the physical examination are eyegrounds, cardiovascular system, and nervous system. Levels of hemoglobin, urinalysis, serum creatinine, glucose, lipids, electrolytes, and an ECG are routine laboratory tests for patients with newly diagnosed hypertension.

CLINICAL BOTTOM LINE

Treatment

What are treatment goals for patients with hypertension?
See Box for blood pressure goals from different guidelines. Goal blood pressure level is less than 140/90 mm Hg in a patient with hypertension without CVD-related comorbid conditions. In patients with comorbid illness or more than a 10% 10-year Framingham risk for cardiovascular events, goal blood pressure is less than 130/80 mm Hg. Key diseases include diabetes; chronic kidney disease; established CVD or CAD equivalents, such as acute coronary syndrome, ST elevation myocardial infarction, stroke, and stable angina (2). In patients with more than 1 g proteinuria, the recommended goal blood pressure target is 125/75 mm Hg or less.

15. Cordain L, Eaton SB, Sebastian A, et al. Origins and evolution of the Western diet: health implications for the 21st century. Am J Clin Nutr. 2005;81:341-54. [PMID: 15699220]

What are the recommended lifestyle modifications for treating hypertension?

Practice guidelines recommend nonpharmacologic treatment of hypertension with lifestyle modification for all patients with hypertension and prehypertension. Although adherence to lifestyle changes can substantially lower blood pressure, these changes—and their benefits—can be difficult to maintain. Physicians must encourage patients to maintain lifestyle changes when drug therapy becomes necessary. Table 4 shows the expected effects of lifestyle modification.

Salt restriction

The effect of salt intake on blood pressure is well-established. Dietary sodium restriction can reduce systolic blood pressure level by 1 to 4 mm Hg. Dietary sodium restriction to less than 2400 mg per day is often the first lifestyle change. The average Western diet contains 3800 mg of sodium per day (15), and patients are often unaware of the high sodium content of many foods (16). Patients should especially avoid processed foods, lunchmeats, soups, Chinese food, and canned processed food.

In TOHP I, adults with diastolic blood pressure levels of 80 to 89 mm Hg and systolic blood pressure levels <160 mm Hg were randomly assigned to 18-month interventions to lose weight or to reduce dietary sodium or to 2 control groups. After 7 years, the incidence of hypertension was 18.9% in the weight loss group and 40.5% in its control group and 22.4% in the sodium reduction group and 32.9% in its control group (6).

The DASH trial randomly assigned 459 adults with systolic blood pressure levels of <160 mm Hg and diastolic blood pressure

Table 4. Lifestyle Modifications to Lower Blood Pressure Level

Lifestyle Modification	Recommendation	Potential Decrease in SBP
Dietary sodium restriction	Restrict dietary sodium to no more than 2400 mg/d or 100 meq/d	2–8 mm Hg
Weight loss	Maintain normal body weight; BMI = 18.5–24.9 kg/m²	5–20 mm Hg per 10 kg weight loss
Aerobic exercise	Engage in regular aerobic exercise, aiming to do 30 min of aerobic exercise on most days of the week. It is suggested that patients walk about 1 mile per day above current activity level	4–9 mm Hg
DASH diet	Diet rich in fruits, vegetables, and low-fat dairy, with reduced content of saturated and total fat	4–14 mm Hg
Limit alcohol intake	No more than 2 mixed drinks, two 12-ounce cans of beer, or two 4-ounce glasses of wine daily for men and one half of this quantity for women	2–4 mm Hg

BMI = body mass index; DASH = Dietary Approaches to Stop Hypertension; SBP = systolic blood pressure

16. Mattes RD, Donnelly D. Relative contributions of dietary sodium sources. J Am Coll Nutr. 1991;10:383-93. [PMID: 1910064]

17. Appel LJ, Moore TJ, Obarzanek E, et al. A clinical trial of the effects of dietary patterns on blood pressure. DASH Collaborative Research Group. N Engl J Med. 1997;336:1117-24. [PMID: 9099655]

18. Bray GA, Vollmer WM, Sacks FM, et al. A further subgroup analysis of the effects of the DASH diet and three dietary sodium levels on blood pressure: results of the DASH-Sodium Trial. Am J Cardiol. 2004;94:222-7. [PMID: 15246908]

19. Whelton PK, Appel LJ, Espeland MA, et al. Sodium reduction and weight loss in the treatment of hypertension in older persons: a randomized controlled trial of nonpharmacologic interventions in the elderly (TONE). TONE Collaborative Research Group. JAMA. 1998;279:839-46. [PMID: 9515998]

20. Xin X, He J, Frontini MG, et al. Effects of alcohol reduction on blood pressure: a meta-analysis of randomized controlled trials. Hypertension. 2001;38:1112-7. [PMID: 11711507]

21. Fagrell B, De Faire U, Bondy S, et al. The effects of light to moderate drinking on cardiovascular diseases. J Intern Med. 1999;246:331-40. [PMID: 10583704]

22. McGuire HL, Svetkey LP, Harsha DW, et al. Comprehensive lifestyle modification and blood pressure control: a review of the PREMIER trial. J Clin Hypertens (Greenwich). 2004;6:383-90.

23. Alexander CN, Schneider RH, Staggers F, et al. Trial of stress reduction for hypertension in older African Americans. II. Sex and risk subgroup analysis. Hypertension. 1996;28:228-37. [PMID: 8707387]

24. Taubert D, Roesen R, Schömig E. Effect of cocoa and tea intake on blood pressure: a meta-analysis. Arch Intern Med. 2007;167:626-34. [PMID: 17420419]

levels of 80-95 mm Hg to 8 weeks of a control diet, a diet rich in fruits and vegetables, or a "combination" diet rich in fruits, vegetables, and low-fat dairy products. The combination diet reduced systolic and diastolic blood pressure levels by 5.5 and 3.0 mm Hg more, respectively, than the control diet (P < 0.001); the fruits-and-vegetables diet reduced systolic blood pressure levels by 2.8 mm Hg more (P < 0.001) and diastolic blood pressure levels by 1.1 mm Hg more than the control diet (P = 0.07). Blood pressure reductions were larger in 133 patients with hypertension than in normotensive patients. A diet rich in fruits, vegetables, and low-fat dairy foods lowers blood pressure (17, 18).

Other lifestyle interventions

Encourage weight loss (to <20% above ideal body weight for height). Systolic blood pressure level falls approximately 1 mm Hg for every kilogram of weight loss. (19). Encourage at least 30 minutes of aerobic exercise on most days of the week. Strongly encourage smoking cessation (it does not directly lower blood pressure but does lower cardiovascular risk). Reduce alcohol intake to no more than 2 mixed drinks, two 12-ounce cans of beer, or two 4-ounce glasses of wine daily for men and one half of this quantity for women (20, 21).

The PREMIER trial randomly assigned 810 participants to behavioral intervention (weight loss, exercise, limited sodium and alcohol intake), the DASH diet plus behavioral intervention, or one-time advice only. Relative to advice-only, systolic blood pressure levels at 6 months declined by 3.7 mm Hg (behavioral change only) and 4.3 mm Hg (behavioral change plus DASH diet) (22).

Several lifestyle changes are of doubtful value. Fish oil, magnesium, and calcium supplementation do not reduce blood pressure. Although patients may consider relaxation therapies, such as meditation and yoga, their effect is short-term (23). Caffeine may transiently increase blood pressure, but caffeine has little sustained effect on blood pressure in patients with hypertension (24).

When is antihypertensive drug therapy indicated and which drugs should clinicians prescribe as initial therapy?

Many patients with stage 1 hypertension will require drug therapy to control blood pressure despite lifestyle modification. The JNC 7 recommends starting all patients on a diuretic unless they have a compelling reason to use another drug (2). Patients with stage 2 hypertension or those requiring a greater reduction than 20/10 mm Hg to reach goal blood pressure levels should start on 2 drugs, one of which should be a diuretic. Table 5 shows the doses, mechanisms, advantages, and disadvantages of a selection of commonly used antihypertensive drugs. The Figure provides an algorithm for treatment of hypertension, and Table 6 elaborates on compelling drug indications.

ALLHAT randomly assigned 44 000 patients age >55 years with hypertension and one additional cardiovascular risk factor to initial treatment with a diuretic (chlorthalidone), an a-blocker (doxazosin), an ACE inhibitor (lisinopril), or a calcium-channel blocker (amlodipine). Addition of a second drug was permitted as needed. The doxazosin group was discontinued when interim results showed that it could not be superior to diuretic and that heart failure was higher with doxazosin. The results with the remaining 3 drugs supported diuretics as first-choice therapy because of their efficacy in reducing cardiovascular death and nonfatal myocardial infarction, superiority in several secondary outcomes (heart failure and stroke), and low cost (25).

Clinicians should strongly consider treating hypertension in very elderly patients.

The HYVET trial randomly assigned 3845 patients older than 80 years with systolic blood pressure levels from 160 to 199 mm Hg to either placebo or diuretic (indapimide, 1.5 mg daily) with the addition of an ACE inhibitor (perindopril, 4-8 mg daily) as needed. The trial was stopped early because of the large benefit of active

Table 5. Drug Treatments for Hypertension*

Drug Class (daily dose, mg)	Advantages	Disadvantages
Diuretics Hydrochlorothiazide (12.5–50) Chlorothiazide (250–500) Chlorothalidone (12.5–50)	Most effective in the elderly, those with isolated systolic hypertension, diabetics, and African Americans, who are likely to be salt-sensitive; inexpensive	May increase glucose, cholesterol, and uric acid levels; hypokalemia; photosensitivity
ACE inhibitors Enalapril (5–40) Fosinopril (10–40) Lisinopril (5–40) Perindopril (4–16) Quinapril (5–80) Ramipril (1.25–20)	Preferred for chronic kidney disease, heart failure, and diabetes. Work well with diuretics. Generic ACE inhibitors are inexpensive	Cough in 15% (switch to an ARB). Can accept up to 30% increase in serum creatinine with ACE inhibitors. Angioedema in 0.1%–0.7%. Contraindicated in pregnancy
Angiotensin-receptor blocker (ARB) Losartan (25–100) Candesartan (16–32) Irbesartan (150–300)	Usually well-tolerated. Angiedema uncommon. Work well with a diuretic; Do not cause cough	Dizziness. Relatively expensive. Contraindicated in pregnancy
Potassium-sparing diuretics Spironolactone (25–100) Triamterene (25–100)	Most useful when a thiazide causes hypokalemia	Hyperkalemia (rare with triamterene); gynecomastia (spironolactone); weak antihypertensives
ß-blockers Atenolol (25–100) Metoprolol (50–300) Propranolol (40–480) Nebivolol (2.5–10) Carvedilol (12.5–50)	Carvedilol is an α- and ß-blocker. Nebivolol is also a vasodilator. Note: Don't use ß-blockers as initial therapy except in heart failure	Bronchospasm, bradycardia, heart failure; masks insulin-induced hypoglycemia; impairs peripheral circulation; insomnia; fatigue; decreased exercise tolerance; hypertriglyceridemia (unless ISA present); several trials show worse outcomes with atenolol than ACE inhibitors, ARBs, and CCBs
CCBs Amlodipine (2.5–10) Diltiazem (120–360) Verapamil (120–480) Nifedipine (30–120)	Well-tolerated and effective. Dihydropyridines, like amlodipine, are quite potent. Relatively inexpensive	Diuretic-resistant edema (lesser problem if ACE inhibitor or ARB added), headache, cardiac conduction defects, constipation, gingival hypertrophy
Reserpine (0.05–0.25)	Inexpensive	Nasal congestion, depression, peptic ulcer
Central ß-agonists Methyldopa (500–3000) Clonidine (0.2–1.2)	Inexpensive	Sedation, dry mouth, bradycardia, withdrawal (rebound) hypertension
Guanethidine (10–50) α-blockers Prazosin (2–30) Doxasosin (1–16) Terazosin (1–20)	Very potent; inexpensive	Postural hypotension; diarrhea Postural hypotension; heart failure increased with doxasin in ALLHAT
Hydralazine (50–300)	Inexpensive	Lupus reaction; headache; edema
Direct renin inhibitor Aliskiren (150–300)	Newly approved. Reduced plasma renin could be therapeutic per se; effective in combination	Diarrhea

ACE = angiotensin-converting enzyme; ARB = angiotensin-receptor blocker; CCB = calcium-channel blocker; ISA = irregular spiking activity.

* For a full listing of drugs, see Oral Antihypertensive Drug Treatment table in PIER hypertension module.

treatment with an expected 30% reduction in fatal and nonfatal stroke and an unexpected 21% reduction in all-cause mortality. This study confirms the value of drug treatment for patients age ≥80 years who have systolic blood pressure levels ≥150 mm Hg (26).

How should clinicians modify choice of antihypertensive treatment based on patient characteristics and comorbid conditions?

Although diuretics are generally the recommended first-choice agent,

25. Major cardiovascular events in hypertensive patients randomized to doxazosin vs chlorthalidone. ALLHAT Collaborative Research Group. JAMA 2000;283: 1967-75. [PMID: 10789664]

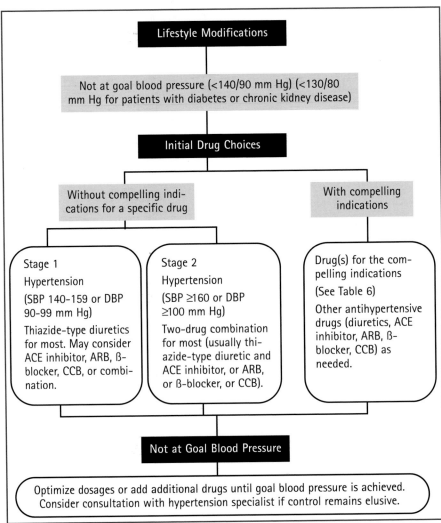

Figure. Algorithm for treatment of hypertension. Adapted from JNC 7 Hypertension Clinical Practice Guidelines (http://www.nhlbi.nih.gov/guidelines/hypertension/express.pdf). ACE = angiotensin-converting enzyme; ARB = angiotensin-receptor blocker; CCB = calcium-channel blocker; DBP = diastolic blood pressure; SBP= systolic blood pressure.

Table 6. Compelling Indications for Individual Drug Classes*

Compelling Indication[†]	Recommended Drugs
Heart Failure	Diuretic, ß-blocker, ACE inhibitor, ARB, aldosterone antagonist
Postmyocardial infarction	ß-blocker, ACE inhibitor, aldosterone antagonist
High coronary disease risk	Diuretic, ß-blocker, ACE inhibitor, ARB + CCB
Diabetes	Diuretic, ß-blocker, ACE inhibitor, ARB, CCB
Chronic kidney disease	ACE inhibitor, ARB
Recurrent stroke prevention	Diuretic, ACE inhibitor

ACE = angiotensin-converting enzyme; ARB = angiotensin-receptor blocker; CCB = calcium-channel blocker.

* Adapted from JNC 7 Hypertension Clinical Practice Guidelines (http://www.nhlbi.nih.gov/guidelines/hypertension/express.pdf).

† Compelling indications for antihypertensive drugs are based on benefits from outcome studies or existing clinical guidelines; the compelling indication is managed in parallel with the blood pressure.

26. HYVET Study Group. Treatment of hypertension in patients 80 years of age or older. N Engl J Med. 2008;358:1887-98. [PMID: 18378519]

27. Yusuf S, Sleight P, Pogue J, et al. Effects of an angiotensin-converting-enzyme inhibitor, ramipril, on cardiovascular events in high-risk patients. The Heart Outcomes Prevention Evaluation Study Investigators. N Engl J Med. 2000;342:145-53. [PMID: 10639539]

clinicians should modify drug selection on the basis of patient characteristics and comorbid conditions.

Elderly and African-American patients tend to be salt-sensitive and respond well to diuretics.

Younger patients with hypertension often respond well to suppression of the renin-angiotensin system and an ACE inhibitor or ARB may be a good initial choice for these patients. ACE inhibitors are helpful in patients with diabetes, particularly if microalbuminuria is present. Patients with heart failure can benefit from ACE inhibitors, diuretics, cardioselective ß-blockers, and ARBs. ß-blockers and ACE inhibitors are good antihypertensive agents for patients who have had a myocardial infarction. Patients with renal insufficiency can benefit from ACE inhibitors, particularly if proteinuria is present.

The HOPE trial randomly assigned more than 9000 patients >55 years old with CVD to ramipril 10 mg at night or placebo and found that those on ramipril had less morbidity and mortality than those on placebo. Because one half of the patients also had hypertension, the authors concluded that an ACE inhibitor is reasonable initial hypertension therapy in patients with vascular disease (27).

In the ASCOT trial, more than 19 000 adults with hypertension and 3 or more CVD risk factors were randomly assigned to either a ß-blocker plus a thiazide-type diuretic (if needed) or to a combination of a calcium-channel blocker (amlodipine) and an ACE inhibitor (perindopril) if needed and, in a factorial design, to either a statin or placebo. After median follow-up of 5.5 years, the trial was stopped because cardiovascular events and total mortality were significantly lower in the group that received the amlodipine-based regimen. Although blood pressure level was well-controlled in both groups, it was lower in the amlodipine group by an average difference of 2.7/1.9 mm Hg. The amlodipine and ACE inhibitor drug combination reduced the risk for stroke by about 25%, for coronary events and procedures by 15%, and for cardiovascular deaths by 25% (28).

What is the role of combination therapies for hypertension?

Combination therapies are gaining popularity. They have several advantages, including better medication adherence. Whether they ultimately cost less for patients than individual prescriptions for each of the drugs depends on the patients' insurance programs.

ACE inhibitors or ARBs combined with hydrochlorothiazide

Many different ACE inhibitors and ARBs are available in combination with a thiazide. This combination is well-tolerated and is often good initial therapy for stage 2 hypertension.

ACE inhibitors and ARBs combined with nonhydropyridine calcium-channel blockers

An ACE inhibitor with amlodipine is available in various doses, including generics. ARBs are not available as generics. Adding an ACE inhibitor or ARB avoids the edema of amlodipine monotherapy.

ACE–ARB combination therapy

ACE–ARB combinations do not seem to have advantages. The recent ONTARGET (Ongoing Telmisartan Alone and in Combination with

Table 7. Drug Therapy for Specific Disease Mechanisms of Hypertension*

Disease Mechanism	Drug Class	Comment
Volume overload	Thiazide; loop diuretic; aldosterone antagonist	
Sympathetic overactivity	ß-blocker	Use to counteract reflex tachycardia from vasodilators or in heart failure
Increased vascular resistance	Angiotensin-converting enzyme inhibitor or angiotensin-receptor blocker	Use in heart failure
Smooth-muscle contraction	Dihydropyridine calcium-channel blockers; ß-blockers; hydralazine	

Adapted from reference 33.

28. ASCOT Investigators. Prevention of cardiovascular events with an antihypertensive regimen of amlodipine adding perindopril as required versus atenolol adding bendroflumethiazide as required, in the Anglo-Scandinavian Cardiac Outcomes Trial-Blood Pressure Lowering Arm (ASCOT-BPLA): a multicentre randomised controlled trial. Lancet. 2005;366:895-906. [PMID: 16154016]

29. ONTARGET Investigators. Telmisartan, ramipril, or both in patients at high risk for vascular events. N Engl J Med. 2008;358:1547-59. [PMID: 18378520]

30. Phillips LS, Branch WT, Cook CB, et al. Clinical inertia. Ann Intern Med. 2001;135:825-34. [PMID: 11694107]

31. Moser M, Setaro JF. Clinical practice. Resistant or difficult-to-control hypertension. N Engl J Med. 2006;355:385-92. [PMID: 16870917]

32. American Heart Association Professional Education Committee. Resistant hypertension: diagnosis, evaluation, and treatment: a scientific statement from the American Heart Association Professional Education Committee of the Council for High Blood Pressure Research. Circulation. 2008;117:e510-26. [PMID: 18574054]

33. Pickering T. Recommendations for the use of home (self) and ambulatory blood pressure monitoring. American Society of Hypertension Ad Hoc Panel. Am J Hypertens. 1996;9:1-11. [PMID: 8834700]

34. Wilson MD, Johnson KA. Hypertension management in managed care: the role of home blood pressure monitoring. Blood Press Monit. 1997;2:201-206. [PMID: 10234118]

Ramipril Global Endpoint Trial) study confirms that ACE inhibitors and ARBs are not additive in combination therapy for hypertension and have more side effects, such as hyperkalemia and slight decline in glomerular filtration rate (29). ACE inhibitor, ARB, and ACE–ARB combination had the same effect on cardiovascular events.

When blood pressure is poorly controlled, how should clinicians decide between increasing dose, adding an additional agent, or switching to another drug class?
When blood pressure is poorly controlled, it is important to avoid clinical inertia (30). The following principles were formulated to deal with a particular form of poorly controlled blood pressure called "resistant hypertension," but they are useful whenever the blood pressure is above the target level. Resistant hypertension is when the blood pressure is above the target level on a rational, full-dose, triple-drug regimen that includes a diuretic (31, 32). If the patient has no target organ damage, consider ambulatory blood pressure monitoring to see if the white coat effect is a contributing factor. Ask about co-medication with blood pressure–raising drugs and excessive alcohol or salt intake. Reconsider secondary causes of hypertension as they are much more common in resistant hypertension. Poor adherence is also common, so carefully evaluate adherence before changing treatment.

Because volume overload is common, start treating uncontrolled hypertension by adding or increasing diuretic therapy with a thiazide (with normal renal function) or a loop diuretic (with abnormal renal function). A key to success is using several different drugs, each of which attacks a different disease mechanism. Table 7 shows physiologic mechanisms and the drug class that counteracts each. If the patient

is taking 2 drugs that attack the same disease mechanism, replace 1 of them with a drug from a different class. If patient is taking 3 drugs and blood pressure remains uncontrolled, ensure that the patient is taking drugs from different classes. Consider adding a potassium-sparing diuretic, such as aldactone or amiloride, in patients taking 3 to 4 drugs if blood pressure is still uncontrolled. Consider a combined α- and ß-blocker, a centrally acting agent, or reserpine (in low doses). If control remains elusive, consider consulting a specialist in hypertension management.

How often should patients with hypertension be seen?
Blood pressure levels and clinical judgment should guide decisions about the frequency of monitoring blood pressure. Suggested recheck intervals for blood pressure levels 140/90 to 159/99 mm Hg are 2 months, and within 1 month if levels are higher. If the systolic and diastolic blood pressure levels fall into different categories, follow recommendations for the shorter follow-up time. After adjusting medications, allow 2 to 4 weeks for the blood pressure level to stabilize before modifying therapy. Clinical opinion rather than evidence determines the interval for seeing patients with stable, well-controlled hypertension; 6- to 12-month intervals are typical practice.

What is the value of home blood pressure level monitoring?
Home blood pressure monitoring is a relatively inexpensive way to monitor blood pressure levels, especially before and after changing therapy. Measurements of home blood pressure levels are more accurate than office blood pressure levels (33). Some patients become obsessed with their blood pressure level, and the physician may have to set limits on how often they take home blood pressure readings, lest

their anxiety over the results raise their blood pressure level. Instruct patients on correct technique of taking blood pressure level and ask them to keep a journal in which they chart their blood pressure level once to twice daily.

Home blood pressure level monitoring can help to confirm a diagnosis of hypertension in an untreated patient (34, 35). Instruct the patient to check at least 2 readings on at least 3 (preferably 7) consecutive days in the morning between 6 and 10 a.m. and to repeat them in the evening between 6 and 10 p.m. If the average home blood pressure level is less than 125/76 mm Hg (after dropping the first day's values), hypertension is very unlikely in an untreated person (36). Average untreated home blood pressure levels of 135/85 mm Hg and higher suggest hypertension. In-between values are an indication for further evaluation by ambulatory blood pressure monitoring.

When should clinicians consider hospitalization or referral to a hypertension specialist?

The main indication for hospitalization because of elevated blood pressure is a hypertensive crisis (see Box). Indications to refer to a hypertension specialist include the following: drug-resistant hypertension uncontrolled on 3 or more drugs; uncertainty about how to evaluate or manage suspected secondary hypertension—especially pheochromocytoma or primary hyperaldosteronism—or assistance needed to assess the extent of target organ damage.

When patients present with markedly elevated blood pressure levels, how should clinicians distinguish between a hypertensive emergency and a pseudocrisis?

A sudden rise in blood pressure level is classified as either hypertensive urgency or a hypertensive emergency (37). Hypertensive urgency is defined as an elevated blood pressure level greater than 180/110 mm Hg without target organ damage. Patients can usually be managed with oral medications as outpatients and sent home after a few hours of observation. A hypertensive emergency is defined as an elevated blood pressure level with impending or acute progressive target organ damage. These patients usually require admission to an intensive care unit and intravenous medication to lower blood pressure level (38). Several drugs lower blood pressure quickly. The choice depends on the physician's level of comfort and experience with the drugs. See the Box for situations in which severe hypertension constitutes a crisis.

Situations in which Severe Hypertension Constitutes a Crisis

Cardiovascular
- Left-ventricular failure
- Myocardial infarction
- Unstable angina
- Aortic dissection
- After vascular surgery or coronary artery bypass grafting

Neurologic
- Hypertensive encephalopathy
- Subarachnoid or intracranial hemorrhage
- Thrombotic stroke

Other
- Severe catecholamine excess, such as clonidine withdrwal, pheochromocytoma, tyramine-MAOI* interaction, or intoxication (cocaine, phenylcyclidine, phenylpropanolamine)
- Eclampsia in pregnancy

MAOI = monoamine oxidase inhibitors.

---

35. Pickering TG, Miller NH, Ogedegbe G, et al. Call to action on use and reimbursement for home blood pressure monitoring: executive summary: a joint scientific statement from the American Heart Association, American Society Of Hypertension, and Preventive Cardiovascular Nurses Association. Hypertension. 2008;52:1-9. [PMID: 18497371]

36. Williams B, Poulter NR, Brown MJ, et al. Guidelines for management of hypertension: report of the fourth working party of the British Hypertension Society, 2004-BHS IV. J Hum Hypertens. 2004;18:139-85. [PMID: 14973512]

37. Townsend R. Hypertensive crisis. In: Lanken PN, ed. The Intensive Care Unit Manual. Vol. 2000. Philadelphia: WB Saunders; 2000:602-14.

38. Lip GY, Beevers M, Beevers DG. Complications and survival of 315 patients with malignant-phase hypertension. J Hypertens. 1995;13:915-24. [PMID: 8557970]

Treatment... The goal blood pressure level should be less than 140/90 mm Hg unless the patient has other cardiovascular risk factors or diabetes, which lowers the target to less than 130/80 mm Hg. Lifestyle modifications can lower the blood pressure level, but most patients also need at least 1 drug to reach goal blood pressure. A diuretic is a good choice for initial therapy absent a compelling indication for another drug (for example, vascular disease is a strong indication to start with an ACE inhibitor). Failure to reach target blood pressure level on a near-maximal dose of one or more drugs is an indication to add a drug that attacks another mechanism for hypertension. Severe hypertension requires urgent treatment, often in the hospital, if acute cardiovascular or neurologic events are present, if the patient is pregnant, or if severe catecholamine excess is present.

CLINICAL BOTTOM LINE

How many patients with hypertension receive treatment, and how well is hypertension controlled in the United States? Of the one third of U.S. adults that have hypertension, only two thirds are aware of their hypertension, and approximately 55% are on treatment. Hypertension control rates are improving: The blood pressure level control rate was 29.2% ± 2.3% in 1999 to 2000 and 36.8% ± 2.3% in 2003 to 2004 (1). The control rates increased substantially in both sexes, non-Hispanic blacks, and Mexican Americans. Among the group of patients age 60 years and older, awareness, treatment, and control rates have all increased significantly (1). Among treated patients with hypertension, control rates approach 65%.

What do professional organizations recommend about the management of patients with hypertension? The advice in this In The Clinic article generally represents the recommendations of the JNC 7 (2), the American Heart Association, the National Kidney Foundation, and the American College of Physicians. Links to the guidelines are listed in the Toolkit.

in the clinic

Tool Kit

Hypertension

PIER Modules

pier.acponline.org
Access the PIER module on hypertension, which provided the up-to-date evidence cited in this In the Clinic article. PIER modules provide evidence-based, current information on prevention, diagnosis, and treatment in an easy-to-use electronic format designed for rapid access at the point-of-care.

Patient Education Resources

www.annals.org/intheclinic
Access the Patient Information material that appears on the following page for duplication and distribution to patients.

Practice Measures

pier.acponline.org/qualitym/index.html
PIER has a list of practice measures, including those of the Physician Quality Reporting Initiative (PQRI). Hypertension quality measures appear under Endocrinology, Diabetes, and Metabolism and under Nephrology.

www.qualityforum.org/pdf/ambulatory/tbAMBALLMeasuresendorsed%2012-10-07.pdf
The National Quality Forum: This influential group's practice measures appear under Diabetes and Hypertension.

www.ama-assn.org/ama1/pub/upload/mm/370/hypertension-8-05.pdf
Practice measures from the Physicians' Consortium for Performance Improvement (PCPI). Among the tools is a good flow sheet for recording key data over time.

Guidelines

hyper.ahajournals.org/cgi/content/full/42/6/1206
The Seventh Report of the Joint National Committee on Prevention, Detection, Evaluation, and Treatment of High Blood Pressure.

circ.ahajournals.org/cgi/reprint/CIRCULATIONAHA.107.183885
Guidelines from the American Heart Association for managing hypertension to prevent atherosclerotic cardiovascular disease.

www.kidney.org/professionals/KDOQI/guidelines.cfm
Guidelines from the National Kidney Foundation for managing hypertension in patients with renal disease.

diabetes.acponline.org/custom_resources/ACP_DiabetesCareGuide_Ch10.pdf?dbp
ACP Guidelines for the care of hypertension in patients with diabetes.

THINGS PEOPLE SHOULD KNOW ABOUT HYPERTENSION

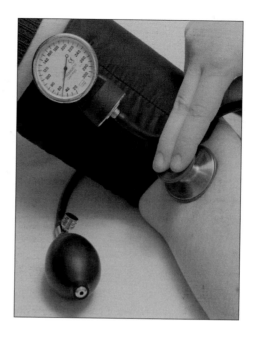

- Hypertension, often called high blood pressure, is a common health problem.

- Most people do not know they have high blood pressure. Some people get headaches or swollen legs due to problems related to hypertension, such as heart failure.

- We don't know what causes hypertension. In a few people who have another disease that causes hypertension, it can be cured. But most people must take medicines to control their blood pressure.

- If you don't get treated for your hypertension, there is a better chance you could have a heart attack, stroke, or kidney failure.

- Just having healthy habits may lower your blood pressure. Follow these healthy habits even if you take blood pressure medicine: Eat less salt, exercise more, eat more fruits and vegetables, lose weight, drink less alcohol, and stop smoking.

- Work with your doctor to have better health habits, measure your blood pressure at home, and take your medicine every day. Keep all of your doctor appointments.

For More Information

American College of Physicians: ACP Special Report: Living with Hypertension

www.doctorsforadults.com/images/healthpdfs/hypertension_report.pdf

American Heart Association: High Blood Pressure

www.americanheart.org/presenter.jhtml?identifier=2114

National Heart, Lung, and Blood Institute: Your Guide to Lowering Blood Pressure

www.nhlbi.nih.gov/health/public/heart/hbp/hbp_low/hbp_low.pdf

National Kidney Foundation: High Blood Pressure (Hypertension)

www.kidney.org/atoz/atozTopic.cfm?topic=1

ACP
AMERICAN COLLEGE OF PHYSICIANS
INTERNAL MEDICINE | *Doctors for Adults*®

Patient Information